The Personality Puzzle

THIRD EDITION

The Personality Puzzle

THIRD EDITION

DAVID C. FUNDER

University of California, Riverside

W. W. NORTON & COMPANY

NEW YORK   LONDON

For my father

W. W. Norton & Company has been independent since its founding in 1923, when William Warder Norton and Mary D. Herter Norton first published lectures delivered at the People's Institute, the adult education division of New York City's Cooper Union. The Nortons soon expanded their program beyond the Institute, publishing books by celebrated academics from America and abroad. By mid-century, the two major pillars of Norton's publishing program— trade books and college texts—were firmly established. In the 1950s, the Norton family transferred control of the company to its employees, and today—with a staff of four hundred and a comparable number of trade, college, and professional titles published each year—W. W. Norton & Company stands as the largest and oldest publishing house owned wholly by its employees.

Editors: Jon Durbin and Aaron Javsicas
Managing Editor, College: Marian Johnson
Production Manager: Ben Reynolds
Editorial Assistant: Andrea Haver

Composition by Matrix.
Manufacturing by Quebecor World—Fairfield Division.
Book design by Good Design Resource.

Library of Congress Cataloging-in-Publication Data

Funder, David Charles.
  The personality puzzle / David C. Funder.—3rd ed.
    p. cm.
  Includes bibliographical references (p.) and indexes.

  ISBN 0-393-97996-2

  1. Personality. I. Title

BF698.F84 2004
155.2—dc22   2003060943

W. W. Norton & Company, Inc., 500 Fifth Avenue, New York, NY 10110
www.wwnorton.com

W. W. Norton & Company Ltd., Castle House, 75/76 Wells Street, London W1T 3QT

3 4 5 6 7 8 9 0

Anybody in science, if there are enough anybodies, can find the answer—it's an Easter-egg hunt. That isn't the idea. The idea is: Can you ask the question in such a way as to facilitate the answer?
—Gerald Edelman

Even if, ultimately, everything turns out to be connected to everything else, a research program rooted in that realization might well collapse of its own weight.
—Howard Gardner

The first step is to measure whatever can easily be measured. That's OK as far as it goes. The second step is to pretend that whatever cannot be easily measured isn't very important. That's dangerous. The third step is to pretend that whatever cannot easily be measured doesn't exist. That's suicide.
—Daniel Yankelovich

There once was an entomologist who found a bug he couldn't classify—so he stepped on it.
—Ernest R. Hilgard

Interpretation is the revenge of the intellect upon art.
—Susan Sontag

CONTENTS IN BRIEF

CONTENTS

11   The Workings of the Unconscious Mind: Defenses and Slips   315

PREFACE TO THE THIRD EDITION

The way a personality course should be taught—and the way its textbook should be written—depends on its purpose. Therefore, any instructor or author needs to ask at the outset, what do I hope to accomplish? Several different answers are possible, all of them legitimate. Each implies a different approach to teaching and to textbook writing.

Goals for a Personality Course

First, an instructor might wish to ensure that his or her students become deeply familiar with the classic theories of personality and learn to appreciate the history of and the intellectual connections among these theories. Such a course in personality can be an important part of a liberal education and fit easily into a "great books" curriculum. This goal is well served by any of the hefty theoretical tomes that have been on the market for many years. But students sometimes end such a course with little idea of what modern personality psychology is all about.

A second, very different goal is to make sure students learn the current activities of modern research psychologists and all of the very latest findings. The classic theories typically are neglected when this goal is pursued, sometimes on the grounds that all of the old theories are false and only modern empirical research has anything worth teaching. (I have actually heard psychology professors say this.) Several recent books seem to have been written with this goal in mind.

But the modern empirical literature is not an infallible source of ultimate truth. Moreover, a textbook or course that focuses exclusively on what modern personality psychologists do is limited to whatever topics current research happens to emphasize. I do not know that any of the answers psychology has provided are eternal, but some of the questions are. And some of those questions are neglected in modern research.

This book serves both of the goals just listed. It covers the main theories of personality and traces some relevant intellectual history. It also includes a large amount of current research, including recent work on biology, cross-cultural psychology, and cognitive processes relevant to personality. But the goal that has driven this book, above all other goals, is to convince the reader that personality psychology matters. To the extent that on the final page the reader ends up believing that personality psychology is intellectually exciting and provides valuable insights into real-life concerns, this book—and, perhaps the personality course of which it may be a part—will have accomplished what it set out to do.

Personality and Life

To convince somebody new to the field that personality psychology matters, an instructor must teach each basic approach in a form that is relevant not just to its historical antecedents or to current research, but to everyday life. Establishing this relevance is the one thing I have tried to do more distinctively than anything else in this book. The result is a presentation that strays from the conventional versions of the basic approaches to personality in favor of a new and modern rendition of each.

This strategy is applied most obviously in the chapters on Freud, where I present a psychoanalytic approach that certainly stems from Freud but departs from orthodoxy in numerous ways and in the end, may not really be Freud anymore. Someone who wants to learn in detail what Freud really said should read a different book. But someone who wants to see how some derivations from Freud's basic ideas can be presented in what I think is a fairly convincing contemporary context might find this book illuminating. Parallel comments could be made about the presentations of the other approaches.

The humorist Dave Barry once wrote a history of the United States that he touted as more interesting than any other because, he said, he left out all

"As a matter of fact, I confess to modest hopes—not wildly unfounded, I trust—that my book may resonate beyond the reaches of academe."

of the boring parts. While I have not gone that far, I have freed myself of the obligation to cover topics just because they are there, or are traditional, or are covered in every other book. I also have included quite a bit of material on topics that some other books either underemphasize or neglect entirely. These topics include person perception, biology (including anatomy, physiology, genetics, and evolutionary theory), cross-cultural studies, and relevant aspects of cognitive psychology.

Topics versus Theories

In broadest outline, this book follows a traditional organization according to "theories" or "paradigms" (I usually call them "approaches"). It begins with a treatment of research methods, and then considers the basic approaches to personality: trait, biological, psychoanalytic, phenomenological, learning, and cognitive.

Some of my colleagues believe this organization is outdated and should be replaced by a scheme that instead focuses on "topics" like aggression, or development, or the self. The components of the several traditional paradigms presumably would be scattered across these topical chapters. The suggested model seems to be social psychology, which in its courses and textbooks almost always follows such a topical organization.

There are several reasons why I believe a topical organization is a mistake for a personality text, however (and it is interesting to note that some authors who tried this approach have abandoned it in later editions). A pragmatic reason is that the basic approaches are complex theoretical systems, and breaking them up across topics seems unlikely to yield a clear understanding of any of them. A more substantive reason is that the topical organization of social psychology represents an intellectual deficit of that field, as compared with personality psychology, rather than any sort of advantage. Social psychology lacks even one organizing, theoretical approach with any scope, as far as I am aware; it organizes itself by topic because it must. Personality psychology, by contrast, has at least five approaches, each of which offers an organized way to cover a wide range of data and theory about human psychology.

A further reason became clearer as I worked on this book. In personality, a "topics" organization and a "basic approaches" organization are not, at a deep level, truly different. A consistent theme throughout this book is that the basic approaches to personality are not different answers to the same question—they are different questions! To put this point another way, each of the basic approaches has a few topics it addresses most centrally, and many others it ignores. The basic topics ignored by each tend to be central concerns of one or more of the others. As a result, a basic approaches organization is a topics organization, to a considerable degree, because each basic approach can be associated with a different basic topic.

Individual differences = trait approach
Biological influences = biological approach
Psychodynamics and the unconscious = psychoanalytic approach
Experience and awareness = phenomenological/humanistic approach (I include cross-cultural psychology here)
Perception, thinking, and behavior change = learning and cognitive approach

I hope this organizational scheme makes this textbook easy to use. It matches in broad outline the way in which most personality courses are now taught. Beyond that, it should not be hard for an instructor using this text to find places where she or he wishes to amplify, supplement, or disagree.

Indeed, the reader will find that I present opinions in this book on nearly every page. An instructor who disagrees with some of these opinions—and surely nobody will agree with me on everything—should be able to put together compelling lectures about those disagreements. The result of this intellectual give-and-take between instructor and author could be, for the student, an exciting introduction to a fascinating subject.

Changes in the Third Edition

Personality psychology is accelerating. The differences in the field between the time of this edition and the Second Edition are vastly greater than those between the Second and First Editions. An increasing number of researchers have been attracted to the field of personality psychology, including psychologists originally trained in other subfields who have discovered that personality is the place where they can best address the issues that interest them the most. As a result, there is a large amount of new research, and the research is increasing in quality as well as in quantity.

For example, the trait approach, too-often limited in the past by an overly exclusive dependence on self-report methodology, is suddenly filled with studies that assess personality through direct behavioral observations, physiological measurements, and imaginative indicators such as music preference and the state of one's bedroom. The biological approach is moving beyond simple reductionism and developing research programs that are truly informative about psychological issues. Psychoanalytic ideas are busily creeping into other areas of the field, especially the cognitive approach, and while they sometimes are relabeled in the process of rediscovery it is fascinating to watch formerly fringe concepts like the unconscious become a routine topic for research. Humanistic psychology was almost dead at the time of the Second Edition, though I believed many of its ideas (and the existential/phenomenological approach behind it) were important to understand anyway. But suddenly there has been an explosion of interest in "positive psychology" and related topics that amount to a rebirth of the field. Cross-cultural psychology was just coming into its own at the time of the Second Edition. Now it is huge. Research activity on cross-cultural issues is not only much more active but it has also become theoretically richer and methodologically innovative. Finally, the cognitive approach has accelerated along with the rest of the field, and seems suddenly much closer to becoming the place where all of personality psychology may someday come together.

The Third Edition of this book reflects these changes. In addition to continued attempts to make the writing clearer and more interesting, a large amount of new and important research is included in almost every chapter. This is especially true of the chapters on the biology of personality (8 and 9) and cross-cultural psychology (14), two areas that have been especially active. In addition, the trait chapters include a new discussion of self-knowledge (Chapter 6) and an overview of personality development (Chapter 7). The psychoanalytic chapters have a new section that considers the classic topic of object relations (Chapter 12). The humanistic chapter (13) adds sections on hardiness and positive psychology. The cognitive chapters (16 and 17) contain a large amount of new research, including innovative methods for investigating unconscious mental processes. The final chapter (18) presents new ideas about the "OBT" (One Big Theory) that may someday integrate the study of personality, and its new concluding section reviews a few key themes I hope the reader will remember long after finishing this book.

The most obvious change is the reorganization of the section on the learning and cognitive approaches. Long-time readers may recall that the First Edition had a single section for learning and cognitive approaches, which included a chapter on behaviorism, one on social learning theory, and one on the (then-new) cognitive approach to personality. As the cognitive approach expanded, the Second Edition divided this into two sections, one for behaviorism and social learning, and one for cognitive research, with two chapters in each. Now in this edition, we are back to one section, with an important change. I have combined the two learning chapters into one that summarizes the implications of both behaviorism and the social learning theories for personality. The two chapters on the cognitive approach to personality have been thoroughly updated and reorganized. I hope the result is a leaner, clearer presentation that focuses better on issues that are truly important.

Acknowledgments

It is with pleasure that I acknowledge some of the help I received with this project over the years and three editions. First of all, my wife, Patti, has been a source of emotional support, clever ideas, and critical comments throughout the process. Her insights and her skepticism about whether psychology is really a science (she was trained as a molecular biologist) helped to keep me on my toes. She was particularly helpful this time around as I labored to bring the Third Edition home under a tight production schedule.

Tiffany Wright, a graduate student at the University of California, Riverside, Chris Langston, a colleague, and Cathy Wick, a former editor at Norton, read the First Edition of this book and made many comments and suggestions, most of which I followed. The encouragement and advice of Paul Rozin was particularly important, and Henry Gleitman was also generous. Traci Nagle carefully copyedited the First Edition, and a little of the prose on which she worked so hard still survives. Mary N. Babcock made an equally important contribution to the Second Edition, and Anne Hellman to the Third Edition. Don Fusting, a former Norton editor, used the softest sell in the history of publishing to convince me to undertake this project in the first place. If not for him, this book would not exist. He has continued to be generous with sage advice. Jon Durbin, my current editor, also provided ideas, encouragement, and the occasional prod, and Aaron Javsicas and the rest of the inimitable Norton crew provided other suggestions and efficiently kept everything on schedule. It was also Aaron's idea to see if I could find a few relevant *New Yorker* cartoons. Finally, Andrea Haver organized the manuscript and completed sundry other necessary tasks.

I am grateful for comments on the First Edition provided by Diane S. Berry, Southern Methodist University; William K. Gabrenya, Florida Institute of Technology; D. Brett King, the University of Colorado, Boulder; Aaron L. Pincus, Pennsylvania State University; Joseph F. Rychlak, Loyola University of Chicago; Drew Westen, Harvard University; and Marvin Zuckerman, University of Delaware. For the Second Edition, I benefited from the comments of Todd Heatherton, Dartmouth College; Denise Newman, University of Virginia; Steven Richards, Texas Tech University; and Michele M. Tomarelli, Texas A&M University. For the Third Edition, help came from Peter Ebersole, California State University, Fullerton; Cindy Hazan, Cornell University; Todd Heatherton, Dartmouth College; Robert Hessling, University of Wisconsin, Milwaukee; Brian Marx, Temple University; Yozan Mosig, University of Nebraska, Kearney; Denise Newman, University of Virginia; Julie Norem, Wellesley College; Gerard Saucier, University of Oregon; Jeanne Tsai, Stanford University; and David Williams, University of Pennsylvania.

I would like to express special appreciation to Todd Heatherton, who helped bring me up-to-date on the biological approach to personality, Jeanne Tsai, who was a fountain of ideas and guidance through recent cross-cultural research, and Julie Norem, for her advice and gentle correction of my presentation of the cognitive approach to personality. I also have been gratified to receive many e-mails from students. Some of these messages arrived late at night—apparently the readers of this book and its author keep the same hours. Many included useful questions, suggestions, and corrections that I have incorporated into this edition. But that wasn't even the best part. I can't adequately express how encouraging it is for an author bogged down at one in the morning to have his computer suddenly beep and yield an e-mail saying, "I really enjoyed your book and just wanted to say thanks." Thank *you.*

Finally, I want to acknowledge the very first person who read the first draft of the First Edition all the way through. He wrote comments on nearly every page. Usually, they were notations like "What does this mean?" or "What are you talking about?" These invariably identified places where I had lapsed into incomprehensible jargon or otherwise failed to make sense. Sometimes his comments were just strong expressions of agreement or disagreement. Over the several years that I worked on the First Edition, I never once had a conversation with him that did not include the question "How is the book coming along?" and some sort of suggestion that I really ought to be working faster. He looked forward to seeing this book in print and didn't miss it by much. My father, Elvin Funder, died in August 1995, just as I was putting the finishing touches on the First Edition. For the Second and Third Editions, I have had to imagine what he would say about some of my observations, but even that was helpful. I rededicate this book to him.

David C. Funder

Riverside, California
September 2003

The Personality Puzzle

THIRD EDITION

THE STUDY OF
THE PERSON

All persons are puzzles until at last we find in some word or act the key to the man, to the woman: straightaway all their past words and actions lie in light before us.

—Ralph Waldo Emerson

You may already have been told that psychology is not what you think it is. Some psychology professors delight in conveying this surprising news to their students on the first day of the term. Maybe you expect psychology to be about what people are thinking and feeling under the surface, these professors expound, maybe you think it's about sexuality, and dreams, and creativity, and aggression, and consciousness, and how people are different from one another, and interesting topics like that. Wrong, they say. Psychology is about the precise manipulation of independent variables for the furtherance of compelling theoretical accounts of well-specified phenomena, such as how many milliseconds it takes to find a circle in a field of squares. If that focus makes psychology boring, well, too bad. Science does not have to be interesting to be valuable.

Fortunately, most personality psychologists do not talk that way. This is because the study of *personality* does come close to being what nonpsychologists intuitively expect psychology to be, and addresses the topics most people want to know about (Block, 1993; Funder, 1998b). Therefore, personality psychologists have no excuse for being boring. Their field of study includes everything that makes psychology interesting.[1]

Specifically, personality psychology addresses all three parts of the **psychological triad**, the combination of how people think, feel, and behave. Each of these phenomena is important in its own right, but they are even more interesting in combination, especially when they conflict. For exam-

---

[1]Thus, if you end up finding this book boring, it is all my fault. There is no reason it should be, given its subject matter.

ple, have you ever experienced a conflict between how you feel and what you think, such as an attraction towards someone you nevertheless *knew* was bad news? Have you ever had a conflict between what you think and what you do, such as intending to do your homework and then going to the beach instead? Have you ever found your behavior conflicting with your feelings, such as doing something that makes you feel guilty (fill in your own example here), and then you kept on doing it anyway? If so (and I know the answer is yes), the next question is, why? The answer is far from obvious.

Inconsistencies between thoughts, feelings, and behaviors are common enough to make us suspect that the mind is not a simple place, and even that understanding oneself—the person we know well above all others—is not necessarily easy. Personality psychology is important not because it necessarily has solved these puzzles of internal consistency and self-knowledge, but because, alone among the sciences and even among the sub-branches of psychology, personality psychologists regard these puzzles as deserving their full attention.

When most people think of psychologists, they think first of the clinical practitioners who treat mental illness and try to help people with a wide range of other personal problems.[2] Personality psychology is not the same thing as clinical psychology, but the two fields do overlap. Some of the most important personality psychologists—both historically and in the present day—had clinical training and treated patients. At many colleges and universities, the person who teaches the courses in "abnormal" or "clinical" psychology also teaches personality. Most important, clinical and personality psychology share a common and fundamental obligation to try to understand whole persons, not just parts of persons, one individual at a time.

In this sense, personality psychology is the largest as well as the smallest subfield of psychology. There are probably fewer doctoral degrees granted in personality than in social, cognitive, developmental, or biological psychology. But personality psychology is allied closely with clinical psychology, which is by far the largest subfield. And again, the most important consideration is that personality psychology is where the rest of psychology comes together. As you will see in this book, personality psychology draws heavily from social, cognitive, developmental, and biological psychology. It contributes to each of these subfields as well, by showing how each part of psychology fits into the whole picture of what people are really like.

---

[2]This is why nonclinical research psychologists sometimes cringe a little when someone asks them what they do for a living.

The Goal of Personality Psychology

Personality refers to an individual's characteristic patterns of thought, emotion, and behavior, together with the psychological mechanisms—hidden or not—behind those patterns. This definition gives personality psychology its unique mission to explain whole persons. Of course, personality psychologists may not always succeed at this job. But that is what they are supposed to be doing—putting the pieces of the puzzle contributed by the various other subfields of psychology, as well as by their own research, back into an integrated view of whole, functioning individuals in their social contexts.

Mission: Impossible

There is only one problem with this mission. It is impossible. In fact, this interesting mission is the source of personality psychology's biggest difficulty. If you try to understand everything about a person all at once, you will immediately find yourself completely overwhelmed. Your mind, instead of attaining a broad understanding, may go blank. This is the problem with trying to see everything at the same time.

The only way out, perhaps ironically, is to choose to limit what you look at. Rather than trying to account for everything all at once, you must

"Do you mind if I say something helpful about your personality?"

search for more specific *patterns*—ways of tying together different kinds of observations. This search will require you to limit yourself to certain kinds of observations, certain kinds of patterns, and certain ways of thinking about these patterns. A systematic, self-imposed limitation of this sort is what I call a **basic approach** (another commonly used term is *paradigm*).

Some personality psychologists focus their efforts on the ways that people differ psychologically from one another and how these differences might be conceptualized and measured. They adhere to the **trait approach** (the reference here is to personality traits). Other psychologists try to understand the mind in terms of the body. That is, they address basic biological mechanisms, such as anatomy, physiology, inheritance, and even evolution, and their relevance for personality. These psychologists adhere to the **biological approach**. Another group of psychologists is concerned primarily with the workings of the unconscious mind, and the nature and resolution of internal mental conflict. These psychologists adhere to the **psychoanalytic approach**. Other psychologists are concerned primarily with people's conscious experience of the world, their "phenomenology," and can be said to follow a **phenomenological approach**. In current research, an emphasis on awareness and experience leads in two directions. One is a program of theory and research, called "humanistic psychology," that pursues how conscious awareness can produce such uniquely human attributes as existential anxiety, creativity, and free will. The other direction is toward an emphasis on the degree to which psychology and the very experience of reality might vary across cultures, leading to an explosion in recent years of research on "cross-cultural" psychology.

Still other psychologists concentrate on the ways in which people change what they do as a result of the rewards, punishments, and other experiences in life, a process called **learning**.[3] Classic "behaviorists" focus tightly on overt behavior and the ways it can be affected by rewards and punishments. Behaviorism was amended by a related subgroup of scientists who study "social learning." Social learning theory attempts to draw inferences about how mental processes such as observation and self-evaluation determine how behaviors are learned and performed. In the past few years, social learning theory has evolved into an influential and prolific new field of cognitive personality research, which is working to apply the insights and methods derived from the study of perception, memory, and thought to the study of personality. Taken together, behaviorism, social learning theory,

---

[3]This narrow use of the term *learning* by behaviorists should not be confused with its broader everyday meaning.

and cognitive personality psychology comprise the **learning and cognitive approaches** to personality.

Competitors or Complements?

The different approaches to personality are often portrayed as competing with each other, and for good reason. The original, famous protagonists of each typically made their mark by announcing to the world that *their* approach was the one that finally accounted for everything anybody would ever want to know about human nature, once and for all, and that all other approaches are worthless. Sigmund Freud, for one, was vocal in claiming that his version of the psychoanalytic approach was the one true path, and even worked to ostracize erstwhile followers, such as Carl Jung, who dared to differ with him on any point. B. F. Skinner, with his very different view of human nature, was not much of an improvement in the modesty department. He announced that behaviorism was sufficient to explain everything relevant to psychology, and he delighted in denouncing all of the other approaches and their presumptions that people might have traits, thoughts, or even freedom and dignity.

This kind of arrogance is not limited to approaches like behaviorism and psychoanalysis that have been closely associated with single, famous founders. Biologically inclined psychologists have been known to proclaim that everything anyone needs to know about personality reduces to a matter of genes, physiology, and brain anatomy. And trait, cognitive, and humanistic psychologists likewise sometimes have insisted their approach is the one that covers it all. In fact, major advocates of every basic approach have claimed frequently and insistently not only that their favored approach can explain anything, but also that all of the others are dead wrong.

Claims like these certainly seem effective, and perhaps they are even necessary to garner attention to a point of view. But their rhetorical smokescreen obscures an important basic fact. It is not obligatory, and I believe it is not helpful, to regard these basic approaches as forever locked in mutually exclusive competition. They complement rather than compete with each other because each addresses a different set of questions about human psychology.

An employer trying to decide whom to hire, for instance, must compare different individuals. The employer's problem is addressed by the trait assessment approach. When a televangelist is arrested for soliciting prostitutes, questions might be raised about his motivation, especially at the unconscious level. A psychoanalytic approach seems called for here. A parent who is worried about aspects of a teenage child's behavior and how the parent's actions might make a difference probably needs a behavioral approach. A philosopher contemplating the vicissitudes of free will or even a student consider-ing career plans and musing upon the meaning of life might find some use-ful insights in the humanistic approach. And so on. Each of the several approaches to personality psychology can be useful for handling its own key concerns.

At the same time, each also and rather disconcertingly tends to ignore the key concerns of all the other approaches (and, as I already mentioned, typically denies they are even important). For example, psychoanalysis has a lot to say about the origin of dreams, but has next to nothing to contribute to our understanding of behavior change. The principles of behaviorism can be used to teach your dog an amazing variety of tricks, but will never explain why he sometimes barks and whines in his sleep.

Distinct Approaches versus the One Big Theory

By now, the following question may have occurred to you: Why doesn't somebody just come up with One Big Theory (you could call it the OBT) that explains everything now accounted for separately by trait, biological, psychoanalytic, humanistic, behavioral, and cognitive approaches? Maybe someday somebody will (and if you become a personality psychologist, it could be you!).

In the meantime, you might do well to consider a time-honored and basic principle of engineering: A device that does one thing well is likely to be relatively poor at doing anything else. A toaster is terrible for making cof-fee. The converse, equally true, is that a device that does many things will probably do none of them especially well. A combination toaster, cof-feemaker, and clock radio will probably not be as good at toasting bread, making coffee, or playing music as an appliance that only tries to serve one of these functions. This principle seems also to be true within psychology, as it describes the inevitable trade-off faced by personality theorists. A theory that accounts for certain things extremely well will probably not do so well at explaining everything else. And a theory that tried to explain almost every-thing—the OBT—would probably not provide the best explanation for any one thing. Maybe dreams, learning curves, free will, and individual differ-ences in job performance could all be squeezed into one theory, but the result might not be a pretty sight.

I will return to these issues in the final chapter, but for now let me assure you that if you are confused, you are in good company. Personality psy-chologists themselves have not worked out a solution to this dilemma. Some really would like to develop the OBT that explains everything at least fairly well. Some believe that their own currently favored approach *is* the OBT (they are wrong). Others, instead of developing a whole new theory, would like to organize all the currently extant approaches into a single elegant system (e.g., Mayer, 1998). Still others, like me, persist in the belief that the different basic approaches address different sets of questions, and that each one has the best answers for the questions it has chosen to address.

If you agree with—or at least understand—this final belief, then you will appreciate why this book for the most part considers each basic approach separately. Personality psychology needs to look at people from *all* of these directions and utilize *all* of these basic approaches because different issues are best viewed from different perspectives. For the present, I believe it is most useful to teach and to apply these approaches one at a time, and in their entirety. Perhaps someday they will become fully integrated. In the meantime, as you will see, each basic approach has many interesting, important, and useful things to say about the aspects of human personality on which it has chosen to focus.

On Advantages as Disadvantages, and Vice Versa

In the introduction to his novel *Mother Night*, Kurt Vonnegut does his readers the unusual service of telling them the moral of the book they are about to read. "I don't think it's a marvelous moral," he writes, "I just happen to know what it is" (Vonnegut, 1966, p. v). My guess is that he hoped to save hundreds of English classes thousands of hours of trying to figure out what he "meant to say." (I doubt he succeeded.)[4]

As a writer I do not much resemble Vonnegut, but I too think I know what the moral of my book is, or at least what one of its major themes is: In life and in psychology, advantages and disadvantages have a way of being so tightly interconnected as to be inseparable. *Great strengths are usually great weaknesses, and surprisingly often the opposite is true as well.* Sometimes I enjoy calling this observation **Funder's First Law** (there will be several other such "laws" in this book).[5] This first law applies to fields of research, theories, and individual people.

Personality psychology provides an excellent example of Funder's First Law. As I already noted, personality psychology's biggest advantage over other areas of psychology is that it has a broad mandate to account for the psychology of whole persons and to be relevant to real-life concerns. This mandate

---

[4]For the record, Vonnegut wrote that the moral of *Mother Night* is "we are what we pretend to be, so we must be careful about what we pretend to be." Come to think of it, this would not be a bad moral for a psychology textbook.

[5]Please do not memorize these laws. I haven't memorized them myself. They are just my attempt to distill into a few aphorisms some observations of which, for some reason, I am particularly fond.

makes the study of personality more inclusive, interesting, important, and even more fun than it would be otherwise. But guess what? This mandate is also personality psychology's biggest problem. In the wrong hands it can lead research to be *over*inclusive, unfocused, or vague. Even in the best of hands, personality psychology can seem to fall far short of what it ought to accomplish. The challenge for a personality psychologist, then, is to maximize the advantages of the field's mandate for breadth and to try to minimize the disadvantages, even though the two are related and therefore may be inseparable.

The same is true about the various approaches within personality psychology. Each is rather good at addressing certain topics and extremely poor at addressing others. (Actually, as we have already discussed, each basic approach usually just ignores the topics it is not good at explaining.) But these two aspects go hand in hand; for example, behaviorism is so effective at changing behavior in part *because* it ignores everything else, whereas the reason the phenomenological approach gives such a nice account of free will is because it ignores how schedules of reinforcement can be shown to shape behavior. The good points come with—and are even sometimes a consequence of—the bad, and vice versa.

This connection between strengths and weaknesses can even occur within individuals. According to one analysis, the personality and ethical "flaws" of various presidents of the United States were precisely the same attributes that allowed them to attain and to effectively use power (Berke, 1998). For example, a certain amount of shiftiness—generally considered a character flaw—might also enable a president to respond flexibly to changing circumstances. A certain amount of stubbornness—also usually considered a flaw—might enable a president to remain steadfast against the temptation to abandon important principles. On the other hand, some traits usually considered virtues, such as truthfulness and consistency, might actually be a handicap in trying to be an effective president.

The same principle may apply to other areas of life, such as basketball coaching. Bobby Knight, the long-time coach at Indiana University (and later at Texas Tech), was once described as vulgar, sarcastic, and intimidating— and also, in the same newspaper article, as "loyal, intelligent, charitable, and [a] principled perfectionist who graduates more players than most college basketball coaches" (Jones, 2003, p. 06E). Are these two aspects of Knight's character connected? They certainly are, in the sense that they belong to the same person; a college that hires one of these Bobby Knights gets the other one for "free." A deeper sense in which they are probably connected is that everybody's personality comes as a package deal. Personality is coherent, and each part stems from and depends upon the others (Block, 2002).

You may or may not ever become president or a Big 10 basketball coach yourself, but take a moment and think about your own strongest point. Now ask, how is it a problem to you? Now think about your own weakest point.

What are its benefits for you? Given the necessary trade-offs, would you *really* like to lose all of your weaknesses and keep all of your strengths? Given the way your strengths and weaknesses are connected to and even grow out of each other, is this even possible?

Personality psychology is perpetually faced with a similar dilemma. If its scope were narrowed, the field would be more manageable and research would become easier to do. But then the study of personality would lose much of what makes it distinctive, important, and interesting. Similarly, each basic approach to personality has made a more or less deliberate decision to ignore some aspects of human psychology. This is a heavy cost to pay, but so far it seems to be necessary in order for each approach to make progress in its chosen area.

The Plan of This Book

This book begins at the beginning, with a brief introduction and an overview of personality psychology that you have almost finished reading. The next two chapters concern how personality psychologists do their research, and will be useful for understanding the material in the chapters that follow. Chapter 2 describes the different kinds of data, or information, that psychologists use to better understand personality, and discusses some of the advantages and disadvantages of each. The chapter's goal is to indelibly engrave the following idea into your psyche: *There are no perfect indicators of personality, there are only clues, and clues are always ambiguous.* Chapter 3 describes some of the ways these data can be analyzed and considers some issues particular to the analysis of personality data.

The second section comprises four chapters that address how people are different from one another, the central concern of the trait assessment approach. Chapter 4 discusses the basic question of whether differences between people are really important (hint: the answer is yes). Chapter 5 describes several ways in which such psychologists measure such differences, the topic of *personality assessment.* Chapter 6 carries that topic further by describing research on personality judgment—how we all do personality assessment in our daily lives. Chapter 7 describes specific examples of how personality traits have been used to understand behavior.

An exciting new direction in psychological research is emerging from rapid, modern advances in biology. These discoveries are beginning to be applied to the study of personality traits and human nature, and some of that research is surveyed in Chapters 8 and 9. Chapter 8 reviews current knowledge about how the architecture and physiology of the nervous system affect behavior and personality. Chapter 9 considers the possibility that personality is inherited to some degree, by looking at two branches of biology: behavioral genetics, which studies how parents might pass on personality traits to their offspring, and evolutionary biology, which tries to find the origins of human nature in the evolutionary history of the species.

The next three chapters consider the psychoanalytic approach, closely identified with Sigmund Freud. Chapter 10 is a basic introduction to psychoanalysis that describes the elements of the structure of the mind and psychological development. Chapter 11 describes how psychoanalytic theory addresses defense mechanisms, mistakes, and humor, and offers an evaluation of this perspective. Chapter 12 concludes the story of psychoanalysis by bringing it into the present day, with some consideration of the "neo-Freudians" (psychoanalysts who came after Freud), object relations theory, and modern research that is relevant to psychoanalytic ideas.

The next pair of chapters considers the topics of thought, experience, and existence. Chapter 13 describes how existential philosophy developed into an approach called *phenomenological* or *humanistic* psychology. The theme is that the particular worldview or set of lenses through which an individual views reality is the central aspect of his or her personality. Chapter 14 takes this point one step further, by considering how individuals' personalities and worldviews—and maybe the whole notion of personality itself—may vary significantly across cultures. Like many people in our society, personality psychologists are becoming increasingly sensitive to cross-cultural issues; some of those are considered in Chapter 14.

The last three substantive chapters describe behaviorism and its modern-day descendants. About seventy years ago, several influential psychologists decided to focus on what people (and animals) actually did rather than on what might be going on in the hidden recesses of their minds. The original psychologists who took this approach were the classic behaviorists, such as John Watson and B. F. Skinner. Over the later decades of the twentieth century, three different derivative theories grew out of behaviorism—theories that increasingly focused on social interaction and even more, on mental (cognitive) processes. Interestingly, all three—the theories of Dollard and Miller, Rotter, and Bandura—were called "social learning theory." Behaviorism and social learning theory are described in Chapter 15. Over time, these theories became increasingly influenced by the rapidly developing separate field of cognitive psychology. The result was research that applies some of the concepts and methods of cognitive psychology to personality. A description of the cognitive system and its relevance for personality is presented in Chapter 16. Some specific applications of cognitive psychology to issues in personality are summarized in Chapter 17.

The final chapter in this book, Chapter 18, offers an overall evaluation of the different perspectives of personality psychology, revisits some of the issues raised in this chapter, and attempts to gaze into the future.

Pigeonholing versus Appreciation of Individual Differences

Personality psychology tends to emphasize how individuals are different from one another. If a critic wanted to be pejorative, he or she could even say that personality psychology tends to categorize, or "pigeonhole," human beings. Some people are uncomfortable with this emphasis, perhaps because they find it implausible, undignified, or both.[6]

Other areas of psychology, by contrast, are more likely to treat all people as if they are the same, or nearly the same. Not only do the various experimental subfields of psychology, such as cognitive and social psychology, tend to ignore differences between people, but also the statistical analyses that are central to their experimental research literally put individual differences into their "error" terms (see Chapter 3).

But here is yet another example of a potential disadvantage working to an advantage (remember that this process can work in either direction, according to Funder's First Law). Although the emphasis of personality psychology often entails categorizing and labeling people, it also leads the field to be extraordinarily sensitive—more sensitive than any other area of psychology—to the fact that people really are different from each other. We do not all like the same things, we are not all attracted to the same people (fortunately), and we do not all desire to enter the same occupation or pursue the same goals in life (again, fortunately). This fact of individual differences is the starting place for all of personality psychology and gives the field a distinctive and humanistic mission of appreciating the uniqueness of each individual.[7] People are different, and it is necessary as well as natural to wonder how and why.

Summary

Personality psychology's unique mission is to try to address the psychological triad of thought, feeling, and behavior, and to explain the psychological functioning of whole individuals. This is an impossible mission, however,

---

[6]I cannot help recalling the old saying that there are two kinds of people in the world: those who think there are two kinds of people in the world, and those who don't.

[7]The focus on individual differences is obvious in the trait and psychoanalytic approaches to personality, which concentrate, respectively, on the quantitative measurement of individual differences and on individual psychological case studies. But less obviously, it is also true— even especially true—about behaviorism, which sees the person as the sum total of his or her unique learning history (see Chapter 15).

so different approaches to personality must limit themselves in various ways. Personality psychology can be organized into five basic approaches: trait, biological, psychoanalytic, phenomenological, and learning/cognitive. Each addresses certain aspects of human psychology quite well and ignores others. The advantages and disadvantages of each approach are probably inseparable. This book is grouped into five sections that survey each basic approach. Sometimes regarded as a field of research that seeks to pigeonhole people, personality psychology's real implication is an appreciation of the ways in which each individual is unique.

PART I

RESEARCH METHODS

A colleague of mine once was selecting the material to include in a general psychology course. She decided to poll her students to find out what they wanted to learn, and listed all the standard topics in psychology she could think of. One topic scored so low it wasn't even funny. The all-time least favorite topic in psychology is . . . research methods.

This finding helps explain why students so often think their psychology professors are strange. Almost without exception, the people who are trained to do psychological research and who teach most college courses seem obsessed with methods. In course after course, hours if not days are spent talking about statistics, data, and research design, leaving some students to wonder, not unreasonably, "What does all this have to do with psychology?" They might even begin to suspect that they are the victims of a diabolical plot to turn a topic—psychology—that should be easy and fun into something that is difficult and boring.

Part of the reason for this, I think, is that research methods are often taught in a narrow and needlessly technical manner that is almost guaranteed to be discouraging. Rules, procedures, and formulas may be thrown at the student with wild abandon and scant explanation until, lost in a sea of confusion, the unfortunate student loses sight of the whole purpose. So, in the next two chapters, I will emphasize two points. First: the basic principles of research methods are neither obscure nor necessarily technical. Second: it is only natural that somebody who wants to learn more about psychology *should* find methods both interesting and useful.

"Oh, if only it were so simple."

To see what I mean, let's imagine an acquaintance who claims he knows how to read minds—he has ESP. Would you be curious to find out whether he really can? Maybe not (what *does* it take to pique your interest?). But if you are, then the next question is, how would you find out? Maybe you can think of a few procedures that would put his claim to the test. You might have him guess which playing card you are thinking of, for example. You might even do this several times and keep track of his right and wrong answers. Suddenly, by choosing what questions to ask and how to ask them, you have ventured into the realm of research design. In effect, you have designed an experiment. By writing down the number of right and wrong answers, you have gathered data. And by trying to interpret the numbers obtained (does twelve right answers out of twenty qualify as ESP?), you have ventured into the world of statistics! Yet all you have done is to apply some good, common sense in order to find something out.

That is what research methods are supposed to do: apply good sense to gather information in order to learn more about questions of interest. The only way to find out something new—about behavior, the mind, or anything else—is to follow a set of procedures that begin with observation—looking at what you want to know about—and end with "data analysis," which means trying to summarize and understand the observations you have recorded.

Chapter 2 presents a detailed account of the kinds of observations that are relevant to understanding personality. All observations are "data," and I categorize these into four basic kinds, called S, I, L, and B data (which can be rearranged to yield the cheerful but misspelled acronym, "BLIS"). Chapter 3 summarizes some issues about the quality of data—their reliability, validity, and generalizability. Chapter 3 also addresses "research design," which is the plan for how one intends to go about gathering data, and then the issue of data analysis I believe to be the most important: how to interpret the "effect size," or strength, of the results that your research has obtained. Finally, Chapter 3 considers ethics in research, an issue relevant to psychology and every other branch of science.

CLUES TO PERSONALITY:
THE BASIC SOURCES
OF DATA

Many years ago, the prominent personality psychologist Henry Murray commented that in order to understand personality, first you have to look at it. This might seem like an obvious comment, but, like many obvious comments, when thought about carefully it raises an interesting question. If you want to "look at" personality, what do you look at, exactly? The answer to this question is the topic of this chapter.

I maintain that to look at an individual's personality, you can do four different things. First, and perhaps most obviously, you can ask the person directly for his or her own opinion about what he or she is like. This is exactly what personality psychologists usually do. Second, you can find out what other people who know the person well say about him or her. Third, you can check on how the person is faring in life. And finally, you can actually look at what the person does, and try to measure his or her behavior as directly and objectively as possible.

In the end, you need to look at personality in all of these ways, because personality is complicated. It is manifested by all of the characteristic ways in which the individual thinks, feels, and behaves—the psychological triad mentioned in Chapter 1. He or she might be deeply afraid of certain things, or attracted to particular kinds of people, or obsessed with accomplishing some highly personal and idiosyncratic goals. Patterns of thought, emotion, and behavior such as these typically are complex and may be revealed in many different areas of behavior and life. Therefore, when you try to learn about or measure personality, you cannot base this endeavor on just one kind of information. You need many kinds.

This brings us to **Funder's Second Law**: *There are no perfect indicators of personality; there are only clues, and clues are always ambiguous.*

Data Are Clues

The observable aspects of personality are best characterized as a set of clues. These clues are always ambiguous because an individual's personality is something that resides, hidden, inside that individual. Because you can never see it directly, you must infer both its existence and its nature, and this inference is forever uncertain.

Inferences about personality must be based on indications that *can* be observed. These might include how a person answers questions, what that person says to his or her psychotherapist, what that person does in daily life, or how he or she responds to certain situations set up in a laboratory. The clues can be almost anything, but it is important to remember that any one of them alone will *always* be ambiguous. The psychologist's task is to piece these clues together, much like pieces of a puzzle, into a convincing and useful portrait of the individual's personality.

In that sense, a psychologist trying to understand an individual's personality is a bit like a detective trying to solve a mystery: clues may abound, but the trick is to correctly interpret what they mean. For example, a detective comes on the scene of a burglary and finds fingerprints on the windowsill and footprints in the flowerbed outside. These are clues. The detective would be foolish to ignore them. But, it might turn out that the fingerprints belong to the careless police officer who first arrived at the scene and the footprints belong to an innocent gardener. These possibilities are not reasons for the detective to ignore the clues, but they are reasons to be wary about their meaning.

The situation is similar for a personality psychologist. The psychologist might look at an individual's behavior, test scores, degree of success in daily living, or responses to a laboratory assessment procedure. These are all clues about personality. The psychologist, like the detective, would be foolish not to gather as many of them as possible. Also like the detective, the psychologist should maintain a healthy skepticism about the possibility that some or all of them might be misleading.

But this skepticism should not go too far. It can sometimes be tempting to conclude that because one kind of clue might be uninformative or misleading, the clue should be ignored. At different times, various psychologists have argued that self-report questionnaires, demographic data, peer's descriptions of personality, "projective" personality tests, summaries of clinical cases, or laboratory assessment procedures should never be used. The reason given? The method can produce misleading results.

No competent detective would think this way. To ignore a source of data because it might be misleading would be like ignoring the footprint under the window because it *might* not belong to the burglar. A much bet-

"Are you just pissing and moaning, or can you verify what you're saying with data?"

ter strategy is to gather all the clues you can with the resources you have. Any of these clues might be misleading; on a bad day, they all might be. This is no excuse to not gather them. The only alternative to gathering information that might be misleading is to gather no information. That is not progress.

Funder's Third Law, then, is this: *Something beats nothing, two times out of three.*

Four Kinds of Clues

Four general kinds of clues can be used to try to understand personality. Each provides vital information, but equally important, each has shortcomings as well. The advantages and shortcomings are probably inseparable (which is no surprise, if you remember Funder's First Law). Before we begin, it is worth emphasizing once again that all of these clues are important and useful, but none is perfect. The imperfections are inevitable and are not a reason to ignore any of these sources of information. Instead, they are precisely the reason you need all of them.

The principle behind the clues is this: To find out what a person is like, you can do any of four different things: (1) You simply ask the person in question for his or her *own* evaluation of his or her personality; (2) you ask his or her acquaintances for their evaluations; (3) you see how the person is faring in life; or (4) you watch, as directly as you can, what the person actually does. Clues of these four types can be called S, I, L, and B data.[1] As you will see, each of them is potentially informative about personality, and each is potentially misleading.

Ask the Person Directly: S Data

If you want to know what a person is like, why not just ask? The easiest way to find out about somebody's personality is to go straight to the source and get his or her own opinion, and personality psychologists often do just that. **S data** are self-judgments. The person simply tells the psychologist (usually on a questionnaire) the degree to which he or she is dominant, or friendly, or conscientious. This might be done on a 9-point scale, where the person indicates a number from 1 ("I am not at all dominant") to 9 ("I am very dominant"). Or, the procedure might be even simpler: The person reads a statement, such as "I usually dominate the discussions I have with others," and then responds true or false. According to most research evidence, the way people describe themselves by and large matches the way they are described by others (Funder, 1999; McCrae, 1982; Watson, 1989). But the principle behind the use of S data is that the world's best expert about your personality is very probably *you.*

It is important to understand that there is nothing the least bit tricky or complicated about S data. S data are straightforward and simple because the psychologist does not interpret what the participant says about himself or herself, or ask about one thing in order to find out about something else. The questionnaires used to gather S data have what is called **face validity**— they are intended to measure what they actually seem to measure, on their face. They ask questions that are directly and obviously related to the construct they are designed to measure.

For instance, right here and now you could make up a face-valid, S-data personality questionnaire. How about a new "friendliness" scale? You might include items such as "I really like most people" (to be answered true or false, a true answer assumed to reflect friendliness), "I go to many parties," and "I think people are horrible and mean" (here answering false would raise the friendliness score). There is nothing subtle or tricky about a scale like this;

---

[1]If you have read the writing of other psychologists, or even the earlier editions of this book, you may notice that these labels keep changing as do, in subtle ways, the kinds of data to which they refer. Jack Block (Block & Block, 1980) also propounded four types of data, calling them L, O, S, and T. Raymond Cattell (Cattell, 1950, 1965) propounded three types called L, Q, and T. T. Moffitt (Moffitt, 1991; Caspi, 1998) proposed five types, called S, T, O, R, and I (or STORI). In most respects, Block's L, O, S, and T data match my L, I, S, and B data; Cattell's L, Q, and T data match my L (and I), S, and B data; and Moffitt's T and O match my B, and her R, S, and I match my L, S, and I, respectively. But the definitions are not exactly equivalent across systems.

the more ways in which the participant describes himself or herself as friendly (or *not* as unfriendly), the higher a friendliness score that person earns. In essence, all our new questionnaire really does is ask, over and over in various phrasings, "Are you a friendly person?"

Another kind of S data can be obtained by asking questions that are more open-ended. For example, one current research project asks participants to list, on a blank sheet of paper, their "personal strivings" (see Chapter 17). These are defined as "objectives you are typically trying to accomplish or attain." Some of the strivings college students have reported include "make my mother proud of me," "be honest in my speech and behavior," and "enjoy life." These responses all constitute S data because they are the participant's own direct descriptions of goals he or she is trying to accomplish, and they are used simply to assess the nature of a person's goals (Emmons & King, 1988; Emmons & McAdams, 1991).

By far, S data are the most frequently used basis for personality assessment. Not only are the questionnaires in *Self* magazine and *Cosmopolitan* (such as "Rate your love potential!") S data, but so are most of the questionnaires used by personality researchers, although the latter are usually more careful in their methods of test construction and validation. (For more on these methods, see Chapter 5.) The reason for the widespread use of S data is obvious: there is no easier and less expensive way to gather so much information about people. If you want S data on five hundred people, all you have to do is print five hundred questionnaires, pass them out to an Introductory Psychology class, and then collect them.

"Next question: I believe that life is a constant striving for balance, requiring frequent trade-offs between morality and necessity, within a cyclic pattern of joy and sadness, forging a trail of bittersweet memories until one slips, inevitably, into the jaws of death. Agree or disagree?"

As a source of information for understanding personality, S data have three advantages and three disadvantages.

ADVANTAGE: BEST EXPERT

Very likely, you are the world's foremost expert about yourself. There are several reasons to expect this is true. First, while some close acquaintances might be with you in many situations in your life, you are present in all of them. In the 1960s, there was a popular book called the *Whole Earth Catalog*, throughout the margins of which were sprinkled small aphorisms. My favorite read, "Wherever you go, there you are." This aphorism describes an important advantage of S data. You live your life in many different settings; even your closest acquaintances see you only within one or at most a few of them. The only person on earth in a position to really know how you act at home, and at school, and at work, and with your enemies, and with your friends, and with your parents is you. This means that you have a unique perspective on the general nature of your personality and that the S data you can provide can reflect complex, general aspects of character that no other data source could access.

A second possible informational advantage of S data is that much, though perhaps not all, of your inner mental life that would be invisible to anyone else is visible to you. You know your own fantasies, hopes, dreams, and fears; you directly experience your emotions. Other people can know about these things only if you reveal them somehow, intentionally or not. To the extent that these aspects of inner, mental life are private and important to an understanding of personality, therefore, S data would seem to provide a unique and indispensable route for finding out about them (Spain, Eaton, & Funder, 2000).

ADVANTAGE: CAUSAL FORCE

Because S data reflect what you think of yourself, they have a way of creating their own truth. What you will attempt to do depends on what you think you are capable of, and your view of the kind of person you are has important effects on the goals that you set for yourself. This idea—the role of what are sometimes called **efficacy expectations**—is considered more fully in Chapter 16. It is also the case that people will work hard to bring others to treat them in a manner that confirms their self-conception, a phenomenon called **self-verification** (Swann & Ely, 1984). For example, if you think you are a friendly person, or intelligent, or ethical, you might make extra efforts to make sure other people see you that way too. Part of the reason S data are important is that your view of yourself does not just reflect what you think about yourself, it may be one of the *causes* of what you do.

ADVANTAGE: SIMPLE AND EASY

As mentioned previously, S data simply cannot be beat for cost-effectiveness. As you will see, other kinds of data require the psychologist to recruit informants, look up information in public records, or find some way to observe the participant directly. These are time-consuming and therefore expensive procedures. But to obtain S data, all the psychologist has to do is write up a questionnaire that asks about what he or she wants to know; for example, how friendly or how conscientious are you? Then the psychologist prints copies of the questionnaire and hands them out to everybody within reach. (Or, nowadays, the psychologist may set each person in front of a computer terminal or post the test on the Internet). The psychologist then will have a great deal of interesting, important information about a lot of people, very quickly and at relatively little cost.

Psychological research is done on a very low budget compared to research in any of the other sciences; the research of many psychologists is "funded" essentially by whatever they can cadge from the university's supply closet along with what they can spare from their own salaries. Even psychologists who do have research grants from the government usually have much less money to spend than their counterparts in fields such as biology, chemistry, and physics.[2] The importance of the inexpensive nature of S data, therefore, is difficult to exaggerate. Sometimes, for very real and compelling reasons, it is the only kind of data you can get.

DISADVANTAGE: MAYBE THEY WON'T TELL YOU

As discussed earlier, an important advantage of S data is that each person is the only one who knows how he or she acts in all of the situations of his or her life, and the only one who knows about the nature of his or her private experience. However, this knowledge only translates into S data if the individual is willing to reveal it. There is no way to force a person to provide an accurate account of his or her own personality if he or she does not want to.

Perhaps the person from whom the psychologist is obtaining S data is ashamed of some aspect of his or her personality or behavior. Perhaps the person wishes to brag, to claim some virtue that he or she does not actually possess. Perhaps the person prefers to keep some aspects of his or her personality private. There is no way to prevent a participant from withholding information for any of these reasons (in fact, one can sympathize with these

---

[2]This discrepancy might make sense (a) if people were easier to understand than cells, chemicals, or particles, or (b) if it were less important to understand people than cells, chemicals, or particles. Both of these presumptions—if indeed anybody holds them—are highly doubtful. Write your congressman.

"Surely you can tell <u>me</u> your secret identity."

reasons), but if the person does choose to withhold information, the accuracy of the S data he or she provides will be compromised. There is little the psychologist can do about it, and in many cases he or she won't even know.

DISADVANTAGE: MAYBE THEY CAN'T TELL YOU

Even if an individual is—for some reason—entirely *willing* to tell a psychologist everything he or she knows about himself or herself, the individual may not be *able* to do it. A person's memory of his or her own behavior (or anything else, for that matter) is finite and imperfect; the information he or she does happen to remember is not necessarily the most important. The Freudians would point out that some particularly important memories may be actively *repressed*; they might be so painful to remember that the ego prevents them from emerging into consciousness (see Chapter 11).

Another factor is simple lack of insight. Some people—maybe all people—lack the perspicacity to see all aspects of their own personality accurately. The self-judgment of personality, like the judgment of personality more generally, can be a complex and difficult undertaking that is unlikely to be 100 percent successful (Funder, 1999). For most if not all people, there are important aspects of their personalities that they are simply the last to know about, even though these aspects might be obvious to everyone else.

For example, research has identified a certain kind of person, called the *narcissist,* who characteristically has an exaggerated idea of his or her own abilities and accomplishments (John & Robins, 1994). As a result, anything he or she says about himself or herself must be taken with a large grain of salt. Do you know anybody like this?

Another, even more common failing of self-judgment stems from what could be called the "fish-and-water" effect (Kolar, Funder, & Colvin, 1996). People are so used to the way they characteristically react and behave that their own actions can stop seeming remarkable. For example, you might have been frugal for so much of your life that you no longer even consider the possibility of spending money. The result is that *frugal* is one of the last terms you would think to use to characterize yourself—you have essentially forgotten that there is any other way to be. But when your acquaintances describe you, one of the first things they may mention is what a cheapskate you are. In this way, the aspects of your behavior that are the most characteristic of you might become invisible over time. You may not know that you have personality traits for roughly the same reason that it is said that fish do not know they are wet.

Concealment, failure of memory, active repression, and lack of insight can cause S data to provide less accurate renditions of personality than psychologists might wish.

DISADVANTAGE: TOO SIMPLE AND TOO EASY

You have already seen that the single biggest advantage of S data, the one that makes them the most widely used form of data in personality psychology, is that they are so cheap and easy to get. If you remember Funder's First Law (about advantages being disadvantages), you can guess what is coming next: S data are so cheap and easy that they are probably overused.

The issue is not that there is anything especially problematic about S data; they have their advantages and disadvantages, just like all of the other types of data. Moreover, Funder's Third Law (about something usually beating nothing) also comes into play here; you definitely should gather S data if that is all your resources will allow. The problem is that S data have been used by so many investigators, to the exclusion of other kinds of data, that some investigators seem to have forgotten that other kinds of data even exist. But there are three other kinds, each with their own special advantages and disadvantages, which I will now consider.

Ask Somebody Who Knows: I Data

A second way to learn about an individual's personality is to gather the opinions of the people who know that person well in daily life. *I* stands for "informant"; **I data** are **judgments**, by knowledgeable human informants, of general attributes of the individual's personality, such as traits. There are many ways to gather such judgments. My own research usually focuses on college students. To gather information about the personalities of these students, I ask each to provide the names and phone numbers of the two people on campus who know him or her the best. These people are then called and asked to come to the lab to describe the student's personality. These informants are asked questions such as "On a 9-point scale, how dominant, sociable, aggressive, or shy is your acquaintance?" The numbers yielded by judgments like these constitute I data.

When I say that these informants are knowledgeable, I mean that they know well the person they are judging. The informants might be the individual's acquaintances from daily life (as in my own research) or they might be co-workers or clinical psychologists who have worked with the individual for an extended period of time. The key aspect of the informants' knowledgeableness is that they know the person well, not that they necessarily have a great deal of formal knowledge about psychology—usually they do not. Moreover, they may not need it; usually close acquaintanceship paired with common sense is enough to allow people to make judgments of each other with impressive accuracy (Funder, 1993). Only when the judgments are of a technical nature (e.g., the diagnosis of a personality disorder) does training in clinical psychology become relevant.

Another important element of the definition is that I data are **judgments;** they derive from somebody observing somebody else in whatever contexts they happen to have encountered them, and then rendering a general opinion (e.g., how dominant the person is) on the basis of such observation. In that sense, I data are judgmental, subjective, and irreducibly human.[3]

I data, or their equivalent, are frequently used in daily life. The ubiquitous "letter of recommendation" that employers and schools often insist on receiving are intended to provide I data—the writer's opinion of the candidate—to the personnel manager or selection committee. Ordinary gossip is filled with I data because few topics of conversation are more interesting. And the first thing some people do, when asked out on a date, is to ask around: do you know anything about him? What's he like? The answers are I data, and these data can be useful.

As a source of information for understanding personality, I data have four advantages and three disadvantages.

ADVANTAGE: LARGE AMOUNT OF INFORMATION

A close acquaintance who provides a description of someone else's personality is in a position, in principle, to base that description on hundreds of behaviors in dozens of situations. The typical informant in my own research

---

[3]Their use is not restricted to describing humans, though. I-data personality ratings have been successfully used to assess the personalities of chimpanzees, gorillas, monkeys, hyenas, dogs, cats, donkeys, pigs, rats, guppies, and octopuses! (Gosling & John, 1999).

is a college roommate. This person would have observed the "target" of his or her judgment working, relaxing, interacting with a boyfriend or girlfriend, reacting to an A grade, receiving medical school rejection letters, and so on. Such behaviors in context not only are commonly observed by acquaintances, but also are very important.

ADVANTAGE: REAL-WORLD BASIS

The second advantage of most I data is that they are derived from the observation of behavior in the real world. Much of the other information about people that psychologists use is not; psychologists often base their conclusions on information that comes from contrived tests of one kind or another, or on the observation of behavior in carefully constructed and controlled environments. The fact that I data ultimately derive from behaviors performed in real contexts may give I data an extra chance of being relevant to important aspects of personality that affect important outcomes.

ADVANTAGE: COMMON SENSE

Recall that I data are not simply counts or mechanical combinations of the behaviors the informant has seen; they comprise the informant's judgments about what the behaviors mean, in general, about the individual's personality. A third advantage of I data derives from this basis in human judgment. In the final analysis, I data are distillations of behavioral observations that are filtered through the informant's common sense. This fact allows I data to take account of the context and the intention of behavior to a degree that no other source of information about people can equal.

An informant with ordinary common sense who transforms an observation of behavior into a judgment of personality will take two kinds of contexts into account (Funder, 1991). The first is the immediate situation. The psychological meaning of an aggressive behavior, for example, can change radically as a function of the situation that prompted it. It makes a difference whether you screamed and yelled at somebody who accidentally bumped you in a crowded elevator, or at somebody who deliberately rammed your car in a parking lot. And, if you see an acquaintance crying, you will—appropriately—draw different conclusions about his or her personality depending on whether the crying was caused by the death of a close friend or by the fact that it is raining and your acquaintance was really hoping to play Ultimate Frisbee today.

A second kind of context is provided by the other behaviors that an informant may know the individual in question has performed. Imagine that you see an acquaintance give a lavish gift to his or her worst enemy. Your interpretation of the meaning of this behavior may (and should) vary depending on whether this acquaintance is someone who, in the past, has been consistently generous, or someone who has been consistently sneaky and Machiavellian. In the first case, the gift may be a sincere peace offering. In the second case, there are grounds for suspecting that some sort of manipulative scheme may be afoot (Funder, 1991). Or say your acquaintance is upset after an argument with a friend. Your interpretation of this reaction, and even your conclusion about how serious the argument was, depends on whether you know this acquaintance to be someone who is easily upset, as opposed to someone who tends to be disturbed only under extreme circumstances.

Applying information about these two kinds of contexts to the judgment of personality is a complex matter. The science of psychology has not come even close to developing a formal set of rules, procedures, or computer programs for interpreting behavioral observations in this manner, and is unlikely to do so anytime soon. The considerations are just too complex; an overwhelming number of possible situational and contextual variations interact with the implications of too many different kinds of behavior. And no catalog of these variations even exists. Yet, surprisingly, integrating diverse information into a coherent impression of personality is not so difficult for the average human judge. The intuitions provided by ordinary common sense seem to do it easily, naturally, and almost automatically.

ADVANTAGE: CAUSAL FORCE

The fourth consideration that makes I data important for understanding personality is quite different from the other three. Because I data are, in a sense, a reflection of the social world of the individual being described—they represent opinions of people who interact with him or her daily—they have an importance that goes beyond their value as a description of the person. I data are the person's reputation, and as one of Shakespeare's characters once noted, reputation may be a person's most important possession (see also Hogan, 1998). In *Othello*, Cassio laments,

> Reputation, reputation, reputation! O, I have lost my reputation! I have lost the immortal part of myself, and what remains is bestial. My reputation, Iago, my reputation![4]

Why does reputation matter so much? The opinions that others have of your personality greatly affect both your opportunities and expectancies. If a person who is considering hiring you believes you to be competent and conscientious, you are much more likely to enjoy the opportunity of getting the job than you would be if that person thought you did not have those

---

[4]Iago was unimpressed. He replied, in part, "Reputation is an idle and most false imposition, oft got without merit, and lost without deserving" (*Othello*, Act 2, Scene 3).

FIGURE 2.1 NATHANIEL PARKER AS CASSIO AND KENNETH BRANAGH AS IAGO   Cassio was worried about his reputation. I data had not been invented yet.

qualities. This will be true no matter how competent and conscientious you really are. Similarly, someone who believes you to be honest will be more likely to lend you money than someone who believes otherwise. Your actual honesty is a separate matter. If you impress people who meet you as warm and friendly, you will develop more friendships than you would if you appeared cold and aloof. If someone you wish to date asks around and gets a good report, your chances of success can rise dramatically—the reverse will happen if your acquaintances describe you as creepy. Again, these appearances may be false and unfair, but their consequences will nonetheless be important.

Moreover, there is evidence (considered in Chapter 6) that to some degree people become what others expect them to be. If others for some reason expect you to be sociable, aloof, or even intelligent, you may tend to become just that! This phenomenon is sometimes called the **expectancy effect** (Rosenthal & Rubin, 1978) and sometimes called **behavioral confirmation** (Snyder & Swann, 1978). By either name, it provides another reason to care about what others think of you.

Now consider some disadvantages of I data as sources of information about personality.

"Of course. Your reputation precedes you, sir."

DISADVANTAGE: LIMITED AMOUNT OF INFORMATION

The first disadvantage of I data is the reciprocal of the first advantage considered. Although the acquaintance who might be a source for I data has seen a person's behavior in a large number and variety of situations, he or she still has not been with that person *all* of the time. There is a good deal that even someone's closest friends do not know. Their knowledge is limited in two ways.

The first limitation is that there is a sense in which each person lives inside a series of separate compartments, and each of those compartments contains different people. For instance, much of your life is probably spent at work or at school, and within each of those environments are numerous individuals whom you might see quite frequently there but no place else. When you go home, you see a different group of people; at church or in a club you see still another group; and so forth. The interesting psychological fact is that you may to some degree be a different person in each of these different environments. As William James, one of the first American psychologists, noted long ago,

> Many a youth who is demure enough before his parents and teachers swears and swaggers like a pirate among his "tough" young friends. We do not show ourselves to our children as to our club-companions, to our customers as to the laborers we employ, to our masters and employers as to our intimate friends. (James, 1890, p. 294)

One telling example of what James was getting at concerns an experience that is typical of modern college students. When a student leaves his or her parents' home to attend college, his or her social environment changes drastically. The essence of the change is not so much that college towns are unique places, though they are to some extent, but that nearly everybody in this new environment is a stranger. The student is suddenly surrounded by a large number of people of about the same age who have no preexisting knowledge of that student; they do not know (yet) whether he or she is the class clown or a workaholic or a jock or a preppy or an artist. (A similar situation can result from joining the military.)

This experience can be disorienting but also extremely liberating, especially for students who have lived for a long time in a small town, with the same group of people, or perhaps in a constraining family. They are suddenly free of the expectations of others and have an opportunity to design a whole new personality for themselves. Many students do just that, trying out new identities that have long been latent within their characters, in front of a new audience of peers who do not know that they are seeing something new. The students who avail themselves of this opportunity learn at least as much from the experience as from any of their classes.

Now consider the first visit home. In many cases, the person who returns for winter break seems very different from the one who left in August. The parents and perhaps even the student's hometown friends may become frustrated and angry when they try to deal in their accustomed way with someone who no longer fits their image of him or her; the student may be equally frustrated and perhaps also anxious about the stability of his or her new identity among people with old expectations. Although this experience can be traumatic, the personality experimentation and growth that it allows are probably good things. If parents, friends, and the student are all patient, they eventually can get used to the "new" person or, in some cases, once the period of experimentation is over the "old" person might return (but they shouldn't get their hopes up). In the present context, the point to appreciate is that neither a description of the student's personality provided by hometown friends and parents nor the description drawn by college friends will tell the whole story of what that student is really like.

Another example of the complexities introduced by the compartmentalization of lives is what happens when people who have adjusted to one identity, developed in and adapted to one life environment, confront the same person in a different environment where he or she may have developed a very different identity. You may be a conscientious and reliable employee much appreciated by your boss, but you will probably be disconcerted if you suddenly encounter him or her at a wild, Friday-night party where you are dancing with a lampshade on your head. (Does anyone actually do this?) At work seeing your boss is not a problem, but at that party, what do you do? In general, people are more comfortable if those who inhabit the compartments of their lives just stay put and not cross over into compartments in which they do not belong.

Occasionally, I am standing with my daughters at the supermarket, contemplating the latest sale on hamburger, when I realize that one of my university students is right next to me, doing exactly the same thing. Although in general I like my students, I think this kind of encounter is mildly upsetting for us both. At best we exchange awkward greetings; more often we continue to gaze vaguely forward and pretend not to have seen each other.

Why? Is either of us really so ashamed to be seen in the supermarket? No, but at the university both of us have well-defined roles that we know how to perform. I know how to relate to a student; most students know how to act with a professor. At the supermarket these roles are irrelevant, so we are left without a script and suddenly neither of us knows quite how to act.

In some cases boundary violation can be upsetting. Once my wife and I hired a babysitter and set out for a romantic dinner. When we arrived at the restaurant, the hostess who seated us was one of my wife's students, who happened to have failed one of her quizzes that very afternoon (and was still teary-eyed about it). Another of my wife's students was sitting at the next table. The evening amounted to less than we had hoped. On another occasion, I was at the university gym, taking a shower. At the next spigot, similarly soaped up, was one of my students. "Dr. Funder," he said, "would it be a problem if I handed in my paper a week late?"

The point here is that people, to a certain degree, are different in different environments. I am not exactly the same person in the classroom as I am at the gym—though surely there is some resemblance—nor are students always as studious as they appear in the lecture hall. Any acquaintance who might provide I data about you is likely to know you in one or, at best, a few of your different environmental compartments. To the extent that you are a different person in these different compartments, the I data provided by any one person will have limited validity as a description of what you are like in general.

The second limitation is that some of every person's life is private in a deep sense, even from a close acquaintance. Each person has an inner mental life that is shared sparingly, if at all. Each has private fantasies, fears, hopes, and dreams. These provide important information about personality, but they can be reflected in I data only to the extent that they have been revealed or shared with somebody. I data provide a view of personality from the outside; information about the inner psychology of thoughts, emotions, and experience must be obtained in some other manner—in most cases, via S data (McCrae, 1994; Spain, Eaton, & Funder, 2000).

DISADVANTAGE: ERROR

Because informants are only human, the judgments of personality that they offer will sometimes be mistaken. The previous section proposed that I data provided by a close acquaintance can be based, in principle, on the observation of hundreds of behaviors in dozens of situational contexts. But that is just in principle. What happens in practice may be a different matter because no informant can remember everything. The capacity of human memory is remarkable, but it is neither infinite nor perfect. Therefore, an informant's judgment is based on what he or she happens to remember about the person being described, and that will necessarily be less than everything that might be relevant.

The behaviors that are most likely to stick in memory are those that are extreme, unusual, or emotionally arousing (Tversky & Kahneman, 1973). This fact could have important consequences for I data. An informant judging an acquaintance might have a tendency to forget the ordinary events he or she observed but remember vividly the fistfight the acquaintance got involved in (once in four years), or the time he or she got drunk (for the first and only time), or how he or she accidentally knocked a bowl of guacamole dip onto the white shag carpeting (perhaps an unusual act by a normally graceful person). The behaviors that a person performs consistently, day in and day out, may be those that are most informative about personality. If this is so, then the tendency by informants to especially remember the unusual or dramatic is likely to lead to judgments that are less accurate than they could be.

DISADVANTAGE: BIAS

Errors are not always so innocent. Personality judgment can be unfair as well as simply mistaken. Because I data consist of acquaintances' and other informants' judgments of personality, they can be affected profoundly by whatever biases these informants may have about the person they are judging. In my own research, as I mentioned, I try to find the two available people who know the person best.

But there are potential pitfalls in this practice. Perhaps the informant I recruit, unbeknownst to me and to the participant, does not like or even detests the person he or she is being recruited to describe. On the other hand, perhaps he or she is secretly in love with the participant! Perhaps the informant is in competition with the participant for some prize, job, boyfriend or girlfriend—all quite common in college. Detesting, loving, or competing with someone can and typically does greatly damage the ability to judge him or her accurately. For this reason, the researcher should always get at least two informants whenever possible. This practice does not solve the problem of potential bias, but it does help.

Biases of a more general type are also potentially important. Perhaps the participant is a member of a minority racial group and the informant is a racist. Perhaps the informant is a sexist who has strong and wrong ideas about what all women are like. If you are a college student, and are from an area where few people go to college, you may find that people have an image of you largely based on this fact. If you are studying psychology, you may have experienced another kind of bias. Your relatives and acquaintances might have all sorts of ideas about your personality based on their knowledge that you are a "psych major." Is there any truth to these ideas?

Life Outcomes: L Data

Have you ever been arrested? Have you graduated from high school? Are you married? How many times have you been hospitalized? Are you employed? What is your annual income? Even, what is your zip code? The answers to questions like these constitute L or "life" data. **L data** are more or less easily verifiable, concrete, real-life outcomes of possible psychological significance.

This type of data can be obtained from archival records such as a police blotter, a medical file, or a tax return, or by asking the participant directly. An advantage of using archival records is that they can be highly accurate and are not prone to the potential biases of self-report or the judgments of others. But the process of getting access to archival data can be tricky and sometimes raises ethical issues concerning privacy. An advantage of asking the participants for this information directly is that access is easier and raises fewer ethical issues, because if they don't want the researcher to know, they don't have to tell. But participants sometimes have faulty memories (e.g., exactly how old were you when you had the measles?) and also may distort their reports of some kinds of information (e.g., why were you arrested? what is your income?).

L data can be thought of as the results or "residue" of personality, rather than directly reflecting personality itself. They are manifestations of how what a person has done has affected his or her world, including important life outcomes, health, and the physical environment. A person who is low in the trait of conscientiousness may perform less well at work and therefore be less likely to be promoted (Barrick & Mount, 1991); his or her L data of annual income will be a lower number. A person who has smoked for many years is likely to have poorer lung health than someone who has managed to avoid acquiring that dangerous habit. Even your zip code can be informative. In California, auto insurance companies use zip codes to predict the probability that the policyholder will get in an accident, and set premiums accordingly. (It is not clear whether accident-prone people move to certain zip codes, or living in certain zip codes makes you accident-prone. The insurance companies don't care.) For a final example, consider the condition of your bedroom. Because you live there, its current state is determined by what you have done in it, which is determined to some degree by the kind of person you are. To the degree the claim I just made is true, then your personality could be assessed through another bit of L data—a survey of your bedroom!

Recent research has attempted to do just that. A study of college students sent observers into their bedrooms to rate their appearances on several different dimensions. These ratings were then compared to personality assessments obtained separately. It turns out that people with tidy bedrooms tended to be conscientious, and people whose rooms contained a wide variety of books and magazines tended to be open to experience (Gosling, Ko, Mannarelli, & Morris, 2002). Conscientious people make their beds. Curious people read a lot. But a person's degree of extraversion cannot be diagnosed from looking at his or her bedroom—the rooms of extraverts and introverts looked about the same.

No matter how they are gathered, as information about human personality, L data have two advantages and one big disadvantage.

ADVANTAGE: INTRINSIC IMPORTANCE

The first reason L data are important is that often—when they concern outcomes more important than the condition of one's bedroom—they constitute exactly what the psychologist needs to know. To an applied psychologist working as a parole officer, a social worker, a school counselor, an insurance underwriter, or a medical researcher, L data are the very justification for his or her professional existence. These professionals are supposed to predict and even influence someone's criminal behavior, employment status, success in school, accident proneness, or health. The goal of every applied psychologist is to predict and even have a positive effect on the real-life outcomes of his or her clients. Those real-life outcomes are L data.

ADVANTAGE: PSYCHOLOGICAL RELEVANCE

The second reason L data are important is that they are in many cases strongly affected by and uniquely informative about psychological variables. Some people have a psychological makeup that makes them more likely than others to engage in criminal behavior. Other psychological attributes, such as a certain amount of conscientiousness, are necessary to hold a job for any length of time or to graduate from school (Borman, Hanson, & Hedge, 1997). As we just learned, conscientious people also keep their rooms neat. And, an increasing amount of research is showing that an individual's personality can have an important effect on his or her health (e.g., Friedman et al., 1995; Horner, 1998; Twisk et al., 1998).

Clinical psychologists have long believed that a simple bit of L data, having never been married by age forty, is a fairly reliable marker of psychopathology. That is to say, people who reach the age of forty having never married are more likely to exhibit one or more forms of mental illness than are those who have been married at least once by then. However, one must be careful with this little nugget of psychological lore. Lots of people who are unmarried at age forty are not mentally ill at all. It is also important to realize that mental illness is quite rare among both married and unmarried forty-year-olds. It just seems to be *less* rare among the unmarried ones. Moreover, there are many reasons besides mental illness why one might never have married by age forty, such as working all day in a single-sex workplace, being economically unable to support a family, or simply having given other goals a higher priority than finding a spouse.

This observation is true about the other varieties of L data as well; they are often influenced by many factors that are *not* psychological. A person's criminal behavior is affected to an important degree by his or her neighborhood and degree of economic opportunity. During a recession, many people lose their jobs for reasons that have nothing to do with their degree of conscientiousness or any other psychological attribute. Whether one graduates from school may depend on finances rather than dedication. It can be very frustrating to be a careful driver who lives in the same zip code as people who are always wrecking their cars. A messy room may be the result of messy guests, not the personality of the inhabitant. And health might be affected by mental outlook, but it is also a function of sanitation, exposure to toxins, and the availability of vaccines, among other things.

"According to my Zip Code, I prefer non-spicy foods, enjoy tennis more than golf, subscribe to at least one news-oriented periodical, own between thirty and thiry-five ties, never buy lemon-scented products, and have a power tool in my basement, but none of that is true."

DISADVANTAGE: MULTIDETERMINATION

These observations bring us directly to the biggest disadvantage of L data: They are sometimes not even slightly informative about psychological attributes. Frequently, L data are influenced by too many other factors to reveal much, by themselves, about a person's psychology.

This disadvantage has an important implication: If your business is to predict L data from an understanding of a person's psychology, no matter how good you are at your job, your chances of success are severely limited. No matter how well you understand an individual's psychological makeup, your ability to predict his or her criminal behavior, employment status, school graduation, health, accidents, marriage, or anything else is constrained by the degree to which any of these outcomes is affected by the individual's personality in the first place.

This fact needs to be kept in mind more often. Psychologists who have the difficult job of trying to predict L data are often criticized severely for their limited success, and they are sometimes even more severe in their criticism of themselves. But even in the absolute best case, a psychologist can only predict something from psychological data to the degree it is psychologically caused. L data often are psychologically caused only to a small degree. Therefore, a psychologist who attains any degree of success at predicting criminality, employment, school performance, health, or marriage has accomplished something rather remarkable.

Watch What the Person Does: B Data

When you are trying to get to know somebody, you will naturally watch his or her actions very closely. This makes sense, because the most visible indication of an individual's personality is what he or she does. The final way to try to learn about someone's personality, therefore, is to observe him or her as directly as possible. One might watch the person's behavior in a setting in real life or in a laboratory experiment. Either way, the information recorded from such direct observation constitutes **B data**; the *B*, as you probably have figured out already, stands for "behavior."

The idea of B data is that participants are found or put into some sort of a situation, sometimes referred to as a "testing" situation, and then their behavior is directly observed.[5] The situation might be a context in the person's real life (e.g., a student's classroom) or some more artificial setting that

---

[5]Other writers, and the First Edition of this book, have called this kind of data T (for "test") data. This label turned out to be hopelessly confusing because most personality tests are not T data, so I have abandoned it.

a psychologist has set up in an experimental laboratory. B data also can be derived from certain kinds of personality tests. What all these cases have in common, as you will see, is that the B data derive from the researcher's *direct* observation and recording of what the participant has done.

B data can be gathered in two kinds of contexts: natural and contrived.

NATURAL B DATA

In principle, it is possible to gather B data from direct observations of the participant's behavior in real life. Ordinary acquaintance with the people we know gives us access to some amount of B data about them, and we indeed do draw conclusions based on these observations. If you see someone do something exceptionally kind, or disturbingly dishonest, or astonishingly energetic, you will naturally conclude something about his or her kindness, integrity, and energy level. But these observations are unsystematic, and also limited to the situations we share with the people we know: maybe this person is usually unkind, honest, or lazy, and we just happened to see him or her on an unusual day. So, ideally, as researchers we would wish for more.

First, B data should be carefully and systematically recorded and each bit of data should refer to a directly observed behavior. The unrealistic ultimate would be to hire a private detective, armed with state-of-the-art surveillance devices and a complete lack of respect for anybody's privacy, to follow the participant around night and day. The detective's report would specify in exact detail everything the participant said and did, and with whom, in all of the contexts of the participant's life. Ultimate, but impossible and unethical too. So, psychologists have to compromise.

One compromise form of B data is provided by diary and experience-sampling methods. Research in my own lab has used both. Participants fill out daily diaries that detail what they did that day: how many people they talked to, how many times they told a joke, how much time they spent studying or sleeping, and so on. In a sense these data are self-reports (S data), but they are not self-judgments; they are reasonably direct indications of what the participant did, described in specific terms. But they are a compromise kind of B data because the participant rather than the psychologist is the one who actually makes the behavioral observations (Spain, 1994).

Experience-sampling methods try to get more directly at what people are doing and feeling moment by moment. The original technique of this sort was called the "beeper" method, (Csikszentmihalyi & Larson, 1992; Spain, 1994) because participants wore radio-controlled pagers that beeped at several randomly selected times during the day. The participants then wrote down exactly what they were doing (and with whom) when the beeper sounded. Recent technological innovations have updated this procedure, so that participants carry around small computers such as Palm Pilots and enter their reports directly into a database (Feldman-Barrett & Barrett, 2001). Either way, one might suspect that participants would edit what they report, producing a sanitized version of their life events. Based on the reports I have read, I think this is unlikely. At least I hope so! A colleague of mine once did a beeper study at his university just after sending his own eighteen-year-old twin daughters to college in another state. After reading the reports of his university students' activities, he came very close to ordering his daughters back home.

Another kind of hybrid B data involves reports of specific behaviors offered by the participant or by one of his or her acquaintances. A person might record how many phone calls he or she made in a day or parties he or she went to in a week, or a close acquaintance or perhaps his or her spouse might provide the same information. But this kind of data is a good distance away from the B-data ideal of having the researcher observe the participant's behavior directly. Now one is forced to rely on the report of the participant or of his or her acquaintance (and thus could be considered mixtures of B data with S data or I data), and therefore are prey to the biases that might stem from that fact (Schwarz, 1999).

For example, when people report on their own behaviors, they may exaggerate the number of socially desirable behaviors they performed. One study asked participants to report the number of their "agreeable" acts during a group discussion (Gosling et al., 1998). This self-report was then compared with a count made by four observers who watched a videotape. In line with the idea that individuals like to exaggerate their good points, most people tended to describe themselves as more agreeable than they really were. Still, for most kinds of acts, the self-reports and the "truth" as revealed by videotape matched fairly well. This last result is encouraging because under real-life circumstances counts of specific behaviors are very difficult to obtain, and researchers have no choice but to settle for reports of "act frequencies" provided by the people who performed them.

Another possibility is to watch what participants do in the not-quite-natural contexts to which a psychologist can gain access. Years ago, I did a study in a nursery school that was operated by a university psychology department. From the children's point of view this place was simply their nursery school. But from a psychologist's point of view it was a gold mine of data. Each classroom was equipped with one-way mirrors and listening devices, and one could observe any of the children unobtrusively, all day long, as they went about their nursery school business. One could gather data that reflected these direct behavioral observations, such as the number of times a child asked a teacher for help, or disagreed with another child, or played with magic markers. These data reflected directly and in quantifiable terms what the child had been observed doing in a specific context, which is the hallmark of B data.

The great thing about B data gathered from real life is that they are realistic; they describe what the participants actually do in their daily activities. The disadvantages of naturalistic B data are their considerable cost—even the compromise forms just described are difficult and expensive—and the fact that some contexts in which one might wish to observe a participant may seldomly occur in the participant's daily life. For both of these reasons, B data derived from laboratory testing contexts are more common than those from natural contexts.

LABORATORY B DATA

Behavioral observations in the laboratory come in three varieties.

Experiments   The first is the psychological experiment. A participant is put into a room, something is made to happen in the room, and the psychologist directly observes what the participant then does.[6] The "something" that happens can be dramatic or mundane. The participant might be given a form to fill out, when suddenly smoke begins pouring under the door. The psychologist, sitting just outside holding a stopwatch, intends to measure how long it will take before the participant goes for help, if he or she ever does (some sit there until they can no longer see their hand in front of their face). If a researcher wanted to assess the participant's latency of smoke response from naturalistic B data, he or she would have to wait a long time for the appropriate situation to come along. In an experiment, the psychologist can make it happen.

Experiments also provide opportunities to find out how people react to very subtle aspects of situations, and the behaviors that are measured can be surprisingly revealing. In one recent study, researchers activated or "primed" subconscious thoughts about old age by having participants solve puzzles that included the words *gray, wise, bingo, forgetful, lonely, retired, wrinkle,* and (I love this one) *Florida* (Hull, Slone, Meteyer, & Matthews, 2002). With these words presumably floating in the participants' heads, they were left to walk away down the hall. The B data recorded was the speed with which they walked. The results showed that people high in the trait of "self-consciousness" walked more slowly (compared to people high in this trait who had read neutral words), whereas people low in this trait were unaffected. The theoretical explanation was that self-conscious people translated these elderly relevant words into thoughts about themselves, and this unconsciously

---

[6]By this definition, nearly all data gathered by social and cognitive psychologists are B data, even though those psychologists are ordinarily not accustomed to classifying their data as such. They also do not usually devote much thought to the fact that their technique of data gathering is limited to just one of four possible types.

caused them to walk as if they were elderly: that is, slower (more will be said about this study in Chapter 17). Admittedly, the chain of inference is complex, but these results imply it might be possible under some circumstances to assess the degree to which someone is self-conscious by measuring how quickly he or she walks!

Experimental situations can also be very straightforward, and intended to be representative of real-life contexts that are difficult to observe directly. In my own research, I often have participants meet partners of the opposite sex and simply engage in a conversation. I assume this is not a completely bizarre situation compared to those of daily life, although it is unusual because the participants know it is an experiment and know it is being video-taped. My purpose is to directly observe aspects of my participants' interpersonal behaviors and styles. In other videotaped situations, my participants compete with each other, cooperate in building a Tinkertoy, or engage in a group discussion. All of these settings are artificial but are designed to allow direct observation of various aspects of the participants' interpersonal behaviors, which would be difficult if not impossible to access otherwise. I put my participants in these situations because I want to see what they will do. My observations become B data (Funder & Colvin, 1991; Funder, Furr, & Colvin, 2000).

(Certain) Personality Tests   Certain kinds of personality tests also yield B data. Many and probably most personality questionnaires simply ask the participants what they are like, and the psychologist essentially chooses to believe whatever the participants say. These kinds of personality tests yield S data. B-data personality tests are different.

For example, the most widely used personality test, the **Minnesota Multiphasic Personality Inventory** (MMPI) is an example of B data (Dahlstrom & Welsh, 1960). The original version of this test (it was recently revised) included this true-false item: "I am a special messenger of the Lord."[7] The presence of an item like this usually signals that the test is looking for B data. Why? Because the psychologist is not actually seeking bearers of heavenly messages. This item was included because people who answer it true tend to be a little unusual. It appeared on the MMPI's schizophrenia scale because schizophrenics are more likely to answer it true than are nonschizophrenics.

Another kind of B-data personality test is the **projective test**, such as the **Thematic Apperception Test** (TAT) (Murray, 1943), or the famous **Rorschach test** (Rorschach, 1921). In the TAT, the participant is shown a picture of some people doing something. In the Rorschach, the participant is shown a blob of ink. In both cases, the participant is asked to describe

---

[7]The item was removed from the revised MMPI because it was deemed an illegal inquiry into assessees' religious beliefs!

what he or she sees. The situation here is much like that in any other sort of contrived psychological experiment; the psychologist puts the participant in a situation in which he or she is confronted with a stimulus that he or she might not otherwise ever have confronted, and then watches the participant closely to see what he or she will say and do. The responses to the TAT or to the Rorschach are carefully recorded and, eventually, interpreted. (More will be said about projective tests in Chapter 5.)

In my experience, students find the distinction between S-data personality tests and B-data personality tests confusing. But the distinction is important. One way to clarify the distinction may be to look at it in the following way: If, on a personality test, a psychologist asks you a question because he or she wants to *know* the answer, the test constitutes S data. If, however, the psychologist asks the question because he or she wants to see *what* you will answer, the test constitutes B data.

In an S-data test, when the psychologist wants to know something about you, he or she simply asks you about it. To diagnose sociability, the psychologist asks you how friendly you are. To assess your goals, she asks you to list them. In a B-data test, by contrast, the psychologist gives you a stimulus—perhaps a question, perhaps a picture—to see how you will respond. Your behavior is directly observed and precisely measured—which makes it B data—but your answer is not necessarily believed. Instead, it is interpreted; your claim that you are a special messenger of the Lord (on the old MMPI) means not that you are such a messenger, but that you may be a schizophrenic. In the case of an S-data test, by contrast, the psychologist will assume that what you say about yourself is basically true.

Physiological Measures   In recent years, another kind of B data has begun to be gathered in laboratory settings increasingly often: physiological measures. These include measures of blood pressure, galvanic skin response (which varies according to moisture on the skin—a.k.a. "sweating"), heart rate, and even highly complex measures of brain function such as pictures derived from CAT scans or PET scans (which detect blood flow and metabolic activity in the brain). In our system, all of these are classified as B data because they are something the participant does—albeit via his or her autonomic nervous sytem—and are measured directly in the laboratory. (In principle, these could be measured in real life as well but the technical obstacles are obvious.) For example, in the same priming study mentioned above the experimenters also showed their participants words meant to evoke thoughts of anger, such as the word "ANGRY" (in capitals), and found that highly self-conscious individuals responded with changes in blood pressure and heart rate, whereas low-self-conscious individuals did not (Hull et al., 2002). Data like these will be discussed further in Chapter 8, but for now the important point is that B data can come directly from physiological measurements

of the biological "behavior" of the participant, and be surprisingly informative about personality.

B data have two advantages and one big disadvantage.

ADVANTAGE: RANGE OF CONTEXTS

Some aspects of personality are regularly manifest in people's ordinary, daily
lives. Your degree of sociability, for instance, is probably evident during many
hours every day. But other aspects are hidden or, in a sense, latent. How do
you know how you would respond to being in a room alone with smoke
pouring under the door unless you are actually confronted with that situation? One important advantage of laboratory B data is that the psychologist
does not have to sit around waiting for the latter situation to happen; if
people can just be enticed into an experiment, the psychologist can make it
happen. Similarly, a psychologist might believe that the way people interpret
certain pictures or inkblots can provide important information about aspects
of their personalities that are ordinarily hidden. In an assessment or research
context, this psychologist can present these stimuli to the participants and
see how they react. The variety of B data that can be gathered are limited
only by the psychologist's resources, imagination, and, perhaps, ethics (see
Chapter 3).

ADVANTAGE: OBJECTIVE AND QUANTIFIABLE

Probably the most important advantage of B data, and the basis of most of
their appeal to scientifically minded psychologists, is this: To the extent that
B data are based on direct observation, the psychologist is gathering his or
her own information about personality and does not have to take anyone
else's word for it. This is an advantage because other people may distort or
exaggerate their reports, as we have already discussed. Perhaps even more
importantly, the direct gathering of data makes it possible for the psychologist to devise techniques to assess them with precision.

Often the measurement of behavior seems so direct that it is possible
to forget that it is an observation. For example, when a cognitive psychologist measures how long it takes, in milliseconds, for a participant to
respond to a visual stimulus flashed on a tachistoscope, this measurement
is simply a behavioral observation: How long did it take the participant to
respond? A biological psychologist can take direct measurements of blood
pressure or metabolic activity. Similarly, when a social psychologist measures a participant's "conformity" or "aggression," the measurement is
essentially an observation of behavior. In my own laboratory, I can derive
from the videotapes taken of my participants' conversations measurements

of how long each one talked, how much each one dominated the interaction, how nervous each one seemed, and so forth (Funder, Furr, & Colvin, 2000). All of these measurements, from cognitive, social, or personality psychology, are expressed in numerical form and, when appropriate care is employed, can be gathered with high reliability (see Chapter 3 for more on reliability).

The combination of direct assessment, numerical expression, and high reliability is almost irresistible. It seems like a direct pipeline to behavioral truth. Of course, this view is naïve. B data have a disadvantage too—a big one.

DISADVANTAGE: UNCERTAIN INTERPRETATION

Whether it reflects a response to an MMPI item, a description of a Rorschach inkblot, a phone call to a friend, a moment of social behavior in the laboratory, a reading of blood pressure, or a measurement of brain activity, a bit of B data is just that: a bit of data. It is usually a number, and a number cannot interpret itself. Worse, when it comes to B data, appearances are often ambiguous or even misleading, and so it is impossible to be entirely certain what they mean.

For example, consider again the situation in which someone gives you an extravagant gift. Do you immediately conclude that this person is generous and/or very much likes you? Perhaps, but you are probably sensible enough to wonder about other possibilities. Are you being manipulated, for example? The conclusion you draw about this behavior will be based on much more than the behavior itself; it depends on the context in which the gift was given and, even more importantly, what else you know about the giver. Is this in fact someone well known to be generous, or someone well known to be sneaky?

Or, consider that strange MMPI item that was mentioned earlier. How do we know what it means when someone claims that he or she is a special messenger of the Lord? Certainly nothing in the content of the item tells us; we need further information, such as the empirical fact that schizophrenics respond true to this item more often than nonschizophrenics. Once we know that, we might conclude, after the fact, that it really is a rather crazy thing to say. But the point is, we cannot conclude that the participant is schizophrenic without further information.

The same thing is true of any kind of behavior seen in real life or the laboratory. The person may give a gift, claim to be a messenger of the Lord, say an inkblot looks like a dragon or some favorite relative, or have a sudden intense spike in heart rate or metabolic activity in the prefrontal cortex; or the person may simply sit and wait a long time for a small reward. These are all behaviors that can be measured with great precision. But what these behaviors might *mean*, psychologically, is another question entirely.

A particular example from a study I did some years ago concerned a behavior called "delay of gratification." A large number of laboratory procedures have been developed for measuring this in children (e.g., Mischel & Ebbesen, 1970). One procedure is to show the child two treats, ask the child which he or she prefers, and then say, "Okay, I am going to leave the room now, but you can bring me back at any time by ringing this bell. If you do, you can have the [less preferred treat]. But if you don't ring the bell, and wait for me to come back by myself, you can have the [more preferred treat]." The measure of the child's delay of gratification is how long, in minutes and seconds, he or she waits before ringing the bell. This measure is a prototypical example of contrived B data.

It is easy to see how this measure of behavior got the label "delay of gratification." That is certainly what it looks like, and seems even to be built into the experimental procedure. If the child waits, he or she gets something better; if the child does not wait, he or she gets something worse. The test is how long the child can wait. What could be more obvious?

However, the measure here is simple only if we are content to regard it purely operationally and therefore nonpsychologically. If we were to call this measurement "delay time," there would indeed be no room for controversy. But if we label this minutes-and-seconds measurement "delay of gratification," we have made a risky move toward making a deeper, psychological claim. We are now claiming, in effect, that what the child is experiencing during that delay time is a psychological tension between desiring the better treat and not wanting to wait, a tension that is mediated according to the child's ability to delay gratification. But, what if the child doesn't mind waiting? Or, what if the child doesn't really like the "better" treat all that much? Then it would seem misguided to call this behavioral measure of waiting time "delay of gratification."

In the study that Daryl Bem and I did some years ago, we put a group of children through the procedure just described and also gathered personality descriptions of the children from their parents. We then analyzed our data to see how the children who waited the longest in our laboratory were described by their parents as acting at home (Bem & Funder, 1978).

The results surprised us: The most notable attribute of the longest-delaying children was not their ability to delay gratification in other contexts—this ability was a correlate, but a relatively minor one. More importantly, the longest-delaying children were likely to be described as helpful, cooperative, obedient, and not particularly interesting or intelligent. Our interpretation of these correlates was that the minutes and seconds of waiting that we measured were not so much a measure of the children's ability to delay gratification, but of their tendency to cooperate with adults. Because these children were offered something better if they waited, they thought we wanted them to wait. (After all, isn't that how life usually works?) The ones inclined to be obedient and cooperative did what they thought we wanted.

This study demonstrated that while a precise behavioral measurement may be easy to make, its meaning can be far from obvious. At the operational level, it is obvious that the minutes and seconds measured in this study did tick off the exact amount of waiting time. It is at the psychological level, when these minutes and seconds are interpreted as a measure of "delay of gratification," that matters suddenly become ambiguous.

The bottom line is that no one can know what a bit of B data means and measures, psychologically, just by looking at it, or even by designing it. (This caution is true of the other kinds of data as well, but it is more frequently forgotten with regard to B data because B data can seem so objective.) To find out what a B-data behavioral measurement means, other information is necessary. The most important information is how the B data correlate with the other kinds: S, I, and L data.

Mixed Types

It is easy to come up with simple and obvious examples of S, I, L, and B data. With a little thought, it is almost as easy to come up with confusing or mixed cases. For example, a self-report of your own behaviors during the day is what kind of data? As mentioned earlier, it seems to be a hybrid of B data and S data. Another hybrid between B data and S data is the kind of data sometimes called "behavioroid," in which participants report what they think they *would* do under various circumstances. (Of course, what people think they would do and what they actually would do might not always be the same.) What about a self-report of how many times you have suffered from the flu? This might be regarded a mixture of L data and S data. What about your parents' report of how healthy you were as a child? This might be a mixture of L data and I data. You can probably invent many more examples on your own.

The point of the four-way classification offered in this chapter is not that now you are supposed to be able to place any kind of data neatly into one and only one category. Rather, the point is to illustrate the wide range of possible types of data that are relevant to personality and to show how any source of data will have both advantages and disadvantages. S, I, L, and B data—and all their possible combinations and mixtures—each provide information missed by the other types, and each type raises its own distinctive possibilities for error.

Conclusion

There are no infallible indicators of personality. There are only clues, and clues are always ambiguous. All four kinds of clues and data for personality psychology are valuable and important. But all four have major disadvantages that cause each to fall far short of being a perfect source of information about personality. The fact that all possible sources of data about personality are incomplete, ambiguous, and even potentially misleading means, ironically, that none of them can be spared. The investigation of personality, and of psychology in general, requires that all of these sources of data be employed. Only then can the different advantages and disadvantages of each type of data begin to compensate for each other. And when all four sources of data begin to point in the same direction, the researcher is probably on to something.

All of which brings us to **Funder's Fourth Law**: *There are only two kinds of data.* The first kind is Terrible Data: data that are ambiguous, potentially misleading, incomplete, and imprecise. The second kind is No Data. Unfortunately, there is no third kind, anywhere in the world.

I am not trying to be cynical here. It is simply a fact, perhaps a sad fact, that no data, no matter what kind, points directly and unerringly towards Truth. But this message does not need to be discouraging. Rather, the potential shortcomings of all kinds of data are precisely what require researchers to always gather every kind they possibly can.

If data are potentially misleading, some people would prefer not to gather them at all. They prefer No Data to Terrible Data. It is tough to be a research psychologist if you have that attitude (consider a career in engineering). My own preference is derived from Funder's Third Law, already expounded: Something will beat nothing, perhaps not always, but two times out of three.

Summary

In order to study personality, first you must look at it: all science begins with observation. The observations a scientist makes are called data. For the scientific study of personality, four kinds of data are available. Each kind has advantages and disadvantages. S data comprise a person's judgments of his or her own personality. The advantages of S data are that each individual is the best expert about herself or himself, that S data also have a causal force all their own, and that S data are simple and easy to gather. The disadvantages are that people sometimes will not or cannot tell researchers about themselves, and that S data may be so easy to obtain that psychologists use them too much. I data comprise the judgments of knowledgeable informants about the personality traits of the person being studied. The advantages of I data include the large amount of information on which informants' judgments typically are based, that this information comes from real life, that informants can use common sense, and that the judgments of people who know the person are important because they have a causal force all their own. The disadvantages of I data are that no informant knows everything about another person, that informants' judgments can be biased or subject to errors such as forgetting, and that not all informants may have common sense. L data comprise observable life outcomes such as being arrested, getting sick, or graduating from college. L data have the advantages of being intrinsically important and psychologically relevant, at least sometimes, but have the disadvantage of not always being psychologically relevant. B or "behavioral" data comprise direct observations of a person doing something in a testing situation. This situation may involve the person's real-life environment, an artificial social setting constructed in a psychological laboratory, a personality test such as the Rorschach inkblot, or a physiological measurement of variables such as heart rate, blood pressure, and even brain activity. The advantages of B data are that they can tap into many different kinds of behaviors, including those that might not occur in normal life, and that B data are obtained through direct observation, and so are in that sense objective. The disadvantage of B data is that for all their superficial objectivity, it is still not always clear what they mean psychologically. Because each kind of data for personality research is potentially valuable and potentially misleading, researchers should gather and compare all of them.

PERSONALITY PSYCHOLOGY AS SCIENCE: RESEARCH METHODS

If data are the ingredients of scientific knowledge, then research methods provide the recipe. These recipes are sometimes quite complex and can take a long time to learn. The topic of research methods ranges very broadly to include specific procedures, sophisticated statistics, and even aspects of the philosophy of science, so obviously the topic involves much more than can be covered fully here. Still, certain aspects of research methodology are particularly important for personality psychology and need to be considered before we begin to study the topic in earnest. This chapter will consider the quality of data, the research designs by which data can be gathered and analyzed, the question of how one knows whether one has a good "strong" result, and, finally, the issue of research ethics.

Psychology's Emphasis on Method

It is sometimes said that the main thing psychologists know is not content, but method. This statement is not usually intended as a compliment. When all is said and done, psychologists do not very often seem to have firm answers to the questions they and others ask about the mind and behavior. What they have instead are methods for generating research aimed at these questions. Indeed, psychologists sometimes seem more interested in the research process itself than in the answers their research is supposed to be seeking.

Such characterizations are not entirely fair, but they do have their kernels of truth. Like other scientists, psychologists never really expect to reach a final answer to any question. For a researcher, the real thrill is in the chase, and the goal is to improve on the tentative answers (hypotheses) constantly being developed, than to settle anything once and for all.

Another kernel of truth in the caricature is that more than any other kind of scientist, psychologists are sensitive and sometimes even self-conscious about research methodology, about the way they use statistics, and *51* even about the basic procedures by which they draw theoretical inferences from empirical data. Issues like these don't seem to worry biologists and chemists so much. They have fewer debates about methodology, and introductory biology or chemistry textbooks usually do not contain an introspective chapter—like this one—on research methods, whereas no psychology text seems complete without one. Why do you think this is?

Sometimes, the emphasis on methods and process is seen as a sign of weakness, even by psychologists themselves. One might even say that many psychologists suffer from "physics envy." But psychology's self-consciousness about method is one of my favorite things about it. I remember beginning to study chemistry and finding that one of my first assignments was to memorize the periodic table of elements. Where did this table come from, I immediately wanted to know, and why should I believe it? But the answers to these questions were not part of the introductory curriculum in chemistry, so no answers were forthcoming. Certain things, at least early in the study of the subject, were just to be accepted—and memorized without question. This was understandable, I suppose, but it did not seem like much fun.

When I took my first psychology course, I discovered that the approach was different. Although I was somewhat disappointed that the professor did not immediately teach me how to read people's minds (even though I was sure he was reading mine), I was engaged by the approach to knowledge he employed. Everything was open to question, and almost no "fact" was presented without both a description of the experiment that found it and a discussion of whether or not the experiment's evidence was actually persuasive. Some students did not like this approach. Why not just tell us the facts, they complained, like the professor does in chemistry class? But I loved it. It allowed me to think for myself. Early in the semester, I decided that some of the facts of psychology did not seem solidly based. Later on, I even began to imagine some ways in which I could find out more myself. I was hooked. It could happen to you. Read on.

Scientific Education and Technical Training

Some people think that psychology is not really scientific because it has so few hard facts, and even the knowledge it has gathered seems always open to question. This view is ironic because it has things precisely backward. Real science is the seeking of *new* knowledge, not the cataloging of facts already known for certain. This distinction is the fundamental difference between scientific education and technical training. Technical training conveys what is already known about a subject, so that the knowledge can be applied. Scientific education, by contrast, teaches not only what is known but also (and much more importantly) how to find out what is not yet known.

By this definition, medical education is technical rather than scientific—it focuses on teaching what is known and how to use it, and so medical doctors learn to be practitioners rather than scientists. Physicians-in-training do an astonishing amount of sheer memorization, and the last step in medical education is an internship, in which the future doctor shows that he or she can apply what he or she has been taught. Scientists-in-training, by contrast, do much less memorization; instead they are taught to question what is already known and how to find out more. The last step in scientific education, including in psychology, is the dissertation, in which the future scientist shows that he or she can make an original contribution to knowledge.

The contrast between technical and scientific training and approaches applies in many other cases, such as the comparison between pharmacists and pharmacologists, gardeners and botanists, or computer operators and computer scientists. The issue is not which of these is "better." They are both necessary, and each depends on the other. The biologist goes to a physician when sick; most of what the physician knows was discovered by biologists. But they are importantly different. Technical training teaches one to use what is already known; scientific training teaches one to explore the unknown. In science, the exploration of the unknown is called **research**. The essential aspect of this exploration is the gathering of data.

"Certainly. A party of four at seven-thirty in the name of Dr. Jennings. May I ask whether that is an actual medical degree or merely a Ph.D.?"

Quality of Data

One of the most famous chefs in the world is Alice Waters, the owner of Chez Panisse in California. Waters is famous for her passion about ingredients. She insists on knowing all of her suppliers personally, and frequently visits the farms and ranches that are the sources of her produce and meats. If the ingredients are good, she believes, superb cooking is possible, but if they are bad, you might as well give up. If we want to learn from her example, before we consider research design—the recipe—we should probably first put some more thought into the ingredients—the data. In Chapter 2 we looked at four basic types of data for personality research: S, I, L, and B data. Each kind can vary in quality. For each of these types and indeed for any type of data, in any field, two aspects of quality are paramount: (1) Are the data reliable? (2) Are the data valid? These two questions can be combined into a third question: (3) Are the data "generalizable"?

Reliability

In science, the term **reliability** has a technical meaning that is narrower than its everyday usage. The question of scientific reliability asks whether your measurement is free of irrelevant influences that might distort your view of the trait or state you are trying to assess. The cumulative effect of such extraneous influences is called **measurement error**, and the less there is of such error the more reliable the measurement is.

The influences that are considered extraneous depend on what is being measured. If you are trying to measure a person's mood—a current and presumably temporary **state**—then the fact that he or she won the lottery ten minutes ago is highly relevant and not at all extraneous. But if you are trying to measure the person's general, or **trait**, level of emotional experience, then this sudden event is extraneous, the measurement will be misleading, and you might choose to wait for a more ordinary day to administer your questionnaire.

When trying to measure a stable attribute of personality—a trait rather than a state—the question of reliability reduces to this: Can you get the same result more than once? A method or an instrument that repeatedly provides the same comparative information is reliable; one that does not is unreliable. For example, a personality test that over a long period of time repeatedly picked out the same individuals as the friendliest in the class, and others as the least friendly, would be a reliable test (although not necessarily valid—that's another matter that we will get to shortly). A personality test that on one occasion picked out one student as the most friendly and on another occasion identified a different student as the most friendly, however, would be unreliable. A test that is unreliable in this way could not possibly be a valid measure of a stable trait of friendliness. Instead it might be a measure of a state or momentary level of friendliness, or (more likely in this case) it might not be a good measure of anything at all.

Reliability is something that can and should be assessed with any scientific measurement, whether the measurement be a personality test, a thermometer reading, the output of a brain-wave scanner, or a blood cell count. This point is not always appreciated. For example, an acquaintance of mine, a research psychologist, had a vasectomy. As part of the procedure, a sperm count was determined before and after the operation. He asked the physician a question that is natural for a psychologist to ask: "How reliable is a sperm count?" What he wanted to know was, does a man's sperm count vary widely according to time of day, or what he has eaten lately, or his mood? Moreover, does it matter which technician does the count, or does the same result occur regardless of who the counter is? The physician, who apparently was trained technically rather than scientifically, failed to understand the question and even seemed insulted. "Our lab is very reliable," he replied. My acquaintance tried to clarify matters with a follow-up question: "What I mean is, what's the error variance of a sperm count?" ("Error variance" refers to the fluctuation of a number around its mean upon repeated measurements, due to uncontrolled influences such as those just listed.) The physician really was insulted now. "We don't make errors," he huffed.

But every measurement includes a certain amount of error variance. No instrument or technique is perfect. In psychology at least four things can undermine reliability. First is low precision. Measurements should be taken as exactly as possible, as carefully as possible. It might seem to go without saying, but nonetheless it is all-important that great care be taken in recording data, scoring it correctly, and entering it carefully into the database. Any experienced researcher has had the nightmarish experience of discovering that a research assistant has wandered away for a drink of water when he or she was supposed to be timing how long it took a participant to solve a problem, or that answers given on a 1–7 scale were entered into the computer as if the scale went from 7 to 1. Things like this happen surprisingly often; be careful.

Second, the state of the participant[1] in the study might vary for reasons that have nothing to do with the study itself. Some participants show up ill, some well, some are happy and others are sad; many college-student participants are amazingly short on sleep. From a research perspective, the problem

---

[1]The term *subjects* is now passé in psychological research. According to the American Psychological Association, we must now call them *participants*, and I try to remember to do so. The change in usage is not uniform, though. The U.S. federal government still enforces voluminous regulations concerning "human subjects."

is that they might have behaved or performed differently, and therefore have given different results for the research, if they were feeling differently or more rested. There is not much researchers can really do about this; variation in the state of the person is a source of error variance or random "noise" in almost every psychological study.

A third potential pitfall for reliability is the state of the experimenter. One would hope that experimenters, at least, would come to the lab well rested and attentive, but alas this is not always the case. Variation due to the experimenter is almost as inevitable as variation due to the participant; experimenters try to treat all participants the same but, being human, will fail to some extent. Moreover, participants may respond differently to an experimenter depending upon whether he or she is male or female, of a different race, or even depending on how he or she is dressed. It is very difficult to control all these things. B. F. Skinner famously got around this problem by having his subjects—rats and pigeons—studied only in the environment of a mechanically controlled enclosure, the famous "Skinner box." But for research with humans, we usually need to have them interact at least to some degree with other humans, including research assistants.

A final potential pitfall is the state of the environment in which the study is done. Experienced researchers have all sorts of stories that never make it into textbooks on research methods, involving fire alarms (even sprinklers) that go off in the middle of experiments, noisy arguments that suddenly break out next door, psychology-building thermostats gone berserk, and so forth. Events like these are relatively unusual, fortunately, and when they happen generally all one can do is cancel the study for the day, throw the data out, and hope for better luck tomorrow. But more minor variations in the environment are constant and inevitable; noise levels and temperature and the weather and a million other factors vary constantly during a research project and provide another potential source of data unreliability.

At least four things can be done to try to enhance reliability. One, obviously, is just to be careful. Double check all measurements, have someone proofread the data-entry sheets (more than once!), and make sure the procedures for scoring data are clearly understood by everyone who works for your project. A second way to improve reliability is to use a constant, scripted procedure for all participants—the procedure that is followed should be the one written on the research protocol no matter what happens. I once did a study in which participants watched a long videotape of a behavioral episode; in another condition other participants watched a much shorter tape. Among the hypotheses of the study was that participants would stop paying attention to a very long episode and so the accuracy of their ratings of that episode would, instead of getting better over time, start to deteriorate. One of our research assistants, eager to go home, watched participants in the long-episode condition until they seemed inattentive. Then he would go in, say

"Well you're not paying attention anyway," stop the tape, and end the experiment! By the time we discovered his procedural innovation, several participants' worth of data was ruined—an expensive error. But the real error was mine. The aspect of the procedure that prescribed "let the tape run to the end even if the participant doesn't seem to be paying attention" seemed so obvious to me that I failed to teach it adequately to at least one of my research assistants. It turns out, nothing is so obvious that it can be taken for granted.

A third way to enhance reliability in psychological research is to measure something that is important, rather than something that is trivial. For example, an attitude about an issue that matters to someone is easy to measure reliably, but if the person doesn't really care (what's your opinion on lumber tariffs?), then the answer is worth little more than the paper the questionnaire is printed on. An experimental procedure that engages participants will yield better data than those that fail to involve them; measurement of big important variables (like the degree of a person's extraversion) will be more reliable than narrow trivial variables (like whether the person is chatting with someone at 1:10 P.M. on Saturdays).

The fourth, most important and generally useful way to enhance the reliability of measurement in *any* domain is **aggregation**, or averaging. When I was in high school, a science teacher whom I now believe to have been brilliant (I failed to be as impressed at the time) provided students in the class with the best demonstration of aggregation that I have ever seen. He gave each of us a meter stick, a piece of wood cut to the length of 1 meter. We then went outside and measured the distance to the elementary school down the street, about a kilometer (1,000 meters) away. We did this by laying our sticks down, then laying them down again against the end of where they were before, and counting how many times we had to do this before we reached the other school.

In each class the counts varied widely—from about 750 to over 1,200, as I recall. The next day, the teacher wrote on the blackboard all the different results. It seemed that the elementary school just would not hold still! To put this observation another way, our individual measurements were quite unreliable. It was hard to keep laying the stick down over and over again with precision, and it was also hard not to lose count of how many times we did it.

But then, the teacher did an amazing thing. He took the thirty-five measurements from the 9:00 class and averaged them. He got 957. Then he averaged the thirty-five measurements from the 10:00 class. He got 959. The thirty-five measurements from the 11:00 class averaged 956. Almost by magic, the error variance had almost disappeared, and we suddenly had what looked like an extremely stable estimate of the distance to the elementary school.

What had happened? The teacher had taken advantage of the power of aggregation. Each of the mistakes we made in laying our sticks down and forgetting what number we were on were essentially random. And over the long haul, random influences tended to cancel one another out (by definition in **psychometrics**, random influences sum to zero—if they didn't, they wouldn't be random!). While some of us may have been laying our sticks too close together, other classmates were surely laying them too far apart. When all the measurements were averaged, the errors canceled each other out. With thirty-five measurements being averaged, the result became pretty stable.

This is a basic and powerful principle of measurement. If you have doubts about the precision of your measurement, take as many measurements as you can, and average them. The **Spearman-Brown formula** in psychometrics quantifies exactly how this works, but the principle is simple: Random errors tend to cancel one another out. So the more error-filled your measurements are, the more of them you need. The "truth" will be in there someplace, near the average. This is the best way to deal with some of the problems discussed above, such as the inevitable fluctuations in the state of the participant, experimenter, and environment. (For further illustrations and discussion of applications of the Spearman-Brown formula to personality measurement, see Chapter 5; also Burnett, 1974; Epstein, 1980; and Rosenthal, 1973c.)

This principle is particularly important if one's goal is to predict behavior. Personality psychology once got into a bitter debate, called the "consistency controversy" (see Chapter 4), just because single behaviors are difficult to predict accurately from personality measurements. That caused some critics to conclude that personality itself did not exist! However, based on the principle of aggregation, it should be much easier to predict the *average* of a person's behavior. Maybe a friendly person *is* more friendly at some times than at other times—everyone has bad days. But the average of the person's behavior over time should be reliably more friendly than that of an unfriendly person (Epstein, 1979).

Validity

Validity, as I indicated earlier, is another matter. It also is a more slippery concept. **Validity** is the degree to which a measurement actually reflects what one thinks, or hopes it does. The concept of validity is slippery for a couple of reasons.

One reason is that for a measure to be valid, it must be reliable. But a reliable measure is not necessarily valid. Should I say this again? A measure that is reliable gives the same answer time after time. If the answer is always changing, how can it be the right answer? So for a measure to be valid, it must first be reliable. But even if a measure is the same time after time, that does not necessarily mean it is *correct*. Maybe it reliably gives the wrong answer (like the clock in my old Toyota, which was correct only twice each day). Reliability is what the logicians call a "necessary but not sufficient condition" for validity.

A second and even more difficult complication to the idea of validity is that the concept seems to invoke a notion of ultimate truth. On the one hand, you have ultimate, true reality. On the other hand, you have a measurement. If the measurement matches ultimate, true reality, it is valid. Thus, an IQ measure is valid if it really measures intelligence. A sociability score is valid if it really measures sociability. But here is the problem: How does anyone know what intelligence or sociability "really" are?

Some years ago, the psychologists Lee Cronbach and Paul Meehl (1955) proposed that attributes like intelligence or sociability are best considered to be **constructs**.[2] A construct, in their terminology, is an *idea* about a psychological attribute, an idea that goes beyond what might be assessed through any particular method of measurement. For example, "intelligence" is a construct. IQ tests attempt to measure intelligence, but the interesting thing about intelligence is not how it affects test scores, but how it affects performance across a wide range of contexts in life. If IQ affected only test scores, and not performance in life, there would be no reason for anybody to care about it. An old-time psychologist once said, "Intelligence can be defined as what IQ tests measure." He was wrong.

Personality constructs are the same as IQ in this sense. They are much more than test scores or any given set of observations. They are ideas about how behaviors hang together and are affected by the same attribute of personality. For example, the construct of "sociability" implies that going to parties, smiling at strangers, and making numerous telephone calls should tend to be correlated with each other—somebody who does one of these behaviors probably does the other two as well. This is because all of these behaviors, and many more, are assumed to be a product of the personality attribute, or trait, of sociability.

As you can now see, using a construct is much the same as proposing a theory (Hogan & Nicholson, 1988). Here, the theory is that sociability is a trait that can affect many different behaviors that all reflect an inclination to be with other people.

Of course, that's just a theory. You need data to test the theory. The process of testing a theory of a construct like intelligence or sociability is called **construct validation** (Cronbach & Meehl, 1955). This research strategy amounts to gathering as many different measurements as you can of the construct you are interested in—such as intelligence or sociability. The

---

[2]Sometimes the term *hypothetical construct* is used, to underline that the existence of the attribute is not known for certain but instead is hypothesized.

measurements that start to hang together—to consistently pick out the same people as intelligent or sociable, for example—begin to validate each other.

For example, you might give participants a sociability test, and ask their acquaintances how sociable they are, and count how many phone calls they make in a week and how many parties they go to. If these four measures correlate—if they all tend to pick out the same individuals as being highly sociable—then you might start to believe that each of them has some degree of validity as a measure of the construct of sociability. At the same time, you would become more confident that this construct makes sense, that sociability is a useful idea for predicting and explaining behavior. Even though you never reach an ultimate truth, you can start to reasonably believe you are measuring something real when you can develop a battery of measurements, all quite different, that yield more or less the same result.

Generalizability

Classic treatments of psychometrics regarded reliability and validity as distinct from one another. When two tests that were supposed to be "the same" were compared, the degree to which they actually yielded the same result indicated their degree of reliability. For example, reliability would be gauged by the degree to which a test given at one time gives the same scores to the same people when exactly the same test is given again, a week later.

The constancy between scores on one form of a test and scores on another form of the same test (maybe consisting of the same items, only slightly rephrased) would also be considered a gauge of reliability. But if the two tests are different, then their relationship is taken to indicate the first test's degree of validity. Here's the rub: How much can a researcher rephrase a test, or change its format, before it changes from the "same" test to a "different" one? If a researcher gives out the Colorado Test of Happiness on Sunday and the Virginia Test of Happiness on Thursday, does the correlation between the two tests reflect the reliability of the measurement of happiness or the validity of the first test as assessed by its correlation with the second test? When one begins to look at it closely, the distinction between which tests should be considered "the same" or "different" turns out to be rather fuzzy.

In recent years, therefore, psychometricians have started to regard the distinction between reliability and validity as also being rather fuzzy. Instead, they view both concepts as aspects of a single, broader concept called **generalizability** (Cronbach et al., 1972). The question of generalizability, applied to a measurement or to the results of an experiment, asks the following: To what else does the measurement or the result generalize? That is, is the result you get with one test equivalent, or generalizable, to the result you would get using a different test? Does your result also apply to other kinds of people than the ones you assessed, or does it apply to the same people at other times, or would you find the same result using different research assistants? All of these questions regard different facets of generalizability.

GENERALIZABILITY OVER PARTICIPANTS

One important facet is generalizability over participants. For example, you might do a case study of a single individual but then wonder about whether what you have found is relevant to people in general or just to this one person. Most psychological research is done by university professors, and most participants in the research are college students. (There tend to be a lot of students near professors, and gathering data from anybody else—such as randomly selected members of the community—is much more difficult and expensive, even when it is possible.) This latter fact raises a basic question of generalizability: To what degree can researchers draw valid conclusions about people in general if all they study are college students? After all, college students are not representative of the broader population. They are somewhat more affluent, more liberal, and less likely to belong to ethnic minorities, among other differences. These facts call into question the degree to which research results found with such students will prove to be true about the wider population of this country, let alone the world (Sears, 1986).

Gender Bias   An even more egregious example of conclusions being based on a limited sample of humanity comes from the fact that until well into the 1960s, it was fairly routine for American psychological research to gather data only from male participants. Some of the classic empirical investigations of personality, such as those by Henry Murray (1938) and Gordon Allport (1937), examined only men. I once had a conversation with one of the major contributors to personality research during the 1940s and 1950s who was still very active years later and who admitted frankly that he was embarrassed to have used only male participants in his research. "It is hard to recall why we did that," he said in 1986. "As best as I can remember, it simply never occurred to any of us to do anything different—to include women in the groups we studied."

In recent years the problem may have reversed, in an ironic way. There is one particular fact about recruiting participants, rarely mentioned in methods textbooks, that nearly all psychologists have known for years: Females are more likely than males to sign up to be in experiments, and once signed up are more likely to actually appear at the scheduled time. This difference is not small. From my desk in the psychology department I used to look directly across the hallway at a sign-up sheet for my own research project, which uses paid, volunteer participants. Because my work needs an exactly equal number of males and females, the sign-up sheet had two columns, one for each. At any hour of any day, there typically would be more than twice as many names in the "women" column as in the "men" column, sometimes as much as five times as many.

This big difference raises a couple of issues. One is theoretical: Why this difference? One hypothesis could be that college-age women are generally more conscientious and cooperative than men in that age range (which I believe is true), or the difference might go deeper than that. A second issue is that this difference raises a worry about the participants researchers do recruit. It is not so much that samples are unbalanced. Researchers can keep them balanced; in my lab, I simply call *all* of the men who sign up and about one in three of the women. Rather, the problem is that because men are less likely to volunteer than women, the men who are in the studies are, by definition, unusual men. They are the kind of men who are willing to be in a psychological experiment. Most men aren't so willing, yet researchers generalize from them to men in general.[3]

Shows versus No-shows   A related limitation of generalizability is that the results of psychological research depend on the people who show up at the laboratory. Anyone who has ever done research knows that a substantial proportion of the participants who are scheduled to be in a study never appear. The results of the research, in the end, depend on the attributes of the participants who do appear. This is a problem if these two groups of people are different.

There is not much research on this issue—it is difficult to study "no-shows," as you might expect—but there is a little. According to one study, the people who are most likely to appear for a psychological experiment at the time they are scheduled are those who adhere to standards of "conventional morality" (Tooke & Ickes, 1988). And most of such people are female. These findings, taken together, suggest that psychological research might more accurately describe the behavioral tendencies of relatively moral women, than of people in general. Immoral males, it seems, don't show up for psychology experiments when they are supposed to.

Cohort Effects   Another possible failure of generalizability stems from the fact that research results may be *historically* limited. It has been argued that much of psychology is really "history," meaning it is the study of a particular group of people in a particular place and time (Gergen, 1973). The research that fills psychological journals today may be interesting as a historical artifact concerning what late-twentieth-century, North American col-

---

[3]It was once suggested to me, quite seriously, that the solution to this problem would be to pay male participants three times as much as female participants. Do you think this is a good idea?

lege students were like, according to this argument, but says little about what people are like in general or, more particularly, what they may have been like across different years and centuries.

Some evidence does indicate that aspects of personality can be affected by the specific historical period in which one lives. One study of Americans who grew up during the Great Depression of the 1930s found that they took from that experience certain attitudes toward work and financial security that were distinct from the outlooks of those who grew up earlier or later (Elder, 1974). Psychologists call the tendency of a group of people who lived at a particular time to be different in some way from those who lived earlier or later a **cohort effect**.

A few other studies have examined differences between people who lived at different times (e.g., Twenge & Nolen-Hoeksema, 2002), but psychologists worry about cohort effects more often than dealing with them directly. The reason is that the necessary research is prohibitively expensive, insofar as it is even possible. The only real way to find out which research results are true across time and which are just characteristics of the cohort being studied is to study other participants from other eras. This is nearly impossible. To some degree one can use old data archives and try to go back a little ways in time. For the future, one must begin new studies, or just wait. None of these tactics is terribly practical, and all of them are expensive.

Ethnic Diversity   A generalizability issue that is receiving increased attention concerns the fact that most modern empirical research in psychology is based on a limited subset of the modern population—specifically, the largely white, middle-class college students referred to earlier. This is becoming a particular issue in the United States, where ethnic diversity has always been wide and where various minority groups are becoming more assertive in their insistence on being included in all aspects of society—including psychological research. The pressure to include minority participants is political as well as scientific. One place to see the result of such political pressure is in the grant application guidelines published by one branch of the U.S. federal government:

> Applications for grants . . . that involve human subjects are required to include minorities and both genders in study populations. . . . This policy applies to *all* research involving human subjects and human materials, and applies to males and females of all ages. If one gender and/or minorities are excluded or are inadequately represented in this research . . . a clear, compelling rationale for exclusion or inadequate representation should be provided. . . . Assess carefully the feasibility of including the broadest possible representation of minority groups. (Public Health Service, 1991, p. 21)

This set of guidelines addresses the representation of *American* ethnic minorities in research funded by the U.S. government. As the tone of this directive hints, such representation is difficult. But notice that even if every goal it espouses were to be achieved, the American researchers subject to its edict would still be restricted to studying residents of a modern, Western, capitalist, postindustrial society. This may be an interesting society to study, but its denizens are a minority, since 70 percent of the world's population lives outside Europe and North America (Triandis, 1994).

THE BURDEN OF PROOF

It is easy to get carried away with these kinds of worries. The concern with generalizability, the degree to which one's research results apply to all people around the world and at all times, is a fundamental issue for psychological research. But two points are worth bearing in mind.

First, getting the facts straight about members of our own culture in our own time seems to be difficult enough, so we should resist making facile and simplistic generalizations about members of other cultures—including jumping to conclusions about ways they might be different from us. To really understand the degree to which and ways in which cultures differ psychologically from one another will require a vast amount of further research more equally spread across cultures and less concentrated in Europe, North America, Australia, and New Zealand. Such research is beginning to appear, but we still have a lot to learn about cross-cultural differences, and even how pervasive they really are (see Chapter 14).

Second, it is one thing to worry, in a general way, that our results or theories might not generalize, and quite another to propose just how and why a particular result or a particular theory might not apply to another culture. Not all of the burden of proof should be put on those who are trying to do research that is generalizable. Some should be put on those who claim it is not generalizable, to show when, how, and why it is not. Simply to observe that psychology's database is limited, and then to conclude that all research and theory are therefore worthless is—as the old saying goes—to throw the baby out with the bathwater.

Research Design

Data gathering must follow some sort of plan, the "research design." No one research design is suitable for all topics—according to what one wants to study, different designs may be appropriate, inappropriate, or even impossible. Research designs in psychology (and all of science) come in three basic types: case, experimental, and correlational.

Case Method

The simplest, most obvious, and most widely used way to learn about something is, as Henry Murray advised, just to look at it. Even seemingly mundane events, when looked at closely, can have important implications. According to legend, Isaac Newton was sitting under a tree when he was hit on the head by an apple, and that got him thinking about laws of gravity. A scientist who keeps his or her eyes and ears open can find all sorts of phenomena to examine that can stimulate new ideas and insights. The **case method** involves closely studying a particular event or person of interest in order to find out as much as possible.

This method is used all the time. When an airliner crashes, the National Transportation Safety Board (NTSB) sends a team to the site and launches an intensive investigation of what happened. For example, in January 2000 an Alaska Airlines plane went down off the California coast; almost three years later the NTSB concluded this happened because a crucial part, the jackscrew assembly in the plane's tail, had not been properly greased (Alonso-Zaldivar, 2002). This conclusion solved the immediate mystery of why this particular crash happened, and also had implications for the way other, similar planes should be maintained (i.e., don't forget to grease the jackscrew!). At its best, the case method yields not only explanations of particular events, but also more general lessons and perhaps even scientific principles.

All sciences use the case method. When volcanoes erupt, geologists rush to the scene with every instrument they can carry. When a fish previously thought long extinct is pulled from the bottom of the sea, ichthyologists stand in line to get a closer look. Medical science has a tradition of "case conferences" where individual patients are presented and discussed at length. Even business schools spend long hours studying cases of companies that succeeded and failed. But the science best known for its use of the case method is psychology, and in particular personality psychology. Freud built his famous theory of personality from his experience with particular patients who offered interesting cases of phobias, weird dreams, and hysterical illnesses (see Chapter 10). Most of psychoanalytic theory from other theorists such as Jung, Adler, and Horney is likewise based on their experience with the cases they treated. Psychologists who are not psychoanalytically inclined have also used cases; Gordon Allport, for example, argued for the importance of studying particular individuals in-depth, and even wrote a whole book about one person (Allport, 1965).[4]

A particularly interesting and important case study could be done on the person who shares your address, name, and social security number. That is,

---

[4]The identity of this person was supposed to be secret. Years later, historians established it was his college roommate's mother.

you. Every person is both complex and unique, and the effort to understand oneself can be a hobby that lasts a lifetime. I am not really recommending that degree of self-absorption, but it is true that understanding why you do things can help you understand why others do what they do. Freud said that an important basis of his theory was his own introspection. We cannot all be theorists of Freud's caliber, but looking into ourselves from time to time to figure out why we think and behave the way we do can help us understand not just ourselves, but other people as well.

The case method has several advantages. One is that, above all other methods, it is the one that feels like it does justice to the topic. A well-written case study is like a short story or even a novel; Freud wrote extensively and well about many of his patients and, in general, the best thing about a case study is that it describes the whole phenomenon and not just isolated variables. A second advantage is that a well-chosen case study can be the source of general ideas. It can illuminate why planes crash and perhaps prevent future disasters, and reveal general facts about the inner workings of volcanoes, the body, businesses, and of course the human mind. These ideas may be ones that would not have occurred to anyone unless the case was studied. Newton's apple got him thinking in a whole new direction; nobody suspected that grease on a jackscrew could be so important, and Freud generated an astounding number of ideas just from examining himself and the people who happened to appear in his consulting room.

A third advantage of the case method is often forgotten: sometimes the method is absolutely necessary. A plane goes down; we *must* at least try to understand why. A patient appears, desperately sick. The physician cannot say "More research is needed"; rather, he or she must try to understand the problem as thoroughly as possible and then do something. Psychologists, too, sometimes must deal with particular individuals, in all their wholeness and complexity, and base their efforts on the best understanding they can quickly achieve.

The big disadvantage of the case method is obvious. It is not controlled. Each case, of any kind, contains numerous and perhaps literally thousands of specific facts and variables. Which of these are crucial, and which are incidental? An insightful scientist might be able to perceive important patterns, but to really become confident about what one has learned from a case requires confirmation from many, many other similar cases, and typically that is not possible.

In sum, therefore, the case method is probably good for two things. First, it can get a researcher interested in a problem in the first place. Newton's apple made him curious about gravity; you may become interested in psychology or a particular topic in psychology because of some specific life episode or some particular person. Second, it can be a source of ideas. New ideas have to come from somewhere, and the best source is probably life and specific events in life, in all their complexity. Once the idea appears, however, it needs to be checked out, and for that the more formal methods of science are required, the **experimental method** and the **correlational method**.

For example, let's say you know someone who has a big exam coming up. It is very important to him, and he studies very hard. He also becomes anxious. He takes the test and freaks out. Even though he knows the subject matter, he performs badly and gets a poor grade. Have you ever seen this happen? If you have (I know I have), then this case might cause you to think of a general hypothesis: anxiety harms test performance. That sounds reasonable, but does this one experience prove that it is true? Not really, but it was the source of the idea. The next step is to find a way to do research to test this hypothesis. You could do this in either of two ways, with an experiment or a correlational study.

An Experimental and a Correlational Study

The experimental way to examine the relationship between anxiety and test performance would be to get a group of research participants and randomly divide them into two groups. It is important that they be assigned randomly because then you can presume that the two groups are more or less equal in ability, personality, and other factors. Now it's time for your experimental procedure. Do something to one of the groups that you expect will make the members of that group anxious, such as telling them, "Your life depends on your performance on this test" (but see the discussion on ethics and deception later in this chapter). Say nothing to the other group (the "control" group). Then give both groups something like a thirty-item math test. If anxiety hurts performance, then you would expect the participants in your "life depends" group to do worse on the test than the participants in the control group, who did not hear this dire message.

To test whether you got the results you predicted, you might write them down in a table like Table 3.1 and then display them on a chart like Figure 3.1. In this example, the mean (average) score of the high-anxiety group indeed seems lower than that of the low-anxiety (control) group. You would then do a statistical test, probably one called a *t*-test in this case, to see if the difference between the means is larger than one would expect from chance variation alone.

The correlational way to examine the same hypothesis would be to measure the amount of anxiety that your participants already have. Give all of them a questionnaire asking them to rate, for example, how anxious they feel right now on a scale of 1 to 7. Then give them the math test. Now the hypothesis would be that if anxiety hurts performance, then those who scored higher on the anxiety measure will score worse on the math test than will those who received lower anxiety scores. The results typically might be presented in a table like Table 3.2 and then a chart like Figure 3.2. Each of the

TABLE 3.1

PARTIAL DATA FROM HYPOTHETICAL EXPERIMENT ON THE EFFECT
OF ANXIETY ON TEST PERFORMANCE

Participants in the High-Anxiety Condition, No. of Correct Answers	Participants in the Low-Anxiety Condition, No. of Correct Answers
Sidney = 13	Ralph = 28
Jane = 17	Susan = 22
Kim = 20	Carlos = 24
Bob = 10	Thomas = 20
Patricia = 18	Brian = 19
Etc.	Etc.
Mean = 15	Mean = 25

Note: Participants were assigned randomly to either the low-anxiety or high-anxiety condition, and the average number of correct answers was computed within each group. When all the data were in, the mean for the high-anxiety group was 15 and that for the low-anxiety group was 25. These results would typically be plotted as in Figure 3.1.

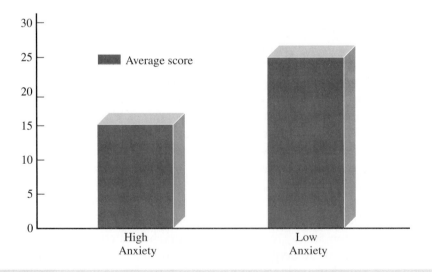

FIGURE 3.1 PLOT OF THE RESULTS OF A HYPOTHETICAL EXPERI-MENT Participants in the high-anxiety condition got an average of 15 out of 30 answers correct on a math test and participants in the low-anxiety condition got an average of 25 correct.

TABLE 3.2

PARTIAL DATA FOR A HYPOTHETICAL CORRELATIONAL STUDY OF THE
RELATIONSHIP BETWEEN ANXIETY AND TEST PERFORMANCE

Participant	Anxiety (X)	Performance (Y)
Dave	3	12
Christine	7	3
Mike	2	18
Alex	4	24
Noreen	2	22
Jana	5	15
Etc.	. . .	. . .

Note: An anxiety score (denoted X) and a performance score (denoted Y) are obtained from each
participant. The results are then plotted in a manner similar to that shown in Figure 3.2.

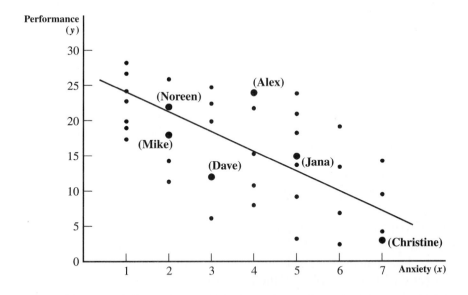

**FIGURE 3.2   PLOT OF THE RESULTS OF A HYPOTHETICAL CORRE-
LATIONAL STUDY**   Participants who had higher levels of anxiety tended to
get lower scores on the math test. The data from the participants represented in
Table 3.2 are included, along with data from other participants not represented in
the table.

points on the chart, which is called a **scatter plot**, represents an individual participant's pair of scores, one for anxiety (plotted on the horizontal or x axis) and one for performance (plotted on the vertical or y axis). If a line drawn through these points leans in a downward direction, then the two scores are "negatively correlated," which means that as one gets higher, the other gets smaller. In this case, as anxiety gets higher, performance tends to get worse, which is what you predicted. A statistic called a **correlation coefficient** (discussed later in this chapter) reflects just how strong this trend is. The statistical significance of this correlation can be checked to see whether it is large enough, given the number of participants in the study, that you can be confident it is different from zero.

Comparing the Experimental and Correlational Methods

The experimental and correlational methods are often discussed as if they were utterly different and diametrically opposed. But I hope this example makes clear that they are neither. Both methods attempt to assess the relation between two variables; in the case just discussed, they were anxiety and performance. A further, more technical similarity is that the statistics used in the two studies are interchangeable—the *t* statistic from the experiment can be converted, using simple algebra, into a correlation coefficient (traditionally denoted by the letter *r*), and vice versa. The only real difference between the two designs is that in the experimental method the presumably causal variable—anxiety—is *manipulated*, whereas in the correlational method the same variable is measured as it already exists.

This single difference is very important. It gives the experimental method a powerful advantage, which is the ability to assess causality. Because the level of anxiety in the experiment was manipulated by the experimenter, and not just measured as it already existed, you know that it was *not* caused by the participant's test performance. The only possible direction of causality is anxiety → performance. In the correlational study, you can't be so sure. The participants' anxiety might have affected their performance, but their past performance on tests might have affected their anxiety. In other words, the causality might have been anxiety → performance, *or* performance → anxiety.[5] You may have heard the statement "correlation is not causality"—it's true. A general problem with all correlational studies is the possibility that either of two correlated variables might have caused the other.

Another possibility is that both variables might be the result of some other, unmeasured factor. For example, perhaps some participants in your correlational study were sick that day, which caused them to feel anxious *and* to perform poorly. Instead of a causal pathway with two variables, that looks like this:

$$\text{Anxiety} \rightarrow \text{Poor performance}$$

the truth of the matter might be more like the three variable case,

$$\text{Illness} \begin{array}{l} \nearrow \text{Anxiety} \\ \searrow \text{Poor performance} \end{array}$$

For obvious reasons, this potential complication of correlational studies is called the "third variable" problem.

The experimental method is not completely free of complications either, however. One problem with the experimental method is that you can never be sure exactly what you have manipulated and, therefore, of where the causality was actually located. In the earlier example, it was presumed that telling participants that their life depends on how they do on the test would make them anxious. The results then confirmed the hypothesis: anxiety hurts performance. But how do you know the statement made them anxious? Maybe it made them angry, or disgusted at such an obvious lie. If so, then it was anger or disgust that hurt their performance. You only know what you manipulated at the most trivial, operational level—you know what you said to the participants. The *psychological* variable that you manipulated, however, the one that actually affected behavior, can only be inferred. (This difficulty is related to the problem with B data that was discussed in Chapter 2.) You might recognize this difficulty as the third variable problem just

---

[5]Strictly speaking, the second possibility is implausible. The actual performance on this test could not have caused the anxiety because the anxiety was measured before the test. But participants' past performances on other tests might have caused them to be anxious on this one. If that is the case, then it would be incorrect to conclude that anxiety affects performance.

discussed. Indeed, the third variable problem affects both correlational and experimental designs, in slightly different ways.

A second complication with the experimental method is that it can create levels of a variable that are unlikely or even impossible in real life. Assuming the experimental manipulation worked as intended, which in this case seems like a big assumption, how often is your life literally hanging in the balance when you take a math test? Any extrapolation from the results of this experiment to the levels of anxiety that ordinarily exist during exams could be highly misleading. Moreover, maybe in real life most people are moderately anxious. But in the experiment, two groups were artificially created: One was highly anxious; the other (again, presumably) was not anxious at all. In real life, both groups may be rare. Therefore, the effect of anxiety on performance may be exaggerated in this experiment, with respect to the degree of importance it has in real life; differences in anxiety level are typically less extreme. The correlational method, by contrast, assesses levels of anxiety that *already* exist in the participants. Thus, these levels are not artificial and they are more likely to represent anxiety as it really exists in average people. Also, notice how the correlational study included seven levels of anxiety (one for each point on the anxiety scale), whereas the experimental study included only two (one for each condition). Therefore, the results of the correlational study may reflect more precisely the degree to which anxiety affects performance in "nature" (i.e., real life).

A third disadvantage particular to the experimental method as opposed to the correlational method is that the experimental method often requires deception. I will discuss deception later, but for now just note that psychological experiments often require experimenters to lie to participants. Correlational studies rarely do.

The final disadvantage of the experimental method is the most important one. Sometimes experiments are simply not possible. For example, if you want to know the effects of child abuse on self-esteem in adulthood, all you can do is try to assess whether people who were abused as children tend to have low self-esteem, and that would be a correlational study. The experimental equivalent is not possible. You *cannot* assemble a group of children and randomly abuse half of them just to see what happens. Moreover, in personality psychology the topic of interest is often the effect of personality traits or other stable individual differences on behavior. You cannot make half of the participants extraverted and the other half introverted; you must accept their traits as the participants bring them into the laboratory.

Despite these disadvantages of experimental research, any researcher on any subject—certainly any personality psychologist—would prefer to do an experiment if he or she could. The certain determination of the direction of causality is a powerful and overwhelming advantage. But because of their topic of study, personality psychologists usually must do correlational studies. They can console themselves, as they do so, with the thought that correlational studies do have a few advantages of their own, relative to experiments.

Representative Design

A great psychologist who studied perception and judgment in the 1940s and 1950s, Egon Brunswik (1956), pointed out another important issue in research design. As was discussed earlier, researchers frequently are concerned whether their research participants are fairly representative of the population to which they wish to generalize their results. Brunswik pointed out that participants are not the only factor across which researchers must generalize. Equally pressing, though less often addressed, are concerns about generalizability across **stimuli** and **responses**. For example, a researcher might use one particular method to induce a state of "anxiety" in participants. The expected results are obtained, but what if a different method had been used to induce anxiety? In the hypothetical example earlier in the chapter, the researcher tried to make participants anxious by saying "Your life depends on your test performance." What if instead the researcher had arranged for an artificial earthquake to hit the testing room, or had parked a cageful of snakes in the corner? Would the effects of these other kinds of "anxiety" be the same? The research cannot say. Or, maybe one particular behavior (perhaps test performance) is measured to detect whether the experimental manipulation has affected how well people perform. Again, good results are obtained, but what if a different method or a different kind of performance test had been used? Does anxiety affect free-throw shooting the same way it effects performance on a math test? Unless both kinds of performance are assessed, the research cannot say.

Brunswik said that the solution to this dilemma should be the use of "representative design"—that is, research should be designed to sample across *all* of the domains to which the investigator will wish to generalize the results. A researcher who wishes to generalize to all people who might serve on juries, for example, ideally should draw participants randomly from a sample of those who are subject for jury duty. It also means that if a researcher intends to generalize his or her experimental manipulation to all methods of producing anxiety, the research should employ a sample of possible methods (it is not necessary to use *all* methods any more than it is necessary to recruit every person on earth to be in the experiment, but the ones that are used should be representative). Representative design further means that in order to generalize results to all ways of assessing performance, research needs to sample from those as well; it should try to affect several different kinds of performance that reflect the range of effects that you think exist in real life.

So a study of the effect of anxiety on performance should include several different ways to induce anxiety, and several different measures of performance.

Perhaps you will be surprised to learn that up to and including the present day, Brunswik's advice is seldom followed. Researchers do tend to sample a group of participants—they usually do not study just one—although they do not often worry about the fact that their college students are not really representative of people in the real world. But at least they use more than one participant. In the other domains of generalizability, sampling is almost nonexistent. The typical experimental study uses *one* kind of experimental manipulation and measures just *one* behavior. This makes the research less generalizable—less broadly relevant—than it might otherwise be.

Brunswik's notion of representative design, though it strikes me as elementary good sense about research, has yet to affect the practice of psychological research in a significant way. One major obstacle is that the employment of representative design, or anything like it, would make research much more expensive and time-consuming. But a small group of psychologists who call themselves "Brunswikians" is working to make his ideas more widely accepted and utilized (see Hammond & Stewart, 2001).

Effect Sizes

Psychologists, being human, like to brag about their results. Often—maybe too often—they describe the effects they have discovered as being "large," "important," or even "dramatic." Nearly always, they describe their results as "significant." These descriptions can be very confusing because there are no rules about how the first three terms can be employed. "Large," "important," and even "dramatic" are just adjectives and unfortunately can be used at will. However, there are formal and rather strict rules about how the term *significant* can be employed.

Problems with Significance Testing

A significant result, in research parlance, is not necessarily large or important, let alone dramatic. But it is a result that probably did not occur by chance. A difference between experimental conditions, or a correlation, that is said to be significant at the "5 percent" level is one that is different from zero to a degree that, by chance alone, would be expected about 5 percent of the time. A difference or correlation significant at the 1 percent level is different from zero to a degree to be expected by chance about 1 percent of

"The figures for the last quarter are in. We made significant gains in the fifteen-to-twenty-six-year-old age group, but we lost our immortal souls."

the time, and so is traditionally considered a stronger result. Various statistical formulas, some quite complex, are employed to calculate the likelihood that experimental or correlational results exceed zero by chance alone. The more unlikely, the better.

For example, the results in Figures 3.1 and 3.2 might be evaluated by calculating the **p-level** (probability level) of the difference in means (in the experimental study) or of the correlation coefficient (in the correlational study). In each case, the p-level would give the probability that the difference in means or the correlation coefficient is really zero. If the result is significant, this means that the statistic probably did not arise by chance; its *real value* (sometimes called the *population value*) is probably not zero.

This traditional method of statistical data analysis, called null-hypothesis significance testing (NHST), is deeply embedded in the psychological research literature and in current research practice. But I would not be doing my duty if I failed to warn you that insightful psychologists have been critical of this method over the years (e.g., Rozeboom, 1960) and the frequency and intensity of this criticism have increased recently (e.g., Loftus, 1996). Indeed, some psychologists have seriously suggested that "significance testing" like this should be banned (Hunter, 1997; Schmidt, 1996)! That may be going a bit far, but there are several serious problems with NHST. This chapter is not the place for an extended discussion, but it might be worth a few words to describe some of the more obvious difficulties (see also Harris, 1997).

One obvious difficulty with the traditional method is that the criterion for a significant result is arbitrary. Why is a result of $p < .05$ significant, when a result of $p < .06$ is not? There is no real answer to this question; it is just an arbitrary convention of unknown origin (though I strongly suspect it has something to do with the fact that we have five fingers on each hand). Another obvious difficulty is that, strangely, the chances of getting a significant result vary with how many participants are in the study. The very same strength of an effect that is nonsignificant with thirty participants might suddenly become highly significant if there are fifty participants. This is worrisome because nature hasn't changed, just the conclusion the scientist reaches about it. Yet another common difficulty is that even experienced researchers too often misinterpret a nonsignificant result to mean "no result". If, for example, the obtained p-level is .06, researchers sometimes conclude that there is no difference between the experimental conditions, or no relationship between two correlated variables. But actually, the probability is only 6 out of 100 that this is the correct conclusion to draw.

This observation leads to the most important difficulty with traditional significance tests: The p-level tells only about the probability of one kind of error, conventionally called a **Type I error**. A Type I error is deciding that one variable has an effect on or a relationship to another variable, when really it does not. The p-level gives the odds of making this kind of error (e.g., a p-level of .05 means you have a 5 percent chance of being wrong if you conclude you have a real effect). But there is another kind of error that can be made, called a **Type II error**. A Type II error is deciding that one variable does *not* have an effect on or relationship with another variable, when it really *does*. Unfortunately, there is no way to estimate the probability of a Type II error without making all sorts of extra assumptions (Cohen, 1994; Gigerenzer, Hoffrage, & Kleinbolting, 1991).

The bottom line is this: When you take a course in psychological statistics, if you haven't done so already, you will have to learn about significance testing and how to do it. But it is probably not as useful a technique as it might look to be at first, and psychological research practice seems to be moving, slowly but surely, away from it (Abelson, Cohen, & Rosenthal, 1996; Wilkinson & the Task Force on Statistical Inference, 1999). What you really want to know from your data is, are your results important? Significance testing was designed to answer this question, but it is not really up to the job.

Correlations

Sometimes on the basis of doubts like these and sometimes not, the psychologists who are better analysts of data do not just stop with significance. They move on to calculate a number that will reflect the size, as opposed to the likelihood, of their result. This number is called an **effect size**. An effect size is much more meaningful than a significance level. Indeed, the latest edition of the *Publication Manual of the American Psychological Association* (which sets the standards that must be followed by almost all published research in psychology), explicitly says that probability value associated with statistical significance does not reflect "the magnitude of an effect or the strength of a relationship. For the reader to fully understand the importance of your findings, it is almost always necessary to include some index of effect size or strength of relationship" (American Psychological Association, 2001, p. 25). Many measures of effect size exist, the most commonly used being the **correlation coefficient**. Despite its name, its use is not limited to correlational studies. The correlation coefficient can be used to describe the strength of the effect in either a correlational *or* an experimental study (Funder & Ozer, 1983).

CALCULATING CORRELATIONS

To calculate a correlation coefficient, in the usual case, you start with two variables. For example, in Table 3.2 the two variables were anxiety and performance. The first step is to arrange all of the scores on the two variables into two columns, with each row containing the scores for one participant. Traditionally, these columns are labeled X and Y, and also traditionally, the variable you think is the cause is put in the X column and the variable you think is the effect is put in the Y column. So, in this example, X is anxiety and Y is performance. Then you apply a common statistical formula found in any statistics textbook to these numbers or, perhaps more commonly these days, punch the numbers into a computer, maybe even a handheld calculator.[6]

The result is a correlation coefficient (the most common kind of correlation coefficient is called the *Pearson* r). This is a number that—if you did the calculations right—is somewhere between -1 and $+1$. If two variables are unrelated, the correlation between them will be near zero. If the variables are positively associated—as one goes up, the other tends to go up too, like height and weight—then the correlation coefficient will be greater than zero, or a positive number. If the variables are negatively associated—as one goes up, the other tends to go down, like anxiety and test performance—then the correlation coefficient will be less than zero, or a negative number.[7] Essentially, if two variables are correlated (positively or negatively), this means that

---

[6]Programs to calculate the correlation coefficient are also available online. For example, excellent and easy-to-use calculators are available at faculty.vassar.edu/lowry/corr_stats.html and calculators.stat.ucla.edu/correlation.php.

[7]Also, if you draw a line through the points on a scatter plot, as in Figure 3.2, and the line slopes up (left to right), the correlation is positive. If the line slopes down, the correlation is negative. If the line is flat (horizontal), the correlation is zero.

one of them can be predicted from the other. For example, Figure 3.2 shows that if I know how anxious you are, then I can predict (to a degree) how well you will do on a math test.

Not everybody knows this, but you can also get a correlation coefficient from experimental studies. For the experiment on test performance, for example, you could just give everybody in the high-anxiety condition a "1" for anxiety and everybody in the low-anxiety condition a "0." These 1's and 0's would go in the X column, and participants' matching levels of performance would go in the Y column. Or, there are formulae to directly convert the statistics usually seen in experimental studies into correlations. For example, the *t* or *F* statistic can be directly converted into an *r*.[8] It is a good practice to do this conversion whenever possible, because then you can compare the results of correlational and experimental studies using a common metric.

INTERPRETING CORRELATIONS

To interpret a correlation coefficient, it is not enough to just use statistical significance. A correlation becomes significant in a statistical sense merely by probably not being zero, which depends as much on how many participants you managed (or could afford) to recruit as on how strong the effect really is. Instead, you need to look at the actual size of the correlation. Some textbooks provide rules of thumb. One that I happen to own says that a correlation (positive or negative) of .6 to .8 is "quite strong," one from .3 to .5 is "weaker but still important," and one from .3 to .2 is "rather weak." (I have no idea what these phrases are supposed to mean. Do you?)

Another commonly taught way to evaluate effect sizes is to square them, which tells "what percent of the variance the correlation explains." This certainly sounds like what you need to know, and the calculation is wonderfully easy. A correlation of .30 means that "only" 9 percent of the variance is explained by the correlation (.30 squared being .09). A correlation of .40 means that "only" 16 percent of the variance is explained. These correlations are often viewed as small, perhaps because the mathematically inclined are quick to calculate that for a .30 correlation, 91 percent of the variance is *un*explained, and for a .40 correlation, 84 percent is unexplained.

---

[8]The most commonly used statistic that reflects a difference between two experimental groups is the *t* (the outcome of a *t*-test). The standard symbol for the commonly used Pearson correlation coefficient is *r*. The experimental *t* can be converted to the correlational *r* using the following formula:

$$r = \sqrt{\frac{t^2}{t^2 + (n_1 + n_2 - 2)}}$$

where n_1 and n_2 are the sizes of the two samples (or experimental groups) being compared.

Despite the wide popularity of this squaring method (if you have taken a statistics course you were probably taught it), I think it is a *terrible* method for evaluating effect size. The real and perhaps only result of this pseudo-sophisticated maneuver is to make correlations seem very small. It is the case that both in correlational research in personality and in experimental research in social psychology, the effect sizes expressed in correlations rarely exceed .40 (Funder & Ozer, 1983). If this result is considered to "explain" (whatever that means) "16 percent of the variance" (whatever that means) leaving "84 percent unexplained," then we are left with the vague but disturbing conclusion that neither sort of research has accomplished much. Yet this conclusion is not correct. It is statistically confusing and substantively misleading (Ozer, 1985). Worst of all, it is almost impossible to understand. What is really needed is a way to evaluate the size of correlations to help understand the strength and, in some cases, the usefulness of the result obtained.

THE BINOMIAL EFFECT SIZE DISPLAY

What is needed is a method, beyond squaring correlations, to demonstrate in some concrete manner how big these effect-size correlations really are. Rosenthal and Rubin (1982) provided a brilliant technique for doing just that, called the **Binomial Effect Size Display** (BESD). Let's use Rosenthal and Rubin's favorite example to illustrate how it works.

Assume you are studying 200 participants, all of whom are sick. An experimental drug is given to 100 of them; the other 100 are given nothing. At the end of the study, 100 are alive and 100 are dead. The question is, how much difference did the drug make?

Sometimes the answer to this question can be reported in the form of a correlation coefficient that is calculated from the data on how many participants lived and died. For example, you may be told that the data show that the correlation between taking the drug or not, and living or dying, is .40. If the report stops here (as it usually does), you are left with the following questions: What does this mean? Was the effect big or little? If you were to follow the common practice of squaring correlations to yield "variance explained," you might conclude that "only 16 percent of the variance is explained" (which does not sound like much) and decide the drug is nearly worthless.

The BESD provides another way to think about the size of a correlation coefficient. Through some further, simple calculations, you can move from a report that "the correlation is .40" to a concrete display of what that correlation means in terms of specific outcomes. For example, as shown in Table 3.3, a correlation of .40 means that 70 percent of those who got the drug are still alive, whereas only 30 percent of those who did not get the drug are still

TABLE 3.3			
THE BINOMIAL EFFECT SIZE DISPLAY			
	Alive	Dead	Total
Drug	70	30	100
No drug	30	70	100
Total	100	100	200

Life and death outcomes for participants in a hypothetical 200-person drug trial, when the correlation between drug administration and outcome $r = .40$.

Source: After Rosenthal & Rubin, 1982.

alive. If the correlation is .30, those figures would be 65 percent and 35 percent, respectively. As Rosenthal and Rubin pointed out, these effects might only explain 16 percent or even 9 percent of the variance, but in either case if you got sick, would you want this drug?

The computational method begins by assuming a correlation of zero, which gives each of the four cells in the table an entry of 50 (i.e., if there is no effect, then 50 participants receiving the drug will live and 50 will die—it does not matter whether they get the treatment or not). Then take the actual correlation (in the example, .40), remove the decimal (.40 becomes 40), divide by two (in this case yielding 20), and add it to the 50 in the upper-left-hand cell (yielding 70). Then adjust the other three cells by subtraction. Because each row and column must total 100, the four cells, reading clockwise, become 70, 30, 70, and 30.

This technique works with any kind of data. Alive and dead can be replaced with any kind of dichotomized outcomes—"better-than-average school success" and "worse-than-average school success," for example. The treatment variables could become "taught with new method" and "taught with old method." Or, the variables could be "scores above average on school motivation," and "scores below average on school motivation," or any other personality variable (see Table 3.4). One can even look at predictors of success by major leage baseball teams (see Figure 3.3).

The fundamental message of the BESD is that correlational effects need to be interpreted more carefully than they usually are. It is both facile and misleading to use the frequently taught method of squaring correlations if the intention is to evaluate effect size (squaring is useful for other, more technical purposes). The BESD, by contrast, shows vividly both how much of an effect an experimental intervention is likely to have, and how well one can predict an outcome from an individual measurement of difference. So, when you read—later in this book or in a psychological research article—that one

TABLE 3.4

THE BINOMIAL EFFECT SIZE DISPLAY USED TO
INTERPET SCHOOL DATA

School Performance

School Motivation	Above average	Below average	Total
Above average	50	50	100
Below average	50	50	100
Total	100	100	200

School performance outcomes for 200 students above and below average on school motivation when correlation between the two variables $r = 0$.

School Performance

School Motivation	Above average	Below average	Total
Above average	65	35	100
Below average	35	65	100
Total	100	100	200

School performance outcomes for 200 students above and below average on school motivation when correlation between the two variables $r = .30$.

variable is related to another with a correlation of .30, or .40, or whatever, you should construct a BESD in your mind and evaluate the size of the correlation accordingly.

Ethics

The Uses of Psychological Research

Like any other human activity, research involves ethical issues. Some of the issues are common to all research. One is the concern that the results may be used for harmful purposes. Just as physicists who build H-bombs should worry about what their invention can do to people, and to the world, so too should psychologists be aware of the consequences of what their research might discover.

For example, one part of psychology—behaviorism—has long aimed to develop a technology to control behavior. The technology is not quite here yet,

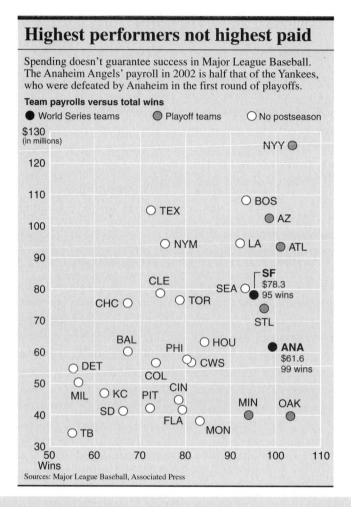

Highest performers not highest paid

Spending doesn't guarantee success in Major League Baseball. The Anaheim Angels' payroll in 2002 is half that of the Yankees, who were defeated by Anaheim in the first round of playoffs.

Team payrolls versus total wins

● World Series teams   ◐ Playoff teams   ○ No postseason

Sources: Major League Baseball, Associated Press

FIGURE 3.3   STATISTICS IN THE NEWSPAPER   An analysis of the relationship between total payrolls of major-league baseball teams and the total number of games won in the 2002 season. This chart appeared in the sports section of the *Los Angeles Times*. Notice the conclusion expressed by the headline. Is it valid? The correlation between payroll and games won is .44, which according to the Binomial Effect Size Display means that a team that pays above-average salaries has a 72 percent chance of winning more than half its games, whereas a team that pays below-average salaries only has a 28 percent chance.

but if it ever comes, it will raise ethical questions about who decides what behaviors to create and whose behaviors should be controlled. The main figure in behaviorism, B. F. Skinner, wrote extensively about these issues (e.g., Skinner, 1948, 1971). Issues of how research is used also sometimes arise in the field of personality assessment. For example, during the 1930s and 1940s some employers used personality tests to try to identify and screen out job applicants inclined to be pro-union (Zickar, 2001). Does this seem ethical to you?

Yet another issue arises when psychologists choose to study racial differences and sex differences. Putting aside whatever purely scientific merits this work might have, it raises a fundamental question about whether its findings are likely to do more harm than good. If some racial group really is lower in intelligence, or if men really are better (or worse) at math than women, do we really want to know? The arguments in favor of exploring these issues are that science should study everything and (on a more applied level) that knowing the basic abilities of a group might help in tailoring educational programs specifically to the needs of its members. The arguments against this research are that such findings are bound to be misused by racists and sexists and therefore can become tools of oppression themselves, and that knowledge of group characteristics is not really very useful for tailoring programs to individual needs.

When the question comes down to whether to study or not to study a given topic, psychologists like other scientists almost always come down on the side of studying it. After all, ignorance never got anybody very far. Still, there are an infinite number of interesting, unanswered questions out there that one could usefully investigate. When a psychologist devotes his or her research time to proving that one race is smarter than another, or that men or women are really superior to the other gender in some respect, it is hard not to wish that he or she had found some other worthwhile topic to investigate instead.

Truthfulness

Truthfulness is another ethical issue common to all research. The past few years have seen a number of scandals in physics, medicine, and psychology in which researchers either plagiarized the work of others or fabricated their own data. Lies cause difficulty in all sectors of life, but they are particularly worrisome in research because science is based on truth and trust. Scientific research is the attempt to seek truth in as unbiased a way as one can manage. Scientific lies, when they happen, undermine the very foundation of the field. Science without truthfulness is completely meaningless.

All scientists *must* trust each other for the process to work. If I report to you some data that I have found, you might disagree with my interpretation—that is fine, and in science this happens all the time. Working through disagreements about what data mean is essential scientific activity. But if you cannot be sure that I really did find those data, then there is no basis for further discussion. Even scientists who vehemently disagree with each other on fundamental issues generally take each other's truthfulness for granted (contrast this with the situation in politics). If they cannot, then science stops dead in its tracks.

Deception

The fundamental reliance of science on truth makes the use of deception in research somewhat worrisome. Quite frequently, psychologists tell their research participants something that is not true.[9] The purpose of such deception usually is to make the research "realistic." A participant might be told— falsely—that a test he or she is taking is a valid IQ or personality test, for example, so that the experimenter can assess the participant's reaction when he or she receives a poor score. Or a participant might be told that another person was described by a "trained psychologist" as "friendly" and "unsociable," to see how the participant resolves this sort of inconsistency. One of the most famous deception experiments was the one in which Stanley Milgram (1975) led participants to believe they were administering fatal electric shocks to an innocent, screaming victim (the "victim" was actually an actor).

The American Psychological Association has developed a detailed set of ethical guidelines that psychological researchers are supposed to follow. Research universities also all have institutional review boards (called *IRBs*) that review the ethics of all procedures conducted with human participants. The decisions made by IRBs, in turn, are increasingly guided by federal regulations. The guidelines used by the American Psychological Association and by most IRBs do allow deception, although the limits are narrower than they used to be. The Milgram experiment probably would not be allowed today, although studies like the other two described are still conducted frequently.

Three arguments are usually given for why deception should be allowed. The first is that participants have given their "informed consent" to be deceived. The second is that the little white lies told to participants usually do no harm. Indeed, some research indicates that participants report enjoying and profiting more from studies where they were deceived than from those in which they were not deceived (Smith & Richardson, 1983). The third argument is that certain topics cannot be investigated without the use of a little deception. For example, if you want to know whether people will stop and help when confronted by an unconscious stranger, the only real way to know is to put such a stimulus (really a confederate of the experimenter) in front of a participant and see what happens (Darley & Batson, 1967; Darley & Latané, 1968).

---

[9]This is not the same as simply withholding information, as in a double-blind drug trial, where neither the patient nor the physician knows whether the drug or placebo is being administered. Deception involves knowingly telling a lie.

You can decide for yourself whether these are convincing arguments. For my part, I do not see how one can give "informed consent" to be deceived; the situation seems oxymoronic (Baumrind, 1985). But more important, I think that excuses for deception that focus on the probable lack of harm to the participant miss the point. Indeed, the experience of being in an experiment is too mild and too infrequent to generate much in the way of consequences for participants. The real victim of a deception experiment, it seems to me, is the psychologist. The problem with lying is that once it begins, you never know when it has stopped. In a deception experiment, one person (a psychologist) has told a lie to another person (the participant). When the experimenter says, "I lied to you, but the experiment is now over," is it really over? (In at least one experiment I know of, it wasn't! See Ross, Lepper, & Hubbard, 1975.) And, on a broader scale, the psychologist has been exposed as somebody who, if for a "right" end, will lie to you. What does this do to the credibility of psychology as a science (Greenberg & Folger, 1988)?

One small way in which I see this harm is in my own research. Although I have not done any deception experiments in a long time (and since I made that decision I have never really felt the lack), often my participants do not believe me! They spend the experimental hour wondering what I am *really* studying. Being sophisticated about psychologists and what they do, my participants find it hard to believe that I am actually studying what I have said I am studying. And I cannot blame them one bit. Until psychologists stop employing deception as a matter of routine, why should anybody believe a word they say? (For a contrary view on this matter, see Sharpe, Adair, & Roese, 1992.)

The most powerful defense of deception in psychological research is that without it, certain topics cannot be investigated. For example, without the use of deception, important research on obedience, bystander intervention, and aggression could never have been conducted. Of course, these and other topics could still be studied in the real world. Instead of showing your participants a hypothetical stimulus person who not only does not exist but also probably never could, let your participants watch and judge somebody who is real. Instead of constructing artificial situations where people are led to think they have succeeded or failed (assuming they believe you), follow them into their real lives where success and failure happen all the time. Obedience, bystander intervention, and aggression can be observed in daily life as well. This could be done, and sometimes is done, but notice how research that follows this advice is restricted to correlational studies. The powerful advantages of the experimental method—its determination of the direction of causality, as discussed earlier—is lost.

The trade-offs are difficult to evaluate. In my own research, as I mentioned, I no longer use deception. But other psychologists have come to other conclusions, and deceptive research is still quite common. I do know this:

The issue of the use of deception in psychological research is not a simple one. There is plenty of room for reasonable disagreement, and my own strong misgivings are fairly rare within the field. Most psychologists believe that with proper controls, the use of deception in research is perfectly safe and ethical. They further believe that deception is necessary to allow psychological research to address certain important issues. If you are reading this book as part of a personality course, your instructor probably has a strong opinion about the permissibility of deception. Why not ask him or her what that opinion is, and why? Then, draw your own conclusions.

Summary

Psychology puts a great deal of emphasis on the methods by which knowledge can be obtained, and in general is more concerned with improving the understanding of human nature than with cataloging specific facts. The essence of science is that its conclusions should be based on data. Data can vary widely in quality, and in personality psychology the important dimensions of data quality are reliability, validity, and generalizability. Reliability refers to the stability or repeatability of measurements. Validity refers to the degree to which a measurement actually measures what it is trying to measure. Generalizability is a broader concept that subsumes both reliability and validity, and refers to the class of other measurements to which a given measurement is related. The plan one uses for gathering psychological data is the research design; the three main types are case, experimental, and correlational. Case studies examine particular phenomena or individuals in detail and can be an important source of new ideas that might apply more generally. To test these ideas, correlational and experimental studies are necessary. Each of these methods has advantages and disadvantages, but the experimental method is the only one that can determine the direction of causality. Representative design is a technique used to maximize the generalizability of research results. The best way to summarize research results is in terms of effect size, which describes numerically the degree to which one variable is related to another. One good measure of effect size is the correlation coefficient, which can be evaluated with the Binomial Effect Size Display. Ethical issues relevant to psychology include the way research results are used, truthfulness in science, and the use of deception in research with human participants.

SUGGESTED READINGS: RESEARCH METHODS

American Psychological Assocation (2001). *Publication manual of the American Psychological Association.* Washington, DC: American Psychological Association.

> *This book is the bible for psychological researchers. It sets the standards that must be followed for all research that is published in journals published by the American Psychological Association, and most other psychological journals also follow it. The book is full of information and advice on the proper conduct, analysis, and reporting of psychological research. Every aspiring psychologist should have a copy.*

Block, J. (1993). Studying personality the long way. In D. C. Funder, R. D. Parke, C. Tomlinson-Keasey, & K. Widaman (Eds.), *Studying lives through time: Personality and development* (pp. 9–41). Washington, DC: American Psychological Association.

> *A survey of his own approach to research by one of the most respected modern personality psychologists. Jack Block describes his approach to data gathering and research design, including longitudinal research (which follows individuals over long spans of time to see how they develop).*

Cronbach, L. J., & Meehl, P. E. (1955). Construct validity in psychological tests. *Psychological Bulletin, 52,* 281–302.

> *A difficult article, but the classic presentation of how personality psychologists think about the validity of their measurements. One of the most influential methodological articles ever published.*

Cronbach, L. J., Gleser, G. C., Nanda, H., & Rajaratnam, N. (1972). *The dependability of behavioral measurements: Theory of generalizability for scores and profiles.* New York: Wiley.

> *If anything, even more difficult than Cronbach & Meehl's article, but nearly as important. This book is the definitive treatment of generalizability theory, which has fundamentally changed the way psychologists think about reliability and validity.*

Rozeboom, W. W. (1960). The fallacy of the null-hypothesis significance test. *Psychological Bulletin, 57,* 416–428.

> *One of the first and still one of the most clear and persuasive of the critiques of the traditional method of hypothesis testing in psychology. After years of being ignored, the issues raised long ago by Rozeboom are finally beginning to receive more attention, but standard research practice still has not changed.*

Rosenthal, R., & Rosnow, R. L. (1991). *Essentials of behavioral research: Methods and data analysis* (2nd ed.). New York: McGraw-Hill.

> *One of the best primers for a beginning researcher. This book includes many topics (such as effect size) not handled well in other methods or statistics texts. You will have to read this book to see what its authors mean by the advice "Think Yiddish, write British."*

Wilkinson, L., & The Task Force on Statistical Inference (1999). Statistical methods in psychology journals: Guidelines and explanations. *American Psychologist, 54*, 594–604.

> *In response to rising controversy about the use of significance testing in psychology, including a proposal to ban such testing altogether, the American Psychological Association put together a task force of distinguished methodologists to examine the issue. This article is their final report. In a subtle but strong way it argues for moving significance testing out of its traditionally central role in psychological data analysis. It includes wise commentary on a number of issues concerning how psychologists analyze their data.*

PART II

HOW PEOPLE DIFFER: THE TRAIT APPROACH

People are different. It is obvious that no two individuals look exactly alike—not even "identical" twins—and it is almost as obvious that no two individuals behave, think, or feel exactly the same way. Everyday language contains many words to describe these differences in personality. Some years ago, the distinguished personality psychologist Gordon Allport sent his assistant, Henry Odbert, to count how many of these words he could find in an unabridged English dictionary. A few weeks later, red-eyed and weary, Odbert reported back the answer: 17,953 (Allport & Odbert, 1936). The words he found included familiar personality traits such as *arrogant, shy, trustworthy,* and *conscientious,* and also more obscure terms such as *delitescent, vulnific,* and *earthbred.* All of these words describe personality traits, and the fact that the dictionary contains so many suggests that traits are an important part of how people naturally talk and think about each other.

The trait approach to personality psychology attempts to build on this intuition by translating the natural, informal language of personality traits into a formal psychology that measures traits and uses them to predict and explain human behavior. The assessment and use of personality traits are the topics of the next four chapters.

I begin by considering a first, basic question about the approach: Do personality traits exist? Unless they did, a trait approach wouldn't make much sense. A debate over this very issue occupied many psychologists for several years, as you will learn in Chapter 4, and the lessons from this debate have important implications for understanding personality. Chapter 5 describes how psychologists construct and use personality tests. Chapter 6 describes how laypersons—nonpsychologists—assess personality in their daily lives without needing to use personality tests, and considers the circumstances under which such everyday assessments are and are not likely to be accurate. Chapter 7 describes the way personality traits have been used to understand several different important kinds of human behavior, including self-control, drug abuse, and racial prejudice, and also considers the following questions: Are all 17,953 personality traits really necessary? Can this list be reduced to just a few that are really essential? The chapter concludes with a brief discussion of the fundamental developmental question: Where do personality traits come from?

The overall goal of the next four chapters is to provide an introduction to the way personality psychologists try to measure and understand, and use their knowledge about, the ways in which people are psychologically different from one another.

PERSONALITY TRAITS
AND BEHAVIOR

Some of the words that describe how people are psychologically different from each other were invented by psychologists. These include terms such as *neuroticism, ego control,* and even more obscure labels like *parmia, praxia,* and *alexithymia.* More often, however, psychologists who follow the trait approach begin with ordinary language and common sense (e.g., Gough, 1995), and their work seeks a theoretical and empirical basis for the scientific measurement of individual differences in more familiar concepts such as sociability, reliability, dominance, nervousness, and cheerfulness (Funder, 1991).

As a result, personality psychology and everyday human observation are in some ways not so very different; both seek to characterize people using similar kinds of terms, and it is even possible to compare one approach to the other. For example, research on accuracy in personality judgment, to be considered in Chapter 6, compares everyday judgments people make of each other to various kinds of research-based personality assessments (Funder, 1995, 1999).

As we begin to consider the trait approach to personality psychology, two points are important to note. The first is that this approach is based on empirical research that is mostly correlational in design (see Chapter 3). Trait psychologists put a great deal of effort into the careful construction of methods, such as personality tests, for accurately measuring how people differ. As we will see, some of these methods have become complex and statistically sophisticated. Whether the method is beguilingly simple or fearsomely complex, however, an ultimate criterion for any measurement of a personality trait is whether it can be used to predict behavior (Wiggins, 1973). If a person scores high on a measure of "dominance," can we accurately predict that he or she will act in a relatively dominant manner (relative, that is, to other people) in one or more life situations? The answer to this question will be indexed, statistically, by the correlation between the score obtained on the measure of dominance and some separate indication of the person's dominant behavior.

The second notable aspect of the trait approach is that it focuses exclusively on individual differences. It does not attempt to measure how dominant, sociable, or nervous anybody is in any absolute sense; there is no zero point on any dominance scale or on any measure of any other trait. The trait approach does try to measure the degree to which a person might be more or less dominant, sociable, or nervous than someone else. (Technically, therefore, trait measurements are made on ordinal rather than ratio scales.[1])

This focus on comparisons is one of the great strengths of the trait approach. It is important to understand and to be able to assess how people differ from one another, as they always do. But as so often happens (remember Funder's First Law), it must also be considered a weakness: The trait approach, by its very nature, is prone to neglect those aspects of human psychology that are common to all people, as well as the ways in which each person is unique. (Other approaches to personality, considered later in this book, do focus on those aspects of human nature.)

The Measurement of Individual Differences

One of my favorite quotes from the personality literature comes from an old chapter by Clyde Kluckhohn and Henry Murray. In elegant, albeit sexist, phrasing, the quote reads:

> Every man is in certain respects (a) like all other men, (b) like some other men, (c) like no other man. (Kluckhohn & Murray, 1961, p. 53)

What Kluckhohn and Murray meant, first, is that *certain* psychological properties and processes are universal. All people have similar, basic needs for food, water, and sex, for example. Their second point is that other properties of people differ but in ways that allow individuals to be grouped. People who are highly dominant, for instance, might be essentially alike in a way

---

[1]A measurement is said to lie on an ordinal scale when its value reflects the rank ordering of each entity measured. For example, three racers would earn values of 1, 2, and 3 if they placed first, second, and third. There is no 0 point on this scale (you can't place "0th"), and the numbers 1 and 3 do not imply that the third-place runner was necessarily three times slower than the first-place runner. A measurement lies on a rational scale if the scale has a true 0 point and the measurement's value can be assessed in terms of ratios with other measurements. For example, one runner might go 3 miles an hour, a second runner 2 miles an hour, and a third (rather slow) runner might go 1 mile an hour. These measurements are rational because there is such a thing as 0 miles an hour, and because the first runner can be said to be going 3 times faster than the third runner. Trait measurements are ordinal rather than rational because there is no such thing as "zero dominance," for example, and if one person has a dominance score of 50 and another has a score of 25, this implies the first person is more dominant than the second but not necessarily twice as dominant, whatever that might mean.

"'Give me liberty or give me death.' Now, what kind of person would say something like that?"

that allows them to be meaningfully distinguished from those who are more submissive (although they might still differ among themselves in other respects). And third, in still other ways each individual is unique and cannot be meaningfully compared to anyone else. Each person's genetic makeup, past experience, and view of the world are different from those of anyone who ever has lived or ever will live (Allport, 1937).

The trait approach comes in at the second, middle level of this analysis, while at the same time and necessarily neglecting the other two. Because the trait approach is based on the ideas that all men are "like *some* other men" and that it is meaningful and useful to assess broad categories of individual difference, it assumes that in some real sense people *are* their traits. Theorists differ on whether traits simply describe how a person acts, are the sum of everything a person has learned, are biological structures, or are some combination of all of these determinants. But for all trait theorists, these dimensions of individual difference are the building blocks of which personality is constructed.

Which raises a fundamental problem.

People Are Inconsistent

You can judge or measure the degree to which someone is shy, conscientious, or dominant, but even minimal experience will reveal that whatever you conclude the truth to be, there will be numerous exceptions. The individual may be shy with strangers but warm, open, and friendly with family members. The individual may be conscientious at work but sloppy and disorganized at home. The individual may be dominant with people of the same sex but deferential to people of the opposite sex, or vice versa. This kind of inconsistency is seen all the time.

Casual observation, therefore, is sufficient to confirm that personality traits are not the only factors that control an individual's behavior; situations are important, as well. Some situations will make a person more or less shy, more or less careful, more or less friendly, and more or less dominant. This is because situations vary according to what people are present and what the implicit rules are (Price & Bouffard, 1974). You act differently at home than you do at work partly because your home is inhabited by your family members, while your workplace is inhabited by your co-workers (and perhaps, competitors). You act differently at a party than at a church because some pretty specific, albeit usually implicit, rules of decorum limit what is acceptable behavior at a church. Parties have implicit rules, too, but they provide more leeway (Snyder & Ickes, 1985).

If situations are so important, then what role does personality play? Some people might answer, not much. Perhaps the behavior of individuals is so inconsistent and apt to change according to the given situation that there is no use characterizing them in terms of broad or global personality traits. If correct, this answer would imply not only that the personality assessments that many professional psychologists do are a colossal waste of time, but also that much of the everyday thinking and talking about people is fundamentally wrong. You should consider the possibility, therefore, that traits do not exist, that people change who they are according to the situation they are in, and that everybody is basically the same.

Do you find this idea outrageous? The answer you give may depend on your age and stage in life. When I teach personality psychology to college undergraduates, who are typically eighteen to twenty-two years old, I find most students nod and calmly accept the possibility raised in the preceding paragraph. The suggestion that people have few consistent attributes to their personality and change who they are from moment to moment depending on the immediate situation sounds about right to them—or at least it does not immediately strike them as preposterous.

Thus, I was somewhat taken aback the first time I presented this same possibility to a night-school class. The course was ostensibly the same as the one I was teaching during the daytime that semester, but the night-school students were for the most part adult, working professionals from the metropolitan area, rather than dorm-dwelling eighteen- to twenty-two-year-olds. These older students had the opposite reaction to the idea that individual differences are not important and that how you act depends on the situation you happen to be in at the moment: "Are you crazy?"

I wish I could document this developmental trend more formally, but I cannot because the relevant study has not been done yet. But it is my strong impression that students who are still financially dependent on their parents, have not yet found spouses or started a family, and perhaps have not yet even settled on a career goal find the idea that people are the same and that how you act depends on the situation to be quite reasonable—indeed, they wonder why anybody would make a fuss about it. After all, their own personalities are still in the design stage. Older students who are on a career track, have started families, and otherwise have undertaken adult roles and responsibilities, by contrast, find the idea outlandish.

What I am proposing, therefore, is that people differ from each other in the degree to which they have developed a consistent personality for themselves (Baumeister & Tice, 1988; Bem & Allen, 1974; Snyder & Monson, 1975). This might be related to age and life experience—older people and those with greater and broader experience may have more consistent personalities. If I am right about this, then the degree to which you find the idea that personality does not exist to be reasonable might depend on whether you have developed a consistent personality yourself!

The Person-Situation Debate

Whether or not it violates your intuition to claim that behavior is so inconsistent that, for all intents and purposes, personality traits do not exist, an argument about just this point occupied a good deal of the attention of a large number of personality psychologists for more than two decades (and it continues to preoccupy some—see Cervone & Shoda, 1999). These psychologists were and are the protagonists in the "person-situation debate," which focuses on this very question: Which is more important for determining what people do, the person or the situation?

To a considerable degree, the debate was triggered by the publication in 1968 of a book by Walter Mischel entitled *Personality and Assessment*.[2] Mischel argued in his book that behavior is too inconsistent from one situation to the next to allow individual differences to be characterized accurately in terms of broad personality traits. Other psychologists—including, not surprisingly, those who were heavily invested in the technology and practice of personality assessment—emphatically disagreed. Thus was the person-situation debate joined.

---

[2]Ironically, given its title, the book usually is interpreted as arguing that personality does not exist and that assessment is impossible.

The rest of this chapter reviews the basis and resolution of this debate. Ordinarily, arguments among psychologists are one of the things I try to spare you in this book. I would rather teach you about psychology itself than about what psychologists do, much less what they argue about. At the risk of sounding defensive, I hope to convince you that this particular argument is different. It is not just a tempest in a teapot, as arguments among specialists so often are. Rather, the consistency controversy goes to the heart of how everybody thinks about people.

There are two issues here. The first is: Does the personality of an individual transcend the immediate situation and moment and provide a consistent guide to his or her actions, or is what a person does utterly dependent on the situation he or she is in at the time? Because our everyday intuitions tell us that people do have consistent personalities (everybody uses personality-trait terms all day long), this question leads to a second issue: Are common, ordinary intuitions about people fundamentally flawed, or basically correct?

When I talk about the debate that was, to some extent, triggered by Mischel's book, I want to avoid the trap of focusing too much on Mischel and his particular arguments, and not enough on the issues that make the debate they triggered both interesting and important. A small cottage industry sprang up within personality psychology during the 1970s, the main activity of which seemed to be to figure out what Mischel did and did not actually say. I was briefly a member of this enterprise myself (Funder, 1983).

But figuring out what Mischel did and did not say is a frustrating way to spend your time, both because the original book contained many qualifying phrases and escape clauses, and because Mischel seems to have changed his position on some fundamental issues during the intervening years (e.g., Mischel & Shoda, 1995). Mischel frequently has claimed that his views are less extreme than portrayed by others. He often protests, for example, that he never meant to say that personality does not exist. At one psychologists' meeting attended by Mischel years ago, the chairman looked up and down the table and then intoned, ironically, "We don't seem to have a Mischelian here with us today" (E. R. Hilgard, personal communication, October 1975).

Nevertheless, the situationist arguments are important, regardless of what Mischel or others now say about them, because they are aimed at the very foundations of the trait approach. In the discussion that follows I believe that my presentation of the situationist position is faithful to its basic tenets.

Stripped to its essentials, the situationist argument has three parts:

1. A thorough review of the personality research literature reveals that there is a limit to how well one can predict what a person will do based on any measurement of any aspect of that person's personality, and this upper limit is a small upper limit.

"Can I call you back, R.B.? I've got a situation here."

2. Therefore, situations are more important than personality traits in determining behavior. (This is the origin of the term *situationism* [Bowers, 1973].)

3. Therefore, not only is the professional practice of personality assessment a waste of time, but also everyday intuitions about people are fundamentally flawed. The trait words used to describe people are not legitimately descriptive, and more generally, people tend to see others as being more consistent across situations than they really are.

Let us consider each part separately.

Predictability

THE SITUATIONIST ARGUMENT

The definitive test of the usefulness of a personality trait is its ability to predict behavior. If you know somebody's level or score on a trait, you should be able to forecast what that person will do in the future. Situationists argue that this ability is severely limited. There is no trait that you can use to predict someone's behavior with very much accuracy.

Mischel's book surveys some of the research concerning the relationships between self-descriptions of personality and direct measurements of behavior, between others' descriptions of personality and direct measurements of behavior, and between one measurement of behavior and another. Or, to use the terms introduced in Chapter 2, Mischel looked at the relationships between S data and B data, between I data and B data, and between B data and other B data. The first two comparisons address the ability of personality trait judgments to predict behavior—for example, can an acquaintance's judgment of your sociability predict how sociable you will be at Friday's party? The third comparison addresses the consistency of behavior across situations—for instance, if you are sociable at Friday's party, will you also be sociable at Tuesday's work meeting?

The data reported in the studies that Mischel reviewed were not, for the most part, taken from real life. Nearly all of the behavioral measurements—the B data—were gathered in laboratory settings. Some studies measured "attitude toward authority" by asking participants for their opinions of photographs of older men, some measured "self-control" by seeing how long children could wait for candy treats provided by the experimenters, and so forth. Only rarely was behavior assessed in more-or-less natural situations, such as measures taken of cheating on games at a summer camp. Such more naturalistic studies were (and remain) rare, primarily because they are so difficult and expensive (see the discussion of B data in Chapter 2). Either way, the critical result is how well a person's behavior in one situation can be predicted either from his or her behavior in another situation or from his or her personality trait scores.

In the research literature, predictability and consistency are indexed by a statistic called a **correlation coefficient**. As you will recall from Chapter 3, a correlation coefficient is a number that ranges between -1 and $+1$ and that indexes the association or relation between two variables, such as a personality score and a behavioral measurement. If the correlation is positive, it means that as one variable increases, so does the other; the higher someone's sociability score, for example, the more parties he or she is likely to attend. If the correlation is negative, it means that as one variable increases, the other decreases; the higher someone's shyness score, for example, the *fewer* parties he or she is likely to attend. Both positive and negative correlations imply that one variable can be predicted from a knowledge of the other. But if the correlation is near zero, it means the two variables are unrelated; perhaps, for example, scores on this particular sociability test have nothing to do with how many parties one attends.

Mischel's original argument was that correlations between personality and behavior, or between behavior in one situation and behavior in another, seldom exceed .30. Another prominent situationist, Richard Nisbett (1980), later revised this estimate upward, to .40. The implication in both cases was that such correlations are small, and that personality traits are unimportant in the shaping of behavior.

This claim concerning the (un)predictability of behavior hit the field of personality psychology in the early 1970s with surprisingly devastating force. Some personality psychologists, and even more psychologists outside the field of personality, concluded that for all intents and purposes, personality did not exist. This conclusion was based on two premises. The first was that situationists are right and .40 is the upper limit for the predictability of behavior from personality variables or behavior in other situations. The other implicit but necessary premise was that this upper limit is a low upper limit.

THE RESPONSE

It took the representatives of the pro-personality side of this debate a few years to get their rebuttals in line, but when they finally did, they came up with three.

Unfair Literature Review   The first counterargument was that Mischel's review of the personality literature, which kicked off the whole controversy, was selective and unfair. After all, the relevant research literature goes back more than sixty years and contains literally thousands of studies. Mischel's review, by contrast, is quite short (only sixteen pages [pp. 20–36] of his book, about the length of a typical undergraduate term paper) and concentrates on a few studies that obtained disappointing results rather than on the— perhaps more numerous—studies that obtained more impressive results.

This is a difficult point to prove or disprove, however. On the one hand, it is obvious that Mischel's review was selective because it is so short. Moreover, it is obvious that he did not go out of his way to find the best studies in the literature; the very first empirical study that Mischel cited (Burwen & Campbell, 1957) was hardly exemplary. The study was filled with methodological and empirical flaws (e.g., a number of the participants deliberately sabotaged the research questionnaires) yet still managed to find a bit of evidence in favor of the trait it examined, which was "attitude toward authority." Many of the other studies Mischel cited were little better; moreover, even some of those managed, despite everything, to find evidence for the consistency of personality and behavior (see Block, 1977).

On the other hand, some studies are bound to find positive results on the basis of chance alone. And although it would be easy to put together a short literature review that looks much more positive than Mischel's, it is not clear how one would prove that such a review were any more fair or less selective. It is extremely difficult to characterize the general findings of entire research literatures (see Rosenthal, 1980), and the literature on behavioral consistency is no exception.

I frankly do not know how to establish whether the literature in general supports consistency with a few exceptions or whether it supports inconsistency with a few exceptions. So, to move the argument along, let me just "stipulate" (as lawyers say) the Mischel-Nisbett figure: Assume that a correlation of about .40 is the upper limit for how well personality traits can predict behavior, as well as for how consistent behavior is from one situation to another.

We Can Do Better   A second counterargument to the situationist critique grants the .40 upper limit, as I just did, but claims that this limit is a result of poor or less-than-optimal research methodology. The weak findings summarized by Mischel do not imply that personality is unimportant; they merely imply that psychologists can and must do better research.

One way in which research could be done better, according to this counterargument, is for research to move out of the laboratory more often. As I mentioned earlier, nearly all of the behavioral measurements that formed the basis for the situationist critique were made in laboratory situations. Some of these situations were probably dull and uninvolving for the participants. How about behavior in real life? Personality is much more likely to become relevant, it has been argued, in situations that are real, vivid, and important to the individual in question (Allport, 1961). For example, when a person in a laboratory is asked to respond to a picture of an older individual, his or her personality may or may not become involved (Burwen & Campbell, 1957). But when a person is about to make his or her first parachute jump, personality seems likely to play a more important role (Epstein, 1980; Fenz & Epstein, 1967).

A second kind of research improvement that frequently has been advocated takes into account that some people might be more consistent than others. *Moderator variables* could be used to identify those people.[3] For example, one study asked participants how consistent they were on the trait of sociability, and found that the behavior of those who said they were consistent was easier to predict accurately than the behavior of those who said they were inconsistent (Bem & Allen, 1974).[4] Research on the trait of self-monitoring suggests that some people, called *high self-monitors,* quickly change their behavior according to the situation they are in, whereas *low self-monitors* are more likely to express their personality consistently from one situation to the next (Snyder, 1987; see also Chapter 7). Finally, some behaviors might be more consistent than others. Elements of expressive behavior, such as how much a person gestures or how loudly a person talks, are likely to be consistent across situations, whereas more goal-directed behaviors, such as trying to impress someone, are more likely to depend on the situation at the moment (Funder & Colvin, 1991; see also Allport & Vernon, 1933).

---

[3]A *moderator variable* is one that affects, or "moderates," the relationship between two other variables.

[4]Although this was an influential finding and an important idea, Chaplin and Goldberg (1985) provided evidence that the finding is difficult to replicate. Later, Zuckerman et al. (1988) surveyed a broad range of research literature and concluded that this effect of self-rated consistency on behavioral predictability is small but probably real.

A third research improvement that has been advocated proposes focusing efforts to predict behavior or general behavioral *trends*, instead of actions at particular moments. Thus, rather than try to predict whether somebody will act in a friendly fashion next Tuesday at 3:00 P.M., one might be better off trying to predict how friendly that person will behave on average over the next year. The basic principle of aggregation, which you will recall from Chapter 3, establishes that such an average can be much more accurately predicted than can a single act at a single time (Fishbein & Ajzen, 1974; Epstein, 1979).

The issue here is more than just a matter of statistics. It concerns the whole meaning and purpose of personality-trait judgments. When you say that somebody is friendly, or conscientious, or shy, are you trying to predict what he or she will do at a specific time and place, or are you expressing a prediction of how that person will generally act over the long haul (McCrae, 2002)? In most cases, I think, the answer is the latter. When you wish to understand someone, or wish to select a roommate or an employee, it is not so critical to know what the person will do at a specific place and time, because that will always depend on the exact situation at the moment. Rather, you need to know how the person will act *in general* across the various relevant situations of life. You understand that somebody might be late on rare occasions because his or her car will not start; you know that anybody can have a bad day and be grouchy. But when choosing an employee or a roommate, what you really need to know is how reliable will the person be in general? Or, how friendly is the person, usually?

These three suggestions—measure behavior in real life, check for moderator variables, and predict behavioral trends rather than single acts—are all good ideas for improving personality research. However, they represent potential more than reality. To follow any of these suggestions is difficult. Real-life behaviors are not easy to assess (see Chapter 2), moderator variables may be subtle and difficult to measure (Chaplin, 1991), and assessment of the prediction of behavioral trends requires, by definition, that the researcher make many direct observations of behavior, not just a few. So, although these suggestions provide good reasons to think that the situationist critique may underestimate the levels of consistency in people's behavior, there is not yet enough research to prove that behavioral consistency can regularly get much higher than what is reflected by the correlations of around .40 that the situationists now concede.

Besides, both of the first two responses to the situationist critique miss a more basic point, discussed next.

.40 Is Not Small   Remember that to be impressed (or depressed) by the situationist critique of personality traits, you must believe two things: (1) A correlation of .40 represents the true, upper limit to which one can predict behavior from personality, or see consistency in behavior from one situation to another; and (2) this upper limit is a small upper limit. The discussion so far has concentrated on responses to point 1. But if for some reason you were to conclude that a correlation of .40 was not small in the first place (point 2), then the limit would cease to be so worrisome, and the force of the situationist critique would largely dissipate.

Thus, it is critical to evaluate how much predictability a correlation in the range granted by the situationist critiques really represents. But to evaluate whether .40 is big or little, or to assess any other statistic, you need a standard of comparison.

Two kinds of standards are possible, absolute and relative. To evaluate this correlation against an absolute standard, you would calculate how many correct and incorrect decisions a trait measurement with this degree of validity would yield in a hypothetical context. To evaluate this correlation against a relative standard, you can compare this degree of predictability conceded for personality traits with the ability of other methods to predict behavior. Let's do both.

An absolute evaluation of a .40 correlation can be obtained from Rosenthal and Rubin's (1982) Binomial Effect Size Display (BESD), which was described in Chapter 3. I won't repeat the description here but will go straight to the bottom line: According to the BESD, a correlation of .40 means that a prediction of behavior based on a personality trait score is likely to be accurate 70 percent of the time (assuming a chance accuracy rate of 50 percent). (This figure should not be confused with the "percentages of variance explained" discussed in Chapter 3, which are computed in a different way and have a far different—and far more difficult—interpretation.) Seventy percent is far from perfect, but it is enough to be useful for many purposes. For instance, an employer choosing who to put through an expensive training program could save large amounts of money by being able to predict with 70 percent accuracy who will or will not be a successful employee at its conclusion.

Let's work through an example. Say a company has 200 employees being considered for further training but the budget only allows for training 100 of them. Let's further assume that, overall, 50 percent of the company's employees could successfully complete the program. The company picks 100 employees at random and spends $10,000 to train each one. But, as I said, only half of them are successful. So the company has spent a total of $1 million to get 50 successfully trained employees, or $20,000 each.

But consider what happens if the company uses a selection test—a test that has been shown to correlate .40 with training success. By selecting the top half of the scorers on this test for training, the company will get 70 successful trainees (instead of 50) out of the 100 who are trained, still at a total cost of $1 million but now at only about $14,300 per successful trainee. In other words, using a test with a .40 validity could save the company $5,700 per successful trainee, or about $400,000. That will pay for a lot of testing.

What about a relative standard? Well, what is the most appropriate basis of comparison when trying to evaluate the predictive ability of personality traits? Situationists, you will recall, believe that the *situation*, not the person, is all important in the determination of behavior. To evaluate the ability of personality traits to predict behavior, therefore, the appropriate comparison to draw would seem to be with the ability of situational variables to predict behavior. That is the topic of the next section.

Situationism

A key tenet of the situationist position is that personality does not determine behavior—situations do. To evaluate the degree to which a behavior is affected by a personality variable, the routine practice is to correlate a measure of behavior with a measure of personality. But how do you evaluate the degree to which behavior is affected by a situational variable?

This question has received surprisingly little attention over the years. When it has been addressed, the usual practice was rather strange: the power of situations was determined by subtraction. Thus, if a personality variable was found to correlate .40 with a behavioral measurement and it therefore "explained 16 percent of the variance," the other 84 percent was assumed, by default, to be due to the situation (e.g., Mischel, 1968).

Of course, this is not a legitimate practice, even if it used to be common. I have already protested the needlessly misleading obscurity of the whole "percent of variance" language (see Chapter 3). But even if you accept this terminology, it would be just as reasonable to attribute the "missing" variance to other personality variables that you did not measure as it would be to attribute it to situational variables that you also did not measure (Ahadi & Diener, 1989). Moreover, to assign variance by subtraction in this way does not allow you to say anything about *which* aspects of the situation might be important, in a way parallel to how trait measures tell you which aspects of personality are important.

It has long seemed remarkable to me that the situationists have been willing to claim that situations are important, yet have been seemingly unconcerned with measuring situational variables in a way that indicates precisely how or how much situations affect behavior. After all, not everybody responds to the same situation in the same way. When situationists claim that situations are important but do not specify what about them is important or to what extent, then, as one trait psychologist pointed out,

> situations turn out to be "powerful" in the same sense as Scud missiles [the erratic weapons used by Iraq during the Persian Gulf wars] are powerful:

They may have huge effects, or no effects, and such effects may occur virtually anywhere, all over the map. (Goldberg, 1992, p. 90)

Moreover, there is no need for the situationists to sell themselves so short—to be so vague about what specific aspects of situations can affect behavior. There is a large and impressive body of psychological research that does allow the effects of situations to be directly calculated. The evidence comprises nearly every study in experimental social psychology (e.g., Aronson, 1972).

In the typical social psychological experiment, two (or more) separate groups of participants are placed, randomly and usually one at a time, into one or another of two (or more) different situations. The social psychologist measures what the participants do. If the average behavior of the participants who are placed in one situation or "condition" turns out to be significantly different (statistically speaking—see Chapter 3) from the average behavior of the participants placed in the other condition, then the experiment is deemed successful.

For example, you might be interested in the effect of incentives on attitude change. In an experiment, you could ask participants to make a statement they do not believe, such as that a dull game was really interesting. Then, you could test to see if they come to believe these statements—that the game was not dull after all. Some of your participants could be offered a large incentive (say, twenty dollars) to make the counter-attitudinal statement, while the rest are offered a smaller incentive (say, one dollar). If the two groups of participants change their attitudes about the game to different degrees, then you can conclude that the difference in incentive between the two conditions was the effective cause of this difference in attitude (although the exact process by which this happened would still be open to question). The way the two situ-

FIGURE 4.1   SCUD   A scud missile that apparently missed its target.

ations were constructed to be different must have led the participants to respond differently, and therefore the experiment demonstrated an effect of a situational variable on behavior (Festinger & Carlsmith, 1959).

The vast literature of experimental social psychology provides a treasure trove of specific examples of situational effects. For the present topic, one needs to ask how large those effects are, compared to the effects of personality variables on behavior. Perhaps surprisingly, social psychologists historically have paid very little attention to the size of the situational effects they study. They have concentrated on statistical significance, or the degree to which their results would not have been expected by chance. As was discussed in Chapter 3, this is a separate matter from effect size or what one might consider "actual" significance, because even a small effect can be highly significant statistically, if one has studied a large-enough number of participants.

Personality psychologists, by contrast, have always focused on the size of the effects. The key statistic in personality research, the correlation coefficient, is a measure of effect size and not statistical significance. The "personality coefficient" of .40 is ordinarily not comparable with the effects found in social psychological studies of situational variables, therefore, because the two styles of research do not employ a common metric.

Fortunately, this difficulty can be remedied easily. As mentioned in Chapter 3, the experimental statistics used by social psychologists can be converted algebraically into correlations of the sort used by personality psychologists. A few years back, Dan Ozer and I did just that (Funder & Ozer, 1983). From the social psychological literature, we chose three prominent examples of the power of situations to shape behavior. We then converted the results of those studies to effect-size correlations.

The first classic study that we chose concerned the "forced compliance" effect demonstrated by Festinger and Carlsmith (1959) in a study similar to the one I just described. Participants were induced to tell innocent, new participants that a dull experiment was actually interesting. The participants were offered either twenty dollars or one dollar for doing this. The counterintuitive result was that the participants paid one dollar actually changed their attitudes, after telling the lie, to believe that the experiment was more interesting than they had originally thought. The participants paid twenty dollars, in contrast, did not change their attitudes—they still thought the experiment had been boring.

This study was one of the early, important demonstrations of the workings of **cognitive dissonance**. The explanation given by Festinger and Carlsmith was that participants felt dissonance as a result of saying something they did not believe, but that a payment of twenty dollars was sufficient to reduce their uneasy feelings. One measly dollar was not enough to make them feel better, however, so the lower-paid participants had to change their own attitudes in order that their words would not be so out of line with their beliefs.

"Obviously, some people here do not appreciate the gravity of our situation."

This effect is a classic of the social psychological literature and perhaps one of the most important and interesting findings in the field. Yet the statistical size of this effect had seldom been reported. Ozer and I performed the simple calculation: the effect of incentive on attitude change following counter-attitudinal advocacy turns out to correspond to a correlation of $-.36$ (the correlation has a negative sign because more incentive leads to less change). This is a direct, statistical measure of how strongly rewards can affect attitude change.

A second important program of research in social psychology has concerned bystander intervention. Darley and his colleagues staged several faked but dramatic incidents in which participants came upon apparently distressed individuals lying helplessly in their path (Darley & Batson, 1967; Darley & Latané, 1968). The research was intended to find out if the participants would stop and help.

The answer turned out to depend, among other things, on whether other people were present and on whether the participant was in a hurry. The more people that were present, the less likely the participant was to stop and help; the correlation indexing the size of this effect was $-.38$. Also, the greater the participant's hurry, the less likely the participant was to help; the correlation indexing the size of this effect was $-.39$.

The third program of research we examined was Stanley Milgram's classic investigation of obedience. In a famous series of studies, Milgram's research assistants ordered participants to give apparently painful and dangerous (but fortunately bogus) electric shocks to an innocent "victim" (Milgram, 1975). If the participants objected, the assistant said "the experiment requires that you continue."

Milgram identified two variables as relevant to determining whether the participants would obey this command. The first was the isolation of the victim. If the victim was in the next room and could not be heard protesting, or could be heard only weakly, obedience was more likely than if the victim was right in front of him or her. The correlation that reflects the size of the effect of victim isolation is .42. The second important variable was the proximity of the experimenter. Obedience was more likely if the research assistant giving the orders was physically present than if he or she gave orders over the phone or on a tape recorder. The correlation that reflects the size of the effect of experimenter proximity turned out to be .36.

Recall that the size of the personality coefficient that was supposed to reflect the maximum relationship that can be obtained between personality variables and behavior is about .40. Now, compare that to the effects of situational variables on behavior, as just surveyed: .36, .38, .39, .42, and .36.

One can draw two different conclusions from these results. This little reanalysis by Ozer and myself has been described by others as implying that neither personality variables nor situational variables have much of an effect on behavior. That was hardly our point! We reanalyzed these particular experiments precisely because, as far as we knew, nobody had ever doubted that each and every one of them demonstrated a powerful, important influence of a situational variable on behavior. These experiments are classics of social psychology—they will be found in any textbook on the subject and have contributed important insights into the bases of social behavior.

We prefer a second conclusion, therefore: that these situational variables are important determinants of behavior, but that many personality variables are important as well. When put on a common scale for comparison, the size of the effects of the person and of the situation are much more similar than many had assumed. And, in this light, calling a correlation of .40 a "personality coefficient" loses a little of its pejorative edge.

Now we are ready to consider the third part of the situationist argument.

Are Person Perceptions Erroneous?

Recall that the situationists argue that the ability of personality variables to predict behavior is limited if not nonexistent; that situations are much more important; and that people's everyday perceptions of one another, which consist to a large degree of judgments of personality traits, are therefore largely erroneous. Now that we have dealt carefully with the first two parts of this argument, the third falls apart of its own weight. The effects of personality on behavior do seem sufficient to be perceived accurately. Despite the situationist critique, our intuitions probably were not that far off base after all.

Both everyday experience and any fair reading of the research literature make one thing abundantly clear: When it comes to personality, one size does not fit all. People really do act differently from each other. Even when they are all in the same situation, some individuals will be more sociable, or nervous, or talkative, or active than others. And when the situation changes, those differences will still be there (e.g., Funder & Colvin, 1991). The 17,953 trait terms in the English language did not appear out of thin air. Ideas about personality traits are an important part of Western culture (and perhaps all cultures; see Chapter 14). Consider Eskimos and snow: It has long been noted that the Eskimo languages have many more words to describe snow than do the languages of those who live in warmer climes (Whorf, 1956; Clark & Clark, 1977).[5] This is assumed to be because snow is important to Eskimos; they build shelters from it, they travel across it, and so forth. (Skiers also have a specialized vocabulary with many different words for snow.) The need to discriminate between many different kinds of snow has led Eskimos to develop words to describe each kind, in order to communicate better with one another about this important topic.

The same thing seems to have happened with the language of personality. People are psychologically different and it is both important and interesting to note just how. Words arose to describe these differences, words that make us more sensitive to the differences and that make it possible to talk about them.

The proliferation of trait words is not finished yet; consider the relatively "new" words *jock, geek, preppy,* and *Val.*[6] Personality psychologists are not leaving the language alone either. They have introduced the terms *self-monitoring, private self-consciousness, public self-consciousness,* and even *parmia* and *threctia* to delineate aspects of personality that they did not believe were described precisely enough by the existing English language (Cattell, 1965).

---

[5]This long-standing, famous claim stirred a controversy when the linguist Geoffrey Pullum (1991) claimed that the Eskimos do *not* have a particularly large number of words for snow. In response, Cecil Adams (2001), author of the newspaper column *The Straight Dope,* reported that he was able to find "a couple of dozen terms for snow, ice and related subjects" in an Eskimo dictionary and that Eskimo languages are "synthetic," meaning new words are constructed as the need arises, making it impossible to count how many snow words actually exist. Another observer counted 49 words for snow and ice in West Greenlandic, including *qaniit* (falling snow), *qinuq* (rotten snow), and *sullarniq* (snow blown in a doorway) (Derby, 1994).

[6]In a bit of regional (California) slang that is probably already passing out of use, a *Val* (short for "Valley Girl") is a teenage girl from the San Fernando Valley (just north of Los Angeles) who is stereotyped as being empty-headed, materialistic, and boy-crazy.

Conclusion

Persons and Situations

The evidence is overwhelming that people are psychologically different from one another, that personality traits exist, and that people's impressions of each others' personalities are based on much more than mere illusion. It is important to be aware of this evidence to be able to counter the argument, still sometimes heard, that traits are little more than illusions. But having achieved this awareness, it is also important to put the relative role of personality traits and situations into perspective. Situational variables are relevant to how people will act *under specific circumstances.* Personality traits are better for describing how people act *in general* (Fleeson, 2001).

For example, consider relationships. Every person you have a relationship with—your parents, your siblings, your friends, the people you date— is different and you will therefore and necessarily act differently with each of them, to some degree. You might date two different people, or have six good friends, and treat no two of them in quite the same way. One might say each of these people presents you with a different situation, and you respond accordingly. At the same time, aspects of your behavior are more general and are likely to remain consistent across relationships. Research has shown that broad traits such as extraversion, sociability, and shyness predict how many friends you usually have overall and the degree to which, in general, you will find yourself in conflict with them (Asendorpf & Wipers, 1998; Reis, Capobianco, & Tsai, 2002). The most general aspect of your relationship behavior might be simply the degree to which you tend to be happy. Three personality variables—a low level of negative emotionality, a high level of positive emotionality, and "constraint"—tend to predict the degree to which people enjoy happy and nonabusive relationships regardless of who the relationship is with (Robins, Caspi, & Moffitt, 2002).

Another good example can be found in the world of the workplace. Every job is a special situation with its own requirements; some require careful attention to detail, some require mechanical skill, some require good relations with customers, and so forth. But as the industrial psychologists Walter Borman and Louis Penner have noted, some aspects of good job performance are general across almost *all* jobs. One of these is a behavioral pattern they call "citizenship performance," in which the employee tries in various ways to promote the goal of the organization. This might include behaviors such as helping to teach new employees their jobs and alleviating conflict in the workplace, being aware of problems and opportunities as they arise and trying to respond to them, and in general having the kind of good attitude that makes everything go better. This kind of behavior is predicted by traits such as conscientiousness, and is a boon to organizational performance regardless of whether the work setting is a store, a factory, or an office (Borman & Penner, 2001).

The specific aspects of how people relate to specific relationship partners are important, as are the special requirements that arise for every type of job. Personality variables are about something else that is also important: the psychological aspects of a person that he or she carries along, consistently and throughout life, from one relationship, job, and situation to the next.

Individual Differences

Late in his career, the distinguished Harvard social psychologist Roger Brown wrote:

> As a psychologist, in all the years . . . I had thought individual differences in personality were exaggerated. I compared personality psychologists to cultural anthropologists who took pleasure in, and indeed derived status from, the exoticism of their discoveries. I had once presumed to say to Henry A. Murray, Harvard's distinguished personologist: 'I think people are all very much the same.' Murray's response had been; 'Oh you do, do you? Well, you don't know what the hell you're talking about!' And I hadn't. (Brown, 1996, p. 169)

FIGURE 4.2 MURRAY AND BROWN The personality psychologist Henry Murray (on the left) once got into an argument with the social psychologist Roger Brown (on the right) over whether everybody was basically the same. Years later, Brown concluded Murray was right: people really are different from each other.

This little exchange captures the person-situation debate in a nutshell. Historically, and even to some extent to the present day, social psychologists have tended to regard individual differences as being relatively unimportant, while personality psychologists of course put such differences front and center. Near the end of his career Roger Brown decided the personality psychologists were right, and in that decision he finally came to agree with what most nonpsychologists have intuitively believed all along, as well as with the central lesson of the person-situation debate: People *are* psychologically different from each other, and these differences matter. This conclusion implies that it is important for psychologists to think long and hard about the best concepts to describe these differences, to develop appropriate technologies to measure them, and finally to find ways to use them to predict and to understand what people do. These are the topics of the next three chapters.

Summary

The trait approach to personality begins by assuming that individuals differ in their characteristic patterns of thought, feeling, and behavior. These patterns are called personality traits. Classifying people in this way raises an important problem, however: people are inconsistent. Indeed, some psychologists have suggested that people are so inconsistent in their behavior from one situation to the next that it is not worthwhile to try to characterize them in terms of personality traits. The controversy among psychologists over this issue is called the person-situation debate. Opponents of traits argue, first, that a review of the personality literature reveals that the ability of traits to predict behavior is extremely limited; second, that situations are therefore more important than personality traits for determining what people do; and third, that not only is personality assessment (the measurement of traits) a waste of time, but also many of people's intuitions about each other are fundamentally wrong. The responses to the first of these arguments are that a fair review of the literature reveals that the predictability of behavior from traits is better than is sometimes acknowledged, that better research methods can make this predictability even higher, and that the putative upper limit for predictability (a correlation of about .40) yields better outcomes than is sometimes recognized. The response to the second of these arguments is that many important effects of situations on behavior are no bigger, statistically, than the documented size of the effects of personality traits on behavior. If the responses to the first two arguments are valid, then the third, that both assessment and people's intuitions are fundamentally flawed, falls apart of its own weight. The many personality-trait terms in the English language give support to the importance of traits, which provide a useful way to predict behavior and understand personality. Situational variables are best-suited for predicting behavior in specific situations, whereas personality traits are more relevant to patterns of behavior that persist across relationship partners, work settings, and other life situations.

PERSONALITY ASSESSMENT I: PERSONALITY TESTING AND ITS CONSEQUENCES

If something exists, it exists in some quantity, and if it exists in some quantity, it can be measured.
—Edward Lee Thorndike (Thorndike, 1905; cited in Cunningham, 1992, p. 35)

If you accept the conclusion of Chapter 4—that personality traits are real and everybody has them—then Thorndike's quote, above, implies that the next task is to measure them. Are you more or less friendly, for example, than the person sitting next to you? To answer this kind of question, or, more broadly, for personality traits to be useful for the scientific understanding of the mind, for the prediction of behavior, or for any other purpose, measurement is essential. The next two chapters explore "personality assessment," the enterprise of trying to accurately measure characteristic aspects of personality.

The Nature of Personality Assessment

Personality assessment is a professional activity of numerous research, clinical, and industrial psychologists, and it is a prosperous business. Clinicians may measure how depressed you are in order to plan treatment, whereas potential employers would probably be more interested in measuring your conscientiousness to decide whether to offer you a job. But there is more to personality assessment than just measuring traits.

An individual's **personality** consists of *any* characteristic pattern of behavior, thought, or emotional experience that exhibits relative consistency across time and situations (Allport, 1937). These patterns include the terms commonly thought of as personality traits that were discussed in Chapter 4, and personality psychology has a long, still active, and still fruitful tradition of conceptualizing and assessing such traits.

But these patterns also include other kinds of variables, including motives, intentions, goals, strategies, and subjective representations (the ways in which people perceive and construct their worlds; see Chapter 17). These variables indicate the degree to which a person desires one goal as opposed to another, or thinks the world is changeable as opposed to fixed, or is generally happy, or is optimistic as opposed to pessimistic, or is sexually attracted to members of the same or the opposite sex. All of these variables, and many others, are relatively stable attributes of the psychological makeup of individuals, and any attempt to measure them necessarily entails personality assessment. As a result, assessment is relevant to an extremely broad range of research, including nearly every topic of interest to personality, developmental, and social psychologists.

Moreover, personality assessment is not restricted to psychologists. The term is usually used to refer to assessments by psychologists in research, in clinics, or in private industry; their results sometimes have important consequences for the individuals involved. But assessments by *non*psychologists are even more widespread, and a good case could be made that they are even more important. These personality assessments are done by you, your friends, your family—and by me, in my off-duty hours—all day long, every day. As mentioned at the beginning of Chapter 4, personality traits are a fundamental part of how we think about each other and about ourselves. We choose who to befriend and who to avoid on the basis of our assessments of them—will this person be reliable, or helpful, or honest—and they make the same judgments and choices concerning us. We even base our feelings about ourselves partly on our beliefs about our personalities—are we competent, or kind, or tough? The judgments we make of the personalities of each other and ourselves are at least as consequential as those that any psychologist will ever make.

Regardless of whether the source of a personality assessment is a psychologist, an acquaintance, or a psychological test, the most important thing to know about it is the degree to which it is right or wrong. And regardless of the source of a personality assessment, it must be evaluated according to the same criteria. When professional personality judgments or personality tests are evaluated, the evaluation is said to be of their *validity*. When amateur judgments are evaluated, the term *accuracy* is generally used instead. Despite the difference in terms, the basis of the evaluation is the same either way. Two basic criteria are available: agreement and prediction (Funder, 1987, 1995, 1999). The agreement criterion asks: Does this judgment agree with other judgments obtained through other techniques or from other judges (whether professional or amateur)? The prediction criterion asks, Can this judgment of personality be used to predict behavior?

The topic of this chapter and the next is personality assessment—how personality is judged by professionals and by amateurs. The remainder of this chapter considers the business of personality assessment and how psychologists construct and use personality tests, as well as some of the consequences of testing. Chapter 6 considers personality assessment by amateurs—people who are not trained or paid to be psychologists but who nonetheless practice psychology every day.

The Business of Testing

Each year the American Psychological Association (APA) holds a convention. It's quite an event. Thousands of psychologists take over most of the downtown hotels in a city such as San Francisco, Boston, or Washington, D.C., for a week of meetings, symposia, and cocktail parties. One of the biggest attractions is always the exhibit hall, where dozens of high-tech, artistically designed booths fill a room that seems to go on for acres. These booths are set up, at great expense, by several kinds of companies. One group is textbook publishers; all the tools of advertising are applied to the task of convincing college professors like me to assign their students to read (and buy) books such as the one you now hold in your hand. Another group is manufacturers of videotapes and various strange gadgets for therapy and research. Yet another group is psychological testers. Their booths typically distribute free samples that include not only personality and ability tests but also shopping bags, notebooks, and even beach umbrellas. These freebies prominently display the logo of their corporate sponsor: the Psychological Corporation, Consulting Psychologists Press, the Institute for Personality and Ability Testing, and so on. These goodies are paid for by what they are intended to sell: personality tests.

You can get a free "personality test" even without going to the APA convention. On North Michigan Avenue in Chicago, on the Boston Common, at Fisherman's Wharf in San Francisco, and in Westwood in Los Angeles, I have seen people distribute brightly colored brochures on which are printed "Are you curious about yourself? Free personality test enclosed." Inside the brochure is something that in many ways looks like a conventional personality test—two hundred questions to be answered true or false (one item reads, "Having settled an argument out do you continue to feel disgruntled for a while?"). But as it turns out, it is really a recruitment pitch. If you take the test and go for your "free evaluation"—which I do not recommend—you will be told two things. First, you are all messed up. Second, the people who gave you the test have the cure: you need to join a certain "church" that will provide the therapy you so desperately need.

The personality testers who distribute free samples at the APA convention and those who hand out free "personality tests" on North Michigan

Avenue have a surprising amount in common. Both are seeking new customers, and both use all the usual techniques of advertising, including free samples. The tests they distribute look superficially alike. And they both trade on what seems to be a nearly universal desire to know more about personality. The brochure labeled "Are you curious about yourself?" asks a pretty irresistible question. The more staid tests distributed at the APA convention likewise offer an intriguing promise of finding out something about your own or somebody else's personality that might be interesting, important, or useful.

But below the surface they are not the same. The tests peddled at the APA convention are, for the most part, well-validated instruments that are useful for many purposes. The ones being pushed at tourist destinations from coast to coast are potentially dangerous frauds. But you cannot tell which is which just by looking at them. To tell a valid test from an invalid one you need to know something about how personality tests and assessments are constructed, how they work, and how they can fail. Read on.

Personality Tests

The personality testing companies that are so well represented at APA meetings do a good business. They sell their product to clinical psychologists, to the personnel departments of large corporations, and to the military, for example. You have most likely taken at least one personality test at some point in your life, and you are likely to take more.

One of the most widely used personality tests is the Minnesota Multiphasic Personality Inventory, or MMPI.[1] This test was designed for use in the clinical assessment of individuals with psychological difficulties, but it has also been widely used for purposes such as employment screening. Another widely used test is the California Psychological Inventory, or CPI; it is similar to the MMPI in many ways but is designed for use with *non-disturbed* individuals. Others include the Sixteen Personality Factor Questionnaire, or 16PF; the Strong Vocational Interest Blank, or SVIB (used for vocational guidance in school settings); the Hogan Personality Inventory, or HPI (used by employers for personnel selection); and many more.

Many personality tests, including those just listed, are "omnibus" inventories designed to measure a wide range of personality traits. The NEO Personality Inventory, for instance, measures five broad traits along with a large number of subscales (Costa & McCrae, 1997).

---

[1]By a tradition of mysterious origin, nearly all personality tests are referred to by their initials—all capital letters, no periods.

Other personality tests are designed to measure just one trait. There are tests to measure shyness, self-consciousness, self-monitoring, empathy, attributional complexity, nonverbal sensitivity, something called "Type A" (a hostile personality pattern that makes the person vulnerable to heart attack), something else called "Type C" (a passive personality pattern that supposedly makes the person vulnerable to cancer), and so on. No one has ever done an exact count, but there are at least thousands of such tests, and new ones are introduced every day.

S-Data Versus B-Data Personality Tests

To use the terms introduced in Chapter 2, many personality tests—probably most—provide S data. They ask you about what you are like, so the score you receive amounts to a summary of how you have described yourself. The shyness scale consists of a bunch of questions that ask how shy you are, the attributional complexity scale asks you how complexly you think about the causes of people's behavior, and so forth. Other personality tests yield B data. The MMPI is a good example. It presents items—such as "I prefer a shower to a bath"—not because the tester is interested in the literal answer, but because answers to this item are informative about some aspect of personality (in this case, empathy—preferring the shower is the empathic response, for some reason) (Hogan, 1969).

Another kind of B-data personality test has been introduced very recently. The "implicit associations test" (IAT) measures how quickly participants can respond to instructions to discriminate between terms that apply to "me" or to "others," and between terms that are relevant, or not, to the trait being measured (Greenwald, McGhee, & Schwartz, 1998). One recent study measured shyness in this way (Asendorpf, Banse, & Mücke, 2002). Participants sat at a computer keyboard and responded as quickly as they could as to whether terms (e.g., "self," "them") referred to "me" or "others," and then to whether other terms (e.g., "inhibited," "candid") referred to "shy" and "nonshy," and finally did both tasks at the same time. The theory is that people who "implicitly" (i.e., not necessarily consciously) know they are shy will have faster associations between "me" and "shy" than between "me" and "nonshy." The same study also gathered more conventional, S-data self-ratings of shyness. Finally, the participants were videotaped as they interacted with an attractive individual of the opposite sex, a task calculated to induce shyness.

The fascinating result was that "controlled" aspects of shyness, such as how long people spoke, could be predicted by the S-data shyness scores. (Shy people speak less.) However, more uncontrolled or spontaneous indicators of shyness, such as facial expressions and tense body posture, were predicted much better by the IAT measure. This result suggests that people are only partially conscious of their own knowledge of their shyness, but that their deeper, underlying knowledge can not only be measured, it can be used to predict behavior (this idea will be discussed further in Chapter 17).

Is intelligence a personality trait? Psychologists have differing opinions about this. Either way, it can be noted that tests of intelligence, or "IQ tests," also yield B data. Imagine trying to assess IQ with an S-data test. Such a test would include questions like "Are you an intelligent person?" and "Are you good at math?" Researchers have actually tried this, but simply asking people whether they are smart turns out to be a poor way to measure intelligence (Furnham, 2001). So instead, IQ tests ask people questions of varying difficulty, such as reasoning or math problems, that they might get right or wrong. The more questions they get right, the higher is their (tested) IQ. These right or wrong answers comprise B data.

In my opinion, the distinction between S-data tests and B-data tests is important, but this distinction is rarely drawn in the conventional literature on personality testing. More common is the distinction between projective and objective tests.

Projective Tests

Projective tests are based on a particular theory of how to see into someone's mind. The theory is this: If somebody tries to describe or to interpret a meaningless, ambiguous stimulus—such as an inkblot—his or her responses cannot come from the stimulus itself, because the stimulus does not, in truth, mean anything. The answer he or she gives must instead come from (be a "projection" of) the inner workings of the person's mind (Murray, 1943). The answer may even reveal something the person does not know about himself or herself.

This is the theory behind the famous Rorschach inkblot test, for instance (Rorschach, 1921; Exner, 1993). The Swiss psychiatrist Hermann Rorschach dropped blots of India ink onto note cards, folded the cards in half, and then unfolded them. The result was a set of symmetrical blots.[2] Over the years, uncounted psychiatrists and clinical psychologists have shown these blots to their clients and asked them what they saw.

Of course, the only literally correct answer is "an inkblot," but that is not considered a cooperative response. Instead, the examiner is interested in whether the client will report seeing a cloud, or a devil, or her mother, or whatever. The idea is that whatever the client sees, precisely because it is not in the card, must reveal something about the contents of his or her mind.

The same logic has led to the development of numerous other projective tests. The "draw-a-person" test requires the client to draw (you guessed it) a

---

[2]According to legend, Rorschach made many blots in this way but kept only the "best" ones. I wonder how he decided which ones those were.

person, and the drawing is interpreted according to what kind of person is drawn (e.g., a man or a woman), which body parts are exaggerated or omitted, and so forth (Machover, 1949). Large eyes might be taken to indicate suspiciousness or paranoia; heavy shading to mean aggressive impulses, and numerous erasures to be a sign of anxiety. The Thematic Apperception Test (TAT) asks clients to tell stories about various pictures (Morgan & Murray, 1935; Murray, 1943). The themes of these stories are held to be informative about the client's motivational state (e.g., McClelland, 1975). If a person looks at a picture of two people and thinks they are fighting, for example, this might reveal a desire for aggression; if the two people are described as in love, this might reflect a need for intimacy; if one is seen as giving orders to the other, this might reflect a need for power.

The idea common to all these tests is interesting and reasonable, and interpretations of actual responses can be fascinating. A large number of practicing clinicians swear by their efficacy. In one survey, 82 percent of clinical psychologists reported using the Rorschach at least occasionally (Watkins, Campbell, Nieberding, & Hallmark, 1995). However, objective research data on the validity of these tests—the degree to which they actually measure what they are supposed to measure—is surprisingly scarce (Lilienfeld, Wood, & Garb, 2000).

It is probably fair to say that only two projective tests have a background of evidence that comes even close to establishing validity according to the standards by which personality tests conventionally are evaluated. One of them is the TAT (McClelland, 1984). This instrument measures "implicit motives," meaning motivations concerning achievement, intimacy, power, and other matters that the participant himself or herself might not be aware of. The TAT continues to be used in current research concerning motivations connected with complex thinking (cognitive complexity), the experiences in life one finds most memorable, and other topics (Woike, 1995; Woike & Aronoff, 1992). It is possible that projective tests and more conventional objective tests (see next section) get at slightly different aspects of personality. One group of researchers has proposed that motives measured by the TAT reflect what people want, whereas traits as measured by questionnaires predict how these motives will be expressed (Winter et al., 1998). For example, the TAT might reveal that a person has a great need for power, whereas a more conventional test might reveal how he or she will go about trying to obtain power.

The other projective test that seems to have a modicum of validity is the Rorschach, when it is scored according to one of two specific techniques (either Exner's Comprehensive System [Exner, 1993] or Klopfer's system [Klopfer & Davidson, 1962]). According to a recent, comprehensive review of research using the Rorschach, the correlation coefficient between scores garnered from one of these systems and various criteria relevant to mental health averaged about .33 (Garb, Florio, & Grove, 1998). As you will recall from Chapter 3, this means that a dichotomous (yes-no) diagnostic decision made using the Rorschach will be correct about 66 percent of the time.[3]

To again use the terminology introduced in Chapter 2, all projective tests provide B data. They are specific, directly observed responses to particular stimuli, whether inkblots, pictures, or instructions to draw somebody. All the disadvantages of B data therefore apply to projective tests. For one thing, they are expensive. It takes around 45 minutes to administer a single Rorschach and another 1.5 to 2 hours to score it (Ball, Archer, & Imhoff, 1994). Compare this to the time needed to hand out a pile of questionnaires and score them with a machine. This is a serious issue because it is not enough for the Rorschach to have some small (and even surprising) degree of validity. For its continued use to make any sense, it should provide *extra* information that justifies its much greater cost (Lilienfeld et al., 2000). But despite hundreds of studies, no evidence has been found that the Rorschach provides information above and beyond that provided by easier, cheaper tests such as the MMPI (Hunsley & Bailey, 1999; Parker, Hunsley, & Hanson, 1999).

The even more fundamental difficulty with projective tests is that, perhaps even more so than other kinds of B data, a psychologist cannot be sure what they mean. What does it mean when somebody thinks an inkblot looks like genitalia, or imagines that an ambiguous picture portrays a murder, or draws a person with no ears? The answer and the validity of the answer depend critically on the test interpreter (Sundberg, 1977). Two different

---

[3]The main point the authors of this review intended to make was that the validity of the MMPI is even higher (the parallel $r = .55$ in their analysis). But in the process they seem to have provided one of the most convincing demonstrations to date that the Rorschach has more than zero validity.

interpreters of the same response might come to different conclusions, unless a standard scoring system is used. Of the projective tests, only the TAT is consistently scored according to a well-developed system (e.g., McAdams, 1984). While, as was mentioned above, scoring systems have been developed for the Rorschach (Exner, 1993; Klupfer & Davidson, 1962), not everybody uses them. Most of the remaining projective tests are interpreted according to the predilections of the individual examiner.

The survival of most projective tests into the twenty-first century is something of a mystery. Even literature reviews that show projective tests to have some degree of validity tend to conclude that other, less expensive techniques work as well or even better (Garb, Florio, & Grove, 1998, 1999; Lilienfeld et al., 2000). As the measurement expert Ann Anastasi wrote more than two decades ago, "projective techniques present a curious discrepancy between research and practice. When evaluated as psychometric instruments, the large majority make a poor showing. Yet their popularity in clinical use continues unabated" (Anastasi, 1982, p. 564).

Perhaps they endure because clinicians have fooled themselves into thinking they are valid. One writer has suggested these clinicians may lack "a skill that does not come naturally to any of us: disregarding the vivid and compelling data of subjective experience in favor of the often dry and impersonal results of objective research" (Lilienfeld, 1999, p. 38). Perhaps, as others have suggested, the validity of these tests is beside the point; instead they simply serve a useful, if nonpsychometric, function of "breaking the ice" between client and therapist by giving them something to do during the first visit. Or, just possibly, there is a real validity to these instruments in actual clinical application, and in the hands of certain skilled clinicians, that cannot be duplicated by other techniques and that has not been captured successfully by controlled research studies.

Objective Tests

The tests that psychologists call "objective" can be detected at a glance. If a test consists of a list of questions to be answered yes or no or true or false or on a numeric scale, and especially if it uses a computer-scored answer sheet, then it is an **objective test**. The term comes from the idea that the questions that make up the test seem more objective than the pictures and blots of projective tests.

VALIDITY AND THE SUBJECTIVITY OF TEST ITEMS

It is not clear that the term *objective* is really justified, however. Consider the first item of the famous MMPI. The item reads "I like mechanics magazines," which is to be answered true or false (Wiggins, 1973). The item may *seem* objective, compared to a question like "What do you see in this inkblot?" But the appearance may be misleading. For instance, does "like" mean interest, fondness, admiration, or tolerance? Does liking such magazines require that you regularly read them? Are *Popular Mechanics* and *High Fidelity* mechanics magazines? How about *Computer World*? Are only popular magazines included in the classification, or does the item also refer to trade journals of professional mechanics, or the research literature produced by professors of mechanical engineering? This example is not an unusually problematic item; it is rather typical. And it illustrates how objectivity is harder to attain than it might seem at first.

It is hard to escape the conclusion that the items on objective tests, while perhaps not as ambiguous as those that constitute projective tests, are still not absolutely objective. Writing truly objective items might be impossible, and even if it were possible, such items might not work. Think about it for a moment: if everybody read and interpreted an item in exactly the same way, then might not everybody tend also to *answer* the item in the same way? If so, the item would not be very useful for the assessment of individual differences. In some cases, the ambiguity of objective items might *not* be a flaw; the interpretation of an item might have to be somewhat subjective in order for responses to it to be informative for personality assessment.

Harrison Gough, the inventor of the CPI, included on his test a scale called "commonality," which consists solely of items that are answered in the same way by at least 95 percent of *all* people. He included it to detect illiterates who are pretending to know how to read and individuals deliberately trying to sabotage the test. The average score on this scale is about 95 percent, but an illiterate answering at random will score about 50 percent (since it is a true-false scale) and therefore will be immediately identifiable, as will someone who (like one of my former students) answered the CPI by flipping a coin—heads true, tails false.

These are interesting and clever uses for a commonality scale, but its properties are mentioned here to make a different point. Gough reported that when individuals encounter a commonality item—one being "I would fight if someone tried to take my rights away" (keyed true)—they do *not* say to themselves, "What a dumb, obvious item. I bet everybody answers it the same way." Instead, they say, "At last! A nonambiguous item I can really understand!" People enjoy answering the commonality items because they do not seem ambiguous.[4] Unfortunately, such items are not very useful for personality measurement, because the items are ones on which few people differ. A certain amount of ambiguity may be a good thing for an item on a personality test (Gough, 1968; Johnson, 1981).

---

[4]Another item from the commonality scale reads, "Education is more important than most people think." Paradoxically, almost everybody responds true.

WHY SO MANY ITEMS?

If you look at an objective test, one of the first things you will notice is how many questions it asks. This number may be very large. Some of the shorter personality tests have around a dozen items, but most have more, and some of the most famous personality tests (e.g., the MMPI, the CPI) have hundreds. To complete a test like the MMPI can take an hour or more, and a fairly tedious hour at that.

Why so many items? The answer lies in the principle of aggregation, which was explained in Chapter 3. The answer an individual gives to any one question might not be particularly informative; it might vary according to exactly how he or she interprets the item or other extraneous factors. In the terminology used in Chapter 3, a single answer will tend to be *unreliable*. But if a group of more or less similar questions is asked, the average of the answers to these questions ought to be much more stable, or *reliable*. All other things being equal, you can make a personality test more reliable simply by making it longer. If the items you add are as good indicators of the trait being measured as the items you already have—something easier said than done, frankly—then the improvement in reliability can be estimated rather precisely using a calculation called the *Spearman-Brown formula*.[5]

As you will recall from Chapter 3, a reliable test is one that gives close to the same answer, time after time. However, you will also recall that while reliability is necessary for validity, it is no guarantee. The validity of an objective test depends on its *content*. The crucial task in test construction, then, is to write and select the right questions. That is the topic of the next section.

Methods of Objective Test Construction

There are three basic methods for constructing objective personality tests: the rational method, the factor analytic method, and the empirical method. Sometimes, a mixture of methods is employed, but let me begin by considering the pure application of each.

---

[5]If you must know, here are some formulas. First, the reliability of a test is measured in terms of "Cronbach's alpha" according to the following formula: If N is the number of items in the test, and p is the average correlation among all of the items, then the reliability (alpha) = $Np/[1 + (p(N - 1))]$ (Cronbach, 1951). The "Spearman-Brown formula," just mentioned, predicts the increase in reliability you get when you add equivalent items to a test (Brown, 1910; Spearman, 1910). If $k = n_1/n_2$, the fraction by which the number of items is increased, then the reliability of the longer test is estimated by

$$\text{alpha (longer test)} = \frac{k \times \text{alpha (shorter test)}}{1 + (k - 1) \text{ alpha (shorter test)}}$$

In both formulas, alpha is the predicted correlation between a score on your test and a score on another test of equivalent content and length.

THE RATIONAL METHOD

Calling one method of test construction "rational" does not mean the others are irrational. It simply means that the basis of this approach is to come up with items that seem directly, obviously, and rationally related to what it is the test developer wishes to measure. Sometimes this is done through careful derivation from a theory of the trait in which the researcher is interested. Thus, test developer Douglas Jackson (1971) wrote items to capture the "needs" postulated years earlier by Henry Murray. Other times, the process of writing the items is less systematic, reflecting whatever comes to mind as something relevant to ask. The data that are gathered are S data (see Chapter 2), or direct and undisguised self-reports.

An early example of a test constructed by the rational method is drawn from World War I. The U.S. Army discovered, not surprisingly, that certain problems arose when individuals who were mentally ill were inducted as soldiers, housed in crowded barracks, and given loaded weapons. To avoid these problems, the U.S. Army developed a structured interview consisting of a list of questions that a psychiatrist could ask each potential recruit. As the number of inductees increased, however, this long interview process became impractical. There were not enough psychiatrists nor was there enough time to interview everybody.

To get around these limitations, a psychologist named R. S. Woodworth (1917) proposed that the questions of a typical interview could be printed on a sheet, and the recruits could check off their answers with a pencil. Woodworth's list, which became known as the Woodworth Personality Data Sheet (or, inevitably, the WPDS), consisted of 116 questions, all of which were deemed relevant to potential psychiatric problems. The questions included "Do you wet your bed?," "Have you ever had fits of dizziness?," and "Are you troubled with dreams about your work?" A recruit who responded yes to more than a small number of these questions was referred for a more personal examination. Recruits who answered no to all the questions were inducted forthwith into the army.

Woodworth's idea of listing psychiatric symptoms on a questionnaire was not unreasonable, yet his technique raises a variety of problems that can be identified rather easily. For the WPDS to be a valid indicator of psychiatric disturbance, and for *any* rationally constructed, S-data personality test to work, *four* conditions must hold (Wiggins, 1973).

First, each item must mean the same thing to the person who fills out the form as it did to the psychologist who wrote it. For example, in the item from the WPDS, what is "dizziness," exactly?

Second, the person who completes the form must be *able* to make an accurate self-assessment. He (only men were being recruited at the time the

WPDS was administered) must have a good enough understanding of what each item is asking about, as well as the ability to observe it in himself. He must not be so ignorant nor so psychologically disoriented that he cannot report accurately on these psychological symptoms.

Third, the person who completes the form must be *willing* to report his self-assessment accurately and without distortion. He must not try to deny his symptoms (e.g., in order to get into the army) or to exaggerate them (perhaps in order to stay out of the army). Modern personality tests used for selecting employees encounter this problem frequently (Rosse et al., 1998).

Fourth and finally, all of the items on the form must be valid indicators of what the tester is trying to measure—in this case, mental disturbance. Does dizziness really indicate mental illness? What about dreams about work?

For a rationally constructed test to measure accurately an attribute of personality, all four of these conditions must be fulfilled. In the case of the WPDS, none of them probably were (although given how inexpensive administering the WPDS was, and how expensive psychiatrists' time was, if it caught just a few serious cases, it may have been cost-effective anyway). In fact, most rationally constructed personality tests fail one or more of these criteria. One might conclude, therefore, that they would hardly ever be used anymore.

Wrong. Up to and including the present day, self-report questionnaires that are little different, in principle, from the WPDS remain the most common form of psychological measurement device. Self-tests in popular magazines are always constructed by the rational method—somebody just thinks up some questions that seem relevant—and they almost always fail at least two or three of the four crucial criteria for validity.

Rationally constructed personality tests appear in psychological journals, too. Such journals present a steady stream of new testing instruments, nearly all of which are developed by the simple technique of thinking up a list of questions that seem relevant. These questions might include measures of health status (how healthy are you?), self-esteem (how good do you feel about yourself?), or goals (what do you want in life?).

For example, research has addressed the differences between college students who follow optimistic or pessimistic strategies in order to motivate themselves to perform academic tasks (such as preparing for an exam). Optimists, as described by this research, motivate themselves to work hard by expecting the best outcome, whereas pessimists motivate themselves by expecting the very worst to happen *unless* they work hard. Both strategies seem to be effective, although optimists may have a more pleasant time of it (Norem & Cantor, 1986) (these strategies are considered in more detail in Chapter 17). For purposes of this chapter, the question is, how are optimists and pessimists identified? The researchers in this study used an eight-item questionnaire, on which participants were asked to respond using an

11-point scale ranging from "not at all true of me" (1) to "very true of me" (11) to questions such as:

- I go into academic situations expecting the worst, even though I know I will probably do OK.
- I generally go into academic situations with positive expectations about how I will do.
- I often think about what I would do if I did very poorly in an academic situation.

The first and third items listed are "pessimism" items (higher scores reflecting a pessimistic strategy) and the second is an "optimism" item (a higher score reflecting an optimistic strategy) (Norem & Cantor, 1986, p. 1211).

By the definitions I have been using, this is a rationally constructed, S-data personality test. And in fact, it seems to work fairly well at identifying students who approach academic life in different ways. So clearly tests like this can be valid, even though the four cautions raised earlier should always be kept in mind.

A slightly different case is presented by the technique used in some research to measure "personal strivings." In this research, participants are asked to list the "objective you are typically trying to accomplish or attain" (Emmons & King, 1988, p. 1042). This measure is rational in the sense that it directly asks about what the researchers are trying to find out. But unlike the rational method considered previously, this measure is open-ended. Instead of answering a set of printed questions by marking true or false, or by choosing a point on an 11-point scale, the participant writes his or her strivings on a blank piece of paper. This assessment technique, like other rational approaches, will only work to the degree a participant can and will report accurately what he or she is trying to accomplish. (Research indicates that most participants can and do accurately report the strivings that guide much of their lives [Emmons & McAdams, 1991].) This technique gets around some of the problems found in other rationally constructed questionnaires that ask participants to answer questions that may be ambiguous or of dubious relevance. Yet it poses a different problem: that of figuring out the relevance and decoding the ambiguity of what the participant has written.

THE FACTOR ANALYTIC METHOD

The factor analytic method of test construction is an example of a psychological tool based on statistics. **Factor analysis** is a statistical method for finding order amid seeming chaos. The factor analytic technique is designed to identify groups of things—such as test items—that seem to be alike. The property that makes these things alike is called a *factor* (e.g., Cattell, 1952).

Factor analysis might seem esoteric, but it is not much different from the way people intuitively group things. Consider the rides at Disneyland. Some—the Matterhorn ride, for example—are fast, scary, and enjoyed by teenagers. Others—the "It's a Small World" ride—are slow, include sweet songs, and are enjoyed by young children. Because certain properties seem to occur together (e.g., the slow rides are usually accompanied by sweet songs) and others rarely occur together (e.g., few rides include sweet songs *and* are scary), the groupings of properties can be seen to constitute factors. The properties of being fast, scary, and appealing to teenagers all go together and form a factor that you might call "excitement." Likewise, the properties of being slow, having sweet music, and appealing to young children form a factor that you might call "comfort." You could now go out and measure all the rides at Disneyland—or even anticipate the score of a new ride—according to both of these factors. And then, you could use these measurements for the purposes of prediction. If a new ride gets a high "excitement" score, you would predict long lines of teenagers waiting to ride it. If it gets a high "comfort" score, you can predict long lines of small children and frazzled parents.

To use this technique to construct a personality test, researchers begin with a long list of objective items of the sort discussed earlier. The items can be from anywhere; the test writer's own imagination is one common source. If the test writer has a theory about what he or she wants to measure, that theory might suggest items to include. Another, surprisingly common way to get new items is to mine them from *old* tests. (Items from the MMPI, in particular, have a way of reappearing on other tests.) The goal is to end up with a large number of items; thousands are not too many.

The next step is to administer these items to a large number of participants. These participants are recruited in any convenient manner, which is why they are often college students. Sometimes, for other kinds of tests, the participants are mental patients. Ideally, they should represent well the kind of people with whom you hope, eventually, to use this test.

After your large group of participants has taken the initial test that consists of these (maybe) thousands of items, you and your computer can sit down together and do the factor analysis. The analysis is based on calculating correlation coefficients (see Chapter 3) between each item and every other item. Many items—probably most—will not correlate highly with much of anything and can be dropped. But the items that do correlate highly (or even somewhat) with each other will begin to group together. For example, if a person answers true to the item "I trust strangers," you might find that he or she is also likely to answer true to "I am careful to turn up when someone expects me" and to answer false to "I could stand being a hermit." Such a pattern of likelihood or co-occurrence means that these three items are correlated. The next steps are to read the items, decide what they have in common, and then name the factor.

The three correlated items just listed, according to Cattell (1965), are related to the dimension "cool versus warm," with a true-true-false pattern of responses indicating a "warm" personality. (Cattell decided on this label simply by reading the items, as you just did). The factor represented by these items, therefore, is "warm-cool," or, if you prefer to name it by just one pole, "warmth." These three items now can be said to form a warmth scale. To measure this dimension in a new participant, you would administer these three items, as well as whatever other items in your original list correlated highly with them, discarding the rest of the thousands you started with.

Factor analysis has been used not only to construct tests, but also to decide how many fundamental traits exist—how many out of the thousands in the dictionary are truly essential. Various analysts have come up with different answers. Cattell (1957) thought there were sixteen. Eysenck (1976) believed there are just three. More recently, McCrae and Costa (e.g., 1987) claimed five; theirs is perhaps the most widely accepted answer at present. These five traits—sometimes called the "Big Five"—are extraversion, neuroticism, conscientiousness, agreeableness, and openness (see Chapter 7).

At one point some psychologists hoped that factor analysis might provide an infallible mathematical tool for objectively locating the most important dimensions of personality and the best questions with which to measure these dimensions. They were disappointed, however. Over the years, it has become clear that the factor analytic technique for constructing personality tests and for identifying important dimensions of personality is limited in at least three important ways (Block, 1995).

The first limitation is that the quality of the solution you get from a factor analysis will be limited by the quality of the items you put into it in the first place—or, as they say in computer science, "GIGO" ("garbage in, garbage out"). In theory, a factor analysis requires an initial set of items that are fairly representative of the universe of all possible items. But how are you supposed to get that? Although most investigators do the best they can, it is always possible that some types of items are overrepresented in the initial sample of items and that other, important types are left out. If either of these things happens—and there is no way to ensure that both do not—then the results will provide a distorted view of which factors of personality are really important.

A second limitation of the factor analytic approach is that once the computer has identified a cluster of items as being related statistically, a human psychologist must still decide how they are related *conceptually*. This process is highly subjective, and so the seeming mathematical rigor and certainty of factor analysis are to some extent an illusion. The items used earlier, for example, could be named "warmth," but they could just as easily be called "sociability" or "interpersonal positivity." Any choice between these labels is a matter of taste as much as of mathematics or science. And disagreements over labels are common. For example, the very same factor called "agree-ableness" by some psychologists has been called "conformity," "likability," "friendliness," or "friendly compliance" by others. Another factor has been called, variously, "conscientiousness," "dependability," "super-ego strength," "constraint," "self-control," and even "will to achieve." These labels are all reasonable, and there are no firm rules for choosing which one is best (Berge-man et al., 1993).

A third limitation of the factor analytic approach is that sometimes the factors that emerge do not make sense, sometimes not even to the psychol-ogist who did the analysis. Years ago, the psychologist Gordon Allport com-plained about one such failure to make sense of a factor analysis:

> Guilford and Zimmerman (1956) report an "unidentified" factor, called C_2, that represents some baffling blend of impulsiveness, absentmindedness, emo-tional fluctuation, nervousness, loneliness, ease of emotional expression, and feelings of guilt. When units of this sort appear [from factor analyses]—and I submit that it happens not infrequently—one wonders what to say about them. To me they resemble sausage meat that has failed to pass the pure food and health inspection. (Allport, 1958, p. 251)

Matters are not usually as bad as all this. But it is not unusual for the personality dimensions uncovered by factor analysis to be difficult to name precisely (Block, 1995). It is important to remember that factor analysis is a statistical rather than a psychological tool. It can identify traits or items that go together. As in the example just described, however, figuring out the psy-chological meaning of this grouping will require some difficult *psychological* thinking.

Factor analysis continues to have important uses. One, which is described in Chapter 7, is to help reduce the long list of personality traits from the dic-tionary down to an essential few that are really useful. Another important use is for the refinement of personality tests, in conjunction with the other techniques of test construction. It is useful to know how many different clus-ters of items are in a new personality test because some tests turn out to mea-sure more than one trait at the same time. A routine step in modern test development, therefore, is to factor analyze the items (Briggs & Cheek, 1986).

THE EMPIRICAL METHOD

The empirical strategy of test construction is an attempt to allow reality to speak for itself. In its pure form, the empirical approach has sometimes been called "dust bowl" empiricism. The term refers to the origin of the technique at Midwestern universities (notably, Minnesota and Iowa) during the Depression, or "dust bowl," years of the 1930s. Intentionally or not, the term also serves to remind one of how "dry" or atheoretical this approach is.

Like the factor analytic approach described earlier, the first step of the empirical approach is to gather lots of items. The methods for doing this can be just as eclectic—or haphazard—as described earlier.

The second step, however, is quite different. For this step, you need to have a group of participants who have *already* and independently been divided into the groups you wish to detect with your test. Occupational groups and diagnostic categories are often used for this purpose. For example, if you wish to measure the aspect of people that makes them good and happy religious ministers, then you need at least two groups of participants— happy, successful ministers and a comparison group. (Ideally the comparison group would be miserable and incompetent ministers, but more typically the researcher will settle for people who are not ministers at all.) Or, you might want a test to detect different kinds of psychopathology. For this purpose, you would need groups of people who have been diagnosed as suffering from schizophrenia, depression, hysteria, and so forth. A group of normal people—if you can find them—would also be useful for comparison purposes. Whatever groups you wish to include, their members must be identified *before* you develop your test.

Then you are ready for the third step: administering your test items to all of your participants. The fourth step is to compare the answers given by the different groups of participants. If schizophrenics answer a certain group of questions differently from the way everybody else does, those items might form a schizophrenia scale. Thereafter, new participants who answer questions the same way diagnosed schizophrenics did would score high on your schizophrenia scale. Thus, you might suspect them of being schizophrenic, too. (The MMPI, which is the prototypical example of the empirical method of test construction, was built using this strategy.) Or, if successful ministers answer some items in a distinctive way, these items might be combined into a minister scale. New participants who score high on this scale, because they answer the way successful ministers do, might be guided to become ministers themselves. (The SVIB was constructed this way.)

The basic assumption of the empirical approach, then, is that certain kinds of people have distinctive ways of answering certain questions on personality inventories. If you answer questions the same way that members of some occupational or diagnostic group did in the original derivation study, then you might belong to that group, too. This philosophy can be used even at the individual level. The developers of the MMPI published an atlas, or casebook, of hundreds of individuals who took this test over the years (Hathaway & Meehl, 1951). For each case, the atlas gives the person's scoring pattern and describes his or her clinical case history. The idea is that a clinical psychologist confronted with a new patient can ask the patient to take the MMPI, and then look up those individuals in the atlas who scored similarly in the past. This might provide the clinician with insights or ideas that he or she might not otherwise have gotten.

Items are selected for empirically derived personality scales solely on the basis of whether they are answered differently by different kinds of people. Then, the scale is cross-validated: If the test can predict behavior, diagnosis, or category membership in new samples of participants, it is deemed ready for use. At each step of the process of test development, the actual content of the items is purposely ignored. In fact, empirical test constructors of the old school sometimes prided themselves on never actually reading the items on the tests they developed!

This lack of concern with item content, or with what is sometimes called face validity, has four implications. The first is that empirically derived tests, unlike other kinds, can include items that seem contrary or even absurd. As I mentioned a few pages back, the item "I prefer a shower to a bath" when answered true is correlated with empathy. Similarly, the item "I like tall women" tends to be answered true by impulsive males. Why? According to the empirical approach to test construction, the reason does not matter in the slightest.

Consider some other examples. People with psychopathic personalities (who have little regard for moral or societal rules and lack "conscience") tend to answer false to the item "I have been quite independent and free from family rule." Paranoids answer false to "I tend to be on my guard with people who are somewhat more friendly than expected." One might surmise they do this because they are paranoid about the question itself, but they also answer true to "I believe I am being plotted against." Even though the relationship between item content and meaning seems counterintuitive, a faithful adherent to the empirical strategy of test construction is not supposed to even care.

Here are a few other examples (all taken from the excellent discussion in Wiggins, 1973): "I sometimes tease animals" is answered false by depressives; "I enjoy detective or mystery stories" is answered false by hospitalized hysterics; "My daily life is full of things to keep me interested" is answered true by dermatitis patients; "I gossip a little at times" is answered true by people with high IQs; "I do not have a great fear of snakes" is answered false by prejudiced individuals, whose prejudice apparently extends even to reptiles. Again, in each case the indicated people are *more likely* to answer in the indicated direction; they do not always do so.

A second implication of this lack of concern with item content is that responses to empirically derived tests are difficult to fake. With a personality test of the straightforward, S-data variety, you can describe yourself the way you want to be seen and that is indeed the score you will get. But because the items on empirically derived scales sometimes seem backward or absurd, it is difficult to know how to answer in such a way as to guarantee the score you want. This is often held up as one of the great advantages of the empirical approach.

The psychologist interpreting a person's responses to an empirically derived personality test does not really care whether the person told the truth in his or her responses. The literal truth does not matter because the answers to the questions on such a test are not considered important for their own sake. They matter only as indicators of what group the person belongs to. Thus, empirically derived personality tests give B data instead of S data.

The third implication of the lack of concern with item content is that even more than tests derived through other methods, empirically derived tests are only as good as the criteria by which they are developed or against which they are cross-validated. If the distinction between the different kinds of participants in the derivation or validation sample was not drawn correctly, the empirically derived test will be fatally and forever flawed. For example, the original MMPI was derived by comparing the responses of patients who had been diagnosed by psychiatrists at the University of Minnesota mental hospitals. If those diagnoses were incorrect in any way, then diagnostic use of the MMPI will only perpetuate those errors. The theory behind the SVIB is that if the participant answers questions the way a successful minister (or member of any other occupation) does, he or she too will make a successful minister (or whatever) (Strong, 1959). But perhaps the theory is false—perhaps new ministers who are too much like the old ministers will not be successful. Or perhaps some of the "successful" ministers in the derivation sample were not really successful. Such difficulties would undermine the SVIB as a source of vocational advice.

A more general problem is that the empirical correlates of item response by which these tests are assembled are those found in one place, at one time, with one group of participants. If no attention is paid to item content, then there is really no valid reason to be confident that the test will work in a similar manner at another time, in another place, with different participants. The test must be continually validated and revalidated over time, for different geographic regions, and for different kinds of participants (e.g., those of different ethnicity or gender mix than the original derivation sample). A particular concern is that the empirical correlates of item response might change over time. The MMPI was developed decades ago and was revised only recently (Butcher, 1999). The revision will take a long time to revalidate before psychologists can be confident it works the same way the old test did.

The fourth and final implication of the empirical approach's lack of concern with item content is that it can cause serious public relations and even legal problems—it can be difficult to explain to a layperson why certain questions are being asked. As was mentioned during the discussion of rationally designed tests, face validity is the property of a test seeming to measure what it is supposed to measure. A similar property is content validity, in which the content of the test matches the content of what it is trying to predict. For example, the WPDS had content validity for the prediction of psychopathology; the MMPI does not. Most psychologists would consider this difference to work to the advantage of the MMPI, but it also has caused problems. A lack of content validity not only can lead to skeptical reactions among the people who take the test, but also can raise legal issues that have become increasingly troublesome in recent years.

The original MMPI, for example, contained questions about religious preference and health status (including bowel habits). According to some readings of antidiscrimination law, such questions can be illegal in applied contexts. In 1993, Target stores had to pay a two-million-dollar judgment to job applicants to whom it had (illegally, the court ruled) asked questions such as "I am very strongly attracted to members of my own sex," "I have never indulged in unusual sex practices," "I have had no difficulty starting or holding my urine," and "I feel sure there is only one true religion" (Silverstein, 1993). (These items all came from a test called the Rodgers Condensed CPI-MMPI Test, which included items from both the MMPI and the CPI.)

As Target found to its dismay, it can be difficult for users of the MMPI, CPI, or similar tests to explain to judges or congressional investigating committees that they are not actually manifesting an unconstitutional curiosity about religious beliefs or bowel habits, and that they are merely interested in the correlates of the answers to these items. Target may have asked these questions not because its management cared about sexual or bathroom habits, but because the scale scores built from these items (and many others—the test they used had 704 items) showed validity in predicting job performance, in this case as a security guard. Indeed, reports from tests like these typically include only total scores and predictions of job performance, so the responses to the individual items might not have even been available to Target's personnel department. Nevertheless, in many cases it would not be difficult for an interested test conductor to extract applicants' responses to individual questions and then to discriminate illegally on the basis of religious or sexual orientation or health status. For this reason, developers of new tests, such as the MMPI-2, are attempting to omit items of this sort, while still trying to maintain validity.

Developers and users of empirically derived tests have come almost full circle over the last fifty years or so. They began with an explicit and sometimes vehement philosophy that item content does not matter; all that mattered was the external validity, or what the test items could predict. As the social and legal climate has changed over time, however, developers of empirical tests have been forced, to some degree against their will, to acknowledge that item content does matter after all. Regardless of how their responses are used, individuals completing any kind of personality test are revealing things about themselves.

A COMBINATION OF METHODS

In modern test development, a surprisingly large number of investigators still use a pure form of the rational method: they ask their participants the questions that seem relevant, and hope for the best. The factor analytic approach still has a few adherents. Pure applications of the empirical approach are rare today. The best modern test developers use a combination of all three approaches.

A good example is the way Douglas Jackson developed the Personality Research Form (known as the PRF, of course). He came up with items based on their apparent relevance to the theoretical constructs he wished to measure (the rational approach), administered them to large samples of participants and factor analyzed their responses (the factor analytic approach), and then correlated the factor scores with independent criteria (the empirical approach) (see Jackson, 1967, 1971). Jackson's approach is probably close to ideal. The best way to select items for a personality scale is not haphazardly, but with the intent to sample a particular domain of interest (the rational approach). Factor analysis should then be used to confirm that items that seem similar to each other actually elicit similar responses from real participants (Briggs & Cheek, 1986). Finally, any personality measure is only as good as the other things with which it correlates or can predict (the empirical approach). To be worth its salt, any personality scale must show that it can predict what people do, how they are seen by others, and how they fare in real life.

Purposes of Personality Testing

If we can assume that a personality test has a modicum of validity, then a further question must be considered: How will this test be used? This is an important question that some psychologists, engrossed in the techniques and details of test construction, may forget to ask. The answer one reaches has practical and ethical implications (Hanson, 1993).

The most obvious uses for personality tests are those to which they are put by the professional personality testers—the ones who set up the booths at APA conventions—and their customers. The customers are typically organizations such as schools, clinics, corporations, or government agencies that wish to know something about the people they encounter. Sometimes this information is desired so that, regardless of the score obtained, the person who is measured can be helped. For example, schools frequently use tests to measure vocational interests to help their students choose careers. A clinician might administer a test to get an indication of how serious a client's problem is, or to suggest a therapeutic direction.

Sometimes the motivation for testing is a little more selfish. An employer may test an individual's "integrity" to find out whether he or she is trustworthy enough to be hired (or even to be retained), or may test to find out about other personality traits deemed relevant to future job performance. The Central Intelligence Agency (CIA), for example, routinely uses personality testing when selecting its agents (Waller, 1993).

Reasonable arguments can be made for or against any of these uses. By telling people what kind of occupational group they most resemble, vocational-interest tests provide potentially valuable information to individuals who may not know what they want to do (Schmidt, Lubinski, & Benbow, 1998). On the other hand, these tests are based on the implicit theory that any given occupation should continue to be populated by individuals like those already in it. For example, if your response profile resembles those obtained from successful mechanics or jet pilots, then perhaps you *should* consider being a mechanic or a jet pilot. But this approach, although it seems reasonable, also could keep occupational fields from evolving and keep certain individuals (e.g., women or members of minority groups) from joining fields from which they traditionally may have been excluded. For example, an ordinarily socialized American woman may have outlooks or responses that are very different from those of the "typical" garage mechanic or jet pilot. Does this mean that women should never become mechanics or pilots?

Similarly, many "integrity" tests administered in pre-employment screenings seem to yield valuable information. In particular, they often provide good measures not so much of integrity, but of the broader trait of conscientiousness. That is, people who score high on integrity scales often also

"Here's a little test I like to give prospective employees, Phil: let's see if you can grab this twenty-dollar bill before I can."

score high on the trait of conscientiousness, which is highly correlated with learning on the job and with performance in many fields (Ones, Viswesvaran, & Schmidt, 1993; see Chapter 7 for a more detailed discussion).

Still, many of these integrity tests ask questions about minor past offenses (e.g., "Have you ever taken office supplies from an employer?"), which puts nonliars into the interesting dilemma of whether they should admit past offenses, thereby earning a lower integrity score for being honest, or deny them and thereby earn a higher integrity score for having lied. Liars, by contrast, experience no such dilemma; they can deny everything and yet earn a nice, high integrity score.

A more general class of objections is aimed at the wide array of personality tests used by many large organizations, including the CIA, major automobile manufacturers, phone companies, and the military. According to one critic, almost any kind of testing can be objected to on two grounds. First, tests are unfair mechanisms through which institutions can control individuals—by rewarding those with the institutionally determined "correct" traits (such as high conscientiousness) and punishing those with the "wrong" traits (such as low conscientiousness). Second, perhaps traits such as "conscientiousness" or even "intelligence" do not matter until and unless they are tested, and in that sense are "constructed" by the tests themselves (Hanson 1993). Underlying these two objections seems to be a more general sense, which I think many people share, that there is something undignified or even humiliating about submitting oneself to a test and having one's personality described by a set of scores.

All of these objections make sense. Personality tests—along with other kinds of tests such as intelligence, honesty, and even drug tests—do function as a part of society's mechanism for controlling people, by rewarding the "right" kind of people (e.g., those who are intelligent and honest and don't do drugs) and punishing the "wrong" kind. It is also correct to note the interesting way in which a trait can seem to spring into existence as soon as a test is invented to measure it. Did traits like "parmia" or even "self-monitoring" (see Chapters 6 and 7) exist before there were scales to measure them? Perhaps they did, but you can see the argument here. Finally, it is undeniably true that many individuals have had the deeply humiliating experience of "voluntarily" (in order to get a badly needed job) subjecting themselves to testing, only to find out that they somehow failed to measure up. It's bad enough to lack the right skills or relevant experience. But to be the wrong kind of person? That hurts.

On the other hand, these criticisms are also overstated. A relatively minor point to bear in mind is that, as we have seen in the preceding sections of this chapter, personality traits are not merely *invented* or *constructed* by the process of test construction, they are also to an important degree *discovered*. That is, the correlates and nature of a trait measured by a new test cannot be presumed, they must be discovered empirically by examining what life outcomes or other attributes of personality the test can predict. For example, psychologists did not know until *after* doing research that integrity tests are better measures of conscientiousness than of integrity, and this finding forced them to change their conception of what they incorrectly had assumed were honesty tests. The fact that the interpretation of psychological tests depends critically on the gathering of independent data undermines the argument that personality traits, or any other psychological measurements, are mere social constructions.

A more basic and important point is that the criticisms that view personality testing as undignified or unethical are criticisms that, when considered, appear rather naïve. These criticisms seem to object to the idea of determining the degree to which somebody is conscientious, or intelligent, or sociable, and then using that determination as the basis of an important decision (e.g., employment). But if you accept the fact that an employer is not obligated to hire randomly anybody who walks through the door, and that the employer only uses good sense in deciding who would be the best person to hire (if you were an employer, wouldn't you do that?), then you also must accept that traits like conscientiousness, intelligence, and sociability are going to be judged. The only real question is *how*. What are the alternatives? One alternative seems to be for the employer to talk with the prospective employee and try to gauge his or her conscientiousness by how well his or her shoes are shined, or hair is cut, or some other such clue. (Employers frequently do exactly that.) Is this method an improvement?

B. Smaller

"Give me a hug. I can tell a lot about a man by the way he hugs."

You may argue that you would rather be judged by a person than by a computer scanning a form, regardless of the demonstrated invalidity of the former and validity of the latter (Ones, Viswesvaran, & Schmidt, 1993). Although that is a reasonable position, it is important to be clear about the choice being made. The choice cannot be for personality never to be judged— that is going to happen even if all of the tests are burned tomorrow. The only real choice here is this: *How* would you prefer to have your personality judged?

Summary

Any characteristic pattern of behavior, thought, and emotional experience that exhibits relative consistency across time and situations is part of an individual's personality. These patterns include personality traits as well as psychological attributes such as goals, moods, and strategies. Personality assessment is a frequent activity of industrial and clinical psychologists and researchers. Everybody also performs personality assessments of the people they know in daily life. An important issue for assessments, whether by psychologists or by laypersons, is the degree to which those assessments are correct. This chapter examined how psychologists' personality tests are constructed and validated. Some personality tests comprise S data and others comprise B data, but a more commonly drawn distinction is between projective tests and objective tests. Projective tests try to gain insight into personality by presenting participants with ambiguous stimuli and recording how the participants respond. Objective tests ask participants specific questions and assess personality on the basis of how the participants answer. Objective tests can be constructed by rational, factor analytic, or empirical methods, and the state of the art is to use a combination of all three methods. Some people are uncomfortable with the practice of personality assessment because they see it as an unfair invasion of privacy. However, because people inevitably judge each other's personalities, the real issue is how personality assessment should be done—through informal intuitions or more formalized techniques.

PERSONALITY ASSESSMENT II: PERSONALITY JUDGMENT IN DAILY LIFE

You don't need a license to practice personality assessment; everybody does it. Trying to figure out what other people are like is one of the most interesting, important, and widespread things that people do. With luck, you might go many years without being assessed by a psychologist. But there is no chance whatsoever that you can long escape being assessed by your friends, enemies, romantic partners—and yourself.

The present chapter is in two parts. The first part considers how and why the assessments others make of your personality and the assessments you make of yourself are important. The second part of this chapter addresses the validity—or, in the synonymous term traditionally used when considering nonprofessional judgments, the *accuracy*—of these assessments. To what degree and under what circumstances do everyday judgments of personality agree with each other? To what degree and under what circumstances can they accurately predict behavior? And finally, how is accurate personality judgment possible? How might we become more accurate in knowing other people, and even ourselves?

Consequences of Everyday Judgments of Personality

The people who practice the daily, informal assessment of your personality fall into two categories: the first category is everybody you know, or everybody who knows you; the second category has only one person in it—you. The opinions of both are important.

Everybody Who Knows You

The judgments other people make of your personality reflect a significant part of your social world. They represent opinions of people who interact with you daily, and so their importance goes beyond their value as accurate (or inaccurate) descriptions. Furthermore, your reputation among those who know you matters because, as was mentioned during the survey of I data in Chapter 2, it greatly affects both opportunities and expectancies.

OPPORTUNITIES

Reputation affects opportunities in numerous ways. If a person who is considering hiring you believes that you are competent and conscientious, you are much more likely to enjoy the opportunity of getting the job than if that person thinks you do not have those qualities. This will be true regardless of how competent and conscientious you really are. Similarly, if someone believes you to be honest, he or she will be more likely to lend you money than if that person believes you to be dishonest. Your *actual* honesty is immaterial. If you impress people who meet you as being warm and friendly, you will develop more friendships than if you seem cold and aloof. These appearances may be false and unfair, but the consequences will be important nonetheless.

Consider the case of shyness. Shy people seem to be quite common in American society; one estimate is that about one person in four considers himself or herself to be chronically shy (Zimbardo, 1977). Shy people are often lonely and may deeply wish to have friends and normal social interactions, but they are so fearful of the process of social involvement that they become isolated instead. The typical consequence is that shy people spend a lot of time by themselves, staying in their rooms and denying themselves the opportunity to develop normal social skills. When they do venture into the world, they are so out of practice that they may not know how to act, and so other people may respond to them negatively, which will only reinforce the shyness that caused these problems in the first place (Cheek, 1990).

A particular problem for shy people is that typically other people do not perceive them as shy. Instead, to most observers they seem cold and aloof. This is understandable when you consider how shy people often behave. A shy person who lives in your dormitory sees you coming across campus, and you see her. She would actually like to talk to you and perhaps even try to develop a friendship, but she is extremely fearful of rejection or even of not knowing quite what to say. (This apprehension may be realistic, given her lack of social skills.) So, she may very well pretend not to see you, or may suddenly reverse course and dodge behind a building. This kind of behavior, if you detect it (and often you will), is unlikely to give you a warm, fuzzy feeling deep inside. Instead, there is a good chance that instead you will feel insulted and even angry. You may be inclined thereafter to avoid *her*.

Thus, shy people are not cold and aloof, or at least they do not mean to be. But that is frequently how they are perceived. That perception, in turn, affects the lives of shy people in important, negative ways and is part of a cycle that perpetuates shyness. This is just one example of how the judgments of others are an important part of the social world and can have a significant effect on personality and life.

EXPECTANCIES

Judgments of others can also affect you through "self-fulfilling prophecies," more technically known as **expectancy effects**, or just **expectancies**.[1] These seem to operate in both the intellectual and the social domain.

Intellectual Expectancies   The classic demonstration of expectancy effects in the intellectual domain is the series of studies by Rosenthal and Jacobson (1968). These investigators gave a battery of tests to a group of schoolchildren and then told their teachers, falsely, that the tests had identified some of the children as "bloomers" who were likely to show a sharp increase in IQ in the near future. These children were actually selected at random. But when the actual IQ of the so-called bloomers was compared to that of other children at the end of the school year, the bloomers had actually bloomed! That is, the first-grade children who were expected by their teachers to show an increase in their IQ actually did, by about fifteen points, and the IQ of the second-graders increased by about ten points, even though these expectations were introduced randomly.

The exact process by which this effect happens has been a matter of some controversy. At least four different theoretical models of expectancy effects have been proposed (Bellamy, 1975; Braun, 1976; Darley & Fazio, 1980; Rosenthal, 1973a, 1973b). The one that has garnered the most evidence in its support seems to be a "four factor" theory proposed by Robert Rosenthal himself, one of the original discoverers of the effect (Harris & Rosenthal, 1985).

According to Rosenthal's theory, four major kinds of teacher behavior cause high-expectancy students to perform better. The first, *climate*, refers to the way that teachers project a warmer emotional attitude toward the students they expect to do well. The second behavior, *feedback*, refers to the way teachers give more differentiated feedback—feedback that varies according to the correctness or incorrectness of a student's

---

[1]As mentioned in Chapter 2, the expectancy phenomenon is also called "behavioral confirmation" by some psychologists.

response—to their high-expectancy students. The third behavior, *input*, refers to the way teachers attempt to teach more material and more difficult material to high-expectancy students. Finally, the fourth behavior, called *output*, reflects how teachers give their special students extra opportunities to show what they have learned. A large number of studies showed convincingly that teachers treat their high-expectancy students differently in these four ways, and that each kind of behavior actually leads such students to perform better (Harris & Rosenthal, 1985). This is important research not only because it helps to explain expectancy effects, but also because it demonstrates some of the basic elements of good teaching: it might be better if *all* students could be treated in the four ways that high-expectancy students are treated.

Social Expectancies   A related kind of expectancy effect has been demonstrated in the social rather than the intellectual realm. Mark Snyder and his colleagues (Snyder, Tanke, & Berscheid, 1977) performed the following remarkable experiment. Two previously unacquainted college students of the opposite sex were brought to two different locations in the psychology building. The experimenter immediately took a Polaroid picture of the female participant, saying, "You are about to meet someone on the telephone, but before you do this I need to give him a picture of you so he can visualize who he is talking to." The male participant was not photographed.

The female's real photograph, just taken, was thrown away. Instead, the experimenter gave the male participant one of two photographs of *other* female undergraduates who previously had been identified as either highly attractive or less attractive. "This is who you will be meeting on the phone," the male participant was told. The telephone connection was then established, and the two students chatted for several minutes as a tape recorder whirred.

Later, the researchers took the tape recording of this chat and erased everything that the *male* student had said. (Remember, he is the one who saw the bogus photograph.) Then they played the edited tape, which contained only the female's voice, for a new group of students, and asked them to rate, among other things, how warm, humorous, and poised she seemed.

The result: If the male had seen an attractive photograph, the female was more likely to have behaved in a manner rated as warmer, more humorous, and more poised than when the male student saw an unattractive photograph. This finding means that the male student had somehow acted toward a woman he *thought* to be attractive in such a way as to cause her to respond in a more warm and friendly manner than she would have if he had thought her to be unattractive. Snyder interpreted this effect as another form of self-fulfilling prophecy: Attractive females are expected to be warm and friendly, and those thought to be attractive are treated in such a manner that they indeed respond that way.[2]

In some ways this is an even more disturbing finding than Rosenthal's results concerning IQ. This study suggests that to some degree our behavior with other people might be determined by how these other people expect us to act, perhaps based on such superficial cues as our physical appearance. Snyder's results imply that to some degree we will actually *become* what other people perceive, or even misperceive, us to be.

Expectancies in Real Life Research on expectancy effects is interesting and important, and the two studies just described are classics of the genre. However, there was another important development in this area of research that I need to tell you about. The psychologist Lee Jussim (1991) asked an important question about expectancy effects that, surprisingly, had seldom been considered previously: Where do expectancies generally come from in real life?

The usual experiments do not address this question because the expectancies they study are induced experimentally; Rosenthal's teachers believed that some kids would improve academically because that is what he had told them they would do. Snyder's male students thought some females would be warm and friendly because they were led to develop that expectation based on the common stereotypes they held about attractiveness along with a misleading photograph.

Jussim suggested that the situation in real life is usually quite different. A teacher who expects a child to do well might base that expectation on the child's actual test results, rather than bogus ones, as well as on his or her observation of the child's performance in previous classes, what he or she has been told about the child by other teachers, and so forth. A male undergraduate who expects a female undergraduate to be warm and charming might base this on how he has seen her act with other people, what he has been told about her by mutual friends, and so forth. Moreover, research has shown that to some degree, physically attractive women really are more

---

[2]Two complications are worth brief mention. The first is that a slightly different process may lie behind the result. Rather than males directly inducing the females to confirm their expectancies, it may be the case that males are more friendly to attractive females because they are hoping for a date, and more cold and aloof with unattractive females for whom they do not have such hopes. The women then respond in kind. Such a process would technically not be an expectancy effect, although the final result would be the same.

A related complication concerns the question of whether this effect works the other way around, when female students see pictures of attractive or unattractive males and the effects on his behavior are examined. A study by Andersen and Bem (1981) addressed this issue. The conclusions were not completely clear, but it did seem to some degree that male and female perceivers could, through what they expected of the other, affect the behavior of both male and female targets.

socially skillful and likable on the telephone (Goldman & Lewis, 1977). Therefore, these expectancies, although false in the lab, might sometimes or often be correct in real life. When this is the case, the self-fulfilling prophecies just described might have the effect of slightly magnifying behavioral tendencies that the participant has had all along.

This observation challenges the traditional interpretation of expectancy effects. It implies that rather than restrict themselves to introducing expectancies in the lab, researchers also should study expectancies in real life, to assess how powerful these effects really are. Research is also needed to learn how strong these effects can be under realistic circumstances. The studies to date show that expectancy effects are consistently greater than zero, but are they ordinarily strong enough to change a low-IQ child into a high-IQ child, or a cold, aloof person into a warm and friendly one, or vice versa? The research suggests that the answer is probably no (e.g., Jussim & Eccles, 1992). However, it is difficult to be sure of this conclusion because most research so far has been concerned more with discovering whether expectancy effects exist than with assessing how important the effects are in relation to other factors that also influence behavior.

Although what can be said about expectancy effects is less tidy than it would have been a few years ago, they remain interesting and important. To some degree, the judgments of personality rendered of you by the people who know you not only reflect what you are like, but also can *lead* you to be what you are like. Moreover, understanding how expectancy effects happen sheds valuable light on the more general question of how people affect each other's performance and social behavior. Rosenthal's research revealed four basic factors that probably ought to be a part of all good teaching. And Snyder's research suggests that if you want to be treated in a warm and friendly manner, it might not be a bad idea to begin by expecting the best, and acting warm and friendly yourself.

Self-Judgments

The judgments you inevitably make about your own personality are, if anything, even more important than those others make of you. You very likely have opinions about how sociable you are, how reliable you are, and even how intelligent you are. In psychological parlance, the assembly of all of the opinions of this sort that you hold is called your **self-concept**, or just *self*. Psychologists who study the self are interested in the opinions and judgments individuals have and make about their own personalities and abilities.

Self-judgments matter because they affect how you evaluate yourself and therefore affect your mood. Your self-esteem plays an important role in how happy or sad you feel. Feelings of worthlessness—extremely low self-esteem—are a classic element of depression. And in interpersonal relations, perhaps the oldest, truest cliché is this: If you don't like yourself first, you won't be able to like anybody else either (Shaver & Clark, 1994). Substitute *love* for *like* in that cliché, and the implications become even deeper.

The consequences of feeling that you are less than you ought to be can vary according to exactly how you feel you have come up short. According to *self-discrepancy theory* (Higgins, 1987), people often compare themselves to two different concepts of what they should be. The "ideal" self is what they hope, wish, and aspire to be. The "ought" self is what people think they would be if they fulfilled all of their duties, responsibilities, and obligations. According to this theory (and some data as well), to the degree that individuals believe they have failed to become their ideal self, they feel disappointed, dissatisfied, and sad. To the degree they believe they have failed to become their "ought" self, they feel threatened, fearful, and restless (see Chapter 17).

Your self-judgments affect your life in other ways. They often determine what you will do or attempt to do. For example, perhaps you had a friend in high school who was just as smart and hardworking as you are. But for whatever reason, your friend thought that he or she could not possibly be a successful college student. If you were a true friend, you might have tried to argue otherwise: "Of course you can do it—if I can, you can too!" But in the face of a negative self-attitude, such arguments are usually ineffective. So you went to college and your friend did not. In a year or two you will graduate, and your friend will still be pumping gas or flipping burgers.[3] The difference was not one of ability or drive—it was in the self. You believed you could do it, while your friend did not have such a positive self-view.

This example shows how important and sometimes devastating one's self-concept can be. It also shows the dangers in persuading people that they cannot do certain things. For example, many young girls pick up the message from society that girls cannot—or should not—be good at math (Hilton & Berglund, 1974; Stipek & Gralinski, 1991). The result? Here's a personal example: I used to teach at a prestigious engineering college. More than 90 percent of the students were male—hardly a result of chance. Similarly, members of certain racial groups and economic classes are taught, usually implicitly but powerfully by the media and other sources, that "their kind" do not go to college or otherwise better themselves. So sometimes these individuals give up, or find other ways—not necessarily constructive—to feel like they have succeeded in life.

Beliefs about one's self and what one can do transcend specific domains. People who have the trait called *internal locus of control* believe that the important forces in their lives come from within or inside themselves, and that they can affect what happens. Those with *external locus of control*, by

---

[3] I am presuming that with your college education, you will find a better job than those.

contrast, believe that most of what happens to them is up to others or is a product of impersonal outside forces. Not surprisingly, "internals" take a much more active role in determining their life outcomes than do "externals," and therefore are more likely to succeed at most things (Rotter, 1954). A related concept, **self-efficacy**, refers to a person's beliefs about what he or she will and will not be able to accomplish (Bandura, 1977) (Rotter's and Bandura's theories are considered in more detail in Chapter 17). For example, you might have the efficacy expectation that you will someday be able to finish reading this book. I myself, as I am writing these words, am trying to maintain the efficacy expectation that I can finish writing this book. In either case, the belief about what a person can do is likely to affect whether that person persists at that activity. Since you are reading this book, we can presume that my efficacy expectations held up. How are yours doing?

Efficacy expectations can interact with or be determined by other kinds of self-judgments. For example, if you think you are extremely attractive to the opposite sex, you are more likely to attempt to date someone in whom you are interested than you would be if you saw yourself as unattractive. To use the terms developed earlier, your self-concept affects your efficacy expectation in this domain. Of course, both of these concepts—your self-concept and your efficacy expectation—can be independent of how attractive you really are. A person's *actual* physical attractiveness might matter less than people sometimes believe; individuals who merely *think* they are attractive often do surprisingly well, it seems.

So far I have emphasized the harm that results from thinking poorly of oneself, and the advantages of improving the self-image. But do you know anyone who has too high an opinion of himself or herself for his or her own good? Some individuals whose self-esteem is better than it should be can become oblivious to the effects their behavior is having on others, with the result that while in the short run these people feel good about themselves, in the long run they are disadvantaged because other people find them increasingly annoying (Colvin & Block, 1994). Extreme cases, called *narcissists*, can in the end be destructive to themselves and others and even dangerous (see Bushman & Baumeister, 2002). Clearly, the psychological problems of dictators such as Hitler, Stalin, and Saddam Hussein did not stem from low self-esteem. More generally, an extremely positive self-image—thinking you are 110 percent wonderful—is associated with antagonism, hostility, arrogance, and the exploitation of others, which is a style that, not surprisingly, sooner or later alienates everybody else (Morf & Rhodewalt, 2001; Rhodewalt & Morf, 1995).

The moral of the story, perhaps, is this: Think well of yourself but don't overdo it. In particular, it might be a good idea to avoid advertising just how wonderful you think you are (Taylor, Lerner, Sherman, Sage, & McDowell, 2003).

We have seen that the judgments other people make of your personality matter a good deal, and the judgments you make of yourself—too unfavorable, too favorable, or just right—probably matter even more. This conclusion raises two further questions: To what degree, and under what circumstances, are these ever-so-consequential judgments accurate? And finally, how is accurate personality judgment possible, and how might it be improved?

The Accuracy of Personality Judgment

Because people constantly make judgments of their own and each others' personalities, and because these judgments are consequential, then it would seem important to know when and to what degree these judgments are accurate. It might surprise you, therefore, to learn that for an extended period of time (about thirty years) psychologists went out of their way to *avoid* doing research on accuracy. Although research on the accuracy of lay judgments of personality was fairly active from the 1930s to about 1955, after that the field fell into inactivity, from which it began to emerge only in the mid-1980s (Funder & West, 1993).

There are several reasons why research on accuracy experienced this lengthy hiatus (Funder & West, 1993; Funder, 1995). The most basic reason is that researchers were stymied by a fundamental problem: By what criteria can the personality judgments made by somebody else be judged to be right or wrong (Hastie & Rasinski, 1988; Kruglanski, 1989)? Some psychologists believe this question to be unanswerable, because any attempt to answer it would simply amount to pitting one person's set of criteria for accuracy against another's. Who is to say which is right?

This point of view is bolstered by the attitude called **constructivism**, which is widespread throughout modern intellectual life (Stanovich, 1991). This attitude—slightly simplified—is that reality, as a concrete entity, does not exist. All that does exist are human ideas or *constructions* of reality. This view finally settles the age-old question, "If a tree falls in the forest with no one to hear, does it make a noise?" The constructivist answer: No. A more important implication is that there is no way to regard one interpretation of reality as accurate and another interpretation as inaccurate, because all interpretations are mere "social constructions" (Kruglanski, 1989).

This point of view—that since there is no reality, judgmental accuracy cannot be assessed meaningfully—is quite fashionable today. Nevertheless, I reject it (Funder, 1995). To regard independent reality as nonexistent and accuracy as meaningless is a nihilistic point of view that withers under serious scrutiny.

I find another philosophical school, called **critical realism**, more reasonable. Critical realism holds that the absence of perfect, infallible criteria for truth should not force one to conclude that all interpretations of reality are equally likely to be correct (Rorer, 1990). Indeed, even psychological researchers who argue that accuracy issues are not meaningful (constructivists) still find themselves choosing between research conclusions they regard as more or less valid—even though their choices might sometimes be wrong. As researchers, they implicitly recognize that the only option is to make such choices as reasonably as possible, based on whatever information is at hand or can be gathered. The only alternative is to cease doing research altogether.

Evaluating a personality judgment is no different. You must gather all the information possible that might help you determine whether or not the judgment is valid, and then make the best determination you can. The task remains perfectly reasonable, even though the outcome will always be uncertain (Cook & Campbell, 1979; Cronbach & Meehl, 1955).

Criteria for Accuracy

There is a simpler way to think of this issue. A personality judgment, rendered by an acquaintance, a stranger, or the self, can be thought of as a kind of personality assessment or even a personality test. If you think of it as a test, then the same considerations discussed in the previous two chapters immediately come into play, and the assessment of the *accuracy* of a personality judgment becomes exactly equivalent to the assessment of the *validity* of a personality test. And there is a well-developed and widely accepted method for assessing test validity.

The method is called **convergent validation**. It can be illustrated by the **duck test**: If it looks like a duck, walks like a duck, swims like a duck, and quacks like a duck, it is very probably (but still not absolutely positively) a duck. (Maybe it's a Disney audio-animatronic machine built to resemble a duck, but probably not.) Convergent validation is arrived at by assembling diverse pieces of information—such as appearance, walking and swimming style, and quackiness—that "converge" on a common conclusion, in this case that it must be a duck. The more items of diverse information that converge, the more confident one is in the conclusion (Block, 1989, pp. 236–237).

For personality judgments, the two primary converging criteria are **interjudge agreement** and **behavioral prediction**. If I judge you to be conscientious, and so do your parents, and so do your friends, and so do you, it is likely that you *are* conscientious. Moreover, if my judgment of you as conscientious converges with the subsequent empirical fact that you arrive on time for all your class meetings for the next three semesters, and thereby demonstrates **predictive validity**, then my judgment of you is even more certainly correct (although 100 percent certainty is never attained).

"Let me through! I'm a quack."

In sum, psychological research can evaluate the accuracy of personality judgments by asking two questions (Funder, 1987, 1995, 1999): (1) Do the judgments agree with one another? (2) Can they predict behavior? To the degree the answers are yes, the judgments are probably accurate.

Moderators of Accuracy

In psychological parlance, a **moderator variable** is one that affects the relationship between two other variables. A moderator of accuracy, therefore, is a variable that makes the correlation between a judgment and its criterion higher or lower. Research on accuracy has focused primarily on four such potential moderators: (1) properties of the judge, (2) properties of the target (the person who is judged), (3) properties of the trait that is judged, and (4) properties of the information on which the judgment is based.

THE GOOD JUDGE

The oldest question in accuracy research is this: Who is the best judge of personality? Clinical psychologists have long postulated that some people are better at judging personality than are others, and numerous studies tackled this question during the old, pre-1955 wave of research on accuracy (Taft, 1955). A satisfying answer has turned out to be surprisingly difficult to reach. Early studies seemed to show that a good judge in one context or of one trait might or might not be a good judge in other contexts or with other traits.

The only somewhat consistent finding seemed to be that highly intelligent and conscientious individuals rendered better judgments—but then again such individuals are good at nearly any task you give them, so it was not clear that these traits were a functional part of any specific ability to judge people. Disappointment with this vague conclusion may be one reason why the first wave of accuracy research waned in the mid-1950s (Funder & West, 1993). But the pessimism may have been premature, because the original research was conducted using inadequate methods (Colvin & Bundick, 2001; Cronbach, 1955; Hammond, 1996).

Recent research has renewed this important topic. One promising study compared personality judgments that college students made of their peers with the students' own self-judgments and with the students' behaviors observed directly in three laboratory situations (Kolar, 1996). Men and women did not differ in their degree of accuracy, but the personality correlates of accuracy were different by sex. The most accurate male judges of personality tended to be extraverted, well-adjusted, and relatively unconcerned by what other people thought of them. The most accurate female judges tended to be open to new experiences, have a wide range of interests, and value their independence. These results suggest that for men, accurate personality judgment is part of an outgoing and confident interpersonal style, whereas for women it is more a matter of deeply understanding people. Either way, the good judge appears to be someone who is invested in developing and maintaining interpersonal relationships, a style sometimes called "communion" (Bakan, 1966). A recent study found that both women and men who were high on communion—who put a particular emphasis on interpersonal relationships—were more accurate judges of personality (Vogt & Colvin, 2003).

The study of the good judge lay dormant for too long. As these intriguing new findings are followed-up and extended, we can expect a rapid increase in our understanding of what makes some people better judges of personality than others.

THE GOOD TARGET

Another potential moderator of accuracy is the flip side of the good judge: the good target. Some people seem to be as readable as an open book, whereas others seem more closed and enigmatic. This observation implies that some individuals are judged more easily than others. As the pioneering personality psychologist Gordon Allport asked in this context, "Who are these people?" (Allport, 1937, p. 443; Colvin, 1993b).

"Judgeable" people are those about whom others reach agreement most easily. Naturally, these tend to be the same people whose behavior is most predictable from judgments of their personalities. As follows from this definition, judgeable people are those for whom "what you see is what you get." Their behavior is organized coherently, in such a way that even different people who know them in different settings describe essentially the same person. Furthermore, the behavior of such people is consistent, which means that we can predict what they will do in the future by taking note of what they have done in the past. We could say that these individuals are stable and well organized, or even that they are psychologically well adjusted (Colvin, 1993b).[4]

Theorists have long postulated that the most psychologically healthy style you can have is to conceal very little from those around you, to exhibit what is sometimes called a "transparent self" (Jourard, 1971). To the extent that you exhibit any kind of psychological facade and that there are large discrepancies between the person "inside" and the person you display "outside," you are likely to experience excessive isolation from the people around you, which can lead to unhappiness, hostility, and depression. There is also evidence that concealing one's emotions can actually be harmful to physical health (Berry & Pennebaker, 1993; Pennebaker, 1992).

Recent research builds on this theory by pointing out that **judgeability** itself—the "what you see is what you get" syndrome—is a part of psychological adjustment precisely because it stems from behavioral coherence and consistency. This is a pattern with roots that reach into early childhood, and the association between judgeability and psychological adjustment appears to be particularly strong among males (Colvin, 1993a).

THE GOOD TRAIT

All traits are not created equal—some are much easier to judge accurately than others. For example, more-visible traits, such as talkativeness, sociability, and other traits related to extraversion, are judged with much higher levels of inter-judge agreement than are less-visible traits, such as cognitive and ruminative styles and habits (Funder & Dobroth, 1987). For example, you are more likely to agree with your acquaintances, and they are more likely to agree with each other, about whether you are talkative than about whether you "tend to worry and ruminate." This finding holds true even when the people who judge you are strangers who have observed you only for a few minutes (Funder & Colvin, 1988; see also Watson, 1989).

This finding might seem rather obvious. I once admitted that the main discovery of the study by Kate Dobroth and me is that more visible traits are easier to see. We needed federal funding to learn that? (Don't worry—our

---

[4]It is reasonable to wonder whether this can go too far. A person who is rigid and inflexible might be judged easily but would not be well adjusted. However, research has not yet identified any real cases of such hypothetical judgeable but maladjusted individuals.

grant was very small.) But it does have some interesting implications. One concerns the basis of personality judgments by acquaintances. Some psychologists, reluctant to concede that peer judgments of personality can have any accuracy at all, have proposed that inter-judge agreement is merely the result of conversations judges have had with one another, or with the participants. Thus, these psychologists conclude, peer judgments are not based on the participants' personalities, but instead on their socially constructed reputations (McClelland, 1972; Kenny, 1991).

This idea seems plausible, but I doubt it is true. If peers based their personality judgments only on reputation and not on observation, then there would be no reason for observable traits to yield any better agreement than unobservable ones. Other people can manufacture a reputation about your ruminativeness just as well as they can about your talkativeness. But while all traits are equally susceptible to being talked about, certain traits are much harder to actually observe. Therefore, the finding that more-observable traits yield better inter-judge agreement implies that peer judgment is based more on direct behavioral observation than on mere reputation (Clark & Paivio, 1989).

Another investigation of visibility addressed a trait the researchers called *sociosexuality,* or the willingness to engage in sexual relations with minimal acquaintanceship with or commitment to and from one's partner (Gangestad et al., 1992). It seems reasonable to speculate that the accurate perception of this trait may have been important across the history of the human species. According to evolutionary theory, the traits and abilities that make individuals more likely to reproduce are more likely to be present in later generations (for a more detailed discussion of this issue, see Chapter 9). A crucial part of reproduction is figuring out who might be willing to mate with you. The hypothesis of this study, therefore, was that for evolutionary reasons people should be particularly good at judging this trait as opposed to other traits presumably less important for reproduction.

The study indeed found that individual differences in this trait, as measured by self-report, were detected more accurately by observers than were traits less directly relevant to reproduction, such as social potency and social closeness. In an interesting corollary, although this finding held true regardless of the sexes of the perceiver and the person perceived, females judging the sociosexuality of males were especially accurate, and males judging the sociosexuality of other males were even more accurate!

This last finding presents a mild problem for the evolutionary explanation: What would be the reproductive advantage for a male to know the mating availability of another male? After thinking about it for a moment, you might be able to come up with an answer to this question. The problem is that it seems doubtful that this is a finding evolutionary theory would have predicted *before* the results were known. (In case you were wondering, males, probably to their eternal regret, were not particularly good at judging the sociosexuality of females.)

GOOD INFORMATION

The final moderator of judgmental accuracy is the amount and kind of information on which the personality judgment is based.

Amount of Information   When it comes to the amount of information, it seems clear that more is usually better. In one study, for example, participants were judged both by close acquaintances (who had known the participants for at least a year) and by strangers (who had viewed the participants only for about five minutes on a videotape). Personality judgments by the close acquaintances agreed much better with the participants' self-judgments than did judgments by strangers (Funder & Colvin, 1988).

But this advantage of longer acquaintanceship did not hold under all circumstances. The videotapes watched by the strangers were of a five-minute conversation that the participant held with a peer of the opposite sex. This observation was the sole basis for their personality judgments. The acquaintances, by contrast, never saw the videotape. Their judgments were based, instead, on their own knowledge of the participant obtained through observations and interactions in daily life over an extended period of time. Interestingly, when the judgments by the strangers and those by the acquaintances were used to try to predict what the participant would do in a further video-taped interaction, with a different opposite-sex peer, the two sets of judgments performed about the same. That is, the advantage of acquaintances over strangers vanishes when the criterion is the ability to predict behavior in a situation similar to one that the strangers have seen but that the acquaintances have not (Colvin & Funder, 1991).

Let me clarify this finding with a personal example. During most academic quarters, I lecture before 150 or more undergraduates two or three times a week. As a result, a lot of people have seen me lecture but have no way of knowing what kind of person I am in other settings. My wife, on the other hand, has known me well for more than twenty years but has never seen me deliver a lecture (this is not uncommon among college professors and their spouses). If one of my students *and* my wife were asked to predict how I will behave in lecture next week, whose predictions will be more accurate? According to Colvin and Funder (1991), the two predictions will be about equally valid. On the other hand, according to Funder and Colvin (1988), if you ask these two people to predict what I might do in any *other* context, my wife will have a clear advantage.

In our 1991 article, Colvin and I called this phenomenon a "boundary" on the acquaintanceship effect, because we seemed to have found the one circumstance under which strangers could provide personality judgments with a predictive validity equal to those offered by close acquaintances. But through a reversed perspective, this finding may be even more remarkable. Even though a close acquaintance—such as a spouse—has never seen you in a particular situation, he or she will be able to generalize from observations of you in *other* situations with accuracy sufficient to predict your behavior in that situation as well as someone who has actually seen you in it. From casual observation in daily life, for example, the acquaintances were able to extract information about the participants' personalities that was just as useful in predicting how they would behave under the gaze of a video camera as was strangers' direct observation of behavior in a highly similar situation. The real news of this research may be this ability of acquaintances to go from their specific experiences to judgments that are generally accurate.

Another recent study added a further wrinkle to understanding the effect of quantity of information on accuracy. It turns out that if judges are given more information, this will improve the agreement between their judgments and the self-judgments of the target himself or herself but *not* their agreement with each other (Blackman & Funder, 1998). Judges watched a series of videotapes of people having conversations with each other. Some judges saw only one five-minute tape, some saw two tapes (for a total of ten minutes), and so on up to judges who saw six tapes for a total of thirty minutes of observation. Then they tried to describe the personality of the person they watched.

The results are illustrated in Figure 6.1. *Consensus,* or the agreement among judges, was almost as good at the beginning as it became by the end; it did not change significantly between the judges who watched five versus thirty minutes of videotape. But *accuracy,* here indexed by the agreement between their descriptions and the targets' own self-descriptions, did improve both noticeably and significantly.

What caused this difference? The reason seems to be that judges' first impressions of their targets agree with each other because they are based on superficial stereotypes and other potentially misleading cues. Because these stereotypes are shared across judges, the judges tend to agree with each other even if they are largely wrong. After coming to observe the target for a period of time, however, they begin to discard these stereotyped judgments and see the person as he or she really is. The result is not so much an increase in agreement among the judges, as it is an improvement in the accuracy of what they are agreeing about.

A hypothetical example may help to clarify what is being said here. Consider two owners of a garage, Sue and Sally. They need a new mechanic and interview an applicant named, let us say, Luther. Luther's hair is neatly combed and his shoes are freshly shined, so they decide he is conscientious and give him the job. Sadly, after a few weeks they realize that he is chroni-

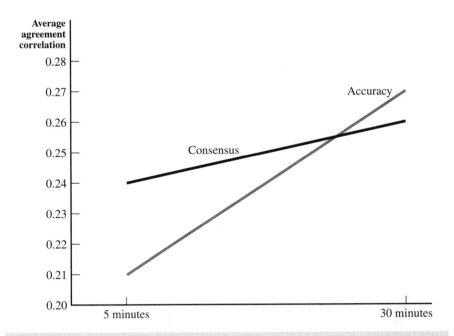

FIGURE 6.1   ACCURACY AND CONSENSUS AT 5 AND 30 MINUTES OF ACQUAINTANCE   Blackman and Funder (1998) evaluated how *consensus* (inter-judge agreement) and *accuracy* (self-other agreement) changed according to the length of time that judges watched videotapes of the target participants' behavior. The results show that while accuracy improved significantly with longer observation, consensus did not. Source: Blackman & Funder, 1998.

cally late for work and leaves his repairs only half done, and that customers are starting to complain about finding beer cans in the back seat. Sue and Sally have a meeting and agree that, contrary to their first impression, Luther is unreliable and must go.

In technical terms, consensus did not change during this story, even though accuracy did. Sue and Sally agreed at the beginning, and they agreed at the end. However, the content of what they agreed about changed dramatically. At the beginning they agreed about an erroneous stereotype; at the end, with the benefit of more information, they agreed about what Luther was really like. This is the kind of process, I believe, that explains why the "accuracy" line leans upward in Figure 6.1, even though the "consensus" line lies almost flat.

Quality of Information   Quantity is not the only variable concerning information that is important to consider. Common experience suggests that sometimes it is possible to learn a lot about someone very quickly, and it is also possible to "know" someone for a long time and learn very little about

*"When you picked up your car, Mr. Ferguson,
after we did the hoses, did you see Luther's shoes?"*

him or her. It appears to depend on the situation, and the information that
it yields. For example, it can be far more informative to observe a person in
a "weaker" situation, in which different people do different things, than in
a "strong" situation where social norms restrict what people do (Snyder &
Ickes, 1985). This is why behavior at a party is more informative than behavior while riding a bus. At a party extraverts and introverts act very differently and it is not difficult to see who is which; on a bus most everybody just
sits there. This is probably also why, according to recent research, unstructured job interviews are more valid than highly structured interviews for
judging an applicant's personality (Blackman, 2002).

A common intuition, and one that is probably correct, is that you learn
something extra about a person if you see him or her in a stressful or emotionally arousing situation. Watching how someone acts in an emergency or
how he or she responds to a letter of acceptance—or rejection—from medical
school, or even participating in a romantic encounter with someone can reveal
things about him or her that you might not have suspected otherwise. By the
same token, it is possible to sit next to a person in a class day after day for
months and know next to nothing about him or her. The best situation for
judging a person is one that brings out the trait you want to judge. To evaluate
a person's approach towards his or her work, the best thing to do is to observe
him or her actually working. To evaluate a person's sociability, observations at
a party might be more informative (Freeberg, 1969; Landy & Guion, 1970).

An interesting start toward evaluating the quality of information was
provided by a study in which everyday judges of personality listened to interviews in which participants were asked either about their thoughts and feel-

ings or about their daily activities. The judges then tried to describe the participants' personalities using a set of one hundred different traits. The researchers found that listening to the thoughts-and-feelings interview "produced more 'accurate' social impressions, or at least impressions that were more in accord with speakers' self-assessments prior to the interviews *and* with the assessments made by their close friends, than did [listening to] the behavioral . . . interviews" (Andersen, 1984, p. 294).

This experimental finding suggests that in real life, knowing someone in a context where you get to know their thoughts and feelings—as a close friend or lover might, for example—is likely to lead to more accurate overall impressions of that person's personality than knowing someone in a setting where you see only what they do—as a co-worker would, for example. This implication has never been tested empirically, however, as far as I know; it deserves future research.

Another way to evaluate the quality of the information on which a judgment is based is to consider how specific observations of behavior are linked to the judgment of specific traits. For example, when a participant is heard to speak in a very loud voice, judges are apt to infer that he or she is extraverted, and that inference is generally correct. However, the loudness of someone's voice has little to do with his or her other traits, such as conscientiousness or agreeableness (Funder & Sneed, 1993; Scherer, 1978).

Other research showed that a glance at someone's face can be sufficient for perceivers to make surprisingly accurate judgments of his or her dominance and submissiveness (Berry & Finch Wero, 1993). The degree to which someone dresses fashionably and has a stylish haircut can lead lay perceivers to infer, with a surprising degree of validity, that he or she is extraverted (Borkenau & Liebler, 1993). People also often assume they can judge a person by the kind of music he or she listens to. They may be right! According to one recent study, people who enjoy reflective, complex music (e.g., new age) tend to be inventive, imaginative, tolerant, and liberal. People who prefer aggressive and intense music (e.g., heavy metal) are more likely to be curious, risk-taking, and physically active. People who like upbeat and conventional music (e.g., pop) are relatively cheerful, outgoing, and helpful, but are not very interested in abstract ideas (Rentfrow & Gosling, in press).

Another recent study examined that most classic of interpersonal cues to personality: the handshake. People often claim to judge people by this cue, and one study found that people with a firm handshake indeed tended to be extraverted and emotionally expressive. People with a weak grip were more likely to be shy and anxious (Chaplin et al., 2000).

The accurate judgment of personality, then, depends on both the quantity and the quality of the information on which it is based. More information is generally better, but it is just as important for the information to be specifically relevant to the traits that one is trying to judge.

The Realistic Accuracy Model

To bring sense and order to the wide range of moderators of accuracy, it is helpful to back up a step and ask how accurate personality judgment is possible in the first place. At least sometimes, people do manage to accurately evaluate one or more of the aspects of the personalities of the people they know. This does not happen by ESP, I presume. So how do they do it? One explanation is in terms of the Realistic Accuracy Model (or RAM) (Funder, 1995).

In order to get from an actual attribute of an individual's personality to an accurate judgment of that trait, according to this model, four things must happen (see Figure 6.2). First, the person being judged must do something *relevant*, that is, informative about the trait to be judged. Second, this information must be *available* to a judge. Third, this judge must *detect* this information. Fourth and finally, the judge must utilize this information correctly.

For example, consider an attempt to judge someone's degree of courage. This may never be possible unless the right situation comes along that allows a courageous person to reveal this trait. But if the target of judgment encounters a burning building, rushes in, and saves the family within, then he or she has now done something *relevant*. Next, this behavior must occur in a manner and place that makes it possible for you, as the judge, to observe it. Someone might be doing something extremely courageous right now, right next door, but if you can't see it, you may never know and never have a chance to accurately assess that person's courage. But let's say you do happen by just as the target of judgment rescues the last member of the family from the flames. Now the judgment has passed the *availability* hurdle. That is still not enough. Perhaps you were distracted, or you are perceptually

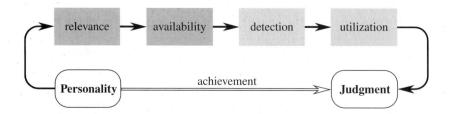

FIGURE 6.2   THE REALISTIC ACCURACY MODEL   For an attribute of an individual's personality to be judged accurately, four things must happen. First, the individual must do something *relevant* to the attribute. Second, this behavioral information must be *available* to the judge. Third, the judge must *detect* this information. Fourth, the judge must *utilize* this information correctly. Source: Funder, 1995.

impaired, or for some other reason you failed to register the dramatic rescue. But if you did notice, then the judgment has passed the *detection* hurdle. Finally, you must accurately remember and correctly interpret the relevant, available information that you have detected. If you infer that this rescue means the target person rates high on the trait of courage, then you have passed the *utilization* stage and achieved, at last, an accurate judgment.

This model of accurate personality judgment has several implications. The first and most obvious implication is that accurate personality judgment is difficult. Notice how all four of the hurdles—relevance, availability, detection, and utilization—must be overcome before accurate judgment can be achieved. If the process fails at any step—the person in question never does something relevant, or does it out of sight of the judge, or the judge doesn't notice, or the judge makes an incorrect interpretation—accurate personality judgment will fail as well.

The second implication is that the moderators of accuracy discussed earlier in this chapter—good judge, good target, good trait, and good information—must be a result of something that happens at one or more of these four stages. For example, a good judge is someone who is good at detecting and utilizing behavioral information. A good target is someone who behaves in accordance with his personality (relevance) in a wide range of situations (availability). A good trait is one that is displayed in a wide range of contexts (availability) and is easy to see (detection). Similarly, knowing someone for a long time in a wide range of situations (good information) can enhance the range of behaviors a judge sees (availability) and the odds that the judge will begin to notice patterns that emerge (detection).

A third implication is the most important. To improve the accuracy of personality judgment, according to RAM there are four different places to intervene. Traditionally, efforts to improve accuracy have focused on attempts to get judges to think better, to use good logic and avoid inferential errors. These efforts are worthwhile but address only one stage—utilization—out of the four stages of accurate personality judgment. Improvement could be sought at the other stages as well (Funder, 2003).

For example, consider the disadvantages of being a "touchy" person. Someone who easily takes offense will find that people tiptoe when he or she is around: they avoid discussing certain topics and doing certain things whenever he or she is present. As a result, his or her judgment of these acquaintances will become stymied at the *relevance* stage—relevant behaviors that otherwise might have been performed will be suppressed—and he or she likely will be unable to judge them accurately. For example, a boss who blows up at bad news will lead employees to hide evidence of their mistakes, thus interfering with the *availability* of relevant information. As a result, the boss will be clueless about the employees' actual performance and abilities.

The situation can also affect judgmental accuracy. Meeting someone under tense or distracting circumstances is likely to interfere with the detection of otherwise relevant and available information, again causing accurate judgment to be stymied. People on job interviews or first dates may not always be the most accurate possible judges of the people they interacted with in those situations.

Being a better judge, then, is much more than a matter of thinking better. You should also try to create an interpersonal environment where other people can be themselves and where they feel free to let you know what is really going on. It may be more difficult to avoid situations where tensions and other distractions cause you to miss what is right in front of you. But it might be worth bearing in mind that your judgment in such situations may not be completely reliable, and to try to remember to calm down and be attentive to the other person as well as to your own thoughts, feelings, and goals.

Self-Knowledge

Most of the same principles derived from the Realistic Accuracy Model also apply to self-knowledge (Funder, 2003). As was mentioned earlier in this chapter, in an important sense you are just one of the people you happen to know, and to some degree you come to know yourself the same way you find out about anybody else: you observe what you do and try to draw appropriate conclusions (Bem, 1972).

KNOWING THE SELF VERSUS KNOWING OTHERS

Knowing yourself might in some respects be even more difficult than trying to figure out someone else. Research does indicate that, not surprisingly, we have better insight into our personal emotional experience than anyone else does (e.g., Spain, Eaton, & Funder, 2000). But when it comes to actual, overt behavior, the picture is somewhat different. In a study that obtained personality judgments from the participants' close acquaintances as well as from the participants themselves, the acquaintances' judgments had *better* validity for predicting behavior than did the self-judgments in nearly every comparison (Kolar, Funder, & Colvin, 1996). For example, acquaintances' judgments of assertiveness correlated more highly with later assertive behavior observed in the laboratory than did self-judgments of assertiveness. The same was true for talkativeness, initiation of humor, physical attractiveness, feelings of being cheated and victimized by life, and several other traits of personality and behavior.

One reason for findings like this may be that attending to the self is actually rather difficult. From the "inside" you spend the day preoccupied with planning your next moves in response to the situations with which you are confronted. And, all you see is what *you* decide to do, not what anybody else would do in the same situation. In terms of RAM, problems arise at both the relevance and detection stages. But when you view somebody else from the "outside," you may be in a better position to compare what he or she does with what others do, and therefore be better able to evaluate his or her personality traits, which as you will recall from Chapter 4 are *relative* constructs. Their very essence entails comparing one person with another. If you can see two different people responding differently to the same situation, this is an ideal opportunity to judge how their personalities might be different.

For example, imagine you are standing in a long line at an airline ticket counter and, when it is finally your turn, the clerk is rushed and somewhat rude to you. You do your best to ignore the clerk's behavior, take your ticket, and leave. Whatever you learn about yourself from this episode is necessarily limited. But now imagine you get a chance to watch two other people who happen to be ahead of you in line. The first talks to the clerk, shrugs his shoulders, takes his ticket, and leaves. The second person begins to talk to the clerk and quickly becomes angry. He gets red in the face and is shaking a finger and raising his voice by the time they finish. Now you are in an excellent position to compare the personalities of these two individuals, who reacted very differently to the same stimulus.

Occasionally, it might be possible to take this sort of "outside" perspective on your own behavior. One such occasion might be when you use your memory to survey your past behaviors and see retrospectively how each of your actions fits into a pattern that may have been invisible to you at the time. You might realize you generally try to get along with people and avoid confrontation whenever you can. To consider another example, when alcoholics are asked to explain the causes of their recent drinking relapses, they tend to attribute them to a stressful day at work, a fight with a spouse, and so on. But the more time has passed, the more likely the alcoholic is to view the relapse as part of the chronic pattern of being an alcoholic (McKay et al., 1989).

One of the great misperceptions many people seem to have about their own behavior is that it is the logical or natural response to the situation at the moment—that it is what anyone would have done (Ross, Greene, & House, 1977). "What else could I do?" you may often hear people ask. Such explanations are somewhat like those of the alcoholic who, after a stressful argument, goes on a bender. The alcoholic might say, "The stress caused me to drink," but of course what he or she forgets is that nonalcoholics find other ways to respond to stress. You probably know people who are hostile, or deceitful, or unpleasant in some way, who similarly believe they are just responding normally to the situations in which they find themselves. As an outside observer, however, you are in a position to see their chronic patterns of behavior, not just the momentary pressures that impinge upon them, and you can also see that other people manage to respond more constructively to similar situations (Kolar, Funder, & Colvin, 1996).

Nor is this phenomenon probably limited to negative behaviors, although the positive end of the effect has not yet been documented by research. You probably know people who are consistently easygoing, kind, or diligent, or brave. When asked about their behavior they seem just as surprised as the alcoholic or hostile person just described: "What else could I do?" they respond. To them, acting in an easygoing, kind, diligent, or brave manner is simply the obvious response to the situations they experience, and they find it hard to imagine themselves or anyone else acting differently. It takes an outsider's perspective to recognize their behavior as consistent across situations, unusual, and even admirable. Perhaps the tendency to overestimate the influence of situation is more pronounced when negative traits like alcoholism are involved. But I suspect that in many cases individuals can be equally blind to their good qualities.[5]

The purpose of psychotherapy is often to try to get perspective on one's own behavior to discover where one's weaknesses and strengths lie. Therapists will often induce the client to review his or her past behavior and seek to identify chronic patterns, rather than continuing to see his or her maladaptive behavior merely as responses to momentary pressures. The alcoholic, for example, must realize that his or her drinking is a chronic and characteristic behavior pattern, and not just a normal response to situational stress. And then he or she must find the inner strengths that can be drawn on to help to overcome this problem.

IMPROVING SELF-KNOWLEDGE

The Realistic Accuracy Model has several implications for how to get to know yourself better. The utilization stage emphasizes the importance of accurate memory for and evaluation of what you have done. The detection stage emphasizes the importance of avoiding distractions—such as worrying too much about how you are coming across to the other person—and focusing

---

[5]Social psychological research on the "false consensus" effect has studied in detail the tendency of people to see their own behavior as more common than it really is (see Ross, Greene, & House, 1977). The present discussion can be compared to research on the "actor-observer effect" (e.g., Jones & Nisbett, 1971), which found that people typically see their own behavior as a response to momentary, situational pressures, whereas they see the behavior of others as consistent and as a product of their personality attributes. The present discussion differs from earlier presentations of the effect in that it does not follow the traditional assumption that the participant is correct in thinking his or her behavior is caused by the situation, and the observer is wrong. I suspect that, more often, the participant tends to be blind to consistencies in his or her own behavior, and that those consistencies are better observed from the external perspective of another person (see Funder, 1982; Kolar, Funder, & Colvin, 1996).

on the person you wish to understand. The availability stage raises fewer issues for self-knowledge, because presumably everything you do is at least in principle available to you, if you can just manage to notice it appropriately.

The most important implications of RAM for self-knowledge probably are at the relevance stage. Just like getting to know another person, you can only really evaluate yourself on the basis of what you have seen yourself do, and this is limited by the situations you have experienced and even by what you have allowed yourself to do. For example, some people test themselves by bungee jumping or going mountain-climbing, thus allowing the performance of behaviors relevant to attributes they might not otherwise have known that they have. I am not really recommending that you go bungee jumping, but it might be worthwhile to consider the possibility that you could learn a lot about yourself by going to new places, meeting new people, and trying new things.

This may be difficult in some circumstances. If you live your whole life in a small town, around the same few people, you may have no idea what you would do—what traits would emerge, what skills would develop—in a broader or different environment. During time I spent in New Zealand—an idyllic country on a set of small islands in the South Pacific—I was interested to see how many college students were desperately anxious to travel. They live in a bit of paradise, but were eager to test themselves against some of the challenges in the wider, more crowded, and even more dangerous worlds of Europe and North America.

A similar kind of limitation of self-knowledge can occur for reasons of family or culture, rather than geography. For example, some families (and some cultural traditions) curb the self-expression of young people to a significant degree (see Chapter 14). One's education, occupation, and even spouse may be chosen by others. More commonly, families may exert strong pressures on children to follow certain educational objectives and career paths. My own university—like many others—is populated by many freshman pre-medical students. Strangely, by the senior year there are far fewer. The most difficult cases are those where a student has been pressured by family expectations to be pre-med and, some time in the junior year, realizes that he or she lacks the skills, the interest, or both. It must feel to the student like he or she has five minutes to decide on a new major, new occupation, and new path in life. This will be even more difficult if in the past he or she has not tried out alternatives—he or she may literally have very little basis for knowing where his or her talents and interests really lie.

So on the level of occupational choice, relationship formation, and every other level, the best advice towards self-knowledge is probably this: Be yourself. It is probably not possible to avoid being influenced by the desires and expectations of our friends, acquaintances, and family members. But it is by searching for your own interests and testing your own abilities that you are most likely to find out who you really are. And it is on the basis of that knowledge that you are most likely to be able to make wise choices about education, occupation, relationship partners, and everything else that matters.

Conclusion

There is no escaping personality assessment. If you manage to evade having your personality judged by tests or by psychologists, you still will find that your personality is judged every hour of every day by your acquaintances, co-workers, friends, and yourself. Furthermore, these judgments will matter just as much and probably more than any that will ever be rendered by tests or psychologists. This is why it matters whether they are accurate. We need to understand others in order to interact with them and make decisions ranging from whom to lend $10 to whom to marry. We need to understand ourselves for even deeper reasons. A person cannot possibly judge what to do in life or whom to associate with unless, first, he or she understands his or her own personality. And a person cannot possibly do that unless he or she has given his or her personality a fair chance to emerge.

Summary

People judge the personalities of each other and of themselves all the time, and these judgments have important consequences. The judgments of a person by others can affect that person's opportunities and can create self-fulfilling prophecies, or expectancy effects. A person's judgments of himself or herself influence what he or she is likely to attempt to accomplish in life. Therefore, it is important to examine when and how judgments of the self and of others are accurate. Recent research evaluated the accuracy of personality judgment in terms of agreement and predictive validity. That is, judgments that agree with judgments from other sources (such as other people) or that are able to predict the people judged are more likely to be accurate than judgments that do not agree with each other or that cannot predict behavior. Research has examined four kinds of variables that seem to affect the likelihood of accurate personality judgment: (1) the good judge, or the possibility that some judges are more accurate than others; (2) the good target, or the possibility that some individuals are easier to judge than others; (3) the good trait, or the possibility that some traits are easier to judge accurately than others; and (4) good information, or the possibility that more or better information about the target makes accurate judgment more likely. This research leads to the Realistic Accuracy Model (RAM) of the process of accurate personality judgment, which describes accuracy as a function of the relevance, availability, detection, and utilization of behavioral cues. This model implies that accurate personality judgment is difficult, helps to explain the four moderators of accuracy, and suggests some ways in which one might be able to judge others more accurately. It also implies many ways to improve self-judgment, the most important of which is: Allow yourself to be yourself.

USING PERSONALITY TRAITS TO UNDERSTAND BEHAVIOR

Traits exist (Chapter 4) and can be assessed by psychologists (Chapter 5) as well as by everybody else in daily life (Chapter 6). So now it is time to ask how traits can be *used* to understand behavior. From a scientific perspective, the main purpose for measuring anything is to move toward an explanation of an important phenomenon. In order to use traits to help explain behavior, psychologists have used four basic methods: the **many-trait approach**, the **single-trait approach**, the **essential-trait approach**, and the **typological approach**.

In the *many-trait approach*, researchers approach the investigation of behavior with long lists of traits, intended to cover the whole domain of personality. These researchers investigate which of these traits correlate with the specific behavior in which they are interested, and then seek to explain the correlations. For example, a researcher might measure how long each member of a group of children can wait for a reward (a behavior technically called *delay of gratification*) and also measure up to one hundred traits in each child. The researcher could then see which of these traits tended to characterize the children who delayed the longest and the shortest lengths of time. As you will see later in this chapter, the results from such an experiment can reveal much about how and why the longest-delaying children were able to do so, as well as illuminate the psychological mechanisms that underlie the tendency to delay.

In the *single-trait approach*, researchers focus on one particular trait and examine its implications in detail. For example, important research programs have examined authoritarianism, conscientiousness, and self-monitoring, to name only three. For each trait, the research question concerns not so much the broader functioning of personality or even the basis of specific behaviors, but how wide-ranging the implications might be of a particular, arguably central, attribute of personality.

The *essential-trait approach*, which has made considerable headway in recent years, is to try to narrow the list of thousands of trait terms in the dictionary into a much shorter list of the ones that really matter. Most prominently, the "Big Five" includes the traits of *extraversion, neuroticism, consci-entiousness, agreeableness,* and *openness.* These five factors have become widely used, but psychologists still debate whether they are sufficient for char-acterizing personality, and whether the number and nature of essential traits might vary from one culture to another.

The *typological approach* is different. It stems from a doubt and a hope. The doubt is whether it is really valid to compare people with each other, quantitatively, on the same trait dimensions. Perhaps they are so qualitatively different—because they are different types of people—that comparing indi-vidual trait scores makes as little sense as the proverbial comparison between apples and oranges. The hope is that researchers can identify groups of peo-ple who resemble each other enough, and are different enough from every-body else, that it makes sense to consider them all to be the same "type." Instead of focusing on traits directly, this approach focuses on the *patterns* of traits that characterize whole persons, and tries to sort these patterns into types of people.

This chapter reviews each of these four approaches to the scientific use of personality traits.

The Many-Trait Approach

A number of personality psychologists—including me—enjoy looking at many traits at once when examining the correlates of behavior. Several more or less comprehensive lists of traits have been developed for this purpose (including Allport and Odbert's list of 17,953, which is a bit long for prac-tical purposes; Allport & Odbert, 1936). My own favorite is the list of one hundred traits called the **California Q-set** (Bem & Funder, 1978; Block, 1978).

The California Q-Set

Maybe *trait* is not quite the right word for the items of the Q-set. The set consists of one hundred phrases printed on separate cards. Each phrase describes an aspect of personality that might or might not be important for characterizing a particular individual. The phrases are more complex than personality traits, which are usually expressed in single words. For example, item 1 reads, "Is critical, skeptical, not easily impressed"; item 2 reads, "Is a genuinely dependable and responsible person"; item 3 reads, "Has a wide range of interests"; and so forth for the remaining ninety-seven items (see Table 7.1 for more examples).

TABLE 7.1

SAMPLE ITEMS FROM THE CALIFORNIA Q-SET

1. Is critical, skeptical, not easily impressed
2. Is a genuinely dependable and responsible person
3. Has a wide range of interests
11. Is protective of those close to him or her
13. Is thin-skinned; sensitive to criticism or insult
18. Initiates humor
24. Prides self on being "objective," rational
26. Is productive; gets things done
28. Tends to arouse liking and acceptance
29. Is turned to for advice and reassurance
43. Is facially and/or gesturally expressive
51. Genuinely values intellectual and cognitive matters
54. Emphasizes being with others; gregarious
58. Enjoys sensuous experiences—including touch, taste, smell, physical contact
71. Has high aspiration level for self
75. Has a clear-cut, internally consistent personality
84. Is cheerful
98. Is verbally fluent
100. Does not vary roles; relates to everyone in the same way

Both the way this list of items is used and the way it originated are rather unusual. Raters use the items to express judgments of personality by sorting them into nine categories ranging from "not characteristic" of the person being described (category 1) to "highly characteristic" (category 9). Items neither characteristic nor uncharacteristic are placed in or near category 5. The distribution is forced, which means that a predetermined number of items must go into each category. The usual distribution is peaked or "normal," meaning that most items are placed near the center and just a few (just five of the one hundred) can be placed on each end (see Figure 7.1).

The rater who does this sorting might be a friend, or a researcher, or a psychotherapist; in these cases the item placements constitute I data. Alternatively, a person might provide judgments of his or her own personality, in which case the item placements constitute S data. The most important advantage of Q-sorting[1] is that it forces the judge to compare all of the items directly against each other within one individual, rather than just relatively across individuals. Furthermore, the judge is restricted to identifying only a few

---

[1]A note on terms: A *Q-set* is a set of items (such as the one hundred items of the California Q-set) that a rater sorts into categories in order to describe someone. A *Q-sort* is this arrangement of the items into categories, once completed, and *Q-sorting* is what one does to turn a Q-set into a Q-sort.

FIGURE 7.1   THE CALIFORNIA Q-SORT   To describe an individual, one places the items of the Q-set into a symmetrical, forced distribution ranging from "not characteristic" (category 1) to "highly characteristic" (category 9). These Q-sorters are in the process of laying the Q-set cards into the prescribed categories. Photos by author.

items as important for characterizing a particular person. Nobody can be described as "all good" or "all bad"; there simply is not enough room to put all the good traits—or all the bad traits—into categories 9 or 1. Finer and subtler discriminations must be made.

The items of the California Q-set were not derived through factor analysis or any other formal, empirical procedure. Rather, they were the result of efforts of a team of clinical practitioners and investigators to come up with a comprehensive set of terms sufficient to describe the diverse, real-life people they saw every day (Block, 1978). After they formulated an initial list, these investigators met regularly to try to use the items to describe their clients and research participants. If an item proved useless or vague, it was revised or eliminated. When the set was "embarrassed" because it lacked an item that was necessary to describe a particular person, a new item was written. The resulting set of one hundred items emerged only after numerous revisions and refinements. Later, other investigators further revised the set so that its sometimes-technical phrasings could be understood and used by nonpsychologists; it is this slightly reworded list that is excerpted in Table 7.1 (Bem & Funder, 1978).

Delay of Gratification

One behavior that has been investigated frequently through the multi-trait, Q-sort approach is delay of gratification. Delay is a classic topic for psychological research because denying oneself immediate pleasure for long-term gain seems opposed to basic human nature, yet it is also necessary in order to do things such as to hold a job, to stay in school, and to invest rather than spend money.

SEX DIFFERENCES

One line of research has focused on sex differences. It has long been known that males in our society are less prone to delay gratification than are females (Block, 1973; Maccoby, 1966). Why?

One study tried to answer this question using the many-trait approach (Funder, Block, & Block, 1983). One hundred sixteen four-year-old children (59 boys and 57 girls) were tested in two delay-of-gratification experiments. In one experiment, each child was shown a festively wrapped gift and promised that he or she would receive it after completing a puzzle. The gift was set down just within reach, and then the researchers measured how long the child was able to resist before reaching out and grabbing it. In the other experiment, each child was told that he or she was forbidden to play with an attractive toy. The experimenters then left the room but secretly observed whether the child approached the toy anyway. The more the child moved toward playing with the forbidden toy, the lower was his or her delay-of-gratification score. The two delay scores were then averaged and correlated with Q-sort personality descriptions obtained when the children were three years old (a year before the delay experiments were conducted), four years old (about the time the delay experiments were conducted), and years later, when the children were seven and eleven years old. The results are shown in Tables 7.2 and 7.3.

These two tables can seem overwhelming at first glance, but please bear with me and take a few minutes to examine them closely. The perusal of tables of correlates like these is a crucial part of the work of many personality psychologists. The most important thing is not the exact correlations or the specific items. Instead, the trick is to look for general patterns. Which items are stable over time? What do those items generally mean? When Tables 7.2 and 7.3 are examined in this way, a couple of clear patterns emerge.

One pattern revealed by both tables is that the personality correlates of a behavior measured when the children were four years old could be detected through personality assessments provided one year earlier and as much as seven years later. This evidence, which some psychologists find surprising, indicates that many aspects of personality remain fairly consistent even across the rapid development and changes that occur during childhood.

Another interesting facet of the information in these tables is the way that the correlates of delay of gratification are similar and different between the sexes. Girls and boys show a similar pattern in that the ones who are planful, reflective, and reasonable and who are *not* emotionally unstable (*labile* is the term on the tables) are likely to manifest the most delay in the experimental tests. However, girls who delay the most are also intelligent,

TABLE 7.2

CHILD Q-SORT CORRELATES OF DELAY OF GRATIFICATION: GIRLS

	Age at Personality Assessment			
Q-set Item	3	4	7	11
Positive Correlates				
Appears to have high intellectual capacity	.27	.51	.27	.24
Is competent, skillful	.37	.28	.39	.19
Is planful; thinks ahead	.38	.28	.32	.16
Is attentive and able to concentrate	.19	.41	.43	.07
Develops genuine and close relationships	.18	.32	.35	.24
Is reflective; thinks before acting	.22	.30	.22	.29
Is resourceful	.37	.23	.18	.18
Uses and responds to reason	.13	.37	.28	.14
Negative Correlates				
Has transient interpersonal relationships	−.24	−.30	−.31	−.41
Is emotionally labile	−.39	−.24	−.43	−.07
Is victimized by other children	−.19	−.17	−.35	−.39
Tries to take advantage of others	−.04	−.23	−.33	−.44
Goes to pieces under stress	−.25	−.25	−.30	−.14
Seeks reassurance from others	−.02	−.39	−.12	−.29
Is easily offended	−.32	−.25	−.11	−.01
Tends to be sulky or whiny	−.30	−.26	−.02	−.09

Source: Funder, Block, & Block, 1983.

competent, attentive, and resourceful—correlates missing among the boys. Boys who delay the most are also shy, quiet, compliant, and anxious—all correlates missing among the girls. This finding can be interpreted in terms of two broader personality attributes called **ego control** (which is also sometimes called *self-control* or *inhibition*) and **ego resiliency** (which is much like healthy psychological adjustment). In both sexes the children who delayed the longest had the highest levels of ego control, just as one would expect. But in the girls—and only in the girls—ego resiliency, or adjustment, was also related to delay. The boys who delayed the most, by contrast, manifested varying levels of psychological adjustment. This difference may arise because in our society girls are taught that they must learn self-control and delay of

---

TABLE 7.3

CHILD Q-SORT CORRELATES OF DELAY OF GRATIFICATION: BOYS

	Age at Personality Assessment			
Q-set Item	3	4	7	11

Positive Correlates

Is shy and reserved	.40	.36	.42	.51
Keeps thoughts and feelings to self	.41	.32	.35	.51
Is obedient and compliant	.24	.25	.53	.34
Prefers nonverbal communication	.26	.08	.47	.53
Is reflective; thinks before acting	.32	.34	.36	.30
Is inhibited and constricted	.38	.23	.25	.46
Withdraws under stress	.31	.41	.18	.42
Is indecisive and vacillating	.14	.35	.32	.45
Is physically cautious	.37	.21	.18	.39
Uses and responds to reason	.20	.22	.36	.19
Is fearful and anxious	.32	.02	.21	.35
Is planful; thinks ahead	.30	.26	.03	.22

Negative Correlates

Is vital, energetic, lively	−.39	−.32	−.44	−.40
Tries to be the center of attention	−.37	−.23	−.39	−.46
Is physically active	−.34	−.15	−.51	−.29
Is self-assertive	−.25	−.21	−.36	−.45
Has rapid personal tempo	−.41	−.28	−.22	−.38
Characteristically stretches limits	−.28	−.16	−.43	−.31
Is emotionally expressive	−.34	−.20	−.36	−.29
Is talkative	−.23	−.10	−.35	−.47
Is curious and exploring	−.21	−.22	−.21	−.39
Is emotionally labile	−.38	−.07	−.39	−.12
Is unable to delay gratification	−.31	−.30	−.17	−.16
Is restless and fidgety	−.27	−.20	−.34	−.16

Source: Funder, Block, & Block, 1983.

gratification, whereas boys do not receive this lesson. The result is that the girls most able to absorb society's lessons—the well-adjusted, resilient ones—accordingly best absorb the lesson about delay and therefore manifest the behavior more. No such lesson is aimed at boys, however, so their adjustment and resiliency end up being irrelevant or even (especially by age eleven) negatively relevant to their tendency to delay gratification (Funder, Block, & Block, 1983).

THE NATURE OF DELAY

Another study compared two different theoretical views of delay of gratification (Funder & Block, 1989). The first view regards delay behavior as one among many by-products of a general psychological tendency to inhibit one's impulses, sometimes called ego control (Block & Block, 1980). The other view regards delay of gratification as a cognitive or intellectual skill, through which one gains the *ability* to control one's impulses when necessary (Mischel, Shoda, & Peake, 1988). The difference is important, because from the ego-control perspective, delay of gratification might sometimes be a by-product of an unfortunate tendency toward overcontrol and inhibition, which might in some cases lead a person to delay more than is good for him or her. From the ability perspective, by contrast, delay of gratification is a flexible and adaptive skill of which a person cannot have too much—just as a person cannot have too much intelligence.

In one experiment, fourteen-year-old participants were offered the choice of being paid a small amount of money after each of several experimental sessions, or being paid a single, larger lump sum after all the sessions were over (Funder & Block, 1989). The results support elements of *both* views. A close look at Tables 7.4 and 7.5 reveals that the adolescents who opted for the larger, delayed payment seem to have been smarter and more ambitious, and at the same time were relatively inhibited and overcontrolled. When a study uses rewards that are strongly desired—such as the money in this study—*and* gives the subjects something to gain by waiting—also as in this study—then both ego control and intelligence will be related to delay (Funder & Block, 1989). But other studies by other investigators suggest that when

"I can tell—you like my being a little out of control."

TABLE 7.4

Q-SORT CORRELATES OF PAYMENT DELAY IN
FOURTEEN-YEAR-OLD FEMALE SUBJECTS

Q-set Item	r
Positive Correlates	
Genuinely values intellectual and cognitive matters	.49
Is a genuinely dependable and responsible person	.48
Is able to see to the heart of important matters	.48
Is socially perceptive of interpersonal cues	.45
Behaves in an ethically consistent manner	.44
Has insight into own motives and behaviors	.43
Has high aspiration level for self	.43
Is productive; gets things done	.40
Tends to arouse liking and acceptance	.40
Has a clear-cut, internally consistent personality	.40
Favors conservative values in a variety of areas	.36
Behaves in a sympathetic or considerate manner	.32
Tends toward over-control of needs and impulses	.32
Has warmth, capacity for close relationships	.32
Appears straightforward, candid	.32
Prides self on being "objective," rational	.31
Is verbally fluent	.31
Appears to have high intellectual capacity	.30
Negative Correlates	
Is unable to delay gratification	−.65
Feels a lack of personal meaning in life	−.50
Is self-indulgent	−.46
Characteristically pushes limits	−.42
Tends to be rebellious and non-conforming	−.41
Is extrapunitive; tends to transfer or project blame	−.41
Has hostility toward others	−.40
Interprets simple situations in complicated ways	−.40
Thinks and associates ideas in unusual ways	−.39
Is over-reactive to minor frustrations, irritable	−.38
Has unpredictable and changeable behavior, attitudes	−.38
Creates and exploits dependency in people	−.38
Is subtly negativistic; undermines and obstructs	−.37
Perceives many contexts in sexual terms	−.37
Is guileful and deceitful; manipulative	−.35
Is basically distrustful	−.35
Expresses hostile feelings directly	−.34
Is sensitive to demands	−.32
Gives up and withdraws from frustration, adversity	−.31
Feels cheated and victimized by life	−.31
Enjoys sensuous experiences	−.30

Note: Items with correlations smaller than .30 have been omitted.

Source: Funder & Block, 1989.

TABLE 7.5

Q-SORT CORRELATES OF PAYMENT DELAY IN
FOURTEEN-YEAR-OLD MALE SUBJECTS

Q-set Item	r
Positive Correlates	
Favors conservative values in a variety of areas	.63
Is a genuinely dependable and responsible person	.60
Is productive; gets things done	.59
Has high aspiration level for self	.57
Has a clear-cut, internally consistent personality	.54
Tends toward over-control of needs and impulses	.52
Behaves in an ethically consistent manner	.52
Genuinely values intellectual and cognitive matters	.49
Is fastidious (perfectionist)	.46
Appears to have high intellectual capacity	.44
Prides self on being "objective," rational	.41
Is moralistic	.39
Judges self and others in conventional terms	.39
Behaves in a sympathetic or considerate manner	.37
Is turned to for advice or reassurance	.35
Appears straightforward, candid	.32
Is able to see to the heart of important problems	.32
Tends to arouse liking and acceptance	.31
Genuinely submissive; accepts domination comfortably	.30
Has a readiness to feel guilt	.29
Negative Correlates	
Is unable to delay gratification	−.69
Has unpredictable and changeable behavior, attitudes	−.62
Tends to be rebellious and non-conforming	−.59
Is self-indulgent	−.58
Characteristically pushes limits	−.50
Has fluctuating moods	−.50
Is guileful and deceitful; manipulative	−.48
Is subtly negativistic; undermines and obstructs	−.44
Is basically distrustful	−.43
Expresses hostile feelings directly	−.42
Has hostility toward others	−.41
Is sensitive to demands	−.38
Feels a lack of personal meaning in life	−.34
Gives up and withdraws from frustration, adversity	−.34
Is self-defeating	−.34
Feels cheated and victimized by life	−.34
Tends to be self-defensive	−.31
Denies unpleasant thoughts and experiences	−.29
Is power oriented	−.29
Perceives many contexts in sexual terms	−.28

Source: Funder & Block, 1989.

rewards are small and unexciting, delay is simply a matter of following instructions, and only intelligence matters. Intelligent kids who are good at following instructions will delay. But when rewards are great, a powerful impulse must be kept in check, thus ego control will matter more. Only those able—or prone—to control their feelings will be able to delay.

The implication of this conclusion for daily life, where the consequences of waiting and acting are much larger than can be simulated in any lab, is that intellect alone will never be sufficient to explain delay of gratification. Deeper tendencies to control or express one's impulses also will prove important. Another implication is that self-control is not a completely unmixed bag. It is good to be able to wait for rewards when such waiting serves a useful purpose, but controlling oneself too much can cause needless self-denial of the pleasures of life. According to other research, "overcontrol" is sometimes associated with negative emotions, disrupted thoughts, and even physical illness (Funder, 1998a; Polivy, 1998).

Other Behaviors

Many other important behaviors have been examined through the many-trait approach using the Q-sort, including drug abuse, depression, and even political orientation.

DRUG ABUSE

One study looked at adolescents who by the age of fourteen were using illegal drugs. These adolescents had been described with Q-sort items nearly a decade earlier, when they were small children, as being relatively restless and fidgety, emotionally unstable, disobedient, nervous, domineering, immature, aggressive, teasing, and susceptible to stress. These correlates imply that whatever might be the immediate effects of peer pressure and other external influences, the adolescents most likely to use drugs suffered from other significant problems that had been visible years earlier. They further imply that some of the effort to prevent drug abuse should be redirected, away from campaigns such as "just say no" and other immediate, short-term interventions, and toward identifying and remedying the longer-term problems and the susceptibility to stress that underlie drug abuse (Block, Block, & Keyes, 1988; Shedler & Block, 1990).

DEPRESSION

Depression is another common problem among young adults that turns out to have deep roots (Block, Gjerde, & Block, 1991). Young women who were seriously depressed at age eighteen had been described as early as age seven by such Q-sort items as shy and reserved, oversocialized, self-punishing, and overcontrolled. Young men who experienced depression at age eighteen had been identified at age seven and even as early as age three as unsocialized, aggressive, and undercontrolled. This pattern implies that women become at risk for depression when they are overcontrolled and never venture outside of the box society has prepared for them. For young men, the risk factor is undercontrol; unless they can somehow get control of their emotions and behavior they may be constantly in trouble and have difficulty finding a useful or comfortable niche in life. These findings show how society's different expectations for women and men can affect their psychological development and their psychological health, and how such expectations can lead personality traits to have opposite implications in the two sexes.

POLITICAL ORIENTATION

The last set of findings I consider in this section compares personality to political orientation. The psychologist Jack Block assessed a group of subjects around the ages of three and four. Years later, when his subjects were twenty-three years old, Block had them complete a questionnaire about their political orientation, which included questions about abortion, expenditures for welfare, national health insurance, rights of criminal suspects, and so forth. From their responses he assigned each subject a score along a dimension from "liberal" to "conservative" and found a remarkable set of personality correlates dating to early childhood. Children who grew into political conservatives, by Block's definition, were likely to have been described at age three or four as easily victimized, easily offended, indecisive, vacillating, fearful, anxious, rigid, and inhibited. Those who grew into liberals, by contrast, were more likely to have been described as developing close relationships, self-reliant, energetic, and dominant. Block so far has refrained from interpreting these correlations, calling them only "food for thought regarding the underpinnings of political values" (Block, 1993, p. 32). What do you think they mean? (For one possibility, see the discussion of the trait of authoritarianism in the next section.)

The Single-Trait Approach

The research summarized in the previous section cast a wide net over personality, as it tried to consider as many as one hundred attributes at once. The next approach employs a fishhook instead. Some of the most important and influential research in personality has focused on the nature, origins, and consequences of *single* traits of special importance.

This section considers three traits. Each of them has been examined in hundreds of studies over several decades. Psychologists view all of them as important, but for different reasons. The first trait, *authoritarianism*, has implications for social problems: it has been theorized to be a basis of racial prejudice and even fascism. The second trait, *conscientiousness*, has turned out to be surprisingly useful for predicting who will be productive employees. The third trait, *self-monitoring*, is important for theoretical reasons: it addresses fundamental issues concerning the relationship between inner reality and the private self, and external reality and the self as presented to others.

Authoritarianism

Racial prejudice and mindless obedience to corrupt government have been persistent problems throughout human history. These phenomena reached particularly horrifying dimensions in Europe in the 1930s and 1940s. The rise of Adolf Hitler and Nazism in Germany produced not only a repressive, dictatorial state bent on conquering its neighbors, but also a massive wave of ethnic oppression that led to the extermination of millions of Jews and members of other disfavored minority groups, such as Gypsies and homosexuals. For this to happen, the German people had to cooperate with or at least accede to atrocities committed by their own government.

Even while this was going on, the philosopher and psychologist Erich Fromm began to wonder how a supposedly civilized people could allow such activities to occur. Fromm formulated an explanation in terms of the influence of history and society. He theorized that the demise of Catholicism and the rise of Protestantism in Germany, combined with the rise of capitalism, gave individuals unprecedented freedom to conceive of God as they wished and to direct their economic activity in any way they chose. But with this freedom came a frightening degree of responsibility, to conceive of God without the comforting certainty of religious dogma and to choose an occupation or trade in which to thrive rather than starve. Many individuals, according to Fromm, fear this degree of freedom and seek to escape it—hence the title of his book, *Escape from Freedom* (1941). To avoid these frightening personal choices, some people turn their will over to external authority, such as a government or church, and take the comforting attitude that "I am just following orders." In turn, such individuals enjoy the experience of *giving* orders—which they expect to be unquestioned—to those who are below them in the hierarchy. Fromm coined the term *authoritarian character* to describe these personalities. It was the widespread presence of such individuals in Germany, Fromm guessed, that could explain how Nazism arose there.

Fromm's analysis concentrated on societal influences that affect people in general. However, he also acknowledged that not everybody becomes an authoritarian under the circumstances he described, not even in 1930s Germany. This observation suggests that personality might be involved. A decade later, the "Berkeley group" of psychologists (Adorno et al., 1950) attempted to understand the difference between authoritarians and nonauthoritarians (Dillehay, 1978). These psychologists had been commissioned (by the American Jewish Committee) to search for the root psychological causes of the anti-Semitism that had produced so much death and suffering during the 1930s and 1940s. Their efforts were detailed in a book called *The Authoritarian Personality*, a classic of psychological research.

The Berkeley group began by constructing a questionnaire to measure anti-Semitism. Called the "A-S scale," it included items such as "Jews seem to prefer the most luxurious, extravagant, and sensual way of living," "In order to maintain a nice residential neighborhood it is best to prevent Jews from living in it," and "The Jews should give up their un-Christian religion with all its strange customs (Kosher diet, special holidays, etc.) and participate actively and sincerely in the Christian religion" (Adorno et al., 1950, pp. 68–69). The people who scored highest and lowest on this scale were singled out for extensive clinical interviews and were given other tests.

The first thing the psychologists noticed was that the same individuals who endorsed anti-Semitic statements also tended to be prejudiced against other minority groups. So the next step was to construct a more broadly worded ethnocentrism scale, called the "E scale." It added items such as "Negroes have their rights, but it is best to keep them in their own districts and schools to prevent too much contact with whites," and "The worst danger to real Americanism during the last 50 years has come from foreign ideas and agitators" (Adorno et al., 1950, p. 142). The researchers found that scores on the E scale were correlated very highly, in the range from .63 to .75, with scores on the A-S scale.

The psychologists of the Berkeley group also believed that a more general political outlook was associated with both anti-Semitism and ethnocentrism, and in an attempt to tap it they developed the "politico-economic conservatism scale" (PEC). It was a short step from the PEC scale to the development of the "California F scale" (*F* meaning "fascism"), which aimed to measure the basic antidemocratic psychological orientation that these researchers believed to be the common foundation of anti-Semitism, racial prejudice, and political *pseudo*conservatism.

The authors of *The Authoritarian Personality* tried carefully to distinguish pseudoconservativism from genuine conservatism. Genuine conservatives, according to Adorno (1950), hold an internally consistent set of political beliefs, all of which support institutions and the traditional social order while seeking to protect individual rights, property, and initiative. There is no necessary connection between these beliefs and racism or psychopathology. Pseudoconservatives, by contrast, "show blatant contradictions between their acceptance of all kinds of conventional and traditional values—by no means only in the political sphere—and their simultaneous acceptance of the more destructive [attitudes] . . . such as cynicism, punitiveness, and violent anti-Semitism" (Adorno, 1950, p. 683). They also often hold radical positions that are anything but truly conservative—that the Bill of Rights should be abolished, for example, or that all taxes should be eliminated or all politicians impeached. This is the sense in which Adorno claimed authoritarians are pseudoconservative rather than genuinely conservative.

The California F scale, one of the most widely researched personality questionnaires ever developed, appears in Table 7.6. (The scoring method is explained in a note at the bottom of the table.) Theoretically, the F scale measures the nine different facets that the Berkeley group believed comprised the essence of authoritarianism (Adorno et al., 1950, pp. 255–57):

1. *Conventionalism*: an unthinking, inflexible tendency to follow mainstream values.

2. *Authoritarian submission*: a tendency to be submissive to and uncritical of societally endorsed moral authorities.

3. *Authoritarian aggression*: a tendency to want to severely punish those who do not obey authority.

4. *Anti-"intraception"*: an active aversion to looking within the self and a general suspiciousness of anything philosophical, humanistic, or subjective.

5. *Superstition and stereotypy*: a belief that fate is determined by mysterious, supernatural forces, combined with a tendency to think in rigid categories.

6. *Power and toughness*: a fascination with the idea of bosses, power, and domination, coupled with awe of powerful individuals and institutions.

7. *Destructiveness and cynicism*: a lack of faith in the value of people and a generally hostile attitude.

8. *Projectivity*: the belief that wild and dangerous things are going on in the world, which the researchers interpreted as an outward projection of the authoritarian's own repressed impulses.

9. *Sexual repression*: a disproportionate concern with sexual issues, especially concerning what supposedly immoral things other people might be doing (recall that the Nazis intended to exterminate not only Jews but also homosexuals).

Taken together, these characteristics make up the syndrome of authoritarianism. Their combination can help explain some patterns of behavior

TABLE 7.6

ITEMS OF CALIFORNIA F SCALE

	Disagree			Agree		
1. Obedience and respect for authority are the most important virtues children should learn.	−3	−2	−1	+1	+2	+3
2. No weakness or difficulty can hold us back if we have enough willpower.	−3	−2	−1	+1	+2	+3
3. Science has its place, but there are many important things that can never possibly be understood by the human mind.	−3	−2	−1	+1	+2	+3
4. Human nature being what it is, there will always be war and conflict.	−3	−2	−1	+1	+2	+3
5. Every person should have complete faith in some supernatural power whose decisions he obeys without question.	−3	−2	−1	+1	+2	+3
6. When a person has a problem or a worry, it is best for him not to think about it, but to keep busy with more cheerful things.	−3	−2	−1	+1	+2	+3
7. A person who has bad manners, habits, and breeding can hardly expect to get along with decent people.	−3	−2	−1	+1	+2	+3
8. What the youth needs most is strict discipline, rugged determination, and the will to work and fight for family and country.	−3	−2	−1	+1	+2	+3
9. Some people are born with an urge to jump from high places.	−3	−2	−1	+1	+2	+3
10. Nowadays when so many different kinds of people move around and mix together so much, a person has to protect himself especially carefully against catching an infection or disease from them.	−3	−2	−1	+1	+2	+3
11. An insult to our honor should always be punished.	−3	−2	−1	+1	+2	+3
12. Young people sometimes get rebellious ideas, but as they grow up they ought to get over them and settle down.	−3	−2	−1	+1	+2	+3
13. It is best to use some prewar authorities in Germany to keep order and prevent chaos.	−3	−2	−1	+1	+2	+3
14. What this country needs most, more than laws and political programs, is a few courageous, tireless, devoted leaders in whom the people can put their faith.	−3	−2	−1	+1	+2	+3
15. Sex crimes, such as rape and attacks on children, deserve more than mere imprisonment; such criminals ought to be publicly whipped, or worse.	−3	−2	−1	+1	+2	+3
16. People can be divided into two distinct classes: the weak and the strong.	−3	−2	−1	+1	+2	+3

TABLE 7.6

ITEMS OF CALIFORNIA F SCALE (CONTINUED)

	Disagree			Agree		
17. There is hardly anything lower than a person who does not feel a great love, gratitude, and respect for his parents.	-3	-2	-1	$+1$	$+2$	$+3$
18. Someday it will probably be shown that astrology can explain a lot of things.	-3	-2	-1	$+1$	$+2$	$+3$
19. Nowadays more and more people are prying into matters that should remain personal and private.	-3	-2	-1	$+1$	$+2$	$+3$
20. Wars and social troubles may someday be ended by an earthquake or flood that will destroy the whole world.	-3	-2	-1	$+1$	$+2$	$+3$
21. Most of our social problems would be solved if we could somehow get rid of the immoral, crooked, and feebleminded people.	-3	-2	-1	$+1$	$+2$	$+3$
22. The wild sex life of the old Greeks and Romans was tame compared to some of the goings-on in this country, even in places where people might least expect it.	-3	-2	-1	$+1$	$+2$	$+3$
23. If people would talk less and work more, everybody would be better off.	-3	-2	-1	$+1$	$+2$	$+3$
24. Most people don't realize how much of our lives are controlled by plots hatched in secret places.	-3	-2	-1	$+1$	$+2$	$+3$
25. Homosexuals are hardly better than criminals and ought to be severely punished.	-3	-2	-1	$+1$	$+2$	$+3$
26. The businessman and the manufacturer are much more important to society than the artist and the professor.	-3	-2	-1	$+1$	$+2$	$+3$
27. No sane, normal, decent person could ever think of hurting a close friend or relative.	-3	-2	-1	$+1$	$+2$	$+3$
28. Familiarity breeds contempt.	-3	-2	-1	$+1$	$+2$	$+3$
29. Nobody ever learned anything really important except through suffering.	-3	-2	-1	$+1$	$+2$	$+3$

Note: Instructions for scoring:
Assign a point value for each item, as follows:
    -3 = 1 point
    -2 = 2 points
    -1 = 3 points
    $+1$ = 5 points
    $+2$ = 6 points
    $+3$ = 7 points
Then add up the total score.

As of 1950, the average score for American women was approximately 3.5; the average for American men was approximately 4.0.

Source: Adorno et al., 1950, pp. 255–258.

"If we can just get beyond this 'I'm the boss' mentality and concentrate on a simple 'What I say goes' outlook, I think this will all work well."

and belief that otherwise might seem perplexing or even paradoxical. For example, authoritarians are extremely deferential to and respectful of people with higher rank than their own. But they act the opposite way with anybody who ranks lower. When I was in graduate school, a departmental administrator was extremely hostile and belittling toward graduate students. Yet we had a hard time convincing the faculty of this because this same administrator was quite respectful toward *them*. Her behavior seemed highly inconsistent and even paradoxical, until it was pointed out (by my own faculty adviser at the time, Daryl Bem) that the administrator was a "classic authoritarian"—worshipful up, contemptuous down. In that sense, her behavior was perfectly consistent. Consider another example. Some people believe that abortion should be outlawed because, they say, fetuses are alive and human life is absolutely sacred. Yet some of these same people also support the death penalty! They also frequently own guns, are fascinated with military topics, and tend to be enthusiastic about the prospect of war—any war.[2] When challenged about their conflicting beliefs, these individuals typically resist the question, show little interest and less insight into the para-

---

[2] I do not want to engage in simplistic stereotyping here. Many people who oppose abortion do not support the death penalty and do not own guns and so are logically consistent (the Pope is a well-known example). Other people have carefully nuanced views that resolve the apparent contradiction (e.g., distinguishing between abortion, seen as murder of the innocent, and the death penalty, seen as justifiable killing of the guilty). Even so, the consistent pro-life position is surprisingly rare. According to the *New York Times*, in the 2000 U.S. House of Representatives, only one member out of 435 (Rep. Chris Smith of New Jersey) opposed both abortion and the death penalty (Sullivan, 2000).

doxical structure of their own beliefs, and become red in the face; they may begin to shout (Meehl, 1992).

The nine authoritarian characteristics just listed can resolve the seeming paradox. The antiabortion stance, despite claims to the contrary, often comes from characteristic 9 ("sexual misbehavior must be punished")—authoritarians not only wish to protect the unborn, but also wish to punish the sexual behavior of any woman who seeks an abortion (Duncan, Peterson, & Winter, 1997). Support for the death penalty and war derives from characteristics 3 ("bad people have broken the rules and must pay") and 6 ("the big, powerful nation of which I am a part cannot be pushed around by these vermin"). Gun ownership, when it is not just for historical interest or target shooting, may derive from characteristics 8 ("there are a lot of dangerous people out there") and 7 ("if I shoot one of them, it serves them right"). Authoritarian individuals seldom notice their contradictory motivations because of characteristic 4 ("I don't want to think about it") (Dillehay, 1978).

It is impressive to see how the idea of authoritarianism accounts for the way an individual can hold a collection of otherwise unrelated or even paradoxical beliefs. This feat is even more impressive when you consider that the concept was first developed in the early 1940s, when anti-Semitism and destructive nationalism were the major issues instead of today's battles over abortion, gun control, and the death penalty. A psychological concept demonstrates real power when it is formulated to account for one set of phenomena, then proves itself able to account for another, unforeseen set of phenomena. Authoritarianism has proved itself remarkably able to do just that (see Jost, Glaser, Kruglonski, & Sulloway, 2003).

More than fifty years after the concept was introduced, research on authoritarianism continues at a steady pace, with more than four thousand articles so far. For example, research has shown that authoritarians tend to be uncooperative and inflexible when playing experimental games, and are relatively likely to obey an authority figure's commands to harm another person (Elms & Milgram, 1966). They also watch more television (Shanahan, 1995)!

Other recent research explored the underlying fearfulness of authoritarians. Their personality is critically involved in how they respond to threat. When society is in turmoil and basic values are threatened, authoritarians become particularly likely to support "strong" candidates for office (McCann, 1997). When they feel their standard of living has declined, that crime is getting worse, and that environmental quality is declining, authoritarians become six times as likely[3] to favor restrictions on welfare and eight times

---

[3]Compared to nonthreatened authoritarians or nonauthoritarians.

as likely to support laws to ban abortions (Rickert, 1998). And when they feel their nation might be in danger, they are eager to go to war.

On the other hand, there seems (perhaps surprisingly) to be no relation between authoritarianism and partisan self-identification. It appears that authoritarians prefer whatever candidate they feel projects the more powerful image, regardless of the candidate's party affiliation (McCann, 1990). Democrats are nearly as likely to be authoritarian as are Republicans—or at least they were forty years ago, when the most recent data available were produced (Campbell et al., 1960). Indeed, even communists can be authoritarian. A study conducted in Romania 10 years after the collapse of communist rule found that people who scored high in authoritarianism still believed in communist ideas (such as government ownership of factories), but also supported fascist political parties and candidates whose positions were at the opposite extreme (Krauss, 2002). The common thread seemed to be that the personalities of these people led them to crave strong leaders and even to be attracted to dictatorship. They almost missed their communist dictators, it seemed, and wouldn't mind trading them in for fascist dictators.

If you completed the authoritarian scale in Table 7.6, you may have noticed that all of its items contribute to a higher score if answered true. This fact led some psychologists to propose that authoritarians are simply people who will answer true to *any* statement, no matter how ludicrous (Peabody, 1966). The tendency to agree with statements regardless of their content is called the **acquiescence response set**. However, other investigators pointed out that acquiescence is unlikely to be the sole basis of authoritarianism scores, because authoritarianism has been found to be related to so many other measures of prejudice and social behavior (Rorer, 1965).

Two points are important to remember about authoritarianism. The first is that authoritarianism is an individual-difference construct, and thus it cannot and is not supposed to explain why Nazism arose in Germany rather than in America, or why it arose in 1932 rather than 1882 or 1982 (Sabini, 1995). Instead, it tries to explain which individuals within any society—whether Germany, Romania, or even America—would be most likely to follow a leader like Hitler. Second, authoritarianism provides an example of how a personality trait can be used to try to understand a complex and important social phenomenon. After all, as I noted, not all Germans became Nazis in the 1930s. An examination of the differences between those who did and those who did not might help us understand who is most and least susceptible, and could also help us understand why some people are dangerously attracted to the charms of leaders who seek to lead them into dictatorship (Krauss, 2002).

Conscientiousness

When employers are selecting new employees, what are they looking for? According to one survey, out of eighty-six possible employee qualities ranked in their importance by over three thousand employers, seven out of the top eight involved conscientiousness, integrity, trustworthiness, and similar qualities (the eighth was general mental ability) (Michigan Department of Education, 1989). When trying to decide whether to hire you, therefore, almost any prospective employer will try to gauge these traits. As job interview workshops repeatedly tell you, employers will examine your haircut, your neatness of dress, and your punctuality. (Showing up late or in ragged jeans is not recommended.)

Sometimes employers go beyond these casual observations in their attempt to assess conscientiousness, by administering formal personality tests. As a broad category, these are sometimes called *integrity tests*, but they are actually purported by their publishers to measure a wide range of qualities, including responsibility, long-term job commitment, consistency, moral reasoning, hostility, work ethics, dependability, depression, energy level, and proneness to violence (O'Bannon, Goldinger, & Appleby, 1989). According to Ones and colleagues (1993), all these attributes may boil down to one broad trait that could simply be called *conscientiousness*.

What is the validity of these various tests of conscientiousness? Ones and co-workers reviewed more than seven hundred studies that used a total of 576,460 subjects in assessing the validity of forty-three different tests. Their estimate of the mean validity of these tests for predicting supervisors' ratings

"I've been up all night drinking to prepare for this interview."

of job performance was equivalent to a correlation of .41. This finding means (recall the discussion in Chapter 3, and the example in Chapter 4) that if a potential employer's prediction of future job performance *without* using one of these tests would be accurate 50 percent of the time, his or her prediction *using* the test would have more than a 70 percent accuracy rate. As we saw in Chapter 4, given the costs of training (and, when necessary, firing) employees, this difference could prove financially significant. Of course, all of this assumes that supervisors' ratings are a reasonable measure of job performance.

The tests do less well at predicting employee theft, with a mean validity of .13 (or about 58 percent accuracy as defined earlier). This may be an underestimate because theft is difficult to detect, so the criteria used in these studies may have been flawed. Still, Ones and co-workers concluded that so-called integrity tests are better viewed more broadly as measures of conscientiousness, rather than more narrowly as tests of honesty, and can serve as impressively valid predictors of job performance. Indeed, according to another review of the literature (which included 117 different studies), "conscientiousness showed consistent relations with all job performance criteria for all occupational groups" (Mount & Barrick, 1998, p. 849). This finding holds in both genders and even after controlling for age and years of education (Costa, 1996).

This finding not only gives employers a potentially useful tool but has other implications as well. One surprising implication is that measuring conscientiousness could help alleviate the effects of bias in testing. It is well known that African Americans, as a group, score lower than white Americans on many "aptitude" tests used by businesses to select employees. (Although a few psychologists believe this difference to be genetic, more believe it to be a by-product of discrimination in educational and social environments; see Sternberg, 1995.) The results of such tests can damage employment prospects and financial well being. Tests of conscientiousness (and most other personality tests), however, typically do *not* show racial or ethnic differences (Sackett, Burris, & Callahan, 1989). Thus, if more employers could be persuaded to use personality tests instead of or at least in addition to ability tests, racial imbalance in hiring could be eliminated, or at least lessened, without affecting productivity (Ones et al., 1993).

For many years, employers and organizational psychologists have tried to find and measure the elusive "motivation variable" that distinguishes good workers from poor ones. The findings of Ones and colleagues suggest that perhaps it has been found. General conscientiousness not only might be a good *predictor* of job performance, but also may be a *cause* of excellence (Schmidt & Hunter, 1992). For example, highly conscientious employees seek out opportunities to learn about the company they work for and to acquire skills and knowledge that go beyond their present job. As a result, guess who gets promoted? Similarly, highly conscientious individuals tend to do well in interviews, not just because they present themselves well in that context, but because they spend more time seeking information and preparing themselves *before* the interview begins (Caldwell & Burger, 1998).

Conscientiousness is currently a hot topic and as research continues to expand the trait is being found to have a surprisingly wide range of implications that go beyond job performance. In economics, theorists have long puzzled over the paradox that the people with the lowest risk are the ones most likely to buy insurance, when it would make more economic sense for high-risk people to do so. One recently suggested resolution is that all is explained by conscientiousness: highly conscientious people both avoid risks and seek to protect themselves from risks that are inevitable, so they are the ones who, for example, drive carefully *and* carry lots of insurance (Caplan, 2003). In education, it has been found that conscientiousness correlates with years of schooling even though it is uncorrelated with IQ (Barrick & Mount, 1991). This finding might imply that years of education can be used as a "signal" of conscientiousness. An employer might be wise to hire someone with more schooling not because it necessarily means he or she has learned anything, but because a person who has managed to complete many years of education is likely to be high in conscientiousness (Caplan, 2003, p. 399). Consider just two more important outcomes. Criminals are low on conscientiousness (Costa, 1996). People high in conscientiousness live longer (Friedman et al., 1993). Clearly, this is one important trait.

Self-Monitoring

Mark Snyder, the developer of the concept and test of self-monitoring, has long been interested in the relations and discrepancies between the inner and outer selves. For example, a person might drink beer at a fraternity party because being a beer drinker is what that situation calls for, but the same person might be studious, serious, and intelligent in a research seminar because that is the kind of person this academic situation calls for. And yet inside, in his or her heart of hearts, this individual might be still another kind of person. Snyder theorized that the degree to which this is true varies across individuals. Some really do vary in their inner and outer selves and in how they perform in different settings. Snyder called these individuals "high self-monitors." Others are largely the same outside as they are inside and do not vary much from one setting to another. Snyder called these individuals "low self-monitors" (Snyder, 1974, 1987).

Consider Table 7.7, which lists twenty-five questions of a personality test that has been used widely for research purposes. Before reading beyond this paragraph, take a moment to answer these questions and then calculate your score according to the key at the bottom of the table.

TABLE 7.7

PERSONAL REACTION INVENTORY

The statements on this page concern your personal reactions to a number of different situations. No two statements are exactly alike, so consider each statement carefully before answering. If a statement is **true** or **mostly true** as applied to you, circle the **T** next to the statement. If a statement is **false** or **usually not true** as applied to you, circle the **F** next to the statement.

T	F	1.	I find it hard to imitate the behavior of other people.
T	F	2.	My attitude is usually an expression of my true inner feelings, attitudes, and beliefs.
T	F	3.	At parties and social gatherings, I do not attempt to do or say things that others will like.
T	F	4.	I can only argue for ideas which I already believe.
T	F	5.	I can make impromptu speeches even on topics about which I have almost no information.
T	F	6.	I guess I put on a show to impress or entertain others.
T	F	7.	When I am uncertain how to act in a social situation, I look to the behavior of others for cues.
T	F	8.	I would probably make a good actor.
T	F	9.	I rarely seek the advice of my friends to choose movies, books, or music.
T	F	10.	I sometimes appear to others to be experiencing deeper emotions than I actually am.
T	F	11.	I laugh more when I watch a comedy with others than when I am alone.
T	F	12.	In a group of people I am rarely the center of attention.
T	F	13.	In different situations and with different people, I often act like very different persons.
T	F	14.	I am not particularly good at making other people like me.
T	F	15.	Even if I am not enjoying myself, I often pretend to be having a good time.
T	F	16.	I'm not always the person I appear to be.
T	F	17.	I would not change my opinions (or the way I do things) in order to please someone else or win their favor.
T	F	18.	I have considered being an entertainer.
T	F	19.	In order to get along and be liked, I tend to be what people expect me to be rather than anything else.
T	F	20.	I have never been good at games like charades or improvisational acting.
T	F	21.	I have trouble changing my behavior to suit different people and different situations.
T	F	22.	At a party I let others keep the jokes and stories going.
T	F	23.	I feel a bit awkward in public and do not show up quite as well as I should.
T	F	24.	I can look anyone in the eye and tell a lie with a straight face (if for a right end).
T	F	25.	I may deceive people by being friendly when I really dislike them.

Key: 1-F, 2-F, 3-F, 4-F, 5-T, 6-T, 7-T, 8-T, 9-F, 10-T, 11-T, 12-F, 13-T, 14-F, 15-T, 16-T, 17-F, 18-T, 19-T, 20-F, 21-F, 22-F, 23-F, 24-T, 25-T.

Source: Snyder, 1974.

The list of questions you have just answered is the original measure of self-monitoring (and its standard title, when it is administered, is indeed "Personal Reaction Inventory" and *not* "Self-monitoring Scale"). In samples of college students, the average score falls between 12 and 14. A score of 14 or more is interpreted as implying high self-monitoring; 12 or below implies low self-monitoring. (If your score is 13, I don't know what to tell you—in theory everybody is either high or low.)

High self-monitors, according to Snyder, carefully survey every situation looking for cues as to the appropriate way to act, and then adjust their behavior accordingly. Low self-monitors, by contrast, tend to be more consistent regardless of the situation, because their behavior is guided more by their inner personality. As a result, one would expect a low self-monitor to be more judgable, in the sense discussed in Chapter 6, and a high self-monitor to be much less judgable (Colvin, 1993b).

Snyder has always been careful not to apply value judgments to high or low self-monitoring. One can say good or bad things about either. High self-monitors can be described as adaptable, flexible, popular, sensitive, and able to fit in wherever they go. They also can be described, just as accurately, as wishy-washy, two-faced, utterly without integrity, and slick. Low self-monitors, for their part, can be regarded as self-directed, as having integrity, and as being consistent and honest. Or they can be described as insensitive, inflexible, and stubborn.

One nice thing about the self-monitoring scale is that you probably got just the score you wanted. If the description of high self-monitors sounded better to you than the description of low self-monitors, the odds are very good that you are in fact a high self-monitor. If you preferred the description of the low self-monitor, then that is probably what you are.

Research has demonstrated a number of ways in which high and low self-monitors differ. Some studies gathered descriptions of these people from those who know them well in daily life. In some of my own research (Funder & Harris, 1986), high self-monitors were more likely than low self-monitors to be described by those who knew them with Q-sort items such as

- skilled in social techniques of imaginative play, pretending, and humor (e.g., is good at charades)
- talkative
- self-dramatizing, histrionic (exaggerates emotion)
- initiates humor
- verbally fluent
- expressive in face and gestures
- having social poise and presence

Low self-monitors, by contrast, were more likely to be described as

- distrustful
- perfectionist
- touchy and irritable
- anxious
- introspective
- independent
- feeling cheated and victimized by life

It is clear from these lists that high self-monitors are described more favorably and are more popular than low self-monitors. However, according to the construct, the difference arises because being positively regarded and popular is more important to high self-monitors. So although the description of low self-monitors might seem more negative, the low self-monitor probably doesn't care—other things such as independence are more important to him or her.

A second kind of research borrows a leaf from the empiricists' book (recall Chapter 5) by comparing the self-monitoring scores of members of different criterion groups—groups that, if the theory of self-monitoring were correct, would be expected to score differently. For instance, Snyder (1974) administered his scale to professional stage actors. Because their profession involves putting on the persona called for by a script, he expected them to score high on his scale—and they did. He also examined hospitalized mental patients, who typically are hospitalized because their behavior has been highly inappropriate. Snyder expected them to get low scores on self-monitoring— and they did. (Please note: this does not mean that low self-monitors are mentally ill!)

Snyder also performed some interesting experiments. He asked his participants to read the following passage into a tape recorder: "I'm going out now, I won't be back all day. If anyone comes by, just tell them I'm not here." Each participant had to read this passage six times, while trying to project one of a number of emotions—happiness, sadness, anger, fear, disgust, and remorse—by using tone of voice, pitch, speed of talking, and so forth. (Try it yourself, right now—unless you are reading at the library.) It turns out to be easier to figure out which emotion is being projected when the reader is a high self-monitor (Snyder, 1974).

Studies have demonstrated relationships between self-monitoring scores and numerous other behaviors. For example, compared to low self-monitors, high self-monitors perform better in job interviews (Osborn, Feild, & Veres, 1998), place themselves in central positions in social networks (Mehra, Kilduff, & Brass, 2001), use more strategies to influence their co-workers (Caldwell & Burger, 1997), are willing to lie in order to get a date (Rowatt,

Cunningham, & Druen, 1998), and even masturbate more often (Trivedi & Sabini, 1998).

Recent research also indicates that self-monitoring is related to the experience of emotion. In one study, men put on headphones and heard a tape of heartbeats that they were told (falsely) were their own, and then were shown a series of pictures of women. High self-monitors reported feeling most attracted to the women whose pictures were shown when they thought their hearts had sped up. Low self-monitors were less likely to be influenced by the bogus heart-rate feedback. In a second study, high self-monitors thought that jokes were funnier if they heard a laugh track along with it; low self-monitors were less prone to this effect (Graziano & Bryant, 1998). These findings imply that high self-monitors look to the environment for clues as to how they are feeling, whereas low self-monitors are more prone to look within.

The concept of self-monitoring has raised some controversy. Critics have factor analyzed (see Chapter 5) the scale and found that its items break apart into three separate factors (Briggs, Cheek, & Buss, 1980). One measures acting ability, one measures extraversion, and one measures "other directed-ness" or a tendency to be concerned about what other people think. The appearance of the latter two factors could be viewed as a serious problem for the self-monitoring construct, because extraverts tend to use an aggressive, assertive style of getting along with others, whereas "other-directed" people try to get along by going along. These are opposite styles and perhaps they are even mutually exclusive,[4] yet either kind of person could score equally high on self-monitoring. This possibility makes scores difficult to interpret. The controversy provides an illustration of the important role that factor analysis plays in the development and interpretation of personality scales (Briggs & Cheek, 1986).

The scale has since undergone further refinement. Mark Snyder recommended that the original twenty-five-item scale be reduced to only eighteen items (Gangestad & Snyder, 1985).[5] A series of complex analyses indicates that this abbreviated scale is a more pure measure of the core idea behind self-monitoring, the degree to which behavior and emotion are controlled by the environment (high self-monitoring) or by the person (low self-monitoring). This revision may be a good idea, but it raises complications. The most important complication is that the vast literature on self-monitoring—more than one thousand studies—is based almost completely on the

---

[4]When I once suggested this in class, a student came up afterwards and said, "It is too possible to both get along and get ahead. I am the highest-selling saleswoman at Nordstrom's, and I am also and *by far* the most popular!" I congratulated her.

[5]See Table 7.7. Snyder recommends that items 2, 7, 9, 10, 11, 15, and 19 now be omitted.

twenty-five-item scale, not the eighteen-item version. A good deal more research will be needed to see if the many behaviors shown to be related to the old scale are similarly related to the "new" self-monitoring.

The Essential-Trait Approach

A thorough survey of the literature of personality and clinical psychology would find measures of thousands of different traits. Recall Allport and Odbert's famous estimate of the number of traits in the dictionary: 17,953. For a long time, many psychologists have suspected that this is entirely too many. As I discussed in the first part of this chapter, some psychologists have been happy to work with a still-lengthy list of one hundred personality characteristics. But several important efforts have been made over the years to dismantle the Tower of Babel of traits by reducing them to the ones deemed truly essential.

Reducing the Many to a Few

More than half a century ago, the psychologist Henry Murray (the inventor of the Thematic Apperception Test described in Chapter 5) theorized that twenty trait terms—he called them *needs*—were essential for understanding personality (Murray, 1938). His list included needs for aggression, autonomy, exhibition, order, play, sex, and so on. Murray came up with this list theoretically—that is, by thinking about it. Later, the psychologist Jack Block developed a theory that proposed two essential characteristics of personality called *ego resiliency* (or *general adjustment*) and *ego control* (or *impulse control*) (Block & Block, 1980; Block, 2002). (These constructs were mentioned earlier, in the discussion of delay of gratification.)

Other psychologists turned to factor analysis (discussed in Chapter 5) because this method seemed like a more empirical, objective way to eliminate the redundancies in the trait lexicon. One of the pioneers, Raymond Cattell, concluded that sixteen traits were essential. These included friendliness, intelligence, stability, sensitivity, and dominance, among others (Cattell & Eber, 1961). Another pioneer, Hans Eysenck, concluded that most of what was essential to know about an individual's personality could be reduced to just three traits: extraversion; neuroticism, or unstable emotionality; and a trait he (rather confusingly) labelled *psychoticism,* a blend of aggressiveness, creativity, and impulsiveness (Eysenck, 1947; Eysenck & Long, 1986) (he believed these traits have biological bases; see Chapter 8).

The Big Five

To date, the most widely accepted factor analytic solution to the problem of reducing the trait lexicon is one offered by several psychologists including Lewis Goldberg (e.g., 2001) and Robert McCrae and Paul Costa (e.g., 1987). Drawing on earlier work by Warren Norman (1963) and others, these investigators analyzed numerous broad personality-measurement instruments and the English language itself and concluded that five broad traits summarize a large part of what can be said about personality.

The traits that make up the so-called Big Five factors are *neuroticism, extraversion, openness, agreeableness,* and *conscientiousness* (the labels vary somewhat from one investigator to the next; rearranged, these terms form the acronym "OCEAN"; John, 1990). Advocates claim that these five traits are "orthogonal," which means that getting a high or low score on any one of these traits implies nothing about the chances of getting a high or low score on any of the others. The further claim is that these five terms are sufficient as a summary of most, if not all, that anybody can say and that any test can measure about personality. For example, as we saw earlier in this chapter, Ones and co-workers were able to reduce numerous, widely varying tests of "integrity" into the single, Big Five trait of conscientiousness, and thereby brought an important degree of order to a previously confusing field of research.

Another Big Five trait with wide implications is neuroticism. It turns out that numerous questionnaires that are supposed to assess happiness, well-being, and physical health correlate strongly (and negatively) with neuroticism (also called *negative emotionality*). The higher the level of neuroticism, the more likely people are to report being unhappy, anxious, and even physically sick (McCrae & Costa, 1991; Watson & Clark, 1984). This finding implies that many of these instruments, despite their different intentions and titles, may be to some degree measuring the same underlying tendency: some people (those high on neuroticism) complain a lot, about a lot; others (those low on neuroticism) complain less.

Sex differences have been found on three of the Big Five. Across several independent samples, women scored consistently higher than men in neuroticism, agreeableness, and conscientiousness. The Big Five also are associated with several different behaviors. Extraverts are consistently rated as more popular and as more physically attractive than introverts (they also exercise more); this may be why they attend more parties, where, incidentally, they drink more alcohol. People high in conscientiousness get better grades—as was noted earlier—and are seen as more honest. People high in openness to experience are more likely to play a musical instrument, and highly agreeable people are consistently found to smoke less (all of these findings are reported by Paunonen, 2003).

Although the Big Five have proved to be useful, they also remain controversial (Block, 1995). One objection is that the Big Five *do* seem to correlate with each other to some degree; in many samples people who score high on extraversion tend to score low on neuroticism, for example. So it is not clear that the Big Five are, as advertised, five "orthogonal"—separate and independent—traits.

A more important objection is that there is more to personality than just five traits. For example, one could summarize authoritarianism, discussed earlier in this chapter, as a combination of high neuroticism, high conscientiousness, low openness, and low agreeableness, but that summary seems to miss the essence of the construct. It fails to account for authoritarians' being deferential and agreeable with those of higher rank but mean and nasty to those of lower rank, and it says nothing about their psychodynamic motivations. Similarly, self-monitoring could be recast as a combination of high extraversion and high agreeableness, but that summary also seems to miss much. Even advocates of the Big Five have acknowledged that they may not encompass attributes such as religiosity, sensuality, frugality, humor, and cunning (Saucier & Goldberg, 1998). However, they also argue that these five factors remain key because they seem to crop up again and again, while other aspects of personality are found more sporadically (Goldberg, 2001; McCrae, 2001). Other psychologists debate this point, too (e.g., Briggs, 1989; McAdams, 1992).

One question that has puzzled many people is: why five? Is there something magical about these particular five dimensions of personality? Why are there not six, or four? Some have suggested it might be because humans have five fingers on each hand, but proponents have offered a different answer:

> Why [are there] . . . five factors, what rationale remains? We believe it is simply an empirical fact, like the fact that there are seven continents on earth or eight American presidents from Virginia. Biologists recognize eight classes of vertebrates (mammals, birds, reptiles, amphibians, and four classes of fishes, one extinct), and the theory of evolution helps to explain the development of these classes. It does not, however, explain why *eight* classes evolved, rather than four or eleven, and no one considers this a defect in the theory. There are, of course, reasons why human beings differ along each of the five personality dimensions—reasons to be found somewhere in evolution, neurobiology, socialization, or the existential human condition. But it is probably not meaningful or profitable to ask why there happen to be just five such dimensions. (McCrae & John, 1992, p. 194)

Another advocate of the Big Five believes they may correspond to five essential, universal questions people need to ask about a stranger they are about to meet:

> (1) Is X active and dominant or passive and submissive (Can I bully X or will X try to bully me)? [This question corresponds to extraversion, also called

surgency.] (2) Is X agreeable (warm and pleasant) or disagreeable (cold and distant)? [agreeableness] (3) Can I count on X (Is X responsible and conscientious or undependable and negligent)? [conscientiousness] (4) Is X crazy (unpredictable) or sane (stable)? [neuroticism] (5) Is X smart or dumb (How easy will it be for me to teach X)? [openness, also sometimes called *intellect*] Are these universal questions? (Goldberg, 1981, p. 161)

Maybe they are. Several attempts have been made to see whether the Big Five can be found in cultures other than American and European and in languages other than English. Personality questionnaires translated into various native languages yielded at least four of the five factors (all except "openness") in the Philippines (Guthrie & Bennett, 1971), Japan (Bond, Nakazato, & Shiraishi, 1975), and Hong Kong (Bond, 1979). All five factors appeared when the questionnaires were translated into German (Ostendorf & Angleitner, 1994), Hebrew (Montag & Levin, 1994), Chinese (McCrae, Costa, & Yik, 1996), Korean (Piedmont & Chae, 1997), and Turkish (Somer & Goldberg, 1999).

An even more ambitious study moved beyond merely translating questionnaires and began with an analysis of the Chinese language to find the terms commonly used to describe personality in that culture (Yang & Bond, 1990). An analysis of personality descriptions by residents of Taiwan yielded five factors labeled *social orientation, competence, expressiveness, self-control,* and *optimism.* While the Chinese five factors seemed to overlap to some degree with the English five factors (e.g., expressiveness in the Chinese solution seems similar to extraversion in the English solution), there was not a one-to-one correspondence across the entire list. The researchers concluded that the central attributes of personality are similar to an important degree, yet are also to an important degree different from one culture to another (see Chapter 14 for a more extended discussion of cross-cultural issues). This conclusion seems rather wishy-washy, but it is probably the only reasonable one possible under the circumstances.

The fact that the Big Five traits of personality keep popping up, again and again, no matter what measures are used or what populations are studied, have led these traits to be characterized as making up the essential "structure" of personality. But, as Costa and McCrae themselves noted,

> The organization of specific traits into broad factors [such as the Big Five] is traditionally called the *structure of personality,* although it refers to the structure of traits in a population, not in an individual. (Costa & McCrae, 1998, pp. 107–8)

In other words, the Big Five are types of *traits,* not of people. Are there types of people, and can their personality structures be characterized? That is the next question we shall consider.

Typological Approaches to Personality

Over the years of successful application of the three trait approaches just summarized, some psychologists have occasionally expressed misgivings about the whole enterprise. First, as just noted, the structure of personality traits across individuals is not the same thing as the structure of personality as it resides *within* people, and it seems a little strange to call the former the "structure of personality." Second, it is at least possible that important differences between people are qualitative, not just quantitative. The trait approach usually assumes that all people can be characterized on a common scale of measurement. You might score high on extraversion, and I might score low, but we are compared on the same scale. But what if some differences between people are matters not of degree but of kind? If your extraversion is fundamentally different from my shyness, then to summarize this difference by comparing our extraversion scores might be a little like comparing apples to oranges by giving both of them scores on "appleness" and concluding that oranges score lower.

Of course, it is one thing to raise doubts like these and quite another to say what the essential types of people really are. To do this, one must "carve nature at its joints" (as Plato reportedly once said) and identify the ways in which people are discretely—not just continuously—different from one another. Repeated attempts at this carving did not achieve notable success over the years, leading one review to summarize the literature in the following manner:

"As an orange, how much experience have you had working with apples?"

Muhammed Ali was reputed to offer this typology: People come in four types, the pomegranate (hard on the outside, hard on the inside), the walnut (hard-soft), the prune (soft-hard), and the grape (soft-soft). As typologies go, it's not bad—certainly there is no empirical reason to think it any worse than those we may be tempted to take more seriously. (Mendelsohn, Weiss, & Feimer, 1982, p. 1169)

However, interest in typological conceptions of personality has revived in the past decade or so (Kagan, 1994; Robins, John, & Caspi, 1998). For example, Mark Snyder and his colleague, Steve Gangestad, proposed—based on an extraordinarily complex set of analyses—that the "trait" of self-monitoring considered earlier in this chapter is actually a type (Gangestad & Snyder, 1985). That is, people do not differ from one another in how high or low they are in self-monitoring, but rather fall into one of two types, high or low. Your self-monitoring score, in this interpretation, does not reflect how much self-monitoring you have, but rather reflects the probability that

The four basic personality types

you are in fact a high self-monitor. The higher your score, the more likely this is. Gangestad and Snyder may or may not be correct in this interpretation, but in any case the typology they offer seems rather limited. Their scheme categorizes people based on how they think and act related to the construct of self-monitoring, which is interesting, but the real challenge of the typological approach is to come up with basic types of people that characterize the whole range of personality.

Avshalom Caspi (1998) reported some surprising progress in this direction. He surveyed several different attempts to find the basic types of people that exist. In each study he examined, psychologists correlated whole descriptions of people with each other. For example, Block (1971) used the one hundred items of the Q-set described earlier in this chapter. He compared each person in his sample to every other person by correlating the one hundred scores that characterized each of them. He then examined the subgroups of people who resembled each other the most and gave them labels. Block identified five personality types among male participants. *Ego-resilients* were well adjusted and interpersonally effective; *vulnerable overcontrollers* were rigid, uptight, and maladjusted; *unsettled overcontrollers* were impulsive and antisocial; *belated adjusters* were maladjusted during childhood but functioning effectively in adulthood; and *anomic extraverts* were well adjusted in childhood but maladjusted as adults.

This is an interesting typology, but as Caspi noted, it was found only among males who were almost all white, intelligent, and relatively affluent. So we would want to look further, at other studies, to see if this typology holds up. It turns out that across seven different studies with varying participants all over the world, three basic types out of the five identified by Block show up again and again. The basic results of this review are summarized in Table 7.8. The terms used by specific researchers to summarize their results have varied, but underneath the same basic three types seem to be the same.

One of the basic types (denoted "Type I" in Table 7.8) is the *well-adjusted person*, who is adaptable, flexible, resourceful, and interpersonally successful. Then there are two maladjusted types. The *maladjusted overcontrolling person* ("Type II") is too uptight for his or her own good, denying himself or herself pleasure needlessly, and being difficult to deal with at an interpersonal level. The *maladjusted undercontrolling person* ("Type III") has the reverse problem. He or she is too impulsive, prone to be involved in activities such as crime and unsafe sex, and tends to wreak general havoc on other people and on himself or herself.

These types have received wide attention by researchers and have been found repeatedly in samples of participants in North America and Europe (e.g., Asendorpf & van Aken, 1999; Asendorpf, Borkenau, Ostendorf, & van Aken, 2001). But recent work has also limited the conclusions about these

TABLE 7.8

SEVEN VIEWS OF THE THREE BASIC TYPES OF PERSONALITY

Types	Block, 1971	Klohnen & Block, 1995	Robins et al., 1996	van Lieshout et al., 1994	York & John, 1992	Caspi & Silva, 1995	Pulkkinen, 1995
I	Ego-resilients	Resilients	Resilients	Resilients	Individuated	Well adjusted	Resilients/individuated
II	Vulnerable overcontrollers	Overcontrollers	Overcontrollers	Overcontrollers	Traditional	Inhibited	Introverts/anxious
III	Unsettled undercontrolled	Undercontrollers	Undercontrollers	Undercontrollers	Conflicted	Undercontrolled	Conflicted/undercontrolled

Source: Adapted from Caspi, 1998.

and other personality types in an important way. When thinking about personality types, one should keep two questions in mind. The first is, are different types of people, as identified by the typological approach, *qualitatively* and not just quantitatively different from each other? That is, are they different from each other in ways that conventional trait measurements cannot capture? The possibility that this was the case—the apple-versus-orange issue—was one basis of the sudden, renewed excitement about personality types. However, it has turned out that the answer to this question is: no. The latest evidence indicates that knowing a person's personality type adds nothing to the ability to predict his or her behavior, above and beyond what can be done by knowing how he or she stands on the traits that define the typology (Costa et al., 2002).

This is a decided blow to the typological approach, but a second question still remains: Is it useful to think about people in terms of personality types? The answer to this question may be yes (Asendorpf, 2002; Costa et al., 2002). Each personality type serves as a summary of how a person stands on a large number of personality traits. The adjusted, overcontrolled, and undercontrolled patterns in the typology described above are all rich portraits that make it easy to think about how the traits within each type tend to be found together, and how they interact. In the same way, thinking of people in terms of whether they are "military types," "rebellious student types," or "hassled suburban soccer mom types" brings to mind an array of traits in each case that would be cumbersome, though not impossible, to summarize in terms of ratings of each dimension. For this reason, it has been suggested that types may be useful in the way they summarize "many traits in a single label" (Costa et al., 2002, p. 573) and make it easier to think about psychological dynamics. Even though traits may add little for conventional psychometric purposes of measurement and prediction, they still may have value as aids in education and in theorizing.

Where Do Traits Come From? The Question of Development

The final question we will consider about the trait approach is, in one sense, the first: Where do personality traits come from? This is the question of *personality development.* It is the basis of a whole field, *developmental psychology*, and it has no easy answers.

The first point to bear in mind when we wonder about where traits come from is that this question has to do with individual differences. As has been mentioned several times already, personality traits describe ways in which people differ from each other, not ways in which they are all the same. This means that when looking for the source of a trait, one must look for an influence that differs across individuals, and so can make one person turn out differently from someone else. For example, if you see a hostile adult, it is not very helpful to say "he's hostile because he grew up in a hostile society." This kind of claim might be useful for explaining why all people in this society tend to be hostile, but *not* for explaining why one person is more hostile than another. A better explanation, therefore, might be something like "he watched much more violent television as a child than other people did." This explanation might be right or wrong, but it is at least in the correct form.

Three kinds of influences can cause one person to turn out differently than another. First, there is the way in which a person was raised, including his or her parents' child-rearing practices and the childhood family environment. A second influence comes from early experiences that were not shared with other family members, such as friends and other people encountered outside the home, and also the way one child may have been treated differently from another by their parents. The third kind of influence is genetic: Increasing amounts of evidence indicate that personality is to some extent biologically inherited (see Chapter 9).

Consider, first, the early family environment. Psychologists are currently engaged in a debate about how much this factor, long assumed to be all-important, really influences the development of personality (Harris, 1998; Eisenberg, Spinrad, & Cumberland, 1998). The debate will be reviewed in Chapter 9, but for the moment I will just say that I am convinced parents' child-rearing styles and the family environment do have important effects on the kind of people their children grow up to be. This influence might be stronger at the bad end than the good end: a truly terrible (or absent) set of parents or a pathological family situation clearly can have disastrous effects on personality development. It is less certain that once these influences are "good enough" that it makes a huge difference whether one has truly excellent parents or just good ones.

A second kind of influence on personality development, the early environment experienced outside the family unit, or experiences within the family that are different for different family members, is called "non-shared environment." The term refers to the fact that not all aspects of early experience are the same, even for siblings who grow up together. For example, you probably grew up with different friends and had different teachers than your brothers or sisters, and it is also likely that your parents treated each of you at least somewhat different. This might help to explain why siblings who grow up in the same family can so often turn out to have widely varying personalities.

The third kind of influence has only recently begun to draw serious attention in psychological research: Traits to some extent appear to come from genes, and so are at least partially biologically inherited. This process will also be described in more detail in Chapter 9, but for the moment I can note that persuasive evidence exists that, for a huge number of personality traits, people are more similar to each other the more closely they are related biologically. Indeed, this may be true for *all* traits (Turkheimer, 1998). This is a major shift in psychological thinking: Just a couple of decades ago it was assumed that the environment was the source of almost all variation in personality, but now it is clear that biology matters too.

To return to one trait that was discussed earlier in this chapter, where does *authoritarianism* come from? Consistent with the usual practice at the time, the psychologists who originally investigated this construct assumed that the explanation must lie in child-rearing styles. They theorized that children who are severely punished on a regular basis end up fearing, obeying, and being unwilling to question authority figures in their adult lives. They also develop the desire to wield power themselves and thereby become ripe to grow into full-fledged authoritarians (Adorno et al., 1950).

This theory of the development of authoritarianism was never really proved correct or incorrect. The necessary research turned out to be extraordinarily difficult to conduct. One major difficulty was that it is hard to get accurate information about the early childhood environments of adult authoritarians, or about anybody else. Another difficulty is that children typically take on the values of their parents, and authoritarian parents tend to have punitive child-rearing styles (Peterson, Smirles, & Wentworth, 1997). Yet another consideration is that parents and children are genetically related (naturally), and so parent-child similarities that seem to arise from child-rearing patterns may really be due to genetic similarity. The authoritarianism scores of parents and their biological children turn out to be correlated about .40, and biological siblings' scores are correlated about .36 (Scarr, 1981). The authoritarianism scores of adoptive parents and siblings, however, are correlated with each other between .00 and .14, a difference that implies some degree of genetic basis for authoritarianism (for more on the heritability of personality traits, see Chapter 9). So, even if a researcher could show an association between parental style and later authoritarianism, determining which of these factors actually caused the authoritarianism—the parental style itself, or simply the parents' own attitudes, or even their own genes, being passed on to their children—is nearly impossible (Sabini, 1995).

Still another possibility is that, as mentioned above, early environmental influences on authoritarianism may come from outside the home. Perhaps teachers, or friends, or even the commentators one happens to hear on the radio affects the development of this trait (imagine a child who grows up listening to Rush Limbaugh every day). It is plausible to assume that this might be important, but again, the evidence is difficult to gather and therefore is lacking. Better evidence is available that once a trait does begin to develop, people will tend to select themselves into environments that will strengthen that trait. According to the *corresponsive principle*, people enjoy experiences that are congruent with their personality traits because they seem validating and engaging, whereas incongruent experiences are unpleasant and alienating. For example, an extravert might choose to become a salesperson, and find that work environment engaging and someplace where he or she can succeed. The result is likely to be an increase in his or her extraversion over time. By the same token, a shy person who happens into or is forced into sales will probably hate the work and not be successful either, an experience that will not only be alienating but also cause him or her to change jobs as soon as possible (Roberts, Caspi, & Moffitt, 2003). In the case of authoritarianism, a budding authoritarian might join a political party, quasi-military organization, or some other kind of group already dominated by authoritarians, and find the experience pleasant, validating, and tending to increase his or her authoritarian tendencies (see Krauss, 2002). For the most part, the people who listen to Rush Limbaugh already agree with him, but he solidifies their attitudes and motivates them into action.

Thus, a person who grows up to be high on the trait of authoritarianism may do so because of how he or she was raised, because of other influences in his or her early life, because of his or her genetics, or (most likely) some combination of all of these influences. Much the same thing could probably be said about almost every other personality trait.

Conclusion

The usefulness of personality assessment goes beyond its ability to predict behavior and performance. When we learn which personality traits are associated with certain behaviors, we can learn much about why people do what they do. We have seen how personality assessment can shed light on how children delay gratification, why some people are prejudiced, use drugs, or are depressed, and other important psychological phenomena. This kind of increase in understanding is the most important goal of science.

Summary

Traits are useful not just for predicting behavior, but for increasing our understanding of the basis of what people do. This chapter examined four basic approaches to the study of traits. The many-trait approach looks at the relationship between a particular behavior and as many different traits as possible. One technique used in this approach, the California Q-sort, assesses one hundred different traits at once. The Q-sort has been used to explore the basis of delay of gratification, drug use, depression, and political ideology. The single-trait approach zeros in on one particular trait deemed to be of special interest and its consequences for behavior; it has been used to study the traits of authoritarianism, conscientiousness, and self-monitoring, among others. The essential-trait approach attempts to identify the few traits, out of the thousands of possibilities, that are truly central to understanding all of the others. The most widely accepted essential-trait approach is the Big Five, which identifies extraversion, neuroticism, conscientiousness, agreeableness, and openness as the essential traits to understand. The typological approach attempts to capture the ways in which people might differ in kind, not just in degree. Recent research has identified three basic types of personality: well-adjusted, maladjusted overcontrolled, and maladjusted undercontrolled. However, while these types may be useful for thinking about how traits work in combination, they add little if any predictive validity over what can be achieved using trait measures. The source of personality traits is a combination of influences including parents and the early childhood environment, other influences from peers, teachers and other members of society, and the individual's genetic endowment.

SUGGESTED READINGS: THE TRAIT APPROACH

Adorno, T. W., Frenkel-Brunwik, E., Levinson, D., & Sanford, N. (1950). *The authoritarian personality.* New York: Harper.

> *The classic work describing the activities of the Berkeley group to understand the psychological underpinnings of Nazism. An important part of this project was the development of the California F scale, which is described in detail.*

Allport, G. W. (1937). *Personality: A psychological interpretation.* New York: Holt, Rinehart, & Winston.

> *The classic and perhaps still best presentation of how trait psychologists think about personality.*

Funder, D. C. (1999). *Personality judgment: A realistic approach to person perception.* San Diego: Academic.

> *A more detailed (and somewhat more technical) presentation of some of the material on personality judgment, the person-situation debate, and personality research that is summarized in Chapters 4 through 7 of the present book.*

Kenrick, D. T., & Funder, D. C. (1988). Profiting from controversy: Lessons from the person-situation debate. *American Psychologist, 43,* 23–34.

> *A review of the person-situation debate written for a general audience of psychologists (not just for specialists in personality). Kenrick and I attempted to declare the person-situation debate finished; it almost worked.*

Megargee, E. I. (1972). *The California Psychological Inventory Handbook.* San Francisco: Jossey-Bass.

> *A summary of the research (to 1972) on the California Psychological Inventory (CPI). This book is at once perhaps the clearest and most thorough presentation of any of the major omnibus psychological tests. It teaches about much more than just the CPI; it serves as an excellent primer in the philosophy and technology of personality test construction.*

Mischel, W. (1968). *Personality and assessment.* New York: Wiley.

> *The book that launched a thousand rebuttals—this is the volume that touched off the person-situation debate. It is well written and, in its key sections, surprisingly brief.*

Ross, L., & Nisbett, R. E. (1991). *The person and the situation: Perspectives of social psychology.* New York: McGraw-Hill.

> *A clearly written exposition of the modern situationist position.*

Snyder, M. (1987). *Public appearances, private realities: The psychology of self-monitoring.* New York: Freeman.

> *A summary, by the test's originator, of the research stimulated by the self-monitoring scale. The book goes beyond test-relevant issues and has much of interest to say about basic topics in social psychology, notably self-presentation.*

Wiggins, J. S. (1973). *Personality and prediction: Principles of personality assessment.* Reading, MA: Addison-Wesley.

> *The classic basic textbook for personality psychologists, including much of methodological as well as substantive interest. The book is now slightly out of date, but like a true classic has lost little of its interest or value with age.*

PART III

THE MIND AND THE BODY: BIOLOGICAL APPROACHES TO PERSONALITY

Let's face it: People are animals. From a biological point of view, a human being is a member of a mammalian species, and the anatomy of the human body, especially its internal anatomy and definitely including the brain and nervous system, has many similarities with the anatomy of other species. One anatomical researcher has concluded that the human brain is made of three parts—one that resembles the brain of a reptile, a second part that resembles the brain of most mammals, and a third, uniquely human part (the "triune brain" hypothesis, MacLean, 1982). Other writers believe this description is vastly oversimplified (Buck, 1999; Fridlund, 1994), but the superficial resemblance across the brains and nervous systems of many species is striking.

The resemblance is chemical as well as anatomical. My elderly dog was once put on a thyroid medication that, it turned out, was identical to one being taken by an equivalently elderly—after the correction for dog years—human relative of mine. (The only difference was that the human version was about 10 times as expensive.) The slightly unsettling fact that most of the same medicines used by veterinarians have similar effects on people serves to remind us that our physiology is not so very different. Humans share with their fellow mammals many of the same, or nearly the same, essential chemicals that sustain and regulate the body and, yes, the mind. The widely prescribed anti-depressant drug Prozac is effective with vervet monkeys (Raleigh, 1987; Raleigh et al., 1991).

A third area of similarity is the way that so much of human nature and personality seems to be biologically inherited. The family resemblance you can see at your next holiday gathering will confirm that traits such as hair and skin color, body size, and perhaps even abilities and behavioral styles are shared among family members and transmitted from one generation to the next. Animal breeders have known for a long time how to accentuate and minimize various traits of appearance and behavior by careful selection of parental matches. Not only will the offspring of two poodles surely have curly fur, but they will also probably have more gentle personalities than the offspring of two rottweilers. Evidence that will be considered in the following chapters suggests that personality traits of humans are to some degree inherited as well.

Finally, and perhaps most controversially, all of life—plant, animal, and human—is the product of a long process of biological evolution. The "theory" of evolution is more than a theory: it is the fundamental principle that organizes biology, systematizes the taxonomy of species, and explains their origin. Evolution has taken millions of generations over hundreds of millions of years to produce the diversity of life we see today, and it continues to change specific characteristics of species (for example, in the case of bacteria that are quickly evolving to become immune to the antibiotics that are too-frequently prescribed to fight them). The implication of evolution for psychology is that attributes of any species—including behavioral patterns in humans—may exist because of the advantage they have had for the survival and reproduction of members of past generations.

The principle of evolution has sometimes evoked opposition because it seems to violate some religious beliefs—or, in the slightly more colorful words of William Jennings Bryan in 1928, the "evolutionary hypothesis . . . takes from man the breath of the almighty and substitutes the blood of a brute." But the underlying issue goes beyond dogma. Bryan also reportedly once offered $100 to anyone who would sign an affidavit that he or she was personally descended from an ape. Apparently he had few if any takers, which illustrates that people are reluctant, to say the least, to think of themselves as merely another species of animal. I confess that I was disturbed, myself, when I found the same medicine in my aunt's medicine chest that I stored at home next to the dog food. Besides the possible loss of dignity in thinking of oneself as an evolved ape (or a dog who walks upright), the topic of evolution returns us to the statement with which I began this section: Are people *really* just animals?

The question brings us directly to one of the oldest issues in philosophy and one that has particular importance for psychology: the mind-body problem. To what degree is the human mind—including behavior, emotion, thought, and all other experience—a direct product of physical, biological processes? This question is more acute than ever for psychology because until about a decade ago so little was known about the biological basis of personality that the issue could be safely ignored. This is no longer possible. Rapidly developing, sophisticated technology is making dramatic discoveries of relations between brain processes and psychological functioning, while at the same time it is becoming apparent that personality traits are to an important degree inherited and that some aspects of human nature can be traced to their evolutionary roots.

These aspects of the intersection between the study of biology and the study of personality—anatomy, physiology, genetics, and evolution—are the topics of the next two chapters. More will be said about the degree to which biology can subsume psychology near the end of Chapter 9, but in the meantime I would urge you to think about the mind-body question as you read. To what degree is human psychology—behavior, emotion, thought, and experience—reducible to processes of the body and the brain? It is not difficult to find writers willing to argue that the answer is 100 percent (this is the *reductionist* position), and others who will maintain that the answer is 0 percent (this is the *humanist* position). I do not pretend to know the answer, myself, but I am certain that both of these answers are too simple.

THE ANATOMY AND PHYSIOLOGY OF PERSONALITY

For a long time, people have suspected that the brain is important for psychology. In the fourth century B.C., the Greek physician Hippocrates maintained that "from the brain and from the brain only arise our pleasures, joys, laughter and tears. Through it, in particular, we think, see, hear and distinguish the ugly from the beautiful, the bad from the good, the pleasant from the unpleasant." However, realizing that the brain is important, and figuring out just how it functions, are two very different matters.

To appreciate the plight of anyone who would seek to understand how the brain works, picture the following scenario: Imagine traveling to ancient Greece and giving Hippocrates a portable compact disc (CD) player equipped with batteries and a music CD. As it blasted forth some of Eminem's additions to the musical canon, we can presume that Hippocrates would be amazed and then perplexed. Then, being curious, he might try to figure out how this remarkable device works.

What would he do? He could try dismantling the CD player, but it is unlikely he would recognize anything he saw inside, and once he took it apart, it is unlikely he would ever get it back together again. But if he were too cautious to probe the CD player's innards, his only course would be to observe it, listen to it, and fiddle with its various controls. Only after the battery wore out might he dare open it up (new batteries being unavailable in ancient Greece). Unfortunately, all he would see would be the inner workings of a mechanism that no longer functioned. Part of Hippocrates' problem here is that his tools would be limited. What if we also used our time-transporter to send him a voltometer and an X-ray machine? Now Hippocrates would begin to have a chance to get somewhere.

In many respects, anyone seeking to understand the physical basis of the mind faces a similar situation. Here stands a living, thinking person who possesses a functioning brain that can do amazing things, more amazing than anything a CD player can do, by far. But how can you figure out how this brain works? You can say or do things to the person and note how he or she replies and what he or she does. This is a little like Hippocrates pushing the "play" button and noticing that he hears music. It is a useful start but tells you little about what is going on inside. Still, sometimes observing from the outside is all you *can* do. You cannot easily open up a person's brain, especially while that person is alive. And even when the brain is opened, all you see is squishy, bloody tissue, the function of which is far from obvious. Again, the problem may lie to some extent in the limitations of the available tools. For decades, indeed for centuries, people curious about brain function have been limited largely to studying people who are already dead, with tools such as scalpels and magnifying glasses. But a dramatic revolution has begun just within the past decade with the invention and availability of new tools to examine processes in living brains, such as EEG machines, PET scanners, fMRI magnets, and other devices that can capture images of the brain in action.

The rapid increase in knowledge about the workings of the brain is largely due to the availability of better tools for studying it. Modern technology allows close examination of two aspects of the brain: its *anatomy* and its *biochemistry*. Anatomical studies examine the function of different parts of the brain and try, as much as is possible, to determine the timing and physical location of various brain processes. Studies of brain biochemistry examine the effects of fundamental chemicals, **neurotransmitters** and **hormones**, on brain processes. These two kinds of research are related to each other; neurotransmitters and hormones have different effects on different parts of the brain, and different parts of the brain secrete and respond to different neurotransmitters and hormones. Differences in aspects of brain anatomy and biochemistry have been found to be related to differences in behavior and personality in many ways. These relations are the topic of this chapter. First we will consider anatomy, and then biochemistry.

The Brain and Personality

The physical basis of personality is the brain and its tentacles, the nerves that reach into every corner of the body right down to the tip of the big toe. Every part of the body constantly sends messages that report what the body is doing and feeling up the sensory, or *afferent*, nerves through the spinal cord and into the brain. In turn, the brain sends messages back down motor, or *efferent*, nerves that direct the actions of all the various organs and muscles of the body. In between are the *interneurons*, which connect nerves to each

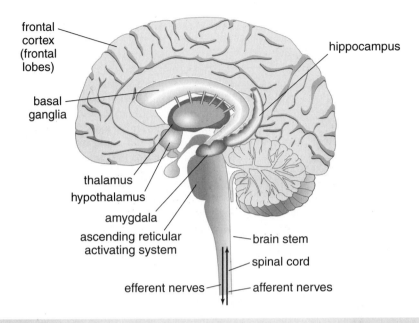

frontal cortex (frontal lobes)

hippocampus

basal ganglia

thalamus
hypothalamus
amygdala
ascending reticular activating system

brain stem

spinal cord

efferent nerves

afferent nerves

FIGURE 8.1 PERSONALITY AND THE BRAIN   Some of the major organs of the brain and nervous system that are relevant to personality.

other; the biggest bundle of these is the large, wrinkled organ known as the brain.

The brain itself is made up of a number of anatomically distinct structures. In the middle are small organs such as the *thalamus* and the **hypothalamus**. The hypothalamus, which is located near the bottom center of the brain, just above the roof of the mouth, is particularly important because it seems to be connected to everything. It has nerves that extend throughout the brain and it also secretes several hormones that affect the entire body. Just behind and above the hypothalamus lie the **amygdala**, which has an important role in emotion, and the **hippocampus**, which seems to be especially important for memory. Wrapped all around and over these inner organs is the **cortex**, which itself is divided into several regions. The most important of these for personality is the **frontal cortex**, which is (not surprisingly) the part of the cortex that lies in front (it is also known as the *cerebral cortex*), and which is the part of the brain that is most different in humans from other animals. The frontal cortex is divided into two *lobes* on the right and left side of the brain. These seem to be crucial for such uniquely human aspects of cognition as the ability to plan ahead, to anticipate consequences, and (perhaps) uniquely human aspects of emotional experience, such as empathy.

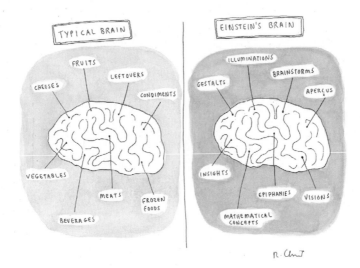

Research Methods for Studying the Brain

Knowledge about the brain comes from three principal sources. The first source, and the oldest, is the study of people who have suffered accidental brain damage. If enough such people are observed, it becomes possible to draw conclusions by keeping track of the specific problems that are caused by damage to different parts of the brain. The second source of knowledge is damage done to brains deliberately; in other words, brain surgery. Parts of the brain are deliberately "lesioned" (damaged) by being cut off from other brain structures or even removed completely. Nearly all of this kind of research has been done with animals such as rats, dogs, and (more rarely) monkeys. This is a reasonable approach because, as we have already mentioned, there are obvious structural and functional similarities in brains across mammalian species. There appear to be psychological similarities as well; for example, it is possible to assess personality traits in chimpanzees, hyenas, dogs, and other animals (Gosling, 1998; Gosling & Vazire, 2002; King & Figueredo, 1997). So knowledge about animal brains is surely relevant to understanding the human brain. In addition, there is a smaller amount of research on the effects of surgery on human brains, some of which we will consider later in this chapter.

A third approach to studying the brain is to attempt to observe its function directly—to see what it is doing, while it is doing it. The oldest technique for doing this is **electroencephalography**, or EEG, in which electrodes are placed on the scalp to pick up electrical signals generated by the brain activity underneath. A much newer but related technique is **magnetoencephalography** (MEG), which uses delicate sensors to detect magnetic (as opposed to electrical) indications of brain activity. Both of these techniques are good at determining *when* the brain is especially active, but are not very specific as to just *where* in the brain the activity is concentrated, or exactly what it is doing. I once heard the analogy that trying to understand brain activity from an EEG is a little like trying to follow a football game by standing in the parking lot outside the stadium and listening to the cheering. It will be easy to tell *when* something important happens, but more difficult to know precisely whether it was a touchdown, an interception, or something else.

More specific localization is possible with another technique, **positron emission tomography** (PET), which was developed in the late 1980s. It creates a map of brain activity by following the location of a harmless radioactive tracer that has been injected into the bloodstream. The brain needs more blood the harder it works, and by following blood flow it is possible to learn where it works hardest when doing various sorts of tasks. The newest way to image the workings of the brain is **functional magnetic resonance imagery** (fMRI), which uses magnetic pulses generated by blood flow to generate an image of the course of blood through the brain and thereby allows the researcher another way to see where the brain is most active at a given moment.

These imaging techniques are mostly quite new and their use is complex. Because all parts of a living brain are always metabolically active to some degree, a researcher has to do more than simply measure what the brain does during a certain task. It is also necessary to come up with a control task so that the *difference* in activation can be measured. To show that a certain brain region is relevant to emotional experience, for example, it is necessary to come up with a task that evokes an emotion (e.g., a photograph of the participant's child) and then a task that is as similar as possible without being emotionally relevant (perhaps, a picture of a stranger). Then the areas where

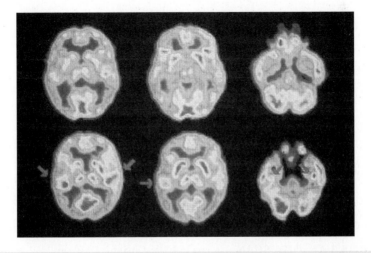

FIGURE 8.2 PET SCAN   A picture of the human brain made by a PET scan.

brain activation is different must be mapped. These areas might be—but very possibly are not—parts of the brain specifically relevant to emotion.

An even more basic difficulty is that as the technology to image brain activity becomes more sophisticated and sensitive, it also becomes more difficult to use and more delicate. An fMRI scan requires that the research participant lie still inside a cramped cylinder filled with loud buzzing noises that might distract him or her from the stimulus to which his or her reaction is being studied. The room in which the scanner is housed must be carefully shielded, and the building itself must be specially constructed with, for example, an extra-solid floor (the machine is almost always found in the basement). Despite all of these precautions, MEG scans, for example, are so sensitive that they can be disrupted by someone elsewhere in the building turning on a light at the wrong moment. Data from these various imaging devices must be carefully analyzed and transformed to eliminate as much noise as possible. It's not like snapping a photograph.

All these difficulties should lead us to two conclusions. First, it is impressive that despite everything psychologists have managed to make rapid progress using these techniques to understand the brain. Second, it is clear that this recently invented technology, for all its sophistication and vast expense, is in its Model-T phase (Logothetis, 2002; Spinney, 2002). All conclusions drawn so far are probably subject to change, and that which will be found in the next few years will far surpass what we think we know now. With all that in mind, let us turn to some of the first conclusions that are being reached concerning the parts of the brain that are relevant to various aspects of personality.

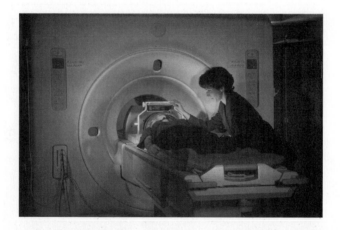

FIGURE 8.3 AN fMRI SCAN   A research participant entering an MRI scanner.

THE FAR SIDE®   By GARY LARSON

"Whoa! *That* was a good one! Try it, Hobbs—just poke his brain right where my finger is."

The Ascending Reticular Activating System (ARAS)

At the point where the spinal cord enters the base of the skull, it grows thicker and more complex, becoming a structure called the *brain stem.* Some of the brain stem is devoted to the maintenance of automatic activities such as breathing and swallowing. Another part, called the *reticular formation,* has connections that lead up into the cerebral cortex and the rest of the brain. A trailblazer in the attempt to relate personality to biology, the British psychologist Hans Eysenck (e.g., 1967, 1987), developed a theory that gives a central role to this structure, which he called the **ascending reticular activating system**, or ARAS. At the core of the theory is a simple basic assumption. The human brain has excitatory and inhibitory neural mechanisms, and important aspects of one's personality are determined by the balance between these mechanisms. Excitatory mechanisms cause an individual to be awake, aroused, and alert. Inhibitory mechanisms have the reverse effect. The balance between the excitatory and inhibitory mechanisms produces the level of psychological arousal at any given moment.

Eysenck hypothesized that this balance is regulated by the ARAS, which some evidence suggests regulates the amount of information and stimulation that goes into the brain. Sometimes the information channels are opened wide (allowing a lot of sensory stimulation to flow into the brain) and sometimes they are closed down (cutting the brain off from sensory stimulation). Eysenck's conjecture is that each individual's ARAS functions differently. Some persons' systems let in a great deal of information and stimulation nearly all the time. Other persons' systems are prone to reduce the amount of sensory stimulation.

Eysenck theorized that this difference is the basis of the difference between introverts and extraverts, although the way it works might seem counterintuitive at first: A person whose ARAS causes him or her to be chronically overaroused is an introvert, whereas one whose ARAS causes him or her to be chronically underaroused is an extravert. The reason for this is that when your ARAS opens you up to a large amount of sensory input, you end up getting more stimulation than you need—perhaps more than you can stand. As a result, you will seek to avoid exciting situations, loud noises, and social stimulation. You may turn down invitations to noisy parties, finding it stimulating enough to stay home with a good book (and perhaps an unexciting book at that).

On the other hand, when your ARAS closes off much of the sensory stimulation your brain would otherwise receive, you find yourself craving more. So you seek out stimulation, perhaps going to as many loud parties as you can find. You might become more generally what is called a "sensation seeker," not only going to parties but taking up activities such as racecar driving or parachute jumping (Zuckerman, 1984). According to Eysenck, you seek such activities just to maintain the level of sensory input that makes you feel good—a requirement that is higher for extraverts than for introverts.

The best-known study supporting Eysenck's theory of extraversion may be the famous "lemon juice test," in which researchers dropped small amounts of lemon juice on the tongues of introverts and extraverts (as assessed by Eysenck's personality questionnaire) and then measured the resulting amount of salivation. (Notice how, using the terms introduced in Chapter 2, the study compared S data with B data). Would you expect introverts to salivate more or less than extraverts? Eysenck predicted that introverts, because of their wide-open ARAS, would experience the sour taste more strongly and as a result would produce more saliva in response. That is the result he found (Eysenck & Eysenck, 1967; Wilson, 1978).

More recent studies have used other techniques such as brain-wave amplitude (measured by EEG), cardiovascular reactivity, and even PET scans to indicate arousal. The results, taken as a whole, are far from clear. Sometimes they support Eysenck's theory, and sometimes they do not (Zuckerman, 1991). In one recent study that did tend to support Eysenck's scheme, researchers identified introverts and extraverts using the Eysenck Personality Questionnaire and then tried to arouse them psychologically by giving them caffeine and making them do demanding tasks such as completing complex puzzles quickly (Bullock & Gilliland, 1993). Then they measured each person's neurological arousal through "brain stem auditory evoked responses"—how quickly and strongly the electrical activity of his or her brainstem, as seen on an EEG, responded to noises. The most important result was that introverts showed faster neural transmission (via their auditory evoked responses) than did extraverts, and the researchers concluded that this finding was consistent with Eysenck's theory that introverts are more sensitive to stimulation.

Taken as a whole, the currently available evidence seems to indicate that Eysenck's theory is about half right. It does not seem to be the case, as Eysenck surmised, that introverts are chronically more aroused than extraverts (Stelmack, 1990). The ARAS is not as general a system as was first believed; it does not just turn neural stimulation to the entire brain on and off like a faucet (Zuckerman, 1991). One part of the brain can be stimulated, aroused, and active at the same time that another part is almost quiescent. In fact, differing levels of arousal across different parts of the brain are more typical than not. On the other hand, there seems to be a good deal of evidence—including the studies just summarized—that introverts react more strongly and often negatively to sensory stimulation, compared to extraverts—a general idea that can be traced back to early work by Ivan Pavlov (1927). In other words, when the environment is quiet and calm, extraverts and introverts are about equally aroused. But when loud, bright, or exciting stimuli are present, introverts react more quickly and more strongly (Zuckerman, 1998). This apparently is what leads them to withdraw—the crowds, the noise, and the excitement are just too much—and exhibit the pattern of behavior that is identified as "introverted." This same level of stimulation may be just what the sensation-seeking extravert needs to perform at his or her best (Geen, 1984)—a need that, according to one writer, can even lead to a life of crime. "The vandal is a failed creative artist," who is bored, needs to be constantly stimulated, and "does not have the intellectual or other skills and capacities to amuse or occupy himself" (Apter, 1992, p. 198; Mealey, 1995).

Indeed, Eysenck argued in some of his later writings that it can be dangerous to have a nervous system that requires extra stimulation. According to the "general arousal theory of criminality," such a person may seek out high-risk activities such as crime, drug use, gambling, and promiscuous sexuality (Eysenck & Gudjonsson, 1989). To prevent these people from becoming dangerous, according to another psychologist, perhaps they should be encouraged to enter stimulating but harmless professions such as stuntman, explorer, skydiving exhibitionist, or radio talk-show host (Mealey, 1995)! Personally, I question this advice. Are radio talk-show hosts really harmless?

The Amygdala

The **amygdala** is a small organ located near the base of the brain, behind the hypothalamus. It is found both in humans and in many other animals, and its function appears to be to link perceptions and thoughts about the world with their emotional meaning (Adolphs, 2001). When the amygdala is surgically removed from rhesus monkeys, they become less aggressive and less fearful, they sometimes try to eat inedible things (even feces and urine), and they may exhibit increased and unusual sexual behavior. Research with humans and other animals indicates that the amygdala has important effects on negative emotions such as anger and fear. The amygdalas of shy people become extremely active when they are shown pictures of people that they don't know, compared to non-shy participants (Birbaumer et al., 1998). Its functioning is also related to positive emotions such as social attraction and sexual responsiveness (Klein & Kihlstrom, 1998). Some psychologists suggest that the amygdala might be the physical basis of human personality traits such as chronic anxiety, fearfulness, sociability, and sexuality (Zuckerman, 1991).

The importance of the amygdala and related structures was dramatically illustrated by an incident at the University of Texas on July 31, 1966. A graduate student named Charles Whitman wrote a letter that read, in part,

> I have been a victim of many unusual and irrational thoughts. These thoughts constantly recur, and it requires a tremendous mental effort to concentrate on useful and productive tasks. . . . After my death I wish that an autopsy would be performed on me to see if there is any visible physical disorder. . . . It was after much thought that I decided to kill my wife, Kathy, tonight after I pick her up from work. . . . I love her dearly, and she has been as fine a wife to me as any man could ever hope to have. I cannot rationally pinpoint any specific reason for doing this. . . . (Johnson, 1972, cited in Buck, 1999, p. 312)

That night, Whitman did kill his wife, and then his mother. The next day he took a high-powered rifle and climbed to the top of a tower at the center of campus and began firing at random, killing fourteen more people and wounding thirty-two before police managed to shoot him. At the autopsy he had wanted, the "visible physical disorder" Whitman suspected was indeed found. He had a malignant tumor in the right hemisphere of his brain, in the basal ganglia next to the amygdala.

This finding implies that "lower" parts of the brain near and including the amygdala may be capable of producing motivations for actions that may even include killing one's wife and mother along with innocent strangers (Buck, 1999). But these motivations, powerful as they are, might not be accompanied by understanding, or even the usual emotional experiences (e.g., rage) usually associated with acts such as killing. For that, other brain structures must become involved. Whitman did not know why he was motivated to do what he did. The rest of his brain did not understand the strange impulses produced by his amygdala any more than outside observers did; in a sense, the rest of his brain *was* an outside observer.

Just as the frontal cortex generally has been viewed as the seat of uniquely human cognitive functions such as thinking and planning, the amygdala and associated structures near the core of the brain have become widely accepted as important for some basic motivations and emotions. The case of Charles Whitman adds an important wrinkle to this idea. In order to understand, to consciously experience or "feel" these emotions in the typical way, other brain structures such as the cerebral cortex may be necessary. The fact that many animals, including reptiles, have an amygdala suggests that the basic foundation of emotional processes is ancient, evolutionarily speaking, and functions similarly across species. But the unique presence of the neocortex in humans suggests that other animals might not understand or experience these emotions in quite the same way.

The Frontal Lobes and Neocortex

The **neocortex** is the outer layer of the brain that is most uniquely human. If it were spread out flat it would be about the size of a sheet of newspaper, but to fit inside the skull it is scrunched around the brain in a way that explains its wrinkled appearance. Psychologists have long accepted the idea that the frontal lobes, the two parts of the neocortex at the left-front and right-front of the brain, are particularly important for "higher" cognitive functions such as speech, planning, and interpreting the world. The two lobes appear to be somewhat specialized. For example, EEG studies suggest that the left frontal lobes are more active when a person experiences pleasant emotions, whereas unpleasant emotions are associated with activity in the right frontal lobes (Davidson et al., 1990). The degree to which the two sides of the brain respond differently—called *brain asymmetry*—may itself be an important individual difference variable associated with emotional sensitivity (Davidson, 1993). An especially active left brain may be associated with a propensity to feel emotions such as happiness and enjoyment, whereas an active right brain seems associated with feelings of disgust and fear (Tomarken, Davidson, & Henriques, 1990; Wheeler, Davidson, & Tomarken, 1993).

Another clue to the importance of the frontal lobes comes from the observed effects of brain injuries. Massive injuries to this area can result in a victim who has very little left of what used to make him or her seem human. More subtle injuries have more subtle effects.

One famous case began in 1848, when a railroad construction supervisor named Phineas Gage stood in the wrong place at the wrong time, near a dynamite explosion that sent a three-and-a-half-foot iron rod through his left cheek, into the frontal lobes of his brain, and out through the top. Remarkably, he survived and lived another fifteen years. According to some preliminary reports, Gage was fine afterward in all respects. He could speak and move normally, and his memories were intact. Some observers noted that he was perhaps a little less emotional than he used to be (Harlow, 1849; Bigelow, 1850).

These early reports had an unfortunately long-lasting influence. A century later, they reassured some surgeons that it was OK to remove large portions of the human brain in attempt to "cure" excessive emotionality (Freeman & Watts, 1950). But these impressions were incorrect (Klein & Kihlstrom, 1998). In his final reports, Gage's physician, who seems to have been an astute observer, recorded that although Gage did retain some reasonable degree of mental functioning, his personality was noticeably changed, and not for the better (Harlow, 1868, 1869). According to this physician, Gage's behavior became "fitful, irreverent, indulging at times in the grossest profanity (which was not previously his custom), manifesting but little deference for his fellows, impatient of restraint or advice, . . . at times pertinaciously obstinate, yet capricious and facillating [sic]. . . . " Overall, Gage had become "a child in his intellectual capacity and manifestations . . . [yet had]

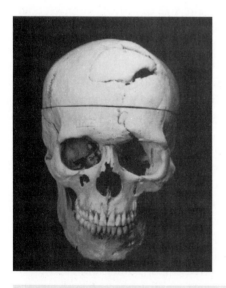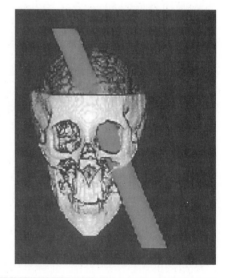

FIGURE 8.4 PHINEAS GAGE   The photograph (left) shows the incredible damage to Phineas Gage's skull. The computer image (right) reconstructs the path of the rod that caused the injury. (*Left:* Courtesy of the Warren Anatomical Museum, Harvard Medical School. *Right:* From Damasio et al., *Science* 264 [1994]: 1102.)

the animal passions of a strong man" (Harlow, quoted in Valenstein, 1986, p. 90).

Indeed, over the long term the outcome for Gage was disastrous. His emotional life seemed flattened out—nothing ever made him either very happy or very upset. And the rest of his life simply fell apart. Before the accident he was one of the most valued employees of the Rutland & Burlington Railroad. Afterward, he was unable to perform his job and never managed to hold another for any length of time. He made unwise decision after unwise decision, and both his professional life and his personal life disintegrated.

Phineas Gage was not the only person in history to suffer accidental brain injury, although his case was surely one of the more notable ones. Gunshot wounds to the head and other injuries have shown that people can live despite having had remarkable amounts of tissue removed or severed. According to some accounts—similar to the first impressions of Gage—when these accidents involved the frontal lobes, the victims could still function but were less excitable and emotional than they had been prior to the injury (e.g., Brickner, 1936).

A particularly fascinating problem that can result from brain damage is called "Capgras syndrome," after one of the first doctors to identify it. An early case was a 53-year-old woman who believed that her husband, daughter, and other important persons in her life had disappeared and had been replaced by doubles who were merely impersonating them (Capgras & Reboul-Lachaux, 1923, cited in Doran, 1990). In a more recent case, a 20-year-old man who received a severe blow to the head subsequently came to believe that his parents and siblings had been taken out and shot by Chinese communist spies, and that the people who were caring for him and worrying about him were imposters (Weston & Whitlock, 1971, cited in Doran, 1990). In yet another case, a victim of severe head injury returned home from the hospital to a wife and four children who, he insisted, were an entirely different family from the one he had before the accident, although he admitted they seemed very similar.

What all of these cases have in common is an injury to the right frontal lobe, which a large amount of evidence now indicates is particularly important in emotional response (Sautter, Briscoe, & Farkas, 1991; Stuss & Levine, 2002). Apparently what happens to these patients is that they see someone who is near and dear to them, and whose form they recognize readily, but then they fail to feel any emotional response to this recognition. Imagine, if you can, seeing your parents, your siblings, or your boyfriend or girlfriend and feeling nothing emotional at all. What would you think? What these patients conclude, it seems, is that these cannot possibly be the people they appear to be, and that the only possible interpretation (one conjured up by the uninjured left frontal lobe) is that they must have been replaced by nearly identical doubles.

Another remarkable case was a patient of the neurologist Antonio Damasio known as "Elliott." Elliott was a good husband and father and held a responsible job in business, when he began to report headaches and an inability to concentrate. His family physician suspected a brain tumor, and unfortunately that turned out to be correct. Elliott had a large tumor right above the nasal cavities, at the midline of the brain, below the ventromedial cortex. The surgery to remove the tumor also had to remove a good deal of that cortical tissue.

After the surgery, Elliott seemed much improved and showed no obvious mental defects. Like Gage, he could move and speak normally, and his memory was unimpaired. But also like Gage, he had become almost peculiarly unemotional—he seemed to not experience strong positive or negative emotions. And over time, it became apparent that something was seriously wrong with his judgment. At a restaurant, he might sit for an hour, unable to decide between different dishes, as he weighed the advantages and disadvantages of each. At work, he might begin to sort through papers for a client, and then stop to read one and spend the rest of the day deeply analyzing that single paper instead of completing his main mission. He seemed unable to allocate his time and effort appropriately between tasks and activities that were really important, and those that were trivial. He lost his job and, in the end, his family as well.

Similar effects to the result of Elliott's surgery have been reported as a result of accidental brain damage. Two different high-level executives suffered damage to their right frontal lobes and afterwards made what seemed like a complete recovery in terms of their ability to speak, remember, and perform other cognitive tasks. They even could recognize some of their own failings, show concern about them, and express intentions to do better. But they could no longer function as executives. They seemed to lack full understanding of the implications of problems that arose, even though they could speak about them almost as if they did, and therefore they were unable to make appropriate decisions or even act wisely in their own self-interest (Stuss & Levine, 2002).

According to Damasio's analysis, Gage's and Elliott's problems in decision making, along with those of the executives just described, and their flattened emotional landscape stemmed from the same neural damage. The damage to tissue in the right frontal lobes impaired their emotional reaction to events and to thoughts. This emotional reaction, according to Damasio's **somatic marker hypothesis**, is what allows humans to tell the difference between what is important and what is not, and between a good outcome of an action and a bad outcome. Without this emotion, Gage and Elliott lost not only an important part of life's experience but also their very ability to make decisions. Everything began to seem equally important (or unimportant); all outcomes were equally valued. As a result, they lost the ability to choose to spend their time on important activities and to choose actions that lead to valued outcomes.

All of these cases—Gage, Elliott, and the Capgras cases—show how cognition and emotion are inextricably intertwined. You can't really have one, fully, without the other. Understanding is important for full emotional experience, and emotional experience is important for real understanding. This fact may help explain why the people who are the best at what they do are involved with their work not just intellectually but emotionally. The best physicists become excited as they talk about black holes, multidimensional space, and string theory. The best football coaches care at a deep level about every step taken by every player during every play. Their emotions motivate their thinking and guide their strategic decision making. On the other hand, people who don't care about what they do are a little like poor Gage and Elliott. Their work is just a job—they punch in, do what they must, and punch out—and the important and trivial parts of it are all the same to them. Obviously, nothing they accomplish will ever be very creative or remarkable. They may have all the IQ points one could want, but something in them— in some cases, perhaps, a deficiency somewhere in the right frontal lobes— prevents them from really feeling anything about what they are doing, and this apathy stands in the way of their ever accomplishing anything truly great.

The Lessons of Psychosurgery

At the 1935 World Congress of Neurology, the Yale psychologist J. F. Fulton told the assembled delegates a story about two laboratory chimps named Becky and Lucy. They were difficult to work with because they were easily frustrated, and when they were frustrated, they became vicious. As part of a study of the function of the brain in learning, an operation was performed that removed part of the chimps' frontal lobes. The effects on learning were inconclusive, but the researchers noticed something else. Becky and Lucy had become relaxed and mellow chimps, placid instead of vicious, a downright pleasure to work with. According to legend, after Fulton presented these results, a Portugese neurosurgeon named António Egas Moniz stood up and asked whether such an operation might be helpful for controlling human psychotics. Fulton was so startled by the question he couldn't answer.

That didn't stop Moniz. Within two years—by 1937—he performed— on a human!—the first *prefrontal leucotomy*, in which small areas of white matter behind each of the frontal lobes were deliberately damaged. The idea was that patients with pathological levels of agitation and emotional arousal had overactive frontal lobes, and that this operation—aimed at the same area as Gage's iron bar—might make them less emotional, more rational, and calmer, like Becky and Lucy.

It is important to note that Moniz only operated on people with severe emotional problems and may even have done most of them some good. Whatever subtle damage was done to their emotional lives or decision-making capabilities may have been outweighed by their relief from a miserable degree of emotional overexcitement (Damasio, 1994). In any case, the operation quickly became popular around the world, especially in the United States, and in 1949 it received the ultimate scientific seal of approval when António Egas Moniz was awarded the Nobel Prize.

But there was a dark side to this popularity. As its use spread, the surgical procedure became increasingly drastic. The standard technique changed from Moniz's relatively modest leucotomy, in which small areas of tissue were damaged, to the more-famous *lobotomy*, in which whole sectors of the frontal lobes were scooped out. The results were similarly more drastic. Some lobotomy patients ended up much worse off than either Gage or Elliott and became almost inert, mere shells of the people they were before. One was Rosemary Kennedy, the mentally retarded elder sister of John, Robert, and Edward Kennedy, who was operated on in 1941 in an attempt to control her "mood swings" (Thompson, 1995). She has been living in an institution—a convent school in Wisconsin—ever since.

Even the leading American advocates of the lobotomy noted,

> It is almost impossible to call upon a person who has undergone [an] operation on the frontal lobes for advice on any important matter. His reactions to situations are direct, hasty, and dependent upon his emotional set at the moment. (Freeman & Watts, 1950, p. 549)

Notice how this observation is wholly consistent with the cases of Gage and Elliott. Evidence from a number of sources converges to suggest that the frontal lobes are centers of cognitive control, serving to anticipate the future and plan for it. The results also suggest that a particular function of the frontal lobes might be to anticipate future negative outcomes and to respond emotionally to their possibility—in other words, worrying. This emotional aspect of forethought seems to be particularly important. Unless you have the appropriate reaction to future possibilities—pleasant anticipation, on the one hand, or worrying, on the other—you will not be able to plan appropriately or make the right decisions about what to do now.

In the midst of all the enthusiasm for what had become a very trendy procedure, nobody paid much attention to this downside. Often psychosurgery (as it was called) was performed with an astonishing disregard for what the long-term results really were. Zuckerman summarized many of the early medical articles on psychosurgery this way:

> The neurosurgeons' reports provide a remarkable contrast between accounts of the precise surgical techniques and the imprecise or totally absent methods

of [subsequent behavioral] evaluation. Control groups were virtually nonexistent and, with the exception of an occasional use of the MMPI [Minnesota Multiphasic Personality Inventory—see Chapter 5], observations of change were based on the crudest kind of clinical observations, with no tests of reliabilities of ratings or single-blind controls. (Zuckerman, 1991, p. 147)

Tens of thousands of lobotomies and other psychosurgeries were performed over a span of more than four decades, but such operations are rare today. The side effects became too obvious to ignore, and began to be widely publicized, not just in medical journals and newspapers but also in works such as *One Flew Over the Cuckoo's Nest*.[1] A perhaps even more important factor in the decline of psychosurgery is that chemical therapies (a.k.a., drugs) were developed to make mentally ill patients manageable, if not cured. Someone like Rosemary Kennedy, who troubled her family with mood swings, would today be tranquilized rather than lobotomized. In other words, her brain would be altered with chemicals, rather than with a knife. Somehow, this seems less drastic and more acceptable. Is it?

The history of psychosurgery can serve as a cautionary tale that illustrates not only the alarming tendency of medical practice to sometimes follow fashion rather than sound research, but also the danger of oversimplifying our still-tentative and incomplete knowledge of the brain. Entirely too many surgeons were willing to jump to the conclusion that because the frontal lobes have something to do with excessive worrying and neuroticism, such problems could be alleviated simply by severing or even removing them.

This conclusion was surely misguided; given what is known about brain function, it is highly unlikely that brain anatomy corresponds to psychological processes or problems in any simple, one-to-one manner (Valenstein, 1986). A more reasonable and more subtle conclusion would be that the frontal lobes include among their functions the regulation of emotional responses to anticipated events. When the frontal lobes are damaged, severed, or removed, this regulatory function is disrupted. Although the result may seem to be "less worry," the evidence indicates that in fact emotional responsiveness and future anticipation become erratic and disorganized. As a result, lobotomized people do not worry when they should and sometimes worry when they should not, and their ability to make decisions and to fully understand reality falls apart, as we saw with Gage, Elliott, and the Capgras patients.

---

[1]*One Flew Over the Cuckoo's Nest* is a popular novel by Ken Kesey, which was made into a play and a motion picture (starring Jack Nicholson), about life in a mental hospital and the disastrous effect of a lobotomy on the main character.

Biochemistry and Personality

Chemical approaches to the study of personality have a long history. The ancient Greek physician Galen (who lived between A.D. 130 and 200, practicing mostly in Rome), building on an earlier proposal by Hippocrates, theorized that personality was dependent on the balance between four *humors,* or fluids, in the body. These humors were blood, black bile, yellow bile (also called *choler*), and phlegm. A person who had a lot of blood relative to the other three humors, Galen conjectured, tended to be *sanguine* (cheerful), ruddy, and robust. An excess of black bile caused a person to be depressed and melancholy; an excess of yellow bile caused a person to be *choleric,* angry, and bitter; and an excess of phlegm made one *phlegmatic,* cold, and apathetic.

The terms *sanguine, melancholic, choleric,* and *phlegmatic* survive in the English language to this day, carrying roughly the same psychological meaning that Galen ascribed. Even more remarkably, this fourfold typology is undergoing something of a revival among health psychologists who find it useful in connecting personality with disease (Friedman, 1991, 1992). The choleric or chronically hostile person, for example, seems to be at extra risk for heart attack. But modern research suggests the basis of this risk is not the person's yellow bile, but rather the stress produced by a life filled with arguments and fights.

The Chemistry of the Mind

The physical basis of behavior is the nervous system. The nervous system is made up of billions of cells, called *nerve cells* or **neurons**, which are connected with one another through complex pathways. The brain is a thick bundle of neurons; other neurons form the brain stem and the spinal cord, which connect the brain to muscles and sensory receptors all over the body. The essence of neuronal activity is communication. The activity of one neuron may affect the activity of many other neurons, transmitting sensations from the far reaches of the body into the brain, connecting these sensations with feelings, memories, and plans in the brain; and sending behavioral instructions back out to the muscles, causing the body to move.

Communication between neurons is based on substances called **neurotransmitters**. As illustrated in Figure 8.5, a bioelectrical impulse causes a release of neurotransmitters at the end of the neuron. These neurotransmitters travel across the **synapse** to the next neuron in line, where they cause a chemical reaction that results in that second neuron firing an impulse that causes the neurotransmitters at its other end to be released, and so on down the neural network. Hormones work slightly differently. They are released

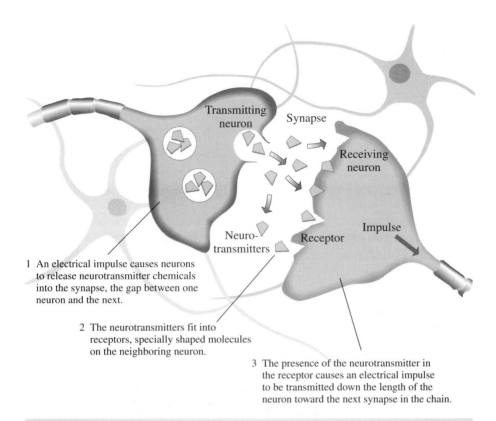

Transmitting neuron

Synapse

Receiving neuron

Neuro-transmitters

Receptor

Impulse

1 An electrical impulse causes neurons to release neurotransmitter chemicals into the synapse, the gap between one neuron and the next.

2 The neurotransmitters fit into receptors, specially shaped molecules on the neighboring neuron.

3 The presence of the neurotransmitter in the receptor causes an electrical impulse to be transmitted down the length of the neuron toward the next synapse in the chain.

FIGURE 8.5 COMMUNICATION BETWEEN NEURONS The transmission of impulses throughout the nervous system is mediated by electrical and chemical processes.

from central locations, such as the hypothalamus and the adrenal glands (located atop the kidneys), and spread throughout the body in the bloodstream. Once they reach the nerve cells that are sensitive to them, they will tend to either stimulate or inhibit their activity. The difference between neurotransmitters and hormones can be confusing because they both affect the transmission of nerve impulses, and some chemicals qualify as belonging to both categories. For example, **norepinephrine**, to be discussed below, functions as a neurotransmitter within the brain but is also a hormone that is centrally released from the adrenal gland in response to stress.

Many neurotransmitters and hormones have been discovered, and more are still being identified—so far researchers have counted about 60 different chemicals that transmit information throughout the brain and body (Gazzaniga & Heatherton, 2003). Different neurotransmitters and hormones are associated with different neural subsystems and so have different effects on behavior. For example, norepinephrine, **dopamine**, and **serotonin** work almost exclusively in the **central nervous system**—the brain and spinal cord. By contrast, very little of the neurotransmitter epinephrine is found in the brain. Epinephrine is found mostly in the **peripheral nervous system**, the neuronal networks that extend all over the body. As another complication, some neurotransmitters cause adjacent neurons to fire, while others inhibit the neuronal impulse. For example, the body's own natural pain-killing system is based on endogenous opiates, or **endorphins**. These special neurotransmitters work by inhibiting rather than facilitating the neuronal transmission of pain.

Many aspects of biochemistry are important in neural communication. As we have just seen, the neurotransmitters themselves play a large role in transmitting impulses. But the chemicals out of which neurotransmitters are made are also important, as are other chemicals that cause neurotransmitters to be broken down into their constituent chemical parts after they have traveled across the synaptic gap. For example, the enzyme monoamine oxidase (MAO) regulates the breakdown of the neurotransmitters dopamine, norepinephrine, and serotonin. Low levels of MAO in the blood, and therefore higher levels of these neurotransmitters, are associated with sensation seeking, extraversion, and even criminal behavior (Zuckerman, 1998). For another example, the antidepression drug Prozac increases the amount of serotonin in the body by inhibiting the activity of the chemical that ordinarily causes serotonin to break down (Kramer, 1993).

I once attended a scientific meeting where I heard the famous psychologist Robert Zajonc cry out, "The brain is not a digital computer, it is a juicy gland!" Indeed, that is what it looks like, and to an important degree that is exactly how it functions—through the chemicals that it secretes and to which it responds.

Neurotransmitters

The functioning of the various parts of the nervous system is affected in important ways by the amounts of various neurotransmitters available at the moment. This availability can vary as a function of what the individual is doing, and indeed can fluctuate quite widely over short periods of time. But people also seem to differ from each other in their average levels of various transmitters, and these differences seem to be associated with various personality traits.

EPINEPHRINE AND NOREPINEPHRINE

Two particularly important neurotransmitters are **epinephrine** (also known as *adrenaline*), and **norepinephrine**. Epinephrine and the neurons that respond to it are found throughout the body, while norepinephrine and its neurons work primarily within the brain itself. The levels of both hormones can rise dramatically and suddenly in response to stress. Heart rate increases, digestion stops, and muscles tense—the well-known "adrenaline rush." At the same time, the brain becomes fully alert and concentrated on the matter at hand.[2] This set of events has long been called the *fight-or-flight response* (Cannon, 1932; Selye, 1956). The idea is that if the threat—such as a predator or an enemy—is one that you have a realistic chance of overcoming, you will stand and fight. If the situation seems hopeless, you will run away. Either way, the body has made you ready to do what needs to be done.

The fight-or-flight response is a well-known phenomenon and has been documented in dozens of studies over the years. However, the psychologist Shelley Taylor and her colleagues recently noted that almost all of these studies—both in animals (usually rats) and in humans—have been conducted on males (Taylor et al., 2000). Why does this matter? According to Taylor and her colleagues, the response to threat may be importantly different in men and women. They point out that—during the prehistoric era that our species evolved—a man under threat had the relatively simply choice to, indeed, either stand and fight or else run away. For a woman, who may be pregnant or nursing helpless infants and caring for children, the choice is not so simple. Either fighting *or* running away might put her children and herself at unacceptable risk. Instead, it might make more sense for her to respond differently, in such a way that helps her to calm everyone down and to band together to fend off the threat—a response Taylor and her colleagues call *tend-and-befriend*. They point out that another hormone in the stress-response cascade is **oxytocin**, which has specific effects, in females, of promoting nurturant and sociable behavior along with relaxation and reduction of fearfulness—the exact opposite of fight-or-flight. One specific effect of oxytocin may be to decrease fear and increase maternal attachment (McCarthy, 1995). This might be why primates—and, apparently, human mothers—rarely if ever abandon their infants under stress.

This is a fascinating argument. On a methodological level, it shows how high the cost can be of limiting research subjects to just one gender. Researchers apparently did this not out of malicious intent, but because they wished to avoid the complications of accounting for estrus and menstrual cycles when conducting their neurobiological assays. But this simplification may have come at the cost of missing a fundamental difference between the sexes. On a substantive level, moving from prehistoric environments to the modern day, Taylor's argument implies that men and women may have fundamentally different responses to threats and attacks. Men evaluate their

---

[2]Mark Twain is said to have remarked that "the imminent prospect of a hanging focuses a man's mind most wonderfully"—a classic effect of norepinephrine.

strength relative to their opponent, and their chances to escape. Then they either fight or run away. Women are more likely to seek out their friends and relatives and "gather their wagons in a circle," as it were. If you can't fight, and can't run, at least there is some safety in numbers.

It is important to remember that to the extent this thesis is correct, it refers to the initial and automatic response to threat. It does not imply that further behavior is completely constrained. Men certainly do form alliances, for example, and women definitely sometimes stand and fight. But Taylor and her colleagues suggest that the first and instinctive responses of men and women to a threatening situation may be fundamentally different.

DOPAMINE

Dopamine is important for the mechanisms that allow the brain to control body movements and also is involved in systems that cause one to respond to reward, and to approach attractive objects and people. (Dopamine is also an important part of the chemical process that produces norepinephrine.) This neurotransmitter has been theorized to be part of the basis of sociability and of general activity level. According to one theory, an inherited inability of the brain to properly use dopamine can produce *reward deficiency syndrome,* characterized by such diverse outcomes as alcoholism, drug abuse, smoking, compulsive overeating, attention-deficit disorder, and pathological gambling (Blum et al., 1996). A severe lack of dopamine is the basis of Parkinson's disease.

In a famous case (shown, with artistic license, in the movie *Awakenings*), a group of patients who developed Parkinson's as a result of an epidemic of encephalitis during World War I were given the new drug L-dopa forty years later, during the 1960s. L-dopa increases the brain's production of dopamine, and for some patients who had been nearly catatonic for years, the results were dramatic. Suddenly they not only could move around much better than before, but also were able once again to experience positive emotions, motivation, sociability, and interest in and awareness of their environments.

Sadly, over time, most of these patients' conditions worsened again. They went from normal enthusiasm and energy levels into hypomanic excitement, restlessness, and grandiosity. Then, like manic-depressive patients, they "crashed" into deep depressions (Sacks, 1983; Zuckerman, 1991). These effects suggest that dopaminergic systems (systems affected by dopamine) also might have something to do with manic-depressive disorder. Perhaps even more important, they suggest that dopamine might be relevant to the personality traits of extraversion, impulsivity, and perhaps some others.

The neuropsychologist Jeffrey Gray has hypothesized that dopamine and the brain structures in the hypothalamus that this neurotransmitter activates are the basis of the tendency to seek out reward, which he calls the *behav-*

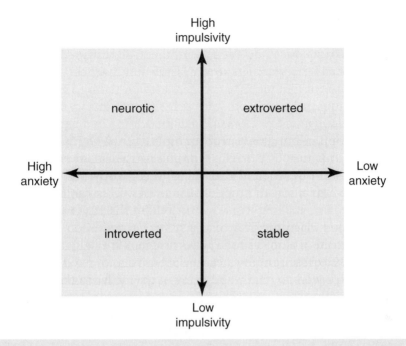

High
impulsivity

neurotic   extroverted

High   Low
anxiety   anxiety

introverted   stable

Low
impulsivity

FIGURE 8.6 GRAY'S TWO-DIMENSIONAL MODEL OF PERSONALITY
According to Gray's theory, impulsivity is mediated by the dopamine-based "Go"
system, and anxiety is mediated by one "Stop" system in the frontal lobes.

ioral activation or "Go" system (Gray, 1981). Someone with a strong and
active Go system will tend to be active and impulsive. This system interacts
with other areas in the brain such as the frontal lobes that assess and respond
to risk, and constitute a *behavioral inhibition or* "Stop" system (Corr, Pickering, & Gray, 1997; these two systems are sometimes called the "BIS" and
"BAS," respectively). Someone with a strong and active Stop system will tend
to be inhibited and anxious. Because these are separate systems, according
to Gray, any combination of these two traits is possible. One could be highly
anxious and impulsive, and thus be deemed neurotic. Or, one could be highly
anxious but not impulsive, and be judged introverted.

A more recent theory focuses directly on the degree to which people have
developed nerve cells that produce and are responsive to dopamine (Depue
& Collins, 1999). These individual differences might have a genetic basis, and
they also may come from experience—people who have had more rewarding experiences, especially early in life, may develop more such cells. As a
result, the dopaminergic part of their nervous system is well-developed and
active, and they are motivated to seek out rewards of all sorts, and capable
of enjoying them strongly. Such people enjoy being with others and are warm

and affectionate, experience a great deal of positive emotion, and also may tend to be rather impulsive. In a word, according to Depue and Collins, they are extraverts—but notice how their use of the word differs somewhat from its meaning for other researchers such as Gray and Eysenck.[3]

SEROTONIN (AND PROZAC)

Serotonin is another important neurotransmitter, one which seems to play a role in the inhibition of behavioral impulses (e.g., in stopping a person from doing something attractive yet dangerous). Serotonin is particularly relevant to the inhibition of emotional impulses. This can be useful. For example, a predator stalking its prey must inhibit the urge to leap before it is close enough to catch the prey. If you have ever watched a cat hunt, you might conclude the typical cat has a lot of serotonin in its system. The ability to inhibit emotional impulses can help humans to avoid worrying too much, being too quick to anger, and being oversensitive to the minor crises and insults of daily life.

But what if a person does not have enough serotonin? Problems, apparently. Violent criminals, arsonists, and people who die by violent methods of suicide have been shown to have low serotonin levels (Virkkunen et al., 1994). According to one author, people with insufficient serotonin suffer from a syndrome called *serotonin depletion* (Metzner, 1994), the symptoms of which include irrational anger, hypersensitivity to rejection, chronic pessimism, obsessive worry, and fear of risk taking (Metzner, 1994).

The effects of serotonin and the reality of the syndrome of serotonin depletion have become a topic of public discussion in recent years. The pharmaceutical company Eli Lilly in 1993 sold $1.2 billion worth of Prozac, which is a selective serotonin reuptake inhibitor (SSRI). By 1999, an estimated twenty-two million Americans—almost one person in ten—had used this drug (Shenk, 1999). The physical effect of Prozac seems fairly clear—it raises the serotonin levels in the nervous system of the person who takes it. The psychological effects, however, are more controversial, as are the implications of those effects.

In his best-selling book, *Listening to Prozac*, psychiatrist Peter Kramer (1993) claimed that Prozac can give many people dramatically improved personalities. It can stop a person from needlessly worrying and from being oversensitive to minor stresses and so provide a newly cheerful outlook on life. Some individuals who take Prozac claim that it makes them more like "themselves"; they don't feel like different people, they feel like *better* peo-

---

[3]The term also does not quite match the use of the word *extraversion* in the Big Five, or "five-factor," model of personality (see Chapter 7).

ple. They get more work done, and even become more attractive to members of the opposite sex. One particularly interesting study showed that normal people—i.e., people with no diagnosable personality disorders in themselves or any of their close relatives—showed noticeable personality change when they took Paxil (paroxetine), a drug closely related to Prozac (Knutson et al., 1998). In as little as one week, these people reported feeling less hostility and fewer negative emotions overall. One participant commented, "I used to think about good and bad, but now I don't; I'm in a good mood" (Knutson et al., 1998, p. 377). On the other hand, the people taking paroxetine in this study *also* reported feeling sleepy and having delayed orgasms!

Kramer raised the possibility that the ability of drugs to change aspects of personality may mean that, in the end, personality is primarily a matter of chemicals. He also suggested that this fact could give rise to "cosmetic psychopharmacology," the psychiatric equivalent of plastic surgery. Just as people with perfectly good noses sometimes go to a surgeon to obtain even better noses (they think), so too might people with perfectly adequate personalities begin to take Prozac and other drugs to obtain even better personalities.

This possibility gives rise to several issues. First, some authorities claim that the term *cosmetic psychopharmacology* is misleading because Prozac does not work on people whose personalities are adequate already (Metzner, 1994). They claim that unless the individual suffers from a disease—serotonin depletion—Prozac will have no effect. Since the diagnosis of this syndrome is far from clear-cut, this claim is difficult to evaluate, but it seems doubtful in light of the study cited above, which showed that the related drug

"Of course your daddy loves you. He's on Prozac—he loves everybody."

Paxil had noticeable effects on people who were perfectly normal (Knutson et al., 1998).

A second issue is that although chemicals clearly influence personality, the idea that personality is based so specifically on chemicals that it can be precisely adjusted is surely an exaggeration. For one thing, the effects of Prozac and related drugs on a given individual are difficult to predict and can change over time. Moreover, these effects can vary according to other factors in the patient's life, including the administration of psychotherapy. Sometimes the drugs have no effect at all, and sometimes they make things worse (Shenk, 1999). Like cosmetic surgery, cosmetic psychopharmacology may have side effects (such as sleepiness, confusion, and sexual dysfunction). Kramer's and other psychiatrists' prescription strategies—by their own accounts—seem to be to give troubled patients some Prozac, see what happens, and then adjust the dosage of the drug accordingly, while also providing some psychotherapy on the side. Most prescriptions for Prozac are not even written by psychiatrists; they are written by primary-care practitioners, sometimes on the basis of little more than a phone call (Shenk, 1999).

Drugs that affect neurotransmitters can be remarkably beneficial for certain individuals, but it is difficult to avoid the conclusion that Prozac and similar drugs have become part of a wider, legal drug culture in which people casually ingest a wide variety of substances, of uncertain effect. They hope the drug will make them feel better, but the ultimate consequences of such

FIGURE 8.7 MICHAEL JACKSON Cosmetic surgery can have side effects. What will be the side effects of cosmetic *psychopharmacology?*

large-scale psychopharmacological intervention are at present unknown. For example, we could question whether the structure of modern society is what leads so many people to seek out drugs to combat depression and anxiety. If it is, then maybe we ought to think a bit about changing the structure of society, rather than just medicating everybody. Finally, it is also worth pondering whether future historians will regard the present enthusiasm for psychoactive drugs such as Prozac much differently than we regard the previous generation's enthusiasm for psychosurgeries such as the lobotomy.

Hormones

A **hormone** is a biological chemical that, by definition, has effects on the body in a location different from where the chemical was produced (Cutler, 1976). As we have already seen, some neurotransmitters, such as norepinephrine, also can be considered hormones because they affect nerve cells far from their origin. The status of other chemicals as hormones is more clear; their main function is to be produced in a central location and broadcast throughout the body, stimulating the activity of neurons in many locations in the brain and body at the same time. Different hormones affect different nerve cells and so influence different neural systems. Hormones that are important for behavior are released by the hypothalamus (part of the limbic system of the brain), the **gonads** (testes and ovaries), and the **adrenal cortex** (part of the adrenal gland that sits atop the kidneys).

TESTOSTERONE

The most studied and probably best-known hormones are the gonadal or sex hormones: **testosterone** in males and **estrogen** in females (although all humans in fact have both kinds of hormone in their bodies). It has long been observed that males seem generally to be more aggressive than females (e.g., Kagan, 1978; Maccoby & Jacklin, 1974), and males certainly have more testosterone in their bodies. To be exact, normal human females have about 40 nanograms of testosterone in each deciliter of their blood; normal males have between 300 and 1,000 nanograms per deciliter, or a ten-times greater concentration.

This set of observations led some psychologists to hypothesize that testosterone is the cause of aggressive behavior, and many studies have pursued this idea. Some of these studies found that human males who have higher levels of testosterone are indeed more likely to have aggressive and other behavioral control problems than are those with lower levels. In one study, male American military veterans were asked about their past behaviors. Those with higher testosterone levels reported more trouble with their parents, teachers, and classmates; a history of assaulting others; more use of hard drugs, marijuana, or alcohol; numerous sexual partners; and a "general tendency toward excessive behavior" (Dabbs & Morris, 1990, p. 209).

It should be noted that findings like these, though provocative, are not always consistent from one study to the next (Zuckerman, 1991). They are also complex. For example, you should bear in mind that nearly all studies in this area—including the one just quoted—measure aggressive or even criminal behavior solely through self-report (S data); they do not account for the people who engage in such activities but do not admit it. A more basic consideration is that while males of many species are more aggressive than females of the same species, this is not always the case. Males are *not* more aggressive than females among gibbons, wolves, rabbits, hamsters, or even laboratory rats (Floody, 1983).

There is yet another important complexity. Although some extreme criminal types (e.g., rapists who also commit other kinds of bodily harm) may be likely to have high levels of testosterone (Rada, Laws, & Kellner, 1976), the reverse does not seem to be true: men with high levels of testosterone are *not* necessarily aggressive, and they are certainly not all aggravated rapists. Furthermore, it has sometimes been reported that the relationship between testosterone level and physical aggression holds only (or holds more strongly) for relatively uneducated men from the lower-economic classes (Dabbs & Morris, 1990). The presumed reason is that more-educated men in the higher classes have been socialized to express their aggressive impulses in less-physical ways (maybe by saying something elegantly sarcastic or initiating a hostile takeover of your company).

Despite its reputation (have you ever heard a woman complain of someone who suffers from "testosterone poisoning"?), the hormone is not all bad. Males with more testosterone are higher in "stable extraversion," that is, sociability, self-acceptance, and dominance. They have more restless energy, spend a lot of time thinking about concrete problems in the immediate present, and become frustrated when they can't get things done (Dabbs, Strong, & Milun, 1997). They smile less, which seems to make them appear more dominant (Dabbs, 1997), and also report having more sexual experience and more sexual partners. But again, higher testosterone levels may be a result rather than a cause of sexual activity (Zuckerman, 1991). Testosterone also has interesting interactions with personality traits. One study found that high-testosterone males who were also conscientious were better emergency medical service (EMS) providers, and high-testosterone males who were extraverted and active were better firefighters. The researchers concluded that testosterone should be thought of as an energizing factor that "appears to facilitate the behavior of individuals along directions they are already inclined to take" (Fannin & Dobbs, 2002, p. 107).

And let's not forget that women have testosterone as well. In women, testosterone is produced by the adrenal cortex and has important behavioral effects. One study showed that female prisoners who had committed "unprovoked" violent crimes had higher levels of testosterone than did women who had been violent after provocation or who had committed nonviolent crimes (Dabbs et al., 1988). Lesbian women who take on the so-called butch role (dressing and acting like men) have higher testosterone than either lesbians who take the "femme" role or heterosexual women (Singh et al., 1999). Other research showed that women with impaired adrenocortical functioning, who therefore produce less testosterone, seem to become less interested in sex. Moreover, the administration of testosterone injections to women can sometimes produce dramatic increases in sexual desire (Zuckerman, 1991). These results suggest that testosterone is a chemical basis of sexual arousal in women as well as in men.

Also similar to the findings among men, higher levels of testosterone in women are associated with higher levels of self-reported sociability and with impulsivity, lack of inhibition, and lack of conformity. In both sexes, higher testosterone is also associated with holding a blue-collar, industrial job as opposed to a white-collar, professional job. Among lawyers, trial lawyers who battle cases in court have higher testosterone levels than do those who work in the back room with law books (Dabbs, Alford, & Fielden, 1998).

Further evidence concerning the effects of testosterone comes from bodybuilders and athletes who take anabolic steroids to promote muscular development (Pope & Katz, 1994). Anabolic steroids are synthetic testosterone; their effects include not only speedier muscle development but also a whole host of troublesome side effects. Steroid users frequently experience erratic and uncontrolled aggressiveness and sexuality. For example, male steroid users may experience erections without stimulation, but also seem to have a lower overall sex drive and to be prone to impotence and sterility. Ben Johnson, the Canadian sprinter whose Olympic gold medal was taken away when he was found (through blood tests) to have used steroids, seemed to experience difficulty controlling aggression: he got into a lot of fights with reporters (then again, maybe that behavior was not abnormal).

What can we conclude from all this? It would be an oversimplification to conclude that testosterone causes either aggression *or* sexuality in any simple or direct way. Instead, it seems that testosterone plays a role in the control and inhibition of aggressiveness and sexuality, including normal assertiveness and perhaps even generalized activity level, as well as the normal range of sexual function and responsiveness in both sexes. Recall the comment quoted earlier that males with high testosterone levels were prone to "excessive" behavior. In general, the evidence suggests that when this hormone is present in abnormally high proportions, such as occurs naturally in certain individuals and artificially in steroid users, aggression and sexuality are not so much enhanced as they are messed up. Both may occur at inappropriate times and fail to occur at appropriate times. But the simple belief that testosterone makes a person either more aggressive or more sexy is probably not true.

Moreover, testosterone is not just a cause of behavior; it is an effect. A particularly good demonstration of this was a study of World Cup soccer fans watching a playoff match (Bernhardt et al., 1998). Testosterone was measured from the fans' saliva before and after the game. Afterward, the testosterone level in fans of the winning team had increased, and the testosterone level in fans of the losing team had decreased. This might help explain why riots so often break out in the city that wins the NBA championship, and at colleges that win football championships, whereas the losers usually just slink silently home (Gettelman, 2002). A more important implication is that this finding may provide insight into testosterone's regulatory function. Imagine winning a fight. Your testosterone level goes up, and you press your advantage. But if you lose, your testosterone level goes down, and you leave the field of battle before you suffer further damage or even get killed. Testosterone is therefore more than a simple or undirectional cause of behavior; it is an important part of the feedback system that affects how people respond to winning and losing.

CORTISOL

In the discussion of the neurotransmitters epinephrine and norepinephrine, above, I described their role in the fight-or-flight response, which in women may be more of a tend-and-befriend response. Another part of this same response is the release of glucocorticoid hormones, also known as **cortisol**. Released into the bloodstream by the adrenal cortex as a response to physical or psychological stress, cortisol is part of the body's preparation for action, and is also an important part of several normal metabolic processes. It can speed the heart rate, raise blood pressure, stimulate muscle strength, and metabolize fat, and has many other effects.

Individuals who suffer from severe stress, anxiety, and depression tend to have chronically high levels of cortisol in their blood. But the rise in cortisol seems to be an effect of stress and depression rather than a cause; injecting cortisol into people does not produce these feelings (Born et al., 1988). Infants with high levels of cortisol tend to be timid and vulnerable to developing social phobias (irrational fears of other people) later in life (Kagan, Reznick, & Snidman, 1988), but again it may be their fearful reactions that stimulate the cortisol production rather than the other way around. Recent evidence even suggests that the excess cortisol production stimulated by experiencing too much fear and anxiety may actually, over time, make one's brain smaller (Knutson et al., 2001)! It seems clear that on both a psychological and physical level, feeling bad all the time is not good for you.

A low level of cortisol entails risks too. It may lead to the underreactivity syndrome that has been noted several times already in this chapter. People with low levels of cortisol may be impulsive sensation seekers who are disinclined to follow the rules of society (Zuckerman, 1991, 1998). This latter pattern may arise because the lack of the normal surge in production of cortisol in response to danger causes such individuals to fail to respond normally to the danger signals associated with such activities as bungee jumping and shoplifting.

Biology, Cause, and Effect

A final note. When looking deeply into the relationships between brain activity, neural chemicals, and behavior, it is tempting to believe that we are finally getting to the "real" causes of things. Since all behavior must have its origins somewhere in the nervous system, some people infer that once the brain is understood, all of behavior will be as well. But the situation is not so simple. The relationship between mind and body works in both directions.

As we saw several times in this chapter, biological processes are *effects* of behaviors or events in the environment as often as they are simple causes. For example, a more stressful environment will raise one's cortisol level, as will feeling depressed or anxious, and the *result* (not the cause) may be a smaller brain! Winning a game will raise one's testosterone level, and behavior and the social environment no doubt affect levels of other hormones and neurotransmitters along with the development and functioning of the brain. Measurable brain activity can be changed by drugs; it can also be changed by psychotherapy (Isom & Heller, 1999). So we will not fully understand the functions of the nervous system until we understand stressful environments, depression, anxiety, psychotherapy, and even why some people win fights while others lose. The workings of the brain help to explain social behavior, but a greater understanding of social behavior will also help us to understand the brain.

Remember Hippocrates' CD player? Let's imagine, clever fellow that he is, he actually manages to figure out how it works. Ah, he realizes, the power comes out of the battery and rotates this disk, the sensor picks up the information and then it is amplified through this transistor and comes out the speaker. If he figured all of this out, it would be a stunning accomplishment comparable to modern attempts to understand the workings of the brain. Then, being *really* clever, Hippocrates might ask, and who is this Eminem person? What does this song mean? Who decided to record music like this, and why do people choose to listen to it? The important questions haven't ended; they are just beginning.

Summary

Both brain anatomy and neurophysiology are relevant to personality. Knowledge about the brain comes from studies of the effects of brain injury and brain surgery, and from newly developed imaging tools such as PET scans and fMRI. The ascending reticular activating system (ARAS), part of the brain stem, was hypothesized by Hans Eysenck to be the basis of extraversion and introversion. According to his theory, people whose ARAS cuts them off from stimulation may seek out exciting people, environments, and activities, perhaps to the point of danger. The amygdala has a special role in emotional response. The frontal lobes are the basis of uniquely human abilities such as language and foresight, and also are important for the understanding and regulation of emotion. Cases such as Phineas Gage, Elliott, and victims of Capgras syndrome show how basic emotional response and cognitive functioning must work together for meaningful experience and adaptive decision making. Psychosurgeries on the frontal lobes, such as lobotomies, may have helped some desperately ill people in the past, but overall seemed to do important damage to patients' ability to reason and to function. The chemical bases of behavior include neurotransmitters and hormones, both of which play a role in communication between and stimulation of the cells of the nervous system. The neurotransmitters epinephrine and norepinephrine are an important part of the fight-or-flight response, which, some psychologists have recently proposed, may in women be a tend-and-befriend response. Dopamine is important for responding to reward and according to Jeffrey Gray may be the basis of the trait of impulsivity. Other evidence suggests its relevance to the broader trait of extraversion. Serotonin aids in emotional regulation and some widely prescribed antidepressant drugs are designed to increase its prevalence in the brain. However, attempts to improve personality-relevant brain functioning through "cosmetic psychopharmacology" may have side effects. The male sex hormone testosterone plays a role in sexuality, aggression, and dominance. Testosterone level is an effect as well as a cause of social behavior; e.g., it rises after the experience of victory over an opponent. Cortisol is an important part of the fight-or-flight response, and its excess production may lead to chronic anxiety and even brain damage, whereas a shortage can lead to dangerously impulsive behavior. In conclusion, it is important to remember that biological processes affect behavior, but both behavior and the social environment affect biological processes. An understanding of each will be helpful for understanding the other.

THE INHERITANCE OF PERSONALITY: BEHAVIORAL GENETICS AND EVOLUTIONARY THEORY

The next baby born in New York's Rockefeller family will be rich. Why? The reason, of course, is *inheritance.* His or her parents are already rich, so the child will belong to a wealthy family and have all of the advantages (and perhaps disadvantages) that go along with large amounts of money. But why are his or her parents rich? Why are *all* the Rockefellers wealthy? The explanation goes back more than a hundred years, to the career of John D. Rockefeller, a fabulously successful and utterly ruthless businessman. Using such tactics as secret buyouts, intimidation, and market manipulation, between 1870 and 1882 he built Standard Oil of Ohio into the Standard Oil Trust, which held a near-monopoly on the U.S. oil business. After many battles with competitors and in court, he retired in 1911 with a fortune of a size almost beyond imagining, and his family name has been a synonym for wealth ever since.

Now consider a question that might at first seem unrelated. Where did your personality come from? Why are you so friendly, or competitive, or stubborn? Maybe the answer is that you have chosen to be this way, but we need also to consider the strong possibility that to some degree the answer concerns inheritance. Are your parents especially friendly, competitive, or stubborn? If the answer to this question is yes, as it might well be, then a further question could be asked. Where did this trait come from in the first place? The answer might lie in the careers of some ancestors who lived a very long time ago.

Two different biologically based approaches consider the ways in which personality might be "inherited"; that is, how characteristic patterns of behavior might be encoded on genes and passed from parents to children across generations. The first of these approaches, *behavioral genetics*, attempts to explain how individual differences in behavior—personality traits—are passed from parent to child, and are shared by biological relatives. The second of these approaches, *evolutionary psychology*, attempts to explain how patterns of behavior that are characteristic of all humans had their origins in the survival value of these characteristics over the history of our species.

These two approaches are directly connected because the evolutionary approach assumes that inherited personality attributes that promoted survival became more prevalent across generations, and the personality attributes we inherited from our ancestors—ancient and recent—are the (currently) final result. Put another way, behavioral genetics concerns how personality can be inherited much like a bank account or a great estate; evolutionary psychology asks, where did all this money come from in the first place?

Behavioral Genetics

You surely look at least somewhat like your parents, and on family reunion days it can be interesting to look around the room and try to figure out in what way all of these aunts, uncles, and cousins share a family resemblance. The similarity is obvious, but can be surprisingly difficult to pin down. The basis of this similarity is of course the genes that biological relatives share with each other. Physical appearance is one thing, but now consider another question: Did you inherit your *personality* from your parents? Are you psychologically similar to your brother or sister because you are biologically related? Questions like these motivate the study of behavioral genetics. This field of research examines the way inherited biological material, that is, *genes*, can influence broad patterns of behavior. A pattern of behavior that is relevant to more than one situation—the only kind of pattern worth considering—is, by definition, a personality trait (Plomin, Chipuer, & Loehlin, 1990). Thus, "behavioral" genetics might more accurately be called "trait" genetics, but I will stick with the traditional term in this chapter.

Controversy

The field of behavioral genetics has been controversial from the beginning, in part because of its historic association with a couple of highly questionable ideas. One is the idea of *eugenics*, that people could be improved through selective breeding. This idea has led to activities ranging from campaigns to keep "inferior" immigrants out of the country to attempts to set up sperm banks stocked with deposits from winners of the Nobel Prize. Another is the idea of *cloning*, that through the miracles of modern technology it might be possible to produce a complete duplicate—psychological as well as physical—of oneself. Both of these ideas have dodgy histories (e.g., Adolf Hitler promoted eugenics), and seem to lead to nightmarish scenarios about the future.

Modern behavioral geneticists are generally (but not quite unanimously) quick to dissociate themselves from these ideas. They view themselves as basic scientists pursuing knowledge for its own sake and invoke the standard (and true) argument that ignorance never got anyone very far (see the discussion of research ethics in Chapter 3). But a more reassuring observation may be that neither eugenics nor cloning turns out to really be very feasible. Because an individual's personality is the result of a complex interaction between his or her genes and his or her environment, as we shall see, the chances of being able to breed people to specification or to duplicate any individual are, thankfully, slim. The real contribution of behavioral genetics is the way it expands our understanding of the sources of personality to include its bases in both genes and the environment.

Calculating Heritabilities

The basic methodology of behavioral genetics is to compare similarities in personality between individuals who are and are not genetically related, or who are related to each other to different degrees. The basic question concerns the degree to which variation in the *phenotype*, the observable traits of a person, can be attributed to variation in the *genotype*, or underlying genetic structure. The classic technique for answering this question is to look at twins. As you probably know, human twins come in two kinds: identical (also called *monozygotic*, or "MZ") twins, and fraternal (also called *dizygotic*, or "DZ") twins. Monozygotic ("one-egg") twins come from a splitting of a single fertilized egg and therefore are genetically identical. Dizygotic ("two-egg") twins come from two eggs fertilized by two different sperm, and so, although born at the same time, they are no more genetically related than any other two siblings.

Humans are highly similar to each other genetically. More than 99 percent of all human genes are identical from one individual to another. (Indeed, 98 percent of these same genes are also found in chimpanzees! See Balter, 2002). Behavioral genetics concentrates on the less than 1 percent of the human genome that does vary. MZ twins are identical in all of these varying genes; DZ twins share about one-half of them, on average. Thus, the statement, for example, that a mother shares 50 percent of her genetic material with her child really means that she shares 50 percent of the material that varies across individuals. This rather technical point highlights an important fact: Like trait psychology (see Chapters 4 to 7), with which it is so closely aligned, behavioral genetics focuses exclusively on aspects of personality that *differ* from one individual to another. The inheritance of "species-specific" traits that all humans share is addressed by evolutionary biology, which is discussed in the second half of this chapter (Tooby & Cosmides, 1990).

Research on behavioral genetics has made great efforts to find twins of both types (MZ and DZ), and also to seek out the rare twins who were separated at birth and reared apart from each other. When such twins are found, their personalities are measured, usually with self-report instruments such as those discussed in Chapters 5 and 6 (the Eysenck Personality Questionnaire and the California Psychological Inventory [CPI] are particular favorites). Recent research has also directly observed twins in laboratory contexts to assess the degree to which they behave similarly (Borkenau, Riemann, Angleitner, & Spinath, 2001). The next step is to compute the correlation coefficients (see Chapter 3) across each pair of twins.[1] The basic assumption of behavioral genetics is that if a trait or a behavior is influenced by genes, then identical (MZ) twins ought to have more similar trait and behavioral scores than fraternal (DZ) twins. Furthermore, closer relatives (e.g., siblings) ought to be more similar on a gene-influenced, inherited trait than are more distant relatives (e.g., cousins).

A statistic called the **heritability coefficient** is computed to reflect this influence (see the hypothetical example in Table 9.1). In the case of twins, one simple formula is $(MZr - DZr) \times 2$ (that is, twice the difference between the correlation among MZ twins compared with the correlation among DZ twins). Across many, many traits, the average correlation across MZ twins is about .60, and across DZ twins it is about .40, when age and gender are controlled (Borkenau et al., 2001, Table 4, p. 661). The difference

---

[1] For technical reasons, a particular statistic called the "intraclass correlation coefficient" is used.

TABLE 9.1

CALCULATING HERITABILITIES

| | Identical Twins | | Fraternal Twins | |
	Score of First Twin	Score of Second Twin	Score of First Twin	Score of Second Twin
Pair #1	54	53	52	49
Pair #2	41	40	41	53
Pair #3	49	51	49	52
. . .	x_4	y_4	x_4	y_4
. . .	x_5	y_5	x_5	y_5
	$r = .50$		$r = .30$	

Calculation: $.50 - .30 = .20$
$.20 \times 2 = .40$
Conclusion: Heritability $= 40\%$

between these figures is .20; multiply that by 2 and you arrive at a heritability coefficient of .40. This means that, according to twin studies, the average heritability of a good many traits of personality is about .40, which is interpreted to mean that the proportion of "phenotypic" (behavioral) variance that can be explained by genetic variance is 40 percent (see also, Plomin, Chipuer, & Loehlin, 1990).

Twin studies are simple and elegant, and the calculations are easy because MZ twins share exactly twice as many variable genes as do DZ twins, but these studies are not the only way to estimate heritabilities. Other kinds of relatives also vary in the degree to which they share genes. For example, children share, on average, 50 percent of their variable genes with their biological parents, whereas adopted children (presumably) share no more of their personality-relevant genes with their adoptive parents than would any other person chosen at random. Full siblings also share, on average, 50 percent of the genes that vary, whereas half-siblings (who have one parent in common) share only 25 percent. Calculating similarities in personality across these different kinds of relatives provides an alternative way to derive heritability estimates. Interestingly, the estimates of heritability for most traits garnered from nontwin studies are about 20 percent, or half that estimated from twin studies (Plomin, Chipuer, & Loehlin, 1990).

Why this difference? One likely explanation is that the effects of genes are interactive and multiplicative rather than additive. That is, the twin-study calculation assumes that because DZ twins share half the genes that MZ twins do, they are half as similar in genetic expression. But if genes act not just by independently adding up, but also by interacting with one another, then DZ twins' similarity in genetic expression will be less than 50 percent. While they share 50 percent of the genes, they share only 25 percent of the 2-way inter-actions among those genes. As a result, in terms of genetic expression, iden-tical twins will be four times as similar to each other as are fraternal twins, instead of just twice as similar. If this line of reasoning is correct, then the 20 percent figure for the heritability of many traits is probably a better esti-mate than the 40 percent figure often quoted.

There is at least one other good reason to conclude that genes interact with each other. The Human Genome Project concluded that the human genome includes somewhere between 30,000 and 40,000 genes. For com-parison, fruitflies have between 13,000 and 14,000 genes; the roundworm *C. elegans* has only 959 cells in its body and over 19,000 genes. The vast differ-ences between humans and these other species, not to mention the vast diver-sity among humans, cannot be accounted for by a simple adding up of genetic effects (Gould, 2001). Genes interact with each other, and with the environ-ment, in complex, often unpredictable ways.

What Heritabilities Tell You

Admittedly these heritability calculations are rather technical, and there is a more basic question that should be asked: Regardless of how you compute it, what does a heritability number tell you? Three things.

GENES MATTER

First, heritabilities tell you that genes matter. For years, psychologists com-monly presumed that all of personality was determined environmentally—that is, by early experiences and parental practices. Heritabilities challenge that presumption whenever they turn out to be greater than zero—and they nearly always do. Indeed, it has been seriously suggested that the observa-tion that nearly *all* heritabilities are greater than zero should be "enshrined as the first law of behavior genetics" (Turkheimer, 1998, p. 786; Turkheimer & Gottesman, 1991). So not all of the determination of personality is envi-ronmental; some of it comes from the individual's genes. This important realization is rather new to psychology. It still is not accepted by everyone, and its far-reaching implications are still sinking in.

INSIGHT INTO ETIOLOGY

Second, heritabilities sometimes can tell you whether specific behavioral or mental disorders are part of the normal range or are pathologically distinctive. One of the more interesting findings to emerge so far from the behavioral genetics literature is that severe mental retardation (defined as an IQ below 50, when 100 is the average) apparently is not heritable—a rare violation of the "first law" just mentioned. The average IQ of the sibling of a severely retarded child is a perfectly normal 103. However, moderate mental retardation (IQs ranging from 50 to 69) does seem to be heritable; the average IQ of the sibling of a moderately retarded child is 85. Moderate retardation runs in families but severe retardation, surprisingly, does not! This finding implies that severe mental retardation comes from something other than simply inheriting a very low IQ. The other factor is probably something that has to do with the environment. For example, perhaps the mother had an infection during pregnancy, or the child suffered some kind of birth trauma or head injury—these are all potential nongenetic causes of severe retardation (Plomin, Chipuer, & Loehlin, 1990).

Other psychological problems appear to be examples of extreme ends of the normal range. One recent analysis examined the relationship between the genetics of personality disorders and the genetics of normal personality (Markon, Krueger, Bouchard, & Gottesman, 2002). Well-adjusted people vary in the degree to which they characteristically experience negative emotions, but when taken to an extreme this can turn into depression. A normal tendency to become absorbed in interesting activities and thoughts can, at the extreme, be related to psychosis. And normal variation in impulsiveness and a tendency to be uninhibited may, at the extremes, have the same genetic roots as criminal behavior and family abuse.

INSIGHT INTO EFFECTS OF THE ENVIRONMENT

A third thing that heritability studies can do is provide a window into how the early environment does—or does not—operate in determining later personality. According to some researchers in this area, the major finding of behavioral genetics so far is this: Growing up together in the same home does not tend to make children similar to each other. The personality traits of adoptive siblings who are raised in the same family resemble each other with a correlation of only .05, which means that a mere 5 percent of the variation in their personalities is due to their common family environment. More important, it seems, is the portion of their early environments that siblings do *not* share with each other. This includes effects of their birth order (e.g., the degree to which firstborns are treated differently from later-borns), friendships outside the home, and other outside interests and activities (Loehlin, Willerman, & Horn, 1985, 1989; Rowe, 1994).

Of course, these are just speculations. Research on behavioral genetics does not tell *which* aspects of a child's early environment are important (Turkheimer & Waldron, 2000). It does suggest that whatever they are, they are not aspects that are shared across members of a family. But there is more to this story.

Does the Family Matter?

If it really is true that the shared family environment has little or no effect on personality development, the implications are stunning. For example, this conclusion implies that aspects of the family environment such as neighborhood, home atmosphere, income, nutritional level, parents' styles of child rearing, and even the presence or absence of one or both parents are *not* important in determining the kind of adult each child grows up to be. Recently, psychologist Judith Rich Harris followed these implications to their logical extreme. She wrote professional articles and a best-selling book arguing that parents—and the rest of the family environment—don't matter at all (Harris, 1995, 1998). As she wrote in one attention-grabbing article:

> Do parents have any important long-term effects on the development of their child's personality? This article examines the evidence and concludes that the answer is no. (Harris, 1995, p. 458)

This seems like a radical statement—and it is!—but it really represents just a small step from the conclusion of the behavioral geneticists, that the shared family environment—such as the fact that all siblings in a family are raised by the same parents—has no identifiable effect on later personality.

You can imagine the stir this statement caused when it hit both the professional literature and the popular media. At one stroke this claim denies all of the fundamental assumptions that have guided the study of development for the past fifty years or more. Even more disconcerting, Harris's claim also seems to say that people might as well not bother trying to be better parents, and could even be taken to imply that there is no real reason to remove children from abusive parents.

A number of questions could be raised about this conclusion, however. First, the evidence from past research is not quite as strong as summaries by Harris and others might make it appear. Several developmental outcomes, including juvenile delinquency, love styles, and aggression, have been found—using standard methods of behavioral genetics—to be affected by the shared family environment (Rowe, Rodgers, & Meseck-Bushey, 1992; Waller & Shaver, 1994).

Second, many decades of research in developmental psychology have documented the effects of child rearing, family environment, and even social class on personality (Baumrind, 1993; Bergeman et al., 1993; Funder et al., 1993; Hetherington, 1983). On the other hand, it must be admitted that research on how parental styles affect children has been confounded, to use a methodological term, by the fact that parents and their children are genetically related. So some of the effects that psychologists have believed were due to the way parents raise their children may instead be due to the genes that parents share with their children. Still, it is difficult to believe that having an alcoholic parent, or living in substandard housing, or having parents who encourage all their children to do well has no importance for how a child turns out. Moreover, experiments have shown that when mothers and fathers are taught how to be better parents, their children both behave better and control their emotions more effectively (Eisenberg, Spinrad, & Cumberland, 1998; Kazdin, 1994).

A third, relatively technical complication is that because they are often screened, chosen, and even arranged by social service agencies, the environments fostered by adoptive families may be more similar to each other than are the environments encountered in families at large. And all of the families in typical heritability studies come from the same culture. To the extent that the families in these studies in fact resemble each other, estimates of the effects of family environment on personality will tend to be underestimates (Mandler, 1997). (The technical reason is that the range has been restricted on the family environment variable, lowering its chance of demonstrating an effect on any other variable.) Indeed, according to one recent reanalysis, when heritability calculations are corrected for the similarities among families, it appears that up to 50 percent of the variance in individual differences such as IQ are accounted for by the shared family environment (Stoolmiller, 1999).

The fourth, final, and most important complication with the claim that shared environments do not matter is it is based on personality measures—mostly self-report scales—that may fail to capture the essence of personality as it emerges from family experience. Perhaps the result of family experience is a view of the world or a set of values not measured by standard personality questionnaires (Shweder & Sullivan, 1990). It is also possible that when twins and other siblings rate their own personalities, they focus on the traits that make them different from each other, rather than on more central traits that would be obvious to outside observers. These reasons may help to explain why the shared family environment has been shown to be important in the development of aggression only when aggression is measured through direct observation (B data, discussed in Chapter 2) rather than through questionnaires (S data) (Miles & Carey, 1997). And the effects of the shared family environment go beyond aggression. One large, recent study obtained ratings of twins' personality traits based on the direct observations of 15 different behaviors, including introducing oneself to a stranger, building a paper tower, and singing a song. The result was that "extraversion was the only trait that seemed not to be influenced by shared environment" (Borkenau et al., 2001, p. 655)—everything else was.

As the authors of this study pointed out, this result has two important implications. The first is that the widely advertised conclusion that the shared family environment is unimportant for the development of adult personality was reached too quickly, on the basis of limited data. For many years behavioral genetics research was based almost exclusively on self-report personality questionnaires, and this S data shows little similarity across siblings raised together. But when personality is assessed by observers who have actually seen their behavior, the shared family environment is seen to have important effects on behavioral similarity. The second conclusion returns us to the message of Chapter 2: Personality can be studied using many different kinds of data, and they all should be used. Conclusions based on only one kind of data are at risk; conclusions based on consistent results across several kinds of data are much more likely to hold up in the long run.

The line between provocative scientific hypothesizing and irresponsible overstatement is both thin and blurry. Some behavioral geneticists danced right up to this line with their enthusiastic claim that the shared family environment has little or no effect on personality development. Judith Harris jumped over it with her claim that parents don't matter. The overwhelming scientific evidence, simply put, is that parents *do* matter (Eisenberg, Spinrad, & Cumberland, 1998; Collins et al., 2000).

Still, the overall discussion is worth having. Research on behavioral genetics research should get credit for having raised this provocative issue, and much further research remains to be done to ascertain how genetic factors interact with environmental factors, including the family environment, in personality development. And criticisms of the overstatements made by some behavioral geneticists cannot deny one basic fact: Personality is partially determined by one's genes, to an extent that psychologists just a couple of decades ago would not have believed possible.

Nature versus Nurture

Ever since scientists realized the effects that heredity might have on behavior, they have longed for a simple number that would resolve the nature-nurture debate by indicating what percentage of any given trait was due to *nature* (or heredity) and what percentage was due to *nurture* (or upbringing and environment). To some, the heritability coefficient has seemed like that number, since it indeed yields a figure between 0 and 100 percent that reflects the percentage of the variation in a trait that is due to variation in genes.

But consider, as an example, the number of arms you have. Was this number determined by your genes or by your childhood environment? Well, let's calculate the heritability of this trait. Looking again at Table 9.1, plug in for the first member of the first pair of twins the number of arms he or she has, which you can presume is 2. Then do the same thing for the other twin of that pair. Then do this for all the other individuals in both parts of the table (you can assume that all of these numbers are 2). Then calculate the correlations. Actually you cannot do that in either case, because the formula to calculate the correlation (not shown in Table 9.1) will require a division by 0, the result of which is undefined in mathematics. So, the difference between these correlations is 0; multiply that by 2 and you still get 0—the heritability of having two arms is 0. Does that mean that how many arms you have is determined entirely by the environment? Well . . .

What went wrong in this calculation? The problem is that on the trait of arm quantity there is practically no variation across individuals; nearly everyone has two. Because heritability is the proportion of *variation* due to genetic influences, if there is no variation, then the heritability will approach zero. Generally, the less variation there is on a trait across individuals, the lower the heritability is likely to be. This means that if a given trait has a high heritability, one of two things is possible: that trait might vary greatly across individuals, or it might be a trait for which genes are important, in an absolute sense. Likewise, if a given trait has a low heritability, that trait might vary *less* across individuals, or it may be a trait that is less dependent on one's genes.

If you are still following this discussion, you might now appreciate that in fact the calculation of the heritability of number of arms did not go wrong at all—it did just what it is supposed to do. If you look around at people, occasionally you will see someone with one arm. Why? Almost always, it will be because he or she has been in an accident of some kind—an environmental event. The *difference* between people with one arm and those with two arms therefore is produced environmentally and not genetically. This is why the heritability for the number of arms people have will be near zero.

How Genes Affect Personality

Here is a fact that may astonish you: To a statistically significant degree, television watching is heritable (Plomin, Corley, De Fries & Fulker, 1990). Does this mean there is a biologically active gene in your DNA that causes you to watch television? Presumably not. Rather, there must be some more basic propensity—perhaps sensation seeking, perhaps lethargy, maybe even a craving for blue light—that has some genetic component. And this component, interacting somehow with early experience, creates in some people a propensity to watch a lot of television. Research has not yet examined any of these interactions, however, and does not offer even a hint as to what exactly is inherited or how it influences television watching. Indeed, as the researchers who presented this finding admitted, "It is likely to be difficult to find specific mechanisms of genetic influence on television viewing because genetic mechanisms have not as yet been uncovered for any complex behavioral trait, including cognitive abilities and personality" (Plomin et al., 1990, p. 376).

Here is another example. It turns out that divorce is heritable: if one or more of your close relatives has been divorced, you are more likely to become divorced yourself than if none of your relatives has been divorced—even if you have never met these relatives (McGue & Lykken, 1992). What does this finding imply about the causes of divorce? Maybe not much (see Turkheimer, 1998). The finding does imply that one or more genetically influenced traits are relevant to divorce. But which traits, or how they influence divorce, behavioral genetics analyses cannot say. It could be that impulsiveness is heritable, and impulsive people have affairs, which causes them to become divorced. Or perhaps homosexuality is heritable, or alcoholism, or depression—any or all of which might cause a person to be more likely to become divorced. Since, as the psychologist Eric Turkheimer (1998, p. 785) pointed out, "everything is heritable," every personality trait that might affect divorce is probably heritable, and as a result divorce will turn out to be heritable as well. But this conclusion does not explain *how* genes influence divorce, and it certainly does not imply that people have a "divorce gene" somewhere deep in their DNA.

In the past few years, the basis of genetic effects on personality has begun to become more clear. A few studies have gone beyond heritability calculations and dived into the actual DNA to see which genes are involved in various behavior patterns. Most of these studies use the **association method**, in which molecular geneticists try to determine whether differences in a trait are correlated with differences in a particular gene across individuals. One pioneering effort explored the genetic basis of homosexuality in males (Hamer & Copeland, 1994; Hamer, 1997). First, it found a group of homosexuals who were related to various degrees. Then, using microbiological techniques, it identified a gene on the X chromosone that most (but not all) of the homosexuals shared but that was not found in heterosexual members of the same family. They concluded that this genetic similarity was one basis of the homosexuality. More recent studies have examined the trait of sensation seeking and its association with a gene called D4DR, which affects the development of dopamine receptors. You may recall from Chapter 8 that dopamine is part of the brain system that responds to reward and some psychologists have theorized that a shortage of dopamine, or an inability to respond to it, may lead people to crave extra stimulation to the point of engaging in risky behavior. One study found that different forms of the D4DR gene were associated with variations in sensation seeking, and so concluded that this gene might be a basis of sensation seeking via its effect on dopaminergic systems (Benjamin et al., 1996; see also Blum et al., 1996).

Of course, this is not the whole story. One limitation, as the authors of the original studies themselves acknowledged, is that not *all* homosexuals shared the same DNA pattern, and the effect of D4DR on sensation seeking is small, and does not always replicate (Plomin & Crabbe, 2000). And the situation is even more complicated than that. Ten different genes, or more, may be involved in sensation seeking, and upwards of 500 genes might be important for other aspects of personality (Ridley, 1999). The chance of finding a single gene with a simple, direct, and easy-to-understand effect on homosexuality, sensation seeking, or any other aspect of personality, therefore, seems very slim. (A theory presented near the end of this chapter attempts to provide a more complete picture of how genes might influence sexual orientation.)

In the final analysis, genes themselves cannot cause anybody to do anything, any more than you can live in the blueprint of your house. The genotype only provides the design, and so affects the behavioral phenotype indirectly by influencing biological structure and physiology as they develop within an environment. The next challenge, therefore, after we figure out which specific aspects of the nervous system are affected by genes, is to understand how those aspects interact with environmental experience to affect behavior.

Gene-Environment Interactions

Genes can influence the development of behavior only in people who live in some kind of environment.[2] Without an environment there would be no behavior, regardless of what genes and brain structures are present. And the reverse is also true: without a person (built by genes) to affect, no behavior can occur, no matter what the environment. The point has been made many times but always seems to need reemphasis: In the determination of personality, genes and the environment *interact*. Neither genes nor environment can do anything without the other.

The environment can even affect heritability itself. For example, in an environment where every child receives adequate nutrition, variance in height will be controlled genetically. Tall parents will have tall children, and short parents will have short children; the heritability of height will be a large number. But in an environment where food is scarce and some children have good nutrition while others do not, variance in height will fall under the control of the environment. Well-fed children will grow to be tall while poorly fed children will be shorter, and the height of the parents will not matter so much; the heritability of height will be a small number.

---

[2]Genes can interact with the environment only via the physical bodies, or the phenotypes, of the individuals the genes inhabit. So, the term *gene-environment interaction* would more precisely be termed *phenotype-environment interaction* (Turkheimer & Waldron, 2000), but for present purposes I will stick with the traditional term.

Consider a more psychological trait, such as IQ. From the logic just used, we could expect that in an environment where intellectual stimulation and educational opportunities vary a lot from one child to the next, IQ might be under the control of the environment. The children who are stimulated and educated will grow up to be more intelligent than those who are not so lucky, and heritability of IQ will be low. But if we could achieve a society where *all* children received sufficient stimulation and education, then the remaining differences in IQ would have to be due to their genes. As the intellectual environment improves for everybody, we should expect the heritability of IQ to go up!

Genes and the environment interact in several other ways (Scarr & McCartney, 1983). For example, a boy who as a result of his genes is shorter than his peers may be teased in school; this teasing could have long-term effects on his personality. These effects are in part due to his genes, but they came about only through an interaction between the genetic expression and the social environment that resulted. Without both, there would have been no effect.

Another way genes and environment can interact is through the way people choose their environments. A person who inherits a tendency toward sensation seeking, for example, may take dangerous drugs as a result. This practice might harm that person's health or involve the person in the drug culture, either of which could have long-lasting effects on his or her experience and the development of his or her personality. Let's say the person develops a criminal personality. This result is only indirectly due to the inherited trait of sensation seeking; it comes about through the interaction of the inherited trait with the environment associated with activities that the person seeks out because of that trait.

The most important way in which genes and environments interact is that the same environment can affect different individuals in different ways. A stressful environment may lead a genetically predisposed individual to develop mental illness, while leaving individuals without that predisposition psychologically unscathed. More generally, the same environmental circumstances might be perceived as stressful, or enjoyable, or boring, depending on the genetic predispositions of the individuals involved; these variations in perception can lead to very different behavioral results and, over time, to the development of different personality traits.

Behavioral genetics sometimes is portrayed as a pessimistic view of human nature, because it is seen as implying that we are what we were born to be, and cannot be changed. The discussion here, however, shows why this is mistaken. When the whole process by which genes influence personality is understood, especially concerning the way in which genetic predispositions interact with the environment, then it should become possible to change the environments of people at risk for various outcomes to help them to avoid them. For example, in Chapter 8 I quoted one psychologist who suggested that persons with a biologically determined tendency toward sensation seeking might be deterred from a life of crime by participating in less damaging occupations that might satisfy their needs for excitement (such as racecar driver or radio talk-show host). Frankly, I'm not sure whether this was a serious suggestion. But it has a point. If we understood an individual's biologically given predispositions, we might be able to help him or her to find an environment where his or her personality and abilities can lead to good outcomes rather than bad ones.

The Future of Behavioral Genetics

The most significant news from the study of behavioral genetics over the past few years is that genes are important in the determination of personality. This extremely important lesson constitutes quite a change from the conventional view held only a few years ago. The future of behavioral genetics, however, does not lie in further documenting this fact (Turkheimer, 1998). Rather, the remaining jobs for behavioral geneticists are, first, to explain how genes create brain structures and aspects of physiology that are important to personality, and second, to explain how a person's genetically determined tendencies interact with his or her environment to determine how he or she behaves. You read in the preceding pages a few important advances in this direction, toward identifying genes associated with behavior patterns, the effects of certain genes on brain structures and behavior, and various ways in which genetically determined tendencies and environmental circumstances interact. Behavioral genetics has proved, beyond a shadow of a doubt, that personality is inherited to an important degree. Its next exciting order of business, in coming years, will be to make further progress in explaining *how*.

Evolutionary Theory

Evolutionary theory is the foundation of modern biology. Modern extensions of the theorizing that began with Charles Darwin's *Origin of the Species* ([1859] 1967) are used to compare one species of animal or plant to another, to explain the functional significance of various aspects of anatomy and behavior, and to understand how animals function within their particular environments. In recent years, an increasing number of attempts have been made to apply the same kind of theorizing and reasoning to the understanding of human behavior and even social structure. One landmark book,

E. O. Wilson's *Sociobiology: The New Synthesis* (1975), applied evolutionary theory to psychology and sociology. Other, earlier efforts, such as Konrad Lorenz's *On Aggression* (1966), also tried to explain human behavior using analogies to animals and their evolution.

In general, the evolutionary approach to human behavior assumes that behaviors seen in people are present because in the evolutionary history of the human species, these behaviors were helpful or necessary for survival. The more a behavior helps an individual to survive and reproduce, according to evolutionary theory, the more likely the behavior is to occur in subsequent generations. The evolutionary approach to explaining personality, therefore, is to identify a common behavior pattern and then ask how that pattern could have been adaptive (i.e., beneficial to survival and reproduction) during the development of the human species (Tooby & Cosmides, 1990).

A wide range of human behavior has been examined through this evolutionary lens. For example, Lorenz (1966) discussed the possibly necessary— and sometimes harmful—role of the instinct toward aggression throughout human history. The biologist Richard Dawkins (1976) closely considered the evolutionary roots of the opposite behavior, altruism, and described how a general tendency to aid and protect other people, especially close relatives, might help ensure the survival of one's own genes into succeeding generations (an outcome called *inclusive fitness*). It pays to be nice to your relatives, according to this analysis, because if the people who share your genes survive, then some of your genes may make it into the next generation through these relatives' children, even if you produce no offspring.

Evolutionary theory has even been used to explain why self-esteem is so important. According to the "sociometer theory of self-esteem" by the psychologist Mark Leary, our feelings of self-esteem evolved to monitor the

"Whenever Mother's Day rolls around, I regret having eaten my young."

degree to which we are accepted by others. Humans are a very social species, and few things are worse—or more dangerous—than being shunned by one's fellows. On the television "reality" program *Survivor,* the dreaded words "the tribe has spoken" may touch a deep, instinctual fear.[3] When we receive cues that indicate we are not adequately valued and accepted by other people, our self-esteem goes down and that motivates us to do things that will cause others to think better of us—and each of us to think better of ourselves. We are the descendants of the people who developed this motive to enhance acceptance by others—the people who did not develop this motive did not survive, and left no descendants (Leary, 1999).

Sex Differences in Mating Behavior

A behavioral pattern that has received particular attention from evolutionary psychologists is the variation in sexual behavior between human males and females. Particular differences can be identified in the behaviors of **mate selection**—what one looks for in the opposite sex—and **mating strategies**—how one handles heterosexual relationships.

MATE SELECTION

First consider mate selection. When seeking someone of the opposite sex with whom to form a relationship, is an average heterosexual more likely to

---

[3]In case you have not seen this program, the host says these words just after a member of the tribe is voted out. He then symbolically extinguishes the member's torch.

be interested in that person's (1) physical attractiveness or (2) financial security? Across a wide variety of cultures, most definitely including early-twenty-first-century North America, men are more likely than women to place a higher value on physical attractiveness (Buss, 1989). In these same cultures, by contrast, women are more likely to value economic security in their potential mates. Indeed, there is some evidence that men and women consider attractiveness and resources, respectively, as *necessary* attributes of potential mates, not just nice things to have (Li, Bailey, Kenrick, & Linsenmeier, 2002).

In addition, heterosexual men are likely to desire (and typically do find) mates who are several years younger than themselves (the average age difference is about three years, and increases as men get older), whereas women end up with mates who are older than themselves (of course). This difference can be documented through marriage statistics and even through personal ads. When age is mentioned, men advertising for women usually specify an age younger than their own, whereas women do the reverse. The other effect also can be found in personals: Men are more likely to describe themselves as financially secure than as physically attractive, whereas women are more likely to describe their physical charms than their financial ones (Kenrick & Keefe, 1992). Presumably, each sex is acting this way because it knows what the other sex is looking for, and is trying to maximize its own appeal.

The evolutionary explanation of these and other differences is that men and women are seeking essentially the same thing: the greatest possible likelihood of mating with someone with whom they will have healthy offspring who themselves will survive to reproduce. But each sex contributes to and seeks this goal differently, and thus the optimal mate for each is different. Women bear and nurse children, and so their youth and physical health are essential. Attractiveness, according to the evolutionary explanation, is simply a display or cue that informs a man that a woman is indeed young, healthy, and fit to bear his children (Buss & Barnes, 1986; Symons, 1979).

A man's biological contribution to reproduction is relatively minimal, in contrast. Viable sperm can be produced by male bodies of a wide range of ages, physical conditions, and appearances. For women, what is essential in a mate is his capacity to provide an environment and resources conducive to her children's survival and thriving until their own reproductive years. Thus, since a woman seeks a mate to optimize her children's chances, she will seek someone with resources (and perhaps attitudes) that will support a family, whereas a man seeks a mate who will provide his children with the optimal degree of physical health.

We can see already that these explanations gloss over some complications. For example, a woman who lacks a certain percentage of body fat will stop menstruating and therefore will be unable to conceive children, yet many women considered by men to be highly physically attractive are thin, nearly to the point of anorexia. In previous eras, much heavier women were considered

"Stupid—yet irresistible."

the ideal of physical attractiveness. Thus, culture does seem to influence concepts of physical attractiveness, and although it is far from clear where those ideas come from, reproductive fitness is not always the sole determinant.

Likewise, male physical attractiveness is more important to many women than the standard evolutionary explanation seems to allow. In other species, male displays of large manes or huge fans of plumage appear to be a sign of health that is important for attracting females. It is not clear why the situation would be so different in humans. However, it must be admitted that physical attractiveness does not seem to be as important to women as it is to men. The general trends in what men and women favor in each other are difficult to deny, despite occasional exceptions and complications.

MATING STRATEGIES

Once they have completed their mutual selection process and have mated, men and women still differ in their subsequent behaviors. According to the evolutionary account, men tend to want to have more sexual partners and are neither particularly faithful nor particularly picky about the women with whom they will mate. In fact, they appear to be prone to certain kinds of wishful thinking, in which they are quick to conclude that women are sexually interested in them, even when they are not (Haselton, 2002). Women, in contrast, are much more selective about their mating partners and, having mated, seem to have a greater desire for monogamy and a stable relationship.

These differences also can be explained in terms of reproductive success. A male may succeed in having the greatest number of children who reproduce to subsequent generations—which evolutionarily speaking is the only important outcome—by having as many children by as many different women as possible. In a reproductive sense, it may be a waste of his time to stay with one woman and one set of children; if he leaves them, they will probably survive somehow and he can spend his valuable reproductive time trying to impregnate somebody else. A woman, however, is more likely to have viable offspring if she can convince the man to stay and provide support for her and the family they create. In that case, her children will survive, thrive, and eventually propagate her genes.

Another, related behavioral difference is found in the ways in which men and women experience sexual jealousy. In one study, men and women were asked to respond to the following vignette (Buss et al., 1992):

> Please think of a serious committed relationship that you have had in the past, that you currently have, or that you would like to have. Imagine that the person with whom you've become seriously involved became interested in someone else. What would distress or upset you more: (Circle only one)
>
> (a) Imagining your partner forming a deep emotional attachment to that person, or
>
> (b) Imagining your partner enjoying passionate sexual intercourse with that person?

In this study, 60 percent of the males chose option (b), whereas 82 percent of the females chose option (a). In a follow-up study, the final question was changed slightly:

> What would upset you more:
>
> (a) Imagining your partner trying different sexual positions with that other person, or
>
> (b) Imagining your partner falling in love with that other person?

Here, 45 percent of the males chose (a), whereas only 12 percent of the females chose (a). In other words, option (b) was chosen by 55 percent of the males and by 88 percent of the females. Notice that this question does not produce a complete reversal between the sexes; most members of each sex find their partner falling in love with someone else more threatening than their partner having intercourse with another person. But this difference is much stronger among women than it is among men.

Why is this? Evolutionarily speaking, a man's greatest worry—especially for a man who has decided to stay with one woman and support her family—is that he might not really be the biological father of the children he is supporting. This makes sexual infidelity in his mate his greatest danger and her greatest sin, from a biological point of view. For a woman, however, the greatest danger is that the development of an emotional bond between her mate and some other woman will cause the support of her and her children to be withdrawn or, almost as bad, that her mate will share resources that would otherwise belong only to her and her children with some other woman and her children. This makes emotional infidelity a greater threat than mere sexual infidelity, from the woman's biological point of view.

A related evolutionary logic can even be used to explain some seeming paradoxes or exceptions to these general tendencies. For example, why are some women attracted to men who are obviously unstable? Consider the situation described by the typical country-western song. Some women prefer to mate with men who may be highly attractive physically (and/or own motorcycles) even when such men have no intention of forming a serious relationship and are just "roaming around." I have no idea how common this situation is, but from an evolutionary standpoint it should never happen, right?

Wrong. The theory is rescued here by what has been called the "sexy son hypothesis" (Gangestad, 1989). This hypothesis proposes that some women follow a reproductive strategy different from that of most other women (Gangestad & Simpson, 1990). Instead of seeking to maximize the reproductive viability of their offspring by mating with a stable (but perhaps unexciting) male, they instead choose to take their chances with an unstable but attractive one. The theory is that if they produce a boy, even if the father then leaves, the son will be just like dad. When he grows up, this "sexy son" will himself spread numerous children (who of course will also be the woman's grandchildren) across the landscape, in the same ruthless and irresponsible manner as his father.

Individual Differences

Evolutionary psychology has, so far, been much more concerned with the origins of general human nature than with individual differences. Indeed, it almost seems to imply that individual differences should be unimportant, because maladaptive behavioral variations should have been selected out of the gene pool long ago (Tooby & Cosmides, 1990). However, it is also true that the mechanism of evolution requires individual differences to be maintained. Species only change through the selective survival into later generations of the genes of the individuals who have been most successful in earlier generations. So not only is it fair to ask a theory-of-everything like evolutionary psychology to also explain individual differences, but such an explanation is essential for the theory itself to be viable.

Evolutionary psychology tries to account for individual differences in at least three ways (Buss & Greiling, 1999). First, the argument is made that behavioral patterns evolve to be reactions to particular environmental experiences. Only under certain conditions does the evolved tendency come "on line," sort of like the way the skin of a Caucasian has a biological tendency to darken if and only if it is exposed to the sun. For example, growing up without a father in the first five years of life may evoke an evolved tendency to act as if family life is not stable, and therefore result in a behavioral pattern of early sexual maturation and frequent changes of sexual partners (Belsky, Steinberg, & Draper, 1991). Second, people may have evolved several possible behavioral strategies and use the one that makes the most sense given their other characteristics. We may have innate abilities to be aggressive and agreeable, for example. The aggressive style only works if we are big and strong; otherwise the agreeable style might be a wiser course. This may be why big, muscular boys are more likely to become juvenile delinquents (Glueck & Glueck, 1956). Third, some biologically influenced behavior may be *frequency dependent*, meaning that it adjusts according to how common it is in the population otherwise. For example, one theory of *psychopathy*—a behavioral style of deception, deceit, and exploitation—is that it is biologically determined in a small number of people (Mealy, 1995). If more than a small number of individuals tried to live life this way, nobody would ever believe anybody, and a psychopathic style would become evolutionarily impossible to maintain.

These are interesting suggestions, but notice how they all seem to boil down to an argument that people are, in the end, evolved to be flexible. I think that is a very reasonable conclusion to reach, but at the same time it tends to undermine the idea that people have evolved specific behavioral tendencies in specific domains such as self-esteem, mate selection, and jealousy—the explanation of which has been the whole point of the evolutionary approach. This is just one reason why the approach is controversial. Psychologists have pointed out several difficulties with an evolutionary approach to human personality, to which we now turn.

Objections and Responses

Many objections have been raised to the evolutionary approach to human behavior. Its account of sexual behavior and sex differences, in particular, seems almost designed to set some people off, and it certainly does. At least five objections to the evolutionary approach to personality can be identified.

METHODOLOGY

The first objection concerns scientific methodology. It is indeed interesting to speculate "backward" in the way that evolutionary theorists do, by wondering about what in the past might have produced a behavioral pattern we see today. But how can such speculations be put to empirical test? What sort of experiment could we do, for example, to see whether men really seek multiple sexual partners in order to maximize their genetic propagation? Or consider the proposals that men have an instinct toward rape because it furthers their reproduction (Thornhill & Palmer, 2000), or that step-parents are prone to child abuse because of the lack of shared genes (Daly & Wilson, 1988). These are stimulating suggestions, to say the least, but they also entail certain problems.

For example, there is something odd about postulating an instinct toward a behavior like rape or child abuse when most men are *not* rapists and most step-parents are *not* abusive. (The primatologist Frans de Waal [2002] calls this the "dilemma of the rarely exercised option," p. 189). Furthermore, it is probably not wise to assume that every genetically influenced trait or behavior pattern has evolved for a purpose. Because of the human genome, people walk upright, and because we evolved from four-legged creatures this design change makes us prone to backache. Apparently, walking upright had enough advantages to counteract the disadvantages, but that does not mean that lower-back pain is an evolved mechanism. In the same way, behavioral patterns such as unfaithfulness, child abuse, and rape, even if they are genetically influenced, may not have evolved for any particular purpose but may be unfortunate side effects of other adaptations. As de Waal noted, "the natural world is rampant with flawed designs" (2002, p. 188).

Evolutionary theorists usually acknowledge that criticisms like these are fair, to a point, but they do have a good response: For any theoretical proposal in science—not just those in evolutionary psychology—alternative explanations are always possible. And, whole, complex theories are seldom subjected to one crucial, "up or down" study. Instead, bits and pieces of these theories are tested as methods to do so become available. Similarly, complex evolutionary theories of behavior may be difficult to prove or disprove in their entirety, and all the alternatives may never be ruled out, but empirical research *can* be designed to address specific predictions from these theories. For example, the evolutionary theory of sex differences yields a further prediction that males should be older than their sexual partners across all cultures, because the evolutionary hypothesis is that this difference is a biological and not a cultural product (Kenrick & Keefe, 1992). In the cultures examined by researchers so far (which have included India, the United States, and many others) the hypothesis seems to have been supported. Even though this finding does not absolutely prove that the reproductive motives described by evolutionary theory are the cause of the age differences, nor rule out all possible alternative explanations, in fairness it must be considered encouraging empirical support.

REPRODUCTIVE INSTINCT

A second objection is that there is something strange about assuming that everybody wants as many children as possible in an age where many people practice birth control and abortion to limit their own reproduction. Evolutionary psychologists have a good response to this objection, too. For evolutionary theorizing about behavior to be correct, it is not necessary for people to be *consciously* trying to do what the theory says they are *ultimately* trying to do (Wakefield, 1989). All that is required is for people in the past who followed a behavioral pattern to have left more children in the present generation than did people who did not follow the pattern (Dawkins, 1976).

Thus, although you might or might not want children, and you might even practice birth control, it cannot be denied that you would not be here unless *somebody* (your ancestors) had children. (Neither sterility nor complete abstinence runs in anyone's family.) The same tendencies (e.g., sexual urges) that caused them to reproduce offspring are also present in you. Thus, your sexual urges are based on a reproductive instinct, whether or not you consciously wish to reproduce. After all, your sexual urges *do* increase your chances of reproducing (birth control methods can sometimes fail). In general, according to evolutionary theory, people have a tendency to do what they do because of the effect similar behavior in past generations has had on reproductive outcomes, not because they necessarily have any current intention to add to the population of the earth.

CONSERVATISM

A third criticism of the evolutionary approach to behavior is that it seems to embody a certain conservative bias (Alper, Beckwith, & Miller, 1978; Kircher, 1985). Because it assumes that whatever tendencies exist in human behavior today evolved because of the past environments experienced by the species, and that these tendencies are biologically rooted, the evolutionary approach seems to imply that the current behavioral order was not only inevitable, but also is probably unchangeable. This conservative implication bothers some people who think that male promiscuity, child abuse, and rape are reprehensible (they are correct, of course), and others who think that human tendencies toward aggression, for example, must and can be changed.

Evolutionary theorists respond that political objections like these are irrelevant from a scientific standpoint (see the discussion of research ethics in Chapter 3). They also observe that with this criticism, opponents of evolutionary theorizing are themselves committing the "naturalistic fallacy" of believing that all that is natural must be good. Critics seem to be saying that evolutionary reasoning, because it claims sex differences (for example) are natural, is also claiming that these sex differences are good. But evolutionary theorists do not draw this inference (Pinker, 1997). As the evolutionary theorist Daniel Dennett stated, "Evolutionary psychologists are absolutely not concerned with the moral justification or condemnation of particular features of the human psyche. They're just concerned with their existence" (Flint, 1995).

HUMAN FLEXIBILITY

A fourth and more powerful objection is that evolutionary accounts seem to describe a lot of complex behavior as genetically programmed into the brain, whereas a general lesson of psychology is that humans are extraordinary flexible creatures with a minimum of instinctive behavior patterns, compared with other species. Indeed, we saw in Chapter 8 that the neomammalian brain (the outer cortex that is unique to humans) has the function of planning and thinking in ways that go beyond fixed action patterns and other simple responses. Yet evolutionary accounts such as that of sex differences seem to come close to postulating built-in patterns of behavior that cannot be overcome by conscious, rational thought.

The issue here is not whether the theory of evolution is correct; the scientific community settled that question to its satisfaction long ago. Rather, the question is whether, in the domain of behavior, people evolved *general* capacities for planning and responding to the environment, or *specific* behavioral patterns or "modules" (Öhman & Mineka, 2001). When it tries to explain behaviors such as mate preference, sex differences in jealousy, and even child abuse and rape, evolutionary psychology seems to favor a modular approach (Harris, 2000). But when it addresses the question of individual differences, it acknowledges that the evolution of the cerebral cortex has given the human brain the ability to respond flexibly to changing circumstances, and even to overcome innate urges. These two kinds of explanation are difficult but perhaps not impossible to reconcile, and debate in the next few years is likely to focus on this issue. What *is* the human evolutionary heritage? Is it a collection of specific responses that are triggered almost automatically by particular circumstances? Or is it the ability to plan, foresee, choose, and even override behavioral impulses?

BIOLOGICAL DETERMINISM OR SOCIAL STRUCTURE?

A final criticism of the evolutionary approach to personality is closely related to the idea that people may have evolved to be flexible. Many behavioral phenomena may be the result not of evolutionary history but of humans flexibly responding to circumstances, especially social structure. For example, the sex differences discussed earlier may be caused not by biological hard-wiring, but by the current structure of society.

The psychologists Alice Eagly and Wendy Wood (Eagly & Wood, 1999; Wood & Eagly, 2002) have provided an alternative to the evolutionary account of the differences in the criteria used by men and women in choosing mates. They hypothesize that because of men's greater size and strength, and women's role in childbearing and lactation, societies have developed around the world in which men and women are assigned different jobs and social roles. Men around the world tend to be the warriors, the rulers, and those holding power. Women are more likely to be restricted near the home, and gain power and

THE FAR SIDE®   By GARY LARSON

"And now, Randy, by use of song, the male sparrow will stake out his territory ... an instinct common in the lower animals."

affluence largely as a function of the men with whom they affiliate. This difference is enough, Eagly and Wood argue, to explain why women value the wealth of a man more than his looks, and why the wealth of a woman matters less to a man. The difference comes not from a specific innate module, but from a reasonable and flexible response to the biologically given facts that men tend to be larger than women, and women play a more central role in childbirth and child-rearing.

Eagly and Woods's argument is important for both theoretical and practical reasons. On a theoretical level it goes to the heart of the question of how much of human nature is evolutionarily determined and biologically inherited. Their argument is important on a practical level because the world is changing. In an industrial culture where physical strength is less important than it was, and alternative child care arrangements are possible, the traditional division of labor between men and women no longer seems as inevitable as it used to. But it continues anyway, because societies are slow to change. What happens next?

According to the evolutionary view, the differences between men and women in mate selection and other behaviors are built in through processes of biological evolution. This view implies that it might be almost impossible to change these differences; at best any change will occur at the speed of evolution, meaning that thousands of years may be required. According to the contrary, social view, as the necessity for a sexual division of labor melts away, societies will change, and sex differences will change (and perhaps lessen) as a result. The process may still be slow (it might take hundreds of years), but much quicker than the processes of biological evolution.

This may be happening already. According to one analysis by Eagly and Wood, in the present-day cultures where women have relatively equal power to men, the sex differences in preference for a wealthy spouse are much smaller than in the cultures where the power difference is still intact. This finding implies—but it does not prove—that if over time societies begin to provide equal power to women, some of the sex differences discussed earlier in this chapter may begin to erode.

The current debate about the implications of evolutionary theory for personality psychology, and particularly its implications for sex differences, is lively and stimulating. It is important to note, for now, that neither side has proved its point conclusively. Even critics such as Eagly and Wood acknowledge that their explanations of the origin of sex differences are about as well supported—or poorly supported—as the explanations offered by evolutionary psychologists. We can expect to see further arguments, evidence, and perhaps even improved understanding over the next few years.

The Contribution of Evolutionary Theory

Researchers will continue to argue about the details of evolutionary theory as applied to human behavior for many years. But one fact is beyond argument: After the introduction of evolutionary thinking into psychology, the field will never be the same (Pinker, 1997). Not every aspect of thought or behavior exists because it specifically evolved. But it has become clear that researchers should probably always consider whether it did. Whenever an investigator is trying to explain a brain structure, thought pattern, or behavior, he or she can no longer avoid asking the question, how might this (brain structure, thought process, or behavior) have promoted survival and reproduction in the past? Does the answer to this question help explain why people today—the descendants of past survivors and reproducers—now have it?

Will Biology Replace Psychology?

Chapter 8 and this chapter reviewed the implications for personality of four different areas of biology: anatomy, physiology, genetics, and evolution. Each of these areas has a lot to say about personality. Indeed, each can be taken to imply that personality is biologically based. This implication was anticipated by Gordon Allport's classic definition of personality, which predated nearly all of the research just surveyed by many years. Allport wrote that personality is "the dynamic organization within the individual of those *psychophysical* systems that determine his [or her] characteristic behavior or thought" (originally offered in Allport, 1937; also in Allport, 1961, p. 18; emphasis added).

The rapid progress made by biological approaches to psychology in recent years led some observers to speculate that, as an independent field of study, psychology is doomed. Because personality is a "psychophysical" system, once everything is known about brain structure and physiology, there will be nothing left for psychology to do! This point of view is called *biological reductionism*—in the final analysis, everything about the mind is reduced to biology.[4]

Obviously I have a vested interest in this issue, but nevertheless I will state that I do not think biology is going to replace psychology. It certainly will not do so soon. As we have seen, there are too many huge gaps in our knowledge about the functioning of the nervous system to use it to replace the other approaches to human personality—yet.

But what about the distant future? I don't think so even then, and the reason is fundamental. Biological approaches to psychology, by themselves, often tell us much more about biology than about psychology. This biology is extremely interesting, but it does not provide a description of how people act in their daily social environments, or of the important consistencies that can be found in their behaviors (topics that were considered in Part II of this book). A purely biological approach to psychology will never describe what psychological conflict feels like, or how such conflict might be revealed through accidental behavior, or what it means to face one's existential anxiety (topics to be considered in Parts IV and V). Nor does a purely biological approach address how an individual's environment can determine what he or she does, nor does it explain how an individual interprets his or her environment or plans a strategy for success (topics to be considered in Part VI). It cannot even say much about what is on your mind at this moment.

For example, the evolutionary process as it has affected males gives them a biological mechanism that makes them tend to be unfaithful to their mates (according to one theory). But what happens inside the male's head at the moment he is being unfaithful? What does he perceive, think, feel, and, above all, want? Evolutionary psychology not only fails to answer this question, it fails to ask it. Similarly, the other biological approaches describe how brain structures, neurochemicals, or genes affect behavior without really addressing the psychological processes that lie between the brain, neurochemicals, or genes on the one hand, and behavior on the other.

---

[4]The Department of Psychology at Dartmouth College recently changed its name to the Department of Psychological and Brain Sciences—a harbinger of the future?

One theme of this book is that the different approaches to personality are not different answers to the same question, but different questions. Thus, there is little danger of any one of them completely taking over—not even the biological approach. The biological approach to personality is important and is becoming more so all the time, and evolutionary theory has the potential to organize a huge range of psychological knowledge (Pinker, 1997). But it will never supersede all of the other approaches by showing how behavior is "really" caused by biological mechanisms (de Waal, 2002; Turkheimer, 1998). The greatest promise of the biological approach lies elsewhere, in the way it can sometimes explain how biology interacts with social processes to determine what people do.

Putting It All Together: Sexual Orientation

Consider sexual orientation, for example. What causes a person to become heterosexual, homosexual, or bisexual? A novel theory by the psychologist Daryl Bem shows how anatomical, neurochemical, evolutionary, and genetic perspectives can be combined with social psychology and even sociology to explain the processes that determine this interesting and important psychological outcome (Bem, 1996).

At the outset, Bem observes that the right question to ask is not what is the cause of homosexuality, but rather, what directs sexual orientation in general? Bem shares this point of view with Freud, who said that homosexuality and heterosexuality were equally difficult to understand, and who also speculated that the same basic processes might underlie both (Freud, [1905] 1962). So Bem's theory tries to account for the development of *all* varieties of sexual orientation. The theory is outlined in Figure 9.1.

First, biological influences such as genes and prenatal hormones produce children with particular childhood personalities (Bem calls them *temperaments*); some children are aggressive and active, while others are more quietly sociable. These temperaments interact with the structure of childhood society, which strongly segregates boy and girl playgroups beginning at about age five. A boy who enjoys rough-and-tumble play will fit in well with groups of other boys. A boy who for reasons of his temperament does not enjoy these activities, however, may seek out the company of girls. So the first boy will grow up around other boys; the second boy will grow up around girls. As a result, the first boy will come to see girls—with whom he has little experience in childhood—as relatively unfamiliar and "exotic" (to use Bem's term). The second boy will come to see other *boys*—with whom he may have as little experience—as exotic.

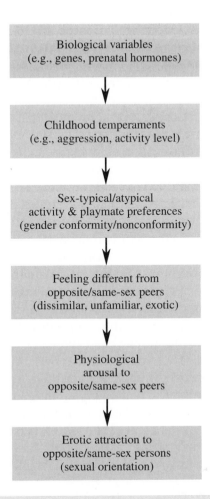

**FIGURE 9.1 BEM'S "EXOTIC BECOMES EROTIC" THEORY OF SEX-
UAL ORIENTATION** This figure describes the sequence of events over the
course of development that produce the sexual orientation of most men and
women in a culture that accentuates sex differences and segregates the sexes during much of childhood. Source: Bem, 1996, p. 321.

At this point psychological mechanisms that are common to all members
of the human species come into play. People are physically aroused by novel
stimuli; when they see something unusual or strange, their heartbeat increases
and blood pressure rises. But people interpret what their arousal *means* based
on the environmental context and who and what is present in it. For example, one classic study showed that men who were aroused by standing on a
high, swaying bridge apparently came to believe they were sexually attracted
to a woman standing on the bridge with them (Dutton & Aron, 1974)!

These processes lead the boy who grew up around other boys to be aroused, later in life, by the novelty of the presence of girls and, as he enters puberty, to label this arousal as sexual attraction. But the boy who grew up around girls is aroused by the novelty of the presence of boys, and through a parallel path comes to label this arousal as sexual attraction. Now you can see why Bem calls this theory "exotic becomes erotic." People who belong to the group (male or female) seen as exotic become seen as erotically stimulating, too. For most people, the exotic sex is the opposite one; for a substantial minority, the reverse is the case.

Notice that Bem's theory has several components, some of which are biological and others of which are social and even sociological. All four of the biological approaches I considered in this chapter and in the preceding chapter are included at least briefly. Bem assumes that hormones and the anatomical structure of the brain produce basic patterns of behavior concerning energy level, activity preferences, and so on. At another level of analysis, he assumes that these basic patterns of behavior are heritable. He also assumes that there are some psychological mechanisms that everybody shares, that are "built in" as the result of evolution—specifically, the mechanisms that cause arousal in response to novel stimuli and that cause arousal to be interpreted according to the situation. The truly novel aspect of Bem's theory is the way he puts all of these components together and integrates them with the experiences of a child who is growing up in the usual cultural context. His theory also makes the point that complex behavioral patterns such as homosexuality may be to some extent biologically determined, but only indirectly, through the inheritance of various more basic traits that make the behavior pattern more likely to develop in a particular social context (Bem, 2001).

The evidence for Bem's theory is reasonably good. Recent evidence from a study of Australian twins indicates that the tendency to enjoy activities conforming to traditional sex roles is biologically heritable (Bailey, Dunne, & Martin, 2000), and this tendency, in turn, is predictive of hetero- and homosexuality. For example, Bem reports that 63 percent of homosexual men report not having enjoyed typical "boy" activities in childhood, while only 10 percent of heterosexual men make the same report. The trend for women is almost as strong. Among lesbian women, 63 percent report not having enjoyed typical "girl" activities in childhood, while this is true of only 15 percent of heterosexual women. Parallel trends are found among many other variables that, according to Bem's theory, ought to be precursors of sexual orientation. The gender nonconformity associated with homosexuality appears to extend into adulthood. One recent study asked people about their occupational preferences, and found that the same choices that were different between men and women also tended to be different between heterosexual and homosexual individuals. For example, women were more likely than men to report wanting to be an interior decorator, beauty consultant, or florist, and homosexual men showed the same pattern in comparison to heterosexual men. At the other end of the scale, men were more likely than women to report wanting to be a mechanical engineer, building contractor, or jet pilot, and homosexual women showed the same pattern compared to heterosexual women (Lippa, 2002).

These findings are consistent with the theory, but they do not prove it. A complete test of Bem's model would require a longitudinal study that followed a sample of boys and girls with varying temperaments, activity preferences, and playmate groups from childhood to adulthood, and tracked their sexual orientation as it developed. Such a study would be difficult to carry out and is not likely to be available any time soon. Moreover, a complete proof of a theory this complex is probably not possible.

But for present purposes, the proof or disproof of Bem's theory of sexual orientation is not really the issue. The most important aspect of Bem's theory may be the way it shows what a biologically informed theory of personality should look like—but almost never does. Notice how many different kinds of elements interact: the child begins with genes and hormones, which produce personality styles, which interact with the structure of society and the formation of childhood groups, which leads to certain feelings about members of the same and opposite sexes, which become eroticized through a universal emotional mechanism, which produces the sexual orientation of the adult. Wow!

Biological approaches to personality have come a long way. Their further progress will come from showing how biological influences interact with behavioral styles, social interaction, and the structure of society to produce the people we become. This could and should be done with many important personality outcomes, not just sexual orientation. Bem has shown us a way to do it.

Conclusion

At the end of Chapter 8, I returned to the problem of Hippocrates' CD player by noting that once he figured out how it works, he would still not have begun to answer questions concerning why people like music, the economics of the music industry, or why some artists achieve fame and others do not, all of which are important if he wants to fully understand the sounds that come out of that box. Let's conclude this discussion of the inheritance of personality by returning to the Rockefellers, and the way they routinely inherit large amounts of money. In the short run, this is easily explained because each new Rockefeller has wealthy parents. In the longer run, the

*"Everything I have, son, I have because your grandfather left it to me.
I see now that that was a bad thing."*

wealth of the extended clan can be traced to one spectacularly successful ancestor. But let's look at little Baby Rockefeller and ask a few more questions. What will she do with all this inherited wealth? Will she spend it on luxury, give it to charity, use it for a career in politics, or fritter it all away on drugs and die broke? Previous Rockefellers have done all of these things. The inheritance is just the beginning; what she will do with it will depend on the society in which she lives, the way she is raised by her parents, and, yes, by her biological genes. The personality you inherited from your parents and from your own distant ancestors may work the same way. It determines where you start, but where you go from there depends on many things, and may ultimately be up to you.

Summary

Behavioral genetics and evolutionary biology concern the degree to which personality is inherited from parents and more distant ancestors. Heritability statistics computed from the study of monozygotic and dyzogotic twins estimate that about 40 percent of the phenotypic variance in many personality traits can be accounted for by genotypic variance, although other studies suggest the real figure may be lower because genes interact. Heritability studies confirm that genes are important for personality, can be informative about whether psychological disorders are distinctive pathologies or extremes on the normal range of variation, and can provide insights into the effects of the environment. Findings that unrelated, adopted children who grow up together do not develop similar personalities led to questioning whether the shared family environment is important for development, but recent analyses and new data suggest that the shared environment has effects on many important traits, especially when they are measured via behavioral observation rather than self-report. Very recent research is beginning to map outthe complex route by which genes determine biological structures that can affect personality; for example, the association of the D4DR gene with dopaminergic systems and the trait of extraversion. The situation is complex because genes interact with each other and their effects on development is critically affected by the environment. Evolutionary psychology attempts to explain behavioral patterns—such as aggression, altruism, mating, and sex differences—by analyzing how they may have promoted survival and reproduction in past generations. Some of these explanations are controversial, and a key issue concerns the degree to which evolutionary processes have produced specific "modular" patterns of behavior, as opposed to general abilities to understand and flexibly respond to changing environments, including culture. Either way, research on evolutionary biology and behavioral genetics implies that biology and genetic inheritance are involved in the determination of human personality. As exemplified by Bem's theory of the development of sexual orientation, the promise of the biological approaches comes from their potential to illuminate the interactions between biological, personality, social, and sociological influences on behavior.

SUGGESTED READINGS: BIOLOGICAL APPROACHES

Damasio, A. R. (1994). *Descartes' error: Emotion, reason, and the human brain.* New York: Putnam.

> *A lively and highly readable summary of one neurologist's view of the relationship between the brain and behavior. It includes several compelling case studies (including Elliot, summarized in Chapter 8 of this book) and the author's "somatic marker hypothesis," in which he argues that emotional feeling is an indispensable component of rational thought.*

Pinker, S. (1997). *How the mind works.* New York: Norton.

> *A far-ranging, stimulating, and engagingly written survey of cognitive and social psychology from an evolutionary perspective. Pinker provides many creative and even startling insights into the way our evolutionary history may have shaped the ways we think.*

Plomin, R., Chipuer, H. M., & Loehlin, J. C. (1990). Behavioral genetics and personality. In L. Pervin (Ed.), *Handbook of personality: Theory and research* (pp. 225–243). New York: Guilford.

> *A good summary of the methods and principal findings of behavioral genetics research.*

Valenstein, E. S. (1986). *Great and desperate cures: The rise and decline of psychosurgery and other radical treatments for mental illness.* New York: Basic.

> A vivid history of psychosurgery, electroshock therapy, and other drastic, biologically based "psychotherapeutic" interventions that have been tried over the years. Along the way, much is taught about both biology and about the sociology of psychology and medicine.

Wilson, E. O. (1975). *Sociobiology: The new synthesis.* Cambridge, MA: Harvard University Press.

> The book that sparked the revival of interest in using evolutionary theory to explain human behavior.

PART IV

THE HIDDEN WORLD OF THE MIND: THE PSYCHOANALYTIC APPROACH

The following dispatch was transmitted by the Associated Press on March 12, 1992. I have changed only the name of the story's protagonist—surely he has suffered enough.

ST. LOUIS—The city's prosecutor, who has crusaded against prostitution and pornography, was charged Thursday with soliciting a prostitute. Circuit Attorney John Smith was charged with soliciting an undercover police officer at the St. Louis Airport Marriott Hotel on Tuesday night, said St. Louis County Prosecutor Robert McCulloch. . . . Smith, 49, at first denied the charge, but on Thursday apologized and said he was "ready for any consequences." . . . But he added he wouldn't step down from the office he's held since 1979. Smith has been a crusader against pornography, and a strong supporter of sting operations to crack down on prostitution in the city. He led a recent crackdown on the rental of pornographic movies at video stores. Last June, the Board of Aldermen adopted mandatory jail terms for prostitutes, pimps and customers on a second conviction. Smith said then that the measure would make the customers of prostitutes "scared to death."

How could this happen? How could someone who is a loud and public opponent of pornography and prostitution, and a professional prosecutor of both, turn out to be a customer of prostitutes himself? This is not an isolated case. In 2003, William Bennett, the morally crusading author of *The Book of Virtues* and *The Children's Book of Virtues,* was forced to acknowledge a long-standing gambling habit at which he had lost millions of dollars. Every few days the news reveals yet another evangelical preacher or sanctimonious politician who turns out to be a regular practitioner of the same vices he (it does usually seem to be a he, but there are exceptions) has made a career of denouncing. Strange and paradoxical cases like these beg to be explained, and that would seem to be a natural job for a psychologist.

It might surprise you, therefore, to learn that most approaches to personality psychology have almost nothing to say about these sorts of paradoxes. More than fifty years ago, the psychologist Henry Murray complained that much of psychology

> is over-concerned with recurrences, with consistency, with what is clearly manifested (the surface of personality), with what is conscious, ordered, and rational. . . . It stops short at the point precisely where a psychology is needed, the point at which it begins to be difficult to understand what is going on. (Murray, 1938, p. 715)

For most areas of psychology, his complaint is equally valid today. There is one approach, however, that has long focused on the challenge of explaining what is going on, when what is going on is difficult to understand. The approach is psychoanalysis, based on the writings of Sigmund Freud. Psychoanalysis is more than just "Freudian" psychology, however; Freud changed his mind at many points during his career, and many other psychologists have continued to translate, interpret, and extend his ideas for nearly a century. These ideas concern the secret part of the mind, the part that is ordinarily hidden from view and, in some cases, seemingly contradictory, irrational, or absurd.

The next three chapters describe the psychoanalytic approach to the study of personality. Chapter 10 provides a general introduction to Freud and to psychoanalytic thought and its view of the structure and development of the mind. Chapter 11 describes some of the workings of the unconscious mind, including defense mechanisms, parapraxes (slips), and humor. Finally, Chapter 12 brings psychoanalysis into the present day by surveying later psychoanalytic work on personal relationships (*object relations*) and other neo-Freudian approaches, as well as some relatively recent empirical research that is relevant to a psychodynamic account of personality.

BASICS OF
PSYCHOANALYSIS

The aim of the psychoanalytic approach, initiated by Sigmund Freud and developed by later, neo-Freudian theorists, is to find out what is really going on in the dark, hidden, unconscious recesses of the human mind. Psychoanalytic theory is very complex and comes in many versions, but in what follows I keep things relatively simple. (I say *relatively* simple; there is no way to talk at all seriously about psychoanalysis without delving into some complex issues.) The present chapter progresses from a description of the key ideas that underlie the psychoanalytic approach and a bit of the history of Freud's life, through an account of how children develop psychologically into adults, to a description of the psychoanalytic model of how the mind is structured and how it thinks, both consciously and unconsciously. It then considers some of the implications of Freudian ideas for psychotherapy and for modern life.

Key Ideas of Psychoanalysis

One of the elegant aspects of the psychoanalytic approach is that all of its complexity is built on a relatively small number of key ideas. The four ideas that make up the foundation of psychoanalysis are psychic determinism, internal structure, psychic conflict, and mental energy.

Psychic Determinism

First and probably most fundamental to the psychoanalytic approach is the assumption of **psychic determinism** (Brenner, 1974). *Determinism,* a basic tenet of science, is the idea that everything that happens has a cause that—in principle, maybe not always in practice—can be identified. The *psychic determinism* at the root of the psychoanalytic approach is the assumption that everything that happens in a person's mind, and therefore everything   *283* that a person thinks and does, also has a specific cause. There is no room for miracles, free will, or even random accidents. If there were, the entire approach would stall at the starting line. The key faith (and that is really what it is—faith) of a psychoanalyst is that even a prostitute-patronizing city prosecutor or a moralizing compulsive gambler can be explained. All it takes is diligence, insight, and, of course, the proper psychoanalytic framework.

The nondeterministic alternative would be to say something like "He just decided to get a prostitute (or go gambling) of his own free will, despite what he said," or "He's just inconsistent." Those statements might be true, but you would never hear either one from a psychoanalyst. Only slightly better, from a psychoanalytic point of view, would be an observation like "This prosecutor is just a politician doing what is popular in order to get elected, but doing whatever he wants to on the side," or "The author of the *Book of Virtues* is a typical hypocrite." These explanations also might be true, but they still beg the questions of why, given the number of law-enforcement issues that a prosecutor might exploit, did this particular prosecutor select prostitution instead of, say, home burglary, and how moral crusading can come out of the same brain as a multimillion-dollar vice. There *must* be a reason, and psychoanalysts would argue that the reason lies somewhere in the structure and dynamics of personality. The only trick is to find it.

From a psychoanalytic perspective, all seeming contradictions of mind and behavior can be resolved and nothing is ever really accidental. There is a reason why you preached one way and acted another; there is also a reason you forgot that name, dropped that dish, or said a word you did not intend to say. The purpose of psychoanalysis is to do the deep digging required to find those reasons, which usually lie in the hidden part of the mind. The assumption of psychic determinism, therefore, leads directly to the conclusion that many of the important processes that go on in the mind are **unconscious**.[1] Modern research tends to support this conclusion—it appears that only some of what the mind does, and perhaps only a small part, is open to conscious awareness (Kihlstrom, 1990; Bornstein, 1999).

Internal Structure

A second key assumption of psychoanalysis is that the mind has an internal structure. For psychoanalysis, it is important to remember the distinction between the *mind* and the *brain*: the brain is a physical organ, whereas the

---

[1]Freud believed that the assumption of psychic determinism led so directly and necessarily to the postulation of unconscious mental processes that to assume one was to assume the other. That is why, following Freud, I do not treat unconscious mental processes as a fifth and separate foundation of psychoanalysis.

mind is the psychological result of what the brain (and the rest of the body) does. The mind is divided into three parts, which will probably sound familiar to you. They are usually given the Latinized labels **id**, **ego**, and **superego**. These terms pertain to the irrational and emotional part of the mind, the rational part of the mind, and the moral part of the mind, respectively,[2] and the interesting problem is that they can work independently and even compete. Our prosecutor's id insisted on seeking out prostitutes even while his superego condemned the activity. *The Book of Virtues* excoriates a long list of unvirtuous behaviors that, strangely (or not so strangely), omits gambling. The author's superego enforced many prohibitions, it appears, but his id insisted on at least one exemption. In both cases, the ego—the rational part of the mind—doesn't seem to have managed to play much of a role in the crossfire between these competing forces.

Modern research in biological and cognitive psychology has not found that the mind is actually divided into three neat parts. However, both kinds of research do support the idea that the mind consists of separate and independent structures that can process different thoughts and motivations at the same time (Gazzaniga et al., 1998; Rumelhart, McClelland, & The PDP Research Group, 1986).

Psychic Conflict (and Compromise)

The third assumption of the psychoanalytic approach stems directly from the second. Because the mind is divided into distinct and independent parts, it can be in conflict with itself, as we saw in the cases of the prosecutor and the book author. But **psychic conflict** is not always so dramatic. For example, right now, maybe your id wants ice cream. Your superego thinks you do not deserve it because you have not studied all week. It might fall to your ego to make a compromise: you get to have ice cream *after* you have finished this chapter.

The idea of **compromise formation** is a key tenet of modern psychoanalytic thought. The ego's main job, psychoanalysts now believe, is to find a middle course between the competing demands of motivation, morality, and practicality, and also among the many different things a person wants at the same time. ("Ego psychology" will be considered again in Chapter 12.) The result of the compromise among all of these competing forces is what the individual consciously thinks and actually does (Westen, 1998). If the

---

[2]The psychoanalyst Bruno Bettelheim (1982) argued that these widely used terms are mistranslations of Freud's original German writing, but it is probably too late to correct that mistake here. Bettelheims' preferred translations for id, ego, and superego are the It, the I, and the Over-I.

prosecutor's ego had been more effective, he might have been able to find some kind of compromise between his sexual motivations and morality that would have kept him out of trouble. The ego of the *Virtues* author failed him by leaving him in the awkward position of campaigning sternly against all modern vices except one. Without the ability to come to a reasonable compromise, these individuals were left to flail between strong and contradictory impulses—first one way, and then the other—with disastrous results.

Mental Energy

The final key assumption of the psychoanalytic approach is that the psychological apparatus of the mind needs energy to make it go. The special kind of energy required is sometimes called **psychic energy**, or **libido**, and only a fixed and finite amount is available at any given moment. Therefore, energy powering one part of the apparatus is not available for any other part; energy that the mind spends doing one thing (such as pushing uncomfortable thoughts out of memory) is unavailable for other purposes (such as having new and creative ideas). The principle of the conservation of energy applies to the mind as it does to the physical world.

This principle seems reasonable, but some implications of psychic energy have not stood the test of time very well. For example, the original formulation assumed that if a psychological impulse was not expressed it would build up over time, like steam pressure building in a boiler. If someone made you angry, unless you expressed your anger the associated psychic energy would build and build until something snapped. This is an interesting idea that seems in accord with some real-life experience (e.g., the meek and mild person who passively allows himself to be pushed around by a bully, then bursts forth in murder), but research suggests that as a generalization it is wrong. Expressing anger typically makes a person more angry, not less, a direct contradiction of the original Freudian idea (Bushman, 2002).

There is another reason not to take the energy metaphor too literally. My first teaching job was at a college of engineering and science (I recommend such a bracing experience to all of my psychologist colleagues). My class of engineers was dozing politely through one of my lectures on Freud when I mentioned psychic energy. They immediately perked up, and one student, grabbing his notebook, asked eagerly, "Psychic energy—in what units is that measured?" Unfortunately, I replied, psychic energy is not something that Freud ever proposed to measure in "units" of any kind. It was just a metaphor that applied in some respects but not in others. And none too precisely in any case. At that answer, the students sighed, slouched back into their chairs, and no doubt privately redoubled their determination to become engineers rather than psychologists.

Modern psychoanalytic theory has moved somewhat away from Freud's original conception of psychic energy. In current thinking, the assumption is that it is the mind's capacity for information, rather than its energy, that is limited (Westen, 1998). This reformulation retains the implication that capacity used up by one purpose is not available for anything else. One goal of psychoanalysis, from the client's perspective, is to free up more psychic energy—or computing capacity—for the challenges of daily living, by removing neurotic conflicts one by one.

Controversy

From its inception the psychoanalytic approach has stirred more controversy than any of the other approaches to personality psychology, and some people have even viewed it as dangerous. Objections to psychoanalysis have changed with the times. The Victorians looked at Freud's emphasis on sex and sexual energy and complained that his theory was "dirty." We more enlightened folk of the twenty-first century look at Freud's emphasis on that which cannot be seen and cannot be conclusively proved and complain that his theory is "unscientific." The bases of the criticisms seem to change, but in every age, it seems, a lot of people just don't like psychoanalysis. And many don't like Freud either. It is interesting to see how often criticisms of psychoanalysis are mixed with *ad hominem* complaints about Freud's ethics, manners, and even personal life (e.g., Crews, 1996; see Westen, 1998, pp. 344–345; more will be said about attacks on Freud in Chapter 12).

Freud anticipated these kinds of attacks and sometimes even seemed to revel in them. He pointed out that Copernicus became unpopular for pointing out that the earth is not the center of the universe and that Darwin was derided for his claim that humans are just another species of animal. His own insights that human nature is largely hidden from view and that the motivations that drive many human behaviors are base and irrational were not ideas he expected would win him any popularity contests, and he was right. Psychoanalysis bothers people.

Let's bring this down to a personal level by considering two cautionary tales. They both exemplify the discomfort that psychoanalytic insights can cause, and the dangers of offering them unsolicited.

The first takes us way, way back to the time when I decided to major in psychology. I broke the news to my family in the traditional fashion. Returning home from college for Thanksgiving break, I waited for the inevitable question: "Have you decided on a major yet?" "Psychology," I replied. As many others making this choice have discovered, my family was not exactly thrilled. After a stunned silence, my sister spoke first. "OK," she said, "but so help me, if you ever psych me out, I will never speak to you again!"

Her comment is highly pertinent. Learning about personality psychology, especially the psychoanalytic approach, can produce irresistible urges to analyze the behavior and thoughts of those around us. It's all part of the fun. The advice you should take from my sister's warning, however, is to keep the fun private. People are typically not grateful to be analyzed. Sharing your insights into why your friends "really" did something can be the start of real trouble. This is true even if your insights are completely accurate—Freud thought this was true *especially* when your insights are completely accurate.

My second tale is a specific example concerning psychoanalysis. When I get to the part of my courses in which I teach about Freud, I try to do so as an advocate. I make the best, most convincing case for psychoanalytic theory that I can. Who knows what effect this sales job has on my students, but one person I never fail to convince is myself. Thus for a few weeks each academic year, I turn into a raving Freudian. One side effect is that I become temporarily unable to avoid analyzing every slip, mistake, and accident I see.

I did this once, years ago, on a date. In the course of a casual conversation, my dinner companion related something she had forgotten to do that day. Being deep in the Freudian phase of my syllabus, I immediately offered a complex (and rather clever, I thought) interpretation of the unconscious anxieties and conflicts that probably caused her memory lapse. My insight was not well received. My date vehemently replied that my interpretation was ridiculous and that in the future I could keep my absurd Freudianisms to myself. Gesturing for emphasis, she knocked a glass of ice water into my lap. Picking up the ice cubes, but still in a Freudian frame of mind, all I could do was acknowledge the vivid, symbolic nature of the warning I had received.[3]

The moral of these two stories is the same: Keep your clever analyses of other people to yourself! If you are wrong, and especially if you are right, it will make them mad. It is a little like what they say at stunt demonstrations: "We are trained professionals. Do not try this at home."

Freud Himself

In this book, I have tried to avoid the trap of writing about psychologists instead of about psychology, because I believe that psychology is much more than simply "what psychologists do." An exception must be made for Freud, though. No other psychological approach is at once so important and influ-

---

[3]Eventually, we married each other anyway.

FIGURE 10.1 Sigmund Freud at work.

ential, and so closely identified with one particular individual. Freud is one of the most interesting and important people to have lived in the past couple of centuries. So let's take a moment and consider Freud and how he developed his ideas.

Sigmund Freud was a medical doctor who practiced in Vienna, Austria, from the 1890s until the 1930s. (He lived from 1856 to 1939.) He was Jewish and had to flee his native country after Hitler came to power in the 1930s; he spent the last few years of his life in London. Freud died in a pessimistic frame of mind, convinced that the impending world war, following so closely on the heels of the unbelievably destructive and tragic First World War, proved that humans had an aggressive, destructive urge that in the end would destroy them.

One of Freud's less profound yet enduring cultural legacies is the collective, stereotypical image of what a psychotherapist should be like. He had a beard and small eyeglasses. He favored three-piece suits, with a watch chain hanging from the vest. When he spoke English it was with a Viennese accent. He had a couch in his office—along with some impressive African art that some of his patients reportedly found distracting.

Freud began his career as a research neurologist. He went to France for a time to study the newly developing field of hypnosis with Jean-Martin Charcot. He gradually moved into the practice of psychiatry, in part so he could

FIGURE 10.2   The outside of Freud's home at Berggasse 19, Vienna. His office and the apartment where he lived with his family were on the second floor. This picture was taken in 1938, shortly after the German army occupied Austria and shortly before Freud fled to London. If you look closely, you can see that someone has affixed a swastika above the door.

make a living and get married. Then, as now, medical practice paid much better than theoretical research. Early in his clinical practice, Freud made a simple but fundamental discovery: when his patients talked about their psychological problems, sometimes that, by itself, was enough to make them better or even cure them. At first, Freud used hypnosis to get his patients to talk about difficult topics. Later, he turned to the use of *free association* (instructing the patient to say whatever comes to mind) for the same purpose. One of Freud's grateful patients dubbed the results of such therapy the "talking cure." The talking cure must be seen as Freud's greatest contribution to psychotherapy. By now, it is ubiquitous. A fundamental assumption of nearly every school of psychotherapy—including many whose followers claim they have nothing in common with Freud—is that "talking about it helps."

Freud thought he knew why talking helps. In part, it is because making one's thoughts and fears explicit by saying them out loud brings them out into the light of day where one's conscious, rational mind can deal with them. (Your crazy thoughts won't make you so crazy once you have had a chance to think them through rationally.) The other reason is that the psychother-

FIGURE 10.3   Freud's famous consulting couch.

apist can provide emotional support during the patient's difficult task of trying to figure out what is going on. (Every psychotherapist keeps a box of tis-
sues handy for clients who cry.) In a letter to Carl Jung, Freud wrote that
"psychoanalysis is in essence a cure through love" (cited in Bettelheim, 1982).
Many non-Freudian schools of psychotherapy have adopted these two ideas
as well.

Freud attracted numerous disciples whom he encouraged to help him
spread the ideas of psychoanalysis. Many of them had strong minds of their
own, however, which led to some famous and bitter quarrels. Carl Jung and
Alfred Adler were the most famous of Freud's followers who eventually split
with their mentor (see Chapter 12).

Freud's ideas came from the patients he treated and even more importantly from his observations of the workings of his own mind. This is something the psychoanalytic approach has in common with the humanistic
approach, which is considered later in this book. Both psychoanalysts and
humanists begin the psychological endeavor with the attempt to know themselves first. (An important part of traditional psychoanalytic training is being
psychoanalyzed oneself.) Other psychologists do not attempt to do this; in
fact, they seem actively to avoid it. Trait psychologists and behaviorists, for
example, generally stay safely outside of their own minds, just as the biological psychologists rarely cut themselves open.

Freud's ideas were certainly influenced by the time and place in which he lived and by the patients he saw. Most were well-to-do women, a surprising number of whom reported having been sexually abused by their fathers when they were young. Freud at first believed them and saw this early abuse as a common source of early-life trauma. Later he changed his mind, and decided that these memories of early abuse were fantasies that, for psychological reasons, had come to seem real.[4]

Now that you have met Freud, let us turn to the basics of the theory he developed. The theory begins with the question of motivation, which asks, what do people want?

Psychoanalysis, Life, and Death

Behind the many and sometimes contradictory things that people want, Freud believed, two motives are fundamental. The first motivation impels toward life, and the other impels toward death. Both motives are always present and forever competing. In the end, death always wins.

The life drive is sometimes called **libido**, and is also referred to as the "sexual drive" (which is what *libido* means in ordinary conversation). In psychoanalytic writings by Freud and by those who came later, libido receives a great deal of attention. But I think it is also widely misunderstood, perhaps in part because so many people are so easily distracted by any reference to sex. In the final analysis, sex is simply life. Sex is necessary for the creation of children (biological interventions aside), and its enjoyment can be an important part of being alive. It is in this sense that libido is a sexual drive— Freud meant that it had to do with the creation, protection, and enjoyment of life and with creativity, productivity, and growth. This fundamental force exists within every living person, Freud believed, and he called this force libido.[5]

Relatively late in his career, Freud posited a second fundamental motive, that toward *death*. He called it **Thanatos** (the Greek word for

---

[4]The critic Jeffrey Masson (1984) argued that this latter conclusion was a fundamental mistake, because it led psychoanalysis to look inside the mind instead of outside at the world for the origin of psychological problems.

[5]Here, as elsewhere, I am reinterpreting Freud in light of later developments in psychoanalytic thought and modern evidence. I think this rendition is true to the spirit of what Freud thought was important about libido. However, I also have to admit that Freud did frequently talk about libido in a literally sexual sense, and that later psychoanalytic thinkers, such as Jung, thought Freud overemphasized sexuality at the expense of a broader interpretation of libido as the life force.

"death"). Although he probably did not mean to claim the existence of a "death wish," he held a fundamental belief in the duality of nature, or the idea that everything contains its opposite. Freud observed that not only do people engage in a good deal of destructive activity that does not seem to have a rational basis (wars are a good example), but also that in the end, everybody does die. It was to account for these facts that he introduced the death drive.

This drive, too, is sometimes misunderstood. Freud probably was not as morbid as his idea of a drive toward death makes him sound. I suspect that Freud really had in mind something like the concept of entropy, the basic force in the universe toward randomness and disorder. Ordered systems tend toward disorder, and this trend is inevitable; local, short-term increases in order only result in widespread, long-term increases in disorder (this is why, according to physics, the universe is doomed). Freud viewed the human mind and life itself in similar terms. We try desperately throughout our lives to make our thoughts and our worlds orderly and to maintain creativity and growth. But the fundamental force of entropy dooms these efforts to failure in the end, although in the meantime we may have a pretty good ride. So, Freud's ultimate view of life was far from morbid; it may be better described as tragic.

The opposition of *libido* and *Thanatos* derives from another basic idea that arises repeatedly in psychoanalytic thinking: the **doctrine of opposites**. This doctrine states that everything implies and even requires its opposite— life requires death, happiness requires sadness, and so forth. One cannot exist without the other.

One application of this doctrine is the idea that extremes on any dimension tend to be more similar to each other than either is to the middle. For example, consider the leaders of antipornography censorship campaigns and pornographers. The doctrine of opposites would claim that they have more in common with each other than either does with people in the middle, for whom pornography is not much of an issue. There may be something to this idea. Pornographers and censorship crusaders share not only extremism, but also a certain fascination with pornographic material and a tendency to spend a lot of time looking at it. Those in the middle, by contrast, may have a distaste for pornography but are not so excited by its existence to make its prohibition one of the burning issues of the age, or to feel compelled to immerse themselves in it all day long. Or consider an antiprostitution crusader and a regular patron of prostitutes. They could not be more different, right? Now reread the Associated Press dispatch on page 279 of this book. Or consider what happens when one person stops loving another. Does his or her new attitude more often move to the middle of the continuum, to "mild liking"— or to the other extreme?

The juxtaposition of the life drive with the death drive is also consistent with the doctrine of opposites. But the death drive came as a sort of afterthought to Freud, and he never worked it fully into the fabric of his theory—most modern analysts do not really believe in it. (Personally, I find the idea useful.) When I talk about psychic energy in the remainder of this book, therefore, the reference is to *life energy*, or libido.

Psychological Development: "Follow the Money"

In the book *All the President's Men*, the reporter Bob Woodward asks his secret source, Deep Throat, how to get to the bottom of the Watergate affair. Deep Throat replies, "Follow the money." By this he means that Woodward should find out who controlled a large sum of secret cash at the Committee to Re-elect the President and find out how that money was spent. Woodward later said that this tip allowed him and Carl Bernstein to crack the case.

When trying to understand the workings and the development of the human mind, Freud gives us similar advice. His version is "follow the energy." For like money, psychic energy is always both absolutely necessary and absolutely limited, so the story of where it goes tends to be the story of what is really happening.

This principle comes into play in Freud's account of how the mind of an infant gradually develops into the mind of an adult. The story of psychological development is the story of how life energy, libido, becomes invested and then redirected over an individual's early years. A new baby fairly bubbles with life energy, but without focus or direction. As the baby develops into a child and an adult, the energy begins to focus, first on one outlet and then another. As the focus shifts and shifts again, the style and type of gratification that the child seeks continually change. But no matter where it is focused at any moment, it is still libido, the same old psychic energy.

The focal points for psychic energy serve to define the stages of psychological development. You have probably heard of them: the oral, anal, phallic, and genital stages. Each stage has three aspects: (1) a physical focus, where energy is concentrated and gratification obtained; (2) a psychological theme, related both to the physical focus and to the demands being made on the child by the outside world as he or she develops; and (3) an adult character type that is associated with being "fixated," or to some degree stalled, in that particular stage, rather than fully developing toward the next one. If an individual fails to resolve the psychological issues that arise at a particular stage, that person will always have some psychological scar tissue in that location, and those issues will continue to be troublesome to him or her throughout life.

Oral Stage

A newborn baby is essentially helpless. It flails its arms and legs around. It cannot see clearly and cannot reach out and grab something it wants. It cannot crawl or even turn over. The lack of motor control and physical coordination is almost total.

Almost. There is one thing a newborn baby can do as well at birth as any grown person will ever be able to do: suck. This is no small matter. The action is quite complex; the baby must develop suction with the muscles of the mouth and bring the resulting food into the stomach without cutting off the air supply. In a full-term baby, the neuronal networks and muscles necessary for doing all of this are present and in working order at the moment of birth. (One of the many problems premature babies can have is that this complex mechanism may not yet be functional.)

So now ask yourself, how does a new baby have any fun? It is not from anything done with the arms or legs because they do not really work yet. The primary source of pleasure for a newborn, and the one place on his or her body where the newborn can meaningfully interact with the environment, is right there in the mouth. It stands to reason, therefore, that the mouth will be the first place psychic energy is focused. The **oral stage** of psychological development lasts from birth to about 18 months. Like every stage, it has a physical focus, a psychological theme, and an associated adult character type.

The physical focus of the oral stage, as just discussed, is on the mouth, lips, and tongue. Freud sometimes said that for an infant these are sexual organs, another remark that seems almost deliberately designed to be misunderstood. What Freud meant was that during this stage the mouth is where the life force and primary feelings of pleasure are concentrated. Eating is an important source of pleasure, but so too are sucking on things and exploring the world with one's mouth.

When a baby begins to get control over the hands and arms, and sees some small, interesting object, what is the first thing he or she does? The baby puts the object in the mouth—often to the distress of the parents. Many parents assume the baby is trying to eat the ball, or the pencil, or the dead cockroach. But that is not the baby's real intention. The baby's hands are simply not developed enough to be much use for exploration. When you pick up something interesting, you fondle it, turn it around, feel its texture and its heft. None of this works for a baby because too many fine-motor skills are required; putting the object in the mouth can be more informative and interesting, because the mouth is more developed than the hands.

The psychological theme of the oral stage is dependency. A small baby is utterly, even pathetically, dependent on others for everything he or she needs to live. The baby is passive in the sense that there is very little the baby can do for himself or herself (though the baby may be far from passive in demands about what others should do). The baby's main psychological experience at this stage, therefore, is lying back and having others either provide everything the baby needs, or not. Either way, there is not much the baby can do about it, besides make plenty of noise. Another way to make more or less the same point is to observe that, at the oral stage, the baby is all id. That is, the baby *wants*, full time: to be fed, to be held, to be changed, to be warm and comfortable, to be entertained. Wanting stuff is the id's specialty. Actually doing something about it is the job of psychological structures that will, along with the necessary physical competencies, develop only later.

If a baby's needs at this stage of life are fulfilled to a reasonable degree, then attention and psychic energy will move along in due course to the next stage. Two things might go wrong, however. One is that the needs might *not* be fulfilled. The caretakers might be so uncaring, incompetent, or irresponsible that the baby is not fed when hungry, covered when cold, or comforted when upset. If this happens, the baby may develop a basic mistrust of the world and never be able to deal adequately with dependency relationships. The idea of depending on other people—or of being betrayed or abandoned by them— will forever make him or her upset, although he or she might not realize why.

A second thing that might happen is that a baby's needs are fulfilled so instantly and automatically that it never occurs to him or her that the world could respond differently. The increasing demands—and poor service—the world later provides, therefore, come as quite a shock. He or she may wish to be back at the oral stage, where all that was necessary was to want something and it immediately and almost magically appeared. Again, any issue that comes up in the baby's later life involving dependency, passivity, and activity might make him or her very anxious, though again he or she may be unaware as to just why.

Here we see the principle of opposites again. (It will resurface many, many times.) Either one extreme kind of childhood experience or its exact opposite, according to Freud, will yield equivalently pathological results. The ideal, Freud believed, was in the middle. For a child-rearing strategy, Freud would recommend that a parent make reasonable efforts to fulfill a child's wants and needs at the oral stage but not go overboard by making sure every wish is instantly gratified, *nor* neglect the child so much that the child starts to doubt that he or she will get what he or she really needs.

I find it surprising that Freud gets so little credit for having been such a consistent and profound moderate. He disliked extremes of any kind—of behavior, of child-rearing styles, of personality types, of attitudes—in part because he saw both ends of most scales as equivalently pathological.[6] Freud's

---

[6]We can see a modern version of this idea in the conclusion of most clinical psychologists that personality disorders are extreme positions on the normal range of personality trait variation (Clark, Livesley, & Morey 1997).

ideal was always the golden mean; his adherence to this ideal is one of the most consistent and praiseworthy aspects of his approach.

The adult personality type Freud thought was the result of either extreme style of childhood experience at this stage is the *oral character*. If you are starting to get used to how Freud thought about things, you will not be surprised to learn that the oral character comes in one of two extreme types. Both share an obsession, discomfort, and fundamental irrationality about any issue related to dependency and passivity. At one extreme are the supposedly independent souls who refuse to accept help from anyone, who are determined to go it alone no matter what the cost. To these people, no accomplishment means anything unless it is done without assistance. At the other extreme are the passive individuals who wait around, seemingly forever, for their ships to come in. They do nothing to better their situation, yet are continually bewildered—and sometimes angry—about their failure to get what they want. To them, wanting something should be enough to make it appear. That is how it works for babies, after all; they feel hunger or some other need and cry, and somebody takes care of them. It is almost as if, as adults, oral characters expect the same strategy to work.

Both types are oral types, and at root they are equivalent, Freud believed. One interesting sign of their equivalence is how these people flip from one type to another. When they change, they go not to the middle but to the other end of the scale, which psychologically is closer to their original position. Someone who is aggressively independent, for example, may suddenly become completely passive and dependent when things do not go right. Someone who is completely passive may one day conclude that things are not going as they should and may move, not to the middle, but to the other extreme, disdaining help and trying to be independent to a degree that is not sensible.

I have a relative who while in his thirties was once described as the world's oldest sixteen-year-old (which is actually an insult to many sixteen-year-olds). He is an intelligent, likable person but he seems utterly unable to connect what he wants with what he must do. A few years ago he announced at a family gathering that he had finally formulated a career goal. We waited to hear what it was with some anticipation. He explained that he had thought about it carefully, worked out all of the figures, and decided that he wanted a job that paid $100,000 a year—*after taxes*. That would be enough to give him everything he wanted. And what would the job be? we asked. He seemed surprised by the question; he had not worked that part through, he said.

This is a classic attitude of an oral character. I think he believed, perhaps at some unconscious level, that all he had to do to get something was to make it clear that he wanted it. The idea that more might be required was somehow foreign. In general, oral characters seem to spend much more time thinking about what they want than about how to get it.

Some students show a related attitude. At the end of the semester, they plead for a higher grade on the grounds that they need it. Often, they make an eloquent case for why they *really* need it. That should be enough, they seem to feel. The idea that attending class and doing the necessary work was the way to get what they wanted, rather than simply demanding it after the course was over, seems not to have occurred to them. Honestly, maybe it never did.

The reverse kind of oral character, the person who is chronically and pathologically independent, seems for some reason to be more rare. Yet I have seen the same relative who I just described disdain even the most minor help in preparing a cookout or fixing a car. Perhaps you know people who insist "I can do it myself" when in the midst of utter failure.

Again, the ideal is the middle. A person who has resolved the oral stage accepts help gracefully but is not utterly dependent on it and understands that people are ultimately responsible for their own outcomes.

Anal Stage

The glory of life at the oral stage is that you do not have to do anything. Because you cannnot take care of yourself in any way, you are not expected to. You do and express whatever you feel like (and whatever you can), whenever you want. Well and truly, this is too good to last.

Many breast-feeding mothers have had the experience of their baby, sucking away, suddenly trying out his or her new teeth with a good, strong bite. You can imagine how mom reacts: she yells, "Yow!" (or something stronger) and instantly pulls the baby off. And you know how the baby reacts: with outrage, anger, frustration, and maybe even fear (if mom yelled loudly enough). The reaction and consequences of its action come to the baby as a rude shock. What do you mean, I can't bite when I feel like it? Moreover, the baby will quickly discover that until he or she can muster enough self-control to stop biting, the groceries will fail to be forthcoming. This experience is an early and ominous forewarning of what later life holds in store.

As the child grows a little older, the demands of the world escalate rapidly. The child becomes expected to do a few things for himself or herself—to control emotions to some degree, for example. As the child begins to understand language, he or she will begin to be expected to follow orders. The child will be taught the word *no*—a new and alarming concept. And—something that famously got Freud's attention—the child begins to be expected to control his or her bowels and processes of elimination. Toilet training begins.

From all of this, the child begins to develop a new psychological structure: the ego. The ego's job is to mediate between what the child wants, and what is actually possible. It is the rudimentary ego that must figure out that breast-feeding only will continue as long as biting ceases, and it is through painful lessons like this that the ego begins to develop a wide range of capabilities—at least sometimes—to control the rest of the mind in a rational manner.

The physical focus of the **anal stage** is the anus and associated eliminative organs. Learning the sensations of "having to go" and dealing with them appropriately are important tasks of this stage. Freud and others pointed out that a good deal of everyday language seems to reveal an emotional resonance with the processes and products of elimination. This includes not only many standard insults and expletives with which I am sure you are familiar, but also descriptions of some people (anal characters as it turns out) as "uptight," or the common advice to "let it all out" (which of course is advice to relax self-control and act "naturally").

But here I am going to bend Freud a bit (in the direction of Eriksonian theory; see Chapter 12). I think in the classic theory there is a misleading degree of emphasis on literal defecation and the supposed physical pleasures thereof. Toilet training is an important part of life during the anal stage and seems to be the source of some powerful symbolic language. But it is just one example, among many, of the increasing demands for obedience and self-control that begin around the age of 18 months. As the child develops the capacity to control his or her bowels, the parents, tired of diapers, are eager to have the child use it. But this escalation of expectation applies to many other circumstances as well, from "get your own drink of water" to "don't touch that!" All of these experiences, happening at once and for the very first time, are part of a dramatic turning point in life, tied to a powerful set of psychological themes.

The primary psychological theme of the anal stage is *self-control* and its corollary, *obedience*. At about 18-months-old, a child begins to locomote efficiently and to be able to do other things for himself or herself; the child also begins to have the ability to control urges, including the urge to defecate, but including other urges as well, such as the urge to cry, or to grab a forbidden object, or to hit a baby sister. Authority figures—usually the parents—begin to insist that the child use his or her new self-control capacities.

There is a lot to learn at the anal stage and things do not always go smoothly. Typically, a child will try to figure out just how much power the authority figures in his or her life really have, as opposed to how much the child gets to decide for himself or herself. The child does this by testing the parents, by repeatedly experimenting to find the boundaries of what he or she can get away with. What happens if the child pulls the cat's tail after being told not to? If the parents say, "No more cookies," what happens if the child sneaks one anyway?

In the folklore of parenthood, this stage of testing is known as the "terrible twos." The child indeed can begin to seem like a little monster. But really, his or her behavior is perfectly rational. How will the child figure out how the world really works without some experimenting? The behavior can be exasperating, but it is normal and probably even necessary.

Two things can go wrong at the anal stage. As always in psychoanalytic thinking, the two mistakes are polar opposites, and the ideal is in the middle. Unreasonable expectations can be traumatic. If demands are insistently made that the child is simply not capable of meeting—for example, that the child never cry, or always obey, or hold bowels longer than the child's physical capability allows—the result can be a psychological trauma with long-lasting consequences. And the opposite—never demanding that the child control urges, neglecting toilet training altogether—can be equally problematic.

As at every stage, the developmental task of the child is to figure out what is going on in the world and how to deal with it. At the anal stage, the child must figure out how and how much to control himself or herself, and how and how much to allow himself or herself to be controlled by those in authority. This is a thorny issue to resolve, even for an adult. A child will never work it through sufficiently if the environment is too harsh *or* too lenient.

Relatively recent research that followed a sample of children from childhood into late adolescence basically confirmed this Freudian view. The parents of these children were classified as authoritarian (extremely rigid and obedience oriented), permissive (weak and lacking control), or authoritative (having found a compromise between firm control and allowing their children freedom). As Freud would have anticipated, it was the authoritative parents—the ones in the middle—whose children fared the best later in life (Baumrind, 1971, 1991).[7]

Psychological mishaps at the anal stage produce the adult *anal character*. The anal character has a personality overly organized around issues concerning control. As always, this might go either of two ways. One way is to become obsessive, compulsive, stingy, orderly, rigid, and subservient to authority. This kind of person insists on trying to control every aspect of his or her life and often seems equally happy to be controlled, in turn, by an authority figure. He or she cannot tolerate disorganization or ambiguity. Long ago, one of my abnormal psychology professors said he had a one-item test for detecting an anal character: Go to that person's room, and you will see on the desk a row of pencils or other items aligned in a perfectly straight line. Reach over casually and turn one of the pencils at a ninety-degree angle. Start timing. If within two minutes the person has quietly reached over and moved the pencil back, he or she is an anal character. (This is too facile, of course, but you get the idea.)

---

[7]This finding may be limited to the Western culture with which Freud was most familiar. Recent evidence suggests that authoritative versus authoritarian parenting may have very different implications and consequences in an Asian cultural context (Chao, 2001).

The other type of anal character is exactly the opposite. This person may have little or no self-control, be unable to do anything on time or because it is necessary, be chaotic and disorganized, and have a compulsive need to defy authority. Freud saw this type of person as psychologically equivalent to the other type of anal character and further believed that it was more likely that such individuals would flip from one anal extreme to the other than that either would attain the ideal position in the middle.

There is a lame joke dating from the 1970s that expresses the equivalence of the two anal types. The two-part joke goes like this:

Q: Why did the short-hair cross the road?
A: Because somebody told him to.
Q: Why did the long-hair cross the road?
A: Because somebody told him not to.[8]

The point of this joke is that crossing the road either because somebody told you to or because somebody told you not to is equally and equivalently foolish. Your behavior is under the control of somebody else in both cases. The ideal is to cross the road because you want to, because *you* have decided it is the most reasonable thing to do.

Freud's point is similar. If you are rigidly organized and obedient because you must be, you have a problem. If you are completely disorganized and disobedient because you cannot help it, you also have a problem—in fact, you have the same problem. Self-control and relations to authority should be means to ends, not ends in themselves. The ideal is to determine how, whether, and to what degree to organize your life and how you relate to authority, in order to move toward the goals that are important to you.

Phallic Stage

The next stage of development begins with a recognition: Boys and girls are different. According to psychoanalytic theory, this fact begins to sink in at around the age of three-and-a-half to four years and dominates psychological development until about the age of seven.

The specific realization that occurs at the **phallic stage**, according to Freud, is that boys have penises and girls do not—hence the name of the stage. (Maybe this is not as universal as Freud thought. I once asked one of my daughters,

---

[8]This joke relies on a stereotypical image from the late 1960s: men with short hair were viewed as conservative and subservient to authority; men with long hair were assumed to be radical and disobedient. Today, hairstyles seem to be less diagnostic of political attitudes.

then not quite four years old, what the difference was between boys and girls. "Boys do not have crotches," she instantly replied.) The basic task of the phallic stage is coming to terms with sex differences and all that they imply.

According to Freud, the physical focus of the phallic stage, for either sex, is the penis. Boys, having noticed that girls do not have one, wonder what happened and if the same thing could happen to them. Girls just wonder what happened.

Hard-core adherents of orthodox psychoanalysis launch into a pretty complicated story at this point. It involves boys' fear of castration by their fathers in a rivalry for the affection of the mother, and girls' grief over a castration that supposedly has already occurred. To resolve this anxiety, or grief, each child identifies with the same-sex parent, taking on many of his or her values and ideals while lessening feelings of rivalry and jealousy that might otherwise reach a critical level. The full story of the Oedipal crisis (referring to the Greek myth of the man who unknowingly killed his father and married his mother) is rich and fascinating, and the summary just presented (which you have noticed was exactly two sentences long) fails to do it justice. Nevertheless, I will not say much more about the Oedipus story here, in part because it is so well told elsewhere. The best rendition in English may be the one provided by Bettelheim (1982). A more important reason for not getting too deeply into the traditional story of the phallic stage is that it has not held up well in the light of empirical research (Sears, 1947). So, I will discuss what happens at this point in development in simpler and more modern terms.[9]

It seems obvious that the realization that the sexes differ must be an important milestone in psychological development. It also seems only natural that with this realization comes the realization that one parent is male and the other female. I do not think it is far-fetched to think that children wonder about the essence of the attraction between their parents, and that they fantasize to some degree about what a relationship with their opposite-sex parent would be like. And, although this may push the envelope a bit, I even think it plausible that children feel guilty to some degree, at some level, about having such fantasies. The fantasies probably seem rather outlandish even to children, and they probably suspect their same-sex parent would not exactly be thrilled if he or she knew what they were thinking.

The psychological theme of the phallic stage is the need to figure out what it means to be a boy or girl. For most children, the best, or at least most obvious, examples in their immediate vicinities are their mothers and fathers. One easy way to be a girl is to act like mom. To be a boy, act like dad. This

---

[9]Here is yet another place where I am straying from what Freud literally said, and substituting a contemporary rendition that strikes me as more sensible in the light of modern knowledge, yet also consistent with the spirit of what Freud meant.

can mean taking on many of their attitudes, values, and ways of relating to the opposite sex. This is the process Freud called **identification**.[10]

Related psychological themes of the phallic stage include love, sexuality, fear, and jealousy. The adult consequences of what happens at the phallic stage include the development of morality, which Freud saw as a by-product of the process of identification; the values of your same-sex parent provide the beginning of your own moral outlook. Another adult consequence is the eventual development of sexuality—what kind of person you find attractive, how you handle sexual competition, and the overall role and importance of sexuality in your life. The most important result of the phallic stage is an image of oneself as masculine or feminine, along with whatever that means to you.

Additional identifications are possible and even likely as well. A child might take on the values and behaviors of an admired teacher, relative, or religious leader or of a rock or sports star. In most cases identifications are with people who are loved and admired, but in some circumstances an individual might identify with someone who is loathed and feared. During World War II, inmates in Nazi death camps reportedly sometimes identified with their guards, making Nazi armbands and uniforms from scraps and giving each other the "Heil Hitler" salute. According to the psychoanalyst Bruno Bettelheim (who was an inmate at Dachau and Buchenwald himself), this seemingly strange behavior was an adaptation to deal with their profound (and realistic) fear of the guards; to become more like the guards was to fear them less (Bettelheim, 1943). I suspect milder forms of this same behavior—trying to become more like the people one most fears—are actually rather common and are probably one basis for the development of the superego. People sometimes identify with a teacher they hate, a coach they fear, an older student who hazes them, or a drill sergeant (or an entire branch of the military) who gives them nothing but abuse. In the process, these characters become less fearful while the person becomes a little more like them.

Wherever they come from, and again the usual source is the parents, the sum total of one's identifications make up the third major psychic structure (after the id and ego): the superego. The superego is the part of the mind that passes moral judgment on the other parts, a moral judgment based on a complex mixture of all the different moral lessons taught, directly and by example, by everybody one has ever identified with. When successfully developed, the superego provides a conscience and a basis for reasonable morality.

---

[10]The personal lives of many students intersect with the content of a personality course at this point. I have been asked many times, "what happens at this stage if a child is raised by a single parent?" Such questions are not merely hypothetical. I wish I had a good answer. The best I can manage is that these children look elsewhere for salient examples of maleness and femaleness, perhaps to relatives, friends, teachers, or (shudder) the mass media.

But as always, the development of the superego is a process that might go too far, or might not go far enough.

An overdeveloped or underdeveloped superego yields the adult character type labeled "phallic." A person who has developed a completely rigid moral code, one that brooks no shades of gray and no exceptions, may be a *phallic type.* So is someone who lacks such a code altogether. A person who is extremely active and promiscuous in his or her sexual behavior might be a phallic type. So too might someone who becomes completely asexual. Male homosexuality might have its roots here, although psychoanalysis, in my opinion, does not offer a very convincing detailed account of just how. (The story basically involves a boy who falls so deeply in love with his mother that all other women become intolerable rivals. To avoid disloyalty to mom, he then turns to members of his own gender for sexual gratification.) An extremely "loose" pattern of sexual behavior might be one manifestation of a phallic character; so too might an overly rigid and puritanical one. As always, Freud was suspicious of the extremes; he viewed the middle as the healthy place to be.

Genital Stage

After the phallic stage, a child gets a chance to take a developmental breath and concentrate on the important learning tasks of childhood, such as learning to read, the names of the state capitals, arithmetic, and all of the other important stuff taught in elementary school. This *latency* phase is a sort of psychological respite to allow the child to do much of the learning he or she will need in adult life. The rest period ends, with a bang, at puberty.

It is no accident, I am sure, that the American school system traditionally moves students to a different school beginning around the sixth or seventh grade. At that time, things are becoming importantly different, and these kids do not really belong with the little ones. Just a couple of years later, some important changes have been completed, and it is necessary to move these kids again, to high school. The American school system doesn't usually advertise itself in this way, but it works like this: elementary school = prepuberty; intermediate school = process of puberty; high school = physically adult (psychological adulthood is another story).

The **genital stage** of development is fundamentally different from all of the others because Freud saw it not as something individuals necessarily pass through, but something they must *attain.* Sometime after physical puberty, if all goes well, a person develops a mature attitude about sexuality and other aspects of adulthood. Freud is not explicit about when this happens; in some people, apparently, it never happens.

The physical focus of the genital stage is the genitals, but notice how this label differs from that for the phallic stage. *Genital* describes not just a physical organ; the word also refers to the process of reproduction or giving life. The genitals, at this stage, become not just organs of physical pleasure, but the source of new life and the basis of a new psychological theme.

The psychological theme of the genital stage is the creation and enhancement of life. True maturity, Freud believed, entailed the ability to bring new life into the world and to nurture its growth. This includes children, but it also can include other kinds of creativity, such as intellectual, artistic, or scientific contributions. The developmental task of the genital stage is to learn how to add something constructive to life and to society, and to take on the adult responsibility to do just that. In that sense, the psychological theme of the genital stage is *maturity*. And, as I mentioned, not everybody attains it. The *genital character* is psychologically well adjusted and—here comes the key term—*balanced*.

Freud made one trip to the United States, early in the twentieth century, where much to his dismay he found himself trailed by newspaper reporters who apparently found some of his sexual theories titillating, especially after they had finished distorting them. Freud's lifelong aversion to America and anything American seems only to have been boosted by this experience. But the trip was not a total loss. At one point, a reporter asked him the following question: "Dr. Freud, what is your definition of mental health?" Freud replied with the single best answer that anybody has ever come up with. The essence of **mental health**, he said, is the ability "to love and to work."

The most important word in this definition is *and*. Freud thought it was important to love, to have a mate and family to care for and nurture. He also thought it was important to work, to do something useful and constructive for society. The good life, Freud thought, would always contain *both*. To do just one was to be an incomplete person. The truly mature person—the one who has attained the genital stage—has learned to balance both kinds of generativity, love *and* work.

Today we hear accounts of the difficulties many women have in balancing families and careers. In our society, one seems to conflict with the other, and to have it all is a nearly insurmountable challenge. Freud would have approved of the way women make this struggle, I think. After all, the balance of those two things is what life is all about.[11]

Consider today's men, by contrast. The word *workaholic* has been coined to describe what many men have become. These men experience little conflict between work and home because they have simply given up on, or delegated, the home part. Are they better off? Freud would not think so. To leave out one of the two things that a person must balance in life is not psy-

---

[11]Actually, perhaps Freud would *not* have approved. In his personal life he seems to have been a typical conservative, Victorian sexist. But I think the spirit of Freudian thought is exactly compatible with what many modern women are trying to accomplish.

chological health—it's arrested development. The balance many women are trying to achieve, therefore, implies that they are psychologically more fully developed than the men who gave up on the struggle before it even started.

I had just finished making this point in class one day when a (female) student startled me by asking, "Does this imply that women are psychologically healthier than men?" I had not thought about it quite that way, but pushed for an answer I said, "Yes." On reflection, I still think that answer is correct. When you consider what the ideal genital character is supposed to be like, more women attain it than men.

Moving Through Stages

As we have seen, an important consequence of movement through the stages of development is the building of the basic psychological structures. At the beginning of the oral stage, the newborn baby is all *id*—a seething pool of wants and needs. As the baby moves into the anal stage, experiences of frustration and delay lead part of the mind to differentiate and separate from the id, taking some of its energy along with it, leading to the formation of the *ego*. The ego has the ability and the duty to control and channel, to some degree, the urges of the id. At the phallic stage, the child forms identifications with important persons in his or her life, principally the parents, and the sum total of these identifications forms the third structure, the *superego*. The superego is the conscience; it sits in judgment on the person's actions and urges, and sometimes tries to stop them.

Freud once used a different analogy, that a mind progressing through the stages of psychological development is a little like an army conquering a hostile territory. Periodically it encounters opposition and difficulty and at that point a battle ensues. To secure the ground after the battle is over, some troops are left behind as the army advances. If the battle was particularly bitter and if the local resistance remains strong, a larger part of the army must be left behind—leaving less with which to advance. Moreover, if the main army encounters severe problems later, it is likely to retreat to one of its strongholds, which will be the site of a former battle.

The store of libido is the army in this analogy. It encounters "battles" at each of the developmental stages. If the battle of the oral or anal or phallic stage is not completely won, libidinal energy must be left behind at that point. The result will be **fixation**. The adult will be dominated by issues from that stage and will tend to retreat there when under stress. Such retreat is called **regression**. An oral character under stress becomes passive and dependent and may even suck his or her thumb. An anal character under stress becomes even more rigid (or even more disorganized) than usual. A phallic character under stress may engage in promiscuous behavior (or become completely

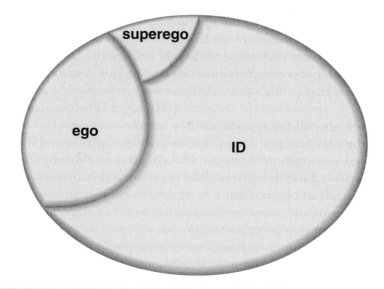

FIGURE 10.4   At birth the baby's psyche is "all id." The ego differentiates from the id at the anal stage, taking some of the id's energy with it. Later, at the phallic stage, the important identifications formed with other people (especially parents) form a third structure, the superego.

asexual). Victory, in this analogy, is making it through all of these stages to the final, genital stage, with as much of one's army as possible still intact. The more libido is left for the final stage of maturity, the better adjusted the adult will be.

Thinking and Consciousness

Underneath the progression through these psychosexual stages, the mind is also undergoing a subtle, profound, but incomplete shift between two kinds of thinking, called **primary process thinking** and **secondary process thinking.** Secondary process thinking is what we ordinarily mean by the word *think.* The conscious part of the ego thinks this way; it is thought that is rational, practical, and prudent and that can delay or redirect gratification. It is "secondary" in two senses. First, it develops only as the ego begins to develop; a newborn has no secondary process thinking. The other sense in which it is secondary is that Freud believed primary process thinking was more interesting, important, and powerful throughout life, not just in infancy.

Primary process thinking is the way in which the unconscious mind operates, and how the infant's (and later adult's) id is said to operate. It is a strange sort of thinking. The fundamental aspect of primary process thinking is that it does not contain the word (or even the idea) *no*. It is thinking without negatives, qualifications, sense of time, or any of the practicalities, necessities, or dangers of life. It has one goal: the immediate gratification of every desire.

Primary process thinking operates by an odd shorthand. It can tie disparate feelings closely together. Your feelings about your family can affect how you feel about your house, for example. Primary process thinking can use **displacement** to replace one idea or image with another: your anger toward your father might be replaced by anger with all authority figures, or your anger toward an authority might be transformed into anger at your father. **Condensation** can cause several ideas to be compressed into one; an image of a house or of a woman might contain within it a complex set of memories, thoughts, and emotions. And through **symbolization**, one thing might stand in for another.

At one point in his career, Freud thought there might be a universal symbolic grammar of the unconscious mind, in which certain symbols meant the same thing to everybody the world over. He thought people could use these symbols to interpret the meaning of dreams, and some of these are included in the little paperback books on dream analysis you can get at the supermarket. They include translations like:

house = human body
smooth-fronted house = male body

house with ledges and balconies = female body
king and queen = parents
little animals = children
children = genitals
playing with children = (you fill in this one)
going on a journey = dying
clothes = nakedness
going up stairs = having sex
bath = birth

Freud later dropped the idea of universal symbols. He decided that their meaning varies for every individual and therefore a general "dictionary" of the unconscious was not really very useful. The idea of unconscious universal ideas was picked up with a vengeance, however, by Carl Jung (see Chapter 12).

Primary process thinking is a very interesting kind of thinking, but one might reasonably ask, where, if it is a property of the unconscious mind, is it ever seen? Freud thought that primary process thinking could emerge into consciousness under several limited circumstances. The conscious thought of very small children operates according to primary process, but because they have developed secondary process thinking by the time they can talk, this idea is difficult to verify (actually it is impossible). He also thought primary process thinking can become conscious during fever deliriums and during dreams. This is consistent with the experience of many people that in dreams (or deliriums) one has no sense of time, one person can change into another, images serve as symbols of other things, and so on. Freud also thought that psychotics sometimes experience primary process thinking; if you ever listen to the speech of a schizophrenic for any length of time, you will see where Freud got this idea.

But instances in which primary process thinking emerges directly into consciousness are relatively rare. More important, Freud believed, are the more ordinary and indirect ways that primary process thinking can be seen to influence conscious thought and overt behavior. The results of primary process thinking often "leak" into slips of the tongue, accidents, lapses of memory, and the like (see Chapter 11).

Freud posited three levels to consciousness in what is sometimes called his *topographic model*. (*Topography* refers to elevation; a topographic map is one that shows the elevations of the hills and valleys over an expanse of territory.) The smallest, topmost, and, Freud thought, least important layer is the **conscious mind**, that part of your mental functioning you can observe when you simply turn your attention inward. A second layer, the **preconscious**, consists of those things you are not thinking about at the

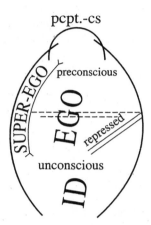

FIGURE 10.5   Freud's own diagram of the relationship between consciousness and the id, ego, and superego. The "pcpt.-cs" is the area of conscious perception. Freud wrote about this diagram, "It is certainly hard to say today how far the drawing is correct. In one respect it is undoubtedly not. The space occupied by the unconscious id ought to have been incomparably greater than that of the ego or the preconscious. I must ask you to correct it in your thoughts" (cited in Funder & Ozer, 2004).

moment, but that you could bring into consciousness easily if you wished. For example, how is the weather outside right now? What did you have for breakfast? Where is your car parked? Who is the president of the United States? None of these things was in your conscious mind until I asked (presumably), but you probably had little trouble bringing them into your conscious awareness.

The third, the biggest, and, Freud thought, the most important layer of the mind is the **unconscious**. The unconscious includes all of the id and superego and most of the ego. The unconscious is buried deep; the only way to bring it to the surface is by digging. One method of digging that Freud used early in his career is hypnosis. Other clues can come from slips of the tongue, accidents, and lapses of memory. All have their causes in mental processes that occur outside of consciousness. Finally, Freud developed the technique of *free association,* in which a person is encouraged to say whatever comes to mind in relation to some concern or issue. Freud thought the wanderings of free association were never random (he never thought *anything* was random), and that the way a person jumps from one thought to another can provide important clues about his or her unconscious.

I know of one psychoanalyst who, following these precepts, explains to his patients that they should tell him whatever comes to mind, because their thoughts, feelings, and motives are all connected with one another along complex networks of associations. We often lack conscious access to these networks, but they can be uncovered. One goal of psychoanalysis is to map these networks to see the context in which a symptom is embedded and to get a better idea of how the patient's mind works (Drew Westen, personal communication, April 28, 1994).

Psychoanalytic Therapy

The core purpose of psychoanalytic therapy is to use all of these various clues to reveal the contents of the unconscious. Freud believed that the problems that make most people anxious and unhappy have their roots in conflicts within the unconscious mind. The way to resolve these conflicts is to bring them into the open, through dream analysis, analysis of slips and lapses, and free association. Once an unconscious conflict is brought into consciousness, the rational part of the ego is able to deal with it and the conflict will no longer pose a problem. In the long run of therapy, Freud believed that the achievement of insight into the hidden parts of the mind would allow a person to take full, rational control of oneself (Freud was nothing if not a rationalist.)

Of course, the process is a bit more complicated than that. Unconscious conflicts must be dealt with not just rationally, but emotionally, which takes

"Why do you think you cross the road?"

time and can be painful. It can even be dangerous. As the psychoanalytic psychologist Robert Bornstein pointed out,

> some patients with a history of severe sexual or physical abuse do not have the psychological resources available to cope adequately with explicit memories of these experiences. For these patients, therapeutic work should focus primarily on bolstering defenses and coping mechanisms. Only when these resources have been strengthened can insight be used productively within and outside of therapy. (Bornstein, 1999, p. 169)

As people bring their conflicts to the surface, they often begin to feel worse anxiety in the short run; the prospect of losing one's neuroses can be surprisingly disconcerting. Many people avoid dealing with their unconscious anxieties for this reason; Freud called the phenomenon of running away from the solution to one's psychological problems the "flight from health." It is very common; it may be the real point every time you hear someone say, "I don't want to talk about it."

To comfort, guide, and support the client through this difficult healing process, Freud believed, there must be an emotional bond between therapist and client. The development of this bond is called the *therapeutic alliance.* This alliance gets its power through **transference**, the tendency to bring ways of thinking, feeling, and behaving that developed with one important person into a later relationship with a different person. One might relate to a teacher in the same way one learned to relate, years earlier, to one's father, for example (see Chapter 12's discussion of *object relations*). Transference is particularly important in psychotherapy, because the emotional relationship the patient develops with the therapist is built on the model of that patient's past relationships with other important people. (The therapist may develop emotional feelings for the patient as well; this is called *countertransference.*)

The development of transference (and countertransference) in therapy is important, but it can also be dangerous. Freud was perhaps the first psychotherapist to note that sexual attractions between clients and psychotherapists are quite common. He was absolutely adamant that it was the duty of the therapist to resist acting on this attraction. The patient *must* get emotionally involved for the therapy to work, Freud believed, and perhaps the therapist as well, but the therapist must *avoid* acting on his or her own involvement at all costs.

Psychoanalysis often is criticized for its allegedly low (or even zero) demonstrable cure rate, and for the fact that it can last for many years and perhaps never end. Many psychoanalysts have become heavily involved in a debate over the therapeutic efficacy of their techniques, but late in his career Freud himself began to see it all as beside the point:

> After forty-one years of medical activities, my self-knowledge tells me that I have not been a physician in the proper sense. . . . [My real interests are] the

events of the history of man, the mutual influences between man's nature, the development of culture, and those residues of prehistoric events of which religion is the foremost representation . . . studies which originate with psychoanalysis but go way beyond it. (From *The Question of Lay Analysis*, as translated by Bettelheim, 1982, p. 48)

In the end, Freud was surprisingly uninterested in psychoanalysis as a medical or therapeutic technique, an attitude that some modern practicing psychotherapists also share (Bader, 1994). He saw its real importance as a tool for better understanding human nature and culture.

Summary

Unlike many other approaches to personality, the psychoanalytic approach concentrates on the cases where the cause of behavior is mysterious and hidden. Psychoanalytic theory is based on a relatively small number of key ideas, including psychic determinism, internal structure, mental energy, and psychic conflict. Psychoanalysis has been controversial throughout its history, although the nature of the controversy has changed with the times. Freud himself was one of the significant geniuses of the twentieth century.

Freud's psychoanalytic theory posits two fundamental motives, a life drive, or libido, and a drive toward death and destruction. Libido produces psychic energy, and the story of psychological development is the story of how this energy is focused in different areas at four different stages of life. Each stage has a physical focus, a psychological theme, and an adult character type that results if development at the stage does not go well. The main issue for the oral stage is dependency; for the anal stage it is obedience and self-control; for the phallic stage it is gender identity and sexuality; and for the genital stage it is maturity, in which ideally one learns to balance "love and work." The different structures of the mind arise during progression through these developmental stages. The newborn baby is "all id." The ego develops at the anal stage as a result of experiences with frustration and delay, and the superego develops at the phallic stage as a result of identifications with significant other people, especially the parents. Fixation occurs when an individual gets to some degree "stuck" in a stage of childhood development; regression is a movement backward from a later psychological stage to an earlier one.

Primary process thinking, assumed by Freud to be present in babies and in the unconscious part of the adult mind, is a primitive style of unconscious thought, characterized by association, displacement, symbolization, and an irrational, uncompromising drive toward immediate gratification. Secondary process thinking, which develops as the child moves toward adulthood, is ordinary, rational, conscious thought. The three layers to consciousness are the conscious mind, the preconscious, and the unconscious, of which Freud thought the conscious mind was by far the smallest. The essence of psychoanalytic therapy, performed through techniques such as dream analysis and free association in the context of a therapeutic alliance between patient and therapist, is to bring the unconscious thoughts that are the source of an individual's problems into the open, where the conscious, rational mind can deal with them.

THE WORKINGS OF THE UNCONSCIOUS MIND: DEFENSES AND SLIPS

Some facts, thoughts, or feelings, if you were to become consciously aware of them, would make you feel uncomfortable or even intolerably anxious, perhaps to the point that you could no longer function. You also have some behavioral urges, Freud believed, that would get you in big trouble if they were ever actually expressed. An important responsibility of the ego, therefore, is to keep these disturbing parts of mental life safely locked up inside the unconscious sectors of the mind. The techniques the ego uses to keep certain thoughts and behavioral impulses hidden, to avoid anxiety, are called the **defense mechanisms**.

Defense mechanisms are not always effective, however. Thoughts, words, and even actions occasionally leak out. You might think something that you do not understand yourself, say something you did not mean to say, or do something against your conscious, better judgment. These "Freudian slips" (also called *parapraxes*; one slip is a **parapraxis**) can be embarrassing and even dangerous, and they also provide important clues about what is going on in the unconscious part of the mind.

Freud believed that the ego also sometimes permits otherwise forbidden thoughts and feelings to leak out into action on purpose, a sort of "venting" that allows the ordinarily forbidden to be enjoyed. The mechanism by which this is accomplished is wit, or humor. A humorous action, statement, or joke is a mechanism that allows an impulse or feeling that is ordinarily seen as dangerous to be enjoyed in safety.

These, then, are the three main topics of this chapter on the unconscious workings of the mind: anxiety and the defense mechanisms, slips, and humor. The chapter concludes with an overall evaluation of Freud's contribution to psychology.

Anxiety

Anxiety is an unpleasant state that can range from a vague and uneasy sense that not all is right with the world to desperate and debilitating terror—the classic "anxiety attack." Anxiety can come from within the mind itself—

this is the kind of anxiety Freud found most interesting—and also from the outside world.

Anxiety from Psychic Conflict

For each of us, there are things we want, things that are possible, and things that are morally the right thing to do. Wouldn't it be wonderful if everything were all three? But of course life is not that simple. To want something we can never have, or to be tempted to do something we know is wrong, is a common human experience. Right now, for example, the odds are you are supposed to be reading this book. If you are a college student, then reading this book is the right thing to do: college students are expected to do their homework, and what are your hard-working parents writing those checks for anyway, if you are so ungrateful as to not even bother to do your reading? (Thus speaks your superego.) Moreover, it is the prudent thing to do. Flunking out is bad; A's are pleasant to receive. The latter becomes more likely relative to the former, the more diligently you do your reading. (Thus speaks your ego.) And yet, and yet . . . there is a party right down the hall. Music is playing, people are laughing, and this chapter seems to be going on *forever.* (Thus speaks your id.) All of these statements are correct, so what will you actually do? The answer is far from certain. The tension among these three aspects of reality—what is right, what is possible, and what we want— is a perpetual fact of existence. If we stay and read, part of us will pine for the party. And, sadly, even if we throw the book down and go to the party, part of us will wish we were back in our room, getting our work done.

We saw in the previous chapter that, according to psychoanalytic theory, the mind is divided into three parts, each with its own specialized function. The id keeps track of (and generates) what we want; the superego provides moral judgment, and the ego tries to figure what is the rational thing to do, with the id and superego both shouting in its metaphorical ear. Because desires, morals, and possibilities are so often in conflict, the id, ego, and superego, likewise—and perhaps typically—are also in conflict. **Psychic conflict** is what goes on in a mind battling itself. The result is *anxiety.*

Suppose you see a small boy, standing with his mother and holding a delicious-looking piece of candy. You may not be aware of the feeling, but your id may immediately want that candy and create an impulse to reach out and grab it. If this happens, both the ego and the superego will swing quickly into action. The ego will realize that grabbing candy from a child in full view of his mother is likely to lead to serious difficulties, such as being yelled at or possibly even arrested. The superego will be horrified at the idea that the id would even think of doing such a despicable thing. Both object, but for different reasons; the ego cares about practical consequences rather than right and wrong, and the superego cares about right and wrong rather than practical consequences.

In this example, both the ego and the superego will probably use their energy to push the id's impulse back down not only below the threshold of action but also below the lower threshold of awareness. You will never even know you were tempted. But consider what might happen if the problematic impulse and its prohibitions were particularly strong. Imagine a married person, deeply committed to his or her family, who experiences strong, lustful impulses toward an attractive, available individual of the opposite sex. This impulse creates problems, because although the temptation is real, the ego will probably calculate that acting on the impulse will cause terrible damage to the person's family and other areas of his or her life. On top of that, the superego may weigh in with the observation that acting on this impulse would violate every value the person holds dear. As a result of these strong oppositions, the impulse might be pushed almost completely out of awareness, although it remains present on some level, and the person might be conscious only of a vague feeling of uneasiness, anxiety, or guilt. Later on, the person might be unable to remember ever having met this attractive individual, or might develop a seemingly inexplicable dislike for him or her. (To remember might cause renewed anxiety; the development of any sort of friendship or liking might cause the forbidden impulse to get stronger.) The person may never know where the anxiety came from, why what seemed like a routine encounter was forgotten so quickly, or even why he or she "just doesn't like" someone who never did him or her any (intentional) harm.

Freud believed one particular conflict to be quite common. He believed that most people at times feel sexual attraction toward members of their own sex and that these latent homosexual feelings are pushed out of action and awareness both by the ego, on practical grounds, and the superego, on moral grounds (most people in Freud's era—as perhaps many are today—were raised with the idea that homosexuality is abhorrent and immoral). This constant but prohibited impulse is a persistent source of anxiety in many individuals, Freud believed, although they may never become consciously aware of the source of their discomfort.

Modern psychoanalysts called **ego psychologists** believe that compromise formation is the most important function of the ego (Brenner, 1982; Westen, 1998). When different parts of the mind want different things, the ego's job is to seek some way that all of them can get a little of what they want. For example, imagine a person whose superego strongly condemns pornography while his id loves the stuff. His ego might formulate a compromise in which he becomes an active antipornography crusader. He then can satisfy his superego by loudly and frequently condemning the evils of pornography, while at the same time collecting and viewing large amounts of pornography, all in reluctant service of the battle against it. This kind of compromise can be brittle, however, as we saw in Chapter 10.

The modern psychoanalyst Drew Westen (1998) described the case of a man who was conflicted about whether to remain in his unhappy marriage. He stayed married for many years, mostly because he would have felt guilty if he left his wife. When he finally did end his marriage, he declined opportunities to date two attractive women who were interested in him and instead continued to live alone in a seedy apartment. According to Westen, in therapy it emerged that his ego had reached the following compromise between the id that wanted freedom and the guilty superego: he allowed himself to leave his wife only if he also did the penance of never enjoying himself afterward, especially with other women. Of course, this compromise was reached unconsciously—he had no conscious idea that this is what he was doing. And while the compromise did work to alleviate his conflicting feelings, to some extent, it wasn't really satisfactory because it left him dissatisfied, unhappy, and vaguely anxious.

Vague anxiety of unknown origin is a quintessential Freudian symptom. When a client presents with the complaint "I feel bad and don't know why;" a psychoanalyst settles into the problem with relish. As we saw in Chapter 10, the whole purpose of psychoanalytic thereapy is to uncover—and eventually to relieve—hidden sources of anxiety.

Realistic Anxiety

To a degree that Freud probably underemphasized, the real world can create plenty of anxiety of its own. First is the unpleasant fact that all of us are mortal and so will die at some point. According to the *terror management theory* of Tom Pyszczynski, Jeff Greenberg, and Sheldon Solomon (1997), many of our thought processes and motivations are based on an effort to deal with (and avoid thinking about) this literally terrifying fact. Other aspects of life can produce anxiety as well. Relationships with other people (does she really love me?), performance in school (will I pass the course?), and career aspirations (will I be able to get a job, or keep the one I have?) are all elements of the real world that can make us realistically anxious. A particular source of anxiety, according to some writers, is any threat to our self-esteem (Cramer, 1998). We sometimes receive information that—looked at objectively—would seem to indicate that we are not as smart, good looking, moral, or lovable as we would like to believe.

None of this anxiety is pleasant, which raises an interesting question. Is it a good thing to experience it? Or should we just avoid these bad feelings any way we can? Psychologists continue to debate this question. According to one perspective, anxiety is something we should avoid even if we have to distort reality to do it (Taylor & Brown, 1988). To be realistic about one's position and chances in life can lead to depression; people who are optimistic to the point of distorting reality are happier and experience better mental health. From another perspective, this idea is dead wrong (Colvin & Block, 1994). The costs of distorting reality can be very high. Anxiety is often a sign that something is not right and needs to be dealt with. If we simply avoid feeling anxious, we might avoid dealing with the underlying problem. For example, some students deal with the anxiety of impending final exams by not thinking about them. In the short run, they are happier than those students who worry about studying, until the moment the exam begins or perhaps when final grades are announced. Then they are less happy. A little anxiety early on can save a lot of anxiety later (Norem & Chang, 2002).

The real trick, apparently, is to keep anxiety within bounds. Too much anxiety and a person can become completely nonfunctional and of no use to anybody. Too little anxiety and a person might fail to deal with real problems in a sensible manner. Sometimes we need to face reality directly; at other times, it seems, a little distortion becomes necessary (Paulhus, 1998). The purpose of defense mechanisms, well used, is to achieve this balance (Block, 2002).

Defense Mechanisms

The ego has a variety of tools at its disposal to keep anxiety within a tolerable range, regardless of whether this anxiety comes from internal, psychic conflict or from stressors in the real world. Sigmund Freud talked about defensive processes but never systematically organized them. It was left to his daughter, Anna, to create an inventory of the tools of psychological defense (A. Freud, 1936).

These tools are not used consciously (that would defeat their whole point); they are deployed by the unconscious part of the ego as soon as it detects a potential source of anxiety beginning to arise. The ego's defense strategies are varied and ingenious. The discussion that follows considers eight of them: *denial, repression, reaction formation, projection, rationalization, intellectualization, displacement,* and *sublimation.*

Denial

Denial is the simplest defense mechanism: one simply denies that the source of anxiety exists, or even fails to perceive it in the first place. This tactic is common and effective in the short run, but if used for very long can lead to a serious lack of contact with reality (Suls & Fletcher, 1985).

At one time my office was located directly across the hall from the location where grades for introductory psychology exams are posted. So I occasionally observed the moment when someone discovered he or she had failed an exam. How could I tell? By the audible defense mechanism of denial: these students would jump back from the grade roster and shout (at themselves more than at anybody else), "No!"

For most of these students, denial is just a temporary tactic. By refusing to believe what they have just seen, they give themselves a psychological breather to collect themselves and make a second run at the problem. As time passes they probably will acknowledge that, yes, they really failed the exam. They may even come back to the grade roster, in a somewhat calmer frame of mind, to double-check their score. At that point they will either deal realistically with the problem—study harder next time, for example— or invoke one or more of the more permanent defense mechanisms to deal with the anxiety produced by academic failure. In the long run, people are likely to take credit for their successes but blame their failures on external circumstances or other people (Zuckerman, 1979). According to several studies, when students perform poorly on a test, they tend to conclude that it is invalid, but if they do well, they think the test is just fine (Schlenker, Weigold, & Hallam, 1990). These skewed interpretations serve to protect one's self-esteem, but they also may prevent learning from one's mistakes.

Denial also can be used to defend against anxiety that comes from within. Suppose you unintentionally blurt out something that is embarrassing or even horrifying. Your next statement might be, "I didn't say that!" Or suppose you do something of which you are ashamed. You might try to deny, even to yourself, that you did it.

Persistent denial may be a sign of serious psychopathology. It is almost the definitive symptom of alcoholism, for example. (Have you ever tried to tell an alcoholic that he or she has a drinking problem?) But, used effectively, the primary purpose of denial is to keep us from being overwhelmed by the initial shock—at something that has happened or at something we have done—as we muster our psychological resources to do something more permanent about it. Elizabeth Kubler-Ross (1969) noted that when people learn they have a fatal illness, their first impulse is to deny that this can possibly be true. Only later are they able to muster other ways of coping with such extreme news.

Repression

The defense mechanism of **repression** is more complex, farther reaching, and longer lasting than denial. Denial generally refers to pushing out of awareness or failing to perceive things that *currently* exist, such as anxiety-

*"Look, call it denial if you like, but I think what goes on in my
personal life is none of my own damn business."*

producing events or feelings. Repression, in contrast, refers to banishing the
past from present awareness and therefore tends to involve less outright nega-
tion of reality. With repression, you do not really deny that something exists,
you just manage not to think about it.

Like denial, the ultimate purpose of repression is to keep out of consciousness and out of action a problematical impulse of the id, an unpleasant thought, feeling, or memory, or something in the real world that is a
potential source of stress.

Freud believed that many forbidden impulses are quite common. For
example, if you are a college student in your early twenties, you may resent
your continued financial dependence on your parents. The ego finds this
feeling problematical, however, because its direct expression (calling your
parents and announcing that you hate them) might endanger your financial
support. Moreover, the superego also finds the resentment problematical
because it seems shamefully ungrateful after all that your parents have sac-
rificed. If the resentment were somehow to become conscious—and even
more if it were to be overtly expressed—its disapproval by both the ego and
superego would cause anxiety. The defense mechanism of repression may
kick in to prevent this from happening.

The most direct action of repression will be to bar from consciousness
any negative thoughts about your parents, which should also prevent any
overt negative behaviors. But repression takes no chances; it may also bar
from consciousness anything that might *remind* you of how you resent your
parents. (In fact, it will build a wider and deeper repressive wall the stronger
and more dangerous the resentment is.) You might find yourself forgetting
to call them as you have promised, because remembering to call them
reminds you they exist, which raises the possibility of becoming aware that

you resent them. Or you might even forget their phone number! It can go further: you might forget your roommate's parents' names, because remembering his or her parents will remind you of your parents, which might remind you of how you resent them. Or you might forget to watch a favorite television show because it is also your father's favorite show—you get the idea. Such elaborate secondary protection from anxiety-arousing stimuli can cause a wide range of slips and memory lapses, and the connection between what is forgotten and what is being defended against can be so indirect that a good deal of psychoanalytic digging can be required to find the cause. For instance, to figure out the real reason you forgot your roommate's mother's phone message might take a long time and a lot of work.

Thus, repression is much more complicated than simple denial. (It is also more difficult to demonstrate with empirical research [Baumeister, Dale, & Sommer, 1998].) The same complex process can work with memories as well. Suppose you did something a month ago, the memory of which would cause you anxiety, perhaps because it was dangerous (an ego judgment), immoral (a superego judgment), or both. Repression might cause you not only to forget what you did, but also to forget other things that might possibly remind you of what you did. If you hate to think about that time you almost got into a stupid accident with your car, for example, you might find that you have forgotten where you parked it.

If the feeling, memory, or impulse is successfully locked away in the unconscious, then you are successfully defended against the anxiety it would otherwise cause. But here is the rub: Such defense does not come free. The ego has a limited store of psychic energy that it has taken from the id.[1] Every forbidden feeling, memory, or impulse has a certain amount of associated id energy that impels toward the surface, toward consciousness and behavioral expression. In repression, the ego must oppose that impulse with an equal amount of its own energy. If the ego runs low on energy or tries to defend against too many impulses at once, it can start to lose the struggle, and these forbidden impulses will work their way toward consciousness again. As they begin to move up, you will feel anxiety, typically without knowing why.

You can imagine the danger of this situation. If ego energy fails for some reason—for example, illness, stress, or some trauma—a whole array of forbidden impulses might suddenly come to consciousness and even action all at once. Or they might burst forth simply because they are too numerous and too strong, as a dam can suddenly break after years of slowly increasing water pressure behind it. The result can be violent lashing out, emotional binges, and a wide variety of irrational behaviors.

---

[1] As was mentioned in Chapter 10, modern psychoanalytic thought holds that it is the mind's capacity for information processing, rather than energy, that is limited (Westen, 1998). The consequences are the same: capacity used for one purpose is not available for other purposes.

"Frankly, I've repressed my sexuality so long I've actually forgotten what my orientation is."

For example, an ordinarily meek and mild man might absorb insults and humiliations for many years. Each insult and humiliation may have been repressed successfully so that he does not have to feel the associated anxiety, until one day it has gone on too long. The defenses fail, the dam breaks, and he goes on a murderous rampage. "He was always so quiet," comment the (surviving) neighbors in the newspaper the next day (see Megargee, 1966).

The danger of repression can be more subtle. The ego's energy store is limited; the more it has tied up in repression, the less it has available for other purposes. A severe shortage of free psychic energy can lead to depression, Freud believed. The more modern interpretation of the same phenomenon would be that a mind preoccupied with the task of keeping certain thoughts and memories out of awareness, has less processing capacity left to deal with anything else. Either way, clinical depression is much more than just being sad all the time. Its hallmark is a near-total lack of motivation and energy. One purpose of psychoanalysis is to locate the loci of repression, remove their causes, and free up more psychic energy for constructive and creative purposes.

Repression, like denial, is a sort of brute-force defense mechanism; it tries to build a psychological dam between the individual and the potential sources of anxiety. But any dam can hold back only so much for so long. Repression is not a defense mechanism that can be used too often, therefore. Fortunately, the ego has several other tactics in its playbook.

Reaction Formation

Reaction formation is an even more complex defense than repression. It keeps forbidden thoughts, feelings, and impulses out of awareness and action by instigating their *opposites*. The ego is particularly likely to use this tactic if the forbidden impulse is very dangerous or very strong, and an extra measure of defense seems necessary. Doing (or thinking) the opposite of the forbidden impulse builds a sort of safety margin, ensuring that the impulse never reaches consciousness or action. This process can protect self-esteem (Baumeister, Dale, & Sommer, 1998). If individuals are concerned that they might have some unacceptable trait, they might act in a way that would imply they have the opposite trait. If someone implies that you are hostile, for example, you might respond with exaggerated efforts to act in an agreeable and peace-loving manner.

Unconscious homosexual impulses again provide a particularly good example. These very common (according to Freud) impulses are considered problematic by both the ego and the superego but ordinarily are suppressed by repression. If the homosexual impulse is particularly strong, however, or if the superego has developed particularly strong prohibitions against it (as might a superego that developed in a rigidly puritanical environment), then reaction formation may become necessary to be sure the impulse is never felt or acted on.

The most obvious manifestation of reaction formation in such a case would be what is called "gay bashing." The person might loudly denounce homosexuals and describe them with epithets; might write "death to queers" on bathroom walls; might tell "fag" jokes frequently and loudly; or in an extreme case might physically attack gays.

The indication that these behaviors might be signs of reaction formation is the disproportion and gratuitousness of the antigay behavior. Reaction formation is *not* revealed by saying something like "some aspects of one common gay lifestyle can lead to serious problems in an age of AIDS." Such a statement might well express a sincere and reasonable attitude. But the demonstrated need to insult, to belittle, to characterize with obscenities, and perhaps even to physically assault is not. *No* reasonable attitude about gays leads to such behaviors. Thus, we are led to suspect a deeper, psychological source.

Consider another example. I lived for several years in a small, peaceful, almost bucolic college town in the Midwest. The local television news one night showed a preacher who was crusading in front of the town's (apparently) one-and-only pornographic bookstore, which was in such an obscure location—even in such a small town—that until I saw it on television I didn't know it existed. The preacher was screaming the dangers of smut. His face was red, his voice was hoarse, the veins stood out on his neck: The store was Sin and it was a Danger!

Again, notice that I am not talking about somebody who is calmly saying, "The images of women and of sexuality in most pornography are not the sorts of things to which we would wish to expose our children." Such a statement, although you might agree or disagree, is certainly reasonable. It is the almost absurd exaggeration of the response to the bookstore that can make one suspicious of the preacher's psychological motives. How big a danger is this store, really? What is it actually doing to the town, if many townspeople do not even know it exists? The vehemence of this crusader's reaction suggests that the source of his emotion is not any danger the store realistically poses, but rather his own temptation to rush in and buy the place out. He effectively prevents himself from doing this, of course, by standing out front with a megaphone and a picket sign. Such is the purpose and mechanism of reaction formation.

The giveaway is always a lack of proportion between the provocation and the response. Homosexuality, pornography, and many other potentially threatening topics are legitimate targets of discussion. But when so much emotion is involved, one is well advised to become suspicious. It can be informative, but also brave to the point of being foolhardy (thus I do not recommend it) to ask such a crusader this question: With so many problems in the world, why do you care about this one so much? The response is unlikely to be reasonable; it will be angry, anxious, and defensive.

An almost universal manifestation of reaction formation, Freud believed, occurs in nearly every family. When a new baby comes home from the hospital, the natural reaction of the older sibling is hate—this is called *sibling rivalry*, and it may be biologically based. But the older sibling soon discovers that his or her parents are protective of the baby and any attempts to harm it are met with punishment and loss of parental love, which is quite threatening. The sibling learns to repress his or her hate for little brother or sister and, if sufficiently threatened (or if the impulse to harm is sufficiently strong), may engage in some elaborate demonstrations of affection. "I love my little brother!" she might say, giving him a big kiss. In this way, she prevents herself from strangling him. The parents may approve of this affectionate behavior, but if they are sensitive they also may realize that it rings a little false. Behavior driven by reaction formation often somehow does not look quite right.

Reaction formation is a slippery phenomenon, but several laboratory experiments have managed to demonstrate something that looks much like it. In one study, female participants completed a questionnaire designed to measure the degree of their "sex guilt." Then they were shown graphic, erotic stimuli and asked to report how they felt. Women who scored higher in sex guilt reported lower levels of arousal in response to the erotic stimuli than did women who scored lower in sex guilt. However, according to physiological measures the former were actually *more* sexually aroused. This discrepancy between self-report (S data) and physiology (B data) suggested to the investigators that the women who experienced the greatest physical arousal were so threatened by it that through the mechanism of reaction formation, they reported (and probably were consciously aware of) the least psychological arousal (Morokoff, 1985).

Apparently—and consistent with Freud's own speculations summarized earlier—much the same thing can happen with men who experience latent homosexual impulses. In one study, a group of men were given a questionnaire to measure their "homophobia," their fear of homosexuals and also their own fear of themselves being homosexual. Then they were shown videotapes of homosexual activity. The men who scored highest on homophobia were the ones who reported the lowest level of sexual arousal from watching the tapes, but these were also the ones who showed the largest degree of physiological arousal (Adams, Wright, & Lohr, 1996). Again, the conscious experience reported of the homophobic men was the opposite to the (forbidden) responses of their bodies. It supports Freud's long-held opinion that homophobia itself is a reaction formation against homosexual impulses, in that it is homophobics who are both the most aroused by homosexual stimuli and the most prone to deny it.

Hamlet's mother said, "Methinks the lady doth protest too much." She was talking about reaction formation.

Projection

Like reaction formation, **projection** is a defense mechanism that protects against unwanted impulses by causing a behavior that, at first glance, appears to be opposite. It is the tactic of attributing a thought or impulse to somebody else that is feared in oneself. You announce, to yourself as much as to anybody else, "It's not me who feels that way (or is like that), it's *him*."

Homosexuality again provides a prototypical example. Freud believed that one way some people deal with threatening, latent homosexual impulses of their own is to project homosexual intent onto everybody else. "Gay bashers" like those described earlier are quick to claim to have spotted "another one" and may even tell you that they can infallibly identify any homosexual at a glance. They are wrong, of course, but it is revealing that they believe this.

Other kinds of self-doubt can lead to projection. People who doubt their own intelligence often deal with the anxiety of realizing their own inadequacy by claiming to be surrounded by morons. It seems to make them feel better, and for the short term the tactic of pointing out other people as stupid is effective in making them seem smarter than they would otherwise appear (Amabile & Glazebrook, 1982).

Current research on projection suggests that the classic psychodynamic view was close to correct, but not quite. In one recent study, participants took a personality test and then were told (falsely) that their scores indicated that they had certain good traits and certain bad ones (Newman, Duff, &

Baumeister, 1997). Then, they were instructed to try not to think about one of the bad traits they had been told that they had. Next, they watched a person on videotape and rated that person on all the same traits on which they had received feedback. They rated that person higher on the one bad trait they were trying not to think about, but not on any of the others. This study's findings suggest that projection—seeing one's own bad traits in another—is specifically the result of trying to suppress a bad thought about oneself. It is not clear that this kind of projection lessens the tendency to see the trait in oneself—which Freud believed—but it does seem to be at least a by-product of the process of trying to deny unpleasant truths.

Not all negative opinions you have of other people are due to projection, of course. But, you should ask yourself this: Do you often characterize other people in a particular way? Are you constantly detecting "jerks," "morons," "lazy freeloaders," or whatever? If so, it is fair to suspect the workings of projection. The negative attribute with which you are tagging other people may be something that you actually (albeit unconsciously) fear characterizes yourself.

Rationalization

Rationalization may be the most widely used defense mechanism of all. Rationalization defends against the anxiety aroused by having done something of which you would otherwise feel ashamed, by concocting a seemingly rational case for why it was something you just had to do. A hit song a couple of decades ago proclaimed, "You've got to be cruel to be kind." That's a rationalization.

Rationalization is everywhere. Parents who harshly punish their children claim it is for their own good. Wealthy people give themselves tax breaks while raising the burden on the poor, then claim this will make things better for everybody. People cheat and tell lies, then claim it was harmless, or even necessary for a greater good.

The remarkable facts about rationalizations like these are that (1) they are obviously rationalizations, and (2) the people who use them seem to believe them anyway. If the reasoning were not so clearly flawed, you might be tempted to think that these people actually believe what they say. It is the ability and even eagerness of otherwise intelligent people to believe the implausible that identifies rationalization. Deep inside, these people are ashamed of themselves. Rationalization protects them from the anxiety they would feel if they realized their shame.

One kind of rationalization is trivialization, a mechanism that was demonstrated in recent research (Simon, Greenberg, & Brehm, 1995). Trivialization amounts to convincing yourself that your shortcomings or your regrettable actions don't matter. In one study, participants were induced to write essays that were contrary to their true beliefs. Ordinarily, such behavior causes a change in the prior attitude, but the experimenters allowed participants the opportunity to dismiss their counterattitudinal essay writing as a trivial exercise that meant nothing. This trivialization had the effect of preventing the attitude change that would otherwise have occurred, because it apparently succeeded in defending participants from the particular brand of anxiety, called *cognitive dissonance,* that is ordinarily triggered by saying things that one does not believe.

Intellectualization

Yet another way to deal with a threatening emotion is to turn the feeling into a thought. This is the defense mechanism of **intellectualization**. Intellectualization can turn a heated and anxiety-provoking issue into something cold, intellectual, and analytical. This can be aided by the development of a technical vocabulary that allows one to talk about horrifying things without using everyday, emotionally arousing language.

You see a lot of intellectualization in war. During modern wars, television screens fill with retired generals and colonels expounding on military strategy. It is remarkable how seldom they use words like *kill* or *die,* even though those are the defining attributes of war. They use words like *suffer* and *bleed* even more rarely. Instead, their analyses deploy maps and charts and pointers to tell an interesting story that has much of the same appeal as a good game of chess. But to truly enjoy the show—and maybe even just to plot strategy—the observer must forget what is really going on.

The medical profession has to do the same thing. Surgeons talk about "this gallbladder" rather than "this person," and their vocabulary is so technical as to be virtually inaccessible. That is on purpose. Physicians are reluctant to talk about pain (they prefer the term *discomfort*) and death (you really just "expire").

I don't mean to belittle the military or medical professions here. When the pretense and technical blather are stripped away, they both deal on a daily basis with situations that are truly horrifying. It is unlikely they could function at all without the defense of intellectualization. If the surgeon thought too directly about the life of the child on whom she is operating, it is doubtful she could get through the operation successfully. A general who dwells too much on the deaths his work will cause might be unable to formulate a winning strategy. Unadorned reality can be too painful to deal with effectively. The purpose of intellectualization and the other defense mechanisms is to build a useful barrier between you and reality, so that you can go on with what you need to do. A recent summary of relevant research supports the idea that creating this kind of a "mental gap or barrier between some threatening cognition and other thoughts and feelings" is an effective tactic for reducing anxiety (Baumeister, Dale, & Sommer, 1998, p. 1099).

All defense mechanisms have costs, however, and intellectualization is no exception. A general who forgets he is killing people might be an effective strategist, but also might sacrifice life needlessly or even come to enjoy war so much as an intellectual exercise that he unnecessarily prolongs it. A physician who finds surgery enjoyable and comes to forget she is cutting real people might also forget that patients have not only physical needs, but also emotional needs that are important components of the healing process.

Intellectualization is a particular occupational hazard of psychologists. I suspect that part of the field's appeal lies in the way it takes potent issues of emotion and experience and puts them into an abstract theoretical framework. This is useful and even necessary; Freud himself seems to have built his theory as a gigantic exercise in intellectualization. But to the extent that it begins to shield one from the realities of everyday mental life, psychology itself can be a defense mechanism.

Displacement

Displacement is a less-intellectual defense mechanism that is based on a property of primary process thinking. Among the attributes of the primary process by which the infantile id operates is a capacity for displacement, or replacing one object of emotion with another. A feeling about your family might be displaced on your house, for example, or a feeling about a parent might be displaced onto a boss, or vice versa. The defense mechanism of displacement relocates the object of an emotional response or desire from an unsafe target to a safe one. A simple example might be the desire, based on a mild fixation in the oral stage, that an adult might have to suck his or her thumb. Of course, this is not acceptable behavior at a business meeting, so displacement might lead the executive to chew thoughtfully, and with impeccable dignity, on a pen or pipe instead.

The direction of displacement depends on two things. Generally an id impulse will be displaced on the available target that is most similar to the actually desired object but that is also socially acceptable. Satisfyingly similar substitutes for sucking one's thumb (itself a displacement from sucking mother's breast) might include both a toe and a pipe stem. However, only the pipe is acceptable in public (it also requires less flexibility), so that is where the impulse relocates.[2]

Aggression frequently is displaced in this manner. You might become angry at your boss but fear losing your job if you confront him. So you go

---

[2]According to legend, Freud was once asked to explain the meaning of the cigars he smoked. He replied, "Sometimes a cigar is just a cigar."

home and kick your dog (especially if your dog looks like your boss). Many student dormitory rooms contain professor dartboards. It is safe and legal to throw darts at a piece of cork decorated with a disliked professor's picture, and dart throwing may partially gratify an aggressive impulse. But it is not the same thing as throwing pointed darts at the actual professor; that is why the behavior is said to manifest displacement.

Like all defense mechanisms, displacement has its uses and its dangers. It is useful in redirecting forbidden and even dangerous impulses onto safe targets. It can be a problem if it becomes a substitute for necessary direct action. Displacement also can be a problem if it causes aggression to be directed onto innocent targets. It is not the dog's fault that your boss is a jerk, and cruelty to animals at home is no solution to difficulties at work.

In addition, displacement is not always effective, if it ever is. Experimental research since the time of Freud suggests that a person who expresses aggression at a displaced target may become *more*, not less, inclined to be aggressive in general (Berkowitz, 1962; Bushman, 2002). This suggests that rather than being one of the ego's defense mechanisms, displacement might be a more primitive function of the id's primary process thinking. People who kick the wall when they are angry at someone may do so not for any functional reason, but because they cannot help it. At a basic and primitive level, they are just built that way. Bad moods and aggressive impulses tend to generalize away from their original targets, but there is little if any evidence that this reduces anxiety (Baumeister, Dale, & Sommer, 1998).

Sublimation

To be sublime is to be elevated and noble. **Sublimation** is the defense mechanism by which base and possibly forbidden impulses are transformed into constructive behaviors. Sublimation is a type of displacement in which the object of an impulse is relocated such that the result is high cultural attainment. For example, Freud believed that the production of great works of art by people such as Leonardo da Vinci and Michelangelo was strongly influenced by psychological traumas they experienced in early childhood. Freud also believed that Leonardo's prolific scientific investigations, in particular, constituted a sublimation of his frustrated sexual passions.[3]

---

[3]Freud's interpretation was presented in a short book entitled *Leonardo da Vinci and a Memory of His Childhood* and is discussed in detail by Gay (1988, pp. 268–277). A recent literature review concluded that no experimental evidence supported the idea of sublimation, but also acknowledged that nobody had figured out a way to test it experimentally (Baumeister, Dale, & Sommer, 1998). So for now we are left with anecdotes, like Freud's story of da Vinci, which you may or may not find convincing.

Occupational choice is a more mundane place to look for sublimation. It can be psychologically useful to channel one's otherwise unacceptable impulses into a lifelong work that will accomplish constructive ends. For example, if you unconsciously want to cut people, poke them with needles, or see them with their clothes off, you might find yourself drawn to a career in medicine, particularly surgery. If your deep urges are to express hostility and to argue, then perhaps you should become a lawyer. If you want to spend your life trying to get everybody to love you, then a career in politics might seem attractive. If you have anally based urges to smear feces (and, via displacement, paint), then you might become an artist. And, if what you really want to do is pry into other people's minds, and ask a lot of questions that are none of your business, then perhaps you should consider a career in clinical psychology.

This can start to sound silly, but there may be a kernel of truth here. Every person has a unique pattern of fixations left over from childhood and as a result has a unique pattern of desires and interests. People who are both wise and lucky may seek constructive careers that allow the expression of these desires and interests. As was discussed in Chapter 8, work you are passionate about is the kind of work you will do best.

It is important to realize that Freud saw sublimation as a *positive* thing. It is a part of normal functioning and a useful way to translate into constructive outcomes urges that otherwise could cause problems. Unlike the other defense mechanisms, sublimation does not have a down side. It is what allows human psychic energy to be channeled into useful pursuits and allows the development of society, culture, civilization, and achievement of all sorts. We need to sublimate more often. To do this, we probably need to know ourselves better.

The Expression of Impulse through Parapraxes and Humor

Defense mechanisms work to prevent forbidden impulses from being acted on or even thought about. But sometimes feelings and thoughts that the ego and superego are trying to suppress make it into the open anyway. This leakage might be uncontrolled and haphazard, or it might be carefully channeled. Uncontrolled, it creates a slip of some kind, or a *parapraxis*. Controlled, it can be the basis of wit and humor.

Parapraxes

A **parapraxis** is another name for what is commonly called a "Freudian slip": a leakage from the unconscious mind into an overt manifestation such as a mistake, accident, omission, or memory lapse. Remember that Freud was a determinist—he thought everything had a cause. This belief comes directly into play when considering the causes of accidents and other slips. Freud was never willing to believe that they just happened.

FORGETTING

Forgetting something is a manifestation of an unconscious conflict revealing itself in your overt behavior. The slip or parapraxis is the failure to recall something you needed to remember or do something you needed to do, either of which can have consequences ranging from embarrassment to much worse. These consequences make the lapse a parapraxis; in service of the suppression of something in your unconscious mind, your slip manages to mess up something in your real life.

Usually this is a result of repression. To avoid thinking about something painful or anxiety producing, you fail to remember it. You make a date and then have second thoughts, so you forget you made it. Although you might have saved yourself some immediate anxiety, when you run into your erstwhile date the next week in the cafeteria, you will have a serious social problem. Many college students manage to forget the times that exams are held and term papers are due. Failing to remember such things may make the students less anxious in the short run but can produce serious problems in the long run. Occasionally a student will make an appointment with me to discuss a difficulty he or she is having in class. I know the odds are no better than 50 percent that the student will actually show up at the appointed time. The explanation is always the same: "I forgot."

These examples are fairly obvious. But Freud insisted that *all* lapses of this kind reveal unconscious conflicts. Now the theoretical going gets a little tougher: What about when you just forget something for no reason? No such thing, according to Freud. The psychoanalytic faith declares that through long psychotherapy using free association, a therapist can eventually (and perhaps at great expense) figure out the cause of *any* memory lapse. The root system may be quite complex: you may have forgotten to do something because it reminds you of something else that through primary process thinking has come to symbolize yet something else, which makes you anxious.

In one case, a psychoanalyst reported that a patient forgot the name of an acquaintance who had the same name as an enemy of his. Moreover, the acquaintance was physically handicapped, which reminded the patient of the harm he wished to do the enemy of the same name. To defend against the superego-induced guilt produced by this wish, he forgot the name of his perfectly innocent acquaintance (Brenner, 1974).

*"And then I say to myself, 'If I really wanted to talk to her,
why do I keep forgetting to dial 1 first?'"*

SLIPS

Slips are unintended actions caused by the leakage of suppressed impulses.
Many of them appear in speech and can be as simple as a failure to suppress
what one really means to say. In one of the first courses on psychoanalysis I
took in college, the professor one day was mentioning the students who visited during his office hours. "When infants come to see me . . . ," he said,
then he stopped, stammered, and his face turned bright red. His students did
not fail to understand this revelation of what he really thought of them.

A more common slip is to say one name when you mean to say another.
Saying the name of one's former boyfriend or girlfriend at important and
delicate moments with one's current boyfriend or girlfriend is a common
and extremely embarrassing slip. Explanations are often demanded: "Why
did you say her name?" "I just made a mistake! It didn't mean anything!"
This reply is no more likely to be accepted by one's current "significant other"
than it would have been by Sigmund Freud himself.

Slips can occur in action as well as in speech. Accidentally breaking something can be a leakage of hostility against the person who owns the object,
who gave the object, or whom the object (for some reason) symbolizes. More
pleasant to think about is the standard interpretation when somebody accidentally leaves something behind at your house after a visit: it means he or
she did not want to leave and hopes to come back.

As already noted, the person who commits these slips of speech or action
may deny that the slip had any meaning. Not only does psychoanalysis not
take such a denial seriously, but the louder and more vehement the person's

denial, the more likely it will be that a Freudian will suspect the presence of a powerfully dangerous and important impulse behind it.

But what about accidents that happen just because a person is tired, not paying attention, in a hurry, or excited? Not accidents, according to Freud. Fatigue, inattention, or excitement might make slips more likely, but they do not cause them. Freud compared the operation of such factors to the way darkness helps a robber. A dark street might make a burglary more likely, but dark streets do not cause burglaries; a burglar is still required. Similarly, fatigue, inattention, and other factors might make it easier for a suppressed impulse to leak into behavior, but they are not the basis of the impulse itself.

Does this mean, then, that there really are no accidents? Freud believed so. Any failure to do something you ordinarily can do—such as drive a car safely—must be due to the leakage of a suppressed impulse, according to Freud. Some examples that seem to fit this description have been quite prominent. In the Winter Olympics a few years ago, a skier on the way to an important downhill race managed to crash into a member of the ski patrol and break her leg. This was an accident, of course, but it is also reasonable to ask, how often does an Olympic-level skier crash into somebody else? How often does any skier crash into a member of the ski patrol? And, of all mornings of this skier's life, why did the accident happen on this morning? One is led to wonder if this skier did not want to show up for her race, and why.

An even more dramatic incident at the 1988 Olympics involved the speed skater Dan Jansen, whose sister died of leukemia just five hours before he was scheduled to compete in the 500-meter event. Jansen was favored for the gold medal, and his sister had insisted he go to the Olympics even though all knew she had not long to live. He fell down just ten seconds into the race. Four days later, in his second event, the 1,000-meter race, he fell again. A psychoanalytic perspective on these accidents makes one wonder whether Jansen might have been ambivalent about coming home bedecked in gold medals at such a time. Had he fully wanted to succeed, it seems unlikely that he would have fallen down in both of the two most important athletic events of his life. (The sports world breathed a sigh of relief when, in the 1994 Olympics, Jansen finally resolved matters, taking the gold medal at 1,000 meters and setting a world record.)

While there may not be many—or any—Freudians in the typical university psychology department, there typically are a lot of them in the physical education department. They may not think about themselves that way, but coaches are often orthodox Freudians. Coaches worry about instilling in their athletes the right mental attitude, a will to win. When an athlete at the free-throw line in a big game misses a shot he or she can make twenty times in a row in practice, any good coach knows the solution is not more free-throw practice; there is something about the athlete's attitude or desire that needs work. If the player had wanted to make the basket, the ball would have gone in. Ask any coach which team will win any given game. The coach will reply, "The team that wants it more." Freud would say, "Exactly right."

The next time you fail to perform to your ability, in sports, in academics, at work, or wherever, take a moment and ask yourself this: Did you *really* want to succeed? Why not?

Humor

Parapraxes are more or less random leaks; they appear wherever defenses are weak. In wit, however, a forbidden impulse comes out in a controlled manner. Freud saw wit as essentially a form of sublimation: an impulse that otherwise would be anxiety provoking or even harmful is vented in such a way that it can be safely enjoyed. Wit, therefore, is the safe expression of evil impulses. It is no accident that the most common themes of humor are the ordinarily forbidden topics of sex, violence, and bodily elimination.

THE PURPOSE OF HUMOR

Humor allows otherwise problematical id impulses to be enjoyed by using the tactic of surprise. In a successful joke, the impulse is disguised until the last possible moment. Then—Bang!—the impulse is expressed and enjoyed before your ego or superego have a chance to inhibit it. A few seconds later, you might even feel a bit sheepish or even guilty about what made you laugh, but the deed is done. The impulse was expressed and enjoyed.

In one of the *Pink Panther* movies, Peter Sellers sees a dog standing next to a desk and asks the clerk, "Does your dog bite?" The clerk answers, "No, never." Sellers reaches down to pet the dog, and his hand is savagely bitten. "I thought you said your dog doesn't bite!" he cries, jumping up and down. "That," replies the clerk, "is not my dog."

Someone who laughs at this scene is enjoying the spectacle of a person being fooled into being physically harmed by an unexpectedly vicious animal. What's funny about that? Everything, apparently. The reason this scene works is that what is going on is concealed carefully until the last moment, when it is revealed suddenly. The situation is enjoyed with a burst of laughter before the superego's censors can point out how reprehensible the whole situation really is.

A comedian named Emo Phillips tells the following story: "When I was a child, my parents always said to me, 'Emo, whatever you do, don't open the cellar door. Never open the cellar door.' But I was curious, and after a few years I finally snuck over and opened the cellar door. What I saw was amazing—things I had never seen before. Trees. Birds. The sky."

"You see? Once more, Wile E. Coyote is restored swiftly and miraculously to health. His potential trauma has been trivialized, and we are yet again amused."

This is a child-abuse joke! What could be funny about locking a child in the basement for the first years of his life? Some evil impulse to enjoy such a situation seems to exist, however, and it leaks out and causes surprised laughter before anyone has a chance to realize that this situation is actually tragic. Moreover, this is a better joke than the Peter Sellers scene for two reasons. First, child abuse is ordinarily more reprehensible than dog bites, so the release of the impulse causes a stronger emotional response. Second (and this is really the key), Emo's disguise around the impulse is deeper than Sellers's. It is less apparent at the beginning where Emo's joke is going, and when I tell it to classes there are always several students who don't get it until someone takes them aside and explains.

The purpose of a joke is to allow a forbidden impulse to be released in such a way that anxiety can be avoided. For this reason, most (maybe all) jokes, when examined closely, are "sick" jokes, based on sexual or hostile impulses. Many involve people being made to look stupid; others express some kind of obscenity in an indirect, disguised, sudden fashion.

BAD JOKES

Not all jokes work. If you do not have the forbidden impulse in the first place, the joke will not be funny to you. Some people enjoy hostile jokes more than others do, for example. Presumably, this is partly because some people have stronger hostile impulses that are seeking expression. The same probably goes for sexual jokes. A particularly noticeable individual difference appears in the enjoyment of racist and sexist jokes. Their enjoyment depends on the existence of underlying hostility toward the targeted minority group or gender. Someone who does not have such underlying hostility may find such jokes mystifying rather than funny. I know someone who is uptight and generally rule-bound—a real "anal" character. Her favorite form of humor? Toilet jokes. Children who are still not far beyond the anal stage themselves also greatly enjoy bathroom humor. But as their libidos move into later stages, most adults find that the appeal of potty humor fades a bit.

Political humor is another problematical area. You are more likely to laugh at jokes about politicians you oppose than those you support. A political humorist, therefore, must choose whether to be a blatant partisan, and thereby limit the audience, or to try to joke about politicians of all persuasions. (Johnny Carson became an American comedy icon to a large degree because he had the rare ability to do just that.)

A joke can also fail by being too direct. If a joke fails to disguise the impulse sufficiently and so fails to surprise the hearer, when the impulse is expressed it will cause discomfort rather than enjoyment. This is why the more times you hear a joke, the less funny it becomes. As the element of surprise is taken away, the impulse can no longer be enjoyed. Some jokes are not even surprising at *first* hearing. If you can see the punch line coming, it won't be very funny.

Some "jokes" do not even try to disguise the impulses they express. They rely simply on saying obscene words or describing sexual acts in graphic terms. Some people find them funny; most do not. Other jokes amount to the almost completely undisguised expression of hostility. Jokes like these are the ones that make most people squirm instead of laugh. That response defeats the whole purpose of humor.

One category of unfunny joke has received increased attention in recent years: sexist jokes that are told in the workplace by male bosses to and about female employees. By commenting lasciviously and loudly on his secretary's physical attributes or personal life, the boss gets to express at least two impulses at once. One is sexual, and the other is a sadistic expression of power. The boss—and those who happen to share his unenlightened attitudes—may laugh loudly; the employee may be miserable.

There are two reasons why such jokes are not funny. The first is that they are usually too obvious. An obscene comment about a subordinate's body lacks the necessary disguise for the safe and enjoyable release of impulse. The second reason is that the impulse may not be shared widely. Surely the subordinate herself is unlikely to enjoy the boss's expression of his needs for sex and power. Co-workers, including male co-workers, who also do not share these impulses toward the employee similarly will find the boss's "humor" unfunny. Pathetically, some of them may laugh loudly anyway, to curry the boss's favor or perhaps so they will seem like "one of the boys."

Practical jokes can be problematical in a similar manner. A harmless prank can express mild hostility in an enjoyable way, but there is a fine line between playing a prank, which can be funny, and seriously harming somebody, which is not. When I was in college, a group of men in my dorm developed a degree of hostility toward a certain female resident. For her birthday, they decided to stage an elaborate surprise party. At its climax they ceremoniously presented her with a gift, which turned out to be an oversized, battery-powered dildo. This was meant to be funny; it was not. It was one of the most depressing and humiliating moments I have ever witnessed. The hostility and contempt that was felt—unfairly—toward this woman was expressed too directly, too publicly, and too cruelly.

A well-known example of the same kind of problem is presented by the long-running television program *America's Funniest Home Videos*. Most of the videos shown on this program portray people, including children, as they fall down, break things, and make huge messes. Some people—myself included—feel uncomfortable rather than entertained by this program. The events portrayed come a little too close to the line that separates a humorous incident from an event that is humiliating, disturbing, or painful.

After these examples, I should reiterate that from the psychoanalytic perspective, humor is *good*. It allows the harmless and even beneficial venting of forbidden impulses that otherwise would have to be repressed or defended against. But humor is also a delicate business. The impulse must be shared, and it must be suitably disguised. To succeed on both of these bases is the fine and difficult art of humor.

Psychoanalytic Theory: A Critique

Throughout the past two chapters, I have tried to sell you Freud. Psychoanalytic theory has much to offer in understanding important aspects of daily life. The theory is dramatic and insightful, it is comprehensive, and it is aesthetic.

Having said that, I still must warn you against taking Freud too seriously. When a student comes up to me after class and says, "What happens to sexual development if a boy is raised solely by his mother in a single-parent family?" (see Chapter 10), what I really want to reply is, "Hey! Don't take this stuff to heart! Freud has a neat theory here, and it's fun to play around with, but don't start using it to evaluate your life." Psychoanalytic theory is far from being received truth. So, having praised Freud, let me now bury him for a bit. There are at least five important shortcomings to psychoanalytic theory.

Lack of Parsimony

First of all, Freud's theory is nonparsimonious (to put it mildly). A basic principle of science, sometimes called *Occam's razor*, is that less is more: all other things being equal, the simplest explanation for something is the best. Suppose you want to explain why small boys take on many of the values and attitudes of their fathers. One possibility is that they look for guides in the world around them and choose the most obvious and prominent. Freud's theory, however, says that boys sexually desire their mothers, they worry that their fathers will be jealous and castrate them in punishment, so they identify with their fathers in order to vicariously enjoy the mother and lessen the threat from the father. This is intriguing, and maybe it is even correct, but is it the simplest possible explanation of the known facts? No way. Even modern theorists who are sympathetic to psychoanalysis have moved away from this story (Westen, 1998).

Case Study Method

A second fundamental tenet of science is that all data must be public. The basis of one's conclusions must be laid out so that scientists can evaluate the evidence together. Classic psychoanalytic theory never did this, and the neo-Freudians and object relations theorists (considered in Chapter 12) have been little different. Their theorizing was based on analysts' (including Freud's) introspections and on insights drawn from working with single therapeutic cases, which are themselves (by law) confidential. Freud himself complained that the real proof of his theory lay in the details of case studies that he could never reveal because of the need to protect his patients' privacy. The fact that this case study method is uncheckable means that it may be biased. This bias may arise out of what psychoanalysts and their patients (such as Freud's turn-of-the-century, Viennese hysterics) are like. Or perhaps the reasoning the theorist employs distorts what really happens in his or her cases. Because the data are forever private, no one can ever be sure. Psychoanalytic theory's historic attitude toward empirical proof could be summarized by this slogan: "Take it or leave it." Only recently have efforts been renewed to test some of its key ideas, some of which are summarized in the next chapter.

Poor Definitions

Another conventional scientific canon is the *operational definition*. In other words, a scientific concept should be defined largely in terms of the operations or procedures by which it can be identified and measured. Psychoanalytic theory almost never does this. Take the idea of psychic energy. I mentioned that a student once asked me what units it was measured in. There are no units, of course, and looked at closely it is not entirely clear what Freud meant by psychic energy at all: Was he being literal, or is energy just a loose metaphor? Exactly how much psychic energy—what percentage, say—needs to be left behind at the oral stage to develop an oral character? As repressions accumulate, at what point will one run out of energy for daily living? And what is the difference, exactly, between denial and repression? Psychoanalytic theory does not come even close to providing specific answers to questions like these.

Untestability

Freud's theory is also untestable. In science, a theory should be "disconfirmable"; that is, a theory should imply a set of observations or results that, if found, would prove it to be false. (This is the difference between religion and science. There is no conceivable set of observations or results that would prove that God does not exist. He always might just be hiding. Therefore, the existence of God is not a scientific issue.) But psychoanalytic theory is so complicated that there is no set of observations that it cannot explain after the fact. Because there is no imaginable experiment that would prove the theory wrong, the theory is in that sense unscientific, and some people have argued that perhaps it should be considered a religion![4]

Still, no single experiment is sufficient to prove or disprove *any* complex theory. So one could conclude that the real question is not whether psychoanalysis is testable in a strict sense, but rather whether the theory leads to hypotheses that can be tested individually. In the case of psychoanalysis, the best answer to this question is sometimes yes and sometimes no.

Sexism

Psychoanalytic theory is sexist. This cannot be denied; even the modern writers who are highly sympathetic to Freud admit it (e.g., Gay, 1988). In psychoanalytic writing it is abundantly clear that Freud considers males to be normal and bases his theorizing on their psychology. He then considers females, if he considers them at all, as aberrations or deviations from the male model. For example, his Oedipal theory of sex typing is much more coherent for males than for females, who seem to have been added almost as an afterthought.

Freud's view of females is that they are essentially castrated males, rather than being whole in their own right. They spend much of their lives griev-

---

[4]Early in his career Freud frequently expressed his desire that psychoanalytic theory be considered scientific. As he grew older, this criterion became less important to him (Bettelheim, 1982). However, he would have been horrified at the idea of psychoanalysis as a religion.

ing for not having a penis. The side effects of being female, in psychoanalytic theory, include having less self-esteem, less creativity, and less moral fiber. Much of a female's life, according to Freud, is based on her struggle to come to terms with the tragedy that she is not male.

Why Study Freud?

So with all these acknowledged problems, why study Freud? I believe there are several reasons. One is simply that Sigmund Freud and the tradition that he initiated continue to have a profound influence on psychology and on modern conceptions of the mind. This is so even though rather few modern research psychologists—including those who teach courses in personality psychology—would consider themselves "Freudians." Freud's continued influence can be seen in many ways.

First and perhaps most obviously, Freud continues to influence the practice of psychotherapy. One survey indicated that about 75 percent of practicing psychotherapists rely to some degree on psychoanalytic ideas (Pope, Tabachnick, & Keith-Spiegel, 1987). For example, even many psychotherapists who consider themselves non-Freudians practice the "talking cure" (the idea that talking about a problem helps), free association (encouraging the client to say whatever comes to mind), and transference (building an emotional relationship between client and therapist to promote healing). (According to legend, Freud also originated the practice of billing clients for their missed appointments!)

Second, many of Freud's ideas have made it into the popular culture and are a routine—and helpful—part of how people think and talk about each other, in ways they might not always recognize. You might find yourself asking, "What's the real reason she did that?" For instance, suppose you give somebody an expensive present. The next time you visit her, the present is nowhere in sight. "Whatever happened to . . . ?" you ask. "Oh," your friend replies nonchalantly, "I broke it, so I threw it away." How does this make you feel? If it makes you feel bad (and of course it does), one reason might be that you have made a Freudian interpretation of your friend's behavior (e.g., she has unconscious hostility toward you) without quite realizing that you have done so.

Sometimes everyday thought is even more explicitly Freudian. Have you ever heard somebody hypothesize that "she only goes out with that older guy because he's a father figure," or "he's all messed up because of the way that his parents treated him when he was little," or "he never dates anybody because his entire soul goes into programming his computer," or "she's got too much invested in him [psychologically] to walk out now"? These are all Freudian interpretations.

So, it is probably the case that you already knew a good deal of psychoanalytic theory even before you read the past two chapters, and you may even use it every day. One result can be that Freud's ideas do not always seem as original as they should. There is an old joke about the person who went to see one of Shakespeare's plays for the first time but walked out halfway through. "It was boring," he complained, "too full of clichés." Of course, much of Shakespeare is full of clichés because so many of his lines (e.g., "To be or not to be") have made it into everyday speech. Some of Freud's most original ideas might sound rather mundane after all these years, for the same unfair reason.

A third consideration is that in very recent years Freudian thought seems to have begun to undergo something of a revival within research psychology (see Chapter 12). After years of inactivity on these topics, psychologists are again researching and publishing articles on defense mechanisms (see Cramer & Davidson, 1998), transference (Andersen & Berk, 1998), unconscious thought (Kihlstrom, 1990; Bornstein, 1999), and other classically Freudian topics (Westen, 1998). Some of these researchers are careful to claim that they are not really Freudian themselves, even though they are researching topics that seem psychoanalytic. If Freud were still alive, he would surely observe that such claims only go to prove his continued and profound influence.

The fourth and perhaps most important way in which Freud continues to be influential is that to the present day, his theory remains the only *complete* theory of personality ever proposed. Freud knew what he wanted to explain: aggression, sexuality, development, energy, conflict, neurosis, dreams, humor, accidents—the list goes on. His theory provides an account of *all* of them. Whether he is right or wrong about every aspect of the theory, it does provide a road map of all the right questions for personality psychology. It is a truism that in science the important thing is not really answering questions but figuring out the right ones to ask. In this regard, Freud's theory of personality is a triumph that may stand for all time.

Among other topics, Freud theorized extensively about how experiences in early life affect personality in adulthood; we saw in Chapter 9 how this issue continues to generate research and controversy. Freud also posed questions concerning such matters as the meaning of dreams and the sources of sexual attraction that psychologists still have not gotten around to investigating seriously. The psychoanalytic psychologist Drew Westen (1990, p. 54) pointed out that "one can read a thousand pages of social-cognitive theory [arguably the dominant paradigm in social psychology today] and never know that people have genitals—or even, for that matter, that they have bodies—let alone fantasies." Freud's function in the Victorian age (as it is today) was to raise questions that others were too uncomfortable to think about.

For all these reasons, no education in psychology—and certainly no education in personality psychology—would be complete without some grounding in psychoanalysis.

Summary

Anxiety can have its origins in the real world or in inner, psychic conflict, such as that produced by an impulse of the id that the ego and superego try to combat. The ego uses several defense mechanisms to protect against the conscious experience of excessive anxiety and its associated negative emotions, such as shame and guilt. These defense mechanisms include denial, repression, reaction formation, projection, rationalization, intellectualization, displacement, and sublimation. They can be useful for lessening anxiety in the short run, but in the long run can produce problems in accurately perceiving and dealing with reality. Forbidden impulses of the id can occasionally be expressed in thought and behavior in two ways. Parapraxes are accidental ventings of forbidden impulses in the kind of accidents of speech or action commonly called Freudian slips. In wit, a forbidden impulse is deeply disguised in such a way as to permit its enjoyment without anxiety. A joke is not funny when the impulse is not shared, or the disguise is insufficient. Psychoanalytic theory has been criticized for its lack of parsimony, its use of the case study method rather than experimentation, its poor definitions of some of its concepts, its untestability, and its sexism. However, it is worth learning about because of its continuing influence on psychotherapy and modern life, because modern experimental evidence is beginning to confirm at least some of its ideas, and because psychoanalysis asks many questions that psychologists are still trying to answer, and raises many more that psychologists are currently ignoring but will someday have to address.

PSYCHOANALYSIS AFTER FREUD: THE NEO-FREUDIANS, OBJECT RELATIONS, AND EMPIRICAL EVIDENCE

Sigmund Freud died in 1939. His theory of the human mind did not die with him, however, nor did his style of theorizing or his general approach to psychodynamics. Academic research psychology—the kind of psychology done at universities by psychology professors—does not currently emphasize Freudian theory and psychoanalysis, and never really did, but more than a few modern psychologists continue to keep Freud's legacy alive. Some reinterpret his theory or extend it into new domains, some do empirical research to test some of his basic ideas, and some keep Freud alive just by continuing to argue about him.

Indeed, more than 60 years after his death, a surprising number of psychiatrists, psychologists, and even professors of English and Sanskrit scholars continue to devote their careers to the neverending project of debunking Freud. Their goal is no less than to prove that he was wrong about absolutely everything, from the beginning (e.g., Crews, 1996). A few years ago a book by the flamboyant psychoanalyst (and Sanskrit scholar) Jeffrey Masson (1984) made a stir in the popular media by using dredged-up material about some of Freud's more questionable friends, to call Freud's whole theory into question.[1] Works with similar intent continue to appear on a regular basis.[2] The most remarkable aspect of many of these efforts is their vehemence and their personal tone. They don't calmly suggest that the modern evidence concerning some of Freud's ideas is weak. No, they argue that Freud was a liar, a cheat, and a fraud, that he was mean to his family, and that he never had an original idea in his life. They stop just short of arguing that all his books should be pulled from the library shelves, stacked in the

---

[1]Masson also received extensive publicity for his lawsuit against the *New Yorker* magazine, which he claimed libeled him in a personality profile. He lost the case.

[2]See, for example, Sulloway (1979) or Crews (1996, 1998). The last-listed reference is a book full of attacks on Freud that, in the words of the ad on its jacket, "decisively (forge) the case against the man and his creation . . . [and] reveal the fumbles and deceptions that led to the 'discovery' of psychoanalysis." On the other side of the debate, Robinson (1993) summarizes the arguments of some of Freud's main critics and offers a defense.

public square, and burned. Recall the discussion of reaction formation in Chapter 11, and what were described as its hallmarks. Are attacks like these a proportionate response?

A more constructive development over the past six decades has been the continuing development of psychoanalytic thought, by a large number of clinical practitioners and theorists who—with varying degrees of acknowledgement of or expressed opposition to the "Big Guy"—have introduced a number of refinements. Some are relatively minor adjustments introduced in the course of summarizing Freud and trying to make sense of his work in a modern context. Other amendments are more drastic. Carl Jung, for example, set up his own version of psychoanalysis that included some mystical ideas that could not be further from the way Freud thought. But Jung's spiritual angle on psychoanalysis—influential as it has turned out to be, with some people—is distinctive. Common to nearly all of the post-Freudian psychoanalysts has been a focus on the interpersonal aspect of life, the way that early relationships, especially with parents, affect the way one perceives and relates to other people. The important insight is that our relationships with other people are mediated through the images we have of them in our mind—which sometimes may not much resemble the way they actually are. The only partially accurate images of other people that we carry in our minds are called "objects," and the modern school of psychoanalysis that deals with the origin and implications of these images is called *object relations theory*.

The aim of this chapter is to bring Freud into the present day by summarizing some of the ways his theory has been reinterpreted and altered by various theorists since the time of his death. We will focus particularly on a few of the more prominent **neo-Freudian** theorists and work in **object relations**. Then we will summarize examples of modern empirical research that

"It's your mother. She wants to remind you again just how difficult and painful your birth was."

has attempted to test psychoanalytic ideas, and conclude with an effort to place psychoanalytic theory into perspective.

Interpreting Freud

Writers who work to make sense of Freud in a modern context may shade their summaries in various ways that try to maintain the spirit, if not the letter, of Freudian law. This is what I did in Chapter 10 when I described how children unsure of their gender roles might look to obvious role models, such as their same-sex parents, for guidance. The dynamic process is different from the one Freud originally envisioned, but the result is still that small boys usually identify with their fathers.

The activities of interpreting and revising a theory are separated only by a fuzzy boundary. Freud wrote hundreds of articles and dozens of books over many years (his career spanned more than six decades, about the length of time that has now passed since his death), and he changed his mind about important issues more than once. So it is no small or insignificant activity to interpret what he said or meant to say, or to determine the overall meaning of his work, or how it can best be summarized. A particular challenge is to interpret Freud's theory in a way that sounds reasonable in the modern context. The original theory is, after all, nearly a century old.

Many psychologists and historians have taken on this task, with widely varying results. Peter Gay's (1988) monumental biography of Freud includes a thorough and insightful survey of the development of Freud's theory and a firm defense of it. Charles Brenner's (1974) very useful outline of psychoanalysis is a complex merging of Freud's original ideas with Brenner's own insights and updates. The preceding two chapters of this book likewise constitute more of an interpretation than a literal rendition of Freud. I merged what Freud said with what I think he meant to say or should have said, and even mixed in some ideas that are probably better traced to later thinkers in the same tradition.

For example, as mentioned, I altered the traditional rendition of the Oedipal crisis because I think the original makes little sense in the light of years of research about socialization. Thus, my version changes (some would say distorts) what Freud actually said. I also reinterpreted *libido* by describing it as the "life drive," rather than limiting it to something exclusively sexual in nature. Again, this changes, and in fact directly contradicts, what Freud said in some of his own writings, but I prefer to interpret what he said in terms of what seems to make sense today. I also changed Freud's description of the stages of personality development to emphasize, as did the great neo-Freudian theorist Erik Erikson (1963), that each stage is associated not just with different bodily sensations but also with different tasks in developing relationships with the social world.

The more you become tempted to "fix" Freud in your rendition, to mix in other thinkers and ideas from other sources, and the more you find yourself having ideas of your own about Freudian theory, the more you become an active developer of psychoanalytic theory yourself. It was Anna Freud, not her father, who wrote the definitive survey of the defense mechanisms (some of these mechanisms were summarized in Chapter 11). It is probably safe to say Sigmund Freud would have approved (he apparently approved of everything his favorite daughter did), as she did not deviate from the spirit of his theorizing. But such an explicit rendering of defenses is not to be found in Freud's own writings. Many other, more minor figures have also continued to write about psychoanalysis in a manner that tries to stay true to Freud's theory, while still extending it in some way.

Latter-Day Issues and Theorists

The theorists who continued the development of psychoanalytic theory after Freud are an impressive crew. They include Anna Freud, Bruno Bettelheim, Erik Erikson, Carl Jung, Alfred Adler, Karen Horney, Harry Stack Sullivan, Melanie Klein, Donald Winnicott, and Henry Murray. You probably have heard of several of them; Erikson, Jung, and Adler, especially, number among the major intellectual figures of the twentieth century. But it is also important to note that every single one of the individuals just named is deceased. Although neo-Freudians still exist and are practicing to this day, the "golden age" of neo-Freudianism seems to have passed.

Most neo-Freudians—including all the ones just mentioned—used the same research "method" as Freud himself. They saw patients, looked into themselves, read widely in history and literature, and drew conclusions. This is just as true of some of Freud's most vehement critics, such as Jung, an early dissenter, and Jeffrey Masson, a recent dissenter, as it is of those more sympathetic to him, such as Bruno Bettelheim and Anna Freud.

This method gives psychoanalysts the ability to cover a lot of theoretical ground and to develop opinions about almost everything. It also invokes a style of argument that more conventionally scientific psychologists find frustrating. When Jung argued with Freud, for example, he basically said that his cases and introspection showed A, and Freud would reply no, his own cases and introspection led clearly to conclusion B, to which Jung would reply that anybody can see it's really A . . . and so forth. Anyone looking for a crucial experiment to settle the matter will search in vain; even if somebody were clever enough to come up with one, neither Freud nor Jung—nor any other neo-Freudian—would admit that a mere experiment could settle such profound matters.

Most neo-Freudians differ from Freud in three major respects. First, sex is less important to them than it was to Freud. Nearly all of them place less emphasis on the libido as the sexual wellspring of all thought and behavior, and instead reinterpret libido as a more general kind of motivation toward life and creativity. You have already seen such a reinterpretation in the preceding chapters of this text. I view this change of emphasis as a permissible modern reinterpretation of an old theory; other theorists view this issue as an example of one place where Freud was simply wrong.

Freud's emphasis on sexuality—even in children—was always one of the most unsettling and controversial aspects of his theory. Thus, it should not be surprising that so many later theorists have been tempted to "clean up" psychoanalysis in this area. Freud himself believed that those who wished to deemphasize the importance of sex did so because of their own anxieties. Their defenses made them unable to directly face the importance of sex and caused them to see the important bases of behavior elsewhere. Maybe he is right, but this kind of argument is not easily settled. If I say you disagree with me because of your own sexual hangups, how can you reply except, perhaps, by saying the same thing about me?

A second deviation by some neo-Freudians is to put less emphasis on the unconscious processes of the mind and more emphasis on the conscious processes of thought. Modern "ego psychologists" are interested in explaining the ego processes behind the perception and conscious comprehension of reality (e.g., Hartmann, 1964; Loevinger, 1976; Rapaport, 1960; Klein, 1970). **Ego psychology** looks a little less like classic psychoanalysis and a little more like the rest of psychology (especially the cognitive approaches considered in Chapters 16 and 17), because instead of focusing on sexuality, psychic conflict, and the unconscious, it focuses on perception, memory, learning, and (rational) thinking. According to Jane Loevinger's influential version, the ego's function is to make sense of everything that a person experiences (Loevinger, 1987). Moreover, the story of development is essentially the story of the development of the ego itself. Early in life the ego struggles to understand how the individual is separate from the world and from his or her mother; later the ego grapples with such issues as how to relate to society, how to achieve personal autonomy, and how to appreciate the autonomy of others. According to a personality test designed by Loevinger to measure individuals' levels of "ego development," most people never get much farther than learning society's basic rules and appreciating that some of those rules have exceptions (Holt, 1980). Very few get to the point of being truly independent people who can appreciate and support the independence of those around them.

A third common deviation of the neo-Freudians is to put less emphasis on instinctual drives and the internal workings of the mind as the source of psychological difficulties, and more on interpersonal relations. By modern psychological standards, Freud was surprisingly uninterested in the daily lives of his patients. Whereas a modern therapist would want to know the details of a client's day-to-day interactions with his or her spouse, Freud would be more interested in the history of that client's relations with his or her opposite-sex parent during childhood. Adler and Erikson both emphasized the way psychological problems can arise from the difficulties people have relating with other people and with society in their present-day lives, and object relations theorists believe that we replay certain key relationship patterns over and over throughout our lives.

Inferiority and Compensation: Adler

Alfred Adler (1870–1937) was the first major disciple of Freud to end up at odds with the master. Like many others at the time and since, Adler thought that Freud was much too focused on sex as the ultimate motivator and organizer of thought and behavior. Of equal or greater importance, Adler thought, was what he called *social interest*, or the desire to relate positively and productively with other people (Adler, 1939).

Adler said that individuals are motivated to attain equality with or superiority over other people, and that they try to accomplish this to compensate for whatever they felt, in childhood, was their weakest aspect. This idea, called **organ inferiority**, leads one to expect that someone who felt physically weak as a child will grow into an adult who strives for physical strength, that a child who feels stupid will grow into an adult obsessed with proving himself or herself to be smarter than everyone else, and so on. It matters little whether the child *was* physically weak or relatively unintelligent; more important is how the child was made to *feel*.

A particular kind of such compensation for the past is seen in the desire of an adult to act and become powerful, as the result of feeling inadequate or inferior. Adler called this kind of overcompensating behavior the **masculine protest**. He applied this term to both men and women, but believed the issue is particularly acute for men. Young boys pick up from society the idea that males are supposed to be the powerful and dominant gender and yet, who is the most powerful person in *their* lives? Mom, obviously. Alder believed this early experience caused some young men to develop a powerful yearning to prove their dominance, power, and masculinity. One way to do this, in modern culture, is to buy a muscle car, or a pickup truck that can only be entered with a ladder, loudly rev the engine, and race up and down the highway and terrify everyone around you. These kinds of tactics always ring a little false. I think most people intuitively understand that someone who is secure in his masculinity does not feel the need to prove it through

"Fill'er up with testosterone."

his choice of vehicle, manner of driving it, or any other superficial means. The masculine protest is a compensation, therefore, a form of inferiority complex.

Adler's point is that everyone felt inferior as a child, in one or probably many respects, and adult behavior can be driven by the quest to overcome these feelings. This quest can help explain behaviors that otherwise do not make much sense—such as driving a race car or an implausibly large truck back and forth to the supermarket—but also much more. Needs for power, for love, and for achievement all have roots in early experience. The various compensations for an individual's perceived childhood inferiorities coalesce into a particular mode of behavior, which Adler called that individual's "style of life." Two familiar terms with roots in Adlerian thought are *inferiority complex* and *lifestyle*.

The Collective Unconscious, Persona, and Personality: Jung

The next major rebel from psychoanalysis was Carl Jung (1875–1961) (see Jung, 1971a, for a collection of his writings). His feud with Freud was even more dramatic and bitter than Adler's, because Freud had high hopes for Jung, who was one of Freud's earliest disciples. Indeed, Jung and Freud had close contacts for many years; they wrote each other numerous letters and even traveled to America together. Freud declared Jung to be his "crown prince," and anointed him the very first president of the International Psychoanalytic Association.

But over the years Jung's theorizing deviated more and more from Freud's, to the point that neither could reconcile their views. Perhaps Jung's most irritating deviation, from Freud's point of view, was his increasing interest in mystical and spiritual matters. Freud, a devout atheist, found Jung's ideas concerning an inner rhythm to the universe ("synchronicity"), transcendental experiences, and a collective unconscious rather hard to take. These ideas became extremely important to Jung, however, and they are an important reason why he remains famous today.

Jung's best-known idea is that of the **collective unconscious**. Jung believed that as a result of the history of the human race as a species, all people share certain inborn "racial" (by which he meant "species-specific") memories and ideas, most of which reside in the unconscious. Some of these are fundamental images, called **archetypes**, which Jung believed went to the core of how people think about the world at both conscious and unconscious levels. They include the earth mother, the hero, the devil, and the supreme being. Images of these archetypes, sometimes disguised behind symbols, show up repeatedly in dreams, in thoughts, in mythology all over the world, and even in modern literature. (Indeed, a school of literary criticism active to this day entails finding Jungian archetypes in novels, plays, and cinema.) This seems like an odd idea, but there may be something to it. Snakes show up frequently in cultural stories, such as the Bible, almost always with a sinister role, and there is some evidence that the human fear of snakes is innate (Öhman & Mineka, 2003).

Another lasting idea of Jung's is the **persona**, which was his term for the social mask one wears in public dealings. He pointed out that to some degree everyone's persona is always a false self, because everyone tries to keep some aspects of their real selves private, or at least fails to advertise all aspects of the self equally. This idea survives in modern social psychology and sociology (e.g., Goffman, 1959), and also influenced object relations theory, which will be considered later in this chapter. The danger, according to Jung, is that individuals might come to identify more with their personas than with their real selves. They may become obsessed with their images instead of who they really are and what they really feel, and thus become shallow with no aims or purposes in life deeper than becoming socially successful. They become creatures of society instead of individuals true to themselves.

Another influential Jungian concept is that of the anima and animus. The **anima** is the idea, or prototypical conceptualization, of the female, as held in the mind of a male. The **animus** is the idealized image of the male as held in the mind of a female. These two images cause members of each sex to have some aspects of the opposite sex in their own psychological makeup: a male's anima is the root of his "feminine side"; a female's animus is the basis of her "masculine side." These concepts also determine how each responds to the other sex: a man understands (or misunderstands) women through the psychological lens of his anima; a woman likewise understands or misunderstands men according to her view through her animus. This can lead to real problems if the idealized woman or man in one's mind turns out to match poorly or not at all with the *real* women and men in one's life. This is a common problem, Jung believed, and daily experience would seem to support him on this.

Another key idea of Jung that survives is his distinction between people who are turned in on themselves (introverts) and those who are oriented outward toward the world and other people (extraverts). As we saw in the trait section of this book, the dimension of extraversion-introversion is one of the Big Five dimensions of personality and has been found again and again in a wide range of psychometric research programs.

Yet another Jungian idea that many people still find useful is his classification of four basic ways of thinking: rational thinking, feeling, sensing, and intuiting. As Jung wrote,

> Sensation establishes what is actually present, [rational] thinking enables us to recognize its meaning, feeling tells us its value, and intuition points to possibilities as to whence it came and whither it is going in a given situation. (Jung, [1931] 1971b, p. 540)

Jung believed that everybody uses all four kinds of thinking, but that people vary in which kind predominates. An engineer might emphasize rational thinking, for example, while an artist emphasizes feeling, a detective emphasizes sensation, and a religious person emphasizes intuition. A modern personality test, the Myers-Briggs Type Indicator (also known as the MBTI) (Myers, 1962), is sometimes used to determine which kind of thinking is dominant in a particular individual. Vocational guidance counselors and personnel departments frequently use this test.

Jung believed that ideally one would achieve a balance between all four types of thinking, although he acknowledged that such an achievement is difficult and rare. (The distinction between Jung and Freud, by the way, could be summed up by saying that Freud emphasized rational thinking, whereas Jung had a more intuitive style.)

Feminine Psychology and Basic Anxiety: Horney

Karen Horney (1885–1952) did not begin writing publicly about psychoanalysis until late in Freud's career, and unlike Adler and Jung she never feuded with the master. She is one of the three most influential women in the history of psychoanalysis (the others were Freud's brilliant and devoted daughter Anna, and the object relations theorist Melanie Klein). Horney wrote widely about psychoanalytical topics, and some of her books are among the best works one can read for an introduction to psychoanalytic thought (see Horney, 1937, 1950). She also wrote about self-analysis, which she thought people could use to help them through their own psychological difficulties at times when the services of a professional psychoanalyst are impractical or impossible to obtain (Horney, 1942).

Horney's principal deviation from Freud is over an aspect of his theory that many other people—especially women—also have found objectionable. She disagreed with Freud's portrayal of women as being obsessed by their "penis envy" and their desire to be male. As mentioned in Chapter 11, in some of his writing Freud seemed to view women as damaged creatures, as men without penises, instead of as whole persons in their own right. Like many others since, Horney found this view implausible and objectionable. If some women wish to be men, she theorized, it is probably because they see men as more free and more able to pursue their own interests and ambitions than women are. Although women might lack confidence and seek self-fulfillment to an excessive degree through their love relationships with men, these are the results of the structure of society rather than of the structure of their bodies.

Horney's other contributions fit better into the conventional Freudian mode. She emphasized how much adult behavior is based on efforts to overcome the basic anxiety acquired in childhood: the fear of being alone and helpless in a hostile world. Attempts to avoid such anxiety can lead to a number of what Horney called *neurotic needs*, needs that people feel but that are neither realistic nor truly desirable. These include the needs to find a life partner who will solve all of one's love-related problems and take over and fix one's life, to be loved by everybody, to dominate everybody, and to be independent of everybody. Not only are these needs unrealistic, they are mutually contradictory. But the mind often unconsciously tries to pursue all of them anyway, which can lead to self-defeating behavior and problems in relating to other people.

Psychosocial Development: Erikson

Erik Erikson (1902–1994) always claimed to be a faithful, orthodox Freudian, but his innovations in psychoanalytic theory make him perhaps the most important of the revisionists (see Erikson, 1963, 1968). For example, he pointed out persuasively that not all conflicts take place in the unconscious regions of the mind—many conflicts are conscious. A person might have to choose between two (or more) activities, two careers, even two lovers. These conflicts can be real, painful, and consequential, as well as completely conscious.

Erikson believed that certain basic kinds of conflict arise at various stages of one's life. This insight led Erikson to develop his own version of Freud's theory of psychological development, in which Erikson emphasized not the physical location of libido at each stage, but rather the conflicts that are experienced and their possible outcomes. For that reason, his theory of development is referred to as *psychosocial* as opposed to Freud's *psychosexual* approach. (Erikson's psychosocial approach heavily influenced the psychoanalytic view of development that I presented in Chapter 10.) Erikson's developmental theory covers not just childhood, but development throughout one's life.

The first stage, according to Erikson, is "basic trust versus mistrust." This corresponds to Freud's oral stage of very early childhood, where the utterly dependent child learns whether his or her needs and wants will be met, ignored, or overindulged. If the appropriate ratio of satisfaction and temporary frustration is experienced, the child develops "hope" (which in Erikson's terminology refers to a positive but not arrogant attitude toward life) and a confidence—but not overconfidence—that his or her basic needs will be met.

The next stage, corresponding to Freud's anal stage, is that of "autonomy versus shame and doubt." As the child becomes able to control his or her bowels and other physical activities, learns language, and begins to receive orders from adult authorities, an inevitable conflict arises: Who's in charge here? On the one hand, adults put strong pressure on a child to obey, but on the other hand, that child has a desire to take control of his or her own life. The outcome can go either way, leading in some cases to the anal character described in Chapter 10.

Erikson's third stage, corresponding to Freud's phallic stage, is that of "initiative versus guilt." The child begins to anticipate and fantasize about what life as an adult might eventually be like. These fantasies inevitably will include sexual ones, as well as various tactics and plans to get ahead in life. Such fantasies are good for a child, Erikson believed, but if not responded to well by adults, they can lead the child to feel guilty and to back off from taking initiative in his or her development toward adulthood. Ideally, the child will begin to develop a sense of right and wrong, derived from adult teachings but also true to the child's developing sense of self. This will lead, in adulthood, to a true and principled morality, in which moral rules are applied with flexibility and wisdom, rather than a merely conformist pseudomorality, in which rigid rules are followed blindly and without exception. You may have noticed that this stage is a reinterpretation of Freud's phallic stage without the full Oedipal crisis (see Chapter 10).

The fourth stage is "industry versus inferiority," during which one begins to develop the skills and attitudes to succeed in the world of work or otherwise make a positive contribution to society, or not. At this time the child must begin to control his or her exuberant imagination and unfocused energy and get on with tasks of developing competence, workmanship, and a way of organizing the various tasks of life. This stage corresponds roughly to Freud's latency period.

At Erikson's fifth stage, development begins to deviate more widely from the path laid out by Freud. The Freudian account of psychological development basically stops with the genital stage, which is reached, if at all, at some unspecified time after puberty. But in Erikson's view, development continues throughout life. The next crisis to be encountered involves "identity versus identity confusion," as the adolescent strives to figure out who he or she is and what is and is not important. The task at this stage is to begin to choose values and goals that are consistent, personally meaningful, and useful.

Close on the heels of the identity conflict comes the conflict of "intimacy versus isolation." The task here, for young adulthood, is to find an intimate life partner to share important experiences and further development, as opposed to becoming isolated and lonely.

As one enters middle age, Erikson said, the next conflict to be faced is "generativity versus stagnation." As a person's own position in life becomes set with increasing firmness, does he or she settle in and become comfortable and passive, or begin to turn his or her concerns to the next generation? The challenge here is to avoid the temptation to simply cash in one's chips and go fishing, and instead to raise and nurture children and more generally to do what one can to ensure the progress of the next generation. I am reminded here of the modern phenomenon of prosperous American retirees who vote overwhelmingly against taxes to support schools. At a younger age, there are "yuppies" (young urban professionals) who either don't have children because they might slow down their career, or do have children but hire other people to raise them because they "don't have time" to do it themselves. Which choice do you think these people have made between generativity and stagnation?

The final crisis in life occurs in late old age, as one begins to face the prospect of death. The choice here is between "integrity" and "despair." Does the person despair about mistakes he or she made in life and feel that, basically, he or she blew it? Or from long experience has the person developed wisdom? The test of that is: After seventy, eighty, or ninety years of life, does the person have anything of interest and value to say to the next generation? Or not?

As we have seen, one progresses from one crisis to another in Erikson's scheme not according to processes of physical or genital maturation, but according to the different developmental tasks that are necessary at different times of life because of the structure of human society. This insight about the societal basis of development is the first of the two major contributions of Erikson's theory of development. The second major contribution is that this scheme is Erikson's pioneering venture into what is now called "life-span development." This idea proposes that development is not something that only little children do; it is a neverending task and opportunity across life, from childhood through middle and old age. Modern developmental psychology is heavily influenced by this idea.

Object Relations Theory: Klein and Winnicott

The most important part of life, the source of most of its pleasures and pains, is probably the relationships we have with other people. In psychoanalytic terms, the emotionally important people in one's life are called "objects," and the analysis of interpersonal relationships is called **object relations theory** (Greenberg & Mitchell, 1983; see also Klein, 1964; Winnicott, 1958, 1965). The key insight of the object relations approach is that we can only relate to other people via the images we hold of them in our minds, and these images do not always exactly match reality. Not surprisingly, mismatch causes problems.

Object relations theory is the most active area of psychoanalytic thinking at present, and has generated a huge literature of its own. A search of the term *object relations* on the PsychInfo® database yields more than 6,000 articles. The core ideas go back (naturally) to Freud himself, who viewed the superego as being built from identifications with important people early in life, and who also thought that important relationships tended to be relived with new people, again and again, through the mechanism of transference. Anna Freud pushed this idea further by examining children and their relationships with their parents. Other important figures in the history of object relations theory include Melanie Klein and D. W. Winnicott. The work of many other theorists, including the neo-Freudians summarized earlier, is also relevant. To the extent that a psychoanalyst addresses problems of interpersonal relations, the more he or she can be considered an object relations theorist (Greenberg & Mitchell, 1983).

Object relations theory comes in many forms, therefore, but almost every version includes four principal themes. The first is the observation that every relationship has in it elements of satisfaction and frustration, or pleasure and pain. Melanie Klein theorized that the first important "object" (literally) in the infant's life is the mother's breast. The infant quickly discovers that this object is a source of great delight, providing nutrition, warmth, and comfort. So the baby adores the breast. At the same time, the breast can be frustrating—it is not always available and not always full. So the baby hates the breast. The baby is not reasonable in its demands—remember the description of the primary process thinking of the id, in Chapter 10. The baby wants everything, now, and when the breast cannot or does not provide this, the baby is angry.

This dichotomy leads to the second theme of object relations: the mix of love and hate. Just like the original object, the breast, the important people in one's life are sources of pleasure and frustration. They may give us love, support, and even sexual satisfaction. So we love them. At the same time, they may express annoyance with us, criticize us, and frustrate us. So we hate them. This sad situation is inevitable, in the view of object relations theory. You cannot satisfy someone without also frustrating him or her at least sometimes. So his or her love for you will never be completely unmixed with frustration and resentment.

The third major theme of object relations is the distinction between parts of the love object, and the whole person. To the baby, the mother *is* the breast, at least at first. This is what interests and attracts the baby, not the mother as an actual person. It is a complex and difficult process, perhaps never completely successful, for the baby to move to appreciating the whole person of his or her mother, rather than just what she gives to the baby. In the same way, the people in our lives are parts and wholes. One might enjoy a partner's sense of humor, intellect, body, or money. To what degree is this the same thing as loving the partner himself or herself? From an object relations perspective, it is quite different. To use a person's attributes for one's own enjoyment is a very different matter than loving the whole person. This is one place where object relations theory intersects with common sense. To love a person's physique or wallet is not the same thing as loving the person herself or himself, and to move beyond appreciating superficial aspects of people to loving them as real and whole persons is a difficult and perhaps rarely accomplished feat.

The fourth major theme of object relations is that, to some degree, the psyche of the baby and the adult is aware of and disturbed by these contradictory feelings. The baby worships the mother's breast, but according to Klein the baby also feels anger (because there is never enough), envy (because the baby wishes to have the breast's power for itself), fear (because the baby does not ever want to lose the breast), and guilt (if the baby were to harm the breast, it could lose it). It may not be particularly plausible to attribute all of these complex reactions to a baby, but the overall theme does strike a chord. Let's say you are fortunate enough to form a relationship with a truly attractive and desirable person. That's great. But the downside may be a set of Kleinian reactions that may be more or less conscious. The very delight in the person's company may make you feel frustrated and even angry that he or she is not available to you all the time. You may envy the power this person now has over you, precisely because of his or her attractiveness. You may fear losing him or her, and the fear is greater the more desirable he or she seems to you. And finally, you may feel guilt over all of these negative reactions, because if you were to express them, you really might lose this person. No wonder relationships can get so messed up.

Melanie Klein developed her theoretical ideas in large part from her work with children; she was one of the earliest psychoanalysts (along with Anna Freud) to attempt psychoanalytic treatment with the very young. Freud himself dealt almost exclusively with adults' memories of themselves as children. One of her innovations in child therapy, still widely used, was to communicate with and diagnose children through play (Klein, 1986/1955). She usually provided a range of toys and watched closely to see which toys a child played with, and how; she believed the child's play was the symbolic expression of emotions such as hate, anger, love, and fear. From watching children play at relations with their parents, for example, she thought she saw signs that children divide or "split" their important love objects into two parts, one good and one bad. The good one is the part of the object that pleases them; the bad is the part that frustrates them. Children wish to destroy the bad part because they fear being destroyed by it (Klein called this the *paranoid position*), and they wish to worship and protect the good part because they fear losing it (Klein called this the *depressive position*).

Naturally, the phenomenon of splitting applies to other love objects as well. The problem, of course, is that people are not neatly divided into good parts and bad parts; they are indivisible wholes. So both desires—to destroy and to worship—are contradictory and irrational. This situation can lead to the development of some common neurotic defenses. For example, to defend against the (more or less hidden) desire to destroy (the bad part of) one's parent, one may idealize him or her. Have you ever heard someone describe his or her mother or father in terms that were, quite literally, too good to be true? Klein believed, in true Freudian fashion, that such idealization is a symptom of underlying hostility, that is being defended against at all costs. This person might not be able to accept that his or her father had flaws, because to do so would expose his or her anger at those flaws and threaten a loss of his love, or the memory of that love. In addition, to the extent that the person has identified with his or her father, he has become a part of the person, and so to criticize him is to criticize oneself. So, one constructs an image of him as having been perfect. It is possible to see people do this with

"I wish I'd started therapy at your age."

descriptions of their parents, their boyfriends and girlfriends, and even their children. The distortion in these descriptions may be obvious to everyone but the person himself or herself.

The pediatrician D. W. Winnicott started out his career in child psychology heavily influenced by Klein, but soon developed ideas of his own that became important additions to object relations theory. One of his ideas that has crossed the boundary into everyday use was his description of what he called the "niffle" (Winnicott, 1996). The term came from a young patient of his named Tom, who at age five had to be hospitalized away from his family and took comfort from sleeping with his "niffle," a small piece of cloth to which he had developed an emotional attachment. Tragically, when he returned home the niffle was lost in transit. This loss was so upsetting that Tom became hostile, stubborn, and annoying to the point that his parents brought him to Winnicott for therapy. From this experience, Winnicott formed the idea of the *transitional object*, often a special blanket, stuffed animal, or "niffle," that the child uses to bridge the gap between private fantasy and reality. These objects become endowed by the child with special emotional meaning, almost magic, and can comfort the child when adult company (or, as Klein would surely say, the breast) is not available. Over time, the object loses its special meaning as the child, becoming an adult, is better able to handle the world without this kind of support.

Objects like these are transitional in two senses. First, they help the child make the change from a time when adults are constantly caring for him or her, to the time when he or she must face the world alone. Second, they exist in an interesting transitional state between fantasy and reality. The objects are always real objects in that there actually is a bear, or a blanket, or whatever (for one of my daughters the role was played for a time by a toy dinosaur). But the child gives it a special magic and, importantly, nobody in the family questions the potency of this magic. Houses have been turned upside down more than once looking for lost "niffles," and for good reason. Objects like this are important, and they are not limited to children. Adults have sentimental attachments to many things that represent important people in their lives. The most obvious example is the family pictures many people perch on their desks and carry in their wallets. The purpose of these pictures and other objects is to compensate in some small way for the fact that we cannot have our loved ones with us all the time, or forever.

Another idea Winnicott added to object relations theory was the notion of the "false self" that children—and later, adults—learn to put on in order to please other people. Winnicott believed that to some degree this is normal and even necessary; ordinary social etiquette and politeness is "false" in a sense but very helpful in smoothing interpersonal relations. He worried more about some particularly charming children who he feared had learned

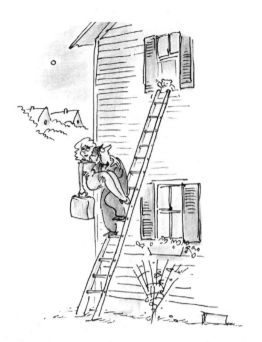

to put on a false act in a desperate attempt to cheer up their depressed mothers, at a high cost to the integrity of their own true selves. In theorizing reminiscent of Jung's thinking about the persona, Winnicott observed that the purpose of the false self is, in a sense, to protect the true self by keeping it invisible. No one can exploit, harm, or even touch the true self if a big enough false front is constructed. The ultimate maneuver of the false self is suicide. If there seems to be no hope that the true self can ever emerge, succeed, and be accepted for what it really is, then the false self prevents its exposure, permanently.

The purpose of psychotherapy, from the perspective of object relations, is to help the true and false self be a little less discrepant and, in general and in the classic Freudian tradition, to help the rational resources of the mind work through its irrational defenses. The goal is for the client to see the important people in his or her life as they really are, not as they are wished or fantasized to be. Likewise, the client may need help to see these people as whole individuals who are a mixture of virtues, vices, and everything in between, rather than "splitting" their images into Jekyll-Hyde twins that are all good on one side, and all bad on the other. Overcoming these illusions is not easy. On some level everybody would prefer it if the important people in one's life were perfect and devoted to one's satisfaction, and perhaps also everyone is on some level outraged that even the most loved people in our lives fall short of perfection and fail to satisfy us sometimes. The faith of object relations theory is the same as the faith of Freud himself: Rationality can win over all. If we just think about things sufficiently clearly, and brush away enough of the neurotic cobwebs, we can do what makes sense and relate to others as real people.

Where Have All the Neo-Freudian Theorists Gone?

As I mentioned earlier, they all seem to be dead. The chapters in personality textbooks that survey Freud and the neo-Freudians are sometimes sardonically called, in the business, the "tour of the graveyard." Certainly no one of the stature of Jung, Adler, Horney, or Erikson, or even Klein or Winnicott, seems to be actively developing psychoanalytic theory today. Their kind of theorizing, based ultimately on informal observation, clinical experience, and insight, is the wave of the past. Instead, the future of psychoanalysis lies in increased attempts to do experimental and correlational research of the more conventional sort in an attempt to scientifically confirm, disprove, or alter psychoanalytic theory on the basis of the same kind of evidence employed by psychology more generally.

Modern Psychoanalytic Research

Almost all conventional psychological research—that is, experimental and correlational studies with data that can be publicly reported—is conducted by academic psychologists with positions at universities or research institutes. Over the years, the relationship between these psychologists and their colleagues who practice psychoanalysis in clinical settings has ranged from uneasy to downright hostile. Most university psychology departments, where researchers are trained, have no Freudians in them at all, so there is a remarkable amount of ignorance about psychoanalysis on the part of many research psychologists. Where would they learn about it? And even when academic psychologists do encounter psychoanalytic research that meets their usual standards of empirical validity, they often seem unprepared to believe any evidence showing any aspect of psychoanalytic thought to have value.

For their part, the psychoanalysts are at least equally guilty (Bachrach et al., 1991; Westen, 1998). They typically have very little interest in conventional scientific research, preferring to exchange anecdotal evidence: "I had a patient once who. . . . " Freud himself thought that psychodynamic processes could only be seen through clinical case study; most modern psychoanalysts likewise seem to regard experimental and correlational research as irrelevant. For example, one modern psychoanalyst wrote the following about experimental research:

> I have been singularly uninterested in, if not contemptuous of, anything that the "number crunchers" had to say. . . . The phrase "meaningful statistical data" was, to me, an oxymoron of hilarious proportions. (Tansey, 1992, p. 539)

The result of this mutual myopia is that psychoanalytic psychologists and nonpsychoanalytic psychologists usually ignore each other, and when they do interact, they typically attack or at best lecture each other without listening to the other side.

This sorry situation may be starting to change, however. A few brave psychologists are pursuing research that is relevant to psychoanalysis, and many more are doing so without realizing that is what they are doing. One of the most important of these new researchers, Drew Westen (1990), has pointed out that while few psychologists research Freud or even psychoanalysis directly, the work of many of them can nevertheless be considered relevant to these topics. He proposes that any research is psychoanalytic to the extent that it includes

1. an examination of independent mental processes that occur simultaneously in the same mind and can conflict with one another;
2. mental processes that are unconscious;
3. compromises among mental processes that are negotiated out of consciousness;
4. self-defensive thought processes and self-deception;
5. the influence of the past on current functioning, especially patterns laid down in childhood that endure into adulthood; or
6. sexual or aggressive wishes as they consciously or unconsciously influence thought, feeling, and behavior.

While very little experimental or correlational research includes *all* of these concerns, a great deal is relevant to at least one or some of them. Westen contends that if a given piece of research addresses any one of these issues, it is at least a little bit psychoanalytic. The more of these issues a piece of research includes, the more psychoanalytic that research becomes—knowingly or not. Westen's observation is extremely important because it implies that conventional, experimental, and correlational research may not be as irrelevant to psychoanalysis as psychologists on both sides of the fence have long assumed.

Testing Psychoanalytic Hypotheses

In light of Westen's argument, it is possible to find a large amount of research in the psychological literature that addresses psychoanalytic hypotheses. Most of this research did not explicitly set out to test psychoanalysis, and sometimes the articles that report this research do not mention psychoanalysis at all. But if one wants to find research documenting some ideas that can be traced back to Freud and the variants on the psychoanalysis he invented, a fair amount of support can be found. I summarized some of this evidence already during the survey of the basic ideas of psychoanalysis in the preceding two chapters (see especially the discussion of defense mechanisms in Chapter 11), but it might be useful to look at a few more instances.

For example, a large amount of research over the years has shown that the unconscious part of a person's mind can perceive some things without the conscious mind being aware of it (Erdelyi, 1974; Bornstein, 1999). It appears that the unconscious mind can keep a perception out of consciousness in order to protect the individual from experiencing anxiety—the classic defense mechanism of denial (see Chapter 11). In one study a "dirty" word—you know what I mean—which presumably might upset the values of the superego, was flashed on a screen. The person reported being unable to perceive what the word was. Then another word, the same length as the first but innocuous rather than obscene, was flashed. The person could read it immediately. This finding implies that some part of the mind recognized that the first word was obscene *before* it was consciously perceived, and apparently decided to keep this recognition out of conscious awareness. Furthermore, people who avoid reporting unpleasant perceptions are not just trying to look good, but appear to be actively pushing their experience of negative emotions out of conscious awareness (Erdelyi, 1974, 1985; Weinberger & Davidson, 1994). This is the process Freud called *denial.*

Many modern cognitive psychologists have concluded that most of what the mind does is unconscious (they usually report their findings without acknowledging Freud, however). As mentioned in Chapter 10, one currently dominant model of cognitive processing, called *parallel distributed processing*, or PDP, posits that the mind does many things at once, all outside of consciousness. Only the result of the compromise between these simultaneous mental processes becomes represented in conscious awareness (Rumelhart, McClelland, & The PDP Research Group, 1986; see Chapter 16). Behavior itself is the result of a similar process of compromise. As the cognitive psychologist Stephen Pinker (1997, p. 42) concluded, "Behavior is the result of an internal struggle among many mental modules." This finding recalls Freud's idea that consciousness is just the tip of the mental iceberg, with most of its determinants hidden from view.

Other psychoanalytic ideas also have been supported by modern research. For example, recently developed techniques can assess the degree to which people unintentionally reveal their use of psychoanalytic defense mechanisms through the way they speak (Feldman-Barrett, Williams, & Fong, 2002). The character traits of the anal personality—stinginess, orderliness, rigidity, and so on—turn out to be correlated with each other just as Freud said they were, and the traits of the oral character also seem to be intercorrelated as Freud predicted, though perhaps to a weaker degree (Westen, 1990). The process Freud called *catharsis*, which involves getting one's psychological disturbances out into the open, has been proved to be helpful for both psychological and even physical health (Erdelyi, 1994; Hughes, Uhlmann, & Pennebaker, 1994).[3] Modern laboratory studies also have demonstrated *transference*, Freud's term for taking patterns of behavior and emotion developed with somebody in the past and applying them to one's relations with somebody new (Andersen & Baum, 1994; Andersen & Berk, 1998).

Not all Freudian ideas have fared so well, however. Notably, as I mentioned earlier, research has failed to support Freud's story of the Oedipal crisis at the phallic stage (Kihlstrom, 1994; Sears, 1947). Apparently this part of Freud's theory is wrong, which is why in Chapter 10 I offered a different account of what happens at the point when children begin to realize that boys and girls are different. Some psychologists claim that the psychoanalytic ideas that have been supported by research, such as the existence of the unconscious, would have been thought of even if Freud had never lived, and that most of the ideas that seem unique to Freud, such as the Oedipal crisis, have been shown to be wrong. These psychologists conclude that Freud has contributed nothing to the modern understanding of human psychology (Kihlstrom, 1994).

This view seems unduly harsh to me. The edifice of Freudian theory has influenced modern thinking and modern psychology in many, many ways. Indeed, it is difficult to imagine what modern psychology would look like had Freud never lived. Moreover, the completeness and persuasiveness of the original Freudian accounts of human nature, along with some of the revisions offered by the neo-Freudians and a bit of modern interpretation, convince me that Freudian theory has a great deal to offer toward trying to understand the complex nature of ourselves and others.

Attachment and Romantic Love

One particularly interesting area of modern research that acknowledges a heavy debt to psychoanalytic thought is the study of attachment and romantic love (Bowlby, 1982; Waters et al., 1991). The English psychoanalyst John Bowlby was heavily influenced by Freud's theory but became frustrated by the sheer speculative way some of his analytic colleagues wrote about the nature of love. He was even more frustrated by what he saw as their failure to understand how a person's early experiences in love—those in infancy, usually with his or her mother—could shape one's entire future outlook on emotional attachments. For this reason, Bowlby is sometimes classified as one of the object relations theorists, discussed earlier in this chapter.

---

[3]Other aspects of the idea of catharis, specifically the prediction that expressing aggressive impulses will "vent" and therefore lessen aggressive drive, have *not* been supported by modern research (Bushman, 2002).

Bowlby's description of the origins of love is similar to some of the theorizing by evolutionary biologists that was described in Chapter 9. Bowlby hypothesized that in the risky environment in which the human species developed over thousands of years, humans (and actually all primates) evolved a strong and basic fear of being alone, especially when in unusual, dark, or dangerous places, and especially when tired, injured, or sick. This fear motivates us to desire someone to protect us, preferably someone who has a particular interest in our survival and well-being. In other words, we want someone who loves us. This desire is especially strong in infancy and early childhood, but it never truly goes away; it is the basis of many of our most important interpersonal relationships (Bowlby, [1969] 1982).

This desire for protection leads us to develop what Bowlby called *attachments*. The first attachment relationship is formed with the child's primary caregiver, usually the mother. The term *primary* implies that a child generally has other caregivers as well, even if one is preferred, and all of those relationships are important. If everything goes well, the attachments the child develops provide both a safe haven from danger and a secure base from which to explore in happier times. This description essentially resembles Freud's account of what is supposed to happen at the oral stage.

Unfortunately everything does not always go well. As a result of his or her interactions with the primary caretaker and other caregivers, and the degree to which they meet his or her basic needs, the child develops expectations about what attachment relationships are like and what can be expected from them. Bowlby pointed out that a child draws two lessons from these early experiences. First, the child develops a belief about whether the people to whom he or she becomes attached will generally be reliable. Second, and perhaps more important, the child develops a belief about whether his or her own self is the kind of person to whom attachment figures are likely to respond in a helpful way. In other words, if a child learns that he or she does not usually receive the necessary amount of love and care, the child might conclude that this is because he or she is not lovable or worth caring about. This inference is not logical, of course: just because a child fails to be loved by a negligent caregiver does not mean the child would not be lovable to others.

The American psychologist Mary Ainsworth tried to make the consequences of these expectations and conclusions concrete and visible. She invented an experimental procedure called the *strange situation*, in which a child is briefly separated from and then reunited with his or her mother. Ainsworth believed that a good deal could be gleaned from observing how the child reacted both to the separation and to the reunion. In particular, one could determine the type of attachment relationship the child had developed (Ainsworth et al., 1978). From her research, Ainsworth classified children into three types, depending on the kinds of expectations they had developed about their primary caregivers and how they acted in the strange situation.

Anxious-ambivalent children come from home situations where their caregivers' behaviors are "inconsistent, hit-or-miss, or chaotic" (Sroufe, Carlson, & Shulman, 1993, p. 320). In the strange situation, these children are vigilant about their mother's presence and grow very upset when she disappears for even a few minutes. In their school situation, they are often victimized by other children and attempt to cling to teachers and peers in a way that backfires—it only drives them away—and leads to further hurt feelings, anger, and insecurity.

Avoidant children come from homes where they have been rebuffed repeatedly in their attempts to enjoy contact or reassurance. According to one study, their mothers tend to dislike hugs and other bodily contact (Main, 1990). In the strange situation, they do not appear distressed, but when their heart rate is measured, one sees definite signs of tension and anxiety (Sroufe & Waters, 1977). When their mother returns from the brief separation, they simply ignore her. In their school situations, these children are often hostile and defiant and manage to alienate both their teachers and their peers. As they grow older, they develop an angry self-reliance and cold and distant attitudes toward other people.

The more lucky ones, secure children, manage to develop a confident faith in themselves and their caregivers. When their mother returns in the strange situation, they greet her happily, with open arms. When upset, they are easily soothed, and they are active in exploring their environment, returning frequently to the primary caregiver for comfort and encouragement. They are sure of the caregiver's support and do not worry about it. This positive attitude carries over into the other relationships in their lives.

One remarkable aspect of these attachment styles is their self-fulfilling nature (Shaver & Clark, 1994). The anxious, clingy child drives people away; the avoidant child makes people angry; the secure child is easy to be with and attracts both caregivers and friends. Thus, a child's developing attachment style affects his or her outcomes throughout life.

In fact, research is beginning to examine in detail what happens to these children as they grow into adults and try to develop satisfying romantic relationships and other elements of a mature life. There are at least twenty-one different methods to assess one's "adult attachment style," the grown-up version of the childhood pattern just described. One of the simplest goes like this:

Which of these descriptions best describes your feelings?

1. I am somewhat uncomfortable being close to others; I find it difficult to trust them completely, difficult to allow myself to depend on them. I am nervous when anyone gets too close, and often, love partners want me to be more intimate than I feel comfortable being.

2. I find that others are reluctant to get as close as I would like. I often worry that my partner doesn't really love me or won't want to stay with me. I want to get very close to my partner, and this sometimes scares people away.

3. I find it relatively easy to get close to others and am comfortable depending on them. I don't often worry about being abandoned or about someone getting too close to me. (Hazan & Shaver, 1987, p. 515)

According to this measure, if you checked item 1, you are avoidant; if you checked item 2, you are anxious-ambivalent; and if you checked item 3, you are secure. When this survey was published in a Denver newspaper, 55 percent of the respondents described themselves as secure, 25 percent as avoidant, and 20 percent as anxious—the same percentages found in American infants studied by Ainsworth in the strange situation (Campos et al., 1983).

More detailed studies found that avoidant individuals are relatively uninterested in romantic relationships, are more likely (than secure individuals) to have their relationships break up, and grieve less after a relationship ends, even though they admit to being lonely (Shaver & Clark, 1994). They like to work alone, and sometimes use their work as an excuse to detach themselves from their emotional relationships. They describe their parents as having been rejecting and cold, or else describe them in vaguely positive ways (e.g., as "nice") without being able to provide specific examples. (For example, when asked, "What did your mother do that was *particularly* nice?" they are typically unable to give a convincing answer.) Avoidant individuals withdraw from their romantic partners when under stress, and instead tend to cope with their stress by ignoring it or denying it exists. They do not often share personal information with other people, and they tend to dislike other people who do share such information.

Anxious-ambivalent adults, in contrast, are obsessed with their romantic partners—they think about them all the time and have trouble allowing them to have their own lives. They suffer from extreme jealousy, report a high rate of relationship failures (not surprisingly), and sometimes exhibit the repeating cycle of breaking up and getting back together with the same romantic partner. Anxious-ambivalent adults tend to have low and unstable self-esteem, like to work with other people, but typically feel unappreciated by their co-workers. They are highly emotional under stress and have to work hard to keep their emotions under control. They describe their parents as having been intrusive, unfair, and inconsistent.

You will be relieved to learn that secure adults tend to enjoy long, stable romantic relationships characterized by deep trust and friendship. They have high self-esteem as well as high regard for others. When under stress, they seek out others and in particular their romantic partners for emotional support. They are also loyal in supporting their romantic partners when they are under stress. They describe their parents in positive but realistic terms, which they are able to back up with specific examples. In sum, they are people who are easy to be with (Shaver & Clark, 1994).

Secure individuals can deal with reality in a direct manner because their attachment experience has been positive and reliable. They have always had a safe refuge from danger and a secure base from which to explore the world. This idyllic pattern does not mean that secure people never cry, become angry, or worry about abandonment. But they do not need to distort reality to deal with their sadness, anger, or insecurity.

According to attachment theory, all of these patterns are learned in early childhood and reinforced in an increasingly self-fulfilling manner across young adulthood. This pattern of transference can persist across a person's entire life span and affect his or her approach to work as well as relationships (Hazan & Shaver, 1990). If an individual is unlucky enough to learn an avoidant or anxious-ambivalent style, change is difficult but perhaps not impossible. Psychotherapists informed by attachment theory try to teach these people the origins of their relationship styles, the way these styles lead to self-defeating outcomes, and constructive, positive ways to relate to others (Shaver & Clark, 1994).

Attachment theory, originated by a psychoanalyst (Bowlby) who considered himself a neo-Freudian, has diverged a long way from its psychoanalytic roots. Indeed, it is possible to say that it is no longer really Freudian (Kihlstrom, 1994). But one can also see it is as an example of how far a group of creatively thinking psychologists can develop a basic Freudian precept. In this case, the Freudian precept is that early relationships with parents form a template for how a person conducts other emotionally important relationships throughout life.

Psychoanalysis in Perspective

It is not easy to come to an overall evaluation of psychoanalytic thought. Freud's own theory, developed and amended over a period of several decades, is complicated enough. Add in Jung, Adler, the neo-Freudians, and 6,000 studies of object relations, and there is clearly no simple answer to the question, is the psychoanalytic perspective valid? Which psychoanalytic perspective? My own suggestion would be to consider carefully what you have learned in the past three chapters, do some extra reading of your own, and come to your own conclusions about which psychoanalytic ideas do and do not make sense.

A valuable contribution towards clearing away some of the difficulty in coming to terms with psychoanalysis was made a few years ago by the analyst and psychologist Drew Westen (1998). We saw earlier in this chapter that he proposed that several common research topics are a "little bit" psy-choanalytic, even if the studies don't acknowledge any debt to Freud. After reviewing a large amount of this research, he concluded that at least five propositions can be regarded as firmly established:

1. Much of mental life, including thoughts, feelings, and motives, is unconscious, which is why people sometimes behave in ways that even they do not understand.
2. The mind does many things at once and so can be in conflict with itself. For example, it is not unusual to want two different and con-tradictory things at the same time.
3. The events of childhood are important in shaping the personality of the adult, especially concerning styles of social relationships (e.g., attachment).
4. Relationships formed with significant other people—such as one's parents—form patterns that tend to be repeated throughout life with new people.
5. Psychological development involves moving from an unregulated, immature, and self-centered state to a more carefully regulated, mature one in which relationships with other people become increas-ingly important.

Not everybody in psychology accepts that these five conclusions have been firmly established, or even accepts that they all are relevant to psycho-analysis. As Freud foresaw from the beginning, psychoanalysis seems doomed to be controversial forever, which means some will always believe it to be not just wrong, but dead wrong.

As you reach your own conclusion about psychoanalysis, I would sug-gest you keep this point in mind: The criterion by which the psychoanalytic approach to psychology and every other approach should be evaluated is not whether it is right or wrong (because all theories are wrong in the end), or even whether it is scientific. Instead you should evaluate it by asking, does the approach raise questions you had not previously considered, and give you insight into things you did not understand as well before? On that ques-tion, I suspect, psychoanalytic theory will get better than a passing grade.

Summary

Freud died more than half a century ago, but his theory lives on in a variety of ways, including continuing to be a source of controversy and argument. Many modern writers have altered Freud's theory in various degrees through their summaries and interpretations. In addition, neo-Freudian theorists have proposed their own versions of psychoanalysis. Most of these revised theories include a lessened emphasis on sex and a greater emphasis on ego functioning and interpersonal relations. Alfred Adler wrote about strivings to overcome early feelings of inferiority. Carl Jung proposed ideas concerning the collective unconscious, the false mask called the "persona," the distinction between extraversion and introversion, and four basic types of thinking. Karen Horney developed a neo-Freudian theory of feminine psychology and also described the nature of basic anxiety and associated neurotic needs. Erik Erikson developed a detailed description of several stages of psychosexual development wherein both children and adults must come to terms with their changing environments. The object relations theorists, notably Melanie Klein and D. W. Winnicott, described the complex relations people have with important emotional "objects," and observed that these relationships often mix pleasure and pain, and love and hate. It is difficult to relate to other people as whole and complex human beings, and people often feel guilty about their mixed emotions and need to defend against them.

Modern psychologists interested in psychoanalysis are trying to bring rigorous research methodology to bear on some of the hundreds of hypotheses that could be derived from psychoanalytic theory. Some of these hypotheses, such as the existence of unconscious mental processes and phenomena like repression and transference, seem to have been confirmed. A particularly fruitful area of research has studied the connection between childhood patterns of attachment and adult patterns of romantic love. In the end, psychoanalysis might best be evaluated not so much in terms of the answers it has offered, but in terms of the questions it alone continues to raise.

SUGGESTED READINGS: PSYCHOANALYSIS

Bettelheim, B. (1988). *A good enough parent.* New York: Vintage.

> *A fascinating look at child-rearing from a psychoanalytic point of view, by one of the more important psychoanalysts of the latter part of this century. It is never blindly orthodox and is filled with nuggets of wisdom that would be of interest to any parent.*

Brenner, C. (1974). *An elementary textbook of psychoanalysis.* Garden City, NY: Doubleday/Anchor.

> *An excellent secondary source for a thorough summary of psychoanalysis.*

Gay, P. (1988). *Freud: A life for our time.* New York: Norton.

> *A masterful, thorough, well-written biography of Freud that includes a tour not just of his life, but of the development of psychoanalytic thought. The author is clearly sympathetic to Freud and psychoanalysis.*

Gay, P. (Ed.) (1989). *The Freud reader.* New York: Norton.

> *An excellent collection of Freud's original writings, including some unusual selections translated for the first time for this volume.*

Horney, K. (1942). *Self-analysis.* New York: Norton.

Horney, K. (1950). *Neurosis and human growth.* New York: Norton.
> *Two books by an important neo-Freudian in her own right that make fascinating reading for their insights into human nature, especially the unrealistic ways people think about themselves and their goals. These are self-help books, but intellectually they are much richer than more recent writings in this category.*

Mitchel, J. (1986). *The selected Melanie Klein.* New York: Free Press.
> *A collection of some of the key short papers by the important object relations theorist, Melanie Klein.*

Westen, D. (1998). The scientific legacy of Sigmund Freud: Toward a psychodynamically informed psychological science. *Psychological Bulletin, 124,* 333–371.
> *A thorough, very up-to-date, and highly readable summary of the modern research evidence that supports many of Freud's key ideas.*

PART V

EXPERIENCE AND AWARENESS: HUMANISTIC AND CROSS-CULTURAL PSYCHOLOGY

Different individuals have different points of view. Fans of opposing teams may watch the same game and come away with drastically different impressions of who fouled whom and which side the referees unfairly favored (Hastorf & Cantril, 1954). Or, more consequential, where one person sees a woman exercising a free choice about whether the circumstances are right for her to start a family, another person, observing exactly the same behavior, may see the murder of an unborn child.

Humanistic psychology, which is the subject of Chapter 13, is based on the premise that to understand a person you must understand his or her unique view of reality. It focuses on *phenomenology,* which comprises everything that a person hears, feels, and thinks, and which is at the center of his or her humanity and may even be the basis of free will. The other basic approaches to personality tend to regard people, implicitly if not explicitly, almost like things that can be put under the psychological

373

microscope and be dispassionately examined. But humanistic psychology emphasizes that the object of the psychologist's scrutiny is a fellow human who can scrutinize right back and form his or her own opinions. Even more centrally, humanistic psychology emphasizes that people feel, think, experience, and choose, and these activities make humans unique.

One interesting question raised by phenomenological considerations is this: If everybody's view of the world is different, which one is right? Or, in the midst of all these shifting perceptions, where is reality? Either way we ask it, the question turns out to be unanswerable, but it is critically important nonetheless. For to ask this question is to acknowledge that none of us has an exclusive ownership of truth, and that other points of view—even those that seem drastically different, foreign, or strange—may have an equal claim to validity.

This latter insight is the basis of the **cross-cultural** study of personality, the topic of Chapter 14. Not only do different individuals have different views of reality, but so do different cultures. A behavior seen as polite by a Japanese may seem horribly inefficient to a North American, and the same action seen as ordinary by an American may seem deeply immoral to an Indian. In recent years, psychologists have paid an increasing amount of attention to the degree to which theories of personality forged in Western culture apply to people in very different cultures around the world. Cross-cultural psychologists are also compelled to address the same issue raised by the phenomenological approach to personality: If different cultures have different views of the world, where is reality?

The following two chapters, therefore, address the same basic phenomenological premise—that the way you view and experience the world is the most important psychological fact about you. The first, Chapter 13, examines this premise at the individual level, and the second, Chapter 14, examines this premise at the cultural level. In both cases, the difficult challenge is to try to see the world the way someone else does, be that someone a close friend or the native of a different culture. From a humanistic, phenomenological perspective, this is the only way to begin truly to understand that person.

EXPERIENCE, EXISTENCE, AND THE MEANING OF LIFE: HUMANISTIC PSYCHOLOGY

The story is told of how Watergate burglar G. Gordon Liddy liked to impress people by holding his hand steadily above a lit candle as his flesh burned. "How can you do that? Doesn't it hurt?" he was asked. "Of course it hurts. The trick," he replied, "is not to care."[1]

Psychology is a funny kind of science, because the object of its scrutiny is the one doing the scrutinizing. Psychologists typically do their best to ignore this fact. Instead, they try to think about people and the human mind as interesting phenomena that can be examined from a distance in the same dispassionate, objective, and precise way that one might examine a rock, a mollusk, or a molecule. Psychologists are eager to have the prestige of "real" scientists, and psychology is even sometimes accused of suffering from "physics envy." Not all psychologists envy physicists, but many do believe that the best way to understand the human mind is through an enterprise modeled on the physical and biological sciences, one that follows the same canons of public data, objective analysis, repeatability, and so on.

The built-in contradiction in this approach once was caricatured by the humanistic psychologist George Kelly in these words:

> I, being a *psychologist,* and therefore a *scientist,* am performing this experiment in order to improve the prediction and control of certain human phenomena; but my subject, being merely a human organism, is obviously propelled by inexorable drives welling up within him, or else he is in gluttonous pursuit of sustenance and shelter. (Kelly, 1955, p. 5)

The goal of *humanistic* psychology is to overcome this paradox by frankly acknowledging and directly addressing the ways in which psychology is unique. Humanistic psychologists vehemently disagree with the idea that the

---

[1]I heard this existential fable from Lily Tomlin, who told it during a performance of *The Search for Signs of Intelligent Life in the Universe,* a play by Jane Wagner. Ms. Tomlin seems reliable on other matters, so perhaps this story is true.

study of the mind is just another science or that it in any way does, could, or should resemble physics or chemistry. As an object of study, they argue, the mind is not just different from things such as molecules or atoms, it is *fundamentally* different.

It is fundamentally different because the human mind is *aware.* It knows it is being studied, for instance, and has opinions about itself that affect the way it is studied. This fact has two implications. First, it means that psychology needs to address the unique phenomenon of awareness rather than brushing it under the rug. Second, and even more important, the fact that people are self-aware brings to the fore many uniquely human phenomena that do not arise when the subject of study is rocks, molecules, or even other animals. These phenomena include will power, conceptual thinking, imagination, introspection, self-criticism, aspirations, creativity, and, above all, free will. It is self-awareness that makes these possible and, interestingly, these are topics that the rest of psychology tends to ignore (Maddi & Costa, 1972; Seligman & Csikszentmihalyi, 2002). That is where the humanistic psychologists come in. Their job, as they see it, is to seek to understand awareness, free will, and the many related aspects of the mind that are uniquely human and that give life meaning.

Phenomenology: Awareness Is Everything

The central insight of humanistic psychology is that one's conscious experience of the world, also called a person's **phenomenology**, is more important— psychologically—than the real world itself. And even that summary may be an understatement. Proponents of *phenomenological* approaches to psychology sometimes assume that immediate, conscious experience is *all* that matters. Everything that has happened to you in the past, everything that is true about you at this moment, and anything that might happen in the future can influence you only in the way that it affects your thoughts and feelings at this moment. Indeed, from a phenomenological viewpoint, the only place and time in which you exist at all is in your consciousness, here, right now. The past, the future, other people, and other places are no more than ideas and, in a sense, illusions. The sense is this: A broader reality might exist, but only the part of it that you perceive—or invent—will ever matter to you. Your hand might be on fire but the trick, as Gordon Liddy observed, is not to care. More importantly, the realization that only your present experience matters is the basis of free will. The past is gone and the future is not here yet. You are here now, and in this moment you can *choose.*

This may all sound rather new age, but phenomenological analysis is not a new idea. The Talmud says, "We do not see things as they are. We see them as *we* are." Epictetus, a Greek Stoic philosopher who lived two thousand years

*"My feeling is that while we should have the deepest respect for reality,
we should not let it control our lives."*

ago, said, "It is not things in themselves that trouble us, but our opinions of
things." More recently, but still more than half a century ago, Carl Rogers (1951,
p. 484) wrote, "I do not react to some absolute reality, but to my perception of
this reality. It is this perception which for me *is* reality" (see McAdams, 1990).

Your own particular experience of the world is called your **construal**.
Because construals are interpretations rather than direct reflections of reality, they can be freely chosen. Your construals will be different from those
of anybody else and are the basis of how you live your life, including the
goals you pursue. So it is through choosing your construal of the world—
deciding how to interpret your experience—that you achieve free will (Boss,
1963). And it is by abdicating this choice, to other people or to society, that
you can lose free will (I'll say more about this later).

Observations such as these imply that psychology has a special duty to
study how people perceive, understand, and experience reality. And, while
some modern psychologists have foresaken and perhaps even forgotten this
duty, some of the earliest research in psychology was begun in an attempt to
understand human experience, as we shall see in the next section.

The Chemistry of Experience

Appreciation of the unique status of the human mind as an object of study
dates back to the very beginning of modern psychology when, in 1879, in
Leipzig, Germany, Wilhelm Wundt founded the first psychological labora-

tory. Over the next several decades, he established a busy research program, trained students, and is credited by some historians as being the scientist who, more than any other single person, is responsible for the emergence of psychology as an independent discipline with its own methods, programs, and institutions (Gardner, 1987).

Wundt worked to set up psychology as a separate field of study precisely because he saw its topic as unique. He noted that while all other sciences study objects of the physical world, they ignore the human experience of these objects. A physicist might note the mass of an iron ball, for example, but has nothing to say about the way it feels "heavy." But Wundt believed it was important also to study this experience of heaviness, and similar experiences arising from human perceptions of and interactions with the physical world. He conceived of psychology as the field that would take on the task of understanding conscious experience as a phenomenon of importance in its own right, quite aside from the physical stimuli that affect it.

There is only one way to study experience, Wundt believed, and that is to observe it closely. Of course, you cannot observe anyone's experience but your own. So Wundt worked to train himself and his team of researchers in the art of **introspection**.

Why was training required? Can't anyone just look inside and tell what he or she is thinking about? Wundt believed the answer to this is a loud No. The problem is that an untrained person will confuse the meaning he or she has learned about an object with perceptions of the object itself. For example, an untrained observer might look at a ball and say, "I see a ball." This is all wrong, according to Wundt; it merely describes an accepted social meaning. He was interested in pure mental *experience*. Thus, a Wundtian observer might say something like, "I see an object with curved boundaries, and a surface that is shiny on the top but shadowed underneath." This description, Wundt believed, is more psychological because it comes closer to describing the information that the perceptual apparatus of the eyes provides to the brain. The interpretation of this information, as meaning that a ball is present, is a later step in the process of perception, but it is not the initial experience.

Wundt spent many years (and wrote ten books) pursuing these ideas (e.g., Wundt, 1894, 1904). His goal was to describe exactly what went on in the mind when one observed various objects, felt other sensations (such as pinpricks), and came to simple decisions (such as whether or not to press a button). For example, in one experiment he instructed an assistant to press a button when he heard a tone. In one condition, the assistant concentrated on the button and his finger on it. In another condition, the assistant listened closely for the tone. Wundt's results showed that the button was pressed more quickly in response to the tone when the assistant focused on the button rather than the tone. Introspection showed that this was because when he listened for the tone, the assistant first had to notice the tone and decide it was necessary to respond by pushing the button, whereas when he focused only on the button, this stage could be skipped. In further studies Wundt found that the response was even slower when the assistant had to listen to several tones, only one of which was the right stimulus for pushing the button. Wundt explained this was because the decision to push the button required "cognition," thinking about whether the tone was correct or not, as well as "perception," recognizing the simple presence of the tone.

The goal of this work was to formulate something like a chemistry of mental life (Gardner, 1987). By closely attending to one's own phenomenology or experience, Wundt believed, it should be possible to identify the simple elements of perception and thought of which all other, more complex, perceptions and thoughts are comprised. A ball might be curved edges and a surface with differing patterns of light reflection, and love might be the experience of attraction plus the experience of pleasure plus a few other elementary sensations. In the end, the goal of phenomenologists like Wundt was to analyze any experience, feeling, or thought into its most basic, irreducible parts.

The enterprise failed. One problem was that it was unclear how useful Wundt's approach could ever be. Once one has analyzed experience into little pieces, then what? Another problem was that apparently some complex perceptions, feelings, and thoughts are themselves irreducible. They cannot be built out of tiny pieces but occur, or not, in their entirety. Love dissected into its component parts is no longer love. But perhaps the most important difficulty with the phenomenological program was the method of introspection itself.

Many scientifically minded psychologists became unsatisfied with a method in which an observer provided data that nobody else could see or verify. Of course, we have already seen that Wundt proceeded a small distance in the direction of observable data in his study of how long it took for his assistant to press buttons. Such "reaction time" is a phenomenon that can be measured objectively (and remains an important part of cognitive psychology to this day). But Wundt still depended heavily on the assistant's introspective report of just what he was thinking as he listened for the tone and decided to press the button. When behaviorism began to dominate psychology in the early twentieth century (see Chapter 15), this sort of introspection was the first thing they discarded.

The behaviorist move away from introspection was extremely influential. Not only was this move the foundation of behaviorism itself, but also it influenced nearly all of the rest of psychology. Modern cognitive science, for example, does try to assess mental activity by measuring reaction time (much as Wundt did), memory recall, and other observable responses. But it almost never simply asks a research participant, "What are you experiencing?" Since the days of Wundt, this question has been out of bounds for nearly everyone except the humanistic psychologists. To put it bluntly, nobody else cares what the subject thinks.

The history of psychology, then, began on an ironic note. The field owes its very existence to an attempt to understand human experience, or phenomenology. The founder of psychology was interested exclusively in this issue. But since that time, most of psychology has turned to other concerns. It has been left to existential philosophers and the humanistic psychologists to keep alive the idea that psychology's ultimate mission is to explain the nature and purpose of human experience.

Existentialism

The attempt to understand human experience and phenomenology goes back even further and deeper than Wilhelm Wundt, to a philosophical school called **existentialism**. Existentialism is not only a ten-dollar word, it is a broad philosophical movement that can be traced to Europe in the mid-1800s. Søren Kierkegaard, the Danish theologian, was one of its early proponents, as were Friedrich Nietzsche, Martin Heidegger, and more recently Ludwig Binswanger, Medard Boss, and Jean-Paul Sartre.

Existentialism arose as a reaction against European rationalism, science, and the industrial revolution. The existentialists thought that by the late nineteenth century, rationality had gone too far in its attempt to account for everything. In particular, they thought that science, technology, and rational philosophy had lost touch with human experience. This point of view began to catch on among European philosophers after World War II. The purpose of existential philosophy was to regain contact with the experience of being alive and aware.

Existential analysis begins with the concrete and specific experience of a single human being *existing* at a particular moment in time and space. An excellent example is you, right now. I mean, then, back when you read the words "right now," although that is already past, so maybe we should concentrate on right now, instead. Too late. The point is, your experience of existence exists only one infinitesimally small moment at a time, which is then gone, to be followed by another.

The key existential questions are the following: What is the nature of existence? How does it feel? And what does it mean?

Three Parts of Experience

We have already seen how the psychological pioneer Wilhelm Wundt attempted to devise a chemistry of phenomenology. Philosophers and others have carried out similar efforts over the years. According to the existential psychologist Ludwig Binswanger, if you look deeply into your own mind, you will find that the conscious experience of being alive has three components (Binswanger, 1958).

The first component is biological experience, or **Umwelt**, which consists of the sensations that you feel by virtue of being a biological organism that is a part of nature. Umwelt includes pleasure, pain, heat, cold, and all the other sensations your body experiences. It also includes the sensations of your eyes, ears, tongue, nose, and skin. Poke your finger with a pin: what you experience is Umwelt.

The second component is social experience, or **Mitwelt**, which consists of what you think and feel as a social being who relates to other people. Your emotions and thoughts about other people, and the emotions and thoughts that you receive from them, make up Mitwelt. Think about someone you love, fear, or admire. What you experience is Mitwelt.

The third component is inner, psychological experience, or **Eigenwelt**. In a sense, this is the experience of experience itself. It consists of how you feel and think when you try to understand yourself, your own mind, and your own existence. Eigenwelt is the experience of introspection (and is something we can presume that Wundt's assistants as well as Binswanger felt strongly when trying to figure out the components of experience). Try to watch yourself having the experience of a pinprick, or the experience of feeling love, or even the experience of reading this paragraph. When you observe your own mind and feelings in this way, the (often confusing) experience you have is Eigenwelt.

"Thrown-ness" and Angst

An important basis of your experience is your **thrown-ness**—Heidegger used the German word *Geworfenheit*. This term refers to the time, place, and circumstances into which you happened to be born (Heidegger, [1927] 1962). A person's experience clearly depends in large part on whether he or she was "thrown" into a medieval slave society, or a seventeenth-century Native American society, or an early-twenty-first-century North American society.

From an existential perspective, this last way of being thrown—yours—is particularly difficult. Existence in modern society is difficult because you have been thrown into a world that seems to have no overarching meaning or purpose. Organized religion plays a relatively small role in providing a meaning to existence, compared to the role it played in the past. Its modern substitutes—science, art, and philosophy—have failed to provide an alternative worldview that can tell you the two things you most need to know:

1. Why are you here?
2. What should you be doing?

"Is this what I want to be doing with my death?"

Indeed, according to existential philosophy, there are no answers to these two concerns beyond those you invent for yourself.

The nearly inevitable failure to answer these questions leads to anxiety about the meaning of life and whether you are spending yours the right way. After all, life is finite, even short, and you get only one—waste it, and you waste everything. The unpleasant feelings you can get from the contemplation of these concerns is called "existential anxiety," or **Angst**. According to Sartre (1965), this Angst can be analyzed into three other sensations: anguish, forlornness, and despair.

Every conscious human must feel anguish because the choices each person inevitably must make are never perfect. A choice to do good in one way will always lead to bad outcomes in other ways. For example, deciding to aid one person can result in harm to others who are not aided. Such trade-offs are inevitable, according to Sartre, and so the resulting anguish is inevitable, too.

Furthermore, nothing and no one—no god, no unquestionable set of rules or values—can guide your choices or let you off the hook for what you have decided. Your choices are yours, and yours alone. (Sartre also says that even if there is a God who will tell you what to do, you still need to decide whether or not to do what God says—and so you are still alone in your choice.) Furthermore, there is no escape from this existential solitude: there you are, *forlorn*, alone with your existential choices.

Finally, any aware person realizes that there are many things and many important outcomes that he or she cannot hope to change or even to affect. These outcomes include some of the most important elements of your life, such as the fate of yourself and your loved ones. If you are honest in acknowledging this momentous and regrettable fact, then you also will feel despair at your inability to change all aspects of the world. This inability, according to Sartre, only redoubles your responsibility to affect those aspects of the world that you can influence.

Bad Faith

What should you do about Angst and all of these other unpleasant-sounding experiences? According to existentialists such as Sartre, you must face them directly. It is a moral imperative, they believe, to face the facts of your own mortality and the apparent meaninglessness of life, and to seek meaning for your existence nonetheless. This is your existential responsibility, which requires existential courage, or what Sartre called "optimistic toughness" (1965, p. 49).

Of course, there is a way out, at least temporarily, which requires neither courage nor toughness: simply avoid the topic and the problem altogether. Quit worrying about what life means, get a good job, buy a big car, and advance your social status. Do not try to think about fundamental issues for yourself. Instead, simply do as you are told by society, convention, your peer group, political propaganda, religious dogma, and advertising. Lead the unexamined life.

Existentialists call this head-in-the-sand approach "living in bad faith." Although the strategy of ignoring existential issues is very common, the existentialists say there are three problems with it.

The first problem, they say, is that to ignore the troubling facts of existence is to live a cowardly lie; it is immoral and amounts to selling your soul for comfort. You are given just one short life to experience, and in a sense you are giving it away by refusing to examine the substance and meaning of that experience. If you surrender your experience of self, you might as well not be alive. Existentially speaking, you might as well be a rock.

In his novel *Cat's Cradle*, Kurt Vonnegut (1963) proposed that a human being is really no more than a pile of lucky mud. After all, the human body is chemically not much different from the dirt on which it walks, plus a lot of water (the body is about 70 percent water). The only difference is that this mass of mud is up and walking around. More important, it has awareness, so it can look around and experience the world. The other mud, that stuff under one's feet, does not get to do that. It just lies there, ignorant of all the interesting things happening above.

And that is Vonnegut's good news. The bad news is that this luck cannot last. Sooner or later (at death), the chemicals that make up the body will break down and turn right back into earth. The Bible says people come from the earth and return to it; that is Vonnegut's point as well.

What is imperative, therefore, is to not blow this brief period of lucky awareness. For as long as you are alive and aware mud, and not just regular mud, your obligation is to experience as much of the world as possible as vividly as possible. In particular, you need to be aware of your luck and know that it won't last—this is the only chance you will get. The tragedy, from an existential perspective, is that many people never do this. They lead the unexamined life, they never realize how lucky they are to be alive and aware, and they eventually lose their awareness, forever, never having realized what a special gift it was.

A second, more pragmatic problem with living in bad faith is that even if you manage to keep yourself unaware of troubling existential issues, you still will not be happy. Even the most smug and unthinking person wakes up occasionally late at night, the existentialists believe, and realizes that he or she will soon be dead without having done anything beyond acquiring material possessions. Indeed, research shows that for most people a meaningful life is much more important than being wealthy (King & Napa, 1998). The person who has chosen the material path, therefore, might occasionally suffer from a brief, tantalizing, frustrating glimpse of what could have been if he or she had made different choices. These dark moments of the soul may pass quickly, but until one has taken one's existential responsibility in hand, and thought seriously about what is *really* important, they will continue to sneak up when least expected.

The third problem with the ostrich approach to existential issues is that it is impossible, because choosing not to worry about the meaning of life and surrendering your choices to external authorities is still a choice. As Sartre (1965, p. 54) put it, "What is not possible is not to choose. . . . If I do not choose, I am still choosing." Thus, there is no exit from the existential dilemma, even if you can fool yourself into thinking that there is.

Authentic Existence

The existentialists' preferred alternative is to courageously come to terms with your existence in the world. Face the facts: you are mortal, your life will be short, and you are master of your own destiny (within those limits). This

STEINBERG

approach is called **authentic existence** (Binswanger, 1963); it entails being honest, insightful, and morally correct.

Authentic existence will not relieve you from loneliness and unhappiness, however; a courageous examination of conscious experience reveals the awful truth that every person is forever alone and doomed to die. Life has no meaning beyond what you give it, which means that any apparent meaning life might have is only an illusion. The essence of the human experience is this discovery: The human being is the only animal that understands it must die.

This is pretty stern stuff. Existentialism is not for wimps (McAdams, 1990). It takes moral courage to peer into the void of mortality and meaninglessness. When the existentialist philosopher Friedrich Nietzsche did this, he decided the only logical response was to rise above it all and become a "superman." This was easier said than done, however: instead of becoming a superman, Nietzsche went insane and died in an asylum.

Jean-Paul Sartre tried to be both more realistic and a little more optimistic. He sometimes expressed annoyance with people who viewed existentialism as a gloomy philosophy, although one wonders what else he could expect, given his claim that the three essential elements of existence are anguish, despair, and forlornness. Sartre lightened this load a little with his claim that only through existential analysis can people regain their awareness of their freedom. He wrote that existential theory "is the only one which gives man dignity, the only one which does not reduce him to an object" (Sartre, 1965, p. 51). The existential challenge, he preached, was not to give up, but to do all you can to better the human condition, even in the face of all its uncertainties. This is how you can regain your dignity and your freedom and still find meaning in life. It is the ultimate benefit of Sartre's optimistic toughness.

Optimistic Humanism: Rogers and Maslow

Sartre did his level best to find a positive message in the midst of an essentially disconcerting existential analysis. But it took two Americans, Carl Rogers and Abraham Maslow, to turn existentialism into an optimistic philosophy of life. Beginning in the early 1950s, they developed related approaches to humanistic psychology that began with the existential assumptions that phenomenology is central and that people have free will, then added a crucial, further idea: that people are basically good, and have an innate need to make themselves and the world better. It is important to bear in mind that this is an added *assumption;* Rogers, Maslow, and other humanists believe it but can offer no proof that it is true. What kind of evidence would be relevant? But all theories begin with assumptions, and this one is not particularly extreme. So let us take a closer look at humanistic psychology and see where it leads.

Self-Actualization: Rogers

Carl Rogers changed the entire tone and much of the message of the classic existential and phenomenological analysis when he proposed that "the organism [by which he means any person] has one basic tendency and striving—to actualize, maintain, and enhance the experiencing organism" (Rogers, 1951, p. 487). According to Rogers's theory, a person can be understood only from the perspective of his or her *phenomenal field,* which is the entire panorama of conscious experience. This is where everything comes together—unconscious conflicts, environmental influences, memories of the past, hopes for the future, and so on. These experiences continually combine in different ways at every moment of a person's life, and the result of their combination is what the person experiences at each moment. So far, this is standard phenomenological fare of the sort we considered earlier.

Rogers added a new aspect, however, when he posited that all people have a basic need to actualize, that is, to maintain and enhance life. (This need has much in common with Freud's notion of libido as it was interpreted in Chapter 10.) The goal of existence is to satisfy this need. This assumption led Rogers to differ sharply with the more traditional existentialists who believed that existence has no intrinsic goal.

The Hierarchy of Needs: Maslow

Abraham Maslow worked at about the same time as Rogers and was almost equally influential (e.g., Maslow, 1987). His version of humanistic psychology theory begins with the same basic assumption: that a person's ultimate need or motive is to self-actualize. However, Maslow claimed that this motive becomes active if and only if the person's other, more basic needs are met first. According to Maslow, human motivation is characterized by a hierarchy of needs (see Figure 13.1). First, one requires food, water, safety, and the other basic elements of survival. When those are in hand, one then seeks sex, meaningful relationships, prestige, and money. Only when enough of those things are in hand does one turn to the quest for self-actualization. In other words, someone starving to death is not particularly concerned with the higher aspects of existence. In this belief, Maslow too is at odds with traditional existentialists who would believe that, even if starving, an individual has free choice in what to concern himself or herself with.

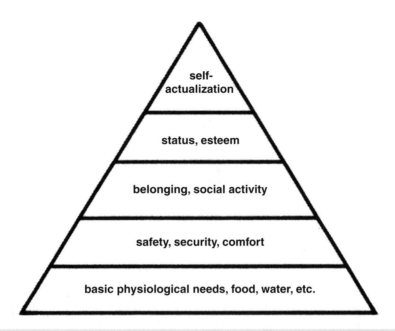

FIGURE 13.1 MASLOW'S HIERARCHY OF NEEDS As an individual's needs lower in the pyramid are fulfilled, the higher needs become more important.

Maslow's theory has practical applications in areas such as career choice and employee motivation. Consider your own ambitions: what kind of career are you seeking? My own parents were children of the Depression of the 1930s, and during their whole lives remained acutely aware of the dangers of being unemployed, homeless, and even starving—not that any of this ever happened to them, but they had lived through an era where these outcomes were a real possibility. As a result, like others of their generation they put a great premium on finding a career path that was, above everything else, safe. Making a lot of money was not really the issue, but rather finding a field where "you can always get a job," as they always said, was the best way to ensure survival and stability. My father always dreamed of being an architect. For most of his career, he worked as an accountant.

You can imagine their reaction when they found out I had declared as a psychology major! But of course, the reason I felt free to do this was precisely because these issues of homelessness and survival never seemed real to me. Thanks to their efforts, I took that level of security for granted, which in Maslow's terms freed me to move up the hierarchy of needs and find a field based on its possibilities for self-expression.

At the university where I teach, a large number of students are children of first- or second-generation immigrants; many are from Asia. Their situation is not very different from mine. Their parents risked much to come to America in search of opportunity and financial security, and they, like my parents, often do not quite understand why their children would choose to major in something so impractical as psychology. But again, when a child of immigrant parents chooses a career because of its opportunities for self-expression rather than financial security, this is the best possible evidence that his or her parents have succeeded. The child takes his or her security for granted and is therefore willing to take risks to accomplish more than just be secure.

Maslow's theory is also often applied to issues of employee motivation. The most expensive part of any organization's budget is its payroll. So it is crucial that employees be motivated to go that extra mile and use their initiative and imagination on behalf of the organization's goals. Smart managers understand two things: (a) Employees will not show initiative and imagination unless they first feel secure. (b) Employees, once they feel secure, want something else besides simply more money: they want to be able to express themselves through their work by identifying with the goals of the organization and feeling that they are contributing to them. As this is written, one of the most successful companies in the United States is Southwest Airlines (and it is almost the only airline not on the brink of bankruptcy). It has never laid off an employee. And while it does not pay as much as some of its competitors, it goes to extraordinary lengths to make employees feel like a real part of the organization, with everything from regular company parties to open meetings with management where anyone at any level can tell the boss how the business should be run. Much more common are companies that do not understand any of this and follow the model that prescribes (a) when in doubt, lay off more people, and (b), if the remaining employees feel overworked and underappreciated, pay them more.

The Fully Functioning Person

Maslow and Rogers shared a belief that the best way to live is to become more clearly aware of reality and of yourself. If you can perceive everything in the world accurately and without neurotic distortion, and if you then take responsibility for the choices you make in life, then you become what Rogers called a fully functioning person, who lives what the existentialists would call an authentic existence, except that the fully functioning person is happy. The only way to accomplish this is to face the world without fear, self-doubt, or neurotic defenses. This becomes possible, Rogers believed, only if you have experienced "unconditional positive regard" from the important people in your life, especially during your childhood. Maslow disagreed slightly with this premise; he believed that anybody from any background could become a fully functioning person. But Rogers thought that if you come to feel that other people value you only if you are smart, successful, attractive, or good, then you will develop "conditions of worth."

Conditions of worth are bad because they limit your freedom to act and to think. If you believe you are valuable only if certain things about you are true, then you will distort your perception of reality to believe that those things are true, even if they are not. If you think you are valuable only if your behavior conforms to certain rules and expectations, then you will lose your ability to choose what to do. Both of these limitations violate the existential imperatives to see the world as it is, to choose freely, and to take total responsibility for all of your actions.

A person who has experienced unconditional positive regard from parents and other important people in his or her life does not develop such conditions of worth. This leads to an existence that is free from anxiety, because that person is confident of his or her value. He or she does not need to follow rules, because his or her innate goodness leads him or her to make the right choices. The experience of a fully functioning person is also rich in emotion and self-discovery, and such a person is reflective, spontaneous, flexible, adaptable, confident, trusting, creative, self-reliant, ethical, open-minded—you get the idea. He or she is also "more understanding of others and more accepting of others as separate individuals" (Rogers, 1951, p. 520).

Psychotherapy

The goal of Rogerian psychotherapy, and humanistic psychotherapy in general, is to help the client to become a fully functioning person. This goal is achieved through the therapist's providing unconditional positive regard. This somewhat infamous technique is sometimes caricatured: the patient says something like, "I would really like to kill you with a knife," and the therapist—reluctant to impose conditions of worth—replies, "You feel you want to kill me with a knife. Uh huh."

This portrayal is probably unfair—Rogers did once state he would stop a murderer—but it captures the basic idea that the therapist's job is (1) to help the client perceive his or her own thoughts and feelings without trying to change them in any way, and (2) to make the client feel appreciated no matter what he or she thinks, says, or does. This process allows insight and the removal of conditions of worth, the theory goes, and the eventual result will be a fully functioning person.

Rogerian psychotherapy requires enormous amounts of time and, on the part of the therapist, the patience (and perhaps also the courage) of a saint. What is the result of this kind of therapy? Although research on the effects of any kind of psychotherapy is extraordinarily difficult, Rogers and his followers have tried to document the effects of his style of treatment.

In a typical study, a group of people about to begin psychotherapy and a group of people who were not interested in undergoing therapy were asked to describe themselves and then to describe their ideal person. (Often these descriptions are rendered using the Q-sort technique, which was described in Chapter 7.) The results showed that these two descriptions diverged more among those who felt they needed therapy. When the therapy group repeated this procedure after completing a program of Rogerian treatment, their real and ideal selves were more closely in alignment—although still not as closely as those of the people who did not seek therapy (Butler & Haigh, 1954).

Results like these—and they have been reported frequently over the years—seem to imply that one result of Rogerian psychotherapy is that people become more like the people they wish they were. But two problems have been noted with this conclusion. First, the results seem to be about equally due to the clients' changing their own self-views as to their changing their ideal views. That is, they not only change what they think they are like, but also change what they wish they were (Rudikoff, 1954). Second, it is not certain that describing oneself as being highly similar to one's idea of a perfect person is always a good measure of psychological adjustment. One study found that paranoid schizophrenics saw themselves as being pretty close to ideal, and so concluded that "to employ a high correlation between the self and ideal-self conceptions as a sole criterion of adjustment would lead to the categorization of many people, particularly paranoid schizophrenics, as adjusted" (Friedman, 1955, p. 73). There is more to mental health than believing that one is the person one wants to be (Wylie, 1974).

Despite this ambiguity about outcome, one important, lasting contribution can be traced directly to Rogerian psychotherapy: the promulgation of the idea that the first job of any psychotherapist is to listen to the client. Although not all therapists will respond "Uh huh" to statements such as those of the hypothetical client mentioned earlier, many have been influenced by the Rogerian example to be more patient in listening and more hesitant to impose their own values than they might have been otherwise.

Personal Constructs: Kelly

Another important phenomenological psychologist, George Kelly, also thought that a person's personal experience of the world was the most important part of his or her psychology. Kelly's unique spin was to emphasize how one's "cognitive" or thinking system builds one's experience of reality out of a unique set of ideas about the world called *personal constructs*. Accordingly, his theory of personality is called *personal construct theory* (Kelly, 1955).

Kelly viewed constructs as bipolar dimensions along which people or objects can be arranged. These constructs can be nearly anything: the idea of good versus bad, or large versus small, or weak versus strong, or conservative versus liberal, for example. If weak versus strong is one of your constructs, you might tend to see everything and everybody in your world in terms of their strength. Each individual has a unique set of constructs that make up his or her personal construct system.

There are many ways to assess your personal construct system, but Kelly favored a method called the Role Construct Repertory Test, or Rep test. The Rep test asks you to identify three people who are or have been important in your life. Then it asks you to describe how any two of them seem to you to be similar to each other and different from the third. Then you do the same with three ideas important to you, three things you admire, and so on. In each case the second question is the same: how are two of these similar to each other and different from the third?

Kelly believed that the ways you discriminate among these objects, people, or ideas reveal the constructs through which you view the world. For example, if you frequently state that two of the objects are strong whereas the third is weak (or vice versa), then strong versus weak is probably one of your important personal constructs. Therefore, because you use it to relate different aspects of the world, this dimension is an important part of how you frame and experience reality.

Recent research showed that certain constructs are more readily brought to mind by certain individuals. These have been called *chronically accessible constructs* (Bargh, Lombardi, & Higgins, 1988). For example, for one person the idea of devastating failure might be chronically accessible, and in everything he undertakes or even considers undertaking, the idea that it will all turn into a catastrophe is never far from his mind. For another person, the idea of interpersonal power might be chronically accessible, and in every relationship she observes or enters, the idea "who is in charge here?" frequently comes to mind and frames her view of these relationships.

Where do these constructs come from? Kelly believed that they come from past experience, although they are not determined by past experience. What does that mean? Kelly leaned heavily on the metaphor that every person is, in a sense, a scientist. A scientist obtains data and tries to come up with a theory that can explain the data. But the data never determine the theory the scientist formulates; any pattern is always consistent with at least two and perhaps even an infinite number of alternative theories. (This observation comes from elementary philosophy of science.) Which theory to use to explain the data, therefore, is always the scientist's *choice*. To be sure, science has developed canons, such as the principle of parsimony (the idea that all other things being equal, the simplest theory is the best). But these canons do not ensure the right choice (sometimes the most complex theory is actually the best). Which theory the scientist chooses is a judgment call.

Kelly believed that everything that has ever happened to you and everything that you have ever seen or heard provide the data from which you must develop an interpretation, or theory, of what the world is like. This theory is your personal construct system, which becomes the framework for your perception of and thinking about the world. This system is determined not by your past experience, therefore, but by your interpretation of past experience, and this interpretation is freely chosen. No matter what has happened to you in the past, you *could* have chosen to draw different conclusions from it than you did. In fact, you still can.

For example, suppose you had a miserable childhood; perhaps you were even abused. You could draw from this history a personal construct system that tells you the world is evil and abusive and there is nothing you can do about it. That would be a conclusion entirely consistent with the data of your life experience. But, just as well, you could draw the conclusion that no matter what life throws at you, you will survive it. That conclusion—since you did survive—is also entirely consistent with your data. Therefore, which conclusion you draw and the worldview you develop is up to you.

A corollary of personal construct theory, which Kelly called the **sociality corollary**, holds that if you wish to understand another person, you must understand his or her personal construct system or view of the world; you must be able to look at the world through that person's eyes. Actions that appear incomprehensible or even evil can make sense, Kelly believed, if you can see them from the point of view of the person who did them. In addi-

"I started my vegetarianism for health reasons, then it became a moral choice, and now it's just to annoy people."

tion, Kelly believed that helping the client to achieve self-understanding was the primary duty of a psychotherapist, and his Rep test was designed to be a tool psychotherapists could use for doing that.

Construals and Reality

The basic lesson of Kelly's theory is that any pattern of experience can lead to numerous construals—perhaps an infinite number. That means the construal you use is one you chose, not one that was forced on you, because others were equally possible. Kelly called this view *constructive alternativism*, which means that your personal reality does not simply exist; it is constructed in your mind. Furthermore, there are always alternative ways you could choose to construct reality, besides the way you happen to be using at this moment.

This lesson has far-reaching implications. Kelly's theory draws on a part of the philosophy of science that scientists themselves sometimes forget. Scientific paradigms are different frameworks for construing the meaning of data. The basic approaches to personality considered in this book—trait, psychoanalytic, phenomenological, and so on—are paradigms in that sense. Each is perfectly sensible, I believe, and each is consistent with the data it regards as important, but each also represents a choice: to focus on some aspects of human psychology and to ignore others. This implies two things about scientific paradigms: (1) the choice between them is not between which is right and which is wrong, but rather of which one addresses the topic you are interested in understanding; and (2) you need all of them because any one of them always leaves out something important.[2]

There are many other systems of constructs, or paradigms, to which the same two lessons also apply. You probably have developed systems of belief that affect how you interpret and understand politics, and morality, and economics, and many other important matters. These belief systems are useful and even necessary, but a myopic devotion to just one paradigm can make you forget (or worse, deny) that other construals of reality—other belief systems—are equally plausible.

My personal favorite example concerns the economic concept of "opportunity costs," which in my opinion (according to my personal belief system) is one of the most harmful ideas ever invented. The concept deals with the question of what something costs. The layperson's answer to this question is that the cost of something is the amount of resources required to get it. A

---

[2]This does not mean they can or should be applied simultaneously; the exercise generally leads only to incoherence. Rather, you need to apply the appropriate paradigm for the question at hand while keeping the rest in reserve, lest the question of interest change.

second and different answer, however, is taught in business schools: The cost of something is the difference between what it brings you and what you could have gotten had you spent your resources on something else. The difference between these two figures is not your ordinary cost, but your opportunity cost.

These two definitions of cost derive from two different construals of the goal of economic life. The first construes the goal as doing what you want as long as you can pay for it. This is sometimes called a "satisficing" goal. The second maintains that you must maximize your gain, and that unless you make as much money as possible, you have failed. This is an "optimizing" goal. Both goals are reasonable, but different, and neither is intrinsically right or wrong. Yet business schools often teach that the second goal is sophisticated and correct, and the first is hopelessly naïve.

The consequences of one's construal can be real and concrete. A few years ago, I read an article in the *Boston Globe* about a mom-and-pop grocery store located on the ground floor of a building in Beacon Hill, which has developed into a fashionable neighborhood in recent years. The grocer, who had been running the store there for decades, was being evicted. The longtime owner of the building had discovered that he could get more rent from a clothing boutique. When neighbors protested, the owner said, apparently with a straight face, "I couldn't afford to keep that grocery store there any longer with property values going up so high."

He may have actually believed what he said, but from another point of view this man's statement is absurd: as long as he could afford to keep the building he could afford to keep the store. He never claimed the grocer paid him less than what he needed to pay for the building or to live well himself. Rather, he focused on the fact that by evicting the grocer he could make more money, and thought of the difference between what he was making and what he could make as a "cost" that he could not "afford."

This viewpoint is the reverse of a remarkably silly television commercial that an automobile maker ran a few years ago. The theme of the commercial was "What will you do with all the money you save (by buying our car)?" In one ad, a happy woman says that with the money she saved, she is going to Hawaii!

I have news for this person: nobody ever went to Hawaii with the money saved by buying a car. The news for the Boston landlord is, nobody ever went broke from opportunity costs. You can *choose* to think about these situations that way, but you are kidding yourself if you think you are getting rich by spending money, or getting poor by not collecting as much money as possible.

The Boston landlord and the car buyer in the commercial had absorbed a particular construct about money and had come to think of that construct as real. The result was a behavior on the part of the landlord that was immoral from the perspective of another construct system, and an action on the part of the car buyer that was silly according to a different construct system. Beware of the construals of reality taught in business school, in science classes, or anywhere else (including in this book); other construals are also possible and you have the ability, the right, and perhaps even the duty to choose your own.

Early in his career, Kelly himself learned something fascinating about construals. He started out as a psychoanalyst, and was conducting an active psychotherapy practice among the plainspoken people of Kansas when he began to doubt some of the Freudian interpretations that he was offering to his patients. As a little experiment, he began offering deliberately random or odd interpretations to his patients, to see how they would react. To his astonishment, he reports, he found that even these interpretations seemed to be helpful! He concluded that the important aspect of psychotherapy was not the content of the intervention, but rather the psychotherapist's role in getting his or her patients to think about, to construe, their reality in a different way (Kelly, 1969). Once the patient has done this, he or she begins to make choices about which construal works best and makes the most sense, and he or she is well on the way to recovery.

Flow: Csikszentmihalyi

The heart of the phenomenological approach is the conscious experience of being alive, moment to moment. The research of Mihalyi Csikszentmihalyi[3] provides a renewed focus on this fundamental concern (Csikszentmihalyi & Csikszentmihalyi, 1988). As a phenomenologist, Csikszentmihalyi believes that your moment-to-moment experience is what really matters in life; his concern is how to make the most of it. His work focuses on "optimal experience"—what it is and how to achieve it.

Csikszentmihalyi investigated the experiences of artists, athletes, writers, and so forth as they did what they enjoy most. He concluded that the best way a person can spend his or her time is in autotelic activities, or activities that are enjoyable for their own sake. The subjective experience a person has during an autotelic activity—the enjoyment itself—is what Csikszentmihalyi calls *flow*.

Flow is not the same thing as joy, happiness, or other more familiar terms for subjective well-being. Rather, the experience of flow is characterized by tremendous concentration, utterly no distractibility, and no thoughts of anything but the activity itself. One's mood is elevated slightly (although not to

---

[3]This name is pronounced "chick-sent-me-high," with the accent on the second syllable.

the point of ecstasy or anything like it), and time seems to pass very quickly. This is what is experienced—when all goes well—by a writer writing, a painter painting, a gardener gardening, or a baseball player waiting for the next pitch. Flow has been reported by surgeons, by dancers, and by chess players in the midst of an intense match. Computers induce flow in many people. Perhaps you have seen an individual playing Sim City on the computer far into the night, seemingly oblivious to any distraction or to the passage of time itself. What he or she is experiencing, I would presume, is flow. I often experience flow when lecturing to a class, and sometimes while writing. To me, a fifty-minute class feels like it ends about a minute and a half after it begins. (I know it does not feel this way to my students.) This sense of losing track of time is one sign that you have been experiencing flow.

According to Csikszentmihalyi, the defining attribute of flow is that it is a focused and ordered state of consciousness that arises when your activity entails a balanced ratio of skills to challenges. If an activity is too difficult or too confusing, you will experience anxiety, worry, and frustration. If the activity is too easy, you will experience boredom and (again) anxiety. But when skills and challenges are balanced, you experience flow.

Csikszentmihalyi thinks that the secret for enhancing the quality of your life is to spend as much time in flow as possible. Achieving flow entails finding something you find worthwhile and enjoyable and becoming good at it. This is not a bad prescription for happiness, come to think of it, whether you are a phenomenologist or not. (Achieving flow also entails staying away from television. Csikszentmihalyi found that watching television disrupts and prevents flow for long periods of time.)

On the other hand, Csikszentmihalyi seems to be describing a rather solitary kind of happiness. In that respect Csikszentmihalyi is a true existentialist, perhaps not dwelling on forlornness like Sartre did, but still regarding experience as something that happens alone. (Csikszentmihalyi does describe flow as it can occur during sexual relations, but the emphasis even here is on the experience of one individual during such an encounter.) The drawback with flow is that somebody experiencing it can be difficult to interact with; he or she may not hear you, may seem distracted, and in general may be poor company. Interrupt somebody engrossed in a novel, or a computer game, and you will see what I mean.

Hardiness: Maddi

Stress has become a bad word. Many people, including psychologists, talk about the sad fact that the modern world is full of stress, assess the bad effects of stress on health and psychological well-being, and seek ways to avoid stress.

According to the modern humanistic psychologist Salvatore Maddi (e.g., 2003), this is all wrong. A life without stress, Maddi argues, would be boring and meaningless. Even worse, he says, is the fact that so many people seek to avoid stress by developing a conformist lifestyle that fits, as much as possible, into the expectations of other people and of society (Maddi, 1985). Get the easy, well-paid (albeit boring) job, hang out with others just like yourself, and be sure to talk only to people who already agree with you.

Despite the seeming safety and ease of a lifestyle choice like this, Maddi believes it is likely to lead to a kind of existential psychological pathology, one that sounds much like Sartre's description of bad faith presented earlier in this chapter. In the words of another humanistic psychologist, R. D. Laing, a conformist lifestyle leads to the development of a false self in which "an individual's acts are no longer self-expressions" (1959, p. 94). According to Maddi, the most severe kind of existential pathology is "vegetativeness," in which the person feels that nothing has meaning and becomes listless and aimless. Slightly less severe, and more common, is "nihilism," in which the person's experience becomes dominated by anger, disgust, and cynicism. Do you know anyone who constantly seeks out the negative, and reacts with disdain and sarcasm to anybody with optimistic expectations or a positive thought? They may be suffering from existential nihilism. (Whatever you do, don't tell them this).

Another potential side effect of the conformist lifestyle is an adventurousness in which only extreme thrills manage to garner one's full attention and succeed in distracting one from deep feelings of meaningless. This kind of "adventurousness"—perhaps too nice a word—can lead to promiscuous sex, involvement in drugs, and other dangerous activities. Whatever form these activities take, their purpose is the same: to fill one's attention so fully that one can remain unaware of the emptiness at the center of life.

Maddi's prescription for curing such bad faith is to develop what he calls "hardiness," a lifestyle that embraces rather than avoids potential sources of stress. Properly approached, stressful and challenging experiences can be sources of learning, growth, and wisdom, and success in dealing with them is an important part of what gives life meaning (King, 2001). Maddi's research has developed self-report scales to measure the trait of hardiness, and has shown that hardy people are in general healthier and more psychologically well-adjusted, even under stressful circumstances (Maddi et al., 2002). Maddi even has helped to set up "hardiness institutes," intended to teach people how to deal properly with stress. But the real importance of his contribution is the way it brings Sartre's notions of bad faith and authentic existence into the twenty-first century, by reminding us that the purpose of life is not the avoidance of anything that might possibly be stressful or disturbing, but rather the development of the capacity to tackle challenges with gusto and to learn and profit from the experience.

Positive Psychology

The past few years have seen an explosion of interest in *positive psychology* (Keyes & Haidt, 2003; Snyder & Lopez, 2002). The purpose of this new field of theorizing and research is to correct what its proponents see as years of overemphasis by psychology on psychopathology and malfunction. Instead, the field seeks to refocus attention on phenonema such as "positive subjective experience, positive individual traits, and positive institutions" in order to "improve quality of life and prevent the pathologies that arise when life is barren and meaningless" (Seligman & Csikszentmihalyi, 2000, p. 5). Sound familiar?

The positive psychology "movement" (as it is also sometimes called) appears to be, to some degree, the long-awaited rebirth of humanistic psychology (Rychlak, 1988). As we saw in this chapter, the humanists have consistently maintained that traditional psychology, because it treats people almost as inanimate objects of study, tends to ignore uniquely human capacities for creativity, love, wisdom, and free will. Perhaps most of all, traditional psychology ignores the question of the meaning of life, which positive psychology places front and center (Baumeister & Vohs, 2002). In a nutshell, positive psychologists usually argue that a good and meaningful life involves happiness, to be sure, but also that true happiness comes from meeting and overcoming important challenges (Ryff & Singer, 2003)—an idea not so different from either Maddi's notion of hardiness or Sartre's conception of optimistic toughness.

The research of positive psychology, however, goes beyond giving a positive spin to existential philosophy. It is busily investigating the traits, processes, and social institutions that promote a good and meaningful life. For example, a good deal of research examines the factors that contribute and detract from happiness or "subjective well-being" (Diener, Lucas, & Oishi, 2002). Beyond a certain level of necessity, money is not important for happiness and overcoming challenges becomes more important, a vindication of Maslow's theory. In addition, some people characteristically think in ways that promote happiness, such as avoiding unproductive rumination about negative events and appreciating the good things in life (Lyubomirsky, 2001). If something is bothering you, this research advises, let it go— admittedly, this is easier said than done.

A specific line of research is investigating the benefits of the tendency to explain and anticipate events with an optimistic viewpoint (Peterson & Steen, 2002). Perhaps not surprisingly, optimistic individuals are less fearful, more willing to take risks, and in general are usually relatively happy. On the other hand, there are hazards to optimism too, such as the possibility that one might take foolish risks or fail to anticipate problems before they arise. For that reason, the psychologist Julie Norem has argued that pessimism also can be part of positive psychology (Norem & Chang, 2002).

The rebirth of humanism is not quite complete in positive psychology. It does not say much about existential anxiety, for example, nor address the difficult dilemmas that can arise because one has free will. Experience is addressed in the form of "subjective well-being," which is basically the degree to which one feels good—a limited sort of phenomenological analysis compared to what the humanists and existentialists have been doing for decades. However, it must also be acknowledged that positive psychology, by that name, is still very new—the most important articles and books have appeared just since the year 2000. As Sartre mordantly observed, the dilemmas of free will and the puzzle of mortality cannot be wished away, so it is probably safe to say that positive psychology will get around to addressing these issues before too long.

Conclusion

At the root of the existential and humanistic approach to psychology is phenomenology, the moment-to-moment experience of a living and aware person. Its emphasis on phenomenology allows humanistic analysis to make two unique contributions. It reminds us of the mystery of experience, and teaches that the only real way that one person can attain understanding of another is to get inside of his or her own view of reality.

The Mystery of Experience

The essential fact that phenomenologists going back to Wundt have always grasped, which all other basic paradigms neglect, is that conscious experience is a basic mystery of life. It cannot be explained or even described very well by science or by words. When words are tried, poetry works better than prose. We may not really be able to describe what it is to be aware and alive, Wundt's efforts notwithstanding, but we all know what it is.

Science and psychology usually choose not to address the fact that something so familiar should also be so difficult to understand; they just ignore the mystery. That is fine, to a point. The point is reached when science and psychology seem to assume that conscious awareness is not important or even pretend it does not exist. It is nearly as bad when psychology treats conscious experience simply as an interesting form of information processing, no different in kind than that done by a computer (Rychlak, 1988). Some theories proposed by cognitive psychologists, for example, claim that consciousness is a higher-order cognitive process that organizes thoughts and allows flexible decision making. Other theories suggest that consciousness is simply a memory tag for "I've been here before." Beyond these functions, say these theories, consciousness is just a feeling (Dennett, 1994; Dennett & Weiner, 1991; Ornstein, 1977).

Of course, to say consciousness is "just a feeling" begs the main question: What does it mean to be able to consciously experience feeling? In fact, conscious awareness is not in the least similar to the kind of information processing that a computer performs, even if it does fulfill some of the same functions. Awareness is a human experience, and science can neither credibly deny that it exists nor explain just what it is or where it comes from. It is only natural, therefore, that phenomenological analysis sometimes drifts into speculations that are not only philosophical, but also religious and spiritual.

Understanding Others

A corollary of the phenomenological view at the heart of humanistic psychology is that to understand another person, you must understand his or her construals (Kelly, 1955). You can only comprehend the mind of someone else to the extent that you can imagine how the world appears from his or her perspective. The adage "Do not judge me until you have walked a mile in my shoes" expresses the general idea.

This principle discourages judgmental attitudes about other people. It implies that if only you could see the world through their eyes, you would realize that their actions and attitudes, which may seem incomprehensible and even evil from your perspective, are the natural consequences of their own view of reality. Furthermore, there is no way to prove that your view of reality is right and other views are wrong. Thus, it is a fundamental mistake to assume that others view the world the same way you do, or that there is only one correct way to view the world. The opinions of others, no matter how strange they may seem, must be considered just as valid as your own. (Extremists such as Thomas Szasz [1960, 1974] have sometimes argued that this is even true about the people usually considered to be mentally ill; they merely have an alternative and equally valid construal of reality. But, this is an extreme position.)

One direct consequence of the phenomenological view is a far-reaching cultural and even moral relativism. You cannot judge the moral codes of other people through your own moral code. For when all is said and done, there is no objective reality—or, if there is, there is no way for anyone to know it. And, you would certainly be unwise to judge the values and practices of other cultures from the perspective of your own. Different cultures see the world very differently, and to understand them, just as to understand another individual person, we need to seek to understand how reality looks from an alternative point of view. The attempt to understand personality and psychology in other cultures is the topic of the next chapter.

Summary

Humanistic psychology concentrates on that which makes the study of humans different from the study of objects or animals, including such issues as experience, awareness, and free will. Wilhelm Wundt founded the first psychological laboratory in an attempt to formulate a phenomenological chemistry, a science that would describe all the elements of experience. Phenomenology is closely related to the philosophical school called existentialism, which breaks experience into three parts (of the world, of others, and of one's own experience) and claims that a close analysis of existence implies that it has no meaning beyond what each person gives it. Philosophers such as Sartre concluded that a failure to face this fact constitutes living in bad faith. A phenomenological perspective also implies that the present moment of experience is all that matters, which means that individuals have free will and that the only way to understand another person is to understand his or her experience of the world.

The modern humanist psychologists added to this existential analysis the further assumption that people are basically good and have an inherent motivation to self-actualize. Rogers and Maslow asserted that a person who faces his or her experience directly can become a fully functioning person; Rogers believed this outcome could only occur for individuals who had received unconditional positive regard from the important people in their lives. Maslow believed that higher needs such as self-actualization could come to the fore only as lower needs related to survival and security became satisfied. Kelly's theory says that each person's experience of the world is organized by a unique set of personal constructs, or general themes. Scientific paradigms have much in common with these personal constructs. Csikszentmihalyi's theory says that the best state of existence is to be in a state of flow, in which challenges and capabilities are well balanced. Maddi argues that people should seek to develop a hardy lifestyle that seeks to embrace the challenges of life, rather than to avoid all stress. Positive psychology, a recent development, may represent a rebirth of humanistic psychology that focuses on the traits and psychological processes that promote well-being and give life meaning. The two main contributions of humanistic psychology's phenomenological approach are its attempt to address the mystery of human experience and awareness and its implications for interpersonal and cross-cultural understanding.

CULTURAL VARIATION IN EXPERIENCE, BEHAVIOR, AND PERSONALITY

What the world actually contains may matter less than how an individual sees or construes it. So, the only real way to understand a person is to understand his or her distinct view of reality. In Chapter 13, we saw the phenomenologists make a pretty good case to this effect. In recent years, psychologists have paid increasing attention to the ways construals of reality vary, not just across individuals, but across cultures. The same behavior that is the epitome of politeness in one culture can be seen as rude by another. The seemingly same idea may take on drastically different meanings in different cultural contexts. And, perhaps most important, cultures seem to differ in some of their most basic values. Cross-cultural differences like these have received increasing attention from psychologists, with a real explosion of interest in recent years.

Few areas of psychology are more challenging, because the job entails grappling with concepts that are often both unfamiliar and difficult. For example, the psychiatrist Takeo Doi reports that the term *amae* is central for understanding personality structure in Japanese culture. *Amae* literally means something like "sweet," but in a family context the word implies both indulgence and dependence, of the sort that may exist between a parent and child. This pattern of benevolent dependence is expected to continue into adult relationships, so that people treat each other thoughtfully and considerately, while appreciating how they depend on each other (Doi, 1962; Tseng, 2003). But it is difficult even to translate the word *amae* into English, much less to fully comprehend its implications. Does this concept have meaning outside of the Japanese context? Would it make any sense, for example, to ask whether your relationship with your parents is sufficiently *amae*, unless you are Japanese? Or is the concept so embedded in the Japanese way of seeing things that it cannot really be exported? Questions like these are difficult and maybe impossible to answer, but the business of cultural psychology is to attempt to address them anyway. The present chapter will survey some of the recent research that is beginning to work through the implications of cultural diversity for personality psychology.

Culture and Psychology

Personality psychology focuses on psychological differences between individuals. Culture comes into play for two reasons. First, individuals may differ from each other to some extent because they belong to different cultural groups. For example, according to one study people in China are on average more emotionally reserved, introverted, fond of tranquility, and considerate than Americans (Cheung & Song, 1989). Second, members of some groups may vary *relative to each other* differently than members of other groups. For example, Dr. Doi described a patient who complained that her son was not as *amae* as he should be, a complaint one would be unlikely to hear from an American parent. An important challenge for personality psychology is to try to understand dimensions of individual differences that differentiate one culture from another, or differentiate between individuals within different cultures.

Cross-Cultural Universals versus Specificity

The big, central issue of cross-cultural psychology is, to what extent are people from different cultures psychologically similar or different? Can they be considered variations on a theme, or are they entirely different symphonies? To put this question one more way, is there a basic and common core to human nature? Or are people from different cultures fundamentally different from each other, perhaps so much so that they cannot even be meaningfully compared? Anthropologists have grappled with these issues for many years and psychologists are relative newcomers to the fray. While in both fields there are plenty of proponents for both the "universal human nature" and "cultural specificity" positions, the bottom line appears to be that this is one of those eternal issues, like the nature-nurture question (Chapter 9) or the consistency debate (Chapter 4) that seems bound to never be entirely settled. In what follows, we will see plenty of evidence that culture has an important influence on how people vary both across and within cultures, and that there may be a common core to human nature as well.

What Is Culture?

The term *culture* refers to psychological attributes of groups, which include, according to one writer "customs, habits, beliefs and values that shape emotions, behavior and life pattern" (Tseng, 2003, p. 1). Culture also may include language, modes of thinking, and perhaps even fundamental views of reality.

All of this is learned, not innate. Genetics cannot be a major basis of cross-cultural differences because, according to recent DNA analyses, individuals within a given ethnic or racial group are as genetically different from one another as are members of different groups (American Anthropological Association, 1999). A child picks up the culture wherever he or she is born (a process called **enculturation**), and a person who moves from one country to another may gradually pick up the culture of his or her new place of residence (a process called **acculturation**).

The idea of the cultural group is a slippery concept. Any group of people that is identifiably, psychologically different from another group can be a candidate for cultural comparison. Traditionally, these groups are ethnic and linguistic, but important cultural differences can be found within national and linguistic borders, as well as across them. Studies have compared North Americans with Asians, Japanese with Chinese, Spanish-speakers with English-speakers, and even residents of Manhattan with residents of Queens (Kusserow, 1999)! Finally, it is important to always remember that psychologists are cultural members, too. Every psychologist speaks a language and lives in a geographic area that inevitably influences his or her own outlook, and it is even possible that being a psychologist itself makes one a member of a certain "culture."

The Importance of Cross-Cultural Differences

Psychologists have three good reasons for being interested in cross-cultural differences.

Possible Limits on Generalizability

The psychological theorizing of Sigmund Freud was largely based on his own introspections added to his experience treating upper-middle-class, hysteric women who lived in turn-of-the-century Vienna. It is not particularly original to observe that his view of humanity may have been skewed by the limited nature of this database.[1] The problem is not limited to Freud, of course. As I discussed in Chapter 3, a basic worry about generalizability concerns the degree to which the results of modern empirical research, obtained in

---

[1] An early tradition in cross-cultural psychology involved trying to interpret different cultures in psychoanalytic terms. For example, Gorer (1943) claimed that Japanese people are anal-compulsive because they subject their children to early and severe toilet training. Theorizing by modern cultural psychologists is very different and seldom Freudian.

large part from college students residing in North America, can be applied to humanity at large. This issue may be particularly acute for personality psychology, because a great deal of evidence now indicates that people in different cultures have importantly different personality characteristics and processes. The only way to deal with this fact is to include in psychological research not only people besides college students, but also people from around the world.

Cross-Cultural Conflict

A second reason to be concerned with cross-cultural differences is that the different attitudes, values, and behavioral styles of members of different cultures frequently cause misunderstandings. The consequences can range from trivial to serious.

Near the trivial end of the spectrum, the cultural psychologist Harry Triandis described a misunderstanding with an Indian hotel clerk that resulted from a contrast between the American practice of putting an X next to the part of a form that does apply, and the Indian practice of putting an X at the part that does not apply. He received a postcard with an X next to "we have no rooms available," and thought he did not have a hotel reservation, when he did (Triandis, 1994). This episode was surely inconvenient, but no major tragedy.

Somewhat more consequential differences include the preference of business people in Thailand to try to save the face of everybody involved in a negotiation, or the traditions in Japan of getting to know a potential business partner well on a personal level before beginning to draw up a contract, and of settling all of the controversial issues that might arise during a meeting in private, before it even starts (Miller, 1999). When these styles encounter the relatively brash, direct, and even insensitive American style of business, the result is more conflict and probably less profit than would have occurred with a little more mutual understanding.

In 1994, an American teenager living with his parents in Singapore learned a hard lesson about cross-cultural differences. After being convicted of spray painting some parked cars, an act that in the United States would be treated as petty vandalism and for which he might not even have been punished if it were his first offense, he was sentenced by the Singapore courts to pay restitution, to spend several months in jail, and—most surprising from an American perspective—to be hit several times with a bamboo cane, which can split open the skin and cause permanent scarring. The sentence caused an international uproar.

Behaviors that are ordinary in other cultures can also stir up a storm if they are practiced in the United States. In 1997, a Danish mother visiting

New York went into a restaurant for dinner and left her 14-month-old daughter parked outside, sleeping in a stroller. Belying their reputation for apathy, alarmed New Yorkers called the police, who arrested the mother and placed the child in temporary foster care. Yet apparently in Denmark this is a common practice. As one Danish writer commented,

> In Denmark, people have an almost religious conviction that fresh air, preferably cold air, is good for children. All Danish babies nap outside, even in freezing weather—tucked warmly under their plump goose-down comforters. . . . In Denmark, her behavior [the mother who parked her baby outside] would have been considered perfectly normal. (Dyssegaard, 1997, p. 2)

Cross-cultural misunderstandings can occur within as well as across international borders. In the inner cities of North America, a subculture of violence, fear, and degradation has led to an extreme valuation being put on receiving proper "respect." Anything that threatens such respect can literally threaten one's life, and so outward tokens such as stylish clothing, a fear-producing appearance, and even an advertised willingness to kill become much more valued than they are in other settings (Anderson, 1994). Nonverbal expressions take on an added meaning, too. For example, to gaze for more than a second or so at a person from this subculture is to express disrespect and invites a violent response. Similarly, recent research has suggested that the American South has a particular "culture of honor" that is different

FIGURE 14.1   A few days after a Danish mother visiting New York was arrested for leaving her baby parked on the sidewalk, this photograph was taken outside of the Café Sommersko in Copenhagen.

from the rest of the United States, and which includes such behaviors as elaborate displays of mutual respect (such as calling people "sir" and "ma'am") and obligations to respond forcefully to any insult (Cohen et al., 1996).

Varieties of Human Experience

A third and more deeply theoretical issue also drives interest in cross-cultural psychology. This issue is phenomenological and stems from a curiosity about the possible varieties of human experience and the degree to which being alive, aware, and human is the same or different across cultures. A moment's reflection is sufficient to tell us that the way we see and construe the world around us is, to a considerable degree, a product of our experience and cultural background. An intriguing possibility to consider is that were we from some other cultural background, the world might look entirely different. Things that are invisible to us now might become visible, and things we see and take for granted might become invisible.

For example, a visitor from a South American rain forest community might look at a tree and immediately "see" the uses to which it, its bark, and its sap might be put. But that same visitor might look at an automobile or a computer and have no idea about how it could be used. A native of Western culture, however, while he or she might immediately "see" the transportation and informational possibilities in the car and the computer, might see little potential on beholding a teak. A ride around the block might be sufficient to acquaint the visitor from the rain forest with the possibilities of cars; getting him or her to understand what computers are for might be a bit more difficult. And if we were to visit their community in the rain forest, there might be artifacts or objects they would find difficult to explain to us. In a similar way, an American might look at a house and ignore which way its door points. To a Chinese raised in the tradition of *feng shui*, this would be one of the first things noticed and would lead him or her to some immediate conclusions concerning the dangers and possibilities that might exist within the house.[2]

Cross-cultural observations like these raise a profound existential question: Does the human experience of life vary fundamentally across cultures? Do people raised and living in different cultural environments see the same colors, feel the same emotions, desire the same goals, or organize their

---

[2]If the American happens to live in California, the difference in perception might not be so wide. For many years, the Sunday real estate section of the *Los Angeles Times* included a *Feng Shui* column with advice on how to align one's home with the unseen forces of the universe. Sadly, the *Times* recently dropped this column.

thoughts in comparable ways? The cultural anthropologist and psychologist Richard Shweder called these aspects of psychology "experience-near constructs" and proposed they are the most fitting subject matter for cultural psychology (Shweder & Sullivan, 1993). In a somewhat more accessible phrase, Harry Triandis (1994, p. 13) claimed "culture imposes a set of lenses for seeing the world." If that description of culture is valid, and it probably is, then the natural next question is, how different are these lenses? Do they lead to views of the world that are fundamentally different, or more or less comparable?

In its ultimate form, this question is probably unanswerable. As we saw in Chapter 13, we can never know for certain what the experience of another individual in our own culture comprises, much less enter fully into the experience of members of a different culture. Still, if you recall Funder's Third Law (Chapter 2) you will know that I prefer something over nothing, usually. In this case, the fact that the basic question of cross-cultural comparability is unanswerable does not mean that it is not worthwhile to study how cultures are psychologically different and similar. And indeed, cross-cultural research is a small but lively and rapidly growing area of psychology.

Cultural Comparison

Until relatively recently, psychologists more or less ignored cross-cultural issues, and many still do. Most of this neglect is fairly benign, of the sort you see in the other chapters of this book. Rather than worry about cross-cultural variation at every step, especially in the absence of much real, relevant data, most psychologists limit themselves to doing their best to describe and explain the phenomenon at hand in the context of their own culture. Freud did not worry too much about cross-cultural concerns; he found hysteric Viennese women complicated enough. Likewise, the measurement of individual differences and the exploration of the laws of behavioral change have proceeded primarily within the Western cultural context. This limited research has proved to be both interesting enough and difficult enough to prevent the international application of these topics from rising to the top of most researchers' agendas.

This attitude of benign neglect is rapidly becoming less tenable as cross-cultural research expands and accelerates. No less an authority than the Surgeon General of the United States has officially announced that "culture counts" for understanding mental health disorders, interventions, and risk factors (Public Health Service, 2001). As psychologists turn their attention to culture, the first question that arises is, how can one culture be compared to another? Or, should it be? The issue is controversial.

Deconstructionism

A widespread modern view in anthropology is that cultures are so fundamentally different that they cannot be compared, because no independent or common frame of reference exists. This view derives from a more general intellectual approach, sometimes called *deconstructionism,* which claims that nothing in the world has any meaning or essence apart from the interpretations invented or "constructed" for it by each observer. The task of deconstructionism is to see beyond these inventions by showing how meaning is essentially arbitrary. In literary theory, for example, it leads to the attitude that the meaning of a "text," such as a novel, lies not in its content or even in the author's intention, but in each reader's interpretation. In cross-cultural psychology, the deconstructionists argue that there is no lens-free way to look at any culture, and that each culture's view of reality is entire in itself and is not judgeable from any other point of view. In the words of prominent advocates of this idea,

> cultural psychology [their name for their preferred approach] has grown up
> in an intellectual climate [deconstructionism] suspicious of a one-sided
> emphasis on fixed essences, intrinsic features, and universally necessary
> truths—an intellectual climate disposed to revalue processes and constraints
> that are local, variable, context-dependent, contingent, and in some sense
> made up. (Shweder & Sullivan, 1993, p. 500)

The Semiotic Subject

The deconstructionist brand of cultural psychology described in the preceding quote conceptualizes people as being "semiotic subjects" who do not have traits, mental states, or psychological processes that are independent from culture. *Semiotic* in this context refers to the human capacity to invent and use symbol systems such as language. To invent a symbol is also to invent the meaning for that symbol, and the fundamental, semiotic human capacity, according to Richard Shweder, one of the most influential of the deconstructionist cross-cultural psychologists, is to decide what the world consists of, what it means, and how to talk and think about it. As language and other symbols change across cultures, so too does human experience.

What, then, can cross-cultural researchers do under this set of assumptions? Two things. The first is to travel among foreign cultures and come back with what they call "thick," detailed reports of how other peoples interpret and symbolize reality. These reports include investigations of how members of different cultures have (or do not have) a sense of self, or how they experience emotions, or whether they believe that individual personalities exist separately from society (e.g., Shweder, 1992; Shweder & Bourne, 1982).

The other activity common to this brand of cross-cultural psychology is to spend some energy berating the rest of psychology for any attempt to understand the whole world through a common set of categories. Each culture must be examined in its own terms, says this argument; to compare one culture to another is profoundly misleading because any system of categorization that allowed such comparison to occur would itself be ethnocentric. Even comparing one individual with another is profoundly misguided, according to this view, because each individual is not a mere "vessel" for psychological states, but a meaning-producing system in his or her own right. Such a semiotic subject, to use that term again, can be understood only in his or her own terms, in regard to his or her unique experience of the world (Shweder & Sullivan, 1990; see also Miller, 1999).

On Categorization

In its essence, the deconstructionist approach to cross-cultural psychology is reminiscent of the argument made by the American personality psychologist Gordon Allport (1937) when he advocated what sometimes is called **idiographic assessment**. No two people ever have the same experiences (or genetic makeup), Allport argued, so it is always to some degree a distortion to see them in common terms, or even to categorize them as varying along common dimensions. As we saw in the preceding chapter, George Kelly (1955) also claimed that no two people have the same personal constructs through which they view the world, and so also believed that it makes little sense to try to classify people or to compare them along common dimensions. When this idiographic approach is followed to its logical extreme, it implies that one individual cannot be compared with another; one culture cannot be compared with another; nothing really can be compared with anything. Everything must be understood in its own terms.

There is some merit to this idea, but it has the downside of coming dangerously close to making cross-cultural psychology impossible. An exclusive focus on the uniqueness of every individual and every culture seems to foreclose any possibility of coming to general understandings about people or cultures. I once heard the psychologist Henry Gleitman exclaim, "If we understood a rose in its own terms, botany would be impossible." He meant that certain things about roses—and even each individual rose—are unique, to be sure. But we can only achieve a general understanding of plants, including roses, by being willing to classify and compare on the basis of important differences, while ignoring some of the small differences.

The deconstructionist approach to cross-cultural psychology tends to leave one in a swirl of details about particular, individual cultures—details that can be very interesting. But because it eschews comparisons between cultures, the approach leads to few broad conclusions beyond the broad conclusion that broad conclusions are impossible. The approach also seems to lend itself more to philosophical debate than to empirical research, as is perhaps already apparent. As a result, recent psychological cross-cultural research, while attempting to acknowledge difficulties such as those raised by Shweder and others, also has become definitely and deeply involved in the enterprise of cross-cultural comparison. This decision may mean the rose will never be *completely* understood, but we need to do some botany. And, as we shall see in the next section, there are many psychological differences between cultures that are both important and fascinating.

Characteristics of Cultures

Cultures can be compared to each other in many different ways that are relevant to personality, including the degree and way in which they control the behavior of their members, and also including the way people who belong to them behave, experience emotion, think, and sense their connection with the larger world. The basic assumption of cultural comparison is that any idea or concept has aspects that are the same across cultures and aspects that are particular to a specific culture (Berry, 1969). The universal components of an idea are called **etics** and the particular aspects are called **emics**.[3] For example, all cultures have some conception of dutifulness in the sense that a person should be responsible for doing what he or she is supposed to do. But beyond this basic, etic idea, different cultures impose different ideas of what one's actual duty is. A dutiful person in New Delhi will probably and "emically" behave differently from an equally dutiful person in New York (McCrae & Costa, 1995). At the same time, a renegade in New Delhi will break rules, as will one in New York, but they will break different rules.

An early approach to cross-cultural psychology, an approach still followed by some, was to attempt to find ways to characterize general differences between whole cultures. One pioneering effort more than half a century ago produced the conclusion that some cultures are "tough" whereas others are "easy" (Arsenian & Arsenian, 1948). Notice the common dimension of tough versus easy is applied here to *all* cultures, and the focus is on how different cultures vary along this common dimension. Tough cultures are strict and demanding, especially on children; easy cultures are more tolerant, and their children seem to have a less stressful time growing up.

---

[3]These terms derive from linguistic terms that refer to "phonetics" (the universal sounds of languge) and "phonemics" (the sounds of a specific language) (Tseng, 2003).

David McClelland (1961) was one of the first personality psychologists to theorize about cultural differences. McClelland assessed cultural attitudes toward achievement by examining the stories that are traditionally told to children. Some cultures, such as in the United States, tell their children many stories along the lines of "The Little Engine That Could," and so reflect a high cultural need for achievement. Other cultures tell more stories in which needs for love or, to use McClelland's term, affiliation, are more prominent. Cultures whose stories manifest a high need for achievement, according to McClelland, can be expected to have more rapid industrial growth than those that manifest less achievement orientation, and data including measures such as electrical production have tended to bear him out. Of course, the correlational nature of these data make the direction of causality unclear. Does reading achievement-oriented stories to children cause them to grow up into adults who build prosperous, electricity-using cultures, or do prosperous cultures create an environment in which children's authors just naturally think up stories with achievement themes?

More recently, Triandis (1994, 1997) proposed that cultures vary along three basic dimensions: complexity, tightness versus looseness, and collectivism versus individualism. One can compare one culture to another by assessing the position of each on these "cultural trait" scales.

Complexity

The first trait describes some cultures as more complicated than others. In particular, Triandis (1997, p. 444) wrote of the difference between "modern, industrial, affluent cultures [and] the simpler cultures, such as the hunters and gatherers, or the residents of a monastery." This difference seems plausible, but be careful. How do we know that modern industrial society is more complex than hunter-gatherer cultures? Although they may not be visible to an outsider, such cultures may have their own patterns of interpersonal relationships and political struggles—when it comes time to choose a new chief, for example—that are themselves fairly complex. It is reasonable to wonder, too, whether monastery life looks as simple from the inside as it does from the outside. While some cultures might indeed be more complex than others, it is not easy to be sure which those are.

Tightness

The tightness versus looseness dimension contrasts cultures in which very little deviation from proper behavior is tolerated (*tight* cultures) with those in which fairly large deviations from cultural norms are allowed (*loose* cultures). Triandis hypothesizes that ethnically homogeneous and densely populated societies tend to be tighter than societies that are more diverse or where the people are more spread out. This is because in order to enforce norms people must be similar enough to one another to agree on what those norms should be, and because strict norms of behavior are more necessary when people must live close together.

The United States, historically a diverse and geographically spread-out society, is a classic example of a loose culture. But even here it varies. Having lived in both places, I can testify that east-central Illinois is a much tighter culture than Berkeley, California, even though both are in the United States. Berkeley is more densely populated than is downstate Illinois, but it is also more diverse. This observation suggests that diversity might be more important than density as a determinant of tightness and looseness.

Boston, where I have also lived, is an even more interesting case. Tightness and looseness can vary by block. In Boston, homogeneous, ethnic Italian and Irish neighborhoods (the North End and South Boston, respectively), where mores are quite tight, abut more diverse neighborhoods (such as Back Bay), where standards are much looser. Again, diversity seems to be key. All of these neighborhoods are about equally crowded. But whereas South Boston and the North End are populated largely by people who were born and raised there, and are each dominated by a particular ethnic group (Irish and Italian, respectively), nearly everybody I met in Back Bay seemed to be from another state—usually California!

An interesting way to index the tightness of a culture is to examine left- and right-handedness. Biologically, about 12 percent of the world's population should be left-handed. But almost all cultures (including American and European) prefer for people to be right-handed and use various tactics to coerce use of the right hand. One cross-cultural survey found that about 10 to 12 percent of Eskimos and Australian Aborigines were left-handed, indicating a minor coercion toward right-handedness in those two relatively loose cultures. In Western European samples the rate was about 6 percent, and in Hong Kong the rate was near 1 percent, suggesting that those cultures are much tighter. Interestingly, the percentage of "lefties" among women enrolled at the University of Hong Kong was zero, suggesting that they are subjected to particularly strong cultural coercion (Dawson, 1974).

Collectivism and Individualism

The dimension of cultural variation that has received the most attention in recent years is the distinction between collectivism and individualism (Markus & Kitayama, 1991). In collectivist cultures, such as Japan, the needs of the group or "collective" are seen as more important than the rights of individuals. In fact, some investigators have claimed that the boundary between the individual self and the others in one's group is relatively fuzzy in such a culture. For example, the Japanese word for "self," *jibun*, refers to "one's portion of the shared life space." Japanese also exhibit a general desire to sink inconspicuously into the group; a Japanese proverb says, "The nail that stands out gets pounded down" (Markus & Kitayama, 1991, pp. 224, 228). This cultural view is related to the perspective of Buddhism, which teaches that the individual self is part of a larger whole, rather than something isolated and apart (more will be said about cross-cultural views of the self, and about Buddhism, later in this chapter).

In individualist cultures, such as the United States, the single person is more important. People are viewed as separate from each other, and independence and individual prominence are important virtues. Individual rights take precedence over group interests, and one has a right—indeed, an obligation—to make moral choices that are independent, not merely guided by cultural tradition. The willingness to stand up for one's rights as an individual is all-important, and an American proverb teaches that "the squeaky wheel gets the grease" (Markus & Kitayama, 1991). As we saw in Chapter 13, an individualist view also leads to phenomena such as existential anxiety, the concern over whether one is living one's individual life in the right way. Because the philosophy of individualism isolates people from each other, members of individualist cultures may be particularly vulnerable to psychological disorders such as loneliness and depression (Tseng, 2003).

Japan, China, and India are the most frequently discussed examples of collectivist cultures, and the United States seems like the most obvious—or glaring—example of an individualist culture. A survey of employees of IBM (which has native employees all over the world) found that natives of Taiwan, Peru, Pakistan, Columbia, and Venezuela were more collectivist and less individualist in outlook than were natives of Australia, Britain, Canada, the Netherlands, and the United States (Hofstede, 1984). Within the United States, Hispanics, Asians, and African Americans are more collectivist than Anglos (Triandis, 1994). Also within the United States, women seem to be more collectivist than men (Lykes, 1985).

Researchers have developed long lists of behavioral and attitudinal differences between individualist and collectivist cultures. For example, more autobiographies are written in individualist countries, and more histories of the group are written in collectivist countries (Triandis, 1997). People from collectivist cultures carefully observe social hierarchies. In India, a person who is even one day older is supposed to receive more respect from the younger friend than the other way around (Triandis, 1997). People in individualist cultures are less attentive to differences in status. In the United States, many students call their professors by their first names; this does not happen in China, Japan, or India. (It also would not have happened in the United States fifty years ago, although it is not clear whether this means that U.S. society is more individualist than it used to be.)

Skiing in groups and social bathing is more common in collectivist cultures; members of individualist cultures prefer these activities alone (Brandt, 1974). In general, members of individualist cultures spend less time with more people; members of collectivist cultures spend more time with fewer people (Wheeler, Reise, & Bond, 1989). The cocktail party, where one is supposed to circulate and meet as many people as possible, is a Western invention. While Easterners may be relatively standoffish and shy at such a gathering, they also tend to have a few relationships, not casually entered into, that are more intimate than usual Western friendships.

Members of individualist and collectivist cultures may experience emotion differently. People in individualist countries report experiencing more self-focused emotions (such as anger), compared with people in collectivist countries, who are more likely to report experiencing other-focused emotions (such as sympathy) (Markus & Kitayama, 1991). Furthermore, Japanese students reported experiencing more pleasant emotional lives when they felt they were fitting well into their group; for American students individual concerns were just as important as this kind of "interdependence" (Mesquita & Karasawa, 2002). In general, emotional experience in collectivist cultures appears to be more grounded in assessments of social worth, to reflect the nature of social reality rather than hidden, inner experience and, perhaps most importantly, to depend upon relationships with other people rather than the individual alone (Mesquita, 2001). Arranged marriages are relatively common in collectivist cultures; members of individualist cultures are expected to marry "for love." The downside of this romantic, individualist approach is that when a married couple falls out of love they may get divorced and cause their family to disintegrate. In collectivist cultures this is much less likely to happen (Tseng, 2003).

Even advertising is different. An ad in a collectivist culture like Korea might say "Our ginseng drink is produced according to the methods of 500-year tradition" or "Seven out of 10 people are using our product." An American ad is more likely to say "Choose your own view," "The Internet isn't for everybody. But then again, you're not everybody," or, simply, "Individualize!" (Kim & Markus, 1999, p. 793).

Cultural Assessment and Personality Assessment

A fairly close analogy can be drawn between assessing a culture along the three dimensions just described and assessing the personality of an individual. Indeed, Triandis's three basic dimensions of cultural variation are also dimensions along which individuals differ. The complexity dimension is analogous to the personality trait of cognitive complexity; cultural tightness resembles the traits of conscientiousness and intolerance for ambiguity; the collectivist versus individualist distinction is analogous to *idiocentrism* vs. *allocentrism*, a dimension of personal values that focuses on whether one believes that the individual is more important than the group, or vice versa. It seems that complexity, tightness, and collectivity are traits of individuals as well as of cultures. As we shall see in the next section, psychologists have also used more familiar personality trait concepts to try to understand cross-cultural differences.

Personality Traits

As we saw in Chapters 4 through 7, personality traits are central concepts in psychology. Apparently, all languages have terms for traits such as *talkative, timid,* and *diligent,* but they differ in how many different terms they include in the lexicon. English has about 2,800 trait terms that are used commonly in everyday speech (Norman, 1967), whereas Chinese has about 557—noticeably less, though still quite a few (Yang & Lee, 1971). So it is not surprising that cross-cultural psychology has tried to address the degree to which traits apply to different cultures. This has been done in two ways. The first is to try to characterize cultural differences by assessing the degree to which members of different cultures vary, on average, across various personality traits. The second is to dive a bit more deeply into the cultures being compared by assessing the degree to which the same traits that characterize people in one culture can meaningfully characterize people in another.

As an example of the first approach, psychologists have translated the MMPI (see Chapter 5) into Chinese and found that, compared to American samples, Chinese on average score higher on emotional reserve, introversion, considerateness, social caution, and self-restraint (Chueng & Song, 1989). Another study, using the NEO Personality Inventory, compared ethnic Chinese living in Canada to those in Hong Kong. It turned out that those who lived in Canada described themselves (S data) as relatively open, cheerful, and agreeable, and that these differences with people in Hong Kong increased the longer they lived in Canada—which suggests that these differences arise because of the different cultural environment (McCrae et al., 1998). In a variant on this approach, psychologists have examined gender differences by administering the NEO Personality Inventory, or translations of it, in 26 cultures to 23,031 individuals (Costa, Terracciano, & McCrae, 2001). They found that in almost all cultures women scored higher than men in neuroticism, agreeableness, warmth, and openness to feelings. Men scored higher than women in assertiveness and openness to ideas. Surprisingly, these differences were actually larger in so-called developed societies such as Belgium, France, and the United States than in less-developed areas such as Zimbabwe and Malaysia.

These are interesting findings, but notice that studies like the ones just summarized depend on a not-so-hidden assumption: they all assume that the same traits are valid for describing people in different cultures—that it makes sense, for example, to compare Americans and Chinese on a common dimension of "self-restraint." The assumption is not unreasonable, but it also seems unlikely to be 100 percent correct. For example, one study found that measures of the Big Five personality traits (see Chapter 7) could be effectively translated into Spanish, but that such translations also missed particular aspects of Spanish personality, such as humor, good nature, and unconventionality (Benet-Martínez & John, 1998, 2000). Therefore, a growing area of cross-cultural research is the attempt to develop personality-trait terms within different cultures, and then see if the same constructs that emerge in one culture also emerge in another.

In one pioneering study, investigators assembled a group of Chinese words that are used to describe personality, and then asked Chinese participants to use these words to rate several other people (I data). The ratings were factor analyzed (see Chapter 3), and five factors were extracted. As I mentioned in Chapter 7, the Chinese Big Five turned out to be social orientation, competence, expressiveness, self-control, and optimism (Yang & Bond, 1990). It is possible to view social orientation as similar to what American psychology often calls "agreeableness"; competence seems related (negatively) to neuroticism; expressiveness seems related to extraversion; self-control is related to agreeableness as well as conscientiousness (the Chinese version of self-control seems to involve the inhibition of negative emotions such as anger); and optimism seems related to both extraversion and (negatively) to neuroticism (compare with McCrae & Costa, 1987). A parallel of this study was conducted in Spain, beginning with personality words taken from an unabridged Castilian Spanish dictionary (Benet-Martínez & Waller, 1997). The conclusion of this study was that Spanish personality terms could be organized into seven factors labeled positive valence, negative valence, conscientiousness, openness, agreeableness, pleasantness (referring to emotional experience), and engagement or "passion."

A group of Chinese psychologists aimed to develop an indigenous Chinese Personality Assessment Inventory (yes, it is called the CPAI). The result was a scale that the researchers concluded measured the factors of neuroticism, conscientiousness, agreeableness, and extraversion in a manner that resembled the same traits as represented in widely used instruments in English (Cheung et al., 1996). But they also found, instead of the "openness to experience" factor often found in Western samples, a factor they interpreted as reflecting an individual's degree of interpersonal relatedness. They also developed factor scores unique to the Chinese context that measured such traits as harmony, face, thrift versus extravagance, and a trait they called *ren qing* ("interpersonal favor").

Thinking

One of the most intriguing and challenging questions facing cross-cultural psychology concerns the degree to which people from different cultures think differently. On one level, it seems safe to assume that because behavioral traits differ across cultures, as we have just seen, the thinking that is associated with behavior must be different too. On another level, it is difficult to specify the exact ways in which thought processes in one culture may differ from those in another, and research attempting to do this is opening an exciting new frontier in psychology, and has important and controversial implications.

For example, one line of research suggests that East Asians think more "holistically" than Americans, explaining events in context rather than in isolation, and seeking to integrate divergent points of view rather than set one against another (Nisbett et al., 2001). This may be related to the collectivism versus individualism difference discussed earlier, in which collectivists feel more a part of their larger social environment than individualists do. A recent study indicates that this difference may reach down to the perceptual level. Japanese participants watched animated underwater scenes, or looked at photographs of wildlife, and in both cases remembered more information about the wider context than did American participants, and also were better able to recognize specific objects when they saw them in their original settings (Masuda & Nisbett, 2001). These results suggest that an American observer may look onto a scene and see a specific object or person, whereas the Japanese observer is more likely to see (and remember) the whole, larger context.

A controversial area of cross-cultural research on thinking concerns the degree to which Asians, compared to Americans, characteristically formulate and express independent and original points of view. Various psychologists and educators have observed that Asian students seem drawn to fields that require rote study and memorization rather than independent thinking, and that they are less willing than European Americans to speak up in class discussion (e.g., Mahbubani, 2002). One Vietnamese-American writer lamented that this occurs because "self-expression is largely discouraged across Asia. . . . Asia is by and large a continent where the ego is suppressed. The self exists in the context of families and clans." On the other hand, he observes, "America still values the maverick, the inventor, the loudmouth class clown, the individual with a vision" (Lam, 2003, p. M6).

Others have offered a different interpretation. One recent study showed that for Asian Americans, thinking is disrupted by trying to talk at the same time, whereas this effect was not found in European Americans (Kim, 2002). Thus, a quiet Asian-American student may be silent because he or she is trying to think. Psychologists have noted that the Confucian philosophy of learning prescribes that the first thing a student should do is learn the basic facts of a field, then analyze, and finally innovate. Early in his or her learning career a student is not supposed to be formulating independent opinions; that should come only later, after he or she has sufficient knowledge (Tweed & Lehman, 2002). Another writer has observed that

> Asians are respectful not because they are afraid of their teachers or because they have no questions, but because they are brought up with the idea that humility ensures better learning. They are taught to listen attentively and to question only after they have understood others. (Li, 2003, pp. 146–147)

The Self

A theme that arises repeatedly in cross-cultural psychology is that different cultures appear to have fundamentally different views of the individual or "self." As we have seen, while individualistic cultures assume the self to have an independent and separate existence, collectivist cultures view the self as imbedded in a larger social context of obligations and relationships. This theme has played out in modern research in two ways. One approach, rooted in anthropological analysis, is to suspect that the "self" is itself a Western cultural artifact that has no meaning in other cultures. The second approach is less extreme, and addresses the way the self and its implications differ across cultural contexts.

IS THE SELF A CULTURAL ARTIFACT?

A particular mistake of most ordinary psychology, from the point of view of some psychological anthropologists, is that it imposes the Western notion of the self on members of other cultures. From their study of the

culture of Hindu India, the anthropologists Richard Shweder and Lyle Bourne (1982) concluded that its holistic outlook leads Indians to think of themselves in a fundamentally different way than members of Western culture. They performed a simple experiment: They asked Hindu Indian and American informants to describe people they knew. The answers differed significantly. While an American might say, "She is friendly," an Indian would say, "She brings cakes to my family on festival days." An American might say, "He is cheap," while an Indian said, "He has trouble giving things to his family." And where an American might say, "He is kind," an Indian is more likely to say, "Whoever becomes his friend he remembers him forever and will always help him out of his troubles." Overall, about 50 percent of the terms Americans used to describe their acquaintances were personality traits such as *friendly, cheap,* and *kind,* but only 20 percent of the terms used by Indians were words like these. The conclusion reached by Shweder and Bourne is that Americans' frequent use of trait terms to describe properties of persons, and even the very idea of self, is not shared by Hindus in India.

The concept of self is extremely important. Every other chapter in this book describes a personality psychology that throughout its diverse approaches uniformly assumes—if it uniformly assumes nothing else—that individuals are separate from one another and from the society of which they are a part. Furthermore, all of personality psychology also assumes that these individuals have properties, whether conceived as traits, learning patterns, or mental structures, which belong to or characterize each of them. Yet if this fundamental idea is an arbitrary artifact of Western culture, then all of Western personality psychology (and much of Western thought, in general) may be little more than an arbitrary social construction.

This kind of sweeping philosophical implication makes it important to take cultural psychology seriously. If this claim is really true, then many ideas that have been taken for granted for many years should be discarded or revised. Among these are the ideas of personality development, self-interest, morality, and personal responsibility, to name a few. It would also be necessary to thoroughly revise all of personality psychology. But before we get started, a few points are worth considering.

First, reconsider the key experiment in which Indian and American subjects were asked to describe people they knew, and in which Americans usually answered with traits while Indians more often used complex and contextualized phrases. As the social psychologist John Sabini (1995, p. 264) pointed out, "It would be rash to impute a very different concept of the self on the basis of this kind of evidence." First of all, the finding that 20 percent of the Indians' descriptions of people were personality-trait terms shows that the idea of individual traits is not exactly foreign to them—if I may be forgiven the pun. Moreover, it is not clear that even the colorful phrases used by the Indian informants are fundamentally different from the Americans' descriptions. They may be just longer and more vivid ways of making the same points.

Sabini recalled the description offered by the former governor of Texas, Ann Richards, of the first President George Bush: "Poor George, he can't help it—he was born with a silver foot in his mouth." Ann Richards is nothing if not Western, and her description is certainly a description—and a vivid one—of an aspect she perceived of Bush's personality.[4] There is nothing Eastern, or fundamentally denying of the separateness of Bush's self, about this description.

Now consider the Indian's description of his kind acquaintance as being someone who "remembers [his friend] forever and will always help him out of his troubles." This description is less caustic than Richards's, but similarly provides a vivid description of the habitual behavioral style—the trait of kindness, in this case—of a person he knows well.

However, the difference between the 20-percent-Indian versus 50-percent-American usage of trait terms remains large enough to deserve attention. It does seem to be the case that in India and some other Eastern cultures, trait terms are used less often than they are in North America and Europe (Bond & Cheung, 1983; Cousins, 1989). As was mentioned earlier, English appears to have several times as many trait terms as does Chinese. Members of different cultures do vary in their ways of describing each other. Traditions of Western philosophy and of Asian philosophy seem to be related to these differences. But do Indians and other Asians have no sense of self or even of personality? The evidence on this point seems doubtful.

INDIVIDUALIST AND COLLECTIVIST SELVES

Rather than rejecting the idea of the self entirely, a less extreme approach is to study how the nature of the self and its implications differ across cultures. A large amount of this sort of research has been conducted in the past few years, and almost all of it is based on the idea, derived from the notions of individualism and collectivism, that the Western self is a relatively separate entity while the Eastern self is more integrated into the social and cultural context. This idea has many implications, some of which we have already discussed, such as the possibility that self-expression, as understood in Western culture, is more limited in Eastern culture.

Self-regard   Another implication is that the individualist's need for positive self-regard may be felt less acutely by a member of a collectivist culture

---

[4]In case a trait translation is necessary, Richards was calling Bush an inarticulate, overprivileged bumbler.

(Heine et al., 1999). Specifically, research has found that Japanese people do not have the pervasive need to think well of themselves that is so characteristic of North Americans, and the theory is that this is because they tie their well-being to a larger group that goes beyond the individual. As a result, Japanese and American students have been found to respond differently to success, failure, and negative self-relevant information. For example, Canadian college students told they had failed on a test of creativity were quick to search for ways to think well of themselves in other contexts, whereas Japanese students showed no sign of this response (Heine, Kitayama, & Lehman, 2001). In another study, Canadians who failed on an experimental task became less persistent on a second task, and denigrated its importance. Japanese participants had the opposite reaction, becoming more persistent and viewing the task as important and something they should strive to do better (Heine et al., 2001). Apparently, this is because they have learned the Confucian view that failure always opens an opportunity for learning.

Consistency   Another basic cross-cultural issue is the matter of "self-determination." The individualist view of the self assumes that the root cause of behavior lies within the person. As a result, an individual's behavior would be expected to be consistent from one situation to the next. Indeed, in American culture, behavioral consistency is associated with mental health (Donahue et al., 1993). The behavior of the more socially imbedded member of a collectivist culture, by contrast, might be expected to be more a function of the particular situation in which he or she finds himself or herself (Markus, Mullally, & Kitayama, 1997). As a result, a member of a collectivist culture might feel less pressure to behave consistently, and less conflicted when he or she behaves inconsistently. This is apparently the basis of the recent finding that among Koreans, unlike among Americans, behavioral consistency is not associated with measures of mental health (Suh, 2002).

A small but increasing amount of evidence suggests that, compared to members of individualist cultures, the behavior and experience of members of collectivist cultures is less consistent from one situation to the next. For example, Koreans describe themselves as less consistent than Americans do, and different observers of a Korean person tend to agree less in their description of his or her personality than different observers of an American (Suh, 2002, but see also Albright et al., 1997). Emotional experience also seems to vary more across situations for Japanese persons than for Americans (Oishi et al., in press).

This latter study adds an important qualification. Consistency can be thought of, and analyzed, in two ways. One way is to focus on the degree to which an individual varies his behavior or experience from one situation to the next—*absolute consistency*. The other is to focus on the degree to which an individual maintains his or her differences from other people across situations—*relative consistency.* For example, even a brave and confident person might be more nervous in a burning house than he or she is in a normal classroom (low absolute consistency), but still might be the most confident person in the room in both situations (high relative consistency) (see also Funder & Colvin, 1991). The study by Oishi et al. found that Japanese had more inconsistent emotional experience than Americans in an absolute sense; their emotions changed more from one situation to the next. But they had equally consistent emotional experience in a relative sense, because a Japanese person who was happier than most other people in one situation would also tend to be happier than most in other situations as well. This finding implies that while it is true that in one sense members of collectivist cultures may be more inconsistent than members of individualistic cultures, individual differences and associated personality traits appear to be equally important in both contexts.

The Buddhist Self   The East-West difference about the self goes deeper than behavioral consistency or the ways people react to success and failure feedback. In Chapter 13 we considered the somewhat gloomy point of view of the European existentialists, who harped on individual isolation, mortality, and the difficulty entailed in finding a meaning to life. Whatever one thinks of this philosophy, it is worth noticing that it is fundamentally European, Western, and individualistic. Notice how it begins with the experience of the single individual at a single moment in time. All else, it claims, is illusion. The fundamental reality is that all you have is your own experience at this moment—the past, the future, and the experience of other people are forever closed off to you.

From the perspective of the Eastern religions that influence most of the people on earth, such as those in China, India, and Japan, and also are often associated with collectivist cultures, this analysis is fundamentally wrong. Consider the perspective of Zen Buddhism (see Rahula, 1974; Mosig, 1989, 1999). The key idea of Buddhism is **anatta**, or "non-self," the idea that the independent, singular self you sense inside your own mind is itself merely an illusion. The French philosopher René Descartes believed that the existence of his own, singular self was the one thing he could be sure of; Buddhism teaches that he was overconfident. What feels like your "self" is merely a temporary composite of many things, including your physiology, environment, social setting, and society, all of which are constantly changing. There is no unchanging soul at the center of all this, just a momentary coming together of all these influences that, in the next moment, is gone, only to be replaced by another. Gertrude Stein once said of Oakland, California, that "there's no there there." That's what Buddha says about the soul.

Furthermore, Buddhism teaches that this illusion of having a separate and independent soul is harmful. It leads to feelings of isolation—such as tormented the existentialists—and an excessive concern with "me" and that which is "mine." The true nature of reality is that everything and everyone are interconnected now and across time. It is not true, Buddhism teaches, that all you have is your own experience, now. Rather, there is nothing special about your own particular experience or about the moment that happens to be labeled the "present." All consciousness and all of time have equal claim to existence, and all are equally important, and time is viewed as flowing not from past to present to future, but from present to present to present (Yozan Mosig, personal communication, November 6, 2000). In a similar fashion, a single person is just one out of many, your existence is no more or less real or important than anyone else's, and the more important fact is that all people are interconnected.

This viewpoint might seem to diminish the importance of the self, but in a way it enhances it. The Buddhist view implies that instead of being forever alone and powerless, you are an integral and interconnected part of the universe. Moreover, you are immortal in the sense that you are part of something larger than yourself that will last forever. You are part of the universe and it is part of you, just as the present moment is made of equal parts past and future.

If you can begin to grasp these ideas, your selfish thoughts and fears about the future will fall away. You will understand the idea of **anicca**, that nothing lasts forever and it is best to accept this fact as the reality it is instead of fighting it. The current moment is not particularly important; all moments in the past and future have equal status. The well-being of others is just as important as your own, because the boundaries between you and them are illusory. These are all difficult ideas to grasp, especially for those raised in Western culture, and to achieve true understanding can be the work of a lifetime. If this understanding is achieved, you are said to be "enlightened." Enlightenment is manifested by caring for others the same as for yourself, which leads to universal compassion, which, according to Buddhism, is the essence of wisdom and leads to a pleasant, selfless state of being, called **nirvana**.

You can probably see the connection between the Buddhist point of view, just described, and the collectivist orientation that tends to characterize regions of the world influenced by Buddhism. Notice how this point of view promotes some values and, in effect, denigrates others. For example, it encourages compassion, sharing, and humility. On the other hand, it discourages independence, individual ambition, and pride. In American culture, at least, these last three attributes are generally considered to be good things, which suggests that the fundamental difference in values between East and West may run deep indeed.

Values

The most difficult issues in cross-cultural psychology concern values. People feel deeply about matters of right and wrong, and may be not merely surprised but also upset and angry when they find that other people do not share their feelings. Sometimes, wars start. Thus, a particular challenge is to try to understand how even seemingly obvious and basic values can vary across cultures, and to formulate an appropriate response to these differences.

For example, styles of moral reasoning are different in collectivist and individualist cultures (Miller, Bersoff, & Harwood, 1990). The individualist cultural ethos emphasizes "liberty," "freedom of choice," "my rights," and "my needs," whereas the collectivist cultural ethos emphasizes obligations, reciprocity, and one's duties to the group (Iyengar & Lepper, 1999; Miller & Bersoff, 1992). The collectivist style of moral reasoning imposes a group norm; the individualist style emphasizes independent and individual choice.

We can see this distinction even within North American culture. For example, even though individualism is often viewed as a Western cultural attribute, the Roman Catholic Church—a Western institution if ever there was one—is profoundly collectivist in outlook. Individualism is really a Protestant, northwestern European idea, whereas collectivism is more Catholic and southeastern European (Sabini, 1995). Martin Luther broke with the Catholic Church over the right of individuals to come to their own interpretation of the Scriptures. The Catholic view was—and still is—that any interpretation must come from the Church itself.

We can hear echoes of this ancient argument, as well as of the distinction between individualism and collectivism, in the modern debate over abortion. The individualist point of view, endorsed by many (though not all) Protestant and Jewish denominations, is that abortion is a matter of individual moral responsibility and choice. One might deplore abortion and regard it as a tragic occurrence but still endorse the idea that it is the pregnant woman who is most centrally involved, and in the end it all comes down to her own, free decision. Those who endorse the right to safe, legal abortions do not like to be called "pro-abortion"; they prefer the term "pro-choice."

The very different, collectivist point of view, strongly espoused by the Catholic Church and some of the more conservative Protestant denominations, is that abortion is morally wrong, period. The unborn fetus is already a person—a member in good standing of the collective, if you will. To kill that fetus with an abortion is to kill a member of the collective, something no individual member—not even the fetus's mother—has a right to do. Indeed, it is the duty of the collective, institutionalized in the church or the state, to prohibit any such act. The matter does not come down to personal choice at all. It comes down to a collectively determined issue of right and wrong.

No wonder this debate shows no signs of subsiding, and no wonder, too, that grounds for reasonable compromise seem nonexistent. In the abortion debate we see a head-on collision between two fundamentally different ways of addressing moral issues. Elements of both coexist, uneasily, in North American culture, but one of them cannot be mapped onto the other. From either a collectivist or individualist point of view on the abortion debate, the other point of view is simply wrong.

The Question of Origin

I am sure it is obvious by now that cross-cultural differences in personality, behavior, and experience are real and profound. Where do these differences come from?

The Deconstructionist Dodge

This obvious and fundamental question seems to have received less attention than it deserves. The deconstructionist cultural psychologists seem particularly prone to avoid this question, probably because their basic approach tends to foreclose any answer to it. Recall that the deconstructionist critique claims that reality cannot be known apart from culturally determined perceptions or constructions of it (e.g., Shweder & Sullivan, 1990). Therefore, one's view of reality must always follow culture; it is not determined before there is any culture. For example, the cultural psychologist Joan Miller is critical of "ecological" views that attempt to find physical or social reasons for cross-cultural differences, and instead argues that differences between cultures must be considered in "symbolic" terms. She wrote:

> Culture is understood as shared meaning systems that are embodied in artifacts and practices and that form a medium for human development. Culture is recognized to be public, in that it depends on intersubjectively held understandings and exists as a socially established reality prior to any specific individual's involvement with it. (Miller, 1999, p. 86; emphasis added)

This "explanation" of cross-cultural differences strikes me as akin to answering the old chicken-or-egg question with "chicken," and then simply ignoring the issue of where that first chicken came from. The existentialists discussed in Chapter 13 would say that even a cultural view of reality is never actually imposed on the individual; it is freely chosen. But the deconstructionist cultural psychologists do not seem to be claiming that cultures have free will, just that their constructions are arbitrary. According to them, the way a culture views reality cannot depend on anything that preceded the culture itself. Frankly, this is not much of an answer to the origin question.

The Ecological Approach

Comparative cultural psychologists have tried to provide serious answers to the origin question, although so far their answers must be classified as speculative rather than proved. Triandis (1994) proposed a straightforward model that can be diagrammed as

Ecology → culture → socialization → personality → behavior.

In this model, behavior comes from personality, which is a result of what one has been taught explicitly and implicitly during one's upbringing (socialization, also called *enculturation* in this context), which is a product of the culture. These steps I have already discussed. The first term in Triandis's model is ecology, by which he means the physical layout and resources of the land where the culture originated, together with the distinctive tasks this culture has needed to accomplish. Part of the collectivist nature of the Chinese culture, for example, might be traceable to their need, thousands of years ago, to develop complex agricultural projects and water systems that required the coordination of many people. In the same historical period, people who lived in hunting or gathering societies did not develop the same collectivist outlook or complex social system. On an even broader scale, the biologist Jared Diamond has argued that European culture became a dominant colonial power around the world because of accidental advantages of the availability of crops and animals that were readily domesticated, and because of the Europeans' development of immunity to germs that were fatal to members of other cultures (Diamond, 1999).

Even small differences in ecology can lead to large differences in personality. Truk and Tahiti, small islands in the South Pacific with cultures dependent on fishing, have evolved different patterns of gender roles and aggressive behavior (Gilmore, 1990). In Truk, fish can only be caught by those who are willing to venture out to sea, which is quite hazardous. The result is a culture in which the men who must do this learn to be brave, violent, and physical, and also dominating of women. In Tahiti, fish can be caught easily in the home lagoon, which is not dangerous at all. The men in this culture tend to be gentle, to ignore insults, to be very slow to fight, and also to be respectful of women. Apparently, all this is merely a result of where the fish are!

Of course, there is no way to prove that this interpretation of the source of the differences between the culture on Truk and Tahiti is correct. If it sounds reasonable to you, fine; if it does not, also fine. Nearly all interpretations of the origins of cross-cultural differences must be taken with a similar grain of salt;

"I don't know how it started, either. All I know is that it's part of our corporate culture."

there are no experiments one can do to prove them right or wrong. But it is still worthwhile to try to formulate such explanations, especially given the fact that the only alternative is to ignore the origin question altogether.

It is also possible to see the development of subcultures within larger cultures as a function of particular conditions experienced by members of that subculture. As I mentioned earlier, extreme poverty and decades of racial discrimination have led some ethnic subcultures within the United States to develop styles of self-presentation (it being essential for young males to appear tough and threatening) and self-definition (through identification with gangs and other sources of social support and physical protection) that stand in strong contrast with that of the mainstream culture (Anderson, 1994). The culture of honor in the American South may have its roots in the agrarian past of that region, where land and possessions had to be personally protected, or else lost (Cohen et al., 1996). Other aspects of minority subcultures in the United States stem from distinct ethnic heritages rooted in Asia, Africa, Latin America, and Europe, which have been more or less imported onto the North American continent.

Issues and Challenges of Cross-Cultural Research

Cross-cultural psychology raises several issues that make research especially challenging, and which are likely to receive increasing attention in the future. Now that we have surveyed some of the recent work on this topic, this might be a good time to review some of those issues.

Ethnocentrism

One central issue for cross-cultural psychology is that any observation made of another culture almost certainly will be colored by the observer's own cultural background, no matter how hard he or she tries to avoid it. A truly objective point of view, free from any cultural bias, is difficult to attain, and some anthropologists argue that such a point of view is impossible in principle. As Harry Triandis (1994) pointed out, researchers are most in danger of committing ethnocentrism (judging another culture from the point of view of their own) when the "real" nature of the situation seems most obvious.

For example, Triandis considered two interviews concerning "a widow in your community [who] eats fish two or three times a week." First, a Hindu Indian was interviewed:

> **Q:** Is the widow's behavior wrong?
> **A:** Yes. Widows should not eat fish, meat, onions or garlic, or any "hot" foods. . . .
> **Q:** How serious is the violation?
> **A:** A very serious violation. . . .
> **Q:** Is it a sin?
> **A:** Yes. It's a "great" sin.
> **Q:** What if no one knew this had been done? It was done in private or secretly. Would it be wrong then?
> **A:** What difference does it make if it is done while alone? It is wrong. A widow should spend her time seeking salvation—seeking to be reunited with the soul of her husband. Hot foods will distract her. They will stimulate her sexual appetite. . . . She will want sex and behave like a whore.

Then an American interview is reported:

> **Q:** Is the widow's behavior wrong?
> **A:** No. She can eat fish if she wants to.
> **Q:** How serious is the violation?
> **A:** It is not a violation.
> **Q:** Is it a sin?
> **A:** No.
> **Q:** What if no one knew this had been done? It was done in private or secretly. Would it be wrong then?
> **A:** It is not wrong, in private or public. (Shweder, Mahapatra, & Miller, 1990, pp. 168–170)

Triandis pointed out that the responses of the Indian informant may seem absurd and somewhat amusing, whereas those of the American informant seem perfectly obvious and even boring. It takes a real intellectual struggle to consider seriously the possibility that the Indian's responses are just as reasonable as the American's, and differ only by starting with an unfamiliar set of cultural assumptions. The principal Indian assumption underlying the conversation is that relationships such as that between a husband and a wife exist for all eternity, whereas the American assumption is that after a husband's death a widow is a free and independent individual. (The Indian interview also contains some assumptions about the aphrodisiac properties of fish and certain other foods.) The American point of view is more familiar, but the Indian one is not necessarily false.

The point of this example is not that we should begin worrying about widows who eat garlic, but that it is difficult, and perhaps impossible, to cast off the lenses on reality provided by our own cultural backgrounds. The whole point of cross cultural psychology is the attempt to do this.

Outgroup Homogeneity Bias

A second potential pitfall of cross-cultural research is to assume that all members of a given culture are alike. Researchers sometimes report that everybody in India, or Japan, or China has a certain view of the world (some even claim that Indians, Japanese, and Chinese all have the same, "Eastern" view of the world), as if it were true that everybody in these cultures thinks in the same way. Given the size and diversity of these populations, any such blanket statement seems extremely unlikely to be correct.

The phenomenon to beware of here is one that social psychologists call the **outgroup homogeneity bias** (e.g., Linville & Jones, 1980; Lorenzi-Cioldi, 1993; Park & Rothbart, 1982). A group to which one belongs naturally seems to contain individuals who differ widely from each other. But members of those groups to which one does not belong seem to be "all the same." Even cross-cultural psychologists and anthropologists, who of all people should know better, sometimes seem to fall into this bias trap. We should remember Western culture contains both individualists and collectivists, for example, and the same is surely true about China or India or anyplace else. Somebody who says that "nobody in India has a sense of the self as separate" is falling into exactly the same trap as somebody who assumes that everybody in the world senses the self as separate. Variations between individuals within a culture are as important as variations between cultures.

Interestingly, to think that variations between individuals within a culture are important is an individualist view. To think that variations between cultures, taken as a whole, are more important, is a collectivist view. Which view is yours?

Cultures and Values

A third issue is that unless one is careful, cultural psychology sometimes has a way of leading to cultural relativism. As we saw in Chapter 13, relativism is the phenomenologically based idea that all cultural views of reality are equally valid, and that it is impossible and presumptuous to judge any of them as good or bad, because any such judgment would inevitably be ethnocentric.

This point of view seems fine until we begin to consider certain examples. In some areas of Africa and Asia, female genitals are mutilated as part of a cultural tradition intended to preserve purity and thereby improve chances for marriage. Typically, elderly village women use a razor blade or piece of glass, under unhygienic conditions and without anesthesia, to remove the clitoris or the clitoris and labia minora of a young girl. Each year, this procedure is performed on about two million girls between the ages of four and fifteen. Opposition expressed by the World Health Organization and some international human rights groups has sometimes been denounced as ethnocentric (Associated Press, 1994). But does our necessarily different cultural perspective truly mean that we have no valid grounds on which to condemn this tradition?

Steven Spielberg's movie *Schindler's List* describes the career of Oskar Schindler, who was by the standards of the dominant culture of his day (the Nazi culture) a misfit and an outlaw. One of the fascinating things about this movie is that it suggests that Schindler might not have been completely well adjusted, psychologically. He is shown as disorganized, deceitful, impulsive, and not very good at calculating risks. Yet it is precisely these traits that allowed him to engage in behavior—a complex and dangerous scheme to save thousands of Jewish lives over a period of several years—that today is regarded as heroic. Being a misfit in one's culture is not always a bad thing.

The dangers of cultural relativism have been compellingly described by the psychologists Jack and Jeanne Block:

> If the absolute definition [of psychological adjustment and of right and wrong] risks the danger of a parochial arrogance, the relative definition may be advocating the value of valuelessness. . . . To the extent that relativism implies one culture is as good as another . . . relativism provides a rationale for tolerance that is also a rationale for perpetuation of what is, rather than what might be. (Block et al., 1971, p. 328)

Subcultures and Multiculturalism

At the beginning of this chapter we saw that the term "culture" was surprisingly difficult to pin down, in part because the definition of a cultural group is necessarily vague. Some groupings are both obvious and oversimplified, such as the difference between East and West (which neatly divides the globe in two), or (almost the same thing) collectivism and individualism. Another way to make groupings is in terms of physical geography, such as one's continent of residence, language, or political boundaries. All of these groupings have turned out to be useful bases of psychological comparison, but it is important to bear in mind that they are also imprecise and to some extent arbitrary, and that people who are members of the same cultural group by one definition may be members of different groups by another definition. Furthermore, cultural groups often contain distinct, identifiable, and important subgroups. For example, much of the research summarized in this chapter treats "Americans" or residents of the United States as a single cultural group that can then be compared with "Asians," Koreans, Japanese, Chinese, Indians, or others. But it may have occurred to Canadian readers that there are subtle but real cultural differences within North America, and to Asian readers that not all Asian groups are alike, either.

Important subcultures exist even within the political borders of the United States. I already mentioned the work on the "culture of honor" that describes how residents of the southern U.S. differ from those in the north. Other recent research has documented that other, ethnic differences can be found within the population sometimes described simply as "European American." One fascinating study compared American-born, second-generation or later descendants of immigrants from Scandinavia, with similarly distant descendants of Irish immigrants. When videotaped reliving episodes of happiness and love, Irish Americans smiled significantly more than Scandinavian Americans, consistent with the different customs of their ancestral culture (Tsai & Chentsova-Dutton, in press). This finding suggests that there may be more ethnic diversity within European-American culture than was previously suspected, and opens the door to future research of this kind.

Another complication to cultural grouping, especially in nations of immigrants such as the United States and Canada, is that some "multicultural" individuals may belong to more than one culture. For example, California includes many young people who were raised in Spanish-speaking households among extended and powerful Mexican-American family groups, who at the same time attended English-speaking schools, watched U.S. television, and in some respects are thoroughly "Americanized." The same is true of many Asian Americans and first-generation children of immigrants from many different lands, not to mention the many children of marriages between individuals from different ethnic or cultural groups. When confronted by the typical university form that demands, "state your ethnicity," what are they supposed to put down?

According to recent research, perhaps some of them should check "all of the above" (or at least check more than one option). One study showed that bicultural Chinese Americans switched quickly between Chinese and American frames of reference, sometimes without necessarily even being aware of doing so, in response to seeing "primes" such as pictures of a Chinese dragon or the Statue of Liberty (Benet-Martínez et al., 2002). But such biculturalism does not always come easy. Some people are able to integrate multiple cultural identities in such a way as to gain the maximum benefit from each, while others experience conflict and even stress (Haritatos & Benet-Martínez, 2002).

Challenges for the Future

The issues just summarized are likely to be critical for cross-cultural psychology in the years ahead. Psychologists will need to think more deeply about the degree to which their own cultural outlook affects their views of other cultures, and find ways to overcome this potential source of bias. While understanding that the collectivist view of the self is profoundly different from the individualistic view, they will also need to avoid the assumption that members of unfamiliar cultures are "all alike," an assumption that opens the door to the worst kind of stereotyping. Psychologists will need to seek to understand and appreciate the profoundly different value systems of different cultures, without imposing on their analysis what Jack and Jeanne Block call the further "value of valuelessness." And cross-cultural psychology is bound to pay increasing attention to the many different kinds and sizes of cultural groups, to the importance of subcultures, and to the unique attributes of multicultural individuals. The pace of research in cultural psychology has accelerated dramatically in just the past few years, and it is sure to become even more important in the future.

The Universal Human Condition

According to the existential philosopher Sartre, discussed in Chapter 13, one universal fact applies across all individuals and all cultures. That fact comprises the "*a priori* limits which outline man's fundamental situation in the universe." Sartre wrote,

> Historical situations vary; a man may be born a slave in a pagan society or a feudal lord or a proletarian. What does not vary is the necessity for him to exist in the world, to be at work there, to be there in the midst of other people, and to be a mortal there. . . . In this sense we may say that there is a universality of man. (Sartre, 1965, pp. 52–53)

And, despite everything we have learned in this chapter, there are other reasons to wonder how different people really are, deep down, from one culture to the next. Differences between cultures in the rules for appropriate behavior might sometimes mask the similar motivations that lie underneath. For example, it is easy to observe that Chinese generally appear to be less extraverted than Americans. They talk less and less loudly, among other differences. However, Chinese culture tends to restrain the inhibition of feelings and to consider their public display to be inappropriate. Thus, it is possible that an extraverted American might laugh twice as much as an equivalently extraverted Chinese and appear different when the two are really the same underneath (McCrae, Costa, & Yik, 1996). In a similar fashion, the same sensations that Americans report as "emotional feelings" are interpreted by members of many other cultures in a more physiological manner. Where an American might report "feeling depressed," a Chinese might report "feelings of discomfort in the heart" (Zheng, Xu, & Shen, 1986), when the underlying experience is the same. Even seemingly obvious cross-cultural differences in behavior may be less pervasive than they appear. The psychologist Laura Miller has commented that

> In presenting the public or outside self to strangers or outgroup members, Japanese will tend to display deferential, hierarchical, and self-effacing conduct. The private personality, in which an individual may display confidence, assertiveness, and directness, will be reserved for interactions with co-workers, friends, and family. Most Americans meet only the public selves of Japan, and interpret these as the "true" personality. (Miller, 1999, p. 225)

In a similar vein, I once heard the psychologist Brian Little relate an unpublished result from a cross-cultural research project. He was interested in the goals or "personal projects" people pursue (see Chapter 17), and the degree to which they might vary cross-culturally. Little teaches at a university in Canada, and it was easy for him to ask his students to describe their current personal projects. At considerable expense and difficulty, he managed to have a group of Chinese students in China surveyed on a similar question. Great pains were taken to translate the question into Chinese, then to "back-translate" it into English to make sure it correctly crossed the cultural divide,[5] and the same efforts were expended on translating the students' answers. Almost uniformly, the results were disappointing for anyone who expected large differences. The goals—get good grades, shop for tonight's dinner, find a new girlfriend—seemed more universal than culturally specific. Then, to his

---

[5]In back translation, the researcher takes a phrase in one language and translates it into a second language, then has a separate person translate it back into the first language. Then, a native speaker of the first language judges whether the original and translated statements mean the same thing (as they should, if the translations were done correctly).

great excitement, Little read one particular Chinese student's response: one of her current projects, she reported, was to "work on my guilt."

Little reported his initial reaction as: Wow, what a profoundly different, non-Western type of goal. What interesting insight a goal like working on one's guilt provides into the fundamentally contrasting, collectivist Chinese worldview. And, not least of all, what a publication this will make!

Then, good scientist that he is, Little did some checking. The statement turned out to be a typographical error. The Chinese student wanted a homemade blanket, so she was trying to find time to work on her *quilt*. Sometimes, cross-cultural differences in personality are surprisingly elusive.

Summary

If, as the phenomenologists claim, a person's construal of the world is all-important, a logical next question concerns the ways in which such construals of reality vary across different cultures. It is important to know whether psychological research and theorizing that originate in one culture can be applied to another, because misunderstandings across cultures can lead to conflict and even war, and because to understand how other peoples view reality can expand our own understanding of the world. Some psychologists ignore cross-cultural issues, while deconstructionists argue that comparing cultures is impossible. Most modern cross-cultural psychologists follow a comparative approach, contrasting etics, or elements that all cultures have in common, with emics, or elements that make them different. Cultures have been compared on emic dimensions including complexity, tightness, and collectivism-individualism. This last dimension has generated a large amount of research comparing behavior, values, and views of the self between members of collectivist (mostly Eastern) and individualist (mostly Western) cultures.

Trait analyses have assessed the degree to which members of cultural groups differ on average, across various personality traits, and also have evaluated the degree to which the same traits that characterize people in one culture can be used to characterize people in another. Analyses of styles of thinking have addressed hypotheses such as that members of collectivist cultures think more holistically and are less prone to self-expression. Some cross-cultural analyses of the "self" have concluded that the idea is a Western cultural artifact, but other research has sought instead to compare the way the self is conceptualized in different cultures, including issues of self-regard and self-determination. Buddhism provides important insights into collectivist views of the self. The most difficult cross-cultural analyses involve values. Collectivist cultures place group values (such as harmony) ahead of individual values (such as freedom); individualist cultures do the reverse.

Deconstructionists avoid the question of where cultural differences originate, but one comparative approach sees the ultimate origin of cultural differences in the differing ecologies to which groups around the world must adapt. It is important to bear in mind that ethnocentrism is a constant hazard, that individuals vary within as well as across cultures, that cultural relativism can be taken too far, that cultures come in many different forms and sizes, and that multicultural individuals may blend influences from more than one culture. Beneath cultural differences may be a universal human condition in an existential sense: everybody everywhere must exist, work, relate to other people, and ultimately die.

SUGGESTED READINGS: EXPERIENCE AND AWARENESS

Keyes, C. L. M., & Haidt, J. (Eds.) (2003). *Flourishing: Positive psychology and the life well-lived.* Washington, DC: American Psychological Association.

   A thorough collection of writings by almost all of the major figures in the modern "positive psychology" movement.

Lee, Y-T., McCauley, C. R., & Draguns, J. G. (Eds.) (1999). *Personality and person perception across cultures.* Mahwah, NJ: Erlbaum.

   An excellent collection of articles on cross-cultural psychology written by psychologists from around the world.

Maslow, A. H. (1987). *Motivation and personality* (3rd ed.). New York: Harper & Row.

   One of the most accessible—and briefest—thorough presentations of American humanistic psychology by one of its two historically most important figures (the other being Carl Rogers). Maslow's writing is passionate and persuasive.

Rogers, C. R. (1961). *On becoming a person.* Boston: Houghton Mifflin.

   The classic statement of the ultimate optimistic phenomenologist.

Sartre, J. P. (1965). *The humanism of existentialism.* In W. Baskin (Ed.), *Essays in existentialism* (pp. 31–62). Secaucus, NJ: Citadel.

   A surprisingly readable and interesting exposition of existentialism, from one of the important historical figures of the approach.

Triandis, H. C. (1994). *Culture and social behavior.* New York: McGraw-Hill.

   A thorough and readable introduction to comparative cross-cultural psychology, now a little out of date.

Tseng, W-S. (2003). *Clinician's guide to cultural psychiatry.* San Diego: Academic Press.

   A very thorough, well-written and up-to-date survey of cross-cultural psychiatry that includes specific case studies. Although it is focused on mental disorders as they vary across cultures, the book includes many insights on the psychology of specific cultures and the difficulties of cross-cultural comparison.

PART VI

THE PERSON AND THE SITUATION: LEARNING AND COGNITIVE APPROACHES TO PERSONALITY

In the very first psychology class I ever took, the professor decided one day to teach us a few things about the power of reward to change behavior. He brought out a basket of slips of paper, on each of which were printed the words, "Good for one extra point on the next exam." Did we want them? Indeed we did. He began a class discussion about what we would be willing to do for an extra point or two, and how our desire for higher grades could be used to manipulate our behavior. From time to time, he would suddenly bestow one of the precious little slips on a student. But it wasn't at all clear when or why. He might call out "Wrong!" in response to a comment, then give the student a slip of paper. He might say "Right!" and give nothing. Slowly, people began to catch on. First one student, then another, gradually realized that he was handing out an extra point every time someone said the word *reinforcement*. Suddenly a critical mass of

awareness was achieved, and we were all screaming, "Reinforcement! Reinforcement! Reinforcement!" Game over.

There were three lessons in this little demonstration. First, behaviors that
are rewarded—*reinforced,* in the behaviorist terminology—become more
likely. I think we were beginning to say "reinforcement" more often even
before we quite realized what the deal was. Second, this fact offers a powerful tool for behavior change. His little slips of paper were enough to
make a room full of legal adults scream the same word over and over—a
pretty weird behavior, when you think about it. The third lesson was a little more subtle. There was a moment, an obvious moment, when everyone
in the class suddenly became aware of the contingency (when we began to
yell "reinforcement!" in unison). This observation shows that awareness is
important. People don't just respond to what is rewarded, they respond to
what they *expect* will be rewarded—a very different matter.

The fact that people base their behavior on their expectations for reward
has several important implications. First, it means that behavior change
can be very sudden—as soon as someone "gets it," or thinks she gets it,
her behavior may change immediately and drastically. Second, it means
that people might sometimes change their behavior for the wrong reason.
We respond to what we *think* will be rewarded, and expectations and reality sometimes, and maybe often, differ. Third, it implies that our behavior
might change not just because we have been rewarded, but because we
have seen other people being rewarded. As soon as my classmates realized
that other students were getting those precious slips just for saying "reinforcement," they immediately began to do it themselves. Fourth, it means
that to understand human behavior, it is not enough to map out the ways
in which people are rewarded and punished. We must also try to understand how people think.

In one fifty-minute class demonstration, my first psychology professor
managed to recreate the entire fifty-year evolution of behaviorism, social
learning theory, and cognitive conceptualizations of personality. This evolution began early in the twentieth century with proud and confident
behaviorist decrees that the basic facts of behavior were very simple, and

that anybody could be made to do or be anything through the proper use of reward and punishment. Then the picture became more complex, as psychologists began to demonstrate that people also learn from watching the rewards and punishments that they see administered to other people, and that the expectations one develops for reward and punishment do not always match reality. These realizations led to the development of social learning theory. Finally, by late in the century social learning theory itself had evolved into an approach that focuses on the entire cognitive system that underlies expectations, goals, plans, and many other psychological phenomena.

This evolution is the topic of the next three chapters. Chapter 15 will review some of the history of behaviorism and how it evolved into social learning theory, and consider the work of the more prominent social learning theorists. Chapter 16 will describe the basic workings of the cognitive system as they are currently understood, and how they are important for behavior and personality. Chapter 17 will focus on cognitively oriented research addressing how we perceive and respond to the world, how we perceive ourselves, and how we choose and pursue the goals that are most important to us.

HOW THE WORLD
CREATES WHO YOU ARE:
BEHAVIORISM AND SOCIAL
LEARNING THEORY

Consider two simple ideas. First, two stimuli—events, things, or people—that are repeatedly experienced together will eventually come to elicit the same response. For example, if someone puffs air into your eye at the same time they ring a bell, before too long the sound of the bell will be enough to make you blink. Second, behaviors that are followed by pleasant outcomes tend to be repeated, and behaviors followed by unpleasant outcomes tend to be dropped. For example, if you find that your hard work is rewarded, you may work even harder; if you find that hard work goes unappreciated, you may figure, why bother?

Both of these ideas can be reduced to a single, even simpler idea: Behavior changes as a result of experience. Whether you blink, or work hard, or do any number of other things in your life depends on what you have experienced in the past. This process—the change of behavior as a function of experience—is called **learning**, and the learning-based approaches to personality attempt to explain all of the phenomena considered in the earlier chapters of this book in terms of this single process.

Learning-based approaches to personality come in two varieties: behaviorism and the social learning theories. By the careful application of one simple idea, learning, to more and more complex situations, psychologists in these two related traditions have built a theory of the basis of personality and behavior, and an effective technology for behavioral change. They also have built an approach to psychology that holds high the scientific values of objectivity, publicly observable data, and tight theoretical reasoning.

This last-named accomplishment—the building of an approach to psychology that seems truly scientific—has been a major attraction for many psychologists. Such researchers believe that psychology is not and should not be art, or literature, or poetry. It is science. And what makes psychology scientific can only be its unique objectivity, its basis in concrete facts rather than personal points of view. The worldview of these scientifically inclined individuals—and certainly their approach to psychology—is exactly the opposite of that of the humanists described in Chapter 13. Indeed, behaviorism **441** was invented, in part, out of frustration with the focus on unobservable events inside the mind propounded by introspectionists such as Wilhelm Wundt.

The desire to bypass introspection and to obtain data that are more objective led the behaviorists to concentrate their science on aspects of the mind and behavior that can be observed directly. Behavioral psychologists try to show how people's behavior is a direct result of their environment, particularly the rewards and punishments that environment contains. However, some researchers eventually grew dissatisfied with its rigidity and with the number of phenomena that behaviorism ignores, and so they extended behaviorism into a closely related approach that yielded the social learning theories. These two approaches are the subject of this chapter.

Behaviorism

Psychology is often regarded as an attempt to "get inside the head." The personality researchers considered so far in this book—the psychoanalysts, humanists, and even most trait theorists and biological psychologists—put great efforts into trying to understand the unseen recesses of the mind. However, behaviorists such as the historical figures John Watson and B. F. Skinner believed that the best angle from which to understand a person is from the outside. Although the behaviorists do not have an official slogan, I will happily make up one for them: "We can only know that which we can see, and we can see everything we need to know."

Consider the two parts of this epigram separately. First, the behaviorist believes that all knowledge worth having can only come from direct, public observation. Introspection, of the sort practiced by Wilhelm Wundt (see Chapter 13), is invalid because nobody else can verify it. Attempting to tap other peoples' thoughts is similarly suspect. The only valid way to know something about somebody is to watch what he or she does—the person's behavior. That is why the approach is called **behaviorism**.

This idea implies that your personality is simply the sum total of everything you do. Nothing else. Personality does not include traits, unconscious conflicts, psychodynamic processes, conscious experiences, or anything else that cannot be directly observed. If such unobservable structures and processes even exist (which behaviorists tend to doubt), they are not important. A behaviorist approach to personality, then, is based exclusively on B data, which were described in Chapter 2.

Close on the heels comes a further belief that the causes of behavior can be observed as directly as behavior itself, because these causes are not hidden away in the mind; they can be seen in the individual's environment. In this context, environment refers not to the trees and rivers of nature, but to the rewards and punishments that are contained in the physical and social world. The goal of behaviorism is a **functional analysis** that maps out exactly how behavior is a "function" of one's environmental situation.

Philosophical Roots of Behaviorism

Behaviorism can be regarded as the American, twentieth-century, scientific manifestation of some very old philosophical ideas. Three ideas in particular are fundamental: empiricism, associationism, and hedonism.

EMPIRICISM

Empiricism is the idea that all knowledge comes from experience. Experience, in this analysis, is not something that exists separately from or that can produce reality, as the phenomenologists described in Chapter 13 would argue. Rather, experience is the direct product of reality itself. The contents of our minds—and, by extension, our behavior—are produced by the contents of the world and how it has impinged on us, producing what we have seen, heard, and felt in life. In this way, the structure of reality determines the structure of the mind.

The opposing view, rationalism, holds that exactly the reverse is true: The structure of the mind determines our experience of reality. We saw this belief in the views of the phenomenologists discussed in Chapter 13, as well as the deconstructionists and some of the cultural psychologists considered in Chapter 14. Empiricism—and behaviorism—is emphatically neither phenomenological nor deconstructionist.

Taken to its logical conclusion, empiricism implies that the mind, at birth, is essentially empty. The nineteenth-century philosopher John Locke called the mind of a newborn baby a *tabula rasa,* or "blank slate," ready to be written on by experience. The twentieth-century psychologist and founder of behaviorism, John Watson, held the same belief. Only as a person encounters reality does he or she begin to accumulate experiences and thereby build a characteristic way of reacting to the world, that is, a personality. Watson once wrote:

> Give me a dozen healthy infants, well-formed, and my own specified world to bring them up in and I'll guarantee to take any one at random and train him to become any type of specialist I might select—doctor, lawyer, artist, merchant, chief and yes, even beggarman and thief, regardless of his talents, penchants, tendencies, vocations, and race of his ancestors. (Watson, 1930, p. 65)

ASSOCIATIONISM

A second key philosophical idea explains how learning happens. **Associationism** is the claim that two things, or two ideas, or a thing and an idea, become mentally associated into one if they are repeatedly experienced close together in time. Often, but not always, this closeness occurs as the result of a cause-and-effect relationship. The lightning flashes and then thunder booms. Thunder and lightning become associated in the mind of all who experience this combination. Other combinations are more psychological: a smile of a certain kind is followed by a kiss. Still other combinations are arbitrary, or even artificially imposed. A bell rings, and then you are fed (try to imagine yourself as a dog for this example). In each of these cases, the two things tend to become one in the mind. The thought of one will conjure up the other, and the way a person reacts to one will tend to become the way he or she reacts to the other.

HEDONISM AND UTILITARIANISM

Taken together, empiricism and associationism form the core of the behaviorist explanation of where personality comes from and of what it is made: it comes from experience and consists of the resulting associations between simple ideas. A third philosophical belief, called **hedonism**, provides the remaining piece of the puzzle: motivation. Hedonism provides an answer for *why* people behave at all.

In this context, hedonism claims that people (and "organisms" in general) learn in order to do just two things: seek pleasure and avoid pain. These fundamental motivations explain why rewards and punishments are able to shape people's behavior. They also form the basis of a value system that guides the technology of behavioral change that is behaviorism's proudest achievement.

Hedonism is not a new idea. Epicurus, a Greek philosopher who lived from 341 to 270 B.C., claimed that the purpose of life is to be free of pain and to pursue what he called "gentle" pleasure, or aesthetic enjoyment and peace of mind. This simple idea led to a surprisingly powerful principle for morality and ethics: Whatever produces the most pleasure for the most people in the long run is good. Whatever does the reverse is bad. Many actions commonly regarded as unethical or immoral fall under this umbrella. Theft, for example, benefits the thief and harms the victim, two outcomes that could be said to cancel each other out, but it also harms the social order that allows commerce and other good things to happen. So theft is, on balance, harmful. In a very different example, marital infidelity might produce short-term pleasure, but it damages a more important marital relationship (thus causing long-term harm to the individual) and may possibly damage an entire family (thus harming the many for the advantage of the few). Lying, cheating, and even more complicated actions such as polluting the environment for short-term profit, or concentrating power and money in the hands of a few at the expense of the many, can be judged immoral by the same pragmatic standard. In general, the Epicurean ideal leads to a social philosophy called **utilitarianism**, which claims that the best society is the social arrangement that creates the most happiness for the largest number of people.

This idea might sound uncontroversial, and in the examples just listed it seems pretty compelling. But it is not without problems of its own. One complication is that utilitarianism puts the goal of the most happiness for the most people above all other goals, including truth, freedom, and dignity. The behaviorist and latter-day utilitarian B. F. Skinner wrote a book, called *Walden Two*, about a fictional utopia (Skinner, 1948). In this utopia everybody was happy, but nobody was free and considerations such as dignity and truth were treated as irrelevant.

Would you give up your freedom to be happy? A utilitarian would (and would believe freedom to be an illusion, anyway). An existentialist, by contrast, surely would not. As you will recall from Chapter 13, the ultimate purpose of life for an existentialist is to understand and to face truth. "Happiness" in the absence of truth, freedom, and meaning would not be worth having.

Three Kinds of Learning

The doctrine of empiricism, as we have seen, asserts that all knowledge comes from experience. The behaviorist idea of learning is similar, except that the focus is on behavior rather than on knowledge. Three types of learning are traditionally identified. They are habituation, classical (or respondent) conditioning, and operant conditioning.

HABITUATION

Sneak up behind someone and ring a bell. The person will probably jump, perhaps high in the air. Then ring it again. The second jump will not be as high. Then ring it again. The third jump (assuming the person has not snatched the bell out of your hand by now) will be still lower. Eventually, the bell will produce almost no response at all.

This kind of learning is called **habituation**. It is the simplest way in which behavior changes as a result of experience. A crayfish, which has only a few neurons, can do it. Habituation can even be seen in amoebas and single neurons. If you repeatedly poke a crayfish or electrically stimulate a neuron, the response diminishes with each repetition, until it disappears almost entirely.

Despite its simplicity, habituation can be a powerful mechanism of behavioral change. When my wife and I moved to Boston some years ago, we had been in our new Back Bay apartment just a few minutes when we heard an ear-splitting whooping and clanging sound outside. I ran to the window and saw a new Mercedes parked across the street, its alarm in full uproar. Nobody was anywhere near. Eventually, the alarm stopped. A few minutes later, it went off again. Again I went to the window, but a little more slowly this time. Then again, a few minutes after that. And again. After a few weeks, only by noticing the looks on our guests' faces did I become aware that another car alarm had gone off.

Experimental research on habituation has shown that a response nearly as strong as the original *can* be maintained, but only if the stimulus is changed or increased with every repetition. Everyone has heard—too often, I'm sure—those car alarms that start with a whooping sound, then go to beeping, then a whistle, and then cycle back to whooping. The purpose of this variation in sound is not to annoy people (although it does this very effectively) but to prevent habituation.

Even the impact of important personal events can lessen over time (Brickman, Coates, & Janoff-Bulman, 1978). For example, people who win millions of dollars in a lottery have a pretty exciting day, but over the long run end up not much happier than they were before. They become habituated to their millionaire status. The reverse effect sometimes happens with people who become paraplegic in accidents. They may habituate even to this change in status and regain more happiness than they might have thought possible. It seems in time you can get used to almost anything.

CLASSICAL CONDITIONING

You moved away ten years ago and have not been back since, but one day you find yourself near the old neighborhood, so you drop by. As you walk down the street you used to travel every day, a host of long-forgotten images and feelings floods your mind. It can be a strange sensation, a little like traveling back in time. You might feel emotions you cannot label but know you have not felt in years; you might surprise yourself with the strength of your reaction to seeing a familiar mailbox or your own old front door; you might even in some hard-to-describe way feel ten years younger! What is going on here? You are experiencing the results of **classical conditioning**.

How Classical Conditioning Works   Classical conditioning is usually described in very different contexts, often involving animals—traditionally dogs. The well-known and nearly legendary story of classical conditioning involves the Russian scientist Ivan Pavlov, who was originally interested in studying the physiology of digestion. (He won a Nobel Prize for his work on that subject in 1904.) His subjects were dogs, which he hooked up to an apparatus that measured their salivation as they were fed.

He discovered such research to be complicated, but in a different way than he expected. He wanted to study how dogs salivated while they were eating, but inconveniently often they started salivating *before* they were fed! They might salivate at the sight of the assistant who usually brought their food, or at the sound of the streetcar that passed outside at feeding time. This finding forced his investigations out of the realm of pure physiology and into psychology. Against the advice of some of his physiological colleagues, Pavlov decided that the psychological issues were more interesting, and turned his attention to the circumstances under which salivation and other physical responses could be elicited with psychological stimuli.

One of his first findings forced an important change in the principle of associationism. It turns out that a bell begins to elicit salivation most quickly and reliably not if it is rung simultaneously with feeding, but if it is rung just slightly before. (If it is rung too early, it also loses its effectiveness.) Associationism had held that two things become combined in the mind by being experienced together; Pavlov's finding, however, showed that conditioning is more than a simple pairing of one stimulus with another; it involves teaching the animal that one stimulus (the bell) is a warning or signal of the other (the food). The difference is subtle but fundamental, because it means that the principle of associationism is slightly wrong. Concepts become associated not merely because they occurred close together in time and place, but because the meaning of one concept has changed the meaning of another. The bell used to be just a sound. Now it means "food is coming."

Classical conditioning can work in a negative direction as well. If you encounter a food under unpleasant circumstances—for example, when you are sick, or if the food itself is dirty or smelly—you may find that forever after you will avoid it whenever you can (Rozin & Zellner, 1985). Or, if you become convinced that smoking cigarettes or eating meat is immoral, you may come to find cigarettes or meat physically disgusting (Rozin, 1999; Rozin, Markwith, & Stoess, 1997).

Classical Conditioning and Physiology   Classical conditioning affects emotional responses and low-level behavioral responses such as salivating, as we have seen. Some research also has suggested that many organs of the body not usually considered to be under psychological control can be classically conditioned. Some "behaviors" that researchers report having been able to classically condition include insulin release by the pancreas, glycogen uptake by the liver, the speed of the heartbeat, and the flow of secretions in the stomach, gallbladder, and endocrine glands (Bykov, 1957; Bower & Hilgard, 1981).

These findings raise some interesting possibilities concerning physical health (Dworkin, 1993; King & Husband, 1991). For example, persons undergoing chemotherapy for cancer, which often creates nausea, may begin to feel nauseated just by entering the room where the chemicals are administered. Unintentional classical conditioning also can change effects of drugs. Injecting heroin into the bloodstream triggers biological "opponent processes" that serve to lessen its effects, which is why addicts tend to require larger doses over time. Through classical conditioning, these opponent processes might be triggered simply by the sight of the needle, or even by entering the room in which the addict usually shoots up. What happens, then, if a heroin addict shoots up in a location where he has not used drugs in the past—such as his parents' house, for example? One possibility is that because this location is not classically conditioned, the opponent processes will fail to kick in before the injection, and a dose that the addict could have tolerated under his usual circumstances may become a fatal overdose (Siegel, 1984; Siegel & Ellsworth, 1986). Apparently, the rock musician Dwayne Goettel (of the band Skinny Puppy) died in this manner (Pervin & John, 1997). Finally, it is possible that eventually we may learn to teach people, through classical conditioning, how to attain control over their own immune systems (Ader & Cohen, 1993).

Learned Helplessness   So far I have considered what happens when a person learns that one stimulus is associated with another. What about the cases where one stimulus is not associated with another—where both seem to happen randomly? This might seem like a nonsensical question; it seems there is nothing to learn in this case. But in fact there is an important lesson here: The world is unpredictable. If you experience occasional, unpleasant shocks, for example, without any stimulus to provide advance warning, you learn this: You are never safe (Gleitman, 1995).

Such a sense of unpredictability not only is unpleasant, but also can have important consequences. If one group of rats is given periodic electric shocks, with each shock preceded by a warning light, and another group of rats is given the exact same shocks at the exact same times, but without any warning, the second (unwarned) group becomes more likely to develop stomach ulcers (Seligman, 1968; Weiss, 1970, 1977). This finding illustrates the difference between fear and anxiety. One feels fear when one knows what the danger is, and has a reason to think that danger is impending. One feels anxiety when it is not clear exactly what the danger is, or when one has no idea when the danger might actually arrive. A chronically anxious person may be somebody who has experienced no more than the usual ration of "hard knocks" but who has never been able to learn when to expect them.

This feeling of unpredictability can also lead to a behavioral pattern called **learned helplessness** (Maier & Seligman, 1976; Peterson, Maier, & Seligman, 1993). Experiments with animals such as rats and dogs, and later with humans, suggest that the experience of random reward or punishment, independent of what one does, can lead to an apparent belief that nothing one does really matters. In turn, this belief can lead to depression (Miller & Seligman, 1975). One long-recognized symptom of depression is the "why bother" syndrome, where everything—including, in extreme cases, even getting out of bed or washing oneself—simply seems like too much trouble. The learned helplessness hypothesis is that this syndrome is the result of a history of unpredictable reward and punishment, leading the person to act as if nothing he or she does matters.

S-R Conception of Personality   Principles of classical conditioning have even yielded a personality theory of sorts. Early American behaviorists such as John Watson derived their understanding of personality directly from Pavlov's ideas. They assumed that the essential activity of life was to learn a vast array of responses to specific environment stimuli, and an individual's personality consists of his or her repertoire of learned "S-R" (stimulus-response) associations. Because everyone has a different learning history, each of these patterns will be idiosyncratic to the individual, and the S-R pattern for a given person need not have any particular structure or coherence. It will depend simply on what he or she has happened to learn. For example, if one has learned to be dominant at home but meek at work, a business meeting might trigger a subservient response, and a home situation might trigger dominance. This conception of personality is not without its influence today, as we shall see near the end of Chapter 16, but it is an old version of behaviorism. B. F. Skinner greatly enriched and expanded basic behaviorism by formulating the idea of operant conditioning, the topic of the next section.

OPERANT CONDITIONING

A good cook likes to experiment. He or she rarely uses the exact same ingredients, cooking times, or methods twice. Nonetheless, every good cook also has a fairly consistent style that evolves from this process of continual experimentation. Things that work are repeated. Things that do not work are dropped. As a result, and through experience, the cook's creations constantly change and constantly improve as he or she develops a distinctive style.

The Law of Effect: Thorndike   This kind of learning from experience is not limited to cooks or even to humans. A classic, early example involved cats. Even before Pavlov began his work with dogs, the American psychologist Edward Thorndike was putting hungry cats in a device he called the puzzle box. The cats could escape only by doing some specific, simple act, such as pulling on a wire or pressing a bar. Doing so would cause the box suddenly to spring open, and the cat would jump out to find a bit of food nearby. Then Thorndike would put the cat back in the box, to try again (Thorndike, 1911).

Thorndike found that gradually, the cat began to escape more and more quickly. What originally took three minutes, after twenty-five trials or so, occurred in less than fifteen seconds. The German psychologist Wolfgang Köhler later argued that the animals he studied, chimpanzees, actually came to understand their situation—to develop "insight." His evidence was that once they learned what would work to get them a banana, they employed it immediately, not gradually (Köhler, 1925; Gleitman, 1995)—like my fellow students, years ago, when they realized that points were being given just for saying "reinforcement." Years later this addition of the idea of insight opened the door for the eventual introduction of social learning theory.

Techniques of Operant Conditioning: Skinner B. F. Skinner (e.g., 1938) pointed out that in the case of Pavlov's dogs, their salivating actually had no effect on their environment. It was a response that, after training, happened to be followed by meat. Even if a dog were not to salivate, the meat would still arrive. But when Thorndike's cats pushed the lever that opened their cage, they changed the state of their world. A door once closed became open, allowing their escape.

Skinner called the first kind of learning **respondent conditioning**, meaning that what is conditioned is an essentially passive response that has no impact of its own. The second kind of learning, which he found much more interesting, he called **operant conditioning**, meaning that the animal learns to operate on its world in such a way as to change it to that animal's advantage.

To work out the laws of operant conditioning, Skinner invented a device that became known as the "Skinner box." In principle, this invention is much like Thorndike's puzzle box, but it is simpler in design and usually is used with simpler animals, such as rats and pigeons. The Skinner box contains little but a bar and a chute for delivering food pellets. Put a pigeon in there and it immediately begins to bump around. It does a little dance, it preens its feathers, and eventually, it pushes the bar. A food pellet immediately rolls down the chute. The pigeon eats it and then—pigeons not being terribly bright—goes back to its pigeon activities. It dances around some more, preens some more, and again eventually hits the bar. Another food pellet. The pigeon dimly begins to catch on. At a steadily increasing rate, the pigeon begins to hit the bar more often, sometimes (depending on the frequency of reinforcement) to the point where it does little else.

"Oh, not bad. The light comes on, I press the bar, they write me a check. How about you?"

    The cook with which I began this section and the pigeon are not all that different, according to the behaviorists. Both learn from experience through operant conditioning. If an animal or a person emits a behavior, and the behavior is followed by a **reinforcement**, the behavior becomes more likely than it was before. If the behavior is followed by a punishment, it becomes less likely (more will be said about punishment later in this chapter).

    Despite Skinner's emphasis on how reinforcement derives from the organism's effect on its environment, the results of operant conditioning are not necessarily logical. It will work on any behavior, regardless of the real connection between it and the consequences that follow. As a little joke, I once rubbed a $10 bill on a colleague's grant proposal "for luck." It was funded. For months after, everyone in my department came by to have me rub money on their grants before they sent them in.

    Skinner worked hard to develop practical techniques for changing behavior that can produce impressive results with both animals and humans. Consider shaping. A sculptor shapes a piece of clay into a statue by gradually shaving here and there until a square block comes to represent a person or an animal. The process is gradual and moves in small steps, but the ultimate result can be amazing. Behavior can be shaped in a similar manner. Reward a pigeon for hitting a bar, then raise the criterion. Now, to get rewarded, the pigeon must step forward and back and *then* hit the bar. (Because a pigeon is constantly emitting different behaviors, it will do this eventually.) The behavior is then rewarded and gradually becomes more frequent. Then the criterion is raised again. Before too long, the pigeon may be doing a fairly complicated dance inside the Skinner box.

According to legend, the same technique was once shown to be effective on Skinner himself. The story, advertised as true when told to me but probably apocryphal, is that his students at Harvard once decided to try out Skinner's principles on their esteemed instructor. They wanted him to stop giving lectures from the podium and instead deliver them from a spot near the door, with one foot out in the hallway. One day, as Skinner began to speak, they looked bored and shuffled their feet. The first time he happened to step away from the podium, they all perked up. When he stepped back, they returned to an apathetic slouch. After Skinner had learned to lecture from a step away, the students raised the criterion. Now they did not look alert until he was *two* steps away from the podium. By the end of the semester, B. F. Skinner was indeed delivering his lectures from the doorway, with one foot in the hall, only running occasionally to the podium to glance at his notes, then back to the doorway to continue.

And now, the punch line. A departmental colleague happened by the class one day. Seeing Skinner later in a faculty lounge, he asked why he had been lecturing from the doorway, instead of from the podium. Skinner replied, "The light is *much* better in the doorway."

Another example, which I know is true because I was there, concerns my old college roommate, Rick. A psychology major long before I was (and now a successful fireman in Idaho—who says you can't have a valuable career with a B.A. in psychology?), Rick was given the assignment of using shaping in a real-life context. He chose the dorm lounge where, every night at 6 P.M., most of the residents gathered to watch *Star Trek*. Rick was a stereo buff as well as a psychology major. He attached a wire to the innards of the television, ran the wire under the carpet to the back of the room, and there connected the wire to a box with a button. When he pressed the button, the television picture scrambled as if the antenna were misaligned.

Now he was ready to strike. That evening, as the crowd gathered to watch *Star Trek,* he silently selected his victim: that person, he decided, was going to stand by the television with one hand on top, one hand raised straight up in the air, and one foot lifted off the floor. It was easy enough to do. As the program began to get interesting, Rick pushed the button and scrambled the picture. Various people leapt up to fix things, but the picture cleared only when his victim stood. It scrambled again when she sat down. After she was standing, he raised the criterion. Now she had to stand closer, and then even closer to the television to clear the picture. Well before 7 P.M., Rick's victim was standing by the television with one hand on top, one up in the air, and one foot off the floor.

After *Star Trek* ended, Rick approached his victim and asked, innocently, why she had been standing like that. "Oh, don't you know," she replied, "the body acts like a natural antenna."

"We reward top executives at the agency with a unique incentive program. Money."

The Causes of Behavior A number of morals can be derived from these stories including, perhaps, the moral that neither psychologists nor their students are to be trusted (see Chapter 3). A deeper moral is that people may do things for very simple reasons without knowing those reasons. They can make up elaborate rationales for their actions that have little or nothing to do with the real causes (Nisbett & Wilson, 1977).

But let's not get too carried away. The human mind has many processes that occasionally lead to errors but usually lead to correct outcomes (Funder, 1987). The fact that sometimes we don't know the real reasons for our actions could be an example. One can fool somebody—like Skinner or the dorm resident—into doing something without knowing the reasons why. But under most circumstances, it is a good bet that we do know why we do certain things. In part, this is because rewards are not usually so hidden. The paycheck that causes many people to go to work is an effective and obvious reinforcement.

Punishment

He that spareth the rod hateth his own son.

—Proverbs 13:24

There is one behaviorist approach that millions of people use every day to try to control behavior: punishment. Despite its wide popularity, it has some definite dangers. Or, to be more precise, punishment works well if it is done right. The only problem is, it is almost never done right.

A **punishment** is an aversive consequence that follows an act in order to stop it and prevent its repetition. Punishment frequently is used by three kinds of people: parents, teachers, and bosses. This may be because people in all three roles have the same goals:

1. start some behaviors
2. maintain some behaviors
3. prevent some behaviors

The usual tactic for achieving goal 1 and goal 2 is to use reward. Teachers use gold stars and grades, parents use allowances and treats, and bosses use raises and bonuses. All of them (if they are good at what they do) use praise. (Praise is an excellent behavior modification tool because it is effective and it is free.) But what about goal 3? Many people believe the only way to stop or prevent somebody from doing something is to punish him or her for doing it.

Wrong. You can use reward for this purpose, too. All you have to do is find a response that is incompatible with the one you are trying to get rid of, and reward that incompatible response, instead. Reward a child for reading, instead of punishing the child for watching television. Or, if you want to stop and prevent drug abuse, provide opportunities for rewarding activities that are not drug related. Provide would-be drug users with recreation, and entertainment, and education, and useful work. Make these other activities as rewarding as possible and drug use will become less attractive.

Consider the famous antidrug campaign, "Just Say No." Saying no to drugs is a pretty limited life unless it also includes saying yes to something else. Yet (if I may editorialize) our society seems more interested in punishing drug use than in providing rewarding alternatives. The reason is not a matter of saving money—it costs taxpayers 1.5 times as much to house a prisoner for a year as it does to house and educate a student at the University of California. Budget savings from closing schools, parks, basketball courts, and community-service programs are more than eaten up in jail construction. I suspect the real reason has to do with a generally punitive attitude, coupled with a profound lack of imagination—and a lack of psychological education. Although I can do nothing about punitive attitudes or lack of imagination, I do what I can about psychological education (writing this book, for example).

Reward also is not used as much as it should be in the workplace. A friend of mine from graduate school now is a psychological consultant for businesses. One of his first clients was a lumber mill. The mill operated along classic, old-style management principles. The supervisor sat in a glass booth high in the rafters, from which he could see the entire production line. He scanned with binoculars until he saw something go wrong. Then he came down, yelled at the worker who was responsible, and sometimes demoted or even fired the worker on the spot. Not surprisingly, the workers dreaded the supervisor's approach. Moreover, they did what they could to conceal their activities from view. Morale was low. Absenteeism and turnover were high. Occasionally even sabotage took place.

My friend's first action was to gather the supervisors together for some instruction. (He charged a high fee, so the company would order them to follow his advice.) He told them they were forbidden to punish workers, effective immediately. Instead, they were to sit in their little glass booths until they saw a worker doing something perfectly. They were then to come down and praise the worker. Occasionally, if the perfection was truly exemplary, they were to award a bonus or a paid day off on the spot.

The supervisors were perplexed by and resistant to this seemingly crazy plan. But they followed corporate orders, and you can guess the results. At first the workers were terrified; they thought they knew what the supervisor's approach meant. But gradually they came to look forward to instead of dread his visits. Then they went one step further: they started to try to show the supervisor what they were doing, in case it might be good enough to merit a reward or just some praise. They started to like the supervisor better, and they started to like their jobs better. Absenteeism and turnover declined. Productivity skyrocketed. My friend earned every cent of his fee.

HOW TO PUNISH

One way to see how punishment works, or fails to work, is to examine the rules that must be followed to apply it correctly. The classic behaviorist analysis says that five principles are most important (Azrin & Holz, 1966).

1. *Availability of alternatives.* An alternative response to the behavior that is being punished must be available. This alternative response must not be punished and should be rewarded. If you want to threaten kids with punishment for Halloween pranks, be certain some alternative activity is available that will not be punished, or will even be rewarding, such as a Halloween party.

2. *Behavioral and situational specificity.* Be clear about exactly what behavior you are punishing and the circumstances under which it will and will not be punished. This rule is the basis of the advice commonly given to parents never to punish a child for being a "bad boy" or "bad girl." (It is also consistent with the religiously based guidance to "hate the sin but love the sinner.") Instead, punish "staying out

after curfew" or "cursing at Grandma." A child who is unsure exactly why he or she is punished may, just to be safe, become generally inhibited and fearful, daring to do little because he or she is not quite sure what is right and what is wrong.

3. *Timing and consistency.* To be most effective—or to be effective at all—a punishment needs to be applied *immediately* after the behavior you wish to prevent, *every* time that behavior occurs. Otherwise, the person (or animal) being punished may not clearly understand exactly what behavior is forbidden. And again, if a person (or animal) is punished but does not understand why, the result will be general inhibition instead of specific behavioral change.

   Have you ever made this mistake? You come home from a hard day at work and discover your dog has dug out the kitchen trash and spread it across the living room. The dog bounds to greet you, and you swat it. This is, one supposes, punishment for scattering trash, but consider the situation from the dog's point of view. The trash scattering occurred hours ago. What the dog did just before being punished was greet you. What behavioral change will result? This kind of error is very common and shows the danger of applying punishment when you are angry. The punishment might vent *your* emotions but is likely to be counterproductive.

4. *Conditioning secondary punishing stimuli.* One can lessen the actual use of punishment by conditioning secondary stimuli to it. I once had a cat who liked to scratch the furniture. I went out and bought a plastic squirt bottle and filled it with water, and then kept it nearby. Whenever the cat started to claw the sofa, I made a hissing noise and then immediately squirted the cat. Soon I did not need the squirt bottle; my "hissss" was sufficient to make the cat immediately stop what she was doing. With people, verbal warnings can serve the same purpose. Many a parent has rediscovered this technique: "If you don't stop, when I get to 3, you'll be sorry. 1, 2 . . . "

5. *Avoiding mixed messages.* This is a particular warning to parents. Sometimes after punishing a child the parent can feel so guilty that he or she picks the child up for a cuddle. This is a mistake. Under the worst circumstances, the child might start to misbehave just to get the cuddle that follows the punishment. If you must punish, then do it. Do not mix your message.

   A variant on this problem occurs when one parent plays off against the other. The father punishes the child, and the child then goes to the mother for sympathy, or vice versa. This can produce the same counterproductive result.

B. Smaller

"What do I think is an appropriate punishment? I think an appropriate punishment would be to make me live with my guilt."

DANGERS OF PUNISHMENT

Punishment will backfire unless all of the rules just listed are followed. Usually, they are not. A punisher has to be extremely careful, for several reasons.

1. *Punishment arouses emotion.* The first and perhaps most important danger of punishment is that it creates emotion. In the punisher, it can arouse excitement, satisfaction, and even further aggressive impulses. The result is that the punisher may get carried away. Anybody who has seen the much-broadcast videotape of the Los Angeles police officers beating Rodney King has seen a good example of punishment getting out of hand. The emotions that beating King aroused in the officers seemed to cause them to lose all semblance of self-control.

   Emotions are aroused in the punishee, too. By definition, a punishment is aversive, which means that the punishee feels pain, discomfort, or humiliation. Punishment also usually arouses fear, hate for the punisher, a desire to escape, and possibly self-contempt. These powerful emotions are not conducive to clear thinking. As a result, the punishee is unlikely to "learn a lesson," which supposedly is the whole point. How well do you learn a lesson when you are fearful, in pain, confused, and humiliated? Often punishers think they are teaching what behavior not to do again. But the punishee is much too unhappy and confused to think much beyond "let me out of here!"

2. *It is difficult to be consistent.* Imagine that, in one day at work, you lost a big account, got yelled at by your boss, spilled ketchup on your

pants, and found a new dent in your car. When you arrive home, your child has thrown a baseball through your living-room window. What do you do?

Now imagine another day, when you landed a big account, got promoted by your boss, and took delivery on a beautiful new car that cost $5,000 less than you had expected. You arrive home and find a baseball through the window. Now, what do you do?

Very few people would react to the child's behavior the same way under both circumstances. (Those who can are saints.) Yet the child's behavior was exactly the same. Punishment tends to vary with the punisher's mood, which is one reason why it is rarely applied with consistency.

3. *It is difficult to gauge the severity of punishment.* Many cases of child abuse have occurred when what a parent thought was a mild but painful slap caused a broken bone or worse. Parents are bigger than children: this is not always easy to take into account, especially when the parent is angry. Words can hurt, too. A rebuke from a parent, teacher, or boss can be a severe humiliation. It can cause more psychological distress than the punisher may imagine and can provoke desires for escape or revenge that will only make the situation worse.

4. *Punishment teaches about power.* Specifically, it teaches that big, powerful people get to hurt smaller, less-powerful people. As a result, the punishee may think, I can't wait to be big and powerful so that I can punish too! Thus, parents who were abused as children may become child abusers themselves (Hemenway, Solnick, & Carter, 1994; Widom, 1989).

5. *Punishment motivates concealment.* The prospective punishee has good reasons to try to conceal anything that conceivably might be punished. Have you ever been in an office where the boss rules through the use of punishment? Nobody talks to anybody, least of all the boss, if they can avoid it, and the boss soon becomes detached from what is really going on in his or her own office. (This was the case in the lumber mill described earlier.)

The use of reward has just the reverse effect. When workers anticipate being rewarded for good work instead of being punished for bad work, they are naturally motivated to bring to the boss's attention everything they are doing, in case it might merit reward. They will have no reason to conceal anything that is going on, and the boss will be in much better contact with the operation he or she is supposed to be running. This works in the home, as well. A child who expects punishment from his or her parent soon cuts off as much contact and communication as possible. A child who expects the reverse, naturally does the reverse. Thus, at home or at work, one important side effect of punishment is that it tends to cut off communication.

THE BOTTOM LINE

Punishment, if used correctly, is an effective technique for behavioral control. But to use it correctly is nearly impossible. Correct application requires that the punisher understand and consistently apply *all* of the rules just listed. It also requires that the punisher's own emotions and other personal needs not affect his or her actions, which is even more difficult. So the bottom line is this: *Punishment works great if you apply it correctly. But to apply it correctly, you may have to be both a genius and a saint.*

Social Learning Theory

Behaviorism can boast of maintaining high standards of scientific rigor and of many practical accomplishments (such as the analysis of punishment we have just reviewed). However, its psychological analysis also has many important omissions.

The most obvious omission is the way behaviorism ignores motivation, thought, and cognition. Behaviorists have sometimes tried to make a virtue of this omission. The writings of B. F. Skinner and his followers typically deny that thinking is important and sometimes have even denied that it exists. They certainly never conduct research on it. Social learning theorists, by contrast, claim that the way people think, plan, perceive, and believe is an important part of learning, and that research must address these processes.

Second, classic behaviorism, to a surprisingly large extent, is based on animals. Much of Skinner's own work was done with rats and pigeons; Thorndike favored cats; Pavlov used dogs. The reason behaviorists so often study animals is that they hope to formulate general laws of learning that are relevant to all species. This is a laudable goal, but according to the social learning theorists it has led behaviorists to concentrate too much on elements of learning that are important for animals, such as reinforcement, and not enough on elements of learning that may be uniquely important to humans, such as solving a problem by thinking about it.

A third shortcoming of classic behaviorism is that it ignores the social dimension of learning. The typical rat or pigeon in the Skinner box is in there alone. It cannot interact with, learn from, or influence any other animal. Ordinary learning by humans, however, tends to be social. We learn by watching others, for example—something an isolated pigeon is in no position to do even if it were capable. The social learning theorists, as their label implies, are highly sensitive to this issue.

A fourth shortcoming of classic behaviorism is that it treats the organism as essentially passive. How does a rat or pigeon get into a Skinner box in the first place? Easy—it is put there. Once there, the contingencies of the

"I don't usually volunteer for experiments, but I'm kind of a puzzle freak."

box are ironclad and may even be automated. The pigeon did not ask to be put in the box, but there it is, and unless it pushes the bar there will be no food pellets. For humans, the situation is different. To an important (if not unlimited) degree, we choose what environments to enter, and these environments then change as a result of what we do in them.

Imagine if rats were allowed to choose which of several Skinner boxes to jump into, and then had a way of changing the reinforcement contingencies once they got inside. For humans, real life is rather like that. A party might bring out certain behaviors you do not emit otherwise, but you can choose whether to go to the party. Moreover, once you are there the party changes as a result of your presence. These facts complicate any analysis of how the environment can affect behavior. This complication is welcomed and focused on by modern social learning theorists.

Three major theories of personality have been invented to expand behaviorism to remedy one or more of these shortcomings. It seems somewhat ironic—and more than a little confusing—that although the three theories are importantly different from each other, all were named *social learning theory* by their inventors. The three different theories were developed by John Dollard and Neal Miller, by Julian Rotter, and by Albert Bandura.

Dollard and Miller's Social Learning Theory

John Dollard and Neal Miller were psychologists at Yale during the 1940s and 1950s. The key idea of their social learning theory is the concept of the **habit hierarchy.** The behavior you are most likely to perform at a given moment resides at the top of your habit hierarchy. Your least likely behavior is at the bottom. For example, at this moment the behavior at the top of your habit hierarchy seems to be "reading." After all, that is what you are doing. Lower on your habit hierarchy—probably a lot lower—is the behavior of "dancing." It is extremely unlikely, although not impossible, that in a moment you will jump up and begin to dance around the room. Somewhat higher in your habit hierarchy might be "snacking"—at any moment you really might put this book down and go get something to eat (especially now that I've mentioned it). Dollard and Miller theorized that the effect of rewards, punishments, and learning is to rearrange the habit hierarchy. If you were to be rewarded for dancing, this behavior might become more likely; if you were punished for reading, then reading might become less likely.

Notice how Dollard and Miller have already deviated from classic behaviorism in a major way. Skinner claimed that the effect of learning is to change *behavior*. Dollard and Miller claimed that the effect of learning is a change in the arrangement of an unobservable, psychological entity, the habit hierarchy. In some cases behavior may not change at all.

MOTIVATION AND DRIVES

What do you want, and why do you want it? These are questions of motivation. According to Dollard and Miller, the answer to this question is to be found in needs, which produce psychological drives. A **drive** is a state of psychological tension that feels good when it is reduced. Pleasure comes from the satisfaction of the need that produced the drive.

Two kinds of drive are important. **Primary drives** include those for food, water, physical comfort, avoidance of physical pain, sexual gratification, and so on. **Secondary drives** include those for love, prestige, money, and power, as well as negative drives such as avoidance of fear and humiliation. In the process of development, according to Dollard and Miller, secondary drives come later. In their own words:

> The helpless, naked, human infant is born with primary drives such as hunger, thirst and reactions to pain and cold. He does not have, however, many of the motivations that distinguish the adult as a member of a particular tribe, nationality, social class, occupation, or profession. Many extremely important drives, such as the desire for money, the ambition to become an artist or a scholar, and particular fears and guilts are learned during socialization. (Dollard & Miller, 1950, p. 62)

According to Dollard and Miller, there can be no reinforcement (and hence no behavioral change) without some kind of drive reduction, whether the drive be primary or secondary. In other words, for a reward to be rewarding, and thereby have the power to make the behavior it rewards more likely, the reward must satisfy a need.

This principle is not as straightforward as it may sound, because it raises an important question: Is the goal of all behavior (and hence of life) really just to satisfy every desire and get to a state of "zero need"? So far, the analysis seems to imply that the ideal state of existence is one in which all needs have been satisfied. At that point, people will have no motivation to do anything and can just sit in an inert, satisfied lump. This is a questionable implication both because that does not really seem like a very desirable state, and because people often seem to go out of their way to *raise* their level of need.

For example, if you are going out this evening for a dinner at a four-star restaurant that will cost you $120, you are unlikely to eat a bag of potato chips at 6 P.M., even if you are hungry. Why not? Because it would "spoil your appetite," as your mother always said. The meal will be less fun and will hardly seem worth the expense if you are not hungry for it. But why would that matter if the goal is simply to attain a state of zero hunger?

Sexual arousal and gratification comprise another obvious example. People go out of their way to seek sexual arousal, not just gratification. The greater the arousal and degree of sexual need, it seems, the more gratifying the ultimate satisfaction of that need will be. Secondary drives also may work this way. Many people not only try to finish the work they have been assigned, for example, but actively seek new work to do. They are constantly creating new needs—starting projects that will need to be finished—as they continue to complete projects they started earlier.

Observations such as these require a modification of drive-reduction theory. Perhaps what is reinforcing is not a state of zero need, but rather the movement from a state of higher need to a state of lower need. It is the distance between the initial and final state that matters, according to this proposition. This principle explains why people might actually try to create new needs in themselves as well as try to increase before seeking to satisfy existing needs.

FRUSTRATION AND AGGRESSION

If your roommate has had a frustrating experience—failing an exam, say, or being turned down for a date—watch out. He or she will be in a bad mood, which means he or she is likely to be angry. It hardly matters at what. It could be at you if you are not careful. If your socks are on the sofa, you will get yelled at. If you present no such opportunity to be the object of anger, then your roommate might just pound the wall instead, or steam loudly about the professor or person who supposedly caused the problem.

Not everybody reacts this way all the time, but such a reaction is not uncommon. When it does happen, the interesting psychological question is, why the anger? Specifically, why does the person vent anger on targets that had nothing to do with the source of the problem, such as an innocent roommate or a wall? Dollard and Miller's classic answer is the **frustration-aggression hypothesis**: The natural, biological reaction of any person (or animal, for that matter) to being blocked from a goal, or frustrated, will be an urge to lash out and injure. The more important the blocked goal, the greater will be the frustration, and the greater will be the aggressive impulse.

The preferred target of the impulse will be the source of the frustration. But Dollard and Miller borrowed Freud's idea of displacement to describe how the aggressive impulse can be redirected elsewhere as well. If your boss unfairly denies you a raise, this might lead to frustration and anger but you are unlikely to vent it at the boss if you want to keep your job. So you might come home and kick the wall or criticize your spouse, all in anger that is displaced from its original target.

PSYCHOLOGICAL CONFLICT

Things that are fun can also be frightening. Take bungee jumping, for example. A while back, a student of mine signed up for a Sunday bungee jump. It cost him money, and he signed up of his own free will, so he must have thought it would be fun. As the day approached, however, he became noticeably more nervous (the funeral plans being made by his fellow students may not have been helpful). In the end it seemed a close call whether he would go or not. In this case he did (and survived, I should add).

This kind of conflict between desire and fear, and how it can change over time, was addressed by Dollard and Miller's theorizing on **approach-avoidance conflict**. (This theorizing can get technical, mind you.) Consider the five key assumptions of this theory:

1. An increase in drive strength will increase the tendency to approach or avoid a goal.
2. Whenever there are two competing responses, the stronger one (the one with greater drive strength behind it) will win out.
3. The tendency to approach a positive goal increases the closer one is to the goal.
4. The tendency to avoid a negative goal also increases the closer one is to the goal.
5. Most important, tendency 4 is stronger than tendency 3. That is, the tendency to avoid a negative goal becomes stronger, with nearness, than does the corresponding tendency to approach a positive goal. To put this technically (I warned you it would get technical), the avoidance gradient is steeper than the approach gradient (see Figure 15.1).

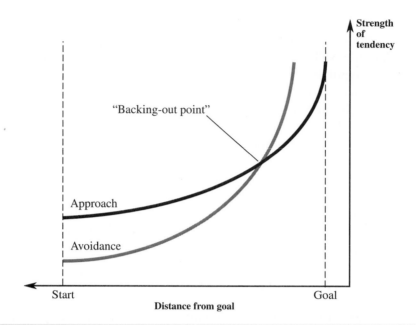

FIGURE 15.1   DOLLARD AND MILLER'S CONCEPT OF APPROACH AND AVOIDANCE   An illustration of how tendencies to approach and avoid a conflicted goal (e.g., a bungee jump) might change over time. According to Dollard and Miller, while tendencies to approach and avoid both increase as the goal gets closer, the avoidance gradient is steeper than the approach gradient. In this example, the person will try to withdraw from, or back out of, the act after the approach and avoidance gradients cross.

This set of principles yields some interesting predictions, particularly involving conflicted goals that have both positive and negative elements. Such a goal might be a bungee jump, an airplane trip you are simultaneously looking forward to (for the vacation) and fearing (because you are afraid of flying), or a talk you have volunteered to give because you need the practice, but that you also dread. Dollard and Miller's five-part theory predicts that in each case you will be relatively willing to commit yourself to these behaviors if they are far off in time. But as the moment of truth approaches, you may start to regret having agreed to do it. Even though the bungee jump, plane trip, or talk seemed like a good idea last week, the negative aspects will become more prominent than the positive aspects. In the end, you may not be able to go through with it.

This can be a useful principle. If you are responsible for arranging a series of speakers before a group, for example, you are wise to schedule your speakers and get ironclad commitments from them as early as possible. Something somebody will commit to six months in advance might be flatly refused if you ask the day before. Dollard and Miller may have discovered the real reason why dentists schedule their appointments so far in advance, and why airlines have made ticket refunds almost impossible.

Rotter's Social Learning Theory

Julian Rotter's version of social learning theory primarily concerns decision making and the role of expectancies (Rotter, 1954, 1982).

EXPECTANCY VALUE THEORY

A woman about to graduate from college scans the list of companies interviewing on campus. She is allowed to interview for one job, and she narrows her choice down to two. One pays $35,000 a year, and the other pays $20,000. Which will she sign up for? Classic behaviorism predicts that she will choose the $35,000 job. But, according to Rotter's social learning theory, there is another factor to consider: What if she does not think she would get the $35,000 job if she interviewed for it, but thinks the chances are excellent that she would get the $20,000 job?

Rotter claimed that her choice can be worked out mathematically. Suppose she thinks her chances of getting the $35,000 job are 50/50, whereas she thinks she is certain to get the $20,000 job. The "expected value" of the $35,000 job then becomes .50 × $35,000, or $17,500. The expected value of the other job is 1 × $20,000, or $20,000. The second job has a higher expected value and, under these circumstances, this is the interview she would be predicted to choose.

The core of Rotter's approach is **expectancy value theory**, which was just illustrated. Its basic assumption is that behavioral decisions are determined not just by the presence or size of reinforcements, but also by beliefs about what the results of behavior are likely to be. Even if a reinforcement is very attractive, according to this theory, you are not likely to pursue it if your chances of success seem slim. Conversely, even something that is not particularly desirable might motivate behavior, if the chances of getting it are good enough.

EXPECTANCY AND LOCUS OF CONTROL

An individual's **expectancy** for a behavior is his or her belief, or subjective probability, about how likely he or she thinks the behavior is to attain its goal. If you ask that person out, what is the probability the person will say yes? If you apply for that job (and forgo others), will you get it? If you go to class, will that really make a difference in how well you do on the final exam?

What are the chances? The expectancy is your belief as to the odds that an action will pay off.

Because an expectancy is a belief, it might be right or wrong. Rotter's theory says that it does not matter whether something is actually likely to succeed or not; if you think it will, you will try. The same goes for something that actually would succeed, if you only gave the effort; if you think it will not work, you will not even try.

Herein lies the key difference with classic behaviorism: The classic view focuses on actual rewards and punishments. Rotter's social learning variant focuses on *beliefs* about reward and punishment. It is these beliefs that shape behavior, Rotter claimed, even when they do not map accurately onto reality. At this point in Rotter's social learning theory, a little wisp of phenomenology—that a person's impressions of reality are more important than reality itself—drifts in (recall Chapter 13).

Rotter claimed that people actually have two kinds of expectancies: specific and general. A specific expectancy is the belief that a certain behavior, at a certain time and place, will lead to a specific outcome. For example, if just after lunch on Tuesday you ask Mary for a date on Friday night, will she say yes? The expected answer may depend on all of the following factors: when the question is asked, who is asked, and when the date is scheduled. In another example, if you attend class this Monday, what are the chances you will pick up something helpful for the exam? From reading the syllabus, you might have reason to think that Monday's material is going to be essential for the exam, but that Wednesday's class can be safely skipped.

At the other extreme, people also have generalized expectancies. These are general beliefs about whether anything you do is likely to make a difference. Some people, according to Rotter, believe that they have very little control over what happens to them; they have low generalized expectancies. Others believe that the reinforcements they enjoy (and the punishments they avoid) are directly a function of what they do; these people have high generalized expectancies. Not surprisingly, people with high generalized expectancies tend to be energetic and highly motivated; those with low generalized expectancies are more likely to be lethargic and depressed. Generalized expectancy is a broad personality variable, and in fact can be considered a trait exactly like those discussed in Chapters 4 through 7.

Specific expectancies and general expectancies feed into each other in complex ways. For example, as you start college, your approach toward studying is likely to be shaped by your generalized expectancy, because you do not yet have relevant experience in the college domain. But as experience accumulates, you will start to develop more specific expectancies about what you can do (e.g., you discover that you are better at chemistry than at psychology), and these will start to take over the direction of your behavior.

The result of this interaction is that people who have generally high or low generalized expectancies might still have lower or higher specific expectancies in different specific situations, depending on their past experience. Rotter sometimes referred to generalized expectancy as *locus of control.* People with *internal* locus of control are those with high generalized expectancies who think that what they do can affect what happens to them. Those with *external* locus of control have low generalized expectancies and tend to think that what they do will not make much difference. Later investigators have emphasized how locus of control (and generalized expectancy) can vary across the domains of one's life. For example, some people have internal academic locus of control (they believe they have control over their academic outcomes), but external locus of control otherwise. Other psychologists have studied health locus of control, which involves the difference between people who believe that their daily actions importantly affect their own health, as opposed to those who think they have very little control over whether they are sick or well (e.g., Rosolack & Hampson, 1991; Lau, 1988). Even dating locus of control can be variable. Maybe you are right to think that not everybody is willing to go out with you, but somebody somewhere is eager to do so.

Bandura's Social Learning Theory

The most recent development that goes by the name "social learning theory" comes from the Stanford psychologist Albert Bandura. Bandura's version of social learning builds directly on Rotter's (Bandura, 1971, 1977). Many of the same ideas appear in both theories, but there are also some important differences. Rotter's concept of generalized expectancies and locus of control leads to theorizing about and measurement of individual differences. Bandura's theory gives less emphasis to stable differences between people— in fact, it generally ignores them. Where Bandura has gone beyond Rotter lies in his emphasis on the social nature of learning and on the way people interact with the situations in their lives.

EFFICACY EXPECTATIONS

What Rotter called *expectancies,* Bandura reinterpreted as **efficacy expectations**. Both terms refer to the belief that one can accomplish something successfully, and carry the phenomenological implication that how one interprets reality matters more than reality itself. The two concepts are not exactly the same, however. Rotter's *expectancy* is the perceived conditional probability that if you do something, you will attain your goal. Bandura's *efficacy* is the perceived nonconditional probability that you can do something in the first place.

Recall the example of the woman deciding which job to seek. Rotter's analysis assumes that she can apply for any job; that is not the issue. To Rotter, the issue is whether she thinks she will get the job if she applies. It is her perception of the probable result of her behavior that determines what she will do.

A more typical case for Bandura's analysis is that of a snake phobic. She wishes not to be so afraid of snakes yet does not believe she could ever get near one. If this belief changes, she will be able to approach snakes and be over her phobia. The issue for Bandura is not what happens after she handles a snake, but rather whether she can get close to a snake in the first place.

What can be seen by comparing Bandura's theorizing to Rotter's is a further step away from the classic behaviorism with which both theories began. Rotter's expectancy is a belief about reinforcement, which was classically seen as the key agent of behavioral change. Bandura's efficacy expectation is a belief about the *self*, about what the person himself or herself is capable of doing.

Bandura emphasized that such efficacy expectations should be the key target for therapeutic interventions. If you can achieve a better match between what you think you can accomplish and what you really can accomplish, Bandura believed, your life will be more rational and productive. Moreover, efficacies can create capacities. A snake phobic who is persuaded, by whatever means, that she *can* handle a snake subsequently *will* be able to handle a snake. The target of therapy, therefore, should not be the behavior of handling a snake, but the client's beliefs about her ability to handle a snake.

Research suggests that increases in self-efficacy can increase both motivation and performance. One study compared leg strength and endurance in men and women as a function of self-efficacy (Weinberg, Gould, & Jackson, 1979). Efficacy was manipulated experimentally. In one condition, participants were told they were competing against someone with a knee injury, a belief that presumably increased their own self-efficacy. In the other condition, participants were told they were competing against a member of the varsity track team, a belief that presumably decreased their self-efficacy. Participants in the high-efficacy condition outperformed those in the low-efficacy condition, even though their actual strength (before the study) was about the same. This effect was quite impressive. In general, men have stronger legs than women. But in this study, the women in the high-efficacy condition demonstrated slightly more leg endurance than the men in the low-efficacy condition—this psychological manipulation was so powerful that it managed to wipe out the usual sex difference in strength.

Increasing efficacy expectations would seem to be a useful approach, therefore. A psychotherapist in Bandura's mold will use whatever tactics can be devised to accomplish this goal, including verbal persuasion ("you can do it!") and modeling, which means allowing the client to watch somebody else (the model) accomplish the desired behavior. Part of the therapy for snake phobics is for them to watch somebody else cheerfully handle a snake. The most powerful technique is to actually have the person perform the behavior. The goal of therapy, therefore, is to build up to the point where the client can actually have the experience of handling a snake. There is no more effective way of convincing him or her that such a thing is possible.

Bandura's prescription for self-change follows the same pattern. If you are afraid to do something, force yourself to do it. You will then become less afraid, and it will be less difficult next time. A small example: suppose you know you should exercise more but do not think you are really the type to exercise. Take control of your life and go exercise anyway. This experience, if you can keep it up, will change your view of yourself in such a way that exercise will come to seem a natural part of your life rather than something strange that you must force yourself to do. In its brilliant way, Madison Avenue created a commercial for an athletic shoe that boiled this principle down to three words: "Just Do It." According to Bandura, that is good advice; the rest will follow, usually.

OBSERVATIONAL LEARNING

One of the most influential aspects of Bandura's theory has been its emphasis on vicarious or observational learning, that is, learning a behavior by seeing someone else do it. It is very different from what happens in a Skinner box. At one time it was believed that only humans could learn from observation, but recent research has indicated otherwise. Learning by songbirds is a frequently cited example. Some species of bird seem to learn their songs simply by listening to adult birds, without any rewards or punishments being involved. We also have all seen those *National Geographic* television specials that show lion cubs learning to hunt by watching their mother. Apparently, some animals do learn by observation, and not always the animals we would expect. Research has shown that pigeons can learn from watching other pigeons (Zentall, Sutton, & Sherburne, 1996), but apes (orangutans) sometimes cannot learn from watching other apes (Call & Tomasello, 1995). The distinctive aspect for humans is that nearly *everything* we learn is by observation.

Bandura provided a classic demonstration of how this process can work with his "Bobo doll" studies (see Figure 15.2). A Bobo doll is a large plastic clown, on a round, weighted base, that bounces back when it is hit. In a series of studies, Bandura showed that a child who watches an adult hit the doll is likely to later hit the doll himself or herself, especially if he or she sees the adult rewarded for the aggressive behavior (Bandura, Ross, & Ross, 1963). The implications for the probable effects of television seem obvious.

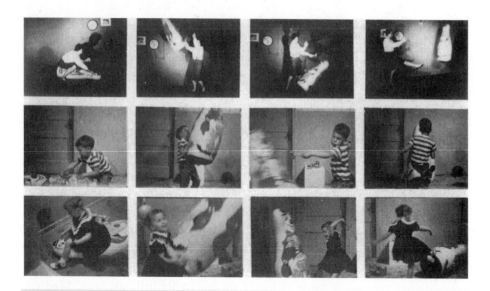

FIGURE 15.2   Photographs from the film *Social Learning of Aggression through Imitation of Aggressive Models*, showing Bandura's classic "Bobo doll" study.

A person—particularly a child—who day after day watches violence glamorized and rewarded may indeed become more likely to engage in such behavior.

The mechanism of observational learning also can be used for positive purposes. A positive role model can provide a whole array of useful and desirable behaviors for a young person to emulate. More specifically in the psychotherapeutic context, Bandura showed that one way to persuade a snake phobic to handle the feared reptile is to let him or her watch a research assistant handling a snake first. This kind of vicarious experience—which, as we have seen, Bandura calls *modeling*—can make the next step, actually handling the snake, easier to take.

RECIPROCAL DETERMINISM AND THE SELF

A third and more recent innovation in Bandura's social learning theory is **reciprocal determinism**, which is an analysis of how people can shape their own environments (Bandura, 1978, 1989). Classic versions of behaviorism, and even Rotter's refinement, tend to view reinforcements and the environments that contain them as influences that are inflicted on people; the people themselves remain basically passive. Bandura's analysis points out that this view is an oversimplification. You are not just placed in the environments in your life, in the way that a rat is placed into a Skinner box. In many circumstances you choose the environments that influence you. If you go to college, all sorts of reinforcement contingencies kick in that will cause you to study, attend class, read books, and do other things you might not do otherwise. But none of these contingencies come into effect until you voluntarily step on the campus (and pay your tuition fees). Similarly, if you join a gang, or the army, or a law firm, environmental rules and contingencies will immediately start to reshape your life. Do not underestimate their power; appreciate the implications of choosing to enter different social environments.

A second aspect of reciprocal determinism is that the social situations in your life are changed, at least a little and perhaps importantly, *because* you are there. The party livens up (or calms down) when you arrive. The class discussion switches to a new topic because of something you contribute. Your home environment is to a large extent a function of what you do there. It is in this sense that you control many of the environmental contingencies that in turn influence your behavior.

The third aspect of reciprocal determinism is perhaps the most important. Bandura's deepest departure from behaviorism is his claim that a *self system* develops that has its own effects on behavior, independent of the environment. Here Bandura forged a middle course between the phenomenologists considered in Chapter 13 and the behaviorists considered earlier in this chapter:

> Unidirectional environmental determinism is carried to its extreme in the more radical forms of behaviorism . . . [but] humanists and existentialists, who stress the human capacity for conscious judgment and intentional action, contend that individuals determine what they become by their own free choices. Most psychologists find conceptions of human behavior in terms of unidirectional personal determinism as unsatisfying as those espousing unidirectional environmental determinism. To contend that mind creates reality fails to acknowledge that environmental influences partly determine what people attend to, perceive, and think. (Bandura, 1978, pp. 344–345)

Think of the self system in reciprocal determinism as a chicken-egg problem. You have the environment affecting the self, which affects the environment, which affects the self. . . . But which came first? Bandura's answer is quite clear, and when boiled down to its essentials, the answer is essentially behaviorist: the environment. Still, social learning theory, and especially Bandura's version, has brought behaviorism a long way. Watson and Skinner emphasized how the environment shapes behavior. Bandura described how behavior shapes the environment. Very little influences you, that you do not influence yourself. Therefore, the causes of what you do cannot be located solely in the world (as the behaviorists would have it) or in your mind (as the humanists would have it); they originate somewhere in the interaction between the two.

Contributions and Limitations of the Learning Approaches

The learning approaches to personality can boast three major achievements.

First, the learning theorists—from Watson and Skinner to Bandura, and everyone in between—conducted admirable programs of research that came close to achieving the dream of establishing psychology as an objective science that can take its place among the other sciences. Their work is characterized by tight theoretical reasoning, careful experimental design, and a style of argument that eschews any statement that cannot be backed up by data. In this way, the learning theorists serve as role models that other psychologists, at times, might wish to emulate.

Second, the learning theorists recognize, better than the adherents of any other approach, how what people do depends on the environment and even the specific situation they are in at the time. Trait theorists emphasize the average of many behaviors people perform over time and across situations; biologists look for physiological and genetic processes that largely occur within the body; psychoanalysts and humanists are interested in how people are influenced by what goes on inside the hidden recesses of their minds. Learning theorists, even latter-day ones such as Bandura, instead emphasize how what we do depends on the rewards and punishments that are present at this moment or—just a little different—the rewards and punishments that we *think* are present at this moment.

It could be argued that the job of each basic approach to personality is to remind us of important influences on psychology that the other approaches forget or neglect. Thus, the trait approach reminds us of the importance of individual differences; the biological approach reminds us of anatomy, physiology, and genetics; the psychoanalytic approach reminds us of the importance of the unconscious; the humanistic approach reminds us of the importance of consciousness. In this list of job descriptions, the task of the learning theorist is clear; to remind us that the physical and social environment, and the specific situation at a given moment, are also important causes of what we do and who we are.

A third contribution of the learning approaches has been the development of a technology of behavior change. The process of learning is all about behavior change, so it was a short step to apply concepts of learning to the treatment of phobias, addictions, and other emotional and behavioral disorders. The evidence seems clear that such techniques work well in the short run, at least.

But what about the long run? Here, the record is less clear and brings us to the first of two important limitations of the learning approaches to personality. It is not clear that the effects of behavioral therapies for phobias, addictions, and other problems are always generalizable and long-lasting (Eysenck

& Beech, 1971; Kazdin & Bootzin, 1972). Consider one example. An acquaintance of mine was once the director of drug treatment services for a county in California. He worked with alcoholics, treating them with a substance called Antabuse (the brand name for disulfiram). Antabuse is a drug that causes nausea when a person drinks alcohol. In the clinic, the therapist could be sure that the patient took the Antabuse regularly. This removed all temptation to drink, and you would think, based on classical conditioning, that after a while the alcoholics would find the very idea of drinking repulsive.

So what happened? Time after time, as soon as a patient was released from the rehab clinic, he or she stopped the car at the first pullout and threw the Antabuse pills into the dumpster. From there, the patient drove to the nearest liquor store. It turns out that people are more complicated than simple theories, like classical conditioning, sometimes acknowledge. These alcoholics weren't stupid. Even though the Antabuse made drinking unpleasant, they knew that as soon as they stopped taking it, they could resume drinking as much as they liked (until the next time they landed back in jail or the clinic, at least).

This observation leads to the second and most important limitation of the learning approaches. They are too simple, and in particular even the social learning theories tend to underappreciate one important fact: People think. Thoughts about rewards can overwhelm the rewards themselves, as the social learning theorists understood. But there is much more. Symbols can be more important than "real" experiences; memories can interfere with or even determine perceptions; and complex processes of comparison, evaluation, and decision making provide important complications that lie between behavior and the environment that learning theorists assume is the ultimate cause of everything we do.

In other words, the learning approaches need to take a more full account of *cognition*, or thought, and in that way push open one door that social learning theory has unlocked. This is the focus of the cognitive approach to personality, considered in the next two chapters.

Summary

Behaviorism's key tenet is that all of behavior is a function of the rewards and punishments in the past and present environment. The philosophical roots of behaviorism include empiricism, a belief that all knowledge comes from experience; associationism, a belief that two stimuli paired together will come to be seen as one; hedonism, the belief that the goal of life is "gentle pleasure"; and utilitarianism, the belief that the best society is the social arrangement that creates the most happiness for the most people. In behaviorist terminology, learning is any change in behavior that results from experience. The basic principles of learning include habituation, classical conditioning, and operant conditioning. Classical conditioning affects emotions and feelings; operant conditioning affects behavior. Punishment is a useful technique of operant conditioning if it is applied correctly, which it almost never is.

Dollard and Miller's social learning theory explains motivation as the result of primary and secondary drives, aggression as the result of frustration, and psychological conflict as the result of the interplay of motivations to approach and avoid a goal. Rotter's social learning theory emphasizes how expectancies of reward can be more important determinants of behavior than reward itself. Bandura's social learning theory focuses on how individuals' expectancies for their own behavioral capacities affect what they will attempt to do, and also develops a detailed analysis of observational learning, in which one learns by watching the behaviors and outcomes of others, and reciprocal determinism, in which one's actions are determined by a self system that originates in the environment, then changes the environment, which in turn affects the self system.

Learning approaches to personality have epitomized objective research, drawn necessary attention to the importance of the environment, yielded a useful technology of behavioral change, and formed the foundation for the cognitive approach to personality.

THE COGNITIVE SYSTEM AND THE PERSONALITY SYSTEM

16

On June 27, 1995, Hugh Grant, popular actor and frequent escort of super-models, was in a parked car engaged in unlawful activities with a local prostitute named Divine Brown, when the Los Angeles police happened to drive by. The result was an arrest followed by a sensational media outcry. Grant went into hiding for weeks. Finally, he emerged to appear on *The Tonight Show,* where Jay Leno immediately asked the obvious question: "What the hell were you *thinking?*"

This was precisely the issue, if one assumes that the cause of a person's behavior is what he or she thinks. To know what was in Grant's mind when he hired the prostitute would be to understand why he did it. This is the logic of the cognitive approach to personality. The explanation of any behavior is its underlying thought process. And the answer for why different people act differently is to be found in the way they think differently. From a cognitive perspective, the reason that no two people are exactly the same, psychologically, is that no two people think exactly the same way.

The cognitive approach to personality is the topic of the next two chapters. The present chapter surveys some basic principles of the cognitive system and illustrates how they are relevant to personality processes, along with an influential, general theory that aims to explain the interaction of the cognitive system and personality. Chapter 17 considers some of the more specific ways in which theory and research in cognitive psychology have addressed cognitive processes relevant to personality, including perception, memory, the organization of the self, and the way people set and pursue important goals in life.

Roots of the Cognitive Approach

Historically, the cognitive approach to personality stems directly from the learning approaches considered in the previous chapter. As we saw, learning theorists sprang onto the scene early in the twentieth century with the bold pronouncement that events inside the head either don't exist or don't matter, and that in either case psychology would be better off ignoring them. Instead, they argued, psychology should focus exclusively on the rewards and punishments in the immediate environment, and how behavior changes as these reinforcements change. But after a few decades, this approach became widely viewed as too limited. It simply leaves too much out that is psychologically important.

This realization opened the door for the social learning theorists, notably Rotter and Bandura. They softened traditional learning theory by acknowledging the importance of learning through observation rather than direct reward and punishment, and the role of mental processes such as interpretation, evaluation, and decision making. You will recall that Rotter's version emphasized how your beliefs about the *environment* can determine your expectations about the probable results of different behaviors; these expectations are in turn the basis for what you decide to do. Bandura's version, subtly different, emphasized that your beliefs about *yourself* determine your expectations of what you are capable of doing in the first place, which also help determine what you will attempt to do. These key components of social learning theory—beliefs about the environment and expectations about the self—are essentially cognitive concepts. Indeed, Bandura (2001) underlined this implication by renaming his approach *social cognitive theory*. The next logical step, then, was to begin to be more specific about how the cognitive system affects personality and behavior, which meant delving into research and theory drawn from cognitive psychology. Thus was born the "cognitive" (also called "social cognitive") approach to personality (Cervone & Shoda, 1999).

Viewed one way, the evolution from behaviorism to social learning theory to the cognitive approach appears perfectly logical. Viewed another way, it seems highly ironic. The historical roots of the cognitive approach to personality lead deep into the discipline that held as its goal, above all other goals, to expunge unobservable thought processes from psychology. Modern cognitive personality psychologists usually ignore this slightly embarrassing history, but it is useful to remember, because vestiges of behaviorism can still be found here and there in the modern field. Stimuli, responses, and reinforcements—or thoughts and ideas (usually called *cognitive representations*) about reinforcements—still play a central role, although often under a different name. Moreover, many cognitive theorists of personality preserve behaviorism's traditional reluctance to see people as characterized by consistent personality traits (e.g., Cervone & Shoda, 1999), even while liberally using mentalistic concepts like "schemas" and "scripts."

Another historical influence on modern cognitive theories of personality is the phenomenological approach considered in Chapter 13, particularly the ideas of George Kelly (1955). Kelly emphasized the way an individual's concepts for thinking about the world—his or her personal constructs—shape his or her personality and behavior. This idea influenced the social learning theories of Rotter and Bandura, as we saw in Chapter 15, and it provides another point where cognitive research has entered personality psychology.

Yet another and perhaps surprising connection can be drawn between some modern cognitive research and psychoanalysis (see Chapters 10 to 12). Various modern theories of the functioning of the cognitive system find counterparts in Freud's notions concerning levels of consciousness, especially those concerning the preconscious and the unconscious, and his idea of compromise among competing psychological subsystems. As we will see, unconscious cognitive processes, in particular, are receiving increasing attention from some proponents of a cognitive approach to personality.

Two Views of the Cognitive System

Modern cognitive psychology includes two different views of the basic architecture of mental activity. The older, more traditional view sees the mind as a "serial" system, one that functions in distinct and ordered steps. In a serial system, first this happens, then this, and then finally that—much as in a FORTRAN or BASIC computer program. The end of this process, its "output," is a single thought or behavior. The newer view sees the mind as a "parallel" system, in which many different processes operate all at once, and the conscious or behavioral output is a constantly changing compromise stemming from the interaction of all these different processes.

At present, cognitive psychology includes research based on both views of the mind, and there is some competition—sometimes heated—between adherents of each. A reasonable middle position is that *both* are necessary; certain aspects of cognitive functioning are best described in serial terms while other aspects are better described in parallel terms (Gardner, 1987). The thinking of personality psychologists has been influenced by both views of the cognitive system.

The Serial System

Most attempts to integrate cognitive theory and personality psychology derive from the basic idea that the cognitive system is a serial mechanism for processing, retaining, and accessing information. In other words, it is a step-by-step system for creating and using memory. This information-processing function intersects in many places with the patterns of perception, thought,

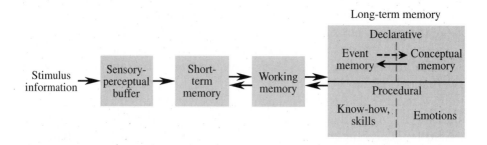

FIGURE 16.1   A GENERIC MODEL OF THE COGNITIVE SYSTEM
This model diagrams a "serial" view of the human cognitive system in terms of the stages and functions of memory. Each arrow represents information transfer (and loss). That is, information is almost always lost in the process of being transferred from one stage of memory to another.

and action that make up personality. A useful way to begin our consideration of the cognitive approaches to personality, therefore, may be to describe in general terms how the cognitive system might work. Figure 16.1 illustrates a typical serial model of cognitive function.

The model is a distillation of the consensus of numerous cognitive psychologists concerning the basic outline of the cognitive system. The essence of mental functioning, from this perspective, is how information enters into the mind, and then is retained or discarded. The process begins with stimuli in the outside world hitting sense organs such as the eyes and ears, then progressing into the sensory-perceptual buffer, short-term memory, working memory, and finally the various parts of long-term memory. In the figure, each arrow represents both information transfer and information loss, because memory is highly selective and most information is probably lost at each of these steps.

This is a model of the mind, not the brain. These boxes are not physical places in the brain or nervous system. They represent stages of mental processing; the physical locations of the organs that perform the functions of each stage might be—and probably are—spread throughout the nervous system.

THE SENSORY-PERCEPTUAL BUFFER

Information comes from the environment in "raw" form via sense organs, the eyes, ears, tongue, nose, and skin. Each of these organs constantly transmits vast amounts of information at a high rate. This stream enters the first stage of processing: the **sensory-perceptual buffer** (sometimes just called the *sensory buffer*).

Most information that enters the sensory buffer is never noticed. As one of my former professors once exhorted his class, "I urge you to consider your backside!" If you are sitting as you read this, then sensations of the chair against your bottom are being steadily transmitted as you read. But as long as you pay attention to what you are reading, those sensations flow right out again, without causing much of a reaction. But if you suddenly shift your attention—consider your backside, now come back to reading, please—you will become aware that you have been ignoring quite a bit of complex information.

The information you notice is determined by the focus of your attention. Attention can be directed at a book, at your backside, or at a noise outside, and make you acutely aware of those stimuli. But, just as everything outside the beam of a spotlight remains in the dark, everything that you do not attend to might as well not exist, phenomenologically speaking (see Chapter 13). Information that comes into the sensory buffer will be lost unless some attention is paid to it.

At one time it was thought that unattended information was not processed at all (Broadbent, 1958). Some fascinating studies of the "cocktail party effect," however, showed that this belief is an oversimplification. You have probably experienced the effect yourself in a crowded room, such as a cafeteria, or at a cocktail party. You are engrossed in talking with the person next to you, oblivious to the general hum of conversation. Suddenly, somebody at the other end of the room speaks your name. What happens? Your attention to your companion lapses for at least a moment as your attention shifts. The interesting thing is that not only do you become immediately aware that your name was included in a conversation to which you *thought* you were not listening, but also you probably can now retrieve the two or three or four words that person spoke *before* saying your name. This information—the words that were spoken before your attention even shifted—was in your sensory buffer.

This effect, which can be demonstrated experimentally (e.g., Moray, 1959; Triesman, 1964), shows two things. First, you constantly monitor "unattended" information at some level. The information is processed to the extent that your mind checks to see if your name was there, for example. Other things are screened as well. If somebody across the room utters an obscenity, your attention is likely to shift. Or you might be driving down the highway, listening to the radio, when suddenly a truck comes at you from an unexpected direction. Your attention is likely to switch immediately—a good thing!

Personality and the Buffer   One interesting aspect of the working of the sensory buffer is that its functioning seems so rapid and automatic. For example, it seems that you almost "can't help" noticing that your name was spoken across the room, even if you were to try to ignore it. One reason is that certain concepts or ideas are experienced or thought about so often that they are never far from the top of awareness. For example, anything having to do with your self-concept is readily activated. Nothing is more central to your self-concept than your name, so it is not surprising that your sensory system will automatically pick out someone who says it even on the other side of a noisy room.

Other aspects of the self are only slightly less central. Consider a shy person who has—she thinks—a long history of people snubbing and avoiding her. Imagine she is talking with someone, at this same cocktail party, and her conversation partner sees someone he knows on the other side of the room and glances that way briefly. Will she see this? A non-shy person, who is not so ready to perceive signs of rejection, very well might not notice at all. A shy person who is constantly on the lookout for any sign that the person she is with would rather be with someone else, however, will probably notice immediately. In this way, a shy person and a non-shy person may end up perceiving the exact same situation in very different ways, with obvious implications for how they will feel and what they will do. In general, to the extent that people with different personality traits, such as shyness, have different ideas of themselves ready to be activated, their attention will be drawn to different perceptual stimuli, and they will inhabit different perceptual worlds (e.g., Downey & Feldman, 1996). The cognitive implications of the self are many and vast; we will return to them several times in this chapter and in Chapter 17.

Perceptual Defense The buffer can screen information out as well, especially, according to some evidence, information that might make you feel anxious or uncomfortable. Indeed, the functions of the sensory buffer have sometimes been viewed as relevant to the psychoanalytic notion of perceptual defense. You will recall from Chapter 11 that this is the idea that the ego will prevent stimuli that the superego finds threatening from entering awareness. Attempts have been made to test this hypothesis experimentally.

In one early experiment, words were presented extremely briefly to subjects by use of a machine called a tachistoscope, which flashes them briefly on a screen. Some of these words were neutral, such as *apple, child,* and *dance.* Others were sexually charged words, such as *penis, rape,* and *whore.* Over successive trials, words of both types were presented for longer and longer durations, beginning with flashes so brief nobody could perceive them, until the exposures were so long that the words became obvious. Subjects' detection of the words was measured two ways. One was simply to ask, "Can you read that?" after each presentation. The minimal amount of exposure time required to perceive each word was recorded. The second way was by measuring the subjects' sweat-gland activity; when they began to sweat in response to a word like *rape,* subjects were assumed to have detected it.

The interesting finding was that these two ways of measuring perception did not exactly coincide. In particular, subjects' sweat glands would react to emotionally charged words sooner than would their verbal reports. In other words, they were claiming, "I can't read that word" at the same time they were physically reacting to it (McGinnies, 1949).

Results like this suggest that something much like an ego defense mechanism, of the sort discussed in Chapter 11, may prevent certain embarrassing stimuli from entering consciousness even while other aspects of the mind are well aware of and responding to them. These results also suggest that we might be able to avoid becoming consciously aware of aspects of the world that might feel threatening, even when they are right in front of us.

Although many investigators have obtained results more or less like the ones just described, their interpretation has been controversial. One obvious possibility is that subjects in fact can read the word *penis* just fine—they are just embarrassed to tell the investigator. It is difficult and perhaps impossible to be 100 percent sure. But, taken as a whole, the evidence seems persuasive that the mind has mechanisms, associated with the sensory buffer, that not only selectively attend to certain stimuli, but also actively screen out other stimuli that could cause anxiety if they were to enter consciousness (Erdelyi, 1974, 1985; Weinberger & Davidson, 1994).

Vigilance and Defense   The examples we have just discussed raise a difficult question. On the one hand, it seems that an important hallmark of personality is that people with different traits have a readiness to perceive different stimuli, such as a shy person vigilant for signs of rejection. On the other hand, the sensory buffer seems to have a capacity to filter out information that might be disturbing or threatening. Why, then, does a shy person tend to see exactly what he or she fears most to see?

One possible answer is suggested by the idea, discussed in Chapter 11, that defense mechanisms exist for a purpose. Although they can be overused, in general they are adaptive functions of the ego that protect the individual from excessive anxiety. One problem of shy people may be that their defense mechanisms don't work well enough. It is possible that the only way to avoid becoming a shy person is to be what clinical psychologists sometimes call "well-defended," to ignore and even fail to perceive small social slights.

Another possible answer is that people vary in the degree to which they are perceptually vigilant versus defensive. Years ago, the psychologist Donn Byrne developed the "repression-sensitization" scale to measure the extent to which people are relatively defensive or sensitive in their perception of potentially threatening information, and this scale has been used in many studies since (Byrne, 1961). A more recent study developed a scale to measure the "need for affect," a related construct that involves the degree to which a person seeks to magnify or minimize emotional experience (Maio & Esses, 2001). Research showed that people high in this

"I'm sorry, I'm not speaking to anyone tonight.
My defense mechanisms seem to be out of order."

"need" tended to hold extreme attitudes, liked to watch emotional movies, and became emotionally involved when they heard about the death of Princess Diana! In this conception, perhaps people with a high need for affect magnify their emotional responses to rejection so much that they become at risk for shyness. Rejection is more upsetting for them than it would be for other people, so some of them develop a style of avoiding social contact altogether.

SHORT-TERM MEMORY

Information that survives through the sensory buffer then moves to the next stage, which is **short-term memory**, or STM. STM is roughly equivalent to consciousness; its contents comprise whatever you have in mind at the moment. Thus, STM is where thinking takes place and is where the ongoing construal of reality, so important to the phenomenologists discussed in Chapter 13, is located.

The capacity of STM is specifically limited. To demonstrate this limit in class, I sometimes read a list of numbers to my students, asking them to hold all of them in memory as I go, and then to raise their hands when their "brains are full." (Try it with a friend; read slowly the numbers 4, 6, 2, 3, 7, 6, 2, 8, 7, . . .) The results are highly consistent. The hands begin to go up after about five numbers, most are up by seven, and by nine I have everybody.

This experiment illustrates the capacity of STM, which is said to be "seven, plus or minus two" (Miller, 1956). The next question, of course, is seven what? The answer is that the capacity of STM is about seven **chunks** of information. A chunk is any piece of information that can be thought of as a unit. It can vary with learning and experience. Seven random numbers, for example, comprise seven chunks. But your own phone number, which also consists of seven numbers, is just one chunk; you know it as one piece of information, not seven pieces. It seems to be about as easy to hold in STM seven phone numbers you have memorized (or forty-nine digits in all) as seven random digits.

STM and Thinking   Chunking can work with ideas, too. If you know what "water pressure" is, or "existential philosophy," or even "short-term memory," these complex ideas can be contained within single chunks. This is important because the limit to STM implies that you can only think about seven things at a time and that all new ideas you have must come from the interaction of these seven things. The more rich and complex each of the ideas in STM is, the more rich and complex your thinking can be.

This is the best argument I know of for education. Education can provide more and better chunks. You learn complicated ideas and concepts one small piece at a time, often slowly and painfully. But when you've finally learned them, complicated patterns of information and thinking become contained within single chunks, which you can now manipulate and contrast in your mind simultaneously with other such chunks. Once you learn all of the many ideas that make up "conservatism" and "liberalism," you will then be in a position to compare the two basic philosophies. By now, you should be able to say something about the basic differences between psychoanalysis and behaviorism, whereas before you understood these ideas you might have been able to compare only one aspect of each at a time. And until you really understand what water pressure is and can use it as a single idea, you will never be able to fix your plumbing.

This is the logic behind **Funder's Fifth Law**: *The purpose of education is not to teach facts, or even ideas. It is to assemble new chunks.* That is the only way to expand your ability to think.

STM and Psychological Health   A danger inherent in the limited capacity of STM is that it might fill up with the wrong things. For example, a shy person, to use that example again, might be thinking, "Do I look like an idiot?", "I bet he'd rather be somewhere else," "Why does nobody like me?", "I wish I were home in bed," and "Argh!" all at the same time, which leaves only a couple of chunks left over to actually carry on a conversation. The result will be that the shy person may seem distracted and confused and either babble incoherently or be unable to say anything at all.

In a related vein, recent research by the psychologist Sonja Lyubomirsky (2001) shows that unhappy people are the ones who fill their heads with comparisons between themselves and others and ruminations about things that have gone wrong or could go wrong. This is the sort of person who obsesses about whether other people make more money, have a bigger office, or drive a nicer car than he or she does, and pointlessly relives unpleasant memories and recycles worries about the future. Much more adaptive, Lyubomirsky's work has found, is to avoid filling your consciousness with thoughts like these and instead to use a few of the chunks of STM to notice and appreciate the good things in life, and save the rest for adaptive planning.

Constructs, Chunks, and Consciousness   Because your thinking consists of the comparison and contrast of the chunks of information and philosophy you have collected from your experience and your education, it will be different from anyone else's. This conclusion is consistent with

Kelly's personal construct theory (Chapter 13), which claimed that the critical aspect of cognition is the "constructs" (perhaps another word for chunks) out of which you build your unique view of the world. These chunk/constructs will also be to a large degree culturally determined (Chapter 14). A Japanese parent whose mind is filled with thoughts of her child's *amae* may be experiencing family life differently than a British parent could even imagine (Tseng, 2003).

The idea of STM as consciousness has interesting parallels in other basic approaches to personality. Freud believed that consciousness was by far the smallest part of the mind. In the usual cognitive model, too, STM is the smallest part—for one thing, it is the only part that has a specifically limited capacity. The phenomenologists believe that all that matters in psychology is what you are conscious of *now*. Research on STM suggests that right now you are conscious of no more than about seven things—a surprisingly exact upper limit to the capacity of human awareness.

WORKING MEMORY

STM is closely connected with **working memory**, which contains a vast store of information that sits just barely out of consciousness. Examples of information in your working memory at this moment (although we will now extract it and move it into STM) are where you last parked your car, whether rain is expected tomorrow, and what you had for breakfast. None of these pieces of information (presumably) was difficult to retrieve into consciousness, even though it is unlikely you were thinking of any of them before I asked. You might recognize working memory as similar to what Freud called the *preconscious* (Chapter 10).

The principal purpose of working memory is to maintain close at hand a constantly updated representation of your current environment. It keeps track of information you might need to know at a moment's notice but that does not need to be kept actively in your consciousness. That is why it holds the information about where your car is parked, for example. You do not need or want to think about it all day, but when you go out to the parking lot at 5:30, it would be nice to be able to remember.

Because it is constantly updated, working memory is a representation of the *current* environment and the various things you need, temporarily, to keep at your mental fingertips. It probably remembers where your car is today but not where you parked it last Tuesday. Working memory also contains a list of the things you are currently trying to accomplish or are worried about.

Current Concerns   Research on individuals' **current concerns** shows that at any given moment people will list around half a dozen matters that frequently come to mind, as thoughts move from working memory to STM and back again (Klinger, 1977). These might include a job you hope to get, a term paper you need to work on, a phone call you expect will be returned soon, and so forth. Some of these current concerns can make you emotionally aroused when you think about them consciously, and you will find many of them drifting into your daydreams (Gold & Reilly, 1985; Nikula, Klinger, & Larson-Gutman, 1993). But what were you trying to accomplish or what were you worried about three weeks ago? It is not the job of working memory to know or to care. Once the concern is resolved—when that person finally calls you back or that problem you were worrying about is finally resolved—working memory can and generally will erase all record of it.

The Cognitive Workbench   The essential difference between working memory and STM is not really one of kind, but of size. Material constantly moves back and forth between them, and the same sorts of chunks likely fill both. So like STM, working memory can be expected to contain personally relevant ideas such as goals and personal constructs; these ideas are both a function and a cause of the kind of person you are.

   One theory describes the process of thinking using the analogy of a workbench. On your workbench is the project you are currently building, and hanging on the wall nearby is an assortment of tools. You take down a tool when you need it, but because the workbench is small, every time you get a tool down you must hang another one up. (The workbench has room for, say, seven tools, plus or minus two.)

   In this analogy, the workbench is STM and the wall where the many other tools are stored is working memory. Information remains in STM only while it is being used, then it goes back to working memory so that another piece of necessary information can be considered. Personal computers work the same way. They have a limited CPU (central processing unit), where all of the computer's "thinking" takes place, but this capacity is expanded through the use of a hard drive that stores information nearby. It constantly swaps information from the CPU onto the hard drive and back again as it needs different data for its analysis. If you observe the machine closely, you will hear the hard drive go whirr (or make rattling or other noises) and the little red light will go on and off repeatedly until the answer is ready. The computer is swapping data from the CPU to the hard drive with each flash of the red light, just as a person (less visibly) swaps information back and forth between STM and working memory.

FROM SHORT-TERM MEMORY TO LONG-TERM MEMORY

Most information that is perceived and even thought about briefly never makes it into the permanent storage locker called **long-term memory** (LTM). The processes by which this can happen, therefore, are important.

Rehearsal and Elaboration An old theory was that if you repeated something over and over in your mind, such *rehearsal* was sufficient to move it from STM into permanent storage. Later research showed that this idea is not quite correct. The only way to get information into LTM, it turns out, is not just to repeat it to yourself, but to really think about it (a process called *elaboration*). The longer and more elaborate the processing that a piece of information receives, the more likely it is to transfer into LTM (Craik & Watkins, 1973; Craik & Tulving, 1975).

This principle of cognitive psychology yields some useful advice about how to study. A common strategy, and one that usually fails dismally, is the rote repetition technique. You all have seen college students with their yellow highlighter pens, marking passages in the textbook they think will be on the exam. To study, they go back through the book and reread everything highlighted; if they have time, they do it again and even again.

A much better strategy would be to take each of these highlighted passages, pause, and ask yourself several questions. Do I agree with this statement? Why? Does this statement remind me of anything in my life? Is it use-

ful for anything? Does it contradict anything else I know from experience or have learned in this course? If you can generate an answer to each of these questions, you are more likely to remember the statement you are asking them about. Moreover, you might learn something.

Self-reference   A particularly good way to remember something, research has shown, is specifically to think about some way that it relates to your self (Symons & Johnson, 1997). The reason for this appears to be that the mental structure of your knowledge of yourself, sometimes called the **self schema** (Markus, 1977), is very rich, well developed, and often used. Any information that becomes tied to this schema in one's memory is likely to be remembered for a long time. A good way to remember something, therefore, is to ask "What does this have to do with me?" (The answer doesn't really matter; the important part is that you have thought about how the information *might* be self-relevant.)

Even more importantly, the real-world memories that stick with you the longest will be the ones that are personally meaningful. These will include tragic events (such as the death of a loved one), major milestones in life (such as graduation day, your wedding day, and the day your child—especially your first child—is born), and other events that for some reason meant something special. Try this right now: Think of a memory from your childhood. Why did this event stay in your mind all of these years? It must mean something special to you—what?

We saw in Chapter 14 that the concept of the "self" appears to have different implications in collectivist cultures, such as China, than it does in individualist cultures, such as the United States. It is reasonable to suspect, therefore, that the self-reference effect might be different in these cultures. A recent study indicates that it is (Qi & Zhu, 2002). In China, information thought about in terms of the self is indeed remembered better, but the same effect is found for information thought about in terms of one's mother or father, leading the authors to conclude that "the self concept might include the concepts of father and mother in Chinese people, supporting the independent/dependent self-concept model in Eastern culture" (Qi & Zhu, 2002, p. 275).

LONG-TERM MEMORY

According to most theories of long-term memory (LTM), this part of the mind is both permanent and of unlimited capacity. It is said that David Starr Jordan, a turn-of-the-century ichthyologist[1] and president of Stanford University, in his later years refused to learn anybody's name. Every time he learned a name, he complained, he forgot a fish.

---

[1]An *ichthyologist* is someone who studies fish.

Apparently, Jordan was a better ichthyologist than he was a cognitive psychologist. The consensus of modern cognitive theories is that any information that makes it into LTM is there forever (although it might be hard to retrieve), and that LTM never runs out of room. In this view, LTM is much like an infinite attic. You can keep storing stuff in there, and you will never fill it. But there is no guarantee that, when you go up there, you will be able to find that snorkel you put away at the end of last summer. Whether you can find anything or not will depend on how well the attic is organized. The same is true about LTM. The better organized its contents, the easier information is to retrieve.

Recall that George Kelly (1955) theorized that your mind is organized by its personal constructs (Chapter 13). These constructs may affect experience, thought, and behavior by their ability to determine what you are and are not able to find in the attic of your mind. To push this attic analogy a little further, imagine your mental attic divided into storage bins, each of which is labeled with a personal construct. Perhaps at the back is a large bin labeled "miscellaneous." Clearly, something that goes in one of the construct-labeled bins will be easier to find than something tossed into the miscellaneous bin. And it will be easier to find things from the construct-labeled bins that are used every day than from bins that are hardly ever used. These facts are important, because the information that is the easiest to find will have the most influence on how you think about the world.

The representation of LTM in Figure 16.1 shows it divided into two parts, each of which is further divided in two. The two main parts are the areas of LTM that contain declarative and procedural knowledge. The distinction comes from the philosopher Gilbert Ryle (1949), who said there were two forms of knowledge, which he called "knowing that" and "knowing how." You might know *that* Little Rock is the capital of Arkansas, but you know *how* to ride a bicycle. These two forms of knowledge are, according to Ryle and modern cognitive theory, fundamentally different (Anderson, 1982; Winograd, 1975).

Declarative Knowledge   **Declarative knowledge** is "knowing that." It includes all of your knowledge you can talk about, or declare. An important property of declarative knowledge is that it is conscious—you know you have it and can, if asked, explain it to others. In Figure 16.1, this kind of knowledge is represented in two kinds of memory, *event* and *conceptual*.

Event Memory   **Event memory** (also called *episodic memory*) contains almost everything you might refer to by saying "I remember . . . " It includes episodes, such as what happened on your first date, as well as specific facts, such as the state capitals, your mother's first name, the number of inches in

"Don't you hate it when you plant evidence but forget where?"

a foot, and (I hope) the essential tenets of psychoanalysis. These are all specific items of information that you can talk about.

Declarative knowledge includes your consciously accessible, "verbalizable" knowledge about yourself (which is not all there is, as we shall see). The important, formative experiences of your life—those you remember— sit here more or less permanently, and have an influence on your personality that can last for many years. As was discussed above, the episodes that make it into LTM are those that mean something to you. Therefore, a particularly traumatic or delightful episode can continue to affect your outlook on life, your emotions, and your behavior, long after it happens.

Conceptual Memory **Conceptual memory** (sometimes called *semantic memory*) contains your more general knowledge of the world. It refers not to specific events or facts about specific things, but rather to the knowledge you have abstracted from experience about how the world works (e.g., Schank & Abelson, 1977).

For example, you probably have never been told explicitly what happens at McDonald's, yet you know the rules. You know that if you sit down, and expect a waiter to come take your order, you might eventually starve to death. From your experience of having gone there many times, you know what to expect and how to follow what some cognitive psychologists call the "McDonald's script." This kind of abstraction from experience is the basis of most of what you do. When you enter a new McDonald's, or a new college classroom, or a new car, you know pretty much what to do even if you have never seen that particular restaurant, classroom, or car before. And if someone else were to ask, you could tell him or her what to do.

Not only have you developed knowledge about all of the specific things you have done in life, but also you have abstracted from those behaviors a general view of the kind of person you are (the *self schema* referred to earlier). This view is made up of beliefs you have formulated about what you are like. These beliefs, in turn, affect what you remember, what you perceive, and what you do. The shy person not only has a good memory for past social disasters, but also has a general—and powerfully influential—view of the self as shy (Cantor, 1990).

Conceptual knowledge is powerful because it often fills gaps in event memory (which is why there is an arrow on Figure 16.1 that leads from conceptual to event knowledge). For example, consider the following scenario: A person walks into McDonald's, orders a hamburger, fries, and a Coke, gets the food, sits down and eats it, then leaves. Now here is a question: Did the person pay for the food? Not only will almost anybody respond yes, after just a few minutes many people will think that they *remember* that the person paid. Of course, they were not told that—they inferred it from their general knowledge that the McDonald's Corporation regards payment as an essential part of every transaction.

It is reasonable to infer that a person eating a burger indeed paid for it, and in general the practice of using conceptual knowledge to fill in gaps in event knowledge is probably quite useful. But it also can lead to errors. For example, someone who has in his or her conceptual knowledge an image of what members of a certain ethnic group are like might "remember" facts about members of that group that never really happened. Trial lawyers and detectives know that eyewitnesses to a crime are likely to confuse what they *actually* saw with what they *assumed* they saw. These assumptions may be based on how they think a bank robbery or mugging usually proceeds, or even on what they expect a person who looks like the suspect to do (e.g., Loftus, 1992; Loftus, Greene, & Doyle, 1989).

Earlier, we considered how a shy person might perceive a social situation differently than a non-shy person would. In a similar manner, even after the situation is over, a shy person might fill in gaps in his or her memory of an unpleasant social encounter with details that did not really happen, but that serve to increase his or her humiliation. For example, he or she might have had a conversation with someone that ended suddenly as the person was pulled away by someone else. The shy person might later use his or her social interaction script, based on past experiences of social awkwardness, to fill in and "remember" added details such as his conversation partner's look of disdain before leaving, or other signs of social rejection—none of which may have actually happened.

Memory is a powerful mental tool, so it is important not to conclude from research such as that on eyewitness testimony that the memory system is deeply flawed. That is not true, and could not be true if we were to survive. But it is the case that our memories of events are complex mixtures of what happened at a specific place and time, and other similar events we may have experienced or even just heard about. This is why someone with a past history of social success is likely to remember a recent social event as possibly more successful than it really was, while someone with a history of failure will have a memory biased in the other direction. And this is precisely where memory intersects with personality: Different kinds of people, with different experiences and outlooks on life, will remember events in different ways.

Correcting Conceptual Knowledge   Our store of conceptual knowledge contains many general scripts and stereotypes. For example, consider these questions concerning a waitress and a librarian: Which one drinks wine and which one drinks beer? Which one drives an old Volvo, and which one drives a pickup truck? Which one likes classical music, and which one prefers country western? Even though no specific person is being referred to, these questions do not seem difficult to answer. We may have abstracted these stereotypes from experience (this is the basis of the arrow leading from event to conceptual knowledge in Figure 16.1) and many of them probably have a kernel of truth (Lee, Jussim, & McCauley, 1995).

Indeed, if all stereotypes were abstractions from firsthand experience, they might not be a problem. Generalizations are useful, after all. But we also form stereotypes and general views of the world from sources that are not valid. One significant source is the mass media. Movies and television programs—including so-called news programs—portray the world as a place where large numbers of people are armed and dangerous and where violence is a frequent event. They also show images that communicate stereotypes about how dangerous people act, how they dress, and to which ethnic groups they belong. An unfortunate recent trend is for politicians to scapegoat stereotyped groups—"illegal immigrants" or "welfare mothers," for example—as the source of society's ills. These images are conveyed repeatedly through the media, and the result is that many citizens think they know all about immigrants and welfare recipients, even if they have never knowingly met an individual of either type. Most worrisome of all, many children watch hours of television every day. Think a moment about the image of reality they must be assembling on the basis of their contact with this violent fantasyland.

In principle, false conceptual knowledge can be undone. The method would be the same by which the knowledge was acquired in the first place—experience. If television shows were to change their portrayal of the world, children's general images might eventually change, too. More powerfully, there is no better way to remove a negative stereotype about an ethnic group than having experience with real, living, breathing members of that group (Pettigrew, 1986). A shy person, given enough successful—or even just nonaversive—social interactions, might become less shy. But the process is likely to be long and difficult, with many setbacks. Recall our description of how a shy person might not just perceive ongoing events in a way consistent with his or her "shy" self-image, but may also misremember past events in a way biased toward making shyness even worse. The same processes no doubt hold true for other personality traits; perception and memory will tend to promote their stability rather than change. So while the situation may not be hopeless, the process by which daily experience and event knowledge might be able to change and correct conceptual knowledge is slow and gradual, at best. That is why a *dotted* arrow connects event to conceptual knowledge in Figure 16.1.

Procedural Knowledge, The Self, and Emotions   Procedural knowledge is what you know but cannot really talk about, even if you want to. Rather than words or statements, it consists of knowledge about ways of doing things, or procedures, which is why it is also called "knowing how." It is knowledge of a special sort—although you know these things, you are not conscious of the knowledge itself and you generally cannot, if asked, explain it to anyone else. (If possible, you may reply with a statement such as "Here, let me show you.") As with declarative knowledge, procedural knowledge can be divided into two parts.

Know-How   The first is simply all of the skills ordinarily called "know-how." Examples include the ability to read, to ride a bicycle, to close a business deal, to analyze a set of data, or to ask someone out on a date. For the most part—by which I mean about 98 percent of the time—these skills are learned by *doing* them and sometimes from watching them. You can talk about each of these skills, and people of course do. But all the talk does not really describe it. If somebody merely tells you, without giving you a chance to actually do it, you will not learn the skill. Furthermore, if you try to describe how you do any of these things, you may find something to say, but your words will fail to capture the essence of the activity.

A classic example is bike riding. I can tell you how to ride a bike: Get on the saddle, grab the handlebars, pump the pedals up and down, and maintain balance so you will not fall off. There might be a little more I could say, but no matter how much I talk, it will never be enough to teach you how to ride a bicycle, or even to let you know what riding one is really like. You can only learn how to ride a bicycle by doing it, and by getting practice and feedback. Social skills are like this too. Despite the prevalence of books with titles like *How to Sell Anything to Anyone* or even *How to Pick Up Girls*, social skills must be acquired through practice.

Relational Selves The usual analysis of procedural knowledge stops here, but the concept can be applied in many different contexts. A very important part of procedural knowledge consists of the general styles and strategies you use to approach life (Cantor, 1990). Everyone has well-practiced routines for dealing with various situations, and sometimes these routines kick in "mindlessly" without conscious intention (Langer, 1992, 1994). In particular, recent theorizing has addressed how we may have "relational" self schemas that are based on past experience and that direct how we relate with each of the important people in our lives (Baldwin, 1999).

For example, as mentioned in Chapter 2, you probably developed over the years some very specific patterns in the way you interact with your parents. You may even forget these patterns exist, until you visit home after a long absence. Before you know it, you are falling into the same old well-rehearsed childhood routine. This is rarely a pleasant experience, so a common response is to try to oppose old patterns by relating to the family as differently from how you used to as possible (Andersen & Chen, 2002). We all know what this can include: odd clothes, tattoos, body piercings, an unsuitable boyfriend or girlfriend, or maybe just a spectacularly bad attitude. All of these behaviors are ways of announcing, "I'm not the child I used to be." This is only natural, but pause a moment, and have a kind thought for the baffled parents.

Despite this example, most of our patterns of relating to other people are deeply ingrained and difficult to change. Even the multiply pierced adolescent may run to Mommy when he or she stubs a toe or feels sick. One reason for the persistence of these patterns is that their roots reach so deep. Attachment theory (e.g., Shaver & Clark, 1994; Sroufe et al., 1993, see Chapter 12) and newer, "relational self" theory (Andersen & Chen, 2002) agree that many of our scripts for relating to others are set early in life. Later,

"Ignore him. He just walks that way to bug his parents."

through "transference," we may find ourselves responding to and treating new people in our lives in a way similar to the people in our past who they remind us of (Andersen & Baum, 1994; Zhang & Hazan, 2002). For example, if you were intimidated by your father and tried to avoid making him mad at all costs, you may find yourself treating your boss the same way. Or, if early romantic relationships did not turn out well for you, you might find yourself, in a self-perpetuating manner, approaching new relationships with implicit expectations of betrayal and disappointment.

Implicit Selves   Another reason why self-relevant behavioral patterns are so resistant to change is that they are not readily accessible to consciousness. Unlike the self schema, which is generally assumed to be consciously accessible and which can be measured readily on straightforward questionnaires (i.e., S data; see Chapter 2), relational selves and other implicit aspects of the self-concept may work unconsciously and powerfully at the same time (Greenwald et al., 2002). In that case, how can they be measured? The psychologist Anthony Greenwald and his colleagues have invented an ingenious method called the Implicit Association Test (or IAT; Greenwald, McGhee, & Schwartz, 1998).

The IAT is a measure of reaction time, in which participants are asked to push one of two buttons as quickly as possible, depending on which of four concepts is displayed to them. To see how this works, imagine that a subject is shown a series of playing cards, and asked to push button A if a heart or diamond is displayed, and button B if a spade or club is displayed. This should be easy, because hearts and diamonds are both red, and spades and clubs are both black, and either attribute can be used to make a correct decision. But now imagine being asked to push button A if a heart or spade is displayed, and button B if a club or diamond is displayed. For most people, this would be more difficult because color is now no help.[2] The idea is that if two categories that are closely associated (e.g., heart-red) share the same button, response will be easy and quick. If two categories that are less associated or negatively associated share the same button (e.g., heart-black), then response will be more difficult and slower. Greenwald's creative idea was to use this principle to measure the degree to which ideas might be associated in an individual's cognitive system, in a way the individual himself or herself might not be consciously aware of (Greenwald & Farnham, 2000).

For example, in a study of "implicit self-esteem," the four concepts were "good," "bad," "me," and "not me." Before the study started, the experimenter obtained from each subject 18 words that he or she considered to be self-descriptive ("me") and 18 words he or she considered to be not

---

[2]Greenwald and his colleagues point out that for an experienced bridge player this might also be easy, because hearts and spades are the higher-ranking suits.

self-descriptive ("not me"). The experimenter also assembled a list of pleasant words (e.g., diamond, health, sunrise) and unpleasant words (agony, filth,
poison). Now the study could begin. In the first part, the subject was asked
to push button A if a "me" word *or* a pleasant word is displayed, and B if a
"not me" word *or* an unpleasant word is displayed. In the second part, the
pairings were switched. Now the subject pushed button A if a "me" word or
unpleasant word was displayed, and button B if a "not me" word or a *pleasant* word was displayed.[3] The logic is that for someone with ordinary, high
self-esteem, reactions should be easier and quicker in the first part of the
study than the second: see something good or self-relevant, push A—that's
easy. But the second part should be harder, and slower: see something self-
relevant or bad; that requires one to slow down and think a bit. The reason
is that good and "me" are implicitly associated in the cognitive unconscious,
as are bad and "not me." Now what about someone with low self-esteem?
For them, the me-good and not me-bad associations might be weaker or
even reversed. If this is true, then the difference in reaction time between the
two parts of the experiment might be usable as a measure of a person's
"implicit" self-esteem—someone with higher self-esteem should be quicker
in part one relative to part two; someone with lower self-esteem should have
a smaller difference or even reverse the difference.

It worked! It turned out implicit self-esteem—and other implicit attributes of the self such as stereotypes and attitudes—could be measured in this
way. The measure was reliable, predicted responses to success and failure
and, perhaps most interesting of all, related only weakly to more traditional,
straightforward, S-data measures of self-esteem. The implication of this
research is that we may have attitudes and feelings about many things, including ourselves, of which we are not entirely conscious, but which nonetheless
can influence our emotions and behaviors perhaps without us even knowing why. To the extent this is true—and it does indeed seem to be true to at
least some extent—then some of the cognitive patterns that guide our behavior are deeply embedded indeed.

Acquiring and Changing Procedural Knowledge Is there any hope for
change, then? The answer is yes, but because implicit knowledge and associated behavioral patterns consist of *procedural* knowledge, not declarative
knowledge, changing them will require more than advice, lectures, or even
well-meaning, conscious intentions to change. As was mentioned earlier, procedural knowledge is both acquired and changed only through doing, specifically *practice and feedback.*

---

[3]The procedure also includes other kinds of counterbalancings to make sure, for example,
that the A and B buttons are used equally for the various possible combinations of stimuli.

Consider how one learns to think (assuming one ever does). A number of colleges now have courses on "how to think," where instructors explain the rules of logic, describe tactics for organizing thinking, teach brainstorming methods, and so on. I am not a big fan of these courses because I believe that in college *all* courses ought to teach you how to think. They teach it (or should teach it) by giving you something to think about. You then formulate ideas and get feedback on them (such as the instructor or a fellow student saying, "Good!" or "Very interesting!"). Practice and feedback are how you learn to think, the same way you learn *how* to do anything else.

Similarly, the main role of an athletic coach is to motivate practice and to provide useful feedback. Teachers of singing, dancing, violin playing, and other forms of procedural knowledge play the same role as coaches. And, in some cases, a psychotherapist trying to help you change your characteristic behavioral patterns may work the same way as well. First, the therapist must motivate his or her clients to practice that which they want to learn to do. (Don't contradict your mother every time she says something you disagree with; practice this restraint as often as possible.) Second, the therapist must provide feedback on how his or her clients are doing.

This is a big difference between declarative and procedural knowledge. The first can be taught by reading or listening to lectures; the second, only through practice and feedback. The first requires a teacher good at what is being taught; you cannot learn Russian history from somebody who does not know the topic. But you can learn to sing from somebody whose own voice is hoarse, or learn to bat from a middle-aged coach with slow reflexes and a beer gut. You might even get some help in developing your personality from someone who has not yet worked out all of his or her *own* personal problems.

Which brings us back to how one acquires and might be able to change procedural knowledge about social behavior and the self. A style of responding to every authority figure with fear, or of expecting and (mis)remembering repeated experiences of social rejection, has its roots in bitter experience, and was not created in a day. Undoing these learning experiences will not be easy, therefore, and verbal exhortation and even willpower are unlikely to be enough. The person, perhaps with help (professional or otherwise), must have the courage to change his or her behavior with authority figures, or in social interaction, or in whatever domain of life where change is sought, and slowly but (hopefully) surely, begin to accumulate countervailing experiences that can eventually generate a new behavioral style and general outlook on life.

And, let us not forget that not all patterns of transference or of characteristic perception and behavior are maladaptive. A child fortunate enough to grow up in a supportive and encouraging environment may be able to face later life with a resilient attitude that can help him or her to bounce back from defeat, rejection, or whatever other disappointments life might have in store. Whether it be explicit or implicit, a strong and consistent self-concept is not necessarily a bad thing.

Emotions   Emotions can be considered a separate category of procedural knowledge. As is true about inner experience in general (see Chapter 13), you cannot fully learn about emotions by reading about them, nor can you really describe emotions in words. But everybody knows what they are.

Knowledge about emotion and feeling is not verbal, nor is it verbalizable, although both psychologists and poets have tried. Scientific verbal descriptions of emotions certainly exist, but always seem somehow to miss the point (Frijda, 1986). Even poetry, when it works, communicates by evoking an emotion in the reader or listener, rather than by actually describing the emotion itself. Emotions cannot be fully described in words because our most important knowledge about them is procedural, not declarative.

Consider the emotion of anger. In the course of experiencing this emotion, a person does a wide variety of things. His heart rate accelerates and his blood pressure rises; he may get red in the face and clench his fist and jaw. His thoughts are taken over by the way the object of his anger mistreated or threatened him, and he makes plans to get even or lashes out without thinking. He may or may not recognize that *everything* he is doing is part of the emotion. That is, he will not necessarily say to himself, "Boy am I angry." But that is what all of the other activities of his body and mind amount to.

Thus, an emotion is a set of procedures of the body and mind. It is something you do, not merely a set of verbal concepts or a passive experience (Ekman & Davidson, 1994). And, like procedural knowledge in general, you learn about emotion by experiencing it, not by talking about it. It may be the most important learning you do.

LIMITATIONS OF THE SERIAL MODEL

The serial model of cognition just described is still alive and well. Many cognitive psychologists do research based on its assumptions, and as we have already seen, it provides a useful framework for accounting for many phenomena relevant to personality. These include perceptual defense and repression, selective perception, biased memory, and the implicit, unconscious, and powerful patterns of behavior that may be unconsciously invoked in relationships and when coming to terms with one's self. However, since about the mid-1980s an increasing number of cognitive psychologists have become dissatisfied with it and sought a new approach.

One reason for dissatisfaction with the serial model is that it seems like a process such as that diagrammed in Figure 16.1 might be too slow to perform many of the ordinary tasks of perception and cognition. For example, raise your eyes from this page and look around the room. You may see a window and a tree outside, a painting on the wall, a chair, perhaps another person, and so forth. According to the traditional, serial model of cognition, in each case the stimuli flowing into your brain from your retina are being brought into STM, compared with prototypes in LTM, evaluated as to the best fit, then interpreted as to what they are (a "window" or a "tree," for example). Then all of these specific stimuli get constructed, in working memory, into a representation of your current environment, all of which might have to change a moment from now when someone new walks into the room. A serial process like this seems too slow and cumbersome to do all of this as quickly as is necessary for survival. Indeed, when psychologists interested in "artificial intelligence" began to try to write computer programs that could identify objects in a room and perform other seemingly simple perceptual tasks, they immediately ran into a serious problem. Serial processing models were so inefficient and used so much processing time that even the largest computers available could not begin to identify simple stimuli within a reasonable period of time (see Haugeland, 1985; Pinker, 1985; Rumelhart, 1989; Winograd & Flores, 1986).

A second reason for dissatisfaction with the serial model of cognition is that a system like that shown in Figure 16.1—with its single stream of boxes and arrows—does not seem to be particularly compatible with what is now known about the architecture of the brain. Cognitive psychology began with the idea that the physical structure of the brain could be safely ignored, because any "software" (cognitive process) could be run on any "hardware" (brain structure). But this is not completely true about computers (did you ever try to run a PC program on a Macintosh?) and may not be true about the brain either. As we saw in Chapter 8, a close look at the brain reveals not distinct structures that resemble anything like "short-term memory" or a "sensory buffer," but a massively interconnected network of billions of neurons that constantly interact with each other.

For these and other reasons, in recent years a new approach to cognition— the "parallel" approach—has become increasingly influential.

The Parallel System

According to the parallel view of cognition (also called *parallel distributed processing*, or PDP), rather than working through the processing of information step-by-step, as depicted in Figure 16.1, the human brain typically processes many different kinds of information all at once. By "many," I mean, maybe, billions! Studies of the electrical activity of the brain indicate that most and perhaps all of its billions of nerve cells are at least a little bit active at any given moment, although their activity level fluctuates up and down over time. One way to interpret this observation is that the brain is—hard as this might be to imagine—constantly looking for *everything* that it knows about. Thus, the structures of the brain that know about windows are always ready to jump the moment they detect anything that looks remotely like a window, the structures that know about trees are equally ready, and so forth. This interpretation also might help to explain why a shy person is so quick to interpret any bump in his or her social life as a humiliating rejection.

IMPLICATIONS OF A PARALLEL SYSTEM

This PDP view of the cognitive system yields three implications right away. First, it helps to explain why perception happens so fast that it feels immediate. All of the various "receivers" for anything we might see or hear are already turned on and ready to respond the instant the appropriate stimulus comes along. Only when we see something new—something we genuinely have not encountered before—will the brain have to stop and think things through.

Second, this view of cognition implies that the receivers that have been activated the most frequently or recently will be "primed" to respond especially quickly, and even issue "false alarms" from time to time. For example, the constantly re-activated self schema of a shy person may include so many concepts related to social rejection and humiliation that thoughts, perceptions, and memories of these concepts are ready to be set off by the slightest hint of a relevant stimulus. Priming can also come from the outside. A person who has just had a financial setback, for example, might suddenly find the prices of objects in the store to be much more salient than they used to be. Even the mass media can, and often does, prime concepts in the whole population. In early 2001, a few shark attacks off of Florida received so much publicity that people around the country were afraid to go swimming, even in lakes! After September 11 of that year, shark mania cooled but people were on the alert for signs of terrorists, not just on airplanes, but also in parks and shopping malls, and people with beards and swarthy complexions found themselves gazed at with deep suspicion. Over time this kind of situational priming fades, fortunately, but the concepts that are constantly primed and re-primed because of their chronic accessibility in our cognitive systems become part of our personalities. As was said at the beginning of this chapter, the main reason people behave differently from each other is that they think differently. And the reason they think differently has much to do with the different concepts that are primed and ready to come to mind (more will be said about priming in Chapter 17).

Third, according to the PDP view the mind is continuously doing many different things at the same time. The ultimate result—what the person actu-

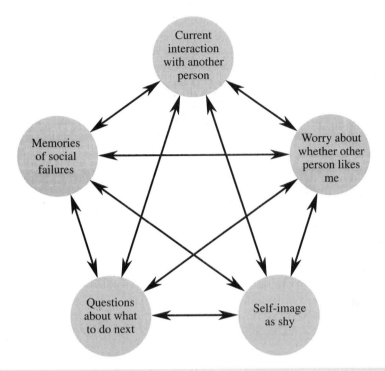

**FIGURE 16.2 A "PARALLEL" MODEL OF SOME OF THE MANY DIF-
FERENT, INTERACTING COGNITIVE PROCESSES IN THE MIND OF
A SHY PERSON DURING A SOCIAL INTERACTION** The person's conscious thoughts and overt behaviors will represent an ongoing compromise
among these simultaneous processes.

ally thinks and does at a given moment—represents a compromise among
all of these different processes (see Figure 16.2). For example, recall how
Freud described the battle among the id, superego, and ego (see Chapter 10).
In a PDP framework, a similar process seems not unreasonable. At any given
moment, we have brain processes that are appraising what we want to do,
what we should do, and what is actually possible. What we finally and actually do will be some sort of compromise among these three processes. Freud
believed it was the special job of the ego to find a reasonable compromise
between all of the competing demands and motivations of the various, independent parts of the mind. The PDP view implies that such a special compromise mechanism may not be necessary. The mind does many things at
once, but there is only room for a few things in consciousness (seven, plus
or minus two), and a person can only do one thing at a time, usually. The
inevitable result is that what one is conscious of, and what one does, has to
be the result of the combination of many influences.

The Cognitive-Affective Personality System (CAPS)

The present chapter has surveyed many examples of where the cognitive system interacts with processes relevant to personality. Research on this interaction amounts to a whole new paradigm for studying personality, called the **cognitive approach** (sometimes called the *social-cognitive approach,* reminding us of its roots in social learning theory). For the most part, this research addresses specific topics involving perceptual, memory, or self-relevant processes (see Chapter 17). Rarer, at this point, are general and integrative theories of the relationship between cognition and personality. To conclude the present chapter, let us take a look at one prominent attempt.

An important intellectual antecedent of the cognitive approach to personality was the "personal construct" theory of George Kelly (1955), described in Chapter 13. Recall that these constructs are the idiosyncratic ideas about the world that guide each individual's perceptions and thoughts. Kelly's theory was essentially cognitive. For example, as described already, personal constructs presumably reside in LTM, affect the formation of chunks in STM, and determine which of the pieces of information that enter the sensory buffer will make it further into consciousness. Kelly's career came before the explosion of research in cognitive psychology in the late 1960s, however, and he never tied his ideas about constructs very closely to the cognitive psychology of his own day.

However, Kelly's theory did inspire one of his students to later develop the cognitive theory of personality that is the most influential at present. This student's name was Walter Mischel—yes, the very same person who triggered the person-situation controversy by claiming that personality traits are not important and that situations are much more powerful determinants of behavior (see Chapter 4). Mischel's approach combines two important ideas. The first is the phenomenological—specifically the Kellyan—idea that the individual's interpretation or construal of the world is all-important. From a phenomenological perspective, to understand a person's thoughts is to understand everything. The second idea is the parallel process or PDP view of the cognitive system, described earlier in this chapter, which describes thought as proceeding simultaneously on multiple tracks that occasionally intersect. The result of the combination of these two ideas is Mischel's theory of the *cognitive-affective personality system,* or CAPS (Mischel, 1999).

Interactions among Systems

Mischel theorizes that the most important aspect of the many different systems of personality and cognition is the way they simultaneously interact. Personality, then, is "a stable system that mediates how the individual selects, construes, and processes social information and generates social behaviors" (Mischel & Shoda, 1995, p. 246). He offers the following example:

> Suppose that while waiting for the results of medical tests, an individual scans for and focuses on a specific configuration of features in the situation, which activate the encoding that this is a health threat to the self, and concurrently trigger anxiety, which activates further scanning of and for those features, and simultaneously feeds back to reactivate the encoded health threat. The perceived threat activates the belief that this situation is uncontrollable, which triggers further anxiety and also negative outcome expectations. Both the negative expectancies and the anxiety concurrently activate defensive plans and scripts that generate a pattern of multiple behaviors at varying levels of strength. These events occur concurrently, in parallel activation within the system. The behaviors ultimately generated depend both on the situational features and on the organization of the network of cognitions and affects that become involved. (Mischel & Shoda, 1995, p. 255)

In other words, a lot of different processes are happening at the same time, and they have many different results. There is not a single output from a single, linear, serial process. How the person feels, what he or she thinks, and what he or she ultimately does, is a compromise among many different processes. Sigmund Freud and Walter Mischel seem to agree about that.

Cognitive Person Variables

The original version of Mischel's theory, proposed in 1973 (when it was called "cognitive social learning theory"), claims that individual differences in personality stem from four "person variables" that characterize properties and activities of the cognitive system.

1. *Cognitive and behavioral construction competencies.* These competencies comprise an individual's mental abilities and behavioral skills and so might include such properties as one's IQ, creativity, social skills, and occupational abilities. In terms of the serial cognitive model described earlier, these would be considered procedural knowledge.

2. *Encoding strategies and personal constructs.* These aspects of personality include a person's ideas about how the world can be categorized (one's Kellyan personal construct system) and efficacy expectations, or beliefs about one's own capabilities (of the sort described by Bandura). They also might include other beliefs about one's self, such as "I am a shy person." These beliefs are usually of the sort that can be verbally described, so they would reside in the declarative knowledge section of LTM in the model described earlier.

3. *Subjective stimulus values.* This idea to some degree resembles the notion of expectancies in Rotter's social learning theory—an individual's beliefs about the probabilities of attaining a goal if it were to be pursued. It also includes the values people put on different rewarding outcomes; for one person money is more important than prestige, for example, whereas another person's priorities might be just the reverse.

4. *Self-regulatory systems and plans.* These are another kind of procedural knowledge in LTM and are closely related to what Bandura called the *self system,* as described in Chapter 15. Recall that Bandura's self system is a set of procedures for the control of behavior, including self-reinforcement, the selection of situations, and the purposeful alteration of situational circumstances. This is more or less what Mischel had in mind, but Mischel was also interested in how one might directly control one's own thoughts.

An example Mischel addressed many times in his research concerned a child who is trying to delay gratification. As described in Chapter 7, most experiments of this sort present a child with two rewards, such as marshmallows and pretzels. The child is told that he or she can have the less-preferred reward immediately, but can have the better reward if he or she is able to wait for a few minutes. Mischel was interested in the strategies the child might use to help himself or herself through the waiting period.

One strategy he proposed to the waiting children was to mentally transform the object that presumably was being so eagerly awaited. For example, if a child's preferred treat was the marshmallow, the child might hardly be able to wait if he or she thought about its "chewy, sweet, soft taste." But if instead the child thought about the marshmallow as a cloud, the waiting period could go much longer without difficulty. If a child's preferred treat was the pretzel, tolerance for waiting would end quickly if the child concentrated on its "crunchy, salty taste." But if he or she thought about the pretzel as a brown log, the waiting was much easier.

Mischel drew from this research not only some pointers on how to help children delay gratification, but also a deeper moral that fits right into the point of view of the phenomenologists considered in Chapter 13:

> The results [of the research just described] clearly show that what is in the children's heads—not what is physically in front of them—determines their ability to delay. (Mischel, 1973, p. 260)

Twenty-two years after his pioneering effort, and after a good deal of progress in cognitive psychology and a great deal of research by many investigators tying cognition to personality, Mischel (and his student Yuichi Shoda) issued an updated version of the theory. Instead of four person variables, the new version had five; the new variable was "affects," or feelings and emotions. This new variable was added because, according to Mischel, by 1995 research had made it "clear that affects and emotions profoundly influence social information processing and coping behavior" (Mischel & Shoda, 1995, p. 252; see also Mischel, 1999).

If and Then

The most important recent addition to Mischel's theory of personality is the idea of what he calls *if . . . then* contingencies. The personality variables summarized above combine in each individual to yield a repertoire of actions that are triggered by particular stimulus situations. For example, one person, when insulted, may simply walk away. Another, with a different *if . . . then* pattern, may respond violently (Shoda, 1999). For every individual, this pattern of *if . . . then* contingencies is unique, and comprises his or her "behavioral signature" (Mischel, 1999, p. 44). In one recent application of this idea, the psychologist Susan Andersen has proposed that the phenomenon of transference, discussed earlier in this chapter (see also Chapter 12), can be conceived of in *if . . . then* terms. If a person encounters someone who reminds her of her father, for example, *then* a behavioral and emotional response might be triggered that resembles the way she used to relate to her father (Andersen & Chen, 2002).

Mischel's goal is for *if . . . then* contingencies to replace personality traits—a concept for which he still has no great love, even after all these years—as the essential units for understanding individual differences in personality. The main advantage of the *if . . . then* idea is its specificity. A trait like "dominance," for example, provides only general guidance for predicting what a dominant person might do. Reconceptualizing it in *if . . . then* terms might allow the specific prediction that *if* a person joins a business meeting, *then* she will quickly take charge. The *if . . . then* idea is also more sensitive to the way people change their behavior across situations. Perhaps the same person who dominates a meeting has a very different style with her family. A trait notion of dominance, in contrast, assumes that a person who is more dominant than most people in one situation is likely to be relatively dominant in other situations, as well. Research shows this to be generally true (see Chapter 4), but the *if . . . then* description is about the exceptions, and focuses more specifically on just which situations would be more and less likely to elicit dominant behavior.

Mischel's *if . . . then* contingencies offer a potential for the integration of personality psychology, but also present an irony. The potential is to integrate trait conceptions of personality with social-learning and cognitive conceptions by redescribing traits, more specifically than previously, as *if . . . then* patterns.

For example, *if* a friendly person meets a stranger, *then* he will probably engage him or her in conversation. *If* a shy person is in a social gathering, *then* he or she will probably be sensitive for any sign of rejection. And so on. For all their demonstrated usefulness, personality traits have tended to be broader and sometimes vaguer than they should be, to be the most useful way to think about behavior. If they can be integrated with the *if . . . then* idea, the possibility exists to make both concepts richer and more useful.

The irony is that Mischel's latest ideas represent something of a pullback from the richly cognitive position of his prior theorizing, and in fact appear to circle back close to the almost-forgotten, ancestral roots of the cognitive paradigm. Recall that the history of the cognitive approach to personality extends to classic behaviorism, such as that of John Watson (Chapter 15), which assumed that personality was a matter of stimulus and response. For every person (or "organism"), his or her pattern of S-R connections would be a function of his or her idiosyncratic learning history, and hence unique. In addition the fact that an individual had learned one S-R connection, leading her to be dominant in meetings, say, would have nothing necessarily to do with any other S-R connections she might have learned, such as whether she is dominant with her family. And here we are almost 80 years later, with personality being described as an idiosyncratic repertoire of learned *if . . . then* responses that have no necessary connection to each other, either. *If . . . then*; stimulus-response. Walter Mischel, meet John Watson.

Conclusion

In current research, many psychologists are pursuing the connections between personality and cognitive psychology. The cognitive approach to personality is based on the serial and parallel models of information processing considered in this chapter, and on other, related ideas such as attention, priming, and the role of the self-concept in memory. The next chapter will consider several specific programs of research in personality that address the implications of perception and the self, and how the cognitive system is organized and motivated.

Summary

An important, relatively new area of research draws connections between personality functioning and the processes of perception and memory long studied by cognitive psychology. This new research derives from social learning theory (which itself derived from behaviorism) and also is influenced by phenomenological theorists such as George Kelly. The *serial* view of the cognitive system views mental functioning as consisting of the flow of information through a sensory buffer into short-term memory, working memory, and in some cases, permanent, long-term memory. The concept of the sensory buffer implies that personality might affect what information is perceived, through processes of perceptual defense as well as vigilance. The concept of short-term memory implies a limit to phenomenological consciousness. The distinction between declarative and procedural memory in long-term memory implies that we might sometimes know something—such as what it means to feel an emotion—without being able to describe it. Important aspects of behavioral patterns and self-views may also reside in procedural memory, and affect what we do without us necessarily being consciously aware of their influence. The *parallel* view of the cognitive system views it as made up of many different systems operating simultaneously. This view is compatible with the psychoanalytic idea of thought and behavior as representing a compromise among competing mental subsystems, as well as with Walter Mischel's modern cognitive-affective personality system (CAPS) theory of personality. Mischel's theory identifies five cognitive person variables that are important for understanding personality and behavior, while reconceptualizing personality in terms of individual repertoires of *if . . . then* behavioral contingencies that are reminiscent of the old idea of stimulus and response.

COGNITIVE PROCESSES
AND PERSONALITY

Our thoughts influence our actions—and our personalities—in three ways. First, there is the way we perceive and interpret the world in which we live. If we perceive the people around us as hostile, and believe that they are plotting to do us in, we may become fearful and hostile ourselves. On the other hand, if we perceive other people as friendly and trustworthy, our interactions with them will tend to be pleasant and productive. Second, there is the way we regard ourselves. For example, if we think that our academic abilities are something that we can improve, we may react to a failure on an exam by studying harder next time. But if we believe that intellectual growth is impossible, our response to failure may be simply to give up. Third, there is the way we set goals and plan to achieve them. For some people, doing well in school is important; for others, their social life comes first. And even among those for whom school is a top priority, different people may use different strategies. Some motivate themselves by anticipating the thrills of victory, others by conjuring the possible agonies of defeat.

In the previous chapter we saw that the cognitive system, described in terms of either a serial or a parallel model, has important implications for personality. This chapter surveys some research that has examined specific cognitive processes that are the basis of how we perceive and respond to the world, how we perceive ourselves, and how we choose and pursue the goals that are most important to us. In other words, it will consider *perceptual processes, self processes,* and *motivational and strategic processes.* All of this research is part of the cognitive approach to personality, which has a lineage that reaches back both to phenomenology (see Chapter 13) and behaviorism (Chapter 15). The final section of this chapter will summarize a different cognitive approach to personality, called *cognitive-experiential self-theory,* which has roots in psychoanalysis and the writings of Sigmund Freud.

Perceptual Processes

Different people are predisposed to perceive the world in different ways. As a result, they behave differently even in the same situation. As the classic trait psychologist Gordon Allport wrote many years ago:

> For some the world is a hostile place where men are evil and dangerous; for others it is a stage for fun and frolic. It may appear as a place to do one's duty grimly; or a pasture for cultivating friendship and love. (Allport, 1961, p. 266)

Priming and Chronic Accessibility

These differences in perception are explained from a cognitive perspective by the mechanism of **priming**, which was mentioned in Chapter 16. From the perspective of the serial model of cognition, primed information is kept at the ready within working memory or the more accessible regions of long-term memory, making it more likely to come to mind and therefore influential. From the perspective of the parallel model, primed information has more numerous connections with other ideas in the cognitive system (more of those double-headed arrows such as in Figure 16.2), and the connections are quicker and smoother. Priming helps explain why shy people are so quick to perceive a social slight and why people watching repeated TV reports of shark attacks are afraid to go swimming in their local lake.

Besides TV programs, what causes a concept to be primed? It is possible that some patterns of priming are built in genetically, for evolutionary reasons (see Chapter 9). For example, we may be preprogrammed to have the concept of "gender" primed; most people are quick to perceive whether other people are male or female and to think about many concepts in terms of their masculinity and femininity.[1] Anthropologists have also speculated that we might be genetically primed to fear snakes (e.g., Öhman & Mineka, 2003), and may even have a built-in tendency, inherited from our ape ancestors, to be especially afraid of falling out of trees!

Other patterns of priming may stem from inborn patterns of individual temperament (see Chapter 9). For example, a person with a temperamental tendency to experience positive emotions may, as part of that pattern, have happy thoughts easily accessible to consciousness, while more disturbing

---

[1]Many languages, including French and Spanish (but not English), denote nearly every noun as either masculine or feminine.

possibilities are buried more deeply. This is someone who is quick to see the good in anyone and anything, and is inclined to be optimistic about the future (Carver & Scheier, 1995). In the same way, a person with a temperamental tendency to experience negative emotions may be equally quick to see other people's less desirable traits and have a more negative view of the future. The first person might say of a new acquaintance, "Well, he's friendly." The second person might reply, "I thought he seemed like a fake." The interesting and important fact is that both perceptions may be equally correct. But different temperaments, and different associated patterns of priming, cause these people to see and interpret the same reality in different ways. Their differing perceptions may have compensating patterns of advantage and disadvantage. The first person may have more friends. The second person is probably harder to fool. Is the glass half-full or half-empty? Really, it's both.

Despite these possibilities for patterns of priming being rooted in evolutionary history or biologically determined temperament, most cognitive theorists operate on the assumption that priming comes about as a result of experience. The effect of experience on priming can be demonstrated experimentally. In one study, participants were asked to read different colored words while holding in memory either the word *stubborn* or the word *persistent* (Higgins, 1999). This procedure was assumed to prime the concept of stubbornness or persistence, respectively, in the participants' minds. Then, the participants completed a seemingly unrelated comprehension task, which included reading passages such as the following:

> Once Donald made up his mind to do something, it was as good as done no matter how long it might take or how difficult the going might be. Only

"Waiter! My glass is half empty."

rarely did he change his mind, even when it might well have been better if he had. (Higgins, 1999, p. 70)

After reading this passage, participants were asked to categorize Donald's behavior—is it "stubborn" or "persistent"? Those who had earlier been primed with the word *stubborn* were more likely to find Donald stubborn, though they did not realize why (Higgins, Rholes, & Jones, 1977). This basic phenomenon has been replicated many times. When it is possible to characterize someone you meet by more than one term, the one you actually use will tend to be whatever has been primed recently (Bargh et al., 1986; Smith & Branscombe, 1987; Srull & Wyer, 1980).

In daily life, and throughout every child's development, some ideas are primed over and over again. For example, if a child's parents strongly value certain attributes of people, the child is likely to grow up hearing these attributes referred to frequently. Every day, or more often, one child might hear someone being described as "honest." Another child, whose parents hold different values, might frequently hear admired people being described as "fearless." Over time, the result will be that different constructs will become chronically accessible to these two children (Bargh, Lombardi, & Higgins, 1988). The first child will grow up to be someone who is alert to any signs of honesty (or the lack thereof) in someone he or she meets; the second will be quicker to make judgments about fearlessness.

The related concepts of priming and **chronic accessibility**, therefore, are important for personality. In the short run, whatever is primed becomes likely to come to mind, given the slightest hint of a relevant stimulus. If one has had a bad scare recently, the next situation one enters may not have to be very dangerous to trigger a fearful response. But if one has recently received a piece of extremely good news, then everyone seems like a nice person, the weather feels perfect, and the world is beautiful. In the long run, different people have a readiness for different concepts to be primed. A person with a positive temperament is built, perhaps at a level of brain architecture and hormonal response, to have positive ideas more readily primed, and the reverse is true for someone with a negative temperament. As a result, different ideas will be chronically accessible, leading to different worldviews and behavior.

Rejection Sensitivity

According to one analysis, chronic accessibility can lead to the personality disposition of "rejection sensitivity" (Downey & Feldman, 1996; Downey et al., 1997). When a person afflicted with this syndrome discusses a relationship problem with a romantic partner, anxious expectations stimulate him or her to scan for suggestions that he or she is about to be rejected. Any indications that are ambiguous will tend to be interpreted as confirming that his or her partner is about to walk out.

You can imagine the result. The slightest expression of irritation or disinterest by the romantic partner leads this person to jump to the conclusion that he or she is being rejected, leading him or her to respond in an anxious or even hostile manner. Of course, the partner then does reject the person (wouldn't you?). In this way, the attribute of rejection sensitivity can itself produce the outcome that the person fears the most.[2] Rejection sensitivity and other forms of chronic accessibility become important when relevant stimuli are present, not otherwise. For example, rejection sensitivity is triggered by any indication—even an ambiguous one—that rejection may be imminent. But in the absence of such indications—perhaps, early in a relationship, when everybody is still being nice all the time—the very same person may be exceptionally caring and supportive. Depending on the circumstances, then, the same person might be "hurtful and kind, caring and uncaring, abusive and gentle" (Mischel, 1999, p. 51).

This observation raises a question: Which person is the "real" one—the kind, caring, and gentle one the partner sees at the beginning of the relationship, or the hurtful, uncaring, and abusive one who appears only later? According to Walter Mischel's CAPS (cognitive-affective personality system) approach, which was summarized in Chapter 16, both are real because behavior patterns stem from the same underlying system, and though they might seem inconsistent, in fact they are meaningfully coherent. As we saw in Chapter 7, a similar line of reasoning was applied many years ago to the construct of "authoritarianism," an attribute that leads a person to be respectful of those higher in the status hierarchy but contemptuous of anyone lower. In the case of rejection sensitivity, authoritarianism, and probably many more attributes of personality, patterns of behavior that seem contradictory may prove, under close analysis, to be manifestations of a single underlying pattern that gives meaning to the whole.

Aggression

Hostility is another behavior pattern related to chronic accessibility (Zelli, Cervone, & Huesmann, 1996). The accessibility of ideas related to hostility can cause hostile people to perceive an ambiguous situation as threatening (Dodge,

---

[2]Notice how this pattern resembles the behavior of the anxious-ambivalent person described in the discussion of attachment theory in Chapter 12. It is possible that the same mechanism of chronic accessibility underlies the readiness of the anxious-ambivalent person to anticipate rejection (see also Zhang & Hazan, 2002).

1993). In one study, aggressive and nonaggressive boys were told the same story about a disagreement between two children. The aggressive boys believed that the children in the story had hostile intentions, while the nonaggressive boys came to a different and more benign interpretation (Dodge & Frame, 1982).

Other research suggests that the memory system of aggressive people may be organized around hostile themes. In one pair of studies, college students were asked to memorize a set of sentences that might have referred to a hostile situation but were basically ambiguous (e.g., "The policeman pushes Dave out of the way"). Those students who were generally hostile—they had reported frequent occasions in which they had punched, kicked, or threatened others—found these ambiguous sentences easier to remember if they were recalled in the presence of "hostility recall cues" (e.g., hostile words, pictures of weapons). Nonhostile students, however, did not find these cues helpful in recalling the sentences. These findings were interpreted as meaning that hostile people tend to remember things in hostile terms, while nonhostile people use other concepts to organize their memory systems (Zelli, Huesmann, & Cervone, 1995; Zelli, Cervone, & Huesmann, 1996).

The result of a cognitive system organized around a theme of hostility is that the theme may come to guide both a person's perceptions and actions. For example, aggressive children in a stressful situation tend to respond in ways that make the situation worse, such as taking a small problem and escalating it. But, if you give them time to think before they act, they can respond much more constructively (Rabiner, Lenhart, & Lochman, 1990).

There is a message of hope in this last result. It implies that even if certain ideas come quickly to mind in a way that causes problems, it still might be possible to avoid responding to situations in life in a preprogrammed manner. Someone with rejection sensitivity or excessive hostility has a chance to over-ride his or her habitual response, if he or she can just remember to slow down and think.

Self Processes

Perhaps the most important of all the concepts that are chronically accessible in your mind are those that pertain to your self. Your "self," from a cognitive perspective, is the assembly of all of the declarative and procedural information (see Chapter 16) that makes up your knowledge of who you are.

Assessing the Self Schema

A good deal of cognitive research in personality has focused on what is often called the **self schema** (e.g., Markus, 1977), which was mentioned in Chapter 16. The self schema is a cognitive structure that is made up of ideas about the self, organized into a coherent system. The self schema can be identified using S data, B data, or both (see Chapter 2). For example, one of the original studies identified college students who were "schematic" for (had self schemas pertaining to) the traits of dependence and sociability by simply asking them to describe themselves on rating scales (Markus, 1977). If these S data indicated that a student saw herself as extremely sociable and that she saw her sociability as important, she was deemed schematic. Otherwise, she was deemed "aschematic." A later study employed the widely used California Psychological Inventory (CPI) (Gough, 1968) to gather self-ratings on the traits of responsibility and sociability (Fuhrman & Funder, 1995). When these S data indicated an exceptionally high score on responsibility, the participant was deemed schematic on that trait.

Both of these studies also gathered B data. In this case, the B data were reaction times. Participants read words such as *friendly* or *responsible* on a computer screen, and then responded by pressing keys labeled "me" or "not me" as quickly as they could. Schematics responded to relevant traits more quickly than did aschematics, whether they were identified using Markus's rating scales *or* the CPI (Markus, 1977; Fuhrman & Funder, 1995).

This research has two important implications. A methodological implication is that the phenomena studied by cognitive personality psychologists, of the sort discussed in this and the previous chapter, and those studied by trait psychologists, of the sort discussed in Chapters 4 through 7, may not be as different as is sometimes presumed. (This implication is discussed further near the end of this chapter.) Having a self schema *or* attaining a high score on a conventional personality inventory such as the CPI seems to have the same implications for response time and other indications of cognitive processing—and they may amount to much the same thing.

A second implication is that one's self-view—conceptualized as a schema or a trait, take your pick—may have important consequences for how one processes information. As the cognitive personality psychologist Nancy Cantor (1990) pointed out, being schematic for a personality trait—such as sociability, or responsibility, or shyness—amounts to being an "expert" about that trait. Research elsewhere in cognitive psychology has shown that experts in any domain—chess or mechanical engineering, for example—can easily remember relevant information in their domain of expertise, tend to see the world in terms dictated by their expertise, and have a ready and almost automatic plan of action that can be invoked in relevant situations (Chase & Simon, 1973; Larkin et al., 1980). This kind of expertise can have some obvious advantages—it can help a person to be a better chess player or engineer—but also can cause that person to limit his or her view of the world, to view things too rigidly, and to fail to test possibilities beyond the limits of his or her expertise. In the same way, your expertise about yourself can cause you to remember a lot of information about yourself and to process this information quickly, but it also may cause you to fail to see beyond the boundaries of what you think you know to be true about yourself.

The knowledge embodied in the self schema, is semantic (again, see Chapter 16) in the sense that it is based on past experience but not on any *particular* past experience. For example, perhaps you have behaved in a kind fashion on many occasions in life, and as a result have developed a view of yourself as a kind person. What would happen if somehow you forgot about all of the occasions on which you were kind, if they were literally erased from your memory? Would your self-view change?

This might seem like an unanswerable question, but in fact a recent case study (Klein, Loftus, & Kihlstrom, 1996) addressed it. A college student sustained a head injury that caused her temporarily to lose all memory of everything she had done during the past year. Yet she was able to describe her own personality perfectly, in a way that agreed with the perceptions of her parents and boyfriend. She could even describe herself in ways that reflected how she had changed during the past year (which happened to be her first year of college), even though, to repeat, she could remember nothing in particular that had happened during the year.[3] This case suggests that the answer to the question asked at the end of the preceding paragraph is no. Once formed, your knowledge of what you are like exists independently of and does not depend on your memory for specific things you have done. Your "self," in that sense, has a life of its own.

Conscious and Nonconscious Self-Conciousness

Another sense in which the self has a life of its own is that its influence on behavior may not always be visible to conscious awareness.

The traditional and usual view of "self-consciousness" is that it amounts to being aware of who one is and what one is doing. A "self-conscious" person in a social interaction might spend so much of his or her cognitive resources worrying about the impression he or she is making that very little is left for actually holding a conversation with anyone, as we saw in Chapter 16. In a more positive light, it has also been suggested (and experimentally demonstrated) that people who are "self-conscious" in the sense that they know who they are, are more self-directed in their behavior (Carver, 1975). That is, their behavior is more likely to be a function of their general attitudes and values rather than the situational pressures of the moment.

Other recent research has shown that self-consciousness may operate on both a conscious and an unconscious level. For example, on a conscious level,

---

[3]This case has a happy ending. Three weeks after the accident, the student recovered all of her memory except for that from a brief period after her fall.

a person might be able to say "I am shy" or "I am not shy," with some degree of validity. On a less conscious or even a nonconscious level, a shy person might tend automatically to associate various ideas differently than a non-shy person would—a form of implicit knowledge of one's own shyness. These two kinds of self-knowledge are not quite the same thing, as was demonstrated in a recent study (Asendorpf, Banse, & Muecke, 2002). The study assessed shyness using conventional self-reports along with the Implicit Associations Test (IAT), described in Chapter 16. The first measure assessed the degree to which subjects explicitly, consciously knew and said they were shy. The second measure was designed to assess the degree to which they implicitly knew they were shy, on some level, not necessarily consciously. The two measures correlated somewhat with each other, but predicted behavior differently. The S-data measure of shyness predicted what the authors called "controlled" behavior such as speech and gestures, while the IAT measure better predicted "spontaneous expressions of shyness" such as facial expressions, body movements, and tense body posture (Asendorpf et al., 2002, p. 386). The conclusion was that some self-relevant behavior is under conscious control and some is not. To predict the first kind of behavior, S-data measures are sufficient, but to predict the second kind, B data seem to be necessary.

Another way in which self-consciousness might not be completely conscious is that some people may automatically tend to process information as if it is relevant to their selves, even if it really is not. This possibility was demonstrated in a remarkable recent study that you may recall from Chapter 2 (Hull et al., 2002). First, college-age subjects were measured as to their degree of self-consciousness using the Private Self-Consciousness Scale (Fenigstein, Scheier, & Buss, 1975). Then, they were asked to unscramble sentences that, in the critical condition, included words relevant to stereotypes of the elderly. These words included *gray, wise, bingo, forgetful, lonely, retired, wrinkle*, and (my favorite) *Florida*. After this, the subjects were dismissed and then "covertly timed" as they walked down the laboratory hallway (Hull et al., 2002, p. 408). It turns out that after this manipulation, the highly self-conscious subjects walked away more slowly—it took them about 2.2 seconds longer to walk a distance of 15.9 meters—whereas, the elderly words had no effect on the walking speed of people low on self-consciousness. The investigators noted that in actual fact, the sentence task and the words in it had no relevance to the subjects' selves—but that highly self-conscious individuals apparently processed them as if they did, with the result that they subsequently walked more slowly. The less self-conscious subjects, by contrast, did not process the words as being self-relevant and so the words had no effect on their behavior. The moral of this story is that highly self-conscious people may tend to respond to *everything* as if it is personally relevant and the effect of this response on their behavior may not even be conscious.

Self-Efficacy and Self-Discrepancy

Because the (conscious) self schema contains our ideas about what we are like and what we are capable of doing (Markus & Nurius, 1986), it affects what we do. If we think we are sociable, we are more likely to seek out the company of others. If we think we are academically capable, we are more likely to go to college. Recall what was said in Chapter 15 about self-efficacy. Our opinions about our capabilities will set the limits to what we are willing to attempt.

Some research indicates that your self schema can affect not only your behavior, but your emotions as well. According to *self-discrepancy theory,* you have not one but three kinds of self-relevant schemas, and their interaction determines how you feel about life (Higgins et al., 1986; Higgins et al., 1994). One kind of self schema is the *actual* self, what you think you are really like. Another kind of self schema is the *ideal* self, which is your view of what you could be at your very best. A third kind of self schema is your *ought* self, which is your view of what you should—as opposed to what you would like—to be. Although they both represent hypothetical ideals, the ideal and ought selves are often different. For example, your ideal self might include an image of yourself as so good-looking that other people have to pause and stare as you walk by. Your ought self might include an image of yourself as somebody who never, ever tells a lie.

Both of these nonactual selves are probably unrealistic. Let's face facts: you are probably neither that good-looking nor that honest. But the discrepancies between these potential selves and the actual self have different consequences, according to the theory. To the extent that you fail to attain your ideal self, you become depressed. To the extent that you fail to attain your ought self, you become anxious.[4]

Why is there this difference? According to the theorist Tory Higgins (1997), the two nonactual selves represent different foci to life. One is reward based and resembles the "go" system hypothesized by Jeffrey Gray (see Chapter 8). To some extent, you live your life in pursuit of pleasures and rewards. The ideal self is the representation of that goal state based on that focus— the state where all of the rewards you could get are finally attained. The other focus is punishment based and resembles Gray's "stop" system. Here the emphasis is on trying to avoid punishments and other bad outcomes. The ought self is the representation of the goal state based on that focus—that state where no punishments or other bad events will occur.

Of course, everybody has both kinds of goals, just as everybody in Gray's theory has a stop system and a go system. And nobody has achieved either final state of perfection described by the ideal or the ought self. But Higgins's

---

[4]The neo-Freudian theorist Karen Horney (see Chapter 12) also wrote extensively about the neurotic consequences of trying to live up to an unrealistic "ideal" self-image (see, e.g., Horney, 1950).

point is that the balance is different in different individuals. If you live your life primarily in pursuit of reward—the ideal self—to the extent you fail to attain your ideal, you will tend to become depressed. If you live your life primarily in avoidance of punishment—the ought self—to the extent you fail to attain your ideal, you will tend to become anxious. The root of depression is disappointment. The root of anxiety is fear.

Self-Change

Once the self schema is formed and spreads out its wide network of influence on thought and behavior, can it ever be changed? Perhaps. In the 1920s, the French pharmacist Emile Coué promoted the idea of what he called "autosuggestion" so successfully that many Americans and Europeans were looking in the mirror every morning and saying "Every day, every way, I am getting better and better" (Coué, 1922/1997). People swore it helped. A more specific possibility is to use one's imagination to conjure up "possible selves," to visualize the other, perhaps better persons one could be (Markus & Nurius, 1986). The possible self can then serve as a goal that directs behavior. Visualize yourself as a more effective and confident person, or just as someone who eats sensibly and gets some exercise every day. Then seek to live up to this new self-image.

A less-pleasant way to change is to experience a serious and upsetting trauma, such as a serious illness or a rape (Janoff-Bulman, 1989). This kind of experience can cause a person to doubt things about the world that were previously taken for granted and can lead to drastic changes in one's self-view. A view of oneself as safe and invulnerable can change in a moment, and a formerly confident person can become fearful and insecure. Self-change is not always positive.

How Many Selves?

According to some theorists, you have not one self schema but many. For example, one theory states that you have many different views of yourself, and that the particular subset of selves that is active in working memory at any given moment depends on where you are and whom you are with (Markus & Kunda, 1986). In this way, your very experience of yourself may shift from moment to moment. You might feel like a student, then like a parent, then like someone who loves ice cream, and then like a hard worker, as the situation and the people in it continue to change all day long.

This continuously changing view of the self is called the *working self-concept* (Markus & Kunda, 1986). A particularly important influence on the current self-concept is the person you are currently with (Ogilvie & Ashmore, 1991; Andersen & Chen, 2002). As was mentioned in Chapter 16, you

MANKOFF

"Look, I can't promise I'll change, but I can promise I'll pretend to change."

may have a different image of yourself—and act differently—when you are with your parents than when you are with your boyfriend or girlfriend. You may also find that with some people you become tense and irritable, and find yourself turning into someone you do not even particularly like. With other people, you find yourself becoming relaxed and charming, and turning into someone you wish you could be all the time. (You should try to spend as much time as possible with this second kind of person.)

On a theoretical level, the claim here is that you are characterized by not one self, but by many selves. As you move into different situations with different people, different selves come into play. This view seems reasonable, but it has its problems, and in fact has been sharply criticized by one of the most important of the cognitive social-learning personality theorists. Albert Bandura argues that psychologists should reject "the fractionation of human agency into multiple selves" for two reasons (1999, p. 194). First, he notes, "a theory of personality cast in terms of multiple selves plunges one into deep philosophical waters." It seems to require a further self that decides which self is appropriate for a given situation, and perhaps another self beyond that to decide which self should decide which self is currently relevant. Another difficulty with the idea of multiple selves is that it raises a perhaps unanswerable question:

> Once one starts fractionating the self, where does one stop? For example, an athletic self can be split into an envisioned tennis self and a golfing self. These separable selves would, in turn, have their subselves. Thus, a golfing self can be subdivided into different facets of the athletic ability to include a driving self, a fairway self, a sand-trapped self, and a putting self. How does one decide where to stop fractionating selves? (Bandura, 1999, p. 194)

Bandura's point is that there is no way to decide. Although we may to some degree seem like different people in different situations or with different others, each of us is, in the end, one person. It is both more parsimonious and philosophically coherent, he believes, to assume that there is one self that interprets experience and decides what to do next.

Motivational and Strategic Processes

The quote by Bandura in the previous section makes the important point that beyond all the processes of perception, information processing, self-comparison, and specific reactions to specific stimuli, there must be a single, overall organization that makes the mind work as a coherent whole. Several investigators have developed theories to describe processes that serve to organize diverse cognitive activities and to maintain coherent patterns of behavior that hold up across time and situations. In current research, two kinds of organizational processes are proposed. The first, **goals**, represent the motivation for what we do. From the cognitive perspective, a goal is a desired end-state that serves to direct perception, thought, and behavior. The second kind of organizational processes, **strategies,** are the methods we use to try to achieve our goals.

Goals

What do you want? The answer to this question reveals your goals, some of which are short term (e.g., find something for lunch) and others of which are long term (e.g., attain a successful career). Much of what you do, and maybe all of what you do, is in the service of some kind of goal. Therefore, the concept of the goal offers the potential to organize much of what has been learned about cognitive processes and behavior. Or, in other words, if you want to understand someone, one of the most useful, all-encompassing ways to do this is to try to understand what he or she wants from life.

A goal can take many different forms. It might be a specific project: I want to finish this paper by Thursday; I want to mow the lawn. Or, it can be more general: I want to be a better person, I want to help the environment; I want to contribute to world peace.

MOTIVATION

The topic of goals is closely related to the topic of motivation. The goal is the end-state; the drive to attain this end-state is the motivation. This is the way in which goals drive behavior. They influence what you attend to, think about, and do (Grant & Dweck, 1999). If you are hungry (and thereby have the goal of food and the motivation of hunger), you will be primed to attend very closely to the slightest whiff of cooking, think about where there might be food, and seek groceries. If you desire a successful career, you will be alert for opportunities to advance, think about how to get ahead, and work hard. (These effects of motivation on perception and thought sometimes can be detected using projective tests, as discussed in Chapter 5.) By the same token, if a person is not alert to opportunities, does not think about how to get ahead, and does not work hard, you might well come to doubt how much he or she really wants to be successful.

The clinical psychologist David Shapiro (1965) once had a patient who continually talked of her desire to move to another city and start a new life. She was convinced that was what she needed, she said, and that was what she was going to do. After a few months of this, Shapiro finally asked, Have you checked the prices of apartments in the new city? Have you called movers? Have you looked at want ads? The answer was no in each case, and Shapiro mildly observed that maybe she didn't think moving was such a good idea after all. Self-contradictions like this are surprisingly common. Many people express desires to get better grades, be promoted, improve their social life, or even leave their spouses, and yet never do the first actual thing toward making these events happen. If you want to know what people want, Shapiro implies, pay no attention to what they say. Watch what they do.

The topic of motivation and goals is one of the oldest in psychology. Most of the early theories proposed that people are characterized by

GIFTS FROM THE
HOUSE OF LOW GOALS

overriding, general motivations. Freud's theory of psychoanalysis (see Chapter 10), for example, is based on sexual motives and, in later versions, aggressive motives as well. Humanistic theorists such as Rogers and Maslow (see Chapter 13) proposed that the goal of "self-actualization" is the driving force in human thought and behavior. Even behaviorism (see Chapter 15) assumes that "organisms" want something, and that it is when they get something they want that their behavior becomes "reinforced."

TYPES OF GOALS

Not all goals are the same. Some are general and all-encompassing; others are more specific and limited in scope. Some goals are *idiographic* or unique to particular individuals; other goals are *nomothetic* or common, in some degree, to almost everyone.

General and Specific Goals Goals can be arranged hierarchically. You might have the goal of impressing your neighbors. Toward that goal, you want a beautiful yard. Toward that goal, you mow your lawn today. Or, perhaps you want to be financially secure. Toward that goal, you must get a good job. Toward that goal, you must graduate from college. Toward that goal, you must pass this course. Toward that goal, you must finish reading this book.

Keeping your eye on a long-term goal can help you to choose wisely and to organize short-term goals. You have probably heard the old story about the two medieval workers who were asked what they were doing. One said, "I'm laying bricks." The other said, "I am building a cathedral." (Of course, they were actually doing the same thing.) The first worker was focused on his specific activity while the second was focused on the ultimate purpose of that activity. When one's goal structures are well organized, life can be lived fairly smoothly and with clear purpose. If you know your general goals, then everything you do on a daily basis can be organized to help reach these goals.

Many people are not so fortunate, however. When a person has few or no general goals, or spends time in activities that do not serve general goals that are important to him or her, then life is chaotic and disorganized, and nothing that really matters seems to get done. Moreover, if you lack general goals or any clear connection between your daily activities and your general goals, your life may seem to lack meaning and your general motivation may suffer. Indeed, you may become depressed.

But the relationship between general and specific goals must not be too one-sided. The potential disadvantage of a general, cathedral-type goal is that you might become too inflexible to accomplish important short-term goals, such as fix the leaky roof on your hut. If your general goal is to promote world peace, you might forget to be kind to your friends. So, it is useful to be able to shift flexibly between long-term and short-term goals (Vallacher & Wegner, 1987).

It is also important to realize that the only way to achieve a long-term goal that might be many years off is to accomplish a series of short-term goals you can achieve every day. President John F. Kennedy liked to tell the story of a German prince who desired more shade next to a lake on his estate. "Plant these trees before the end of the week," he told his groundskeepers. "But prince," they replied, "those trees won't give any shade for 100 years." "In that case," said the prince, "better plant them today."

Idiographic Goals   Some goals are unique or "idiographic" to the individuals who pursue them. Different researchers have conceptualized idiographic goals in somewhat different terms.

Current Concerns   The psychologist Eric Klinger (1987) proposed that daily life is characterized by what he called *current concerns*. A current concern is the ongoing motivation toward a goal that persists in the mind until the goal is either attained or abandoned. Examples include visiting a friend, keeping a dental appointment, losing weight, saving money, and finding a job. At any given moment, a person has many different current concerns, and these concerns constantly change. Some are narrow and some are broad, and a given concern may last from a few seconds to a lifetime.

Not all current concerns are conscious at the same time, and some of them seldom become conscious. According to one study, the more a current concern is valued, committed to, and under threat, the more frequently a person will think about it (Klinger, Barta, & Maxeiner, 1981). Moreover, if words that are related to a person's current concerns are quickly presented on a computer screen, his or her thought processes become momentarily disrupted (Young, 1988). These findings suggest that current concerns are represented in working memory and quickly move into short-term memory or consciousness if something arises to remind the person of them.

Personal Projects   Another kind of idiographic goal is the psychologist Brian Little's idea of the *personal project* (Little, 1989). Where a current concern is something you think about, a personal project is something you do. It is made up of the efforts that people put into projects like "going to the prom with Brad," "finding a part-time job," "shopping for the holidays" or, as you may recall from Chapter 14, "working on my quilt" (Little, 1983). This idea is similar to *life tasks*, conceptualized by Nancy Cantor and her colleagues as the important goals people pursue at particular times of their life. For example, a college student who has recently moved away from home for the first time might be pursuing the life task of attaining independence (Cantor &

Kihlstrom, 1987). Later in life, this task will cease to be so important, and others will rise to the fore.

Personal Strivings   A somewhat broader kind of idiographic goal is Robert Emmons's (1996) idea of *personal strivings*, which are long-term goals that can organize broad areas of a person's life. For example, a person may be "trying to appear attractive to the opposite sex," "trying to be a good listener to his or her friends," or "trying to be better than others."

The personal strivings that a person reports can provide useful insights into what he or she is like. One of Emmons's research participants, who called herself "Crocodile Dundee,"[5] said that her personal strivings included "always appear cool," "always amuse others," "always keep physically fit," and "dress fashionably" (Emmons, 1989, p. 38). Another participant, who called herself "0372," expressed the personal strivings to "please others," "tell the truth," and "be productive in work." It turned out that Crocodile Dundee scored high on a test of the personality trait of "narcissism," which measures the tendency to be self-centered and exploitative of others (see Chapter 6). The person called 0372, as her relatively modest nickname perhaps suggests, scored low on this dimension.

Strivings are important in other ways as well. It is not uncommon for people to report two or more strivings that are inconsistent with each other. I mentioned in Chapter 7 that the goal to "get ahead" (of others) and the goal to "get along" (with others) are often in conflict. If you strive to rise to the top, it is difficult to have everyone—such as the people you defeat—continue to like you. On the other hand, if you put all of your efforts into making other people like you, you are unlikely to get ahead. One study found that people whose strivings are in conflict tend to experience more psychological distress and even more physical illness than those whose strivings are mutually compatible (Emmons & King, 1988).

Properties and Limitations of Idiographic Goals   All of these concepts—current concerns, personal projects, life tasks, and personal strivings—have several elements in common. They are conscious at least some of the time. Indeed, typically they are measured by asking participants to list their concerns, projects, tasks, or strivings on a sheet of paper. They describe thoughts and behaviors aimed at fairly specific goals. They are changeable over time—an important personal project one day, might be forgotten and irrelevant a few weeks later. Finally, an individual's various concerns, projects, tasks, or goals are assumed to be independent of each other. If you have the goal to

---

[5]Emmons asked his participants to give themselves pseudonyms so that they could be anonymously identified for follow-up studies.

be better looking, for example, this fact is not assumed to have implications for the other goals you might also have.

This last-named limitation is important (Grant & Dweck, 1999). Concerns, projects, tasks, or goals (by whatever label) can organize thought and behavior, but they are not themselves theoretically organized. For example, the strivings that characterize a particular person typically are presented in a simple, unordered list (e.g., Emmons, 1989). To some researchers, this seems an unsatisfactory state of affairs. Can the many different goals that people might pursue be organized into a smaller number that can organize our understanding of what people seek in life? The attempt to answer this question leads researchers to seek to formulate nomothetic goals, a relatively small number of essential motivations that are pursued by almost everyone.

Nomothetic Goals   Some investigators have attempted to reduce the almost infinite number of possible idiographic goals to a relatively small number of "nomothetic," or generally applicable goals. The hope is to give order to the domain of goals, much as the Big Five has served to organize thousands of personality traits (see Chapter 7).

The Big Three, or Five, or Two   According to the psychologist David McClelland (1985) and his colleagues, three primary motivations drive human behavior: the need for achievement, the need for affiliation (or intimacy), and the need for power. Research on these motives usually has assessed their presence by themes that emerge in stories people tell in response to the pictures of the Thematic Apperception Test (TAT, see Chapter 5).

Achievement motivation is a recurrent tendency to direct one's thoughts and tendencies toward a striving to attain excellence. People high in this motive set standards for themselves and then work hard to attain them. *Affiliation motivation* is the tendency to direct thoughts and behavior toward the effort to find and maintain close and warm emotional relationships. People high in affiliation motivation seek the close company of others for its own sake, not as a means to any end (McAdams, 1980). *Power motivation* is the tendency to direct thoughts and behavior toward attempts to feel strong and to have an impact on others. People high in power motivation put great efforts into seeking prestige and status, prefer friends who are low in power motivation (whom presumably they can dominate), and are relatively promiscuous in their sexual behavior (Winter & Stewart, 1978).

What proportion of the goals that people follow in life can be organized around these three, achievement, intimacy, and power? At present, only a general answer can be offered: Surely many of our goals fall into one of these categories, but not all of them. For example, according to one research survey, five—not three—categories of goals emerged repeatedly in a number of different studies (Emmons, 1997). The five goals are (1) enjoyment, (2) self-assertion, (3) esteem, (4) interpersonal success, and (5) avoidance of negative affect. You can see for yourself where these five goals do and do not overlap with McClelland's three. According to another analysis, many different goals generated by a group of college students could be boiled down to about two classes, goals related to work (in this case, academic work) and those related to social interaction (e.g., friendships, romantic relationships) (Kaiser & Ozer, 1999). This last finding is particularly interesting because it is reminiscent of Freud's formulation of the complete life (see Chapter 10), which was "to love and to work."

Judgment Goals and Development Goals   The psychologist Carol Dweck and her colleagues claim that two kinds of goals underlie the whole motivational system (see Grant & Dweck, 1999). One kind she calls *judgment goals*. Judgment, in this context, refers to the goal of seeking to judge or validate an attribute in oneself. For example, you might have the goal of convincing yourself that you are smart, beautiful, or popular. The other kind she calls *development goals*. A development goal is the desire to improve oneself, to become smarter, more beautiful, or more popular.

At first glance, these goals might seem highly similar. Don't people want both to see themselves as smart and to be smart, for example? Indeed, Dweck notes that everybody pursues both kinds of goals; "both are natural and important in our everyday lives" (Grant & Dweck, 1999, p. 350). But the balance between them can shift from one person to another, or even within the same person from one situation to the next or across time. And, if you think about it for a moment, it is not difficult to find situations in which the two goals lead to different outcomes.

For example, consider the plight of a teacher trying to correct a student. Have you ever been in this situation? Let's say you are trying to help a high-school student learn algebra. You look at his work, find a mistake, and point it out. You take a piece of paper and patiently begin to explain the right way to solve the problem. You are surprised when the student interrupts you. "This problem is unfair and too hard," he says, "and the whole test is stupid. And what makes you so smart anyway?"

Why is the student responding in such a negative manner? According to Dweck's perspective, he is pursuing a judgment goal instead of a development goal. He is anxious to demonstrate that he is smart and knows what he should. He is so anxious to do this that when he makes a mistake, he belittles the test, the teacher, and perhaps the whole topic ("algebra is stupid"). This attitude has its uses, to be sure. If he can succeed in convincing himself that the test is unfair, the teacher no smarter than he is, and the topic pointless, he will feel better about the fact that he has failed algebra. But he will still have failed algebra, and with that attitude, he will never pass.

Contrast this with the student who listens carefully to what you have to say, who eagerly tries out the new technique you have taught, and immediately asks that his new work be corrected as soon as possible. This student, according to Dweck, is acting in accord with a development goal. He is less interested in proving that he is smart, at this moment, than he is in becoming smarter. So he sets aside any news that he "failed" this particular problem and instead focuses on how to do better next time. This student may have no greater intrinsic mathematical ability than the first student, but his chances of eventually learning algebra are much, much greater.

Let's bring this a little closer to home. Think about the most recent exam in which you scored lower than you had hoped. What was your reaction? Did you argue that the test was unfair, the teaching bad, and the topic pointless? Or did you try to find out what you could do differently to score better next time? Your response may identify the degree to which you are pursuing judgment as opposed to developmental goals, and also may predict how successful you will be in the future.[6]

From the perspective of Dweck's theory, these two goals are important in many areas of life because they produce different reactions to failure, and everybody fails sometimes. A person with a development goal will respond to failure with what Dweck calls "mastery-oriented" behavior, in which he or she tries even harder the next time. The student might get a poor grade on her paper but be eager to take what she has learned from the experience to do a better job on her next paper. In contrast, a person with a judgment goal is vulnerable to respond to failure with what Dweck calls the "helpless" pattern: Rather than try harder in response to failure, this individual simply concludes "I can't do it," and gives up. Of course, this kind of response only guarantees future failure.

Entity and Incremental Theories   Where do these dramatic differences in behavior come from? Dweck believes they originate in fundamentally different implicit theories—personal constructs, if you will (see Chapter 13)—about the nature of the world. Some people hold what Dweck calls **entity theories**, and believe that personal qualities such as intelligence and ability are fixed and unchangeable, leading them to respond helplessly to any indication that they do not have what it takes. Other people hold what Dweck calls **incremental theories**, and believe that intelligence and ability can change over time and with experience. Their goal, therefore, is not to prove their competence but to increase it. One young boy in Dweck's research, following a failure to solve an experimental puzzle, "pulled up his chair, rubbed

---

[6]Sometimes the test really is unfair, the teaching poor, and the topic pointless. Still, you can only expect your situation to improve if you focus, instead, on how to do better next time.

his hands together, smacked his lips, and exclaimed, 'I love a challenge!'" (Dweck & Leggett, 1988, p. 258).

Research and Measurement   Nearly all of the research on Dweck's theory has occurred in academic contexts, or simulations of such contexts. For example, the responses of children to their failure to solve word puzzles have been examined repeatedly. Dweck and her students have consistently found that children who are incremental theorists, as just described, do better in the face of failure than do entity theorists (e.g., Diener & Dweck, 1978; Goetz & Dweck, 1980).

How are these young "theorists" identified? In the time-honored method of trait psychology, identification is accomplished using a self-report questionnaire (S data). For example, subjects have been asked to choose between options such as:

1. Smartness is something you can increase as much as you want to, or
2. You can learn new things, but how smart you are stays pretty much the same.

If you choose the first option, you are an incremental theorist; if you choose the second, you are an entity theorist (Dweck & Leggett, 1988, p. 263). Another method is to give subjects a questionnaire that describes a series of hypothetical social situations, all of which involve rejection. For example, a subject might be asked, "Suppose you move to a new neighborhood. A person you meet does not like you very much. Why would this happen to you?" If the subject responds that the likely reason is that he or she is socially incompetent, then the subject is assumed to be an entity theorist (Goetz & Dweck, 1980).

The goals that children pursue also can be manipulated experimentally. In one study, fourth- and fifth-grade children were asked to participate in a "pen-pal tryout" (Erdley et al., 1997). They wrote letters to a potential pen pal, and were told that the letters would be rated to decide whether each child could join the pen-pal club. Every child was told, at first, that the rater was "not sure whether to have you in the club" and was asked to write another letter. After that, all children were told they could join.

The experimental manipulation came before the children wrote the first letter. Half were told, "We'd like to see how good you are at making friends," which was intended to set up a judgmental goal. The other half were told, "This is a chance to practice and improve how you make friends," to set up a development goal. The second letter (that came after the initial failure) was then rated by independent coders, who found that letters written by children in the first, judgment condition were shorter and of lesser quality than those written by children in the second, development condition. Apparently, the first group of children came to believe they were socially inadequate and might as well give up; the second group saw a chance to improve.

The results of this research led to three conclusions. First, the kind of goal that a person pursues—judgment or development—can have important implications for how he or she responds to failure. (And, again, we all fail sometimes.) A judgment goal can lead to helplessness and withdrawal; a development goal can lead to renewed and improved effort. Second, this effect seems to occur in social as well as in academic (and presumably work-related) realms. If a person fails on an exam, or fails to close a deal at work, or fails to get a prospective date to say yes, he or she has two options. One—if the person pursues a judgment goal—is to decide he or she is inadequate, inept, or unattractive, and simply give up. Another option—if the person pursues a development goal—is to try to learn from the failure and figure out what to do differently next time. The third implication is that which goal he or she pursues can be determined from within, or from without. In most of Dweck's research, people have been assumed to be either entity theorists or incremental theorists, and therefore to characteristically pursue judgment or development goals. But the study by Erdley and colleagues, just described, and other research suggest that sometimes the goal can be determined by the way the task is structured by others. This final point has obvious and important implications for teaching: Teachers should be sure that their students see class as a place to improve, not merely a place to "succeed" or "fail."

Strategies

In the previous chapter I discussed the concept of *scripts*. For example, recall the "McDonald's script." Your knowledge of what happens at McDonald's is not based on any particular visit; it is an abstraction derived from the usual pattern across many visits. Next time you go you will probably follow this script without having to think about it. The "how to get fed at McDonald's" script can be thought of as a strategy. It is a sequence of activities toward a goal, in this case to be fed. However, it is not a very interesting strategy. From the perspective of personality psychology, the more important strategies are the broad ones that pursue important goals in life and that organize a wide range of activities.

We have already seen a couple of examples of such broad strategies. Recall the discussion of *rejection sensitivity,* the maladaptive strategy of automatically responding with fear and hostility to the slightest sign of disinterest from a significant other person. The strategy deploys in a wide variety of situations—all that is needed is the slightest threat of rejection—and with anybody with whom the person has developed an important relationship. In a similar fashion, the authoritarian personality responds to any situation and any person where authority relationships are present with a style of behavior that is obsequious to those of higher rank and contemptuous to those of lower rank.

STRATEGIES AND TRAITS

Many personality traits probably can be explained in a similar manner. For example, the trait theorists Robert McCrae and Paul Costa (1995) developed a theory that describes how the Big Five personality traits, described in Chapter 7, produce what they call "characteristic adaptations," which are essentially generalized scripts. For example, the person high on the trait of "agreeableness" will typically act according to a script that directs him or her to be warm, friendly, approachable, and slow to anger. This conceptualization is similar to Mischel's notion of *if . . . then* patterns, described in Chapter 16. *If* a person is agreeable, for example, *then* he will probably not get angry in response to a mild insult. So far, however, only a few efforts have been made to explain personality traits in terms of characteristic scripts or *if . . . then* patterns, and vice versa. Trait theory and cognitive theory are still like two trains chugging down different tracks. But integrating the two approaches offers an exciting—and almost wide-open—field for future research.

Such integration will be complicated, however. One reason is that different behavioral patterns may be due to the same strategy (as we saw with rejection sensitivity and authoritarianism), while the same behavioral outcomes may sometimes be the product of different strategies as well as goals. For example, one person may work to make friends as part of a strategy to form a network of useful business associates, whereas another person may follow the exact same behaviors as part of a plan to achieve a pleasant social life. Both people might appear "sociable," but this similarity in behavioral style could mask a difference in their goals and underlying strategies.

DEFENSIVE PESSIMISM

At present, only a few generalized strategies have received close attention in research. One of the most interesting of these is the strategic difference between optimists and pessimists. At a general level, the optimistic strategy for life is to always assume that the best will happen. This assumption can produce a positive outlook and motivate goal-seeking behavior that is maintained by the cheerful assumption that if you do your part, all will be well. The pessimistic strategy is the reverse. Assume that the worst is quite likely to happen. This assumption produces a negative outlook on life but also can motivate goal-seeking behavior, driven in this case by a desperate attempt to avoid almost certain doom.

The difference between people who employ these contrasting strategies is examined in an important program of research by the psychologist Julie Norem (Norem, 1989, 2002). One early study focused on the different strategies used by college students in dealing with their academic work. Some college students (the *optimists*) deal with anxiety about exams by expecting to do their best. Others expect the worst, so they can be pleasantly surprised when the worst does not happen (Norem calls these latter individuals *defensive pessimists*). Norem's interesting finding is that both kinds of student seem to succeed about equally well in coping with anxiety and with exam performance (although, admittedly, the optimists seem to enjoy life more). The two strategies represent different routes to a common goal. Indeed, if a researcher only examined the outcome, and not the strategy by which it is attained, the important difference between these two kinds of people would be masked.

Optimistic and pessimistic strategies apply to more than academic life. Several years ago, a friend of mine was waiting anxiously for his wife to have a baby. The pregnancy had been difficult, and the delivery was expected to be complicated. Many people would deal with this situation by hoping for the best, convincing oneself that the mother was a strong person who would do fine, that the doctors can take care of everything, and so on. My friend did just the reverse. An extremely defensive pessimist, he expected nothing but the worst from the very beginning. The night before the baby was born, he cornered the pediatrician and demanded, "What is the worst that could possibly happen?" Understandably, the pediatrician was taken aback, but under continued prodding he finally acknowledged that, well, the worst that could happen would be for the mother to die and for the baby to be born dead. My friend seemed strangely satisfied with this answer.

The next day, all did not go smoothly, but nor did the worst transpire. My friend seemed to maintain his own equilibrium through his constant awareness that things could be worse. And when, in the end, mother and baby came through fine, he seemed to have gotten through the trauma not much worse for the wear. Apparently, his insistence on focusing on the negative was just an exaggerated version of the strategy pursued by Norem's defensive pessimists. He reduced the anxiety that might be produced by bad news by imagining, in advance, the very worst possible news. Then, even as unpleasant news arrived, he could always compare it against this worst-case scenario and feel relieved. I am not sure that this is a wise strategy, but perhaps it does work for some people.

Two important questions arise in connection with these different strategies. The first is, how general are optimistic and pessimistic strategies? Does someone who employs an optimistic strategy in the academic domain also act in an optimistic manner while pursuing his or her social life? According to the available evidence, the answer is yes, sort of. Correlations between the degree to which one uses an optimistic or pessimistic strategy in one context and uses the same strategy in another context range from about .30 to .40 (Norem & Chang, 2001). This means that these styles are generally consistent (see Chapters 3

"What I'll miss most is his indefatigable optimism."

and 4 on interpreting correlations). I can note that the friend whose reaction to his wife's childbirth I described earlier tends to evince gloomy and pessimistic attitudes about all aspects of his life—not just genuine crises like that one. But a consistency correlation in the range of .30 to .40 leaves plenty of room for people to use an optimistic strategy in one domain, and a pessimistic strategy in another. Some people are optimists in their personal relationships, but pessimists in their academic life, for example.

The second question is, which is better, optimism or pessimism? Cultural values in the United States certainly appear to value an optimistic outlook, but pessimism has its virtues too. An optimistic, self-enhancing style may help motivate individual achievement, but interfere with achieving emotional intimacy and interpersonal sensitivity. Pessimism may be a more adaptive approach than optimism in cultures that emphasize these more collectivistic values (Norem, 2002; also, see Chapter 14). Furthermore, too much optimism can be dangerous, and lead to carelessness and needless risk-taking (Norem & Chang, 2002). Finally, the general fact—and it does seem to be a fact—that optimists are generally happier than pessimists should not be taken necessarily to mean that pessimists would be happier if they changed their strategic style. Both optimists and defensive pessimists may have found strategies that work for them, and trying to change them is not necessarily a good idea. Indeed, Norem's research has shown that some people perform worse if they are forced to think optimistically because negative thinking is their way of managing anxiety.

Cognitive-Experiential Self-Theory (CEST)

For the most part, the cognitive approach to personality just summarized stems historically from a mixture of behaviorist ideas and Kelly's humanistic emphasis on conscious experience, phenomenology, and rational thought. A final approach to consider is very different, and stems ultimately from Freud. Seymour Epstein's *cognitive-experiential self-theory* (CEST) seeks to explain unconscious processing and the seemingly irrational, emotion-driven sectors of the mind (Epstein, 2003). According to CEST, people use two major psychological systems—both at the same time—to adapt to the world (Epstein, 1973, 1994). The *rational* system is a relatively recent innovation and includes language, logic, and systematized, factual knowledge. It resembles Freud's conception of secondary process thinking (Chapter 10). The *experiential* system is evolutionarily older, tied closely to emotion, and assumed to be the way that other animals think (and that our distant, pre-human ancestors also thought). It resembles Freud's conception of primary process thinking.

The two systems differ from each other in many ways, some of which are summarized in Table 17.1. The rational system is analytic and breaks a situation into its constituent pieces so it can be carefully analyzed; the experiential system is "holistic" and tends to react to a whole situation all at once. Rational thought is slow and deliberate; experiential thought is fast and sometimes almost instantaneous. Rational thought is effortful. It feels like work. Experiential thought is effortless. Indeed, sometimes it occurs when we don't want it to, such as when we "can't help but think that. . . . "

The rational system includes everything that we are aware of and can talk about. The experiential system, in contrast, operates outside of consciousness and is something we cannot talk about directly—evolutionarily speaking, it is older than language itself. I am sure you can see already how this maps onto the distinction, discussed earlier in this chapter, between declarative and procedural knowledge. Declarative knowledge is conscious and verbalizable; procedural knowledge—knowing how—is the reverse (recall also the discussion of emotion as a kind of procedural knowledge). When Jay Leno asked Hugh Grant to explain his behavior with Divine Brown, this is how he replied:

> I think you know in life what's a good thing to do and what's a bad thing, and I did a bad thing. And there you have it.

In other words, nobody could understand what his motivation was, and he didn't have a clue, either. In Epstein's terms, Grant's rational system—the one that had to decide what to say on television—did not have access to

TABLE 17.1	
Rational System	**Experiential System**
1. Analytic	1. Holistic
2. Resembles Freud's "secondary process thinking"	2. Resembles Freud's "primary process thinking"
3. Logical: driven by what is sensible	3. Affective: driven by what feels good
4. Behavior affected by conscious appraisal of events	4. Behavior driven by "vibes" from past experience
5. Thinks in terms of abstract symbols, words, and numbers	5. Thinks in terms of vivid images, metaphors, and stories
6. Operates at slower speed, designed for deliberate action	6. Operates at very high speed, designed for immediate action
7. Can change rapidly, at speed of logical thought	7. Slow to change, needs repetitive or intense experiences for change
8. Effortful and deliberate (e.g., sitting down to do some serious thinking)	8. Effortless and automatic (e.g., being seized by one's emotions)
9. Requires justification via logic and evidence	9. Self-evidently valid: "experiencing is believing"
10. Knowledge	10. Wisdom

Source: Adapted from Epstein (1994, p. 71).

the workings of the experiential system that set up the consequential encounter with Ms. Brown. (Or, if it did, he wasn't telling.)

The experiential system is likely to dominate when you are under the sway of your emotions, and the rational system will dominate when you are calm. This is why people sometimes give advice such as "Get a grip on yourself. You're too emotional to think straight. Once you calm down, you will see things differently" (Epstein, 1994, p. 710). The two systems may generate different decisions. As was mentioned way back in Chapter 1, it is possible to feel intensely attracted to someone who, you just know, is bad news. It is as if one part of your mind—the emotion-based experiential system—has one opinion, and the other part of your mind—the more logical cognitive system—has another opinion. Which will win? As we all know, the outcome varies. Hugh Grant apparently knew on some level what he was doing was unwise, but he did it anyway.

The experiential system is more than just a source of trouble, however. According to Epstein, it is also the source of intuition, insight, and wisdom. The distinction is a bit like the classic one between the styles of Captain Kirk and Mr. Spock on the original *Star Trek* series. Kirk was dominated by his experiential system. He was emotional, intuitive, and often surprisingly creative. Mr. Spock was obviously much smarter—he had a more developed rational system—but in episode after episode he was shown to be less resourceful than his captain.

How does one gain wisdom? Again, the distinction between declarative and procedural knowledge is relevant. Declarative knowledge—the knowledge of the rational system—can be obtained from books, lectures, and lessons. Procedural knowledge—the knowledge of the experiential system—can only be obtained through experience (e.g., practice and feedback). According to thinkers as far back as Aristotle, while one can gain declarative knowledge at any age, true wisdom comes only later in life:

> While young men become geometricians and mathematicians and wise in matters like these . . . a young man of practical wisdom cannot be found. The cause is that such wisdom is concerned not only with universals but with particulars, which become familiar with experience, but a young man has no experience. (Aristotle, quoted by McKeon, 1947, cited by Epstein, 1994, p. 712)

The preceding quote makes more sense to me with every passing year.

Epstein believes that the rational and experiential systems interact. Recall the cases of Phineas Gage and of Elliott, recounted in Chapter 8. When they lost contact with their emotional experience, their ability to make good judgments fell apart. In Epstein's terms, they may have lost part of their experiential system, or its ability to communicate with the rational system, to the detriment not just of their emotional experience but of their ability to make reasonable decisions.

An interesting experiment by Epstein himself showed how the two systems can work at the same time. The experiment followed up on an earlier study that asked participants to imagine the following scenario: Two people both get stuck in traffic on the way to the airport and arrive at the gate 30 minutes after their planes' scheduled departure. Person A is told, "Sorry, your flight left on time." Person B is told, "Sorry, your flight left 29 minutes late—it's gone now." Who is more upset, A or B? The typical result is that people will report that person B is much more upset, even though both persons, A and B, experienced the same outcome for the same reason. The conclusion drawn was that people are basically irrational (Tversky & Kahneman, 1983).

Epstein's wrinkle on this study was to ask research participants two questions. The first was the same in the original study: how would A and B actually feel? The second question was, how would A and B respond if they were being rational? Everybody agreed that B would be more upset than A, but also everybody seemed to realize that this reaction was irrational—their answer to the second question was that A and B *should* feel the same (Epstein et al., 1992). This result suggests that the human cognitive system is not simply irrational, as the original investigators had assumed; people have two cognitive systems, one of which may respond emotionally while at the same time another system draws the logically appropriate conclusion. It is possible—and perhaps you have had the experience—that one can have a crazy thought and at the same time *know* it is crazy.

The Cognitive Approach and Its Intersections

The cognitive approach to personality was considered here, near the end of the book, for several reasons. The first reason is that the cognitive approach to personality is the newest. It generates much if not most of the empirical research currently being done on personality. A more important reason is that perhaps because it is the most recently developed one, the cognitive approach to personality makes the most reference to all of the other approaches. As we have seen, it intersects at various points with the trait, behaviorist, social learning, and even psychodynamic, phenomenological, cross-cultural, and biological approaches. As a result, it would be difficult to understand the cognitive approach without studying these others first.

Moreover, a consideration of the cognitive approach brings us nearly full circle. Recall that the first basic approach to personality presented in this book was the trait approach, which describes consistent differences between people and patterns of behavior that individuals exhibit across the different situations of their lives. We have seen in this chapter, and the previous one, that cognitive approaches to personality do much the same thing, but at a different level of analysis. Dweck's description of people who pursue judgment versus development goals, Norem's description of optimists and defensive pessimists, and cognitive accounts of rejection sensitivity or aggression, to name just a few, explain ways in which people are different from each other and consistent with themselves from one situation to the next.

Therefore, the trait approach and the cognitive approach would seem like natural candidates for integration. The trait approach has a well-developed technology for assessing individual differences and a vast literature on how these differences are related to each other. The newer, cognitive approach has developed theories of the mental processes that might help to explain the basis of these individual differences, and also help to predict the situations in which these differences will and will not prove to be important.

Sadly, however, some cognitive personality psychologists go out of their way to reject proposals for integration. Their objections seem to be rooted in the behaviorist ancestry of the cognitive approach, which always had an aversion to the idea that people could be described in terms of general patterns of behavior. For example, one cognitive personality psychologist wrote,

> The merger of trait and social-cognitive theories is appealing at first. However
> . . . this merger is generally not accepted by social-cognitive theorists. Indeed,
> a number of contributors [to social-cognitive theory] . . . explicitly reject the
> contention that "trait" approaches . . . provide an adequate foundation for
> understanding social-cognitive processes or for building a personality theory.
> (Cervone & Shoda, 1999, p. 10)

This is not a very hopeful remark, but the writer does not speak for all social-cognitive theorists. Consider the more accommodating stance of one of the most important of them all, Walter Mischel:

> Two goals—to identify and clarify personality dispositions or personality
> processes—have been pursued in two increasingly separated (and warring)
> subdisciplines with different agendas that seem to be in conflict with each
> other. [However] . . . both goals may be pursued in concert with no necessary
> conflict or incompatibility because . . . dispositions and processing dynamics
> are two complementary facets of the same phenomena and of the same uni-
> tary personality system. (Mischel, 1999, pp. 56–57)

In this internecine debate, I agree wholeheartedly with Mischel (Funder, 2001). Both the cognitive approach and the modern trait approach to personality are not only valuable but also more similar than they are different. Both continue to generate a large amount of empirical research that documents the complex nature of individual differences in behavior. Both try to outline the psychological processes that produce those differences. And both try to come to terms with the origin of these differences, in genetics, experience, and culture. So in that way, this book nears its end in a place not so different from where it began.

Summary

Several cognitive processes are important for personality. Perceptual processes, such as priming, affect what we notice in the environment and how we respond to it. Chronically accessible concepts can influence behavioral patterns such as rejection sensitivity and aggressiveness. Self processes guide perception, thought, behavior, and emotion by organizing them around a person's knowledge of who he or she is and what he or she is capable of. People more readily will process information that is relevant to their self-schemas, and some of the effects of self-consciousness can occur out of awareness. Emotional states such as depression and anxiety may depend on how an individual's self schema contrasts with their images of who he or she would like to be or thinks he or she ought to be. Some theorists maintain that people have many different self schemas used in different contexts; others contest this idea. Goals and strategies give coherence to many different cognitive and behavioral phenomena. Goals are desired end-states that motivate thought and behavior. Goals can be arranged hierarchically and can be conceived of in terms of current concerns, personal projects, life tasks, or personal strivings. At a broader level, theorists have proposed that a small number of basic goals are particularly important, such as the goals to love and to work (originally Freud's idea). Dweck's cognitive approach to motivation distinguishes between judgment goals and development goals, which have important consequences for persistence in the face of failure. Strategies are sequences of thought and behavior in the service of goals. Norem describes how optimists and pessimists use distinctively differently strategies for managing anxiety and motivating behavior. Most cognitive research on personality is influenced by a combination of behaviorism and phenomenology, but another approach, called cognitive experiential self-theory, has its roots in the thinking of Freud. The theory posits two psychological systems, called the experiential system and the rational system, which sometimes oppose each other but each of which serves important functions. In the final analysis, the cognitive approach is more similar to than different from the trait approach. Both approaches aim to describe patterns of individual differences in behavior and the psychological processes behind them.

SUGGESTED READINGS: THE PERSON AND THE SITUATION: LEARNING AND COGNITIVE APPROACHES TO PERSONALITY

Bandura, A. (1977). *Social learning theory.* Englewood Cliffs, NJ: Prentice-Hall.
> *This book, along with those listed below by Miller and Dollard and by Rotter, is one of three principle presentations of the three different theories that all go by the same name, "social learning theory." In many ways these theories are the same (in more than just name), but each of them also tackles unique topics and provides some unique insights.*

Epstein, S. (1998). *Constructive thinking: The key to emotional intelligence.* Westport, CT: Praeger.
> *Based on Epstein's cognitive-experiential self-theory (CEST), a summary of the nature of constructive thinking along with advice and exercises to get better at it.*

Gardner, H. (1987). *The mind's new science: A history of the cognitive revolution.* New York: Basic.
> *A lively introduction to the most important ideas and research in modern cognitive psychology. This book includes a good deal of philosophy and history along with summaries of research studies. It may be the only book on cognitive psychology ever written that one could hope to succeed in reading at the beach.*

Miller, N. E., & Dollard, J. (1947). *Social learning and imitation.* New Haven, CT: Yale University Press.

Norem, J. (2001). *The positive power of negative thinking: Using defensive pessimism to manage anxiety and perform at your peak.* New York: Basic.

> *A highly readable introduction to Julie Norem's defense of a pessimistic outlook on life. The book summarizes research in a user-friendly fashion and is full of useful advice.*

Rotter, J. B. (1954). *Social learning and clinical psychology.* Englewood Cliffs, NJ: Prentice-Hall.

Skinner, B. F. (1966). *The behavior of organisms: An experimental analysis.* New York: Appleton-Century-Crofts. (Originally published 1938.)

> *Nearly every college or university library has a copy of this book (either the original or the reprinted edition), and it is worth seeking. It is the original and still the best comprehensive survey of the thinking of this preeminent behaviorist and one of the major intellectual figures of the twentieth century.*

CONCLUSION: LOOKING BACK AND LOOKING AHEAD

Personality is my favorite topic in psychology because it includes most of what makes the subject interesting. It is where all of the other strands of psychology come—or should come—together into a complete account of what people think, how they feel, and what they do. This is the psychological triad I mentioned in Chapter 1, and we saw across the following 16 chapters that research attempting to get at these issues sometimes leads into theories that are deep and complex, and into empirical methodologies that are sophisticated, complicated, and difficult. This complexity and rigor is all well and good, but makes it easy to forget why the research was done in the first place. After one has waded through the deep thicket of a theoretical derivation or a set of research results, and come out on the other side, it is important to remember to ask, "What do I know about people that I didn't know before?"

Psychologists attempting to learn about personality have taken several different approaches, and each of those approaches was the subject of a section of this book. Here at the end I will say little more about why personality has so many different approaches, do some crystal ball-gazing into the future of the field, and conclude by identifying some of the general lessons about personality that I hope you will remember.

The Different Approaches

This book began with the observation that personality is the study of the whole person and everything that is important about his or her psychology. A problem with this goal was identified immediately, however: It is overwhelming. In fact, it is impossible. We cannot really account for everything all at once; we must limit ourselves to a certain perspective and to questions and variables that seem most important. The only alternative to such self-limitation, probably, is hopeless confusion.

For this reason, each basic approach to personality focuses on a limited number of key concerns and pretty much ignores everything else. The trait approach focuses on individual differences, the personality traits that make people psychologically different from one another and every individual unique. The biological approach concentrates on the architecture and function of the nervous system and on the inheritance and evolutionary history of behavioral patterns. The psychoanalytic approach focuses on the unconscious mind and the complicated ways in which motivations and conflicts of which we are not even aware might affect what we think, feel, and do. The humanistic approach focuses on the moment-to-moment conscious experience of being alive, and how the fact that we experience life one moment at a time might give us free will and the ability to choose how we see reality. It also leads to an appreciation of the way cross-cultural differences amount to differing construals of reality. The learning and cognitive approaches focus on how rewards and punishments in the environment shape behavior, and how their effect is mediated through processes of perception, memory, and thought.

Which One Is Right?

Anybody with the experience of teaching a course in personality psychology, after a semester of presenting these approaches in sequence, has had a bright but confused student approach and ask, "Yes, but which one is right?" By now, you probably can predict that professors flounder around when they try to answer this question, because it is not really answerable. To be able to say which one is "right," the different approaches of personality psychology would have to be different answers to the same question. But they are not. Rather, they are different questions. Each lives or dies not by being right or wrong, because in the end, all theories are wrong, but rather by being useful in accounting for a delimited area of known facts, for having application in the real world, and for clarifying important facets of human nature.[1]

Thus, we cannot choose between the different approaches to personality on the grounds of which one is right. A better criterion for evaluating a psychological approach is this: Does it offer us a way to seek an answer to a question we feel is worth asking? The trait approach asks about individual differences; the psychoanalytic approach asks about the unconscious; the biological approach asks about physical mechanisms; the humanistic approach asks about consciousness, free will, and individual construals of reality; the learning and cognitive approaches ask about behavioral acquisition and

---

[1] The statistician G. E. P. Box once commented, "All models are wrong but some are useful."

change, and the mental processes that underlie behavioral coherence. Which do you need or want to know about? The answer to this question tells you which approach to use.

The Order of Approaches

One interesting decision that any author of a book like this gets to make—amid much conflicting advice—is the order in which to present the chapters. This might seem like a trivial decision, but it can reveal much about the author's view of the field of personality.

One surprisingly common method is to begin with the author's least favorite approach, and end by describing the author's most favorite approach. But such books leave the impression that the whole world was just marking time until the right approach came along. In the final chapter, the author can triumphantly announce, at last, the truth was discovered!

I have already explained why I am not a fan of such invidious comparisons. Portraying one approach as right and the others as wrong misses the whole point of why different approaches continue to exist. So it should not be surprising that I did not choose this strategy of chapter arrangement.

A second common strategy is more even-handed. The author arranges the chapters in more or less historical order. I say "more or less" because it is not an easy matter to settle which are the older and which are the newer approaches. The philosophical tradition behind behaviorism is extremely old, but the research is comparatively new; the reverse could be said about psychoanalysis. One problem with this strategy is that a strict chronological ordering (assuming one can be settled on) is not necessarily intellectually coherent. Another problem is that such a book tends also to acquire the "psychology marches on" flavor that I think is somewhat misleading.

The final strategy I will mention—and not coincidentally the one I chose—is to arrange the approaches in the order in which they are most teachable. It is sometimes claimed that unlike other sciences, psychology is not cumulative; its findings do not build in an orderly manner, one on the other, as they do in physics, for example.[2] But psychology is cumulative in another way. The approaches branch off from, react to, and interact with each other in such a way that does suggest an order in which to present them.

So I began this book with a review of the data and research methods of personality psychology. This laid a base for everything that followed. Then, I presented the trait approach first, because it raises a basic issue (does personality exist?) that logically precedes all others, and because its focus

---

[2] I think this claim simultaneously underestimates the cumulativeness of psychology and overestimates the cumulativeness of physics, but that is another story.

on how people differ can be presented without much reference to the other approaches. The biological approaches I considered next are direct outgrowths of the trait approach; they examine how neurostructure, biochemicals, genes, or evolutionary histories produce the broad patterns of behavior called *personality traits.*

By then, an attentive reader could begin to suspect that these trait and biological approaches neglect some of the more mysterious aspects of the mind, such as the workings of the unconscious (recall that this was Henry Murray's complaint about the trait approach). So I presented the psychoanalytic approach next. The psychoanalytic view of behavior as driven by irrational and mysterious impulses is countered in an interesting way by the humanistic approach, which I considered in the following section. The humanists believe people can (even must) consciously choose their construals of reality. We also saw that the essence of the psychological difference between cultures is a matter of how members of different cultures construe reality differently.

The next set of chapters presented learning and cognitive approaches to personality. First I considered classic behaviorism, then looked at the social learning theories that grew directly out of behaviorism, and finally considered the modern cognitive approaches that grew out of social learning, but which also are influenced by trait, psychoanalytic, and even humanistic perspectives. I ended with cognitive research in personality because, as I mentioned in Chapter 17, to appreciate it fully I think you need some familiarity with all of these other approaches. I also think that considering the cognitive approach last brings us full circle, because (whether cognitive theorists admit it or not) it has so much in common with the trait approach. Both approaches describe individual differences and patterns of behavioral coherence and attempt to explain them.

No Single Approach Accounts for Everything

I have been saying this all along, and by now I hope you know what I mean. Einstein's theory of relativity unified physics. Darwin's theory of evolution unified biology. But psychology has no Darwin or Einstein—yet. The most comprehensive theory probably belongs to Freud, but you have already seen the problems there. As broad as Freud's theory is, it still does not address the key concerns of the other approaches, such as conscious experience, free will, individual differences, or learning from experience. It also has not been particularly successful in generating supporting empirical research.

The lack of a single unifying perspective for psychology is often lamented and is an important source of the "physics envy" so often suffered by psychologists. So let me rock the boat a little: I think it's a good thing. I say this for two reasons.

"I'm a social scientist, Michael. That means I can't explain electricity or anything like that, but if you ever want to know about people I'm your man."

The first reason is that any approach that tried to account for all of the key concerns of what are now five basic approaches would almost inevitably be unwieldy, confusing, incoherent, and incomplete. The limitations that each basic approach imposes on observation and theorizing are not faults; these limitations are the very purpose of these approaches. The purpose of the self-limitation is to avoid becoming overwhelmed and confused, and it also allows each basic approach to focus on providing a thorough account of, and useful knowledge about, the phenomena it is designed to address.

The second reason is that the existence of alternative basic viewpoints can keep us open-minded toward phenomena that any one of them may fail to include. Intellectual competition is good. It can prevent dogmatism and closed minds. No matter how emphatically a Freudian or a behaviorist or a biological psychologist believes that his or her approach accounts for everything, he or she also knows that a substantial number of psychologists believe him or her to be dead wrong. That kind of knowledge is intellectually bracing.

I even fantasize, sometimes, that biology and physics might be better off if they had not settled so firmly, so soon, on a single, unifying approach. What phenomena are being missed today because they do not happen to fit current views of relativity or evolutionary theory? Biologists and physicists might never find out what their theories and methods neglect because, as we have seen in this book, adherence to one basic approach tends to blind researchers to many things that are perfectly obvious from other perspectives. For my part, I enjoy personality psychology's lack of a single, basic, unifying approach. This lack leaves a lot of room for free thought and theorizing. Other sciences have always seemed a bit too closed for my taste. If you feel the same way, you might enjoy being a personality psychologist, too.

Choosing a Basic Approach

I believe that it is particularly important to learn each of the basic approaches to personality independently of each other, as they were presented in this book, so that you can get a sense of the full scope and flavor of each. And for most purposes—even the purpose of becoming a personality researcher—it is probably the most profitable as well as easiest course to choose a single paradigm to work within—the trait, biological, psychoanalytic, humanistic, behaviorist, or cognitive approach. As the cognitive scientist Howard Gardner (1987, p. 222) noted, "Even if, ultimately, everything turns out to be connected to everything else, a research program rooted in the realization might collapse of its own weight."

The choice of which approach to pursue cannot be based on which one is right or wrong, because all of them are right and wrong. Rather, the choice should be made on the basis of two (perhaps three) criteria. The first is, what do you want to understand—free will, individual differences, the unconscious mind, or the shaping of behavior? The second is even more personal: Which approach is the most interesting to you? If one of them really turns you on, maybe you should become a personality psychologist. And if you do become a personality psychologist, then a third criterion comes into play: Which basic approach offers you the best potential to do interesting work that can add to knowledge?

My own choice has been the trait approach, mostly on the basis of this third criterion. As much as I admire psychoanalysis, for example, and even find it useful in daily life, I find it hard to imagine what kind of research can tell us more about it, and the case study method is, to me, unsatisfying. The trait approach, by contrast, has managed to keep me busy in a research career for the past two decades and will continue to do so, I hope, for many years to come.

Maintaining an Awareness of Alternative Approaches

Nevertheless, I try to take a vacation from my favored approach now and then. An occasion for such a trip is when I teach a personality course, or work on this book. I get the opportunity, for a time, to look once more at the psychological world through several different sets of unaccustomed lenses. I think about questions I usually ignore—like, what is free will?—and entertain alternative visions of reality. I think this variation is good for me, and it is also fun.

No matter which basic approach you choose, there are five reasons why you should maintain an awareness and knowledge of the alternatives. The first is simply to avoid arrogance and to prevent starting to think that you know it all. The second is to understand the proper basis for evaluating alternative approaches. Remember that each of the basic approaches to personality, brilliant though it is, tends to look irrelevant and even foolish from the point of view of the other approaches. The third reason is to have a way of dealing with those psychological phenomena you will run across, from time to time, that do not fit into your favorite approach. I once heard the psychologist E. R. Hilgard say that we must not be in the position of the entomologist who found a bug he could not classify, so he stepped on it. The fourth reason is to give yourself the chance to change your mind later. If your interests change, if your goals change, or if the phenomena you encounter keep refusing to fit your favorite approach, you will have some place to go.

Finally, the fifth reason: At some point, it really might make sense to try to integrate at least some of the different paradigms of personality psychology, and to do this one will have to be aware of the nature of each of the paradigms being integrated. In Chapter 1 I mentioned the dream of some psychologists to develop what I called the OBT (one big theory) that would explain absolutely everything. And, recent years have seen increasing progress—some deliberate, some accidental—in combining the issues that traditionally have belonged to different approaches.

For example, in Chapter 17 I discussed how the trait approach and cognitive approach seem to address many of the same phenomena, but to view them from different (and not incompatible) angles. The cognitive approach itself has close ties to (and historical roots in) the humanistic and behaviorist approaches. The cognitive approach also is being applied to issues—such as the nature of unconscious thought—that were long restricted to theorists within the psychoanalytic approach. And, more so with each passing year, the biological approach has an increasing amount of influence on everybody. Evolutionary reasoning is used increasingly often to answer questions as to why the mind works the way it does, and genetic, biochemical, and neurological knowledge is beginning to be applied to theories of how mental processes function and where they ultimately originate.

So, in the end, you may not have to choose. Out there, on the horizon, dimly glimmering, is a hint of what an overall integrated theory of personality—the ultimate OBT—might someday look like. I will say a bit more about this possibility in the next section.

The Future of Personality Psychology

No personality textbook seems quite complete without some predictions for the future. A Confucian proverb says, "To find the future in the present, find the present in the past." So one strategy for predicting the future is to identify recent changes and then extrapolate forward.

Trait Approach

The trait approach—always my own personal favorite—has become even more interesting in the past few years. Despite the wide range of fascinating topics it has addressed, trait psychology has sometimes been afflicted with methodological narrowness. This was not true at the beginning; Gordon Allport, the founder of the modern trait approach, gathered data ranging from measurements of the length of a person's stride to the content of a mother's letters to her son. But for several decades the field was dominated by the technology of the self-report personality inventory, to the point where I began to suspect, quite frankly, that some trait psychologists had forgotten that other methods were possible. In the past few years this has changed dramatically. Suddenly we see a wide range of research examining personality traits as they are observed directly in social behavior, as they are expressed in life stories, and even as they are revealed by the state and contents of one's bedroom!

"Those who do not learn from the future are destined to make mistakes in it."

In the next few years we will see further creative expansion in personality assessment techniques, which will provide a larger and clearer window on the implications of traits for behavior. Some of this expansion will come from creative thinking, such as the work described in Chapter 6 that diagnosed personality from assessing music preference or the strength of one's handshake. Other developments will be technologically based. Instruments such as the Behavioral Q-sort will be developed for the richer and more complete recording of behavior (Funder et al., 2000). At a more electronic level, one recent innovation is the development of "virtual realities," in which it might soon be possible to see what people with different personality traits will do in a wide range of artificial situations (Blascovich et al., 2002). The technology for using computers to analyze speech and nonverbal behavior also is just becoming widely available and user friendly, and its potential for personality assessment is almost untapped. How do extraverts move and talk differently from introverts? What are the characteristic speech patterns of someone high in self-monitoring? Biological technology is also changing rapidly. How does the brain of an extravert differ from the brain of an introvert? What happens in the amygdala of a hostile person contemplating a violent act? We are beginning to find out.

Biological Approach

As was just mentioned, biological technology is developing rapidly and is providing many potential routes towards understanding how the anatomy and functioning of the nervous system is related to personality. This development is impressive and bound to accelerate. Look for more color pictures of the nervous system in action, in the personality textbooks of the future.

Other changes will be more subtle, but even more important. I have found that the work at the intersection of biology and personality has become more interesting in the past few years. I complained in an earlier edition of this book that too much biological psychology was all biology and hardly any psychology. There is a research style that seems to think it is finished when it is able to announce, "Left frontal hemisphere damage is associated with impulsiveness," or "Testosterone makes people aggressive." But these are not psychological insights, and sometimes I read articles like this and am tempted to say, "So what?" But such research is not as dominant as it used to be, and more often the literature yields studies of biology and personality that are interesting on a psychological and not just on a biological level. These include studies of testosterone that explain how its interrelated effects include energy and positive emotion as well as aggressiveness and sexuality, and how its production may be part of a feedback loop that regulates the behavioral response to success and failure. I also am fascinated by the anatomical work that reveals how full emotional experiences as well as plain good judgment are dependent on well-functioning links between the "cognitive" frontal lobes and the more "emotional" and in some sense primitive emotional organs in the base of the brain.

The exciting potential for the biological approach to personality is to integrate the two trends of technological advance and theoretical richness. It will have to resist the reductionist temptation to think that a behavior is fully explained when we know which synapse fired to make it happen. Instead, biology has the potential to teach us much about the bases of the psychological triad—thought, feeling, and behavior. At the same time, a greater understanding of thought, feeling, and behavior will provide useful guidance for appropriate research in biology.

Psychoanalysis

Freud lives. While the orthodox psychoanalysts are an inbred and dying breed, the core ideas of psychoanalysis continue to influence a wide swath of personality psychology. A motivational concept resembling "libido" underlies much of humanistic psychology (recall that the humanists call it *self-actualization*), and I don't know how one could get through daily life, much less conduct research on personality, without drawing upon the notion of defense mechanisms. The most central psychoanalytic idea concerns the vast and until recently underestimated influence of unconscious mental processes. Recall the study of unconscious self-consciousness described in Chapter 17 (Hull et al., 2002). Would this study have been possible if Freud had never lived? Maybe. What is certain is that ideas that seem familiar to anyone who has studied psychoanalysis will continue to resurface, in many guises in many areas of personality psychology, for years to come.

Humanistic Psychology

At the time I wrote the previous edition of this book, it seemed that humanistic psychology was all but dead. What a difference a few years make. Suddenly the psychological world is full of talk of what is now called "positive psychology," a paradigm that strikes me as remarkably similar to the humanistic psychology of Rogers and Maslow and even Sartre, without some of the excess baggage. Some of this recent work is a bit flaky and seems to reduce to well-meaning but useless advice to accentuate the positive. But more often it draws on modern cognitive psychology to examine the psychological bases of well-being, such as how happy people think differently from unhappy people, and it also increasingly often addresses the importance of meeting challenges in order to have a meaningful life—a development that would make Jean-Paul Sartre proud.

Cross-Cultural Psychology

Of all the areas of personality psychology, cross-cultural study has accelerated the most in the past few years. The time-honored idea of collectivism versus individualism as a way for contrasting cultural points of view remains useful, but what is really impressive is the sudden diversity in the cultures examined and the methods employed. Cultural differences are not just "East versus West" but are also found among different Asian groups, between different kinds of European Americans, and even among residents of the same city. Research methods have moved beyond the ubiquitous questionnaire to include direct behavioral observations and some truly fascinating studies of cognitive processing. And, research is just beginning to address the intriguing puzzle of the multicultural individual, the ever-more-common person who moves from one continent to another, or grows up in a home with two languages and cultural traditions, or marries someone from a different culture and begins to create a new kind of family.

The cross-cultural study of personality is bound to accelerate even more, because the possibilities are endless and still barely touched, and because the topic is critically important. Multicultural societies such as the United States must understand and appreciate the psychological differences among its people in order to survive. It is just as urgent for the world as a whole to work against global scourges such as war and terrorism by learning how to regard different cultural views as alternate realities to be understood and appreciated, rather than threats to be eradicated.

The Cognitive Approach and the OBT

As I mentioned near the end of Chapter 17, the cognitive approach was considered last because it makes the most contact with all of the other approaches. Now I will go a step beyond and make a pronouncement, new to this edition, that startles even me: The cognitive approach to personality may be the OBT (one big theory), or at least offer the beginnings of one. But first, its practitioners will have to get over some bad habits. Or perhaps (and more likely) new people, free of some of the shackles of the past, will begin to do research in this area.

The potential of the cognitive approach comes precisely from its numerous ties, realized and potential, with other areas. Historically, two sources of the cognitive approach are behaviorism's emphasis on the effects of experience and learning, and humanism's emphasis on construal and cognitive processes of perception and thinking. We also saw cognitive research that addressed what Freud would call defense mechanisms and the unconscious, and which is tied to recent advances in the biology of thought. Even cross-cultural research is suddenly gaining a strong cognitive flavor, as it addresses how multicultural individuals can be primed by cultural cues to think like a member of one culture or another. A thorough understanding of topics such as priming, perception, memory, and the self may lead them to become fully integrated with each other, and that integration in turn has the potential to tie together the rest of personality psychology.

But first, one obstacle will have to be overcome. The cognitive approach to psychology is going to have to discard its historical, traditional, and now self-limiting aversion to acknowledging the importance of behavioral consistency and personality traits. The cognitive personality psychologists are proud of their focus on how behavior changes across situations. They need to acknowledge that cognitive mechanisms underlie consistencies to behavior as well. The main reason that dominant people are different from submissive people, and shy people are different from sociable people, and all the rest of it, is that people with different traits *think* differently. The trait approach to psychology, and the cognitive approach to psychology, will each reach their full potential, and will begin to integrate the field as a whole, when psychologists in both areas finally realize they are studying the same thing.

What Have We Learned?

One of my colleagues has on his office door a cartoon that depicts a student cramming for exams. "It's not what you know," the caption reads, "it's when you know it." The view implicit in this cartoon is that most of what one learns in a college course, or reads in a 600-page book, is forgotten soon after finals week. That view is not cynical, it is realistic. What then, is retained from the experience of taking a personality course or reading a book like this one? One lasting benefit, I hope, is that you became a little smarter. The reason for this hope was explained in Chapter 16, where I described thinking as a procedural skill that can only be learned via practice and feedback. I hope you thought about the material in this book, whether you agreed or disagreed with my point of view, and that you received feedback from your instructor and fellow students. Most of all, I hope you thought about how this material pertains to yourself because, as also was explained in Chapter 16, that is the most effective way to learn it—as well as the most interesting thing you can do with psychological knowledge.

Another realistic possibility is after taking a course and reading a long book, one retains (past the final exam) not specific details of theories and experiments, surely, but a few general themes that have emerged again and again. Let me try to identify a few of the major themes that I hope you will remember.

Cross-Situational Consistency and Aggregation

People remain who they are regardless of the situation. We have seen that psychologists still argue about this question of "behavioral consistency," but the evidence is clear and comes from all directions. Someone who dominates a business meeting will probably dominate a party; someone who is pessimistic about his career will probably also be pessimistic about the outcome of his wife's childbirth; and someone who has "issues" about her father is likely to bring them to bear in her relationships with many of the men she encounters in life. The three examples I just gave came from three different basic approaches. The consistency of dominance has been demonstrated by research in the trait paradigm. The consistency of pessimism has been demonstrated by research in the cognitive paradigm. And the consistency of "transference" of relationship patterns has been demonstrated by both the psychoanalytic *and* cognitive paradigms.

Let's consider consistency another way. If you were dropped off alone on a desert island, you would be in a unique situation with no expectations for your behavior from anybody else. You would nonetheless be who you are, and whether you respond to this situation with fear, or resourcefulness, or loneliness, or joy at the peace and quiet, depends on your personality. Personality is baggage you always have with you.

Consistency is real and important, but it has two major limitations. First, behavior surely does change from one situation to the next. I once did a two-session experiment in which I found that the participants were much less nervous in the second session than they were in the first session, an obvious effect of the familiarity of the setting (Funder & Colvin, 1991). But the same people who were the most nervous at the first session were the same ones who tended to be the most nervous at the second session. To give another example, the most cheerful person at a party will surely become much less cheerful at a funeral. The consistency of her personality implies only that she will probably still be the most cheerful person compared to everybody else at the funeral, *not* that she will be equally cheerful in both situations. Behavior changes over time, but individual differences are maintained. This idea is not obvious at first glance, and not even all psychologists quite grasp it, but it is important.

A second limitation is that behavioral consistency is not strong enough to predict a single action in a single situation with any great fidelity. Recall the personality coefficient of around .30 to .40 (Chapter 4), which means a dichotomous behavioral prediction is likely to be right about two times out of three. This is a useful level of accuracy that includes a lot of errors. Behavioral consistency only becomes truly worthy of the name if the target for prediction is the average or aggregate of several behaviors. Will your roommate greet you cheerfully when you come home next Tuesday at 4:30 P.M.? Who knows? But if she is a cheerful person you can confidently predict that, on the average of the 30 times you arrive home next month, her greeting will be more pleasant than that of your other, crabbier roommate.

The Biological Roots of Personality

As we saw in Chapters 8 and 9, biological research relevant to personality is progressing at a rapid and accelerating pace. It is clear, and the other approaches (such as the learning/cognitive approaches) no longer try to deny, that the consistent patterns of behavior that manifest personality are rooted in evolutionary history, DNA, anatomical structures such as the frontal lobes and the amygdala, and chemicals such as neurotransmitters and hormones. The philosopher John Locke thought that the human mind started out at birth like a "blank slate," or *tabula rasa*. Nice idea, but he was wrong. The behaviorist John Watson thought he could take any baby and with the proper training produce a "doctor, lawyer, beggar man, or thief." Another nice idea, but he was wrong too.

The Unconscious Mind

The psychological unconscious is no longer an exotic, implausible idea kept alive by Freudian diehards. It has entered the mainstream. We saw evidence across almost all of the chapters of this book that the unconscious part of the mind—the part we cannot describe or explain in words, and the part that can occasionally surprise us—is important in many ways. Indeed, we saw in Chapter 16 that consciousness can only hold about 7 ideas at a time anyway (plus or minus two), so the idea that all of the mind's activities are conscious is itself implausible.

Recall just a few examples. Biological research has shown that the connections between the emotional and more rational areas of the brain are sometimes damaged or severed to the point that people have thoughts that make no emotional sense, or emotions that they cannot explain. Psychoanalytic theory provides many examples of how people "defend" against perceptions and thoughts they would find too anxiety provoking to experience immediately or directly. The cognitive approach to personality has produced demonstrations of how perception, memory, and thought can be "primed" in ways we may not be aware of. Indeed, in Chapter 17 we saw how self-consciousness itself might be, to some degree, unconscious!

Free Will and Responsibility

Because psychology tries 99 percent of the time to behave like a "real," deterministic science, it tends to ignore the idea of free will and the related concept of responsibility. We saw psychologists as diverse as Freud and B. F. Skinner unite behind the idea that behavioral freedom is an illusion. The most valuable contribution of humanistic psychology (Chapter 13) is to provide a reasonable way to think about free will. Behavior is determined only up to a point, after which choices become possible. Kelly's theory of constructive alternativism implies that even an abused child could reasonably conclude either (1) the world is a horrible place full of people who cannot be trusted, *or* (2) I can survive anything, even abuse, because both conclusions are consistent with his or her experience. The secret of psychological success may be to recognize the choice points in one's own life, and to take the responsibility to make the most of them.

Another contribution from the humanists, and parts of the related modern *positive psychology* movement, is to remind us that the goal of life is not to achieve a state of zero stress. A totally stress-free life would be boring and meaningless. A healthy life involves seeking out difficult but reasonable and meaningful challenges and, when they are accomplished, to seek more.

Behavior Change

Rewarded behaviors become more likely, and punished behaviors become less likely (duh). This fact is true of amoebas *and* humans. The edifice of behaviorism and social learning theory is based on this key idea, but the most important thing to remember is that you often can choose which set of rewards and punishments you will be subject to. Imagine a rat choosing his own Skinner box. Now think of someone choosing (or not) to enroll in medical school, or to enter a law firm, or to enlist in the military. What will be the consequences of the rewards and punishments in each of those environments? I mentioned choice points a moment ago. The most important choice points in life are those that select an environment and its associated rewards and punishments. These choices include where to go to school, what career to enter, and whom to marry. Much of who you will turn out to be will depend on these decisions.

And there is more. Once you are in an environment, it changes just because you are there, and it changes again because of what you do. If you ever find yourself in an unsatisfactory situation—a hostile work environment, an exploitative relationship—then ask yourself, is any aspect of this situation the result of what I am doing? Maybe the answer is no. In that case, leave. But maybe the answer is yes. In that case, do something about it.

Construals

It is not things that matter, but our opinions of things. This Talmudic insight is a theme not only of existential philosophy and humanistic psychology, but also is at the core of psychoanalytic, cross-cultural, and cognitive approaches to personality. Psychoanalysis emphasizes how unrealistic or fantasized views of reality can cause us to act in a neurotic, self-defeating manner. From a humanistic perspective, the choice of a point of view is the core existential obligation. The only way to understand another person, or a member of another culture, is to try to understand how reality appears from his or her perspective. The cognitive approach to personality does not often use the word *construal,* but almost all research in that approach is intended to explain the origins and consequences of individuals' differing views of reality.

Indeed, it could be argued that the whole of psychology boils down to the moment of construal. All of one's past experiences, biological processes, needs, ambitions, and perceptions combine to yield your view of reality, right now. Then, you decide what to do.

The Quest for Understanding

Remember S, I, L, and B data (Chapter 2)? To learn about a person we have no alternative but to watch what he or she does and listen to what he or she says. These are behaviors, and in the end must be the basis of what we conclude about personality, whether our approach is trait, biological, psychoanalytic, behaviorist, cognitive, or even humanistic. By the same token, if we think we understand an individual's personality, the only way to find out whether we are right or wrong is to use our understanding to explain (and sometimes to predict) what the person does or says. Again, this is true no matter which basic approach we follow.

Our minds are forever sealed off from each other. We can only know each other from watching what we each do. From that observation, we can try to infer the nature of each others' personalities. And that inference, in turn, is the basis of how we try to understand each other. So personality psychology is, in the final analysis, a quest for mutual understanding.

Summary

Each of the approaches to personality has aspects of the person it explains well, and other aspects it does not explain or ignores entirely. Thus, the choice between them depends not on which one is right, but what we wish to know, and we should try to stay open to alternative approaches. In the future, expect the trait approach to develop an ever-wider range of assessment methods, the biological approach to become more psychological, and the key ideas of psychoanalysis—especially the unconscious mind—to continue to have an impact. Cross-cultural psychology will accelerate rapidly and turn to addressing a wider range of cultures, cognitive processes relevant to cultural outlook, and the special situation of multicultural individuals. The cognitive approach might just develop into the OBT (one big theory), if psychologists who follow the cognitive approach and those who follow the trait approach finally realize they are studying the same thing.

It is unreasonable to expect to remember many of the details in a long book such as this, but certain recurring themes are important to retain. These include the nature of behavioral consistency, the biological roots of personality, the workings of the unconscious mind, the issues of free will and responsibility, the sources of behavior change, especially the effect of choosing and changing one's environment, and the central importance of construals. In the final analysis, personality psychology is an attempt to turn our observations of each other into mutual understanding.

GLOSSARY

acculturation The process of social influence by which a person partially or fully acquires a new cultural outlook, either by having contact with or by living in a different culture from his or her culture of origin.

acquiescence response set In personality testing, the tendency to respond "true" regardless of the content of the item.

adrenal cortex The outer layer of the adrenal gland, atop the kidneys, that secretes several behaviorally important hormones.

aggregation The combination of different measurements, such as by averaging them.

amygdala A structure located near the base of the brain that is believed to play a role in emotion, especially negative emotions such as anger and fear.

anal stage In psychoanalytic theory, the stage of psychosexual development, from about eighteen months to three-and-a-half or four years of age, in which the physical focus of the libido is located in the anus and associated eliminative organs.

anatta In Zen Buddhism, the fundamental idea that the single, isolated self is an illusion.

Angst In existential philosophy, the anxiety that stems from doubts about the meaning and purpose of life.

anicca In Zen Buddhism, the recognition that all things are temporary and that therefore it is best to avoid attachments to them.

anima In Jung's version of psychoanalysis, the idea of the typical female as held in the mind of a male.

animus In Jung's version of psychoanalysis, the idea of the typical male as held in the mind of a female.

approach-avoidance conflict In Dollard and Miller's social learning theory, the conflict induced by a stimulus that is at once attractive and aversive.

archetypes In Jung's version of psychoanalysis, the fundamental images of people that are contained in the collective unconscious, including the earth mother, the hero, the devil, and so forth.

ascending reticular activating system (ARAS) A part of the upper brain stem through which information flows into the brain and stimulates it.

associationism The idea that all complex ideas are combinations of two or more simple ideas.

association method In molecular behavioral genetics, the attempt to link genes to personality by comparing the DNA of people who score high and low on trait scales and behavioral measures.

authentic existence In existential philosophy, living with an awareness of the dilemmas concerning the meaning of life, mortality, and free will.

basic approach (to personality) A theoretical view of personality that focuses on some phenomena and ignores others. The basic approaches are trait, biological, psychoanalytic, phenomenological, behavioral, and cognitive.

B data "Behavioral data," or direct observations of another's behavior that are translated directly or nearly directly into numerical form. B data can be gathered in natural or contrived (experimental) settings.

behavioral confirmation The "self-fulfilling prophecy" tendency for a person to become the kind of person others expect him or her to be. Also called the *expectancy effect*.

behavioral prediction The degree to which a judgment or measurement can predict the behavior of the person in question.

behaviorism (or *behavioristic approach*) The theoretical view of personality that focuses on overt behavior and the ways in which it can be affected by rewards and punishments in the environment. A modern variant is the social learning approach, which adds a concern with how behavior is affected by observation, self-evaluation, and social interaction. Also called *learning approach*.

Binomial Effect Size Display (BESD) One method for displaying and understanding more clearly the magnitude of an effect reported as a correlation.

biological approach The view of personality that focuses on the way behavior and personality are influenced by neuroanatomy, biochemistry, genetics, or evolution.

California Q-set A set of one hundred descriptive items (e.g., "is critical, skeptical, not easily impressed") that comprehensively cover the personality domain.

case method Studying a particular phenomenon or individual in depth both to understand the particular case and in hopes of discovering general lessons or scientific laws.

central nervous system The brain and spinal cord.

chronic accessibility The tendency of an idea or concept to come easily to mind for a particular individual.

chunk Any piece of information that can be thought of as a unit. It can vary with learning and experience. The capacity of short-term memory is 7 chunks, plus or minus 2.

classical conditioning The kind of learning through which a response elicited by an unconditioned stimulus becomes elicited also through a new, conditioned stimulus.

cognitive approach The theoretical view that focuses on the ways in which basic processes of perception and cognition affect personality and behavior.

cognitive dissonance The unpleasant feeling that one is holding two conflicting attitudes at the same time. This feeling is held by some theorists to be an important mechanism underlying attitude change.

cohort effect The tendency for a research finding to be limited to one group or "cohort" of people, such as people all living during a particular era or in a particular location.

collective unconscious In Jung's version of psychoanalysis, the proposition that all people share certain unconscious ideas because of the history of the human species.

compromise formation In modern psychoanalytic thought, the main job of the ego, which is to find a compromise among the different structures of the mind and the many different things the individual wants all at the same time. What the individual actually thinks and does is the result of this compromise.

conceptual memory The section of declarative memory that stores what a person knows about general aspects of the environment (e.g., what happens at McDonald's, or what an extravert is).

condensation In psychoanalytic theory, the method of primary process thinking in which several ideas are compressed into one.

conscious (mind) That part of the mind's activities of which one is aware.

construal An individual's particular experience of the world or way of interpreting reality.

construct An idea about a psychological attribute that goes beyond what might be assessed through any particular method of assessment.

constructivism The philosophical view that reality, as a concrete entity, does not exist and that only ideas or "constructions" of reality exist.

construct validation The strategy of establishing the validity of a measure by comparing it to a wide range of other measures.

convergent validation The process of assembling diverse pieces of information that converge on a common conclusion.

correlational method Research technique that establishes the relationship (not necessarily causal) between two variables, traditionally denoted X and Y, by measuring both variables in a sample of participants.

correlation coefficient A number between -1 and $+1$ that reflects the degree to which one variable, traditionally called "Y," is a linear function of another, traditionally called "X." A negative correlation means that as X goes up, Y goes down; a positive correlation means that as X goes up, so does Y; a zero correlation means that X and Y are unrelated.

cortex The outside portion of an organ; in the context of this book, the reference is to the outer layers of the brain.

cortisol A collective term for the glucocorticoid hormones, which are released into the bloodstream by the adrenal cortex as a response to physical or psychological stress.

critical realism The philosophical view that the absence of perfect, infallible criteria for truth does not imply that all interpretations of reality are equally valid; instead, one can use empirical evidence to determine which views of reality are more or less likely to be valid.

cross-cultural psychology Psychological research and theorizing that attempts to account for the psychological differences between and within different cultural groups.

current concern A goal, hope, or worry that resides in working memory and tends to periodically come into consciousness.

declarative knowledge The part of long-term memory that includes verbalizable information; sometimes called "knowing that."

defense mechanisms In psychoanalytic theory, the mechanisms of the ego that serve to protect an individual from experiencing anxiety produced by conflicts with the id, superego, or reality.

denial In psychoanalytic theory, the defense mechanism that denies that a current source of anxiety exists.

displacement In psychoanalytic theory, the defense mechanism that redirects an impulse from a dangerous target to a safe one.

doctrine of opposites In psychoanalytic theory, the idea that everything implies or contains its opposite.

dopamine A neurotransmitter in the brain that plays an important role in positive affect and response to reward.

drive In learning theories, a state of psychological tension, the reduction of which feels good.

duck test If it looks like a duck, sounds like a duck, and acts like a duck, it probably *is* a duck.

effect size A number that reflects the degree to which one variable affects or is related to another.

efficacy expectation In Bandura's social learning theory, one's belief that one can perform a given goal-directed behavior.

ego In psychoanalytic theory, the relatively rational part of the mind that takes on the job of balancing competing claims of the id, the superego, and reality.

ego control In Jack Block's personality theory, the psychological tendency to inhibit the behavioral expression of motivation and emotional impulse. At the extremes, people may be either undercontrolled or overcontrolled.

ego psychology The modern school of psychoanalytic thought that believes that the most important aspect of mental functioning is the way the ego mediates between and formulates compromises among the impulses of the id and the superego.

ego resiliency In Jack Block's personality theory, the ability to vary one's level of ego control in order to respond appropriately to opportunities and situational circumstances.

Eigenwelt In Binswanger's phenomenological analysis, the experience of experience itself; the result of introspection.

electroencephalography (EEG) A technique for measuring brain electrical activity by placing electrode sensors on the outside of the skull.

emics The locally relevant components of an idea. In cross-cultural psychology, the reference is to aspects of a phenomenon that are specific to a particular culture.

empiricism The idea that everything a person knows comes from experience.

enculturation The process of socialization through which an individual acquires his or her native culture, mainly early in life.

endorphins The body's own pain-killing chemicals, which operate by blocking the transmission of pain messages.

entity theory In Dweck's theory of motivation, an individual's belief that abilities are fixed and unchangeable.

epinephrine A neurotransmitter in the brain and also a hormone that is released by the adrenal gland as part of the body's response to stress.

essential-trait approach The research strategy that attempts to narrow the list of thousands of trait terms into a shorter list of the ones that really matter.

estrogen The female sex hormone.

etics The universal components of an idea. In cross-cultural psychology, the reference is to phenomena that all cultures have in common.

event memory The section of declarative memory that stores what a person remembers about specific events and facts.

expectancy In Rotter's social learning theory, an individual's subjective probability for how likely a behavior is to attain its goal.

expectancy effect The tendency for a person to become the kind of person others expect him or her to be. Also known as a "self-fulfilling prophecy."

expectancy value theory Rotter's theory of how the value and perceived attainability of a goal combine to affect the probability of a goal-seeking behavior.

experimental method Research technique that establishes the causal relation between an independent variable (X) and dependent variable (Y) by randomly assigning participants to experimental groups characterized by differing levels of X, and measuring the average behavior (Y) that results in each group.

existentialism The approach to philosophy that focuses on conscious experience (phenomenology), free will, the meaning of life, and other basic questions of existence.

face validity The degree to which an assessment instrument, such as a questionnaire, on its face appears to measure what it is intended to measure. For example, a face-valid measure of sociability might ask about attendance at parties.

factor analysis A statistical technique for finding clusters of related traits, tests, or items.

fixation In psychoanalytic theory, leaving a disproportionate share of one's libido behind at an earlier stage of development.

frontal cortex The front part of the cortex of the brain; divided left and right into two "lobes" (the frontal lobes), this part of the brain is associated with cognitive functioning such as planning, foresight, and understanding.

frustration-aggression hypothesis In Dollard and Miller's social learning theory, the hypothesis that frustration automatically creates an impulse toward aggression.

functional analysis In behaviorism, a description of how a behavior is a function of the environment of the person or animal that performs it.

functional magnetic resonance imagery (fMRI) A technique for imaging brain activity by using a powerful magnet to help detect blood flow in the brain.

Funder's First Law Great strengths are usually great weaknesses, and surprisingly often the opposite is true as well.

Funder's Second Law There are no perfect indicators of personality; there are only clues, and clues are always ambiguous.

Funder's Third Law Something beats nothing, two times out of three.

Funder's Fourth Law There are only two kinds of data, Terrible Data and No Data.

Funder's Fifth Law The purpose of education is not to teach facts, or even ideas. It is to assemble new "chunks."

generalizability The degree to which a measurement can be found under diverse circumstances, such as time, context, subject population, and so on. In modern psychometrics, this term subsumes both reliability and validity.

genital stage In psychoanalytic theory, the final stage of psychosexual development, in which the physical focus of the libido is the genitals, with an emphasis on heterosexual relationships. The stage begins at about puberty, but is only fully attained when and if the individual achieves psychological maturity.

goal In cognitive approaches to personality, a desired end-state that serves to direct perception, thought, and behavior.

gonads The glands, testes in men and ovaries in women, that produce the sex hormones testosterone and estrogen, respectively.

habit hierarchy In Dollard and Miller's social learning theory, all of the behaviors an individual might do ranked in order from most to least probable.

habituation The decrease in response to a stimulus on repeated applications; this is the simplest kind of learning.

hedonism The idea that people are motivated to seek pleasure and avoid pain.

heritability coefficient A statistic that reflects the percentage of the variance of a trait that is controlled by genetic factors.

hippocampus A complex structure deep within the brain, behind the hypothalamus, that plays an important role in memory processes.

hormone A biological chemical that affects parts of the body some distance from where it is produced.

humanistic psychology The approach to personality that emphasizes aspects of psychology that are distinctly human. Closely related to the *phenomenological* and *existential* approaches.

hypothalamus A complex structure near the lower center of the brain that has direct connections to many other parts of the brain and is involved in the production of psychologically important hormones; thought to be important for mood and motivation.

id In psychoanalytic theory, the repository of the drives, the emotions, and the primitive, unconscious part of the mind that wants everything *now*.

I data "Informants' data," or judgments by knowledgeable human informants of general attributes of an individual's personality.

identification In psychoanalytic theory, taking on the values and worldview of another person (such as a parent).

idiographic assessment Personality assessment centered on individuals taken one at a time, rather than on differences between two or more individuals. Contrasts with *nomothetic assessment.*

incremental theory In Dweck's theory of motivation, an individual's belief that abilities can increase with experience and practice.

intellectualization In psychoanalytic theory, the defense mechanism by which thoughts that otherwise would cause anxiety are translated into cold, analytic, nonarousing terms.

inter-judge agreement The degree to which two (or more) judges of the same person provide the same description of his or her personality.

introspection The task of observing one's own mental processes.

judgeability The extent to which an individual's personality can be judged accurately by others.

judgments Data that derive, in the final analysis, from someone using his or her common sense and observations to rate personality or behavior.

L data "Life data," or more-or-less easily verifiable, concrete, real-life outcomes of possible psychological significance.

learned helplessness A belief that nothing one does matters, derived from an experience of random or unpredictable reward and punishment, and theorized to be a basis of depression.

learning In behaviorism, a change in behavior as a result of experience.

learning approach The theoretical view that focuses on how behavior changes as a function of rewards and punishments. Also called *behaviorism*.

libido In psychoanalytic theory, the drive toward the creation, nurturing, and enhancement of life (including but not limited to sex), or the energy stemming from this drive.

long-term memory (LTM) The final stage of information processing, in which a nearly unlimited amount of information can be permanently stored in an organized manner; this information may not always be accessible, however, depending on how it was stored and how it is looked for.

magnetoencephalography (MEG) A technique for using delicate magnetic sensors on the outside of the skull to detect brain activity.

many-trait approach The research strategy that focuses on a particular behavior and investigates its correlates with as many different personality traits as possible, in order to explain the basis of the behavior and to illuminate the workings of personality.

masculine protest In Adler's version of psychoanalysis, the idea that one particular urge in adulthood is to compensate for the powerlessness one felt in childhood.

mate selection What a person looks for in the opposite sex.

mating strategies How individuals handle heterosexual relationships.

measurement error The variation of a set of measurements around their true mean.

mental health According to Freud's definition, the ability to love and to work.

Minnesota Multiphasic Personality Inventory (MMPI) A widely used test derived through the empirical method. Originally designed for the diagnosis of psychopathology, it is used today to measure a wide range of personality attributes.

Mitwelt In Binswanger's phenomenological analysis, social experience; feelings and thoughts about others and oneself in relation to them.

moderator variable A variable that affects the relationship between two other variables.

neocortex The part of the cortex of the brain regarded as uniquely human.

neo-Freudian psychology A general term for the psychoanalytically oriented work of many theorists and researchers who are influenced by Freud's theory.

neuron A cell of the nervous system.

neurotransmitters The chemicals that allow one neuron to affect, or communicate with, another.

nirvana In Zen Buddhism, the state of selfless being that is the pleasant result of having achieved enlightenment.

norepinephrine The main neurotransmitter in the sympathetic nervous system; in the brain it is associated with responses to stress.

objective test A personality test that consists of a list of questions to be answered by the subject as true or false or on a numeric scale.

object relations theory The psychoanalytic study of interpersonal relations, including the unconscious images and feelings associated with the important people ("objects") in a person's life.

operant conditioning Skinner's term for the process by which an organism's behavior is shaped by the consequences for the organism of that behavior's effect on the environment.

oral stage In psychoanalytic theory, the stage of psychosexual development, from birth to about eighteen months of age, in which the physical focus of the libido is located in the mouth, lips, and tongue.

organ inferiority In Adler's version of psychoanalysis, the idea that one is motivated to succeed in adulthood in order to compensate for whatever one felt, in childhood, was his or her weakest aspect.

outgroup homogeneity bias The socio-psychological phenomenon by which members of a group to which one does not belong seem more alike than members of a group to which one does belong.

oxytocin A hormone that may have specific effects in women of emotional attachment and calming.

parapraxis An unintentional utterance or action caused by a leakage from the unconscious parts of the mind; a "Freudian slip."

peripheral nervous system The system of nerves running throughout the body, not including the brain and spinal cord.

persona In Jung's version of psychoanalysis, the social mask one wears in public dealings.

personality An individual's characteristic patterns of thought, emotion, and behavior, together with the psychological mechanisms behind those patterns.

phallic stage In psychoanalytic theory, the stage of psychosexual development, from about four to seven years of age, in which the physical focus of the libido is the penis (or for girls, their lack thereof).

phenomenological approach The theoretical view of personality that emphasizes experience, free will, and the meaning of life. Closely related to the humanistic approach and the existential approach.

phenomenology The study of conscious experience. Often, conscious experience itself is referred to as an individual's "phenomenology."

_p_-level In statistical data analysis, the probability that the obtained correlation or difference between experimental conditions is due to chance alone.

positron emission tomography (PET) A technique for creating images of brain activity by injecting a radioactive tracer into the blood and then finding with a scanner where in the brain the blood is metabolized.

preconscious Thoughts and ideas that temporarily reside just out of consciousness but can be brought to mind quickly and easily.

predictive validity The degree to which one measure can be used to predict another.

primary drive A drive that is innate to an organism, such as the hunger drive.

primary process thinking In psychoanalytic theory, the term for the strange and primitive style of unconscious thinking manifested by the *id*.

priming The activation of a concept or idea by repeatedly perceiving it or thinking about it. The usual result is that this concept or idea comes to mind more quickly and easily in new situations.

procedural knowledge What a person knows but cannot really talk about; sometimes called "knowing how."

projection In psychoanalytic theory, the defense mechanism of attributing a thought or impulse that is feared in oneself to somebody else.

projective test A test that presents a subject with an ambiguous stimulus, such as a picture or inkblot, and asks him or her to describe what is seen. The answer is held by some psychologists to reveal inner psychological states or motivations of which the subject may be unaware.

psychic conflict The phenomenon of one part of the mind being at cross-purposes with another part of the mind.

psychic determinism The assumption that everything psychological has a cause that is, in principle, identifiable.

psychic energy In psychoanalytic theory, the energy that allows the psychological system to function. Also called *libido*.

psychoanalytic approach The theoretical view of personality, based on the writings of Sigmund Freud, that emphasizes the unconscious processes of the mind.

psychological triad The three essential topics of psychology: how people think, feel, and behave.

psychometrics The technology of psychological measurement.

punishment An aversive consequence that follows an act in order to stop the act and prevent its repetition.

rationalization In psychoanalytic theory, the defense mechanism that produces a seemingly logical rationale for an impulse or thought that otherwise would cause anxiety.

reaction formation In psychoanalytic theory, the defense mechanism that keeps an anxiety-producing impulse or thought in check by producing its opposite.

reciprocal determinism Bandura's term for the way people affect their environments even while their environments affect them.

regression In psychoanalytic theory, a movement back to an earlier stage of psychosexual development.

reinforcement In operant conditioning, a reward that, when applied following a behavior, increases the frequency of that behavior. In classical conditioning, this term refers to the pairing of a conditioned stimulus with the unconditioned stimulus.

reliability In measurement, the tendency of an instrument to provide the same comparative information on repeated occasions.

repression In psychoanalytic theory, the defense mechanism that banishes the past from current awareness.

research The exploration of the unknown; finding out something that nobody knew before one discovered it.

respondent conditioning Skinner's term for *classical conditioning*.

response Anything a person or animal does as a result of a stimulus.

Rorschach test A projective test that asks subjects to interpret blots of ink.

scatter plot A diagram that shows the relationship between two variables by displaying points on a two-dimensional plot. Usually the two variables are denoted "X" and "Y"; each point represents a pair of scores and the X-variable is plotted on the horizontal axis while the Y-variable is plotted on the vertical axis.

schema A mental structure of knowledge.

S data "Self-judgments," or ratings that people provide of their own personality attributes or behavior.

secondary drive A drive that is learned through its association with primary drives—for example, the drive for prestige.

secondary process thinking In psychoanalytic theory, the term for rational and conscious processes of ordinary thought.

self-concept A person's knowledge and opinions about himself or herself.

self-efficacy A person's beliefs about the degree to which he or she will be able to accomplish what he or she sets out to do, if he or she tries.

self schema The cognitive structure that is hypothesized to contain a person's knowledge about himself or herself and to direct self-relevant thought.

self-verification The process by which people try to bring others to treat them in a manner that confirms their self-conceptions.

sensory-perceptual buffer The first stage of information processing in which nearly all stimulus information is held, in unprocessed form, for a very short period of time (also called *perceptual buffer*).

serotonin A neurotransmitter within the brain that plays an important role in the regulation of emotion and motivation.

short-term memory (STM) The second stage of information processing, in which the person is consciously aware of a small amount of information (about seven "chunks") as long as that information continues to be actively processed.

single-trait approach The research strategy of focusing on one particular trait of interest and learning as much as possible about its behavioral correlates, developmental antecedents, and life consequences.

sociality corollary In Kelly's personal construct theory, the principle that to understand another person it is necessary to understand his or her unique view of reality.

somatic marker hypothesis Neurologist Antonio Damasio's idea that the bodily (somatic), emotional component of thought is a necessary part of problem solving and decision making.

Spearman-Brown formula In psychometrics, a mathematical formula that predicts the degree to which the reliability of a test can be improved by adding more items.

state A temporary psychological event, such as an emotion, thought, or perception.

stimulus Anything in the environment that impinges on the nervous system. The plural form is *stimuli*.

strategy In cognitive approaches to personality, an organized series of activities in pursuit of a goal.

sublimation In psychoanalytic theory, the defense mechanism that turns otherwise dangerous or anxiety-producing impulses toward constructive ends.

superego In psychoanalytic theory, the location of conscience and the individual's system of internalized rules of conduct, or "morality."

symbolization In psychoanalytic theory, the process of primary process thinking in which one thing stands for another.

synapse The space between two neurons across which impulses are carried by neurotransmitters.

testosterone The male sex hormone.

Thanatos In psychoanalytic theory, another term for the drive toward death, destruction, and decay.

Thematic Apperception Test (TAT) A projective test that asks subjects to make up stories about pictures.

thrown-ness In Heidegger's existential analysis, the era, location, and situation into which a person happens to be born.

trait A relatively stable and long-lasting attribute of personality.

trait approach The theoretical view of personality that focuses on individual differences in personality and behavior, and the psychological processes behind them.

transference In psychoanalytic theory, the tendency to bring ways of thinking, feeling, and behavior that developed with one important person into later relationships with different persons.

Type I error In research, the mistake of thinking that one variable has an effect on or relationship with another, when really it does not.

Type II error In research, the mistake of thinking that one variable does not have an effect on or relationship with another, when really it does.

typological approach The research strategy that focuses on identifying types of individuals. Each type is characterized by a particular pattern of traits.

Umwelt In Binswanger's phenomenological analysis, *biological experience*; the sensations a person feels of being a live animal.

unconscious (mind) Those areas and processes of the mind of which a person is not aware.

utilitarianism The idea that the best society is that which creates the most happiness for the largest number of people.

validity In measurement, the degree to which a measurement actually reflects what it is intended to measure.

working memory The third stage of information processing, which contains a large amount of information, including a representation of the current environment, in easily accessible form that is just out of consciousness.

REFERENCES

Abelson, R., Cohen, J., & Rosenthal, R. (Chairs) (1996). *Initial report of the task force on statistical inference.* Washington, DC: Board of Scientific Affairs, American Psychological Association.

Adams, C. (2001, Feb. 2). Are there nine Eskimo words for snow [Electronic version]? *The Straight Dope.* Retrieved July 15, 2003, from www.straightdope.com/columns/010202.html

Adams, H. E., Wright, L. W., & Lohr, B. A. (1996). Is homophobia associated with homosexual arousal? *Journal of Abnormal Psychology, 105,* 440–445.

Ader, R., & Cohen, N. (1993). Psychoneuroimmunology: Conditioning and stress. *Annual Review of Psychology, 44,* 53–85.

Adler, A. (1939). *Social interest.* New York: Putnam.

Adolphs, R. (2001). The neurobiology of social cognition. *Current Opinion in Neurobiology, 11,* 231–239.

Adorno, T. W. (1950). Politics and economics in the interview material. In T. W. Adorno, E. Frenkel-Brunswik, D. Levinson, & N. Sanford (Eds.), *The authoritarian personality* (pp. 654–726). New York: Harper.

Adorno, T. W., Frenkel-Brunswik, E., Levinson, D., & Sanford, N. (1950). *The authoritarian personality.* New York: Harper.

Ahadi, S., & Diener, E. (1989). Multiple determinants and effect size. *Journal of Personality and Social Psychology, 56,* 398–406.

Ainsworth, M. D. S., Blehar, M. C., Waters, E., & Wall, S. (1978). *Patterns of attachment: Assessed in the strange situation and at home.* Hillsdale, NJ: Erlbaum.

Albright, L., Malloy, T. E., Dong, Q., Kenny, D. A., & Fang, X. (1997). Cross-cultural consensus in personality judgments. *Journal of Personality and Social Psychology, 72,* 558–569.

Allport, G. W. (1937). *Personality: A psychological interpretation.* New York: Holt, Rinehart, & Winston.

Allport, G. W. (1958). What units shall we employ? In G. Lindzey (Ed.), *Assessment of human motives* (pp. 239–260). New York: Rinehart.

Allport, G. W. (1961). *Pattern and growth in personality.* New York: Holt, Rinehart, & Winston.

Allport, G. W. (1965). *Letters from Jenny.* New York: Harcourt, Brace, & World.

Allport, G. W., & Odbert, H. S. (1936). Trait-names: A psycho-lexical study. *Psychological Monographs: General and Applied, 47,* 171–220. (1, Whole No. 211).

Allport, G. W., & Vernon, P. E. (1933*). Studies in expressive movement.* New York: Macmillan.

Alper, J., Beckwith, J., & Miller, L. G. (1978). Sociobiology is a political issue. In A. L. Caplan (Ed.), *The sociobiology debate: Readings on ethical and scientific issues* (pp. 476–488). New York: Harper.

Alonso-Zaldivar, R. (2002, December 11). Jet crash probe is concluded. *Los Angeles Times, 122* (8), B1.

Amabile, T. M., & Glazebrook, A. H. (1982). A negativity bias in interpersonal evaluation. *Journal of Experimental Social Psychology, 18,* 1–22.

American Anthropological Association (1999). AAA statement on race. *American Anthropologist, 100,* 712–713.

American Psychological Assocation (2001). *Publication manual of the American Psychological Association.* Washington, DC: American Psychological Association.

Anastasi, A. (1982). *Psychological Testing.* New York: Macmillan.

Andersen, S. M. (1984). Self-knowledge and social inference: II. The diagnosticity of cognitive/affective and behavioral data. *Journal of Personality and Social Psychology, 46,* 294–307.

Andersen, S. M., & Baum, A. (1994). Transference in interpersonal relations: Inferences and affect based on significant-other representations. *Journal of Personality, 62,* 459–499.

Andersen, S. M., & Bem, S. L. (1981). Sex typing and androgyny in dyadic interaction: Individual differences in responsiveness to physical attractiveness. *Journal of Personality and Social Psychology, 41,* 74–86.

Andersen, S. M., & Berk, M. S. (1998). The social-cognitive model of transference: Experiencing past relationships in the present. *Current Directions in Psychological Science, 7,* 109–115.

Andersen, S. M., & Chen, S. (2002). The relational self: An interpersonal social-cognitive theory. *Psychological Review, 109,* 619–645.

Anderson, E. (1994). The code of the streets. *Atlantic Monthly, 273,* 80–94.

Anderson, J. R. (1982). Acquisition of cognitive skill. *Psychological Review, 89,* 369–406.

Apter, M. J. (1992). *The dangerous edge: The psychology of excitement.* New York: Free Press.

Aronson, E. (1972). *The social animal.* San Francisco: Freeman.

Arsenian, J., & Arsenian, J. M. (1948). Tough and easy cultures: A conceptual analysis. *Psychiatry, 11,* 377–385.

Asendorpf, J. B. (2002). Editorial: The puzzle of personality types. *European Journal of Personality, 16,* 51–55.

Asendorpf, J. B., Banse, R., & Mücke, D. (2002). Double dissociation between implicit and explicit personality self-concept: The case of shy behavior. *Journal of Personality and Social Psychology, 83,* 380–393.

Asendorpf, J. B., Borkenau, P., Ostendorf, F., & van Aken, M. A. G. (2001). Carving personality description at its joints: Confirmation of three replicable personality prototypes for both children and adults. *European Journal of Personality, 15,* 169–198.

Asendorpf, J. B., & van Aken, M. A. G. (1999). Resilient, overcontrolled, and un-dercontrolled personality prototypes in childhood: Replicability, predictive power, and the trait-type issue. *Journal of Personality and Social Psychology, 77,* 815–832.

Asendorpf, J. B., & Wipers, S. (1998). Personality effects on social relationships. *Journal of Personality and Social Psychology, 74,* 1531–1544.

Associated Press (1994, May 5). African emigrants spread practice. Online: Prodigy service.

Azrin, N. H., & Holz, W. C. (1966). Punishment. In W. K. Honig (Ed.), *Operant behavior: Areas of research and application* (pp. 380–447). New York: Apple-ton-Century-Crofts.

Bachrach, H. M., Galatzer-Levy, R., Skolnikoff, A., & Waldron, S. (1991). On the efficacy of psychoanalysis. *Journal of the American Psychoanalytic Association, 39,* 871–916.

Bader, M. J. (1994). The tendency to neglect therapeutic aims in psychoanalysis. *Psychoanalytic Quarterly, 63,* 246–269.

Bakan, D. (1966). *The duality of human existence.* Chicago: Rand McNally.

Bailey, J. M., Dunne, M. P., & Martin, N. G. (2000). Genetic and environmental influences on sexual orientation and its correlates in an Australian twin sam-ple. *Journal of Personality and Social Psychology, 78,* 524–536.

Baldwin, M. W. (1999). Relational schemas: Research into social-cognitive aspects of interpersonal experience. In D. Cervone & Y. Shoda (Eds.), *The coherence of personality: Social-cognitive bases of consistency, variability and organization* (pp. 127–154). New York: Guilford.

Ball, J. D., Archer, R. P., & Imhof, E. A. (1994). Time requirements of psychological testing: A survey of practicioners. *Journal of Personality Assessment, 64,* 213–228.

Balter, M. (2002). What made humans modern? *Science, 295,* 1219.

Bandura, A. (1971). *Social learning theory.* New York: General Learning Press.

Bandura, A. (1977). *Social learning theory.* Englewood Cliffs, NJ: Prentice-Hall.

Bandura, A. (1978). The self system in reciprocal determinism. *American Psycholo-gist, 33,* 344–358.

Bandura, A. (1989). Human agency in social cognitive theory. *American Psycholo-gist, 44,* 1175–1184.

Bandura, A. (1999). Social cognitive theory of personality. In D. Cervone & Y. Shoda (Eds.), *The coherence of personality: Social-cognitive bases of consistency, variability and organization* (pp. 185–241). New York: Guilford.

Bandura, A. (2001). Social cognitive theory: An agentic perspective. *Annual Re-view of Psychology, 52,* 1–26.

Bandura, A., Ross, D., & Ross, S. A. (1963). Imitation of film-mediated aggressive models. *Journal of Abnormal and Social Psychology, 66,* 3–11.

Bargh, J. A., Bond, R. N., Lombardi, W. J., & Tota, M. E. (1986). The additive na-ture of chronic and temporary sources of construct accessibility. *Journal of Personality and Social Psychology, 50,* 869–878.

Bargh, J. A., Lombardi, W. J., & Higgins, E. T. (1988). Automaticity of chronically accessible constructs in person x situation effects on person perception: It's just a matter of time. *Journal of Personality and Social Psychology, 55,* 599–605.

Barrick, M. R., & Mount, M. K. (1991). The Big Five personality dimensions and job performance: A meta-analysis. *Personnel Psychology, 44,* 1–26.

Baumeister, R. F., Dale, K., & Sommer, K. L. (1998). Freudian defense mechanisms and empirical findings in modern social psychology: Reaction formation, projection, displacement, undoing, isolation, sublimation, and denial. *Journal of Personality, 66,* 1081–1124.

Baumeister, R. F., & Tice, D. M. (1988). Metatraits. *Journal of Personality, 56,* 571–598.

Baumeister, R. F., & Vohs, K. D. (2002). The pursuit of meaningfulness in life. In C. R. Snyder & S. J. Lopez (Eds.), *Handbook of positive psychology* (pp. 608–618). London: Oxford University Press.

Baumrind, D. (1971). Current patterns of parental authority. *Developmental Psychology, 4,* 1–103.

Baumrind, D. (1985). Research using intentional deception: Ethical issues revisited. *American Psychologist, 40,* 165–174.

Baumrind, D. (1991). The influence of parenting style on adolescent competence and substance use. *Journal of Early Adolescence, 11,* 56–95.

Baumrind, D. (1993). The average expectable environment is not good enough: A response to Scarr. *Child Development, 64,* 1299–1317.

Bellamy, G. T. (1975). The Pygmalion effect: What teacher behaviors mediate it? *Psychology in the Schools, 12,* 454–461.

Belsky, J., Steinberg, L., & Draper, P. (1991). Childhood experience, interpersonal development, and reproductive strategy: An evolutionary theory of socialization. *Child Development, 62,* 647–670.

Bem, D. J. (1972). Self-perception theory. In L. Berkowitz (Ed.), *Advances in experimental social psychology* (Vol. 6, pp. 1–62). New York: Academic Press.

Bem, D. J. (1996). Exotic becomes erotic: A developmental theory of sexual orientation. *Psychological Review, 103,* 320–335.

Bem, D. J. (2001). Exotic becomes erotic: Integrating biological and experiential antecedents of sexual orientation. In A. R. D'Augelli & C. J. Patterson (Eds.), *Lesbian, gay and bisexual identities and youth: Psychological perspectives* (pp. 52–68). London: Oxford University Press.

Bem, D. J., & Allen, A. (1974). On predicting some of the people some of the time: The search for cross-situational consistencies in behavior. *Psychological Review, 81,* 506–520.

Bem, D. J., & Funder, D. C. (1978). Predicting more of the people more of the time: Assessing the personality of situations. *Psychological Review, 85,* 485–501.

Benet-Martínez, V., & John, O. P. (1998). Los Cinco Grandes across cultures and ethnic groups: Multitrait-multimethod analyses of the Big Five in Spanish and English. *Journal of Personality and Social Psychology, 75,* 729–750.

Benet-Martínez, V., & John, O. P. (2000). Toward the development of quasi-indigenous personality constructs: Measuring Los Cinco Grandes in Spain with indigenous Castilian markers. *American Behavioral Scientist, 44,* 141–157.

Benet-Martínez, V., Leu, J., Lee, F., & Morris, M. (2002). Negotiating biculturalism: Cultural frame switching in biculturals with oppositional versus compatible cultural identities. *Journal of Cross-Cultural Psychology, 35,* 492–516.

Benet-Martínez, V., & Waller, N. G. (1997). Further evidence for the cross-cultural generality of the Big Seven Factor model: Indigenous and imported Spanish personality constructs. *Journal of Personality, 65,* 567–598.

Benjamin, J., Li, L., Patterson, C., Greenberg, B. D., Murphy, D. L., & Hamer, D. H. (1996). Population and familial association between the D4 dopamine receptor gene and measures of novelty seeking. *Nature Genetics, 12,* 81–84.

Bergeman, C. S., Chipuer, H. M., Plomin, R., Pedersen, N. L., McClearn, G. E., Nesselroade, J. R., Costa, P. T., Jr., & McCrae, R. R. (1993). Genetic and environmental effects on openness to experience, agreeableness, and conscientiousness: An adoption/twin study. *Journal of Personality, 61,* 159–179.

Berke, R. L. (1998, September 27). The good leader: in presidents, virtues can be flaws (and vice versa). *New York Times, 148*(4), col 1.

Berkowitz, L. (1962). *Aggression: A social psychological analysis.* New York: McGraw-Hill.

Bernhardt, P. C., Dabbs, J. M., Jr., Fielden, J. A., & Lutter, C. D. (1998). Testosterone changes during vicarious experiences of winning and losing among fans at sporting events. *Physiology and Behavior, 65,* 59–62.

Berry, D. S., & Finch Wero, J. W. (1993). Accuracy in face perception: A view from ecological psychology. *Journal of Personality, 61,* 497–520.

Berry, D. S., & Pennebaker, J. W. (1993). Nonverbal and verbal emotional expression and health. *Psychotherapy and Psychosomatics, 59,* 11–19.

Berry, J. W. (1969). On cross-cultural comparability. *International Journal of Psychology, 4,* 119–128.

Bettelheim, B. (1943). Individual and mass behavior in extreme situations. *Journal of Abnormal and Social Psychology, 38,* 417–452.

Bettelheim, B. (1982). *Freud and man's soul.* New York: Vintage.

Bettelheim, B. (1988). *A good enough parent.* New York: Vintage.

Bigelow, H. J. (1850). Dr. Harlow's case of recovery from the passage of an iron bar through the head. *American Journal of Medical Sciences, 19,* 13–22.

Binswanger, L. (1958). *The case of Ellen West.* In R. May, E. Angel, & H. F. Ellenberger (Eds.), *Existence* (pp. 237–364). New York: Basic.

Binswanger, L. (1963). *Being-in-the-world: Selected papers of Ludwig Binswanger.* New York: Basic.

Birbaumer, N., Grodd, W., Diedrich, O., Klose, U., Erb, M., & Lotze, M. (1998). fMRI reveals amygdala activation to human faces in social phobics. *Neuroreport, 9,* 1223–1226.

Blackman, M. C. (2002). Personality judgment and the utility of the unstructured employment interview. *Basic and Applied Social Psychology, 24,* 241–250.

Blackman, M. C., & Funder, D. C. (1998). The effect of information on consensus and accuracy in personality judgment. *Journal of Experimental Social Psychology, 34,* 164–181.

Blascovich, J., Loomis, J., Beall, A. C., Swinth, K. R., Hoyt, C. L., & Bailenson, J. N. (2002). Immersive virtual environment technology as a methodological tool for social psychology. *Psychological Inquiry, 13,* 103–124.

Block, J. (1971). *Lives through time.* Berkeley, CA: Bancroft.

Block, J. (1977). Advancing the science of psychology: Paradigmatic shift or improving the quality of research? In D. Magnusson & N. S. Endler (Eds.), *Personality at the crossroads: Current issues in interactional psychology* (pp. 37–64). Hillsdale, NJ: Erlbaum.

Block, J. (1978). *The Q-sort method in personality assessment and psychiatric research.* Palo Alto, CA: Consulting Psychologists Press. (Originally published 1961.)

Block, J. (1989). Critique of the act frequency approach to personality. *Journal of Personality and Social Psychology, 56,* 234–245.

Block, J. (1993). Studying personality the long way. In D. C. Funder, R. D. Parke, C. Tomlinson-Keasey, & K. Widaman (Eds.), *Studying lives through time: Personality and development* (pp. 9–41). Washington, DC: American Psychological Association.

Block, J. (1995). A contrarian view of the five-factor approach to personality description. *Psychological Bulletin, 117,* 187–215.

Block, J. (2002). *Personality as an affect-processing system: Toward an integrative theory.* Mahwah, NJ: Erlbaum.

Block, J., Block, J. H., & Keyes, S. (1988). Longitudinally foretelling drug usage in adolescence: Early childhood personality and environmental precursors. *Child Development, 59,* 336–355.

Block, J., Block, J. H., Siegelman, E., & von der Lippe, A. (1971). Optimal psychological adjustment: Response to Miller's and Bronfenbrenner's discussions. *Journal of Consulting and Clinical Psychology, 36,* 325–328.

Block, J., Gjerde, P. F., & Block, J. H. (1991). Personality antecedents of depressive tendencies in 18-year-olds: A prospective study. *Journal of Personality and Social Psychology, 60,* 726–738.

Block, J. H. (1973). Conceptions of sex role: Some cross-cultural and longitudinal perspectives. *American Psychologist, 28,* 512–526.

Block, J. H., & Block, J. (1980). The role of ego-control and ego-resiliency in the organization of behavior. In W. A. Collins (Ed.), *Development of cognition, affect, and social relations: The Minnesota symposia on child psychology* (Vol. 13, pp. 40–101). Hillsdale, NJ: Erlbaum.

Blum, K., Cull, J. G., Braverman, E. R., & Comings, D. E. (1996). Reward deficiency syndrome. *American Scientist, 84,* 132–146.

Bond, M. H. (1979). Dimensions of personality used in perceiving peers: Cross-cultural comparisons of Hong Kong, Japanese, American, and Filipino university students. *International Journal of Psychology, 14,* 47–56.

Bond, M. H., & Cheung, T. (1983). College students' spontaneous self-concept: The effect of culture among respondents in Hong Kong, Japan, and the United States. *Journal of Cross-cultural Psychology, 14,* 153–171.

Bond, M. H., Nakazato, H., & Shiraishi, D. (1975). Universality and distinctiveness in dimensions of Japanese person perception. *Journal of Cross-cultural Psychology, 6,* 346–357.

Borkenau, P., & Liebler, A. (1993). Consensus and self-other agreement for trait inferences from minimal information. *Journal of Personality, 61,* 477–496.

Borkenau, P., Riemann, R., Angleitner, A., & Spinath, F. M. (2001). Genetic and environmental influences on observed personality: Evidence from the German observational study of adult twins. *Journal of Personality and Social Psychology, 80,* 655–668.

Borman, W. C., Hanson, W., & Hedge, J. (1997). Personnel selection. *Annual Review of Psychology, 48,* 299–337.

Borman, W. C., & Penner, L. A. (2001). Citizenship performance: Its nature, antecedents and motives. In B. W. Roberts & R. Hogan (Eds.), *Personality psychology in the workplace.* Washington, DC: American Psychological Association.

Born, J., Hitzler, V., Pietrowsky, R., Pairschinger, P., & Fehm, H. L. (1988). Influences of cortisol on auditory evoked potentials and mood in humans. *Neuropsychobiology, 20,* 145–151.

Bornstein, R. F. (1999). Source amnesia, misattribution, and the power of unconscious perceptions and memories. *Psychoanalytic Psychology, 16,* 155–178.

Boss, M. (1963). *Psychoanalysis and daseinsanalysis.* New York: Basic.

Bower, G. H., & Hilgard, E. R. (1981). *Theories of learning* (5th ed.). Englewood Cliffs, NJ: Prentice-Hall.

Bowers, K. S. (1973). Situationism in psychology: An analysis and critique. *Psychological Review, 80,* 307–336.

Bowlby, J. (1982). *Attachment and loss: Vol. I. Attachment* (2nd ed.). New York: Basic. (Originally published 1969.)

Brandt, V. S. (1974). Skiing cross-culturally. *Current Anthropology, 15,* 64–66.

Braun, C. (1976). Teacher expectation: Sociopsychological dynamics. *Review of Educational Research, 46,* 185–213.

Brenner, C. (1974). *An elementary textbook of psychoanalysis.* Garden City, NY: Doubleday/Anchor.

Brenner, C. (1982). *The mind in conflict.* New York: International Universities Press.

Brickman, P., Coates, D., & Janoff-Bulman, R. (1978). Winners and accident victims: Is happiness relative? *Journal of Personality and Social Psychology, 36,* 917–927.

Brickner, R. M. (1936). The intellectual functions of the frontal lobes. New York: Macmillan.

Briggs, S. R. (1989). The optimal level of measurement for personality constructs. In D. Buss & N. Cantor (Eds.), *Personality psychology: Recent trends and emerging directions* (pp. 246–260). New York: Springer-Verlag.

Briggs, S. R., & Cheek, J. M. (1986). The role of factor analysis in the development and evaluation of personality scales. *Journal of Personality, 54,* 106–148.

Briggs, S. R., Cheek, J. M., & Buss, A. H. (1980). An analysis of the Self-Monitoring Scale. *Journal of Personality and Social Psychology, 38,* 679–686.

Broadbent, D. E. (1958). *Perception and communication.* London: Pergamon.

Brown, R. (1996). *Against my better judgment: An intimate memoir of an eminent gay psychologist.* New York: Harrington Park.

Brown, W. (1910). Some experimental results in the correlation of mental abilities. *British Journal of Psychology, 3,* 297–301.

Brunswik, E. (1956). *Perception and the representative design of psychological experiments.* Berkeley: University of California Press.

Buck, R. (1999). The biological affects: A typology. *Psychological Review, 106,* 301–336.

Bullock, W. A., & Gilliland, K. (1993). Eysenck's arousal theory of introversion-extraversion: A converging measures investigation. *Journal of Personality and Social Psychology, 64,* 113–123.

Burnett, J. D. (1974). Parallel measurements and the Spearman-Brown formula. *Educational and Psychological Measurement, 34,* 785–788.

Burwen, L. S., & Campbell, D. T. (1957). The generality of attitudes toward authority and nonauthority figures. *Journal of Abnormal and Social Psychology, 54,* 24–31.

Bushman, B. J. (2002). Does venting anger feed or extinguish the flame? Catharsis, rumination, distraction, anger and aggressive responding. *Personality and Social Psychology Bulletin, 28,* 724–731.

Bushman, B. J. & Baumeister, R. F. (2002). Does self-love or self-hate lead to violence? *Journal of Research in Personality, 36,* 543–545.

Buss, D. M. (1989). Sex differences in human mate preferences: Evolutionary hypotheses tested in 37 cultures. *Behavioral and Brain Sciences, 12,* 1–49.

Buss, D. M., & Barnes, M. F. (1986). Preferences in human mate selection. *Journal of Personality and Social Psychology, 50,* 559–570.

Buss, D. M., & Greiling, H. (1999). Adaptive individual differences. *Journal of Personality, 67,* 209–243.

Buss, D. M., Larsen, R. J., Westen, D., & Semmelroth, J. (1992). Sex differences in jealousy: Evolution, physiology and psychology. *Psychological Science, 3,* 251–255.

Butcher, J. N. (1999). *A beginner's guide to the MMPI-2.* Washington, DC: American Psychological Association.

Butler, J. M., & Haigh, G. V. (1954). Changes in the relation between self-concepts and ideal concepts consequent upon client-centered counseling. In C. R. Rogers & R. F. Dymond (Eds.), *Psychotherapy and personality change: Coordinated studies in the client-centered approach* (pp. 55–76). Chicago: University of Chicago Press.

Bykov, K. M. (1957). *The cerebral cortex and the internal organs* (W. H. Gantt, Trans.). New York: Chemical Publishing.

Byrne, D. (1961). The repression-sensitization scale: Rationale, reliability, and validity. *Journal of Personality, 29,* 334–349.

Caldwell, D. F., & Burger, J. M. (1997). Personality and social influence strategies in the workplace. *Personality and Social Psychology Bulletin, 23,* 1003–1012.

Caldwell, D. F., & Burger, J. M. (1998). Personality characteristics of job applicants and success in screening interviews. *Personnel Psychology, 51,* 119–136.

Call, J., & Tomasello, M. (1995). The use of social information in the problem-solving of orangutans and human children. *Journal of Comparative Psychology, 109,* 301–320.

Campbell, A., Converse, P. E., Miller, W. E., & Stokes, D. E. (1960). *The American voter.* New York: Wiley.

Campos, J. J., Barrett, K., Lamb, M. E., Goldsmith, H. H., & Stenberg, C. (1983). Socioemotional development. In M. M. Haith & J. J. Campos (Eds.), *Handbook of child psychology: Vol. 2. Infancy and psychobiology* (pp. 783–916). New York: Wiley.

Cannon, W. B. (1932). *The wisdom of the body.* New York: Norton.

Cantor, N. (1990). From thought to behavior: "Having" and "doing" in the study of personality and cognition. *American Psychologist, 45,* 735–750.

Cantor, N., & Kihlstrom, J. F. (1987). *Personality and social intelligence.* Englewood Cliffs, NJ: Prentice-Hall.

Capgras, J., & Reboul-Lachaux, J. (1923). L'illusion des "sosies" dans un delire systematize chronique [The illusion of doubles as a chronically systematized delusion]. *Bulletin de la Societé Clinique de Medicine Mentale, 11,* 6–16.

Caplan, B. (2003). Stigler-Becker versus Myers-Briggs: Why preference-blind explanations are scientifically meaningful and empirically important. *Journal of Economic Behavior and Organization, 50,* 391–405.

Carver, C. S. (1975). Physical aggression as a function of objective self-awareness and attitudes toward punishment. *Journal of Experimental Social Psychology, 11,* 510–519.

Carver, C. S., & Scheier, M. F. (1995). The role of optimism versus pessimism in the experience of the self. In A. Oosterwegel & R. A. Wicklund (Eds.), *The self in European and North American culture: Development and processes* (pp. 193–204). Dordrecht, Netherlands: Kluwer Academic.

Caspi, A. (1998). Personality development across the life course. In N. Eisenberg (Ed.), *Handbook of child psychology: Vol. 3. Social, emotional and personality development* (pp. 311–388). New York: Wiley.

Caspi, A., & Silva, P. A. (1995). Temperamental qualities at age 3 predict personality traits in young adulthood: Longitudinal evidence from a birth cohort. *Child Development, 66,* 486–498.

Cattell, R. B. (1950). *Personality: A systematic, theoretical and factual study.* New York: McGraw-Hill.

Cattell, R. B. (1952). *Factor analysis.* New York: Harper.

Cattell, R. B. (1957). *Personality and motivation structure and measurement.* New York: World Book.

Cattell, R. B. (1965). *The scientific analysis of personality.* Baltimore: Penguin.

Cattell, R. B., & Eber, H. W. (1961). *The Sixteen Personality Factor Questionnaire* (3rd ed.). Champaign, IL: Institute for Personality and Ability Testing.

Cervone, D., & Shoda, Y. (1999). Beyond traits in the study of personality coherence. *Current Directions in Psychological Science, 8,* 27–32.

Cervone, D., & Shoda, Y. (1999). Social-cognitive theories and the coherence of personality. In D. Cervone & Y. Shoda (Eds.), *The coherence of personality: Social-cognitive bases of consistency, variability and organization* (pp. 3–33). New York: Guilford.

Chao, R. (2001). Extending research on the consequences of parenting style for Chinese Americans and European Americans. *Child Development, 72,* 1832–1843.

Chaplin, W. F. (1991). The next generation of moderator research in personality psychology. *Journal of Personality, 59,* 143–178.

Chaplin, W. F., & Goldberg, L. R. (1985). A failure to replicate the Bem and Allen study of individual differences in cross-situational consistency. *Journal of Personality and Social Psychology, 47,* 1074–1090.

Chaplin, W. F., Phillips, J. B., Brown, J. D., Clanton, N. R., & Stein, J. L. (2000). Handshaking, gender, personality, and first impressions. *Journal of Personality and Social Psychology, 79,* 110–117.

Chase, W. G., & Simon, H. A. (1973). The mind's eye in chess. In W. G. Chase (Ed.), *Visual information processing* (pp. 215–281). New York: Academic.

Cheek, J. M. (1990). Shyness, self-esteem, and self-consciousness. In H. Leitenberg (Ed.), *Handbook of social and evaluation anxiety* (pp. 47–82). New York: Plenum.

Cheung, F. M., Leung, K., Fan, R. M., Song, W. S., Zhang, J. X., & Zhang, J. P. (1996). Development of the Chinese Personality Assessment Inventory. *Journal of Cross-cultural Psychology, 27,* 181–199.

Cheung, F. M., & Song, W. (1989). A review of the clinical applications of the Chinese MMPI. *Psychological Assessment, 1,* 230–237.

Clark, H. H., & Clark, E. V. (1977). *Psychology and language: An introduction to psycholinguistics.* New York: Harcourt Brace.

Clark, J. M., & Paivio, A. (1989). Observational and theoretical terms in psychology: A cognitive perspective on scientific language. *American Psychologist, 44,* 500–512.

Clark, L. A., Livesley, W. J., & Morey, L. (1997). Personality disorder assessment: the challenge of construct validity. *Journal of Personality Disorders, 11,* 205–31.

Cohen, D., Nisbett, R. E., Bowdle, B. F., & Schwartz, N. (1996). Insult, aggression and the southern culture of honor: An "experimental ethnography." *Journal of Personality and Social Psychology, 70,* 945–960.

Cohen, J. (1994). The earth is round (p. 05). *American Psychologist, 49,* 997–1003.

Collins, W. A., Maccoby, E. E., Steinberg, L., Hetherington, E. M., & Bornstein, M. H. (2000). Contemporary research on parenting: The case for nature and nurture. *American Psychologist, 55,* 218–232.

Colvin, C. R. (1993a). Childhood antecedents of young-adult judgability. *Journal of Personality, 61,* 611–635.

Colvin, C. R. (1993b). "Judgable" people: Personality, behavior, and competing explanations. *Journal of Personality and Social Psychology, 64,* 861–873.

Colvin, C. R., & Block, J. (1994). Do positive illusions foster mental health? An examination of the Taylor and Brown formulation. *Psychological Bulletin, 116,* 3–20.

Colvin, C. R., & Bundick, M. J. (2001). In search of the good judge of personality: Some methodological and theoretical concerns. In J. A. Hall & F. J. Bernieri (Eds.), *Interpersonal sensitivity: Theory and measurement* (pp. 47–65). Mahwah, NJ: Erlbaum.

Colvin, C. R., & Funder, D. C. (1991). Predicting personality and behavior: A boundary on the acquaintanceship effect. *Journal of Personality and Social Psychology, 60,* 884–894.

Cook, T. D., & Campbell, D. T. (Eds.). (1979). *The design and analysis of quasi-experiments for field settings.* Chicago: Rand-McNally.

Corr, P. J., Pickering, A. D., & Gray, J. A. (1997). Personality, punishment and procedural learning: A test of J. A. Gray's anxiety theory. *Journal of Personality and Social Psychology, 73,* 337–344.

Costa, P. T., Jr. (1996). Work and personality: Use of the NEO-PI-R in industrial/organizational psychology. *Applied Psychology: An International Review, 45,* 225–241.

Costa, P. T., Jr., Herbst, J. H., McCrae, R. R., Samuels, J., & Ozer, D. J. (2002). The replicability and utility of three personality types. *European Journal of Personality, 16,* 573–588.

Costa, P. T., Jr., & McCrae, R. R. (1997). Stability and change in personality assessment: The Revised NEO Personality Inventory in the year 2000. *Journal of Personality Assessment, 68,* 86–94.

Costa, P. T., Terracciano, A., & McCrae, R. R. (2001). Gender differences in personality traits across cultures: Robust and surprising findings. *Journal of Personality and Social Psychology, 81,* 322–331.

Coué, E. (1997). *Self-mastery through conscious autosuggestion—1922.* Kila, MT: Kessinger Publishing. (Originally published 1922).

Cousins, S. D. (1989). Culture and self-perception in Japan and the United States. *Journal of Personality and Social Psychology, 56,* 124–131.

Craik, F. I. M., & Tulving, E. (1975). Depth of processing and the retention of words in episodic memory. *Journal of Experimental Psychology: General, 104,* 268–294.

Craik, F. I. M., & Watkins, M. J. (1973). The role of rehearsal in short-term memory. *Journal of Verbal Learning and Verbal Behavior, 12,* 599–607.

Cramer, P. (1998). Defensiveness and defense mechanisms. *Journal of Personality, 66,* 879–894.

Cramer, P., & Davidson, K. (Eds.). (1998). Defense mechanisms in contemporary personality research (Special Issue). *Journal of Personality, 66,* 879–1157.

Crews, F. (1996). The verdict on Freud. *Psychological Science, 7,* 63–67.

Crews, F. (Ed.) (1998). *Unauthorized Freud: Doubters confront a legend.* New York: Viking.

Cronbach, L. J. (1951). Coefficient alpha and the internal structure of tests. *Psychometrika, 16,* 297–334.

Cronbach, L. J. (1955). Processes affecting scores on "understanding of others" and "assumed similarity." *Psychological Bulletin, 52,* 177–193.

Cronbach, L. J., Gleser, G. C., Nanda, H., & Rajaratnam, N. (1972). *The dependability of behavioral measurements: Theory of generalizability for scores and profiles.* New York: Wiley.

Cronbach, L. J., & Meehl, P. E. (1955). Construct validity in psychological tests. *Psychological Bulletin, 52,* 281–302.

Csikszentmihalyi, M., & Csikszentmihalyi, I. S. (Eds.). (1988). *Optimal experience: Psychological studies of flow in consciousness.* New York: Cambridge University Press.

Csikszentmihalyi, M., & Larson, R. (1992). Validity and reliability of the Experience Sampling Method. In M. V. deVries (Ed.), *The experience of psychopathology: Investigating mental disorders in their natural settings* (pp. 43–57). Cambridge, England: Cambridge University Press.

Cunningham, D. J. (1992). Assessing constructions and constructing assessments: A dialogue. In T. M. Duffy & D. H. Jonassen (Eds.), *Constructivism and the technology of instruction: A conversation* (pp. 34–44). Hillsdale, NJ: Erlbaum.

Cutler, A. G. (Ed.). (1976). *Stedman's medical dictionary.* Baltimore: Williams & Wilkins.

Dabbs, J. M., Jr. (1997). Testosterone, smiling, and facial appearance. *Journal of Nonverbal Behavior, 21,* 45–55.

Dabbs, J. M., Jr., Alford, E. C., & Fielden, J. A. (1998). Trial lawyers and testosterone: Blue-collar talent in a white-collar world. *Journal of Applied Psychology, 28,* 84–94.

Dabbs, J. M., Jr., & Morris, R. (1990). Testosterone, social class, and antisocial behavior in a sample of 4,462 men. *Psychological Science, 1,* 209–211.

Dabbs, J. M., Jr., Ruback, R. B., Frady, R. L., Hopper, C. H., & Sgoritas, D. S. (1988). Saliva testosterone and criminal violence among women. *Personality and Individual Differences, 9,* 269–275.

Dabbs, J. M., Jr., Strong, R., & Milun, R. (1997). Exploring the mind of testosterone: A beeper study. *Journal of Research in Personality, 31,* 577–587.

Dahlstrom, W. G., & Welsh, G. S. (1960). *An MMPI handbook: A guide to use in clinical practice and research.* Minneapolis: University of Minnesota Press.

Daly, M., & Wilson, M. (1988). Evolutionary social-psychology and family homicide. *Science, 242,* 519–524.

Damasio, A. R. (1994). *Descartes' error: Emotion, reason, and the human brain.* New York: Putnam.

Darley, J., & Fazio, R. (1980). Expectancy confirmation processes arising in the social interaction sequence. *American Psychologist, 35,* 867–881.

Darley, J. M., & Batson, C. D. (1967). "From Jerusalem to Jericho": A study of situational and dispositional variables in helping behavior. *Journal of Personality and Social Psychology, 27,* 100–108.

Darley, J. M., & Latané, B. (1968). Bystander intervention in emergencies: Diffusion of responsibility. *Journal of Personality and Social Psychology, 28,* 377–383.

Darwin, C. (1967). *On the origin of the species by means of natural selection, or the preservation of favoured races in the struggle for life.* New York: Modern Library. (Originally published 1859.)

Davidson, R. J., Ekman, P., Saron, C. D., Senulis, J. A., & Frisesen, W. V. (1990). Approach/withdrawal and cerebral asymmetry: Emotional expression and brain physiology. *Journal of Personality and Social Psychology, 58,* 330–341.

Davidson, R. J. (1993). The neuropsychology of emotion and affective style. In M. Lewis & J. M. Haviland (Eds.), *Handbook of emotions* (pp. 143–154). New York: Guilford.

Dawkins, R. (1976). *The selfish gene.* New York: Oxford University Press.

Dawson, J. L. M. (1974). Ecology, social pressures toward conformity, and left-handedness: A bio-social psychological approach. In J. L. M. Dawson & K. W. J. Lonner (Eds.), *Readings in cross-cultural psychology* (pp. 124–149). Hong Kong: University of Hong Kong Press.

Dennett, D. C. (1994). Real consciousness. In A. Revonsuo & M. Kamppinen (Eds.), *Consciousness in philosophy and cognitive neuroscience.* Hillsdale, NJ: Erlbaum.

Dennett, D. C., & Weiner, P. (1991). *Consciousness explained.* Boston: Little, Brown.

Depue, R. A., & Collins, P. F. (1999). Neurobiology of the structure of personality: Dopamine, facilitation of incentive motivation, and extraversion. *Behavioral and Brain Sciences, 22,* 491–569.

Derby, S. P. (1994, Nov. 2). Eskimo words for snow derby [Electronic version]. *The AFU and Urban Legend Archive.* Retrieved July 15, 2003, from www.urbanlegends.com/language/eskimo_words_for_snow_derby.html

De Waal, F. B. M. (2002). Evolutionary psychology: The wheat and the chaff. *Current Directions in Psychological Science, 11,* 187–191.

Diamond, J. (1999). *Guns, germs and steel: The fates of human societies.* New York: Norton.

Diener, C. I., & Dweck, C. S. (1978). An analysis of learned helplessness: Continuous changes in performance, strategy and achievement cognitions following failure. *Journal of Personality and Social Psychology, 36,* 451–462.

Diener, E., Lucas, R. E., & Oishi, S. (2002). Subjective well-being: The science and happiness of life satisfaction. In C. L. M. Keyes & J. Haidt (Eds.), *Flourishing: Positive psychology and the life well-lived* (pp. 463–473). Washington, DC: American Psychological Association.

Dillehay, R. C. (1978). Authoritarianism. In H. London & J. E. Exner (Eds.), *Dimensions of personality* (pp. 85–127). New York: Wiley.

Dodge, K. A. (1993). Social-cognitive mechanisms in the development of conduct disorder and depression. *Annual Review of Psychology, 44,* 559–584.

Dodge, K. A., & Frame, C. L. (1982). Social cognitive biases and deficits in aggressive boys. *Child Development, 53,* 620–635.

Doi, T. (1973). Amae—A key concept for understanding Japanese personality structure. In R. J. Smith & R. K. Beardsley (Eds.), *Japanese culture: Its development and characteristics* (pp. 132–139). Chicago: Aldine.

Dollard, J., & Miller, N. E. (1950). *Personality and psychotherapy: An analysis in terms of learning, thinking, and culture.* New York: McGraw-Hill.

Donahue, E. M., Robins, R. W., Roberts, R. W., & John, O. P. (1993). The divided self: Concurrent and longitudinal effects of psychological adjustment and social roles on self-concept differentiation. *Journal of Personality and Social Psychology, 64,* 834–846.

Doran, J. M. (1990). The Capgras syndrome: Neurological/neuropsychological perspectives. *Neuropsychology, 4,* 29–42.

Downey, G., & Feldman, S. I. (1996). Implications of rejection sensitivity for intimate relationships. *Journal of Personality and Social Psychology, 70,* 1327–1343.

Downey, G., Freitas, A., Michaelis, B., & Khouri, H. (1997). The self-fulfilling prophecy in close relationships: Rejection sensitivity and rejection in romantic partners. *Journal of Personality and Social Psychology, 75,* 545–560.

Duncan, L. E., Peterson, B. E., & Winter, D. G. (1997). Authoritarianism and gender roles: Toward a psychological analysis of hegemonic relationships. *Personality and Social Psychology Bulletin, 23,* 41–49.

Dutton, D., & Aron, A. (1974). Some evidence for heightened sexual attraction under conditions of high anxiety. *Journal of Personality and Social Psychology, 30,* 510–517.

Dweck, C. S., & Leggett, E. L. (1988). A social-cognitive approach to personality and motivation. *Psychological Review, 95,* 256–273.

Dworkin, B. R. (1993). *Learning and physiological regulation.* Chicago: University of Chicago Press.

Dyssegaard, E. K. (1997, May 17). The Danes call it fresh air. *New York Times,* p. 19:2.

Eagly, A. H., & Wood, W. (1999). The origins of sex differences in human behavior: Evolved dispositions versus social roles. *American Psychologist, 54,* 408–423.

Eisenberg, N., Spinrad, T. L., & Cumberland, A. (1998). The socialization of emotion: Reply to commentaries. *Psychological Inquiry, 9,* 317–333.

Ekman, P., & Davidson, R. J. (Eds.). (1994). *The nature of emotion: Fundamental questions.* New York: Oxford University Press.

Elder, G. (1974). *Children of the Great Depression.* Chicago: University of Chicago Press.

Elms, A. C., & Milgram, S. (1966). Personality characteristics associated with obedience and defiance toward authoritative command. *Journal of Experimental Research in Personality, 1,* 282–289.

Emmons, R. A. (1989). Exploring the relations between motives and traits: The case of narcissism. In D. M. Buss & N. Cantor (Eds.), *Personality psychology: Recent trends and emerging directions* (pp. 32–44). New York: Springer-Verlag.

Emmons, R. A. (1996). Striving and feeling: Personal goals and subjective well-being. In P. M. Gollwitzer & J. A. Bargh (Eds.), *The psychology of action: Linking cognition and motivation to behavior* (pp. 313–337). New York: Guilford.

Emmons, R. A. (1997). Motives and life goals. In R. Hogan, J. Johnson, & S. Briggs (Eds.), *Handbook of personality psychology* (pp. 485–512). San Diego: Academic.

Emmons, R. A., & King, L. A. (1988). Conflict among personal strivings: Immediate and long-term implications for psychological and physical well-being. *Journal of Personality and Social Psychology, 54,* 1040–1048.

Emmons, R. A., & McAdams, D. P. (1991). Personal strivings and motive dispositions: Exploring the links. *Personality and Social Psychology Bulletin, 6,* 648–654.

Epstein, S. (1973). The self-concept revisited, or a theory of a theory. *American Psychologist, 28,* 404–416.

Epstein, S. (1979). The stability of behavior: I. On predicting most of the people much of the time. *Journal of Personality and Social Psychology, 37,* 1097–1126.

Epstein, S. (1980). The stability of behavior: II. Implications for psychological research. *American Psychologist, 35,* 790–806.

Epstein, S. (1994). Integration of the cognitive and the psychodynamic unconscious. *American Psychologist, 49,* 709–724.

Epstein, S. (1998). *Constructive thinking: The key to emotional intelligence.* Westport, CT: Praeger.

Epstein, S. (2003). Cognitive-experiential self-theory of personality. In T. Millon & M. J. Lerner (Ed.), *Handbook of psychology: Personality and social psychology* (pp. 159–184). New York: Wiley.

Epstein, S., Lipson, A., Holstein, C., & Huh, E. (1992). Irrational reactions to negative outcomes: Evidence for two conceptual systems. *Journal of Personality and Social Psychology, 62,* 328–339.

Erdleyi, M. H. (1974). A "new look" at the New Look in perception. *Psychological Review, 81,* 1–25.

Erdelyi, M. H. (1985). *Psychoanalysis: Freud's cognitive psychology.* San Francisco: Freeman.

Erdelyi, M. H. (1994). Commentary: Integrating a dissociation-prone psychology. *Journal of Personality, 62,* 669–680.

Erdley, C. A., Cain, K. M., Loomis, C. C., Dumas-Hines, F., & Dweck, C. S. (1997). The relations among children's social goals, implicit personality theories, and responses to social failure. *Developmental Psychology, 33,* 263–272.

Erikson, E. (1963). *Childhood and society.* New York: Norton.

Erikson, E. (1968). *Identity: Youth and crisis.* New York: Norton.

Exner, J. E., Jr. (1993). *The Rorschach: A comprehensive system: Vol. 1. Basic foundations* (3rd ed.). New York: Wiley.

Eysenck, H. J. (1947). *Dimensions of personality.* London: Routledge & Kegan Paul.

Eysenck, H. J. (1967). *The biological basis of personality.* Springfield, IL: Charles C. Thomas.

Eysenck, H. J. (1976). *Sex and personality.* Austin: University of Texas Press.

Eysenck, H. J. (1987). Arousal and personality: The origins of a theory. In J. Strelau & H. J. Eysenck (Eds.), *Personality dimensions and arousal* (pp. 1–13). New York: Plenum.

Eysenck, H. J., & Beech, H. R. (1971). Counter conditioning and related methods. In A. E. Bergin & S. Garfield (Eds.), *Handbook of psychotherapy and behavior change* (pp. 543–611). New York: Wiley.

Eysenck, H. J., & Gudjonsson, G. H. (1989). *The causes and cures of criminality.* New York: Plenum.

Eysenck, S. B. G., & Eysenck, H. J. (1967). Salivary response to lemon juice as a measure of introversion. *Perceptual and Motor Skills, 24,* 1047–1053.

Eysenck, S. B. G., & Long, F. Y. (1986). A cross-cultural comparison of personality in adults and children: Singapore and England. *Journal of Personality and Social Psychology, 58,* 281–291.

Fannin, N., & Dabbs, J. M., Jr. (2002). Testosterone and the work of firefighters: Fighting fires and delivering medical care. *Journal of Research in Personality, 37,* 107–115.

Feldman-Barrett, L., & Barrett, D. J. (2001). An introduction to computerized experience sampling in psychology. *Social Science Computer Review, 19,* 175–185.

Feldman-Barrett, L., Williams, N. L., & Fong, G. T. (2002). Defensive verbal behavior assessment. *Personality and Social Psychology Bulletin, 28,* 776–788.

Fenigstein, A., Scheier, M. F., & Buss, A. H. (1975). Public and private self-consciousness: Assessment and theory. *Journal of Consulting and Clinical Psychology, 43,* 522–527.

Fenz, W. D., & Epstein, S. (1967). Gradients of physiological arousal of experienced and novice parachutists as a function of an approaching jump. *Psychosomatic Medicine, 29,* 33–51.

Festinger, L., & Carlsmith, J. M. (1959). Cognitive consequences of forced compliance. *Journal of Abnormal and Social Psychology, 58,* 203–210.

Fishbein, M., & Ajzen, I. (1974). Attitudes toward objects as predictors of single and multiple behavioral criteria. *Psychological Review, 81,* 59–74.

Fleeson, W. (2001). Toward a structure- and process-integrated view of personality: Traits as density distributions of states. *Journal of Personality and Social Psychology, 80,* 1011–1027.

Flint, A. (1995, October 25). Stone age weighs us down today. *Press-Enterprise* (Riverside, CA), p. D1.

Floody, O. R. (1983). Hormones and aggression in female mammals. In B. B. Svare (Ed.), *Hormones and aggressive behavior* (pp. 39–89). New York: Plenum.

Freeberg, N. E. (1969). Relevance of rater-ratee acquaintance in the validity and reliability of ratings. *Journal of Applied Psychology, 53,* 518–524.

Freeman, W., & Watts, J. W. (1950). *Psychosurgery: In the treatment of mental disorders and intractable pain* (2nd ed.). Springfield, IL: Charles C. Thomas.

Freud, A. (1936). *The ego and the mechanisms of defense.* New York: Hogarth.

Freud, S. (1962). *Three essays on the theory of sexuality.* New York: Basic. (Originally published 1905.)

Fridlund, A. J. (1994). *Human facial expression.* San Diego: Academic.

Friedman, H. S. (1992). Disease-prone and self-healing personalities. *Hospital and Community Psychiatry, 43,* 1177–1179.

Friedman, H. S. (Ed.). (1991). *Hostility, coping, and health.* Washington, DC: American Psychological Association.

Friedman, H. S., Tucker, J. S., Schwartz, J. E., Tomlinson-Keasey, C., Martin, L. R., Wingard, D. L., & Criqui, M. H. (1995). Psychosocial and behavioral predictors of longevity. *American Psychologist, 50,* 69–78.

Friedman, H. S., Tucker, J. S., Tomlinson-Keasey, C., Schwartz, J. E., Wingard, D. L., & Criqui, M. H. (1993). Does childhood personality predict longevity? *Journal of Personality and Social Psychology, 65,* 176–185.

Friedman, I. (1955). Phenomenal, ideal, and projected conception of self. *Journal of Abnormal and Social Psychology, 51,* 109–120.

Frijda, N. H. (1986). *The emotions.* Cambridge, England: Cambridge University Press.

Fromm, E. (1941). *Escape from freedom.* New York: Holt, Rinehart, & Winston.

Fuhrman, R. W., & Funder, D. C. (1995). Convergence between self and peer in the response-time processing of trait-relevant information. *Journal of Personality and Social Psychology, 69,* 961–974.

Funder, D. C. (1982). On the accuracy of dispositional versus situational attributions. *Social Cognition, 3,* 205–222.

Funder, D. C. (1983). Three issues in predicting more of the people: A reply to Mischel and Peake. *Psychological Review, 90,* 283–289.

Funder, D. C. (1987). Errors and mistakes: Evaluating the accuracy of social judgment. *Psychological Bulletin, 101,* 75–90.

Funder, D. C. (1991). Global traits: A neo-Allportian approach to personality. *Psychological Science, 2,* 31–39.

Funder, D. C. (1993). Judgments as data for personality and developmental psychology: Error vs. accuracy. In D. C. Funder, R. D. Parke, C. Tomlinson-Keasey, & K. Widaman (Eds.), *Studying lives through time: Personality and development* (pp. 121–146). Washington, DC: American Psychological Association.

Funder, D. C. (1995). On the accuracy of personality judgment: A realistic approach. *Psychological Review, 102,* 652–670.

Funder, D. C. (1998a). On the pros and cons of delay of gratification. *Psychological Inquiry, 9,* 211–212.

Funder, D. C. (1998b). Why does personality psychology exist? *Psychological Inquiry, 9,* 150–152.

Funder, D. C. (1999). *Personality judgment: A realistic approach to person percep-tion.* San Diego: Academic.

Funder, D. C. (2001). Personality. *Annual Review of Psychology, 52,* 197–221.

Funder, D. C. (2003). Towards a social psychology of person judgments: Implica-tions for person perception accuracy and self-knowledge. In J. Forgas, W. von Hippel, & K. Williams (Eds.), *Social judgments: Implicit and explicit processes.* (pp. 115–133).

Funder, D. C., & Block, J. (1989). The role of ego-control, ego-resiliency, and IQ in delay of gratification in adolescence. *Journal of Personality and Social Psy-chology, 57,* 1041–1050.

Funder, D. C., Block, J. H., & Block, J. (1983). Delay of gratification: Some longi-tudinal personality correlates. *Journal of Personality and Social Psychology, 44,* 1198–1213.

Funder, D. C., & Colvin, C. R. (1988). Friends and strangers: Acquaintanceship, agreement, and the accuracy of personality judgment. *Journal of Personality and Social Psychology, 55,* 149–158.

Funder, D. C., & Colvin, C. R. (1991). Explorations in behavioral consistency: Properties of persons, situations, and behaviors. *Journal of Personality and So-cial Psychology, 60,* 773–794.

Funder, D. C., & Dobroth, K. M. (1987). Differences between traits: Properties as-sociated with inter-judge agreement. *Journal of Personality and Social Psychol-ogy, 52,* 409–418.

Funder, D. C., Furr, R. M., & Colvin, C. R. (2000). The Riverside behavioral Q-sort: A tool for the description of social behavior. *Journal of Personality, 68,* 450–489.

Funder, D. C., & Harris, M. J. (1986). On the several facets of personality assess-ment: The case of social acuity. *Journal of Personality, 54,* 528–550.

Funder, D. C., & Ozer, D. J. (1983). Behavior as a function of the situation. *Jour-nal of Personality and Social Psychology, 44,* 107–112.

Funder, D. C., & Ozer, D. J. (2001). *Pieces of the personality puzzle: Readings in theory and research.* New York: Norton.

Funder, D. C., Parke, R. D., Tomlinson-Keasey, C., & Widaman, K. (Eds.). (1993). *Studying lives through time: Personality and development.* Washington, DC: American Psychological Association.

Funder, D. C., & Sneed, C. D. (1993). Behavioral manifestations of personality: An ecological approach to judgmental accuracy. *Journal of Personality and So-cial Psychology, 64,* 479–490.

Funder, D. C., & West, S. G. (1993). Consensus, self-other agreement, and accuracy in personality judgment: An introduction. *Journal of Personality, 61,* 457–476.

Furnham, A. (2001). Self-estimates of intelligence: Culture and gender differences in self and other estimates of both general (g) and multiple intelligences. *Per-sonality and Individual Differences, 31,* 1381–1405.

Gangestad, S. W. (1989). The evolutionary history of genetic variation: An emerg-ing issue in the behavioral genetic study of personality. In D. Buss & N. Can-tor (Eds.), *Personality psychology: Recent trends and emerging directions* (pp. 320–332). New York: Springer-Verlag.

Gangestad, S. W., & Simpson, J. A. (1990). Toward an evolutionary history of female sociosexual variation. *Journal of Personality, 58,* 69–96.

Gangestad, S. W., Simpson, J. A., DiGeronimo, K., & Biek, M. (1992). Differential accuracy in person perception across traits: Examination of a functional hypothesis. *Journal of Personality and Social Psychology, 62,* 688–698.

Gangestad, S. W., & Snyder, M. (1985). "To carve nature at its joints": On the existence of discrete classes in personality. *Psychological Review, 92,* 317–349.

Garb, H. N., Florio, C. M., & Grove, W. M. (1998). The validity of the Rorschach and the Minnesota Multiphasic Personality Inventory: Results from meta-analyses. *Psychological Science, 9,* 402–404.

Garb, H. N., Florio, C. M., & Grove, W. M. (1999). The Rorschach controversy: Reply to Parker, Hunsley, and Hanson. *Psychological Science, 10,* 293–294.

Gardner, H. (1987). *The mind's new science: A history of the cognitive revolution.* New York: Basic.

Gay, P. (1988). *Freud: A life for our time.* New York: Norton.

Gay, P. (Ed.) (1989). *The Freud reader.* New York: Norton.

Gazzaniga, M. S., Ivry, R. B., & Mangun G. R. (1998). *Cognitive neuroscience: The biology of the mind.* New York: Norton.

Gazzaniga, M. S., & Heatherton, T. F. (2003). *Psychological science: Mind, brain and behavior.* New York: Norton.

Geen, R. G. (1984). Preferred stimulation levels in introverts: Effects on arousal and performance. *Journal of Personality and Social Psychology, 46,* 1303–1312.

Gergen, K. (1973). Social psychology as history. *Journal of Personality and Social Psychology, 26,* 309–320.

Gettleman, J. (2002, December 1). A fall tradition: Rooting and rioting for the home team. *New York Times Week in Review,* p. 2.

Gigerenzer, G., Hoffrage, U., & Kleinbolting, H. (1991). Probabilistic mental models: A Brunswikian theory of confidence. *Psychological Review, 98,* 506–528.

Gilmore, D. D. (1990). *Manhood in the making.* New Haven, CT: Yale University Press.

Gleitman, H. (1995). *Psychology* (4th ed.). New York: Norton.

Glueck, S., & Glueck, E. (1956). *Physique and delinquency.* New York: Harper.

Goetz, T. E., & Dweck, C. S. (1980). Learned helplessness in social situation. *Journal of Personality and Social Psychology, 39,* 246–255.

Goffman, E. (1959). *The presentation of self in everyday life.* Garden City, NY: Doubleday (Anchor).

Gold, S. R., & Reilly, J. P. (1985). Daydreaming, current concerns and personality. *Imagination, Cognition and Personality, 5,* 117–125.

Goldberg, L. R. (1981). Language and individual differences: The search for universals in personality lexicons. In L. Wheeler (Eds.), *Review of personality and social psychology* (Vol. 2, pp. 141–166). Beverly Hills, CA: Sage.

Goldberg, L. R. (1992). The social psychology of personality. *Psychological Inquiry, 3,* 89–94.

Goldberg, L. R. (2001). Analyses of Digman's child-personality data: Derivation of Big-Five factor scores from each of six samples. *Journal of Personality, 69,* 709–743.

Goldman, W., & Lewis, P. (1977). Beautiful is good: Evidence that the physically attractive are more socially skillful. *Journal of Experimental Social Psychology, 13,* 125–130.

Gorer, G. (1943). Themes in Japanese culture. *New York Academy of Sciences, 5,* 106–124.

Gosling, S. D. (1998). Personality dimensions in spotted hyenas (Crocuta crocuta). *Journal of Comparative Psychology, 112,* 107–118.

Gosling, S. D. & John, O. P. (1999). Personality dimensions in nonhuman animals: A cross-species review. *Current Directions in Psychological Science, 8,* 69–75.

Gosling, S. D., John, O. P., Craik, K. H., & Robins, R. W. (1998). Do people know how they behave? Self-reported act frequencies compared with on-line codings by observers. *Journal of Personality and Social Psychology, 74,* 1337–1349.

Gosling, S. D., Ko, S. J., Mannarelli, T., & Morris, M. E. (2002). A room with a cue: Personality judgments based on offices and bedrooms. *Journal of Personality and Social Psychology, 82,* 379–398.

Gosling, S. D., & Vazire, S. (2002). Are we barking up the right tree? Evaluating a comparative approach to personality. *Journal of Research in Personality, 36,* 607–614.

Gough, H. G. (1968). An interpreter's syllabus for the California Psychological Inventory. In P. McReynolds (Ed.), *Advances in psychological assessment* (Vol. 1, pp. 55–79). Palo Alto, CA: Science and Behavior.

Gough, H. G. (1995). Career assessment and the California Psychological Inventory. *Journal of Career Assessment, 3,* 101–122.

Gould, S. J. (2001, February 19). Humbled by the genome's mysteries. *New York Times.* Retrieved April 20, 2003, http://www.nytimes.com/2001/02/19/opinion/19GOUL.html

Grant, H., & Dweck, C. S. (1999). A goal analysis of personality and personality coherence. In D. Cervone & Y. Shoda (Eds.), *The coherence of personality: Social-cognitive bases of consistency, variability and organization* (pp. 345–371). New York: Guilford.

Gray, J. A. (1981). A critique of Eysenck's theory of personality. In H. J. Eysenck (Ed.), *A model for personality* (pp. 246–276). New York: Springer-Verlag.

Gray, J. A. (1987). *The psychology of fear and stress* (2nd ed.). Cambridge, England: Cambridge University Press.

Graziano, W., & Bryant, W. H. (1998). Self-monitoring and the self-attribution of positive emotions. *Journal of Personality and Social Psychology, 74,* 250–261.

Greenberg, J., & Folger, R. (1988). *Controversial issues in social research methods.* New York: Springer-Verlag.

Greenberg, J. R., & Mitchell, S. A. (1983). *Object relations in psychoanalytic theory.* Cambridge, MA: Harvard University Press.

Greenwald, A. G., & Farnham, S. D. (2000). Using the implicit association test to measure self-esteem and the self-concept. *Journal of Personality and Social Psychology, 79,* 1022–1028.

Greenwald, A. G., McGhee, D. E., & Schwartz, J. L. K. (1998). Measuring individual differences in implicit cognition. The implicit association test. *Journal of Personality and Social Psychology, 74,* 1464–1480.

Greenwald, A. G., Banaji, M. R., Rudman, L. A., Farnham, S. D., Nosek, B. A., & Mellott, D. S. (2002). A unified theory of implicit attitudes, stereotypes, self-esteem, and self-concept. *Psychological Review, 109,* 3–25.

Guilford, J. P., & Zimmerman, W. S. (1956). Fourteen dimensions of temperament. *Psychological Monographs, 70,* no. 417.

Guthrie, G. M., & Bennett, A. B. (1971). Cultural differences in implicit personality theory. *International Journal of Psychology, 6,* 305–312.

Hamer, D. (1997). The search for personality genes: Adventures of a molecular biologist. *Current Directions in Psychological Science, 6,* 111–113.

Hamer, D. H., & Copeland, P. (1994). *The science of desire: The search for the gay gene and the biology of behavior.* New York: Simon & Schuster.

Hammond, K. R. (1996). *Human judgment and social policy: Irreducible uncertainty, inevitable error, unavoidable injustice.* New York: Oxford University Press.

Hammond, K. R., & Stewart, T. R. (2001). *The essential Brunswik: Beginnings, explications, applications.* New York: Oxford University Press.

Hanson, F. A. (1993). *Testing testing: Social consequences of the examined life.* Berkeley: University of California Press.

Haratitos, J., & Benet-Martínez, V. (2002). Bicultural identities: The interface of cultural, personality, and socio-cognitive processes. *Journal of Research in Personality, 36,* 598–606.

Harlow, J. M. (1849). Letter in "medical miscellany." *Boston Medical and Surgical Journal, 39,* 506–507.

Harlow, J. M. (1868). Recovery from the passage of an iron bar though the head. *Publications of the Massachusetts Medical Society, 2,* 327–347.

Harlow, J. M. (1869). *Recovery from the passage of an iron bar through the head.* Boston: Clapp.

Harris, C. R. (2000). Psychophysiological responses to imagined infidelity: The specific innate modular view of jealousy reconsidered. *Journal of Personality and Social Psychology, 78,* 1082–1091.

Harris, J. R. (1995). Where is the child's environment? A group socialization theory of development. *Psychological Review, 102,* 458–489.

Harris, J. R. (1998). *The nurture assumption: Why children turn out the way they do.* New York: Free Press.

Harris, M. J., & Rosenthal, R. (1985). Mediation of interpersonal expectancy effects: 31 Meta-analyses. *Psychological Bulletin, 97,* 363–386.

Harris, R. J. (Ed.) (1997). Special section: Ban the significance test? *Psychological Science, 8,* 1–20.

Hartmann, H. (1964). *Essays on ego psychology: Selected problems in psychoanalytic theory.* New York: International Universities Press.

Haselton, M. G. (2002). The sexual overperception bias: Evidence of a systematic bias in men from a survey of naturally occurring events. *Journal of Research in Personality, 37,* 34–47.

Hastie, R., & Rasinski, K. A. (1988). The concept of accuracy in social judgment. In D. Bar-Tal & A. W. Kruglanski (Eds.), *The social psychology of knowledge* (pp. 193–208). Cambridge, England: Cambridge University Press.

Hastorf, A. H., & Cantril, H. (1954). They saw a game: A case study. *Journal of Abnormal and Social Psychology, 47,* 574–576.

Hathaway, S. R., & Meehl, P. E. (1951). *An atlas for the clinical use of the MMPI.* Minneapolis: University of Minnesota Press.

Haugeland, J. (1985). *Artificial intelligence: The very idea.* Cambridge, MA: Bradford/MIT Press.

Hazan, C., & Shaver, P. (1987). Romantic love conceptualized as an attachment process. *Journal of Personality and Social Psychology, 52,* 511–524.

Hazan, C., & Shaver, P. (1990). Love and work: An attachment-theoretical perspective. *Journal of Personality and Social Psychology, 59,* 270–280.

Heidegger, M. (1962). *Being and time.* New York: Harper. (Originally published 1927.)

Heine, S. J., Lehman, D. R., Markus, H. R., & Kitayama, S. (1999). Is there a universal need for positive self-regard? *Psychological Review, 106,* 766–794.

Heine, S. J., Kitayama, S., & Lehman, D. R. (2001). Cultural differences in self-evaluation: Japanese readily accept negative self-relevant information. *Journal of Cross-Cultural Psychology, 32,* 434–443.

Heine, S. J., Kitayama, S., Lehman, D. R., Takata, T., Ide, E., Leung, C., & Matsumoto, H. (2001). Divergent consequences of success and failure in Japan and North America: An investigation of self-improving motivations and malleable selves. *Journal of Personality and Social Psychology, 81,* 599–615.

Hemenway, D., Solnick, S., & Carter, J. (1994). Child-rearing violence. *Child Abuse & Neglect, 18,* 1011–1020.

Hetherington, E. M. (Ed.). (1983) *Socialization, personality, and social development.* New York: Wiley.

Higgins, E. T. (1987). Self-discrepancy: A theory relating self and affect. *Psychological Review, 94,* 319–340.

Higgins, E. T. (1997). Beyond pleasure and pain. *American Psychologist, 52,* 1280–1300.

Higgins, E. T. (1999). Persons and situations: Unique explanatory principles or variability in general principles? In D. Cervone & Y. Shoda (Eds.), *The coherence of personality: Social-cognitive bases of consistency, variability and organization* (pp. 61–93). New York: Guilford.

Higgins, E. T., Bond, R., Klein, R., & Strauman, T. J. (1986). Self-discrepancies and emotional vulnerability: How magnitude, accessibility and type of discrepancy influence affect. *Journal of Personality and Social Psychology, 51,* 1–15.

Higgins, E. T., Rholes, W. S., & Jones, C. R. (1977). Category accessibility and impression formation. *Journal of Experimental Social Psychology, 13,* 141–154.

Higgins, E. T., Roney, C. J. R., Crowe, E., & Hymes, C. (1994). Ideal versus ought predilections for approach and avoidance: Distinct self-regulatory systems. *Journal of Personality and Social Psychology, 66,* 276–286.

Hilton, T. L., & Berglund, G. W. (1974). Sex differences in mathematics achievement: A longitudinal study. *Journal of Educational Research, 67,* 231–237.

Hofstede, G. (1984). The cultural relativity of the quality of life concept. *Academy of Management Review, 9,* 389–398.

Hogan, R. (1969). Development of an empathy scale. *Journal of Consulting and Clinical Psychology, 33,* 307–316.

Hogan, R. (1998). Reinventing personality. *Journal of Social and Clinical Psychology, 17,* 1–10.

Hogan, R., & Nicholson, R. A. (1988). The meaning of personality test scores. *American Psychologist, 43,* 621–626.

Holt, R. R. (1980). Loevinger's measure of ego development: Reliability and national norms for male and female short forms. *Journal of Personality and Social Psychology, 39,* 909–920.

Horner, K. L. (1998). Individuality in vulnerability: Influences on physical health. *Journal of Health Psychology, 3,* 71–85.

Horney, K. (1937). *The neurotic personality of our time.* New York: Norton.

Horney, K. (1942). *Self-analysis.* New York: Norton.

Horney, K. (1950). *Neurosis and human growth.* New York: Norton.

Hughes, C. F., Uhlmann, C., & Pennebaker, J. W. (1994). The body's response to emotional trauma: Linking verbal text with autonomic activity. *Journal of Personality, 62,* 565–586.

Hull, J. G., Slone, L. B., Meteyer, K. B., & Matthews, A. R. (2002). The nonconsciousness of self-consciousness. *Journal of Personality and Social Psychology, 83,* 406–424.

Hunsley, J., & Bailey, J. M. (1999). The clinical utility of the Rorschach: Unfulfilled promises and an uncertain future. *Psychological Assessment, 11,* 266–277.

Hunter, J. E. (1997). Needed: A ban on the significance test. *Psychological Science, 8,* 3–7.

Isom, J., & Heller, W. (1999). Neurobiology of extraversion: Pieces of the puzzle still missing. *Behavorial and Brain Sciences, 22,* 524.

Iyengar, S. S., & Lepper, M. R. (1999). Rethinking the value of choice: A cultural perspective on intrinsic motivation. *Journal of Personality and Social Psychology, 76,* 349–366.

Jackson, D. N. (1967). *Personality Research Form manual.* Goshen, NY: Research Psychologists Press.

Jackson, D. N. (1971). The dynamics of structured personality tests: 1971. *Psychological Review, 78,* 229–248.

James, W. (1890). *Principles of psychology* (Vol. I). London: Macmillan.

Janoff-Bulman, R. (1989). Assumptive worlds and the stress of traumatic events: Applications of the schema construct. *Social Cognition, 7,* 113–136.

John, O. P. (1990). The "Big Five" factor taxonomy: Dimensions of personality in the natural language and in questionnaires. In L. Pervin (Ed.), *Handbook of personality: Theory and research* (pp. 66–100). New York: Guilford.

John, O. P., & Robins, R. W. (1994). Accuracy and bias in self-perception: Individual differences in self-enhancement and narcissism. *Journal of Personality and Social Psychology, 66,* 206–219.

Johnson, J. A. (1981). The "self-disclosure" and "self-presentation" views of item response dynamics and personality scale validity. *Journal of Personality and Social Psychology, 40,* 761–769.

Johnson, R. G. (1972). *Aggression in man and animals.* Philadelphia: Saunders.

Jones, E. E., & Nisbett, R. E. (1971). *The actor and the observer: Divergent perceptions of the causes of behavior.* Morristown, NJ: General Learning Press.

Jones, T. (2003, February 1). On eve of 800th win, Knight's antics still fan flames of debate. *Columbus Dispatch,* Sports, Page 06E.

Jost, J. T., Glaser, J., Kruglanski, A. W., & Sulloway, F. J. (2003). Political conservatism as motivated social cognition. *Psychological Review, 129,* 339–375.

Jourard, S. M. (1971). *Self-disclosure: An experimental analysis of the transparent self.* New York: Wiley.

Jung, C. G. (1971a). *The portable Jung* (J. Campbell, Ed.). New York: Viking.

Jung, C. G. (1971b). A psychological theory of types. In H. Read, M. Fordham, & G. Adler (Eds.), *Collected works of C. G. Jung* (Vol. 20, pp. 524–541). Princeton, NJ: Princeton University Press. (German originally published 1931.)

Jussim, L. (1991). Social perception and social reality: A reflection-construction model. *Psychological Review, 98,* 54–73.

Jussim, L., & Eccles, J. (1992). Teacher expectations II: Construction and reflection of student achievement. *Journal of Personality and Social Psychology, 63,* 947–961.

Kagan, J. (1978). Sex differences in the human infant. In T. E. McGill, D. A. Dewsburg, & B. D. Sachs (Eds.), *Sex and behavior* (pp. 305–316). New York: Plenum.

Kagan, J. (1994). *Galen's prophecy: Temperament in human nature.* New York: Basic.

Kagan, J., Reznick, J. S., & Snidman, N. (1988). Biological bases of childhood shyness. *Science, 240,* 167–171.

Kaiser, R. T., & Ozer, D. J. (1999). *The structure of personal goals and their relation to personality traits.* Unpublished manuscript, University of California, Riverside.

Kazdin, A. E. (1994). Interventions for aggressive and antisocial children. In L. D. Eron, J. H. Gentry, & P. Schlegel (Eds.), *Reason to hope: A psychosocial perspective on violence and youth* (pp. 341–382). Washington, DC: American Psychological Association.

Kazdin, A. E., & Bootzin, R. R. (1972). The token economy: An evaluative review. *Journal of Applied Behavior Analysis, 5,* 343–372.

Kelly, G. A. (1955). The psychology of personal constructs (Vols. 1 and 2). New York: Norton.

Kelly, G. A. (1969). The autobiography of a theory. In B. Maher (Ed.), *Clinical psychology and personality: Selected papers of George Kelly* (pp. 46–65). New York: Wiley.

Kenny, D. A. (1991). A general model of consensus and accuracy in interpersonal perception. *Psychological Review, 98,* 155–163.

Kenrick, D. T., & Funder, D. C. (1988). Profiting from controversy: Lessons from the person-situation debate. *American Psychologist, 43,* 23–34.

Kenrick, D. T., & Keefe, R. C. (1992). Age preferences in mates reflect sex differences in human reproductive strategies. *Behavioral and Brain Sciences, 15,* 75–91.

Keyes, C. L. M., & Haidt, J. (Eds.) (2003). *Flourishing: Positive psychology and the life well-lived.* Washington, DC: American Psychological Association.

Kihlstrom, J. (1990). The psychological unconscious. In L. Pervin (Ed.), *Handbook of personality: Theory and research* (pp. 445–464). New York: Guilford.

Kihlstrom, J. F. (1994). Commentary: Psychodynamics and social cognition: Notes on the fusion of psychoanalysis and psychology. *Journal of Personality, 62,* 681–696.

Kim, H. S. (2002). We talk, therefore we think? A cultural analysis of the effect of talking on thinking. *Journal of Personality and Social Psychology, 83,* 828–842.

Kim, H. S., & Markus, H. R. (1999). Deviance or uniqueness, harmony or conformity? A cultural analysis. *Journal of Personality and Social Psychology, 77,* 785–800.

King, L. A. (2001). The hard road to the good life: The happy, mature person. *Journal of Humanistic Psychology, 41,* 51–72.

King, L. A., & Napa, C. K. (1998). What makes a life good? *Journal of Personality and Social Psychology, 75,* 156–165.

King, J. E., & Figueredo, A. (1997). The five-factor model plus dominance in chimpanzee personality. *Journal of Research in Personality, 31,* 257–271.

King, M. G., & Husband, A. J. (1991). Altered immunity through behavioral conditioning. In J. G. Carlson & A. R. Seifert (Eds.), *International perspectives in behavioral psychophysiology and medicine* (pp. 197–204). New York: Plenum.

Kircher, P. (1985). *Vaulting ambition: Sociobiology and the quest for human nature.* Cambridge, MA: MIT Press.

Klein, G. S. (1970). *Perception, motives, and personality.* New York: Knopf.

Klein, M. (1964). *Contributions to psychoanalysis, 1921–1945.* New York: McGraw-Hill.

Klein, M. (1975). *Envy and gratitude and other works, 1946–1963.* New York: Delacorte.

Klein, M. (1986). The psycho-analytic play technique: Its history and significance. In J. Mitchell (Ed.), *The selected Melanie Klein* (pp. 35–54). New York: Free Press. (Originally published 1955).

Klein, S. B., & Kihlstrom, J. F. (1998). On bridging the gap between social-personality psychology and neuropsychology. *Personality and Social Psychology Bulletin, 2,* 228–242.

Klein, S. B., Loftus, J., & Kihlstrom, J. F. (1996). Self-knowledge of an amnesic patient: Toward a neuropsychology of personality and social psychology. *Journal of Experimental Psychology: General, 125,* 250–260.

Klinger, E. (1977). *Meaning and void: Inner experience and the incentives in people's lives.* Minneapolis: University of Minnesota Press.

Klinger, E. (1987). The interview questionnaire technique: Reliability and validity of a mixed idographic-nomothetic measure of motivation. In J. N. Butcher and C. D. Spielberger (Eds.), *Advances in personality assessment* (pp. 311–319). Hillsdale, NJ: Erlbaum.

Klinger, E., Barta, S. G., & Maxeiner, M. E. (1981). Current concerns: Assessing therapeutically relevant motivation. In P. C. Kendall & S. Hollon (Eds.), *Assessment strategies for cognitive-behavioral interventions* (pp. 161–195). New York: Academic.

Klohnen, E., & Block, J. (1995). Unpublished data, University of California, Berkeley.

Klopfer, B., & Davidson, H. H. (1962). *The Rorschach technique: An introductory manual.* New York: Harcourt, Brace, & World.

Kluckhohn, C., & Murray, H. A. (1961). Personality formation: The determinants. In C. Kluckhohn, H. A. Murray, & D. M. Schneider (Eds.), *Personality in nature, society, and culture* (2nd ed., pp. 53–67). New York: Knopf.

Knutson, B., Momenan, R., Rawlings, R. R., Fong, G. W., & Hommer, D. (2001).

Negative association of neuroticism with brain volume ratio in healthy humans. *Biological Psychiatry, 50,* 685–690.

Knutson, B., Wolkowitz, O. M., Cole, S. W., Chan, T., Moore, E. A., Johnson, R. C., et al. (1998). Selective alteration of personality and social behavior by serotonergic intervention. *American Journal of Psychiatry, 155,* 373–379.

Köhler, W. (1925). *The mentality of apes* (E. Winter, Trans.). New York: Harcourt, Brace, & World.

Kolar, D. W. (1996). *Individual differences in the ability to accurately judge the personality characteristics of others.* Unpublished doctoral dissertation, University of California, Riverside.

Kolar, D. W., Funder, D. C., & Colvin, C. R. (1996). Comparing the accuracy of personality judgments by the self and knowledgeable others. *Journal of Personality, 64,* 311–317.

Kramer, P. D. (1993). *Listening to Prozac.* New York: Viking.

Krauss, S. W. (2002). Romanian authoritarianism 10 years after communism. *Personality and Social Psychology Bulletin, 28,* 1255–1264.

Kruglanski, A. W. (1989). The psychology of being "right": The problem of accuracy in social perception and cognition. *Psychological Bulletin, 106,* 395–409.

Kubler-Ross, E. (1969). *On death and dying.* New York: Macmillan.

Kusserow, A. (1999). De-homogenizing American individualism: Socializing hard and soft individualism in Manhattan and Queens. *Ethos, 27,* 210–234.

Laing, R. D. (1959). *The divided self.* Baltimore: Penguin.

Lam, A. (2003, June 15). Let the I's have it: Think for yourselves, a writer from Vietnam tells Asian American students. *Los Angeles Times,* p. M6.

Landy, F. J., & Guion, R. M. (1970). Development of scales for the measurement of work motivation. *Organizational Behavior and Human Performance, 5,* 93–103.

Langer, E. J. (1992). Matters of mind: Mindfulness/mindlessness in perspective. *Consciousness and Cognition, 1,* 289–305.

Langer, E. J. (1994). The illusion of calculated decisions. In R. C. Schank & E. Langer (Eds.), *Beliefs, reasoning, and decision making: Psycho-logic in honor of Bob Abelson* (pp. 33–53). Hillsdale, NJ: Erlbaum.

Larkin, J. H., McDermott, J., Simon, D. P., & Simon, H. A. (1980). Models of competence in solving physics problems. *Science, 200,* 1335–1342.

Lau, R. R. (1988). Beliefs about control and health behavior. In D. S. Gochman (Ed.), *Health behavior: Emerging research perspectives* (pp. 43–63). New York: Plenum.

Leary, M. R. (1999). Making sense of self-esteem. *Current Directions in Psychological Science, 8,* 32–35.

Lee, Y-T., Jussim, L. J., & McCauley, C. R. (Eds.) (1995). *Stereotype accuracy: Toward appreciating group differences.* Washington, DC: American Psychological Association.

Lee, Y-T., McCauley, C. R., & Draguns, J. G. (Eds.). (1999). *Personality and person perception across cultures.* Mahwah, NJ: Erlbaum.

Li, J. (2003). The core of Confucian learning. *American Psychologist, 58,* 146–147.

Li, N. P., Bailey, J. M., Kenrick, D. T., & Linsenmeier, J. A. W. (2002). The necessities and luxuries of mate preferences: Testing the tradeoffs. *Journal of Personality and Social Psychology, 82,* 947–955.

Lilienfeld, S. O. (1999). Projective measures of personality and psychopathology: How well do they work? *Skeptical Inquirer, 23,* 32–39.

Lilienfeld, S. O, Wood, J. M., & Garb, H. N. (2000). The scientific status of projective techniques. *Psychological Science in the Public Interest, 1,* 27–66.

Linville, P., & Jones, E. E. (1980). Polarized appraisals of out-group members. *Journal of Personality and Social Psychology, 38,* 689–703.

Lippa, R. A. (2002). Gender-related traits of heterosexual and homosexual men and women. *Archives of Sexual Behavior, 31,* 83–98.

Little, B. R. (1983). Personal projects: A rationale and method for investigation. *Environment and Behavior, 15,* 273–309.

Little, B. R. (1989). Personal projects analysis: Trivial pursuits, magnificent obsessions, and the search for coherence. In D. M. Buss & N. Cantor (Eds.), *Personality psychology: Recent trends and emerging directions* (pp. 15–31). New York: Springer-Verlag.

Loehlin, J. C., Willerman, L., & Horn, J. M. (1985). Personality resemblances in adoptive families when the children are late-adolescent or adult. *Journal of Personality and Social Psychology, 48,* 376–392.

Loehlin, J. C., Willerman, L., & Horn, J. M. (1989). Personality resemblance in adoptive families: A 10-year follow-up. *Journal of Personality and Social Psychology, 53,* 961–969.

Loevinger, J. (1976). *Ego development: Conceptions and theories.* San Francisco: Jossey-Bass.

Loevinger, J. (1987). *Paradigms of personality.* New York: Freeman.

Loftus, E. F. (1992). When a lie becomes memory's truth: Memory distortion after exposure to misinformation. *Current Directions in Psychological Science, 1,* 121–123.

Loftus, E. F., Greene, E. L., & Doyle, J. M. (1989). The psychology of eyewitness testimony. In D. C. Raskin (Ed.), *Psychological methods in criminal investigation and evidence* (pp. 3–45). New York: Springer-Verlag.

Loftus, G. R. (1996). Psychology will be a much better science when we change the way we analyze data. *Current Directions in Psychological Science, 5,* 161–170.

Logothetis, N. K. (2002). The neural basis of the blood-oxygen-level-dependent functional magnetic resonance imaging signal. *Philosophical Transactions: Biological Sciences, 357,* 1003–1037.

Lorenz, K. (1966). *On aggression.* New York: Harcourt, Brace, & World.

Lorenzi-Cioldi, F. (1993). They all look alike, but so do we . . . sometimes: Perceptions of in-group and out-group homogeneity as a function of sex and context. *British Journal of Social Psychology, 32,* 111–124.

Lykes, M. B. (1985). Gender and individualistic vs. collectivist bases for notions about the self. *Journal of Personality, 53,* 356–383.

Lyubomirsky, S. (2001). Why are some people happier than others? The role of cognitive and motivational processes in well-being. *American Psychologist, 56,* 239–249.

Maccoby, E. (1966). Sex differences in intellectual functioning. In E. Maccoby (Ed.), *The development of sex differences.* Stanford, CA: Stanford University Press.

Maccoby, E. E., & Jacklin, C. N. (1974). *The psychology of sex differences.* Stanford, CA: Stanford University Press.

Machover, K. (1949). *Personality projection in the drawing of the human figure.* Springfield, IL: Charles C. Thomas.

MacLean, P. D. (1982). On the origin and progressive evolution of the triune brain. In R. G. Grenell & S. Gabay (Eds.), *Biological foundations of psychiatry* (pp. 177–198). New York: Raven.

Maddi, S. R. (1985). Existential psychotherapy. In S. J. Lynn & J. P. Ganske (Eds.), *Contemporary psychotherapies: Models and methods* (pp. 191–219). Columbus, OH: Merrill.

Maddi, S. R. (2003). Hardiness: An operationalization of existential courage. *Journal of Humanistic Psychology,* in press.

Maddi, S. R., & Costa, P. T. (1972). *Humanism in psychology: Allport, Maslow and Murphy.* Chicago: Aldine.

Maddi, S. R., Khoshaba, D. M., Perisico, M., Lu, J., Harvey, R., & Bleecker, F. (2002). The personality construct of hardiness: II. Relationships with comprehensive tests of personality and psychopathology. *Journal of Research in Personality, 36,* 72–85.

Mahbubani, K. (2002). *Can Asians think? Understanding the divide between East and West* (Revised and expanded for North America). S. Royalton, VT: Steerforth.

Maier, S. F., & Seligman, M. E. (1976). Learned helplessness: Theory and evidence. *Journal of Experimental Psychology: General, 105,* 3–46.

Main, M. (1990). Parental aversion to infant-initiated contact is correlated with the parent's own rejection during childhood: The effects of experience on signals of security with respect to attachment. In K. E. Barnard & T. B. Brazelton (Eds.), *Touch: The foundation of experience* (pp. 461–495). Madison, CT: International Universities.

Maio, G. R., & Esses, V. M. (2001). The need for affect: Individual differences in the motivation to approach or avoid emotions. *Journal of Personality, 69,* 583–615.

Mandler, G. (1997). *Human nature explored.* New York: Oxford University Press.

Markon, K. E., Krueger, R. F., Bouchard, T. J., Jr., & Gottesman, I. I. (2002). Normal and abnormal personality traits: Evidence for genetic and environmental relationships in the Minnesota study of twins reared apart. *Journal of Personality, 70,* 661–693.

Markus, H., & Kunda, Z. (1986). Stability and malleability of the self-concept. *Journal of Personality and Social Psychology, 51,* 858–866.

Markus, H. R. (1977). Self-schemata and processing information about the self. *Journal of Personality and Social Psychology, 35,* 63–78.

Markus, H. R., & Kitayama, S. (1991). Culture and the self: Implications for cognition, emotion, and motivation. *Psychological Review, 98,* 224–253.

Markus, H. R., & Nurius, P. (1986). Possible selves. *American Psychologist, 41,* 954–969.

Markus, H. R., Mullally, P. R., & Kitayama, S. (1997). Selfways: Diversity in modes of cultural participation. In U. Neisser & D. Jopling (Eds.), *The conceptual self in context: Culture, experience, self-understanding* (pp. 13–60). New York: Cambridge University Press.

Maslow, A. H. (1987). *Motivation and personality* (3rd ed.). New York: Harper.

Masson, J. M. (1984). *The assault on truth: Freud's suppression of the seduction theory*. New York: Farrar, Straus, Giroux.

Masuda, T., & Nisbett, R. E. (2001). Attending holistically versus analytically: Comparing the context sensitivity of Japanese and Americans. *Journal of Personality and Social Psychology, 81*, 922–934.

Mayer, J. D. (1998). A systems framework for the field of personality. *Psychological Inquiry, 9*, 118–144.

McAdams, D. P. (1980). A thematic coding system for the intimacy motive. *Journal of Research in Personality, 14*, 413–432.

McAdams, D. P. (1984). Scoring manual for the intimacy motive. *Psychological Documents, 14*, 1. (Ms. no. 2613.)

McAdams, D. P. (1990). *The person*. San Diego, CA: Harcourt Brace.

McAdams, D. P. (1992). The five-factor model of personality: A critical appraisal. *Journal of Personality, 60*, 329–361.

McCann, S. J. (1990). Authoritarianism and preference for the presidential candidate perceived to be higher on the power motive. *Perceptual and Motor Skills, 70*, 577–578.

McCann, S. J. (1997). Threatening times, "strong" presidential popular vote winners, and the victory margin. *Journal of Personality and Social Psychology, 73*, 160–170.

McCarthy, M. M. (1995). Estrogen modulation of oxytocin and its relation to behavior. In R. Ivell & J. Russell (Eds.), *Oxytocin: Cellular and molecular approaches in medicine and research* (pp. 235–242). New York: Plenum Press.

McClelland, D. C. (1961). *The achieving society*. Princeton, NJ: Van Nostrand.

McClelland, D. C. (1972). Opinions reflect opinions: So what else is new? *Journal of Consulting and Clinical Psychology, 38*, 325–326.

McClelland, D. C. (1975). Love and power: The psychological signals of war. *Psychology Today, 8*, 44–48.

McClelland, D. C. (1984). *Motives, personality, and society*. New York: Praeger.

McClelland, D. C. (1985). How motives, skills and values determine what people do. *American Psychologist, 40*, 812–825.

McCrae, R. R. (1982). Consensual validation of personality traits: Evidence from self-reports and ratings. *Journal of Personality and Social Psychology, 43*, 293–303.

McCrae, R. R. (1994). The counterpoint of personality assessment: Self-reports and observer ratings. *Assessment, 1*, 159–172.

McCrae, R. R. (2001). Trait psychology and culture: Exploring intercultural comparisons. *Journal of Personality, 69*, 819–846.

McCrae, R. R. (2002). The maturation of personality psychology: Adult personality development and psychological well-being. *Journal of Research in Personality, 36*, 307–317.

McCrae, R. R., & Costa, P. T., Jr. (1987). Validation of the five-factor model of personality across instruments and observers. *Journal of Personality and Social Psychology, 52*, 81–90.

McCrae, R. R., & Costa, P. T., Jr. (1991). Adding Liebe und Arbeit: The full five-factor model and well-being. *Personality and Social Psychology Bulletin, 17,* 227–232.

McCrae, R. R., & Costa, P. T., Jr. (1995). Trait explanations in personality psychology. *European Journal of Personality, 9,* 231–252.

McCrae, R. R., Costa, P. T., Jr., & Yik, M. S. M. (1996). Universal aspects of Chinese personality structure. In M. H. Bond (Ed.), *The handbook of Chinese psychology* (pp. 189–207). Hong Kong: Oxford University Press.

McCrae, R. R., & John, O. P. (1992). An introduction to the five-factor model and its applications. *Journal of Personality, 60,* 175–215.

McCrae, R. R., Yik, M. S. M., Trapnell, P. D., Bond, M. H., & Paulhus, D. L. (1998). Interpreting personality profiles across cultures: Bilingual, acculturation, and peer rating studies of Chinese undergraduates. *Journal of Personality and Social Psychology, 74,* 1041–1055.

McGinnies, E. (1949). Emotionality and perceptual defense. *Psychological Review, 56,* 244–251.

McGue, M., & Lykken, D. T. (1992). Genetic influence on risk of divorce. *Psychological Science, 3,* 368–373.

McKay, J. R., O'Farrell, T. J., Maisto, S. A., Connors, G. J., & Funder, D. C. (1989). Biases in relapse attributions made by alcoholics and their wives. *Addictive Behaviors, 14,* 513–522.

McKeon, R. A. (1947). *Introduction to Aristotle.* New York: Modern Library.

Mealey, L. (1995). The sociobiology of sociopathy: An integrated evolutionary model. *Behavioral and Brain Sciences, 18,* 523–599.

Meehl, P. E. (1992). Factors and taxa, traits and types, differences of degree and differences in kind. *Journal of Personality, 60,* 117–174.

Megargee, E. I. (1966). Undercontrolled and overcontrolled personality types in extreme antisocial aggression. In E. I. Megargee & J. I. Moranson (Eds.), *Psychological monographs.* New York: Harper.

Megargee, E. I. (1972). *The California Psychological Inventory handbook.* San Francisco: Jossey-Bass.

Mehra, A., Kilduff, M., & Brass, D. J. (2001). The social networks of high and low self-monitors: Implications for workplace performance. *Administrative Science Quarterly, 46,* 121–146.

Mendelsohn, G. A., Weiss, D. S., & Feimer, N. R. (1982). Conceptual and empirical analysis of the typological implications of patterns of socialization and femininity. *Journal of Personality and Social Psychology, 42,* 1157–1170.

Mesquita, B. (2001). Emotions in collectivist and individualist contexts. *Journal of Personality and Social Psychology, 80,* 68–74.

Mesquita, B., & Karasawa, M. (2002). Different emotional lives. *Cognition and Emotion, 16,* 127–141.

Metzner, R. J. (1994, March 14). Prozac is medicine, not a miracle. *Los Angeles Times,* p. B7.

Michigan Department of Education (1989). *The Michigan employability survey.*

Miles, D. R., & Carey, G. (1997). Genetic and environmental architecture of human aggression. *Journal of Personality and Social Psychology, 72,* 207–217.

Milgram, S. (1975). *Obedience to authority.* New York: Harper.

Miller, G. A. (1956). The magical number seven plus or minus two: Some limits on our capacity for processing information. *Psychological Review, 63,* 81–97.

Miller, J. G. (1999). Cultural psychology: Implications for basic psychological theory. *Psychological Science, 10,* 85–91.

Miller, J. G., & Bersoff, D. M. (1992). Culture and moral judgment: How are conflicts between justice and interpersonal responsibilities resolved? *Journal of Personality and Social Psychology, 62,* 541–554.

Miller, J. G., Bersoff, D. M., & Harwood, R. L. (1990). Perceptions of social responsibilities in India and in the United States: Moral imperatives or personal decisions? *Journal of Personality and Social Psychology, 58,* 33–47.

Miller, L. (1999). Stereotype legacy: Culture and person in Japanese/American business interactions. In Y-T Lee, C. R. McCauley, & J. G. Draguns (Eds.), *Personality and person perception across cultures* (pp. 213–232). Mahwah, NJ: Erlbaum.

Miller, N. E., & Dollard, J. (1947). *Social learning and imitation.* New Haven, CT: Yale University Press.

Miller, W. R., & Seligman, M. E. (1975). Depression and learned helplessness in man. *Journal of Abnormal Psychology, 84,* 228–238.

Mischel, W. (1968). *Personality and assessment.* New York: Wiley.

Mischel, W. (1973). Toward a cognitive social learning reconceptualization of personality. *Psychological Review, 80,* 252–283.

Mischel, W. (1999). Personality coherence and dispositions in a cognitive-affective personality system (CAPS) approach. In D. Cervone & Y. Shoda (Eds.), *The coherence of personality: Social-cognitive bases of consistency, variability and organization* (pp. 37–60). New York: Guilford.

Mischel, W., & Ebbesen, E. (1970). Attention in delay of gratification. *Journal of Personality and Social Psychology, 16,* 329–337.

Mischel, W., & Shoda, Y. (1995). A cognitive-affective system theory of personality: Reconceptualizing situations, dispositions, dynamics, and invariance in personality structure. *Psychological Review, 102,* 246–268.

Mischel, W., Shoda, Y., & Peake, P. K. (1988). The nature of adolescent competencies predicted by preschool delay of gratification. *Journal of Personality and Social Psychology, 54,* 687–696.

Mitchel, J. (Ed.). (1986). *The selected Melanie Klein.* New York: Free Press.

Moffitt, T. E. (1991). *An approach to organizing the task of selecting measures for longitudinal research.* Technical report, University of Wisconsin, Madison.

Montag, I., & Levin, J. (1994). The five-factor personality model in applied settings. *European Journal of Personality, 8,* 1–11.

Moray, N. (1959). Attention in dichotic listening: Affective cues and the influence of instructions. *Quarterly Journal of Experimental Psychology, 11,* 56–60.

Morf, C. C., & Rhodewalt, F. (2001). Unraveling the paradoxes of narcissism: A dynamic self-regulatory processing model. *Psychological Inquiry, 12,* 177–196.

Morgan, C. D., & Murray, H. A. (1935). A method for investigating fantasies: The Thematic Apperception Test. *Archives of Neurology and Psychiatry, 34,* 289–306.

Morokoff, P. J. (1985). Effects of sex guilt, repression, sexual "arousability," and sexual experience on female sexual arousal during erotica and fantasy. *Journal of Personality and Social Psychology, 49,* 177–187.

Mosig, Y. D. (1989). Wisdom and compassion: What the Buddha taught. *Theoretical and Philosophical Psychology, 9,* 27–36.

Mosig, Y. D. (1999). Zen Buddhism. In Engler, B., *Personality theories* (5th ed., pp. 451–474). Boston: Houghton Mifflin.

Mount, M. K, & Barrick, M. R. (1998). Five reasons why the "Big Five" article has been frequently cited. *Personnel Psychology, 51,* 849–857.

Murray, H. A. (1938). *Explorations in personality.* New York: Oxford University Press.

Murray, H. A. (1943). *Thematic Apperception Test manual.* Cambridge, MA: Harvard University Press.

Myers, I. B. (1962). *The Myers-Briggs Type Indicator.* Princeton, NJ: Educational Testing Service.

Newman, L. S., Duff, K., & Baumeister, R. F. (1997). A new look at defensive projection: Suppression, accessibility, and biased person perception. *Journal of Personality and Social Psychology, 72,* 980–1001.

Nikula, R., Klinger, E., & Larson-Gutman, M. K. (1993). Current concerns and electrodermal reactivity: Responses to words and thoughts. *Journal of Personality, 61,* 63–84.

Nisbett, R. E. (1980). The trait construct in lay and professional psychology. In L. Festinger (Ed.), *Retrospections on social psychology* (pp. 109–130). New York: Oxford University Press.

Nisbett, R. E., & Wilson, T. D. (1977). Telling more than we can know: Verbal reports on mental processes. *Psychological Review, 84,* 231–259.

Nisbett, R. E., Peng, K., Choi, I., & Norenzayan, A. (2001). Culture and systems of thought: Holistic versus analytic cognition. *Psychological Review, 108,* 291–310.

Norem, J. K. (1989). Cognitive strategies as personality: Effectiveness, specificity, flexibility, and change. In D. M. Buss & N. Cantor (Eds.), *Personality psychology: Recent trends and emerging directions* (pp. 45–60). New York: Springer-Verlag.

Norem, J. K. (2002). Defensive self-deception and social adaptation among optimists. *Journal of Research in Personality, 36,* 549–555.

Norem, J. K., & Cantor, N. (1986). Defensive pessimism: "Harnessing" anxiety as motivation. *Journal of Personality and Social Psychology, 51,* 1208–1217.

Norem, J. K., & Chang, E. C. (2001). A very full glass: Adding complexity to our thinking about the implications and applications of optimism and pessimism research. In E. C. Chang (Ed.), *Optimism and pessimism: Implications for theory, research and practice* (pp. 347–367). Washington DC: American Psychological Association.

Norem, J. K., & Chang, E. C. (2002). The positive psychology of negative thinking. *Journal of Clinical Psychology, 58,* 993–1001.

Norman, W. T. (1963). Toward an adequate taxonomy of personality attributes: Replicated factor structure in peer nomination personality ratings. *Journal of Abnormal and Social Psychology, 66,* 574–583.

Norman, W. T. (1967). *2800 personality trait descriptors: Normative operating characteristics for a university population.* Ann Arbor, MI: University of Michigan.

O'Bannon, R. M., Goldinger, L. A., & Appleby, G. S. (1989). *Honesty and integrity testing.* Atlanta, GA: Applied Information Resources.

Ogilvie, D. M., & Ashmore, R. D. (1991). Self-with-other representation as a unit of analysis in self-concept research. In R. C. Curtis (Ed.), *The relational self* (pp. 282–314). New York: Guilford.

Öhman, A., & Mineka, S. (2001). Fears, phobias, and preparedness: Toward an evolved module of fear and fear learning. *Psychological Review, 108,* 483–522.

Öhman, A., & Mineka, S. (2003). The malicious serpent: Snakes as a prototypical stimulus for an evolved module of fear. *Current Directions in Psychological Science, 12,* 5–9.

Oishi, S., Diener, E., Scollon, C. N., & Biswas-Diener, R. (in press). Cross-situational consistency of affective experience across cultures. *Journal of Personality and Social Psychology.*

Ones, D. S., Viswesvaran, C., & Schmidt, F. L. (1993). Comprehensive meta-analysis of integrity test validities: Findings and implications for personnel selection and theories of job performance. *Journal of Applied Psychology, 78,* 679–703.

Ornstein, R. E. (1977). *The psychology of consciousness* (2nd ed.). New York: Harcourt Brace.

Osborn, S. M., Feild, H. S., & Veres, J. G. (1998). Introversion-extraversion, self-monitoring and applicant performance in a situational panel interview: A field study. *Journal of Business and Psychology, 13,* 143–156.

Ostendorf, F., & Angleitner, A. (1994, July). *Psychometric properties of the German translation of the NEO Personality Inventory (NEO-PI-R).* Paper presented at the Seventh Conference of the European Association for Personality Psychology, Madrid, Spain.

Ozer, D. J. (1985). Correlation and the coefficient of determination. *Psychological Bulletin, 97,* 307–315.

Park, B., & Rothbart, M. (1982). Perceptions of out-group homogeneity and levels of social categorization: Memory for the subordinate attributes of in-group and out-group members. *Journal of Personality and Social Psychology, 42,* 1051–1068.

Parker, K. C. H., Hunsley, J., & Hanson, R. K. (1999). Old wine from old skins sometimes tastes like vinegar: A response to Garb, Florio, and Grove. *Psychological Science, 10,* 291–292.

Paulhus, D. L. (1998). Interpersonal and intrapsychic adaptiveness of trait self-enhancement: A mixed blessing? *Journal of Personality and Social Psychology, 74,* 1197–1208.

Paunonen, S. V. (2003). Big Five factors of personality and replicated predictions of behavior. *Journal of Personality and Social Psychology, 84,* 411–422.

Pavlov, I. P. (1927). (Translated by G. V. Anrep). Conditioned reflexes: An investigation of the physiological activity of the cerebral cortex. *Classics in the History of Psychology.* Retrieved July 16, 2003, psychclassics.yorku.ca/Pavlov/lecture23.htm

Peabody, D. (1966). Authoritarianism scales and response bias. *Psychological Bulletin, 65,* 11–23.

Pennebaker, J. W. (1992). Inhibition as the linchpin of health. In H. S. Friedman (Ed.), *Hostility, coping, and health* (pp. 127–139). Washington, DC: American Psychological Association.

Pervin, L. A., & John, O. P. (1997). *Personality: Theory and research* (7th ed.). New York: Wiley.

Peterson, B. E., Smirles, K. A., & Wentworth, P. A. (1997). Generativity and authoritarianism: Implications for personality, political involvement, and parenting. *Journal of Personality and Social Psychology, 72,* 1202–1216.

Peterson, C., Maier, S. F., & Seligman, M. E. (1993). *Learned helplessness: A theory for the age of personal control.* London: Oxford University Press.

Peterson, C., & Steen, T. A. (2002). Optimistic explanatory style. In C. R. Snyder & S. J. Lopez (Eds.), *Handbook of positive psychology* (pp. 244–256). London: Oxford University Press.

Pettigrew, T. F. (1986). The intergroup contact hypothesis reconsidered. In M. Hewstone & R. Brown (Eds.), *Contact and conflict in interpersonal encounters* (pp. 169–195). Oxford, England: Basic Blackwell.

Piedmont, R. L., & Chae, J. H. (1997). Cross-cultural generalizability of the five-factor model of personality. *Journal of Cross-Cultural Psychology, 28,* 131–155.

Pinker, S. (Ed.). (1985). *Visual cognition.* Cambridge, MA: Bradford/MIT Press.

Pinker, S. (1997). *How the mind works.* New York: Norton.

Plomin, R., Chipuer, H. M., & Loehlin, J. C. (1990). Behavioral genetics and personality. In L. Pervin (Ed.), *Handbook of personality: Theory and research* (pp. 225–243). New York: Guilford.

Plomin, R., Corley, R., DeFries, J. C., & Fulker, D. W. (1990). Individual differences in television viewing in early childhood: Nature as well as nurture. *Psychological Science, 1,* 371–377.

Plomin, R., & Crabbe, J. (2000). DNA. *Psychological Bulletin, 126,* 806–828.

Polivy, J. (1998). The effects of behavioral inhibition: Integrating internal cues, cognition, behavior, and affect. Psychological Inquiry, 9, 181–204.

Pope, H. G., & Katz, D. L. (1994). Psychiatric and medical effects of anabolic-androgen steroid use: A controlled study of 160 athletes. *Archives of General Psychiatry, 51,* 375–382.

Pope, K. S., Tabachnick, B., & Keith-Spiegel, P. (1987). Ethics of practice: The beliefs and behaviors of psychologists as therapists. *American Psychologist, 42,* 993–1006.

Price, R. H., & Bouffard, D. L. (1974). Behavioral appropriateness and situational constraint as dimensions of social behavior. *Journal of Personality and Social Psychology, 30,* 579–586.

Public Health Service (1991). *Application for Public Health Service grant* (PHS 398; OMB No. 0925-0001). Washington, DC: U.S. Government Printing Office.

Public Health Service (2001). *Mental health: Culture, race and ethnicity. A supplement to mental health: A report of the Surgeon General.* Washington, DC: U.S. Government Printing Office.

Pulkkinen, L. (1995). *A person-centered approach to the analysis of personality.* Unpublished manuscript, University of Jyvaeskylae, Finland.

Pullum, G. K. (1991). *The great Eskimo vocabulary hoax, and other irreverent essays on the study of language.* Chicago: University of Chicago Press.

Pyszczynski, T., Greenberg, J., & Solomon, S. (1997). Why do we need what we need? A terror management perspective on the roots of human social motivation. *Psychological Inquiry, 8,* 1–20.

Qi, J., & Zhu, Y. (2002). The self-reference effect of Chinese college students. *Psychological Science (China), 25,* 275–278.

Rabiner, D. L., Lenhart, L., & Lochman, J. E. (1990). Automatic versus reflective social problem solving in relation to sociometric status. *Developmental Psychology, 26,* 1010–1016.

Rada, R. T., Laws, D. R., & Kellner, R. (1976). Plasma testosterone levels in the rapist. *Psychosomatic Medicine, 38,* 257–258.

Rahula, W. (1974). *What the Buddha taught.* New York: Grove.

Raleigh, M. J. (1987). Differential behavioral effects of tryptophan and 5-hydroxy-tryptophan in vervet monkeys: influences of catecholaminergic systems. *Psychopharmacology, 93,* 44–50.

Raleigh, M. J., McGuire, M. T., Brammer, G. L., Pollack, D. B., & Yuwiler, A. (1991). Serotonergic mechanisms promote dominance acquisition in adult male vervet monkeys. *Brain Research, 559,* 181–190.

Rapaport, D. (1960). *The structure of psychoanalytic theory: A systematizing attempt.* New York: International Universities.

Reis, H. T., Capobianco, A., & Tsai, F. (2002). Finding the person in personality relationships. *Journal of Personality, 70,* 813–850.

Rentfrow, P. J., & Gosling, S. D. (in press). The Do Re Mi's of everyday life: Examining the structure and personality correlates of music preferences. *Journal of Personality and Social Psychology.*

Rhodewalt, F., & Morf, C. C. (1995). Self and interpersonal correlates of the Narcissistic Personality Inventory: A review and new findings. *Journal of Research in Personality, 29,* 1–23.

Rickert, E. J. (1998). Authoritarianism and economic threat: Implications for political behavior. *Political Psychology, 19,* 707–720.

Ridley, M. (1999). *Genome: The autobiography of a species in 23 chapters.* New York: HarperCollins.

Roberts, B. W., Caspi, A., & Moffitt, T. (2003). Work experiences and personality development in young adulthood. *Journal of Personality and Social Psychology, 84,* 582–593.

Robins, R. W., Caspi, A., & Moffitt, T. (2002). It's not just who you're with, it's who you are: Personality and relationship experiences across multiple relationships. *Journal of Personality, 70,* 925–964.

Robins, R. W., John, O. P., & Caspi, A. (1998). The typological approach to studying personality. In R. B. Cairns & L. R. Bergman (Eds.), *Methods and models for studying the individual* (pp. 135–160). Thousand Oaks, CA: Sage.

Robins, R. W., John, O. P., Caspi, A., Moffitt, T. E., & Stouthamer-Loeber, M. (1996). Resilient, overcontrolled, and undercontrolled boys: Three replicable personality types. *Journal of Personality and Social Psychology, 70,* 157–171.

Robinson, P. (1993). *Freud and his critics.* Berkeley: University of California Press.

Rogers, C. R. (1951). *Client-centered therapy: Its current practice, implications, and theory.* Boston: Houghton Mifflin.

Rogers, C. R. (1961). *On becoming a person.* Boston: Houghton Mifflin.

Rorer, L. G. (1965). The great response-style myth. *Psychological Bulletin, 63,* 129–156.

Rorer, L. G. (1990). Personality assessment: A conceptual survey. In L. Pervin (Ed.), *Handbook of personality: Theory and research.* New York: Guilford.

Rorschach, H. (1921). *Psychodiagnostik.* Bern, Switzerland: Huber.

Rosenthal, R. (1973a). The mediation of Pygmalion effects: A four-factor "theory." *Papua New Guinea Journal of Education, 9,* 1–12.

Rosenthal, R. (1973b). *On the social psychology of the self-fulfilling prophecy: Further evidence for Pygmalion effects and their mediating mechanisms.* New York: MSS Modular Publications, Module 53.

Rosenthal, R. (1973c). Estimating effective reliabilities in studies that employ judges' ratings. *Journal of Clinical Psychology, 29,* 342–345.

Rosenthal, R. (Ed.). (1980). *Quantitative analysis of research domains. New directions for methodology of social and behavioral science,* no. 5. San Francisco: Jossey-Bass.

Rosenthal, R., & Jacobson, L. (1968). *Pygmalion in the classroom: Teacher expectation and pupils' intellectual development.* New York: Holt, Rinehart, & Winston.

Rosenthal, R., & Rosnow, R. L. (1991). *Essentials of behavioral research: Methods and data analysis* (2nd ed.). New York: McGraw-Hill.

Rosenthal, R., & Rubin, D. B. (1978). Interpersonal expectancy effects: The first 345 studies. *Behavioral and Brain Sciences, 1,* 377–415.

Rosenthal, R., & Rubin, D. B. (1982). A simple, general purpose display of magnitude of experimental effect. *Journal of Educational Psychology, 74,* 166–169.

Rosolack, T. K., & Hampson, S. E. (1991). A new typology of health behaviors for personality-health predictions: The case of locus of control. *European Journal of Personality, 5,* 151–168.

Ross, L., Greene, D., & House, P. (1977). The false consensus phenomenon: An attributional bias in self-perception and social perception processes. *Journal of Experimental Social Psychology, 13,* 279–301.

Ross, L., Lepper, M. R., & Hubbard, M. (1975). Perseverance in self perception and social perception: Biased attribution processes in the debriefing paradigm. *Journal of Personality and Social Psychology, 32,* 880–892.

Ross, L., & Nisbett, R. E. (1991). *The person and the situation: Perspectives of social psychology.* New York: McGraw-Hill.

Rosse, J. G., Stecher, M. D., Miller, J. L., & Levin, R. A. (1998). The impact of response distortion on preemployment personality testing and hiring decisions. *Journal of Applied Psychology, 83,* 634–644.

Rotter, J. B. (1954). *Social learning and clinical psychology.* Englewood Cliffs, NJ: Prentice-Hall.

Rotter, J. B. (1982). *The development and applications of social learning theory: Selected papers.* New York: Praeger.

Rowatt, W. C., Cunningham, M. R., & Druen, P. B. (1998). Deception to get a date. *Personality and Social Psychology Bulletin, 24,* 1228–1242.

Rowe, D. C. (1994). *The limits of family influence: Genes, experience, and behavior.* New York: Guilford.

Rowe, D. C., Rodgers, J. L., & Meseck-Bushey, S. (1992). Sibling delinquency and the family environment: Shared and unshared influences. *Child Development, 63,* 59–67.

Rozeboom, W. W. (1960). The fallacy of the null-hypothesis significance test. *Psychological Bulletin, 57,* 416–428.

Rozin, P. (1999). The process of moralization. *Psychological Science, 10,* 218–221.

Rozin, P., Markwith, M., & Stoess, C. (1997). Moralization and becoming a vegetarian: The transformation of preferences into values and the recruitment of disgust. *Psychological Science, 8,* 67–73.

Rozin, P., & Zellner, D. (1985). The role of Pavlovian conditioning in the acquisition of food likes and dislikes. *Annals of the New York Academy of Sciences, 443,* 189–202.

Rudikoff, E. C. (1954). A comparative study of the changes in the concepts of the self, the ordinary person, and the ideal in eight cases. In C. R. Rogers & R. F. Dymond (Eds.), *Psychotherapy and personality change: Co-ordinated studies in the client-centered approach* (pp. 85–98). Chicago: University of Chicago Press.

Rumelhart, D. E. (1989). The architecture of the mind: A connectionist approach. In M. I. Posner (Ed.), *Foundations of cognitive science* (pp. 133–159). Cambridge, MA: MIT Press.

Rumelhart, D. E., McClelland, J. L., & The PDP Research Group (1986). *Parallel distributed processing: Explorations in the microstructure of cognition: Vol. 1. Foundations.* Cambridge, MA: MIT Press.

Rychlak, J. F. (1988). *The psychology of rigorous humanism* (2nd ed.). New York: New York University Press.

Ryff, C. D., & Singer, B. (2003). Flourishing under fire: Resilience as a prototype of challenged thriving. In C. L. M. Keyes & J. Haidt (Eds.), *Flourishing: Positive psychology and the life well-lived* (pp. 15–36). Washington, DC: American Psychological Association.

Ryle, G. (1949). *The concept of mind.* New York: Harper.

Sabini, J. (1995). *Social psychology* (2nd ed.). New York: Norton.

Sackett, P. R., Burris, L. R., & Callahan, C. (1989). Integrity testing for personnel selection: An update. *Personnel Psychology, 42,* 491–529.

Sacks, O. W. (1983). *Awakenings.* New York: Dutton.

Sartre, J. P. (1965). The humanism of existentialism. In W. Baskin (Ed.), *Essays in existentialism* (pp. 31–62). Secaucus, NJ: Citadel.

Saucier, G., & Goldberg, L. R. (1998). What is beyond the Big Five? *Journal of Personality, 66,* 495–524.

Sautter, S. W., Briscoe, L., & Farkas, K. (1991). A neuropsychological profile of Capgras syndrome. *Neuropsychology, 5,* 139–150.

Scarr, S. (1981). *Race, social class, and individual differences in IQ.* Hillsdale, NJ: Erlbaum.

Scarr, S., & McCartney, K. (1983). How people make their own environments: A theory of genotype-environment interactions. *Child Development, 54,* 424–435.

Schank, R. C., & Abelson, R. P. (1977). *Scripts, plans, goals, and understanding.* Hillsdale, NJ: Erlbaum.

Scherer, K. R. (1978). Personality inference from voice quality: The loud voice of extraversion. *European Journal of Social Psychology, 8,* 467–487.

Schlenker, B. R., Weigold, M. F., & Hallam, J. R. (1990). Self-serving attributions in social context: Effects of self-esteem and social pressure. *Journal of Personality and Social Psychology, 58,* 855–863.

Schmidt, D. B., Lubinski, D., & Benbow, C. P. (1998). Validity of assessing educational-vocational preference dimensions among intellectually talented 13-year-olds. *Journal of Counseling Psychology, 45,* 436–453.

Schmidt, F. L. (1996). Statistical significance testing and cumulative knowledge in psychology: Implications for training of researchers. *Psychological Methods, 1,* 115–129.

Schmidt, F. L., & Hunter, J. E. (1992). Development of causal models of processes determining job performance. *Current Directions in Psychological Science, 1,* 89–92.

Schwarz, N. (1999). Self-reports: How questions frame the answers. *American Psychologist, 54,* 93–105.

Sears, D. O. (1986). College students in the laboratory: Influences of a narrow data base on social psychology's view of human nature. *Journal of Personality and Social Psychology, 51,* 515–530.

Sears, R. R. (1947). *Survey of objective studies of psychoanalytic concepts.* New York: Social Science Research Council.

Seligman, M. E. P. (1968). Chronic fear produced by unpredictable electric shock. *Journal of Comparative and Physiological Psychology, 66,* 402–411.

Seligman, M. E. P., & Csikszentmihalyi, M. (2000). Positive psychology: An introduction. *American Psychologist, 55,* 5–14.

Selye, H. (1956). *The stress of life.* New York: McGraw-Hill.

Shanahan, J. (1995). Television viewing and adolescent authoritarianism. *Journal of Adolescence, 18,* 271–288.

Shapiro, D. (1965). *Neurotic styles.* New York: Basic.

Sharpe, D., Adair, J. G., & Roese, N. J. (1992). Twenty years of deception research: A decline in subjects' trust? *Personality and Social Psychology Bulletin, 18,* 585–590.

Shaver, P. R., & Clark, C. L. (1994). The psychodynamics of adult romantic attachment. In J. M. Masling & R. F. Bornstein (Eds.), *Empirical perspectives on object relations theory* (pp. 105–156). Washington, DC: American Psychological Association.

Shedler, J., & Block, J. (1990). Adolescent drug use and psychological health: A longitudinal inquiry. *American Psychologist, 45,* 612–630.

Shenk, J. W. (1999, May). America's altered states. *Harper's, 298,* 38–52.

Shoda, Y. (1999). Behavioral expressions of a personality system: Generation and perception of behavioral signatures. In D. Cervone and Y. Shoda (Eds.), *The coherence of personality: Social-cognitive bases of consistency, variability, and organization* (pp. 155–181). New York: Guilford.

Shweder, R. A. (1992). The cultural psychology of the emotions. In M. Lewis & J. Haviland (Eds.), *Handbook of the emotions.* New York: Guilford.

Shweder, R. A., & Bourne, E. J. (1982). Does the concept of person vary cross-culturally? In A. J. Marsella & G. M. White (Eds.), *Cultural conceptions of mental health and therapy* (pp. 97–137). London: Reidel.

Shweder, R. A., Mahapatra, M., & Miller, J. G. (1990). Culture and moral development. In J. W. Stigler, R. A. Shweder, & G. Herdt (Eds.), *Cultural psychology* (pp. 130–204). New York: Cambridge University Press.

Shweder, R. A., & Sullivan, M. A. (1990). The semiotic subject of cultural psychology. In L. A. Pervin (Ed.), *Handbook of personality: Theory and research* (pp. 399–416). New York: Guilford.

Shweder, R. A., & Sullivan, M. A. (1993). Cultural psychology: Who needs it? *Annual Review of Psychology, 44,* 497–523.

Siegel, S. (1984). Pavlovian conditioning and heroin overdose: Reports by over-dose victims. *Bulletin of the Psychonomic Society, 22,* 428–430.

Siegel, S., & Ellsworth, D. W. (1986). Pavlovian conditioning and death from apparent overdose of medically prescribed morphine: A case report. *Bulletin of the Psychonomic Society, 24,* 278–280.

Silverstein, S. (1993, July 10). Target to pay $2 million in testing case. *Los Angeles Times,* pp. D1–D2.

Simon, L., Greenberg, J., & Brehm, J. (1995). Trivialization: The forgotten mode of dissonance reduction. *Journal of Personality and Social Psychology, 68,* 247–260.

Singh, D., Vidaurri, M., Zambarano, R. J., & Dabbs, J. M., Jr. (1999). Lesbian erotic role identification: Behavioral, morphological, and hormonal correlates. *Journal of Personality and Social Psychology, 76,* 1035–1049.

Skinner, B. F. (1938). *The behavior of organisms: An experimental analysis.* New York: Macmillan.

Skinner, B. F. (1948). *Walden Two.* New York: Macmillan.

Skinner, B. F. (1966). *The behavior of organisms: An experimental analysis.* New York: Appleton-Century-Crofts. (Originally published 1938.)

Skinner, B. F. (1971). *Beyond freedom and dignity.* New York: Knopf.

Smith, E. R., & Branscombe, N. R. (1987). Procedurally mediated social inferences: The case of category accessibility effects. *Journal of Experimental Social Psychology, 23,* 361–382.

Smith, S. S., & Richardson, D. (1983). Amelioration of deception and harm in psychological research: The important role of debriefing. *Journal of Personality and Social Psychology, 44,* 1075–1082.

Snyder, C. R., & Lopez, S. J. (Eds.) (2002). *Handbook of positive psychology.* London: Oxford University Press.

Snyder, M. (1974). The self-monitoring of expressive behavior. *Journal of Personality and Social Psychology, 30,* 526–537.

Snyder, M. (1987). *Public appearances, private realities: The psychology of self-monitoring.* New York: Freeman.

Snyder, M., & Ickes, W. (1985). Personality and social behavior. In G. Lindzey & E. Aronson (Eds.), *Handbook of social psychology* (3rd ed., Vol. 2, pp. 883–948). Reading, MA: Addison-Wesley.

Snyder, M., & Monson, T. C. (1975). Persons, situations, and the control of social behavior. *Journal of Personality and Social Psychology, 32,* 637–644.

Snyder, M., & Swann, W. B. (1978). Confirmation in social interaction: From social perception to social reality. *Journal of Experimental Social Psychology, 14,* 148–162.

Snyder, M., Tanke, E. D., & Berscheid, E. (1977). Social perception and interpersonal behavior: On the self-fulfilling nature of social stereotypes. *Journal of Personality and Social Psychology, 44,* 510–517.

Somer, O., & Goldberg, L. R. (1999). The structure of Turkish trait-descriptive adjectives. *Journal of Personality and Social Psychology, 76,* 431–450.

Spain, J. (1994). *Personality and daily life experience: Evaluating the accuracy of personality judgments.* Unpublished Ph.D. dissertation, University of California, Riverside.

Spain, J., Eaton, L. G., & Funder, D. C. (2000). Perspectives on personality: The relative accuracy of self vs. others for the prediction of behavior and emotion. *Journal of Personality, 68,* 837–867.

Spearman, C. (1910). Correlation calculated from faulty data. *British Journal of Psychology, 3,* 271–295.

Spinney, L. (2002, Sept. 21). The mind readers. *New Scientist,* p. 38.

Sroufe, L. A., Carlson, E., & Shulman, S. (1993). Individuals in relationships: Development from infancy through adolescence. In D. C. Funder, R. D. Parke, C. Tomlinson-Keasey, & K. Widaman (Eds.), *Studying lives through time* (pp. 315–342). Washington, DC: American Psychological Association.

Sroufe, L. A., & Waters, E. (1977). Heart rate as a convergent measure in clinical and developmental research. *Merrill-Palmer Quarterly, 23,* 3–27.

Srull, T. K., & Wyer, R. S., Jr. (1980). Category accessibility and social perception: Some implications for the study of person memory and interpersonal judgments. *Journal of Personality and Social Psychology, 38,* 841–856.

Stanovich, K. E. (1991). Cognitive science meets beginning reading. *Psychological Science, 2,* 70–81.

Stelmack, R. M. (1990). Biological bases of extraversion: Psychophysiological evidence. *Journal of Personality, 58,* 293–311.

Sternberg, R. J. (1995). For whom the bell curve tolls. [Review of *The Bell Curve.*] *Psychological Science, 6,* 257–261.

Stipek, D. J., & Gralinski, J. H. (1991). Gender differences in children's achievement-related beliefs and emotional response to success and failure in mathematics. *Journal of Educational Psychology, 83,* 361–371.

Stoolmiller, M. (1999). Implications of the restricted range of family environments for estimates of heritability and nonshared environment in behavior-genetic adoption studies. *Psychological Bulletin, 125,* 392–409.

Strong, E. K., Jr. (1959). *Strong Vocational Interest Blank.* Palo Alto, CA: Consulting Psychologists Press.

Stuss, D. T., & Levine, B. (2002). Adult clinical neuropsychology: Lessons from studies of the frontal lobes. *Annual Review of Psychology, 53,* 401–433.

Suh, E. M. (2002). Culture, identity consistency, and subjective well-being. *Journal of Personality and Social Psychology, 83,* 1378–1391.

Sullivan, A. (2000, May 21). The double-life crusade. *New York Times, 149*(6), pp. 20–22.

Sulloway, F. J. (1979). *Freud: Biologist of the mind.* New York: Basic.

Suls, J., & Fletcher, B. (1985). The relative efficacy of avoidant and nonavoidant coping strategies: A meta-analysis. *Health Psychology, 4,* 249–288.

Sundberg, N. D. (1977). *The assessment of persons.* Englewood Cliffs, NJ: Prentice-Hall.

Swann, W. B., & Ely, R. J. (1984). A battle of wills: Self-verification versus behavioral confirmation. *Journal of Personality and Social Psychology, 46,* 1287–1302.

Symons, C., & Johnson, B. T. (1997). The self-reference effect in memory: A meta-analysis. *Psychological Bulletin, 121,* 371-394.

Symons, D. (1979). *The evolution of human sexuality.* New York: Oxford University Press.

Szasz, T. S. (1960). The myth of mental illness. *American Psychologist, 15,* 113–118.

Szasz, T. S. (1974). *The myth of mental illness: Foundations of a theory of personal conduct* (rev. ed.). New York: Harper & Row.

Taft, R. (1955). The ability to judge people. *Psychological Bulletin, 52,* 1–23.

Tansey, M. J. (1992). Countertransference theory, quantitative research, and the problem of therapist-patient sexual abuse. In J. W. Barron, M. N. Eagle, & D. L. Wolitzky (Eds.), *Interface of psychoanalysis and psychology* (pp. 539–557). Washington, DC: American Psychological Association.

Taylor, S. E., & Brown, J. D. (1988). Illusion and well-being: A social psychological perspective on mental health. *Psychological Bulletin, 103,* 193–210.

Taylor, S. E., Klein, L. C., Lewis, B. P., Gruenewald, T. L., Gurung, R. A. R., & Updegraff, J. A. (2000). Biobehavioral responses to stress in females: Tend-and-befriend, not fight-or-flight. *Psychological Review, 107,* 411–429.

Taylor, S. E., Lerner, J. S., Sherman, D. K., Sage, R. M., & McDowell, N. K. (2003). Portrait of the self-enhancer: Well adjusted and well liked or maladjusted and friendless? *Journal of Personality and Social Psychology, 84,* 165–176.

Thompson, C. (1995, July 19). Kennedy secretary writes of Rosemary. *Press-Enterprise,* p. A2.

Thorndike, E. L. (1911). *Animal intelligence.* New York: Macmillan.

Thornhill, R., & Palmer, C. T. (2000). *A natural history of rape: Biological bases of sexual coercion.* Cambridge, MA: MIT Press.

Tomarken, A. J., Davidson, R. J., & Henriques, J. B. (1990). Resting frontal brain asymmetry predicts affective responses to films. *Journal of Personality and Social Psychology, 59,* 791–801.

Tooby, J., & Cosmides, L. (1990). On the universality of human nature and the uniqueness of the individual: The role of genetics and adaptation. *Journal of Personality, 58,* 17–67.

Tooke, W. S., & Ickes, W. (1988). A measure of adherence to conventional morality. *Journal of Social and Clinical Psychology, 6,* 310–334.

Triandis, H. C. (1994). *Culture and social behavior.* New York: McGraw-Hill.

Triandis, H. C. (1997). Cross-cultural perspectives on personality. In R. Hogan, J. Johnson, & S. Briggs (Eds.), *Handbook of personality psychology* (pp. 440–464). San Diego: Academic.

Triesman, A. M. (1964). Selective attention in man. *British Medical Bulletin, 20,* 12–16.

Trivedi, N., & Sabini, J. (1998). Volunteer bias, sexuality, and personality. *Archives of Sexual Behavior, 27,* 181–195.

Tsai, J. L., & Chentsova-Dutton, Y. (in press). Variation among European Americans in emotional facial expression. *Journal of Cross-Cultural Psychology.*

Tseng, W-S. (2003). *Clinician's guide to cultural psychiatry.* San Diego: Academic.

Turkheimer, E. (1998). Heritability and biological explanation. *Psychological Review, 105,* 782–791.

Turkheimer, E., & Gottesman, I. I. (1991). Is $H^2 = 0$ a null hypothesis anymore? *Behavioral and Brain Sciences, 14,* 410–411.

Turkeimer, E., & Waldron, M. (2000). Nonshared environment: A theoretical, methodological, and quantitative review. *Psychological Bulletin, 126,* 78–108.

Tversky, A., & Kahneman, D. (1973). Availability: A heuristic for judging frequency and probability. *Cognitive Psychology, 5,* 207–232.

Tversky, A., & Kahneman, D. (1983). Extensional versus intuitive reasoning: The conjunction fallacy in probability judgment. *Psychological Review, 90,* 1124–1131.

Tweed, R. G., & Lehman, D. R. (2002). Learning considered in a cultural context: Confucian and Socratic approaches. *American Psychologist, 57,* 89–99.

Twenge, J. M., & Nolen-Hoeksesma, S. (2002). Age, gender, race, socioeconomic status and birth cohort differences on the children's depression inventory: A meta-analysis. *Journal of Abnormal Psychology, 111,* 578–588.

Twisk, J. W. R., Snel, J., Kemper, H. C. G., & van Mechelen, W. (1998). Relation between the longitudinal development of personality characteristics and biological and lifestyle risk factors for coronary heart disease. *Psychosomatic Medicine, 60,* 372–377.

Valenstein, E. S. (1986). *Great and desperate cure: The rise and decline of psychosurgery and other radical treatments for mental illness.* New York: Basic.

Vallacher, R., & Wegner, D. (1987). What do people think they're doing? Action identification and human behavior. *Psychological Review, 94,* 3–15.

Van Lieshout, C. F. M., & Haselager, G. J. T. (1994). The big five personality factors in Q-sort descriptions of children and adolescents. In C. F. Halverson, A. M. Gedolph, & R. P. Martin (Eds.), *The developing structure of temperament and personality from infancy to adulthood* (pp. 293–318). Hillsdale, NJ: Erlbaum.

Virkkunen, M., Rawlings, R., Tokola, R., Poland, R. E., Gulidotti, A., Nemeroff, C., Bissette, G., Kalogeras, K., Karonen, S. L., & Linnoila, M. (1994). CSF biochemistries, glucose metabolism, and diurnal activity rhythms in alcoholics, violent offenders, fire setters, and healthy volunteers. *Archives of General Psychiatry, 51,* 20–27.

Vogt, D. S., & Colvin, C. R. (2003). Interpersonal orientation and the accuracy of personality judgment. *Journal of Personality, 71,* 267–295.

Vonnegut, K., Jr. (1963). *Cat's cradle.* New York: Holt, Rinehart, & Winston.

Vonnegut, K., Jr. (1966). *Mother night.* New York: Delacorte.

Wakefield, J. C. (1989). Levels of explanation in personality theory. In D. Buss & N. Cantor (Eds.), *Personality psychology: Recent trends and emerging directions* (pp. 333–346). New York: Springer-Verlag.

Waller, D. (1993, April 12). A tour through "hell week." *Newsweek, 33.*

Waller, N. G., & Shaver, P. R. (1994). The importance of nongenetic influences on romantic love styles: A twin-family study. *Psychological Science, 5,* 268–274.

Waters, E., Kondo-Ikemura, K., Posada, G., & Richters, J. E. (1991). Learning to love: Mechanisms and milestones. In M. R. Gunnar & L. A. Sroufe (Eds.), *Self processes and development* (pp. 217–255). Hillsdale, NJ: Erlbaum.

Watkins, C. E., Campbell, V. L., Nieberding, R., & Hallmark, R. (1995). Contemporary practice of psychological assessment by clinical psychologists. *Professional Psychology: Research and Practice, 26,* 54–60.

Watson, D. (1989). Strangers' ratings of five robust personality factor: Evidence of a surprising convergence with self-report. *Journal of Personality and Social Psychology, 57,* 120–128.

Watson, D., & Clark, L. A. (1984). Negative affectivity: The disposition to experience aversive emotional states. *Psychological Bulletin, 96,* 465–490.

Watson, J. B. (1930). *Behaviorism* (rev. ed.). New York: Norton.

Weinberg, R. S., Gould, D., & Jackson, A. (1979). Expectations and performance: An empirical test of Bandura's self-efficacy theory. *Journal of Sport Psychology, 1,* 320–331.

Weinberger, D. A., & Davidson, M. N. (1994). Styles of inhibiting emotional expression: Distinguishing repressive coping from impression management. *Journal of Personality, 62,* 587–614.

Weiss, J. M. (1970). Somatic effects of predictable and unpredictable shock. *Psychosomatic Medicine, 32,* 397–408.

Weiss, J. M. (1977). Psychological and behavioral influences on gastrointestinal lesions in animal models. In J. D. Maser & M. E. P. Seligman (Eds.), *Psychopathology: Experimental models* (pp. 232–269). San Francisco: Freeman.

Westen, D. (1990). Psychoanalytic approaches to personality. In L. Pervin (Ed.), *Handbook of personality: Theory and research* (pp. 21–65). New York: Guilford.

Westen, D. (1998). The scientific legacy of Sigmund Freud: Toward a psychodynamically informed psychological science. *Psychological Bulletin, 124,* 333–371.

Weston, M. J., & Whitlock, F. A. (1971). The Capgras syndrome following head injury. *British Journal of Psychiatry, 119,* 25–31.

Wheeler, L., Reise, H. T., & Bond, M. H. (1989). Collectivism-individualism in everyday social life: The Middle Kingdom and the melting pot. *Journal of Personality and Social Psychology, 57,* 79–86.

Wheeler, R. E., Davidson, R. J., & Tomarken, A. J. (1993). Front brain asymmetry and emotional reactivity: A biological substrate of affective style. *Psychophysiology, 30,* 82–89.

Whorf, B. L. (1956). Science and linguistics. In J. B. Carroll (Ed.), *Language, thought, and reality* (pp. 207–219). Cambridge, MA: MIT Press.

Widom, C. S. (1989). The cycle of violence. *Science, 244,* 160–166.

Wiggins, J. S. (1973). *Personality and prediction: Principles of personality assessment.* Reading, MA: Addison-Wesley.

Wilkinson, L., & The Task Force on Statistical Inference, APA Board of Scientific Affairs (1999). Statistical methods in psychology journals: Guidelines and explanations. *American Psychologist, 54,* 594–604.

Wilson, E. O. (1975). Sociobiology: The new synthesis. Cambridge, MA: Harvard University Press.

Wilson, G. D. (1978). Introversion/extraversion. In H. London and J. E. Exner (Eds.), *Dimensions of personality.* New York: Wiley.

Winnicott, D. W. (1958). *Through paediatrics to psycho-analysis.* London: Hogarth.

Winnicott, D. W. (1965). *The maturational process and the facilitating environment.* New York: International Universities.

Winnicott, D. W. (1996). The niffle. In R. Shepherd, & H. Jones (Eds.), *Thinking about children* (pp. 104–109). Reading, MA: Addison-Wesley.

Winograd, T. (1975). Frame representations and the declarative-procedural controversy. In D. G. Bobrow & A. M. Collins (Eds.), *Representation and understanding: Studies in cognitive science* (pp. 185–210). New York: Academic.

Winograd, T., & Flores, F. (1986). *Understanding computers and cognition.* Norwood, NJ: Ablex.

Winter, D. G., & Stewart, A. J. (1978). The power motive. In H. London & J. E. Exner, Jr. (Eds.), *Dimensions of personality* (pp. 391–448). New York: Wiley.

Winter, D. G., John, O. P., Stewart, A. J., Klohnen, E. C., & Duncan, L. E. (1998). Traits and motives: Toward an integration of two traditions in personality research. *Psychological Review, 105,* 230–250.

Woike, B. A. (1995). Most-memorable experiences: Evidence for a link between implicit and explicit motives and social cognitive processes in everyday life. *Journal of Personality and Social Psychology, 68,* 1081–1091.

Woike, B. A., & Aronoff, J. (1992). Antecedents of complex social cognitions. *Journal of Personality and Social Psychology, 63,* 97–104.

Wood, W., & Eagly, A. H. (2002). A cross-cultural analysis of the behavior of women and men: Implications for the origins of sex differences. *Psychological Bulletin, 128,* 699–727.

Woodworth, R. S. (1917). *Personal Data Sheet.* Chicago: Stoelting.

Wundt, W. (1894). *Lectures on human and animal psychology* (J. E. Creighton & E. B. Titchener, Trans.). New York: Macmillan.

Wundt, W. (1904). *Principles of physiological psychology* (Vol. 1, E. B. Titchener, Trans.). New York: Macmillan.

Wylie, R. E. (1974). *The self concept* (Vols. 1 and 2). Lincoln: University of Nebraska Press.

Yang, K. S., & Bond, M. H. (1990). Exploring implicit personality theories with indigenous or imported constructs: The Chinese case. *Journal of Personality and Social Psychology, 58,* 1087–1095.

Yang, K. S. & Lee, P. H. (1971). Likeability, meaningfulness and familiarity of 557 Chinese adjectives for personality trait description. *Acta Psychologica Taiwanica, 13,* 36–37. (In Chinese.)

York, K. L., & John, O. P. (1992). The four faces of Eve: A typological analysis of women's personality at midlife. *Journal of Personality and Social Psychology, 63,* 494–508.

Young, J. (1988). *The role of selective attention in the attitude-behavior relationship.* Unpublished doctoral dissertation, University of Minnesota, Minneapolis.

Zelli, A., Cervone, D., & Huesmann, L. R. (1996). Behavioral experience and social inference: Individual differences in aggressive experience and spontaneous versus deliberate trait inference. *Social Cognition, 14,* 165–190.

Zelli, A., Huesmann, L. R., & Cervone, D. (1995). Social inference and individual differences in aggression: Evidence for spontaneous judgments of hostility. *Aggressive Behavior, 21,* 405–417.

Zentall, T. R., Sutton, J. E., & Sherbune, L. M. (1996). True imitative learning in pigeons. *Psychological Science, 7,* 343–346.

Zhang, F., & Hazan, C. (2002). Working models of attachment and person perception processes. *Personal Relationships, 9,* 225–235.

Zheng, Y., Xu, L., & Shen, Q. (1986). Styles of verbal expression of emotional and physical experience: A study of depressed patients and normal controls in China. *Culture, Medicine, and Psychiatry, 10,* 231–243.

Zickar, M. J. (2001). Using personality inventories to identify thugs and agitators: Applied psychology's contribution to the war against labor. *Journal of Vocational Behavior, 59,* 149–164.

Zimbardo, P. G. (1977). *Shyness.* New York: Jove/Harcourt Brace.

Zuckerman, M. (1979). Attribution of success and failure revisited; or, the motivational bias is alive and well in attribution theory. *Journal of Personality, 47,* 245–287.

Zuckerman, M. (1984). Sensation seeking: A comparative approach to a human trait. *Behavioral and Brain Sciences, 7,* 413–471.

Zuckerman, M. (1991). *Psychobiology of personality.* Cambridge, England: Cambridge University Press.

Zuckerman, M. (1998). Psychobiological theories of personality. In D. F. Barone, M. Hersen, & V. B. Van Hasselt (Eds.), *Advanced personality* (pp. 123–154). New York: Plenum.

Zuckerman, M., Koestner, R., DeBoy, T., Garcia, K. T., Maresca, B. C., & Sartoris, J. M. (1988). To predict some of the people some of the time: A reexamination of the moderator variable approach in personality theory. *Journal of Personality and Social Psychology, 54,* 1006–1019.

ART AND PHOTO CREDITS

NAME INDEX

SUBJECT INDEX

summer nightgown. She was heating up some milk in a little pan. Mrs. Zimmermann always had to drink hot milk to calm down after parties. She hated the taste of the stuff, but it was the only way she could get to sleep.

"Some party, eh, Rosie?" she said, stirring the milk.

"Yeah. It sure was."

"You know," said Mrs. Zimmermann slowly, "I didn't even want there to be a party."

Rose Rita was startled. "You didn't?"

"Nope. I was afraid your feelings would be hurt. Even more than they already were, I mean—by Lewis's running out on you."

Rose Rita had not told Mrs. Zimmermann how she felt about Lewis's going away. She was amazed at how much Mrs. Zimmermann understood about her. Maybe it all went with being a witch.

Mrs. Zimmermann tested the milk with her finger. Then she poured it into a mug that was decorated with little purple flowers. She sat down across from Rose Rita and took a sip.

"Ugh!" said Mrs. Zimmermann, making a face. "I think the next time I'll slip myself a mickey. But back to what we were talking about. You're pretty mad at Lewis, aren't you?"

Rose Rita stared at the table. "Yeah, I sure am. If I hadn't liked you and Uncle Jonathan so much, I don't think I'd've showed up at all."

Mrs. Zimmermann chuckled. "It didn't look as if you

and he were on the best of terms tonight. Do you have any idea of why he's going to camp?"

Rose Rita crumbled up her cookie and thought. "Well," she said at last, "I guess he's tired of palling around with me and so he wants to be a big eagle scout or something."

"You're about half right," said Mrs. Zimmermann. "That is, he does want to be a boy scout. But he isn't tired of being your friend. I think Lewis wishes very much that you could be going to camp with him."

Rose Rita blinked back her tears. "He does?"

Mrs. Zimmermann nodded. "Yes, and I'll tell you something else. He can't wait to get back and tell you about all the great new things he's learned to do."

Rose Rita looked confused. "I don't understand. It sounds all mixed up. He likes me so he's going away so he can tell me how much fun it was not to have me around."

Mrs. Zimmermann laughed. "Well, when you put it that way, my dear, it does sound mixed up. And I will admit that it's all mixed up in Lewis's head. He wants to learn how to tie knots and paddle canoes and hike through the wilderness, and he wants to come back and tell you so you'll think he's a real boy and like him even more than you do now."

"I like him just the way he is. What's all this dumb stuff about being a real boy?"

Mrs. Zimmermann sat back and sighed. There was a

long silver case lying on the table. She picked it up and opened it. Inside was a row of dark brown cigars.

"Do you mind if I smoke?"

"Nope." Rose Rita had seen Mrs. Zimmermann smoking cigars before. It had surprised her at first, but she had gotten used to it. As she watched, Mrs. Zimmermann bit the end off the cigar and spat it into a nearby wastebasket. Then she snapped her fingers and a match appeared out of thin air. When the cigar was lit, Mrs. Zimmermann offered the match back to the air, and it disappeared.

"Saves on ashtrays," she said, grinning. Mrs. Zimmermann took a few puffs. The smoke trailed off toward the open window in long graceful swirls. There was a silence. Finally Mrs. Zimmermann spoke again. "I know it's hard for you to understand, Rose Rita. It's always hard to understand why someone is doing something that hurts us. But think of what Lewis is like; he's a pudgy shy boy who's always got his nose stuck in a book. He isn't good at sports, and he's scared of practically everything. Well. Then look at you. You're a regular tomboy. You can climb trees, you can run fast, and the other day when I was watching you, you struck out the side in that girls' softball game. You can do all the things that Lewis can't do. Now do you see why he's going to camp?"

Rose Rita couldn't believe what she was thinking. "To be like me?"

Mrs. Zimmermann nodded. "Exactly. To be like you,

so you'll like him better. Of course, there are other reasons. For instance, he'd like to be like other boys. He wants to be normal—most bright kids do." She smiled wryly and flicked cigar ashes into the sink.

Rose Rita looked sad. "If he'd've asked me, I would've taught him a lot of stuff."

"No good. He can't learn from a girl—it would hurt his pride. But look, all this talk is beside the point. Lewis is going off to camp tomorrow, and you're stuck here in New Zebedee with nothing to do. Well now, it just so happens that the other day I received a most surprising letter. It was from my late cousin Oley. Have I ever mentioned him to you?"

Rose Rita thought a second. "Gee, no, I don't think so."

"I didn't think I had. Well, Oley was a strange old duck, but . . ."

Rose Rita cut in. "Mrs. Zimmermann, you said 'late.' Is he . . ."

Mrs. Zimmermann nodded sadly. "Yes, I'm afraid Oley has gone to glory. He wrote me a letter while he was dying, and . . . well, see here now, why don't I just go get it and show it to you? It'll give you some idea of the kind of person he was."

Mrs. Zimmermann got up and went upstairs. For a while Rose Rita heard her banging around and shuffling papers in her large untidy study. When she came down-stairs, she handed Rose Rita a wrinkled piece of paper with several little holes punched in it. There was writing on the paper, but it was very sloppy and shaky. Ink had been spilled in several places.

"This letter came with a bunch of legal documents for me to sign," said Mrs. Zimmermann. "It's all a very odd business and I'm not sure I know what to think of it. Anyhow, there's the letter. It's a mess, but you can read it. Oh, by the way, Oley always wrote with a quill pen when he felt he had something important to say. That's what made all those holes in the paper. Go ahead. Read it."

Rose Rita picked up the letter. It said:

May 21, 1950

Dear Florence,

This may well be the last letter I ever write. I fell ill suddenly last week, and do not understand it, since I have never had a sick day in my life until now. I don't believe in doctors, as you know, and have been trying to cure myself. I bought some medicine at the store down the road, but it hasn't helped a bit. So, as they say, it looks as if I am on my way out. In fact, when you get this letter, I will be dead, since I have left instructions for it to be sent to you with my will in case I kick off, as they say.

Now then, on to business. I am leaving you my farm. You are my only living relative, and I've always liked you, though I know you haven't cared

that much for me. Anyway, let's let bygones be by-
gones. The farm is yours, and I hope you enjoy it.
And here is one final very important note. You
remember the Battle Meadow? Well, I was digging
there the other day, and I came across a magic
ring. I know you will think I'm kidding, but when
you handle the thing and try it on, you will know
I was right. I haven't told anyone about the ring,
except for a neighbor down the road. Maybe I am
a little funny in the head, but I know what I know,
and I think the ring is magic. I have locked the
ring in the lower left-hand drawer of my desk, and
I am going to have my lawyer send the key to you,
along with the key to the front door of the house.
So I guess that is all I have to say for now. With
luck I'll see you again some day, and if not, well,
I'll see you in the funny papers as they say, ha, ha.

Your cousin,
Oley Gunderson

"Wow!" said Rose Rita, as she handed the letter back
to Mrs. Zimmermann. "What a weird letter!"

"Yes," said Mrs. Zimmermann, shaking her head sadly,
"it's a weird letter from a rather weird person. Poor
Oley! He lived all his life up there on that farm. Completely alone. No family, no friends, no neighbors, no
nothing. I think it must have affected his mind."

Rose Rita's face fell. "You mean . . ."

Mrs. Zimmermann sighed. "Yes, my dear. I'm sorry to

disappoint you about that magic ring, but Oley was right when he said he was a little funny in the head. I think he made things up to make his life more interesting. That part about the Battle Meadow is right out of his childhood. A little bit of make-believe that he saved up. The trouble is, he saved it so long that he got to believing it was true."

"I don't get what you mean," said Rose Rita.

"It's all very simple. You see, when I was a girl, I used to go up to Oley's farm a lot. His dad Sven was alive then. He was a very generous sort, and was always inviting cousins and aunts up to stay for long periods of time. Oley and I used to play together, and one summer we found some Indian arrowheads in a meadow by a stream that runs out behind this farmhouse. Well, you know how kids are. On the basis of this little discovery we made up a story about how this had been a place where a battle had been fought between some settlers and a band of Indians. We even gave names to some of the Indians and pioneers who were involved in the battle, and we named the little field where we played the Battle Meadow. I had forgotten all about the Battle Meadow until Oley sent me this letter."

Rose Rita felt very disappointed. "Are you sure the part about the ring isn't true? I mean, sometimes even crazy people tell the truth. They really do, you know."

Mrs. Zimmermann smiled sympathetically at Rose Rita. "I'm sorry, my dear, but I'm afraid I know more about Oley Gunderson than you do. He was completely batty. Batty as a bedbug. But, batty or not, he left me his farm, and there are no other relatives around to contest the will on the grounds of insanity. So I'm going up there to have a look at the farm and sign a few papers. The farm is near Petoskey, right up at the tip of the Lower Peninsula, so after I've taken care of the legal folderol, I'm going to take the ferry across to the Upper Peninsula and drive all over the place. I haven't been on a really long car trip since gas rationing ended, and I've just bought a new car. I'm itching to go. Would you like to go with me?"

Rose Rita was overjoyed. She felt like jumping across the table and hugging Mrs. Zimmermann. But then a disturbing thought came to her. "Do you think my folks'd let me go?"

Mrs. Zimmermann smiled her most businesslike and competent smile. "It's all arranged. I called up your mother a couple of days ago to see if it would be all right with her. She said it sounded like a fine idea. We decided to save the news for you as a surprise."

There were tears in Rose Rita's eyes now. "Gee, Mrs. Zimmermann, thanks a lot. Thanks a whole lot."

"Don't mention it, my dear." Mrs. Zimmermann glanced at the kitchen clock. "I think we'd better be getting off to bed if we're going to be in any shape for tomorrow. Jonathan and Lewis will be coming over here for breakfast. Then off goes Lewis to camp, and off goes we to the wilds of Michigan." Mrs. Zimmermann got up and stubbed out her cigar in the kitchen sink. She went into the front room and started turning out lights. When she returned to the kitchen, she found Rose Rita still sitting at the table with her head in her hands. There was a dreamy look on her face.

"Still mooning about magic rings, eh?" said Mrs. Zimmermann. She laughed softly and patted Rose Rita on the back. "Rose Rita, Rose Rita," she said, shaking her head, "the trouble with you is, you've been hanging around with a witch, and you think magic is going to sprout up out of the cracks in the sidewalk, like dandelions. By the way, did I tell you? I don't have a magic umbrella anymore."

Rose Rita turned and stared at Mrs. Zimmermann in disbelief. "You *don't?*"

"Nope. As you recall, my old one got smashed in a battle with an evil spirit. It's totally done for. As for the new one, the one Jonathan bought me for Christmas, I haven't been able to do anything with it. I'm still a witch, of course. I can still snap matches out of the air. But as for the more serious, more powerful kinds of magic . . . well, I'm afraid I'm back in the bush leagues. I can't do anything."

Rose Rita felt awful. She had seen Mrs. Zimmermann's magic umbrella in action. Most of the time it just looked like a ratty old black umbrella, but when Mrs. Zimmermann said certain words to it, it turned into a tall rod topped by a crystal sphere, a sphere with a purple star burning inside it. It was the source of all Mrs. Zimmermann's greater powers. And now it was gone. Gone for good.

"Isn't . . . isn't there anything you can do, Mrs. Zimmermann?" Rose Rita asked.

" 'Fraid not, my dear. I'm just a parlor magician like Jonathan now, and I'll have to make the best of it. Sorry. Now, run up to bed. We've got a long day of traveling ahead of us."

Sleepily Rose Rita climbed the stairs. She was staying in the guest room. It was a very pleasant room, and, like most of the rooms in Mrs. Zimmermann's house, it was full of purple things. The wallpaper was covered with little bouquets of violets, and the chamber pot in the corner was made of purple Crown Derby china. Over the bureau hung a painting of a room in which almost everything was purple. The painting was signed "H. Matisse." It had been given to Mrs. Zimmermann by the famous French painter during her visit to Paris just before the First World War.

Rose Rita lay back on her pillow. The moon hung over Jonathan's house and cast a silver light on turrets and gables and steep slanted roofs. Rose Rita felt dreamy and strange. Magic umbrellas and magic rings were chasing each other around in her head. She thought about Oley's letter. What if there really was a magic ring up there, locked in his desk? That would sure be exciting. Rose Rita sighed and turned over on her side. Mrs. Zimmermann was a smart person. She usually knew what she was talking about, and she was probably right about that old ring. The whole story was just a lot of baloney. But as she drifted off to sleep, Rose Rita couldn't help thinking how nice it would be if Oley's letter were telling the truth.

CHAPTER TWO

Next morning Mrs. Zimmermann made popovers for breakfast. Just as she was pulling the pan out of the oven, the back door opened, and in walked Jonathan and Lewis. Lewis was pudgy and round-faced. He was wearing his brand-new boy scout uniform and a bright red neckerchief with BSA on the back. His hair was neatly parted and plastered down with Wildroot Cream Oil. Behind him came Jonathan. Jonathan always looked the same, summer or winter: red beard, pipe in mouth, tan wash pants, blue work shirt, red vest.

"Hi, Pruny!" said Jonathan, cheerfully. "Are those popovers ready yet?"

"The first batch is, Weird Beard," snapped Mrs. Zimmermann, as she dumped the heavy iron pan on the table. "I'm only making two pans. Think you can hold yourself down to four?"

"I'll be lucky if I get one, the way you grab them, Haggy. Watch out for her fork, Lewis. She stabbed me right here in the back of the hand last week."

Jonathan and Mrs. Zimmermann went on trading insults until breakfast was ready. Then, together with Lewis and Rose Rita, they sat down to the silent business of eating. At first Lewis didn't dare meet Rose Rita's eyes—he still felt bad about leaving her in the lurch. But then he noticed that she had a very smug look on her face. Jonathan noticed it too.

"Oh, all right!" said Jonathan, when he felt that he couldn't stand the suspense any longer. "What's the big secret? Rose Rita's got canary feathers all over her face."

"Oh, nothing much," said Rose Rita, grinning. "I'm just going up to explore around an old abandoned farm with Mrs. Zimmermann. The farm is supposed to be haunted, and there's a magic ring hidden somewhere in the house. It was put there by a madman who hanged himself later in the barn."

Lewis and Jonathan gaped. Rose Rita was embroidering a bit on the truth. It was one of her faults. Usually she was quite truthful, but when the occasion seemed to call for it, she could come out with the most amazing stuff.

Mrs. Zimmermann gave Rose Rita a sour look. "You ought to write books," she said dryly. Then she turned to Lewis and Jonathan. "Despite what my friend here claims, I am not running a Halloween Tourist Agency. My cousin Oley—you remember him, Jonathan—he died, and he left me his farm. I'm going up to see the place and drive around a bit, and I've asked Rose Rita to come with me. I'm sorry I didn't tell you about this before, Jonathan, but I was afraid you'd slip and spill the beans to Lewis. You know how good you are at keeping secrets."

Jonathan made a face at Mrs. Zimmermann, but she ignored him. "Well!" she said, sitting back and smiling broadly at Rose Rita and Lewis. "Now you both have something to do this summer, and that's how it should be!"

"Yeah," said Lewis sullenly. He was beginning to wonder if maybe Rose Rita wasn't getting the better deal after all.

After breakfast Lewis and Rose Rita volunteered to do the dishes. Mrs. Zimmermann went up to her study and brought down Oley's letter for Jonathan to see. He read it pensively while Rose Rita washed and Lewis wiped. Mrs. Zimmermann sat at the kitchen table, humming and smoking a cigar. When he had finished the letter, Jonathan handed it back to Mrs. Zimmermann without saying anything. He seemed thoughtful, though.

A few minutes later Jonathan got up and went next door to his house. He backed his big black car out of the driveway and pulled it up next to the curb. The back seat was full of Lewis's boy scout stuff: bed roll, pack, scout manual, hiking shoes, and a Quaker Oats box full of Mrs. Zimmermann's specialty—chocolate chip cookies.

Rose Rita and Mrs. Zimmermann stood at the curb. Jonathan was behind the wheel, and Lewis sat next to him.

"Well, good-by and *bon voyage,* and all that," said Mrs. Zimmermann. "Have a good time at camp, Lewis."

"Thanks, Mrs. Zimmermann," said Lewis, waving back.

"You two have a good time too, up there in the wilds of Michigan," said Jonathan. "Oh, by the way, Florence."

"Yes? What is it?"

"Just this: I think you ought to check out Oley's desk to see if there really is anything hidden away there. You never can tell."

Mrs. Zimmermann laughed. "If I find a magic ring, I'll send it to you by parcel post. But if I were you, I wouldn't hold my breath till it arrived. You've met Oley, Jonathan. You know how screwy he was."

Jonathan took his pipe out of his mouth and stared straight at Mrs. Zimmermann. "Yes, I know all about Oley, but just the same, I think you ought to watch out."

"Oh, sure, I'll watch out," said Mrs. Zimmermann carelessly. She really didn't feel that there was anything to worry about.

There were more good-bys and waves, and then Jonathan drove off. Mrs. Zimmermann told Rose Rita to run home and pack while she went inside to get her own things together.

Rose Rita ran off down the hill to her house. She was really excited by now, and impatient to get started. But just as she was opening the front door of her house, she heard her father say, "Well, I wish next time you'd consult me before you let our daughter go gallivanting off with the town screwball. For God's sake, Louise, don't you have any—"

Mrs. Pottinger cut him off. "Mrs. Zimmermann is not the town screwball," she said firmly. "She's a responsible person who's been a good friend to Rose Rita."

"Responsible, ha! She smokes cigars and she hobnobs around with old what's-his-name, the bearded character with all the money. The one who does magic tricks, you know his name . . ."

"Yes, I certainly do. And I would think that after your daughter had been the best friend of old what's-his-name's nephew for a solid year, the least you could do would be to learn his name. But I still can't see why . . ."

And on it went. Mr. and Mrs. Pottinger were arguing out in the kitchen, behind a closed door. But Mr. Pot-

tinger had a loud voice, even when he was talking normally, and Mrs. Pottinger had raised her voice to match
his. Rose Rita stood there a moment, listening. She knew
from past experience that it would not be good to butt in
on the argument. So she tiptoed quietly upstairs and
started to pack.

Into the worn black valise that she used as a traveling
bag Rose Rita threw underwear, shirts, jeans, tooth-
brush, toothpaste, and anything else she thought she
would need. It felt great not to have to pack dresses and
blouses and skirts. Mrs. Zimmermann never made Rose
Rita get all dressed up—she let her wear what she liked.
Rose Rita felt a sudden sense of hopelessness when she
remembered that she wouldn't be able to be a tomboy
forever. Skirts and nylons, lipsticks and powder puffs,
dating and dancing were all waiting for her in Junior
High. Wouldn't it be nice if she were really a boy?
Then she could . . .

Rose Rita heard a horn beeping outside. That had to
be Mrs. Zimmermann. She zipped up the valise and
dashed downstairs with it. When she stepped out the
front door, she found her mother standing there smiling.
Her father was gone, so apparently the storm had blown
over. Out at the curb was Mrs. Zimmermann. She was at
the wheel of a brand-new 1950 Plymouth. It was high
and boxy, and had a humpy sort of trunk. A strip of
chrome divided the windshield in two, and the little
square letters on the side of the car said CRANBROOK—

that was the name of that particular model. The car was bright green. Mrs. Zimmermann was angry about that, because she had ordered maroon, but she had been too lazy to send the car back.

"Hi, Rose Rita! Hi, Louise!" Mrs. Zimmermann called, waving to both of them. "Good day for traveling, eh?"

"I should say," said Mrs. Pottinger, smiling. She was genuinely happy that Rose Rita could be going on a trip with Mrs. Zimmermann. Mr. Pottinger's job kept the family in New Zebedee all through the summer, and Mrs. Pottinger had some idea of how lonely her daughter was going to be without Lewis. Fortunately Mrs. Pottinger did not know anything about Mrs. Zimmermann's magical abilities, and she distrusted the rumors she heard.

Rose Rita kissed her mother on the cheek. " 'Bye, Mom," she said. "See you in a couple of weeks."

"Okay. Have a good time," said Mrs. Pottinger. "Drop me a card when you get to Petoskey."

"I will."

Rose Rita ran down the steps, threw her valise in the back seat, and ran around to climb into the front seat beside Mrs. Zimmermann. Mrs. Zimmermann put the car in gear and they rolled off down Mansion Street. The trip had started.

Mrs. Zimmermann and Rose Rita took U.S. 12 over to U.S. 131, which runs straight north through Grand

Rapids. It was a beautiful sunny day. Telephone poles and trees and Burma-Shave signs whipped past. In the fields farm machines were working, machines with names like John Deere and Minneapolis-Moline and International Harvester. They were painted bright colors, blue and green and red and yellow. Every now and then Mrs. Zimmermann had to pull off onto the shoulder to let a tractor with a long cutting bar go by.

When they got to Big Rapids, Mrs. Zimmermann and Rose Rita had lunch in a diner. There was a pinball machine in the corner, and Mrs. Zimmermann insisted on playing it. Mrs. Zimmermann was a first-rate pinball player. She knew how to work the flippers, and—after she had been playing a particular machine for a while—she knew how much she could bang on the sides and the top without making the TILT sign light up. By the time she was through she had won thirty-five free games. She left them to be played off by the patrons of the diner, who were watching, open-mouthed. They had never seen a lady play a pinball machine before.

After lunch Mrs. Zimmermann went to the A&P and a bakery. She was planning to have a picnic supper at the farmhouse when they got there. Into the big metal cooler in the trunk she put salami, bologna, cans of deviled ham, a quart of vanilla ice cream, a bottle of milk, three bottles of pop, and a jar of pickles. Into a wooden picnic hamper she put two fresh loaves of salt-rising bread and a chocolate cake. She bought some crushed ice at a gas station and put it in the cooler to keep the food from spoiling. It was a hot day. The thermometer on the billboard that they passed on the way out of town said ninety.

Mrs. Zimmermann told Rose Rita that they were going to drive straight up to the farm now, without stopping. As they got farther and farther north, the hills began to grow steeper. Some of them looked as if the car would never be able to get up them, but it was funny how the hills seemed to flatten out under you as the car climbed. Now, all around her, Rose Rita saw pine trees. The wonderful fresh smell of them drifted in through the car windows as they sped along. They were approaching the vast forests of northern Michigan.

Late that afternoon Rose Rita and Mrs. Zimmermann were cruising slowly along a gravel road, listening to the weather report on the car radio. Without warning, the car began to slow down. It rolled to a halt. Mrs. Zimmermann turned the key and pumped the accelerator. All she got was the *rr-rr* sound of the starting motor trying to get the engine to turn over. But it wouldn't catch. After about the fifteenth try, Mrs. Zimmermann sat back and swore softly under her breath. Then she happened to glance at the gas gauge.

"Oh, don't *tell* me!" groaned Mrs. Zimmermann. She leaned forward and began hitting her forehead against the steering wheel.

"What's wrong?" asked Rose Rita.

Mrs. Zimmermann sat there with a disgusted expression on her face. "Oh, not much. We're just out of gas, that's all. I meant to fill up at that place where we bought the ice in Big Rapids, but I forgot."

Rose Rita put her hand to her mouth. "Oh no!"

"Oh yes. However, I know where we are. We're only a few miles from the farm. If you're feeling energetic, we could ditch the car and walk, but we don't even have to do that. There's a gas station a little ways up the road. At least, there used to be one."

Mrs. Zimmermann and Rose Rita got out of the car and started to walk. It was almost sunset. Clouds of midges hovered in the air, and the long shadows of trees lay across the road. Little patches of red light could be seen here and there among the roadside trees. Up and down hills the two travelers plodded, kicking up white dust as they went. Mrs. Zimmermann was a good walker, and so was Rose Rita. They reached the station just as the sun was going down.

Bigger's Grocery Store was surrounded on three sides by a dark forest of pines. The store was just a white frame house with a wide plate glass window in the front. Through the window you could see rows of stacked groceries and a cash register and counter in the rear. Some green letters on the window had once spelled SALADA, but now they just said ADA. Like many rural grocery stores, Bigger's was also a gas station. Out in front stood two red gas pumps, and near them was a white sign with a flying red horse on it. The horse was on the circular ornament on top of each pump too. In a weedy field next to the store stood a chicken coop. The coop stood in a fenced enclosure, but there were no chickens to be seen in the chicken yard. The tarpaper roof of the coop was caved in at one place, and the water pan in the yard had a thick green scum on it.

"Well, here we are," said Mrs. Zimmermann, wiping her forehead. "Now, if we can get Gert to come out and wait on us, we're all set."

Rose Rita was surprised. "Do you know the lady that runs this store?"

Mrs. Zimmermann sighed. "Yes, I'm afraid I do. I haven't been up this way for some time now, but Gert Bigger was running this store when I last came up to visit Oley. That was about five years ago. Maybe she's still there, and maybe not. We'll see."

As Rose Rita and Mrs. Zimmermann got closer to the store, they noticed a small black dog that was lying on the steps out in front. As soon as it saw them, it jumped to its feet and started to bark. Rose Rita was afraid it might try to bite them, but Mrs. Zimmermann was calm. She strode up to the steps, put her hands on her hips, and yelled, "Git!" The dog stood its ground and barked louder. Finally, just as Mrs. Zimmermann was getting ready to aim a good hard kick at the dog, it jumped sideways off the steps and ran off into the shrubbery at the end of the driveway.

"Dumb mutt," grumbled Mrs. Zimmermann. She walked up the steps and opened the door of the shop.

Ting-a-ling went the little bell. The lights in the shop were on, but there was no one behind the counter. Minutes passed as Mrs. Zimmermann and Rose Rita stood there waiting. Finally they began to hear some clumping and bumping around in the back of the shop. A door rattled open, and in walked Gert Bigger. She was a big rawboned woman in a shapeless sack of a dress, and she had an angry face. When she saw Mrs. Zimmermann, she looked startled.

"Oh, it's *you!* You haven't been up this way in quite a while. Well, what do you want?"

Gert Bigger sounded so nasty that Rose Rita wondered if maybe she had a grudge against Mrs. Zimmermann.

Mrs. Zimmermann answered in a quiet voice. "I'd just like some gas, if it won't trouble you too much. We ran out down the road a bit."

"Just a minute," snapped Gert.

She marched down the main aisle of the store and out the door, slamming it as she went.

"Gee, what an old crab!" said Rose Rita.

Mrs. Zimmermann shook her head sadly. "Yes, she gets worse every time I see her. Come on, let's get our gas and get out of here."

After a good deal of fussing around and cursing, Gert Bigger found a five-gallon gasoline can and filled it. Rose

Rita liked the smell of gasoline, and she liked to watch the numbers on the pump whirl. When the numbers stopped, Gert shut off the pump and announced the price. It was exactly twice what it said on the pump.

Mrs. Zimmermann looked hard at the woman. She was trying to figure out if Gert was kidding. "Are you having a little joke, Gertie? Look at those numbers there."

"It's no joke, dearie. Pay up, or you walk to the farm." She added, in a sneering voice, "It's my special price for friends."

Mrs. Zimmermann paused a minute, wondering what to do. Rose Rita was hoping she would wave her hand and turn Gert Bigger into a toad or something. Finally Mrs. Zimmermann heaved a deep sigh and opened her pocketbook. "There! Much good may it do you. Now come on, Rose Rita, let's get back to the car."

"Okay."

Mrs. Zimmermann picked up the gas can, and they started back down the road. After they had rounded the first bend, Rose Rita said, "What's the matter with that old lady, anyway? How come she's mad at you?"

"She's mad at everybody, Rosie. Mad at the world. I knew her when I was younger, back when I used to come up here and spend summers at the old farm. In fact one summer, when I was eighteen, she and I fought over the same boy friend, a guy named Mordecai Hunks.

/ 34 /

I won the fight, but he and I didn't go together very long. We broke up at the end of the summer. I don't know who he married."

"Was Gertie mad at you for taking away her boy friend?"

Mrs. Zimmermann chuckled and shook her head. "You bet she was! And you know what? She's *still* mad! That woman is an expert grudge carrier. She remembers things people said years and years ago, and she's always planning to get even with somebody. I must say, though, that I've never seen her act quite the way she did tonight. I wonder what got into her?" Mrs. Zimmermann stopped in the middle of the road and turned. She looked back in the direction of Gert Bigger's store, and she rubbed her chin. She seemed to be thinking. Then, with a shrug, she turned and walked on toward the car.

It was dark now. Crickets chirped in the roadside weeds, and once a rabbit darted across their path and disappeared into the bushes on the other side. When Mrs. Zimmermann and Rose Rita finally got back to the car, it was sitting there in the moonlight, patiently waiting for them. Rose Rita had gotten to thinking of the car as a real person. For one thing, it had a face. The eyes were starey, like the eyes of cows, but the mouth was fishlike— mournful and heavy-lipped. The expression was sad, but dignified.

"The Plymouth is a nice car, isn't it?" said Rose Rita.

"Yes, I guess I'll have to admit that it is," said Mrs. Zimmermann, scratching her chin thoughtfully. "For a green car, it's not half bad."

"Can we give it a name?" said Rose Rita suddenly.

Mrs. Zimmermann looked startled. "Name? Well, yes, I suppose so. What kind of name would you like to give it?"

"Bessie." Rose Rita had once known a cow named Bessie. She thought Bessie would be a good name for this patient starey-eyed car.

Mrs. Zimmermann emptied the five-gallon can of gasoline into Bessie. When she turned the key in the ignition, the car started immediately. Rose Rita cheered. They were on their way again.

When they got to Mrs. Bigger's store, Mrs. Zimmermann stopped just long enough to stand the empty gas can next to the pumps. As the car chugged along toward the farm, Rose Rita noticed that the forest that ran behind Gert Bigger's store continued on down the road.

"That's a pretty big woods, isn't it, Mrs. Zimmermann?" she said, pointing off to the right.

"Uh-huh. It's a state forest, and as you say, a pretty big one. It runs all the way out to Oley's farm and then up north for quite a ways. It's a nice place, but I'd hate to get lost in it. You could wander around for days, and nobody'd find you."

They drove on. Rose Rita began to wonder what Oley's farm would be like. She had been daydreaming about the farm on the ride up, and she already had in her mind a very clear idea of what the place ought to look like. Would it really be that way? She'd see in a minute. Up a few hills, down a few hills, around a few curves, then down a long narrow rutty road overhung with trees. And then, suddenly, there was old Oley's farm.

It didn't look like Rose Rita's daydream, but it was nice. The barn was long and painted white. Like Bessie, it had a face: two windows for the eyes, and a tall door for a mouth. Near the barn stood the house. It was plain and square, with a square little cupola on top. The place looked totally deserted. Tall grass grew in the front yard, and the mailbox was beginning to get rusty. One of the windows in the barn was broken. As Rose Rita watched, a bird flew in through the hole. Off in the distance the forest could be seen.

Mrs. Zimmermann drove right up to the barn door and stopped. She got out and then, with Rose Rita's help, she rolled back the heavy door. A faint smell of manure and hay drifted out into the chilly air. There were two long rows of cattle stalls (both of them empty) and overhead Rose Rita could see hay. Some old license plates were nailed to the beams that supported the hay mow. When Rose Rita looked at them, she saw that they had dates like 1917 and 1923. Up among the rafters the shadowy form of a bird flew back and forth. Rose Rita and Mrs. Zimmermann stood there silent under the high roof. It was almost like being in church.

It was Mrs. Zimmermann who finally broke the spell. "Well, come on," she said. "Let's get the picnic hamper and the cooler and unlock the house. I'm starved."

"So am I," said Rose Rita. But when Mrs. Zimmermann opened the front door of the farmhouse and turned on the lights, she got a shock. The house looked as if a whirlwind had passed through it. Things were scattered everywhere. Drawers had been pulled out of dressers and cabinets, and the contents had been dumped out on the floor. Pictures had been taken down off the walls, and every book had been pulled out of a small narrow bookcase that stood in the front hall.

"Good Lord!" said Mrs. Zimmermann. "What on earth do you suppose . . ." She turned and looked at Rose Rita. They were both thinking the same thing.

Rose Rita followed Mrs. Zimmermann to the room that Oley Gunderson had used as his study. Against one wall of the room stood a massive roll-top desk. The top was rolled up, and all the cubbyholes at the back of the desk were empty. There were finger marks in the dust on the surface of the desk, and the pencils had been dumped out of the pencil jar. All the drawers of the desk had been pulled out and lay scattered around on the floor. The wood around the place where the bottom left-hand drawer had been was scarred and splintered— apparently it was the only drawer that had been locked. Near the desk lay a drawer with a badly chipped front, and in the drawer lay a Benrus watchcase covered with black leather.

Mrs. Zimmermann knelt down and picked up the watchcase. When she opened it, she found inside a small square ring box covered with blue velvet. Without a word, Mrs. Zimmermann opened the little blue box and looked inside. Rose Rita leaned over her shoulder to see.

The bottom half of the box held a black plush cushion with a slit in it. The slit appeared to have been widened, as if something too big for it had been crammed into the box. But whatever the something was, it was gone.

CHAPTER THREE

Mrs. Zimmermann knelt there on the littered floor, staring at the empty ring box. Suddenly she laughed.

"Ha! That's a good joke on whoever our burglar was!"

Rose Rita was dumbfounded. "I don't get what you mean, Mrs. Zimmermann."

Mrs. Zimmermann got up and brushed dust off her dress. She pitched the ring box contemptuously into the empty drawer. "It's all very simple, my dear. Don't you see? Oley must have blabbed around that ridiculous story about a magic ring. Someone must have believed him and figured that there was something valuable hidden here in the house. After all, you wouldn't have to think a ring was magic to want to steal it. Rings are usually made of precious metals, like gold and silver, and some of them are set with diamonds and rubies and suchlike. After Oley died, someone must have broken in. I can imagine what he found! Probably an old faucet washer. Well, it could be worse. They might have set fire to the place. The house is a mess though, and you and I will have to do some tidying up. Now then . . ."

Mrs. Zimmermann went on chattering as she straightened up Oley's desk, putting the pencils in the pencil jar and erasers into cubbyholes. Who the heck does she think she's fooling? Rose Rita thought. She could tell from the way Mrs. Zimmermann was acting that this was all just a cover-up. She had seen Mrs. Zimmermann's hand tremble as she opened the little box. She had seen how pale she looked. So there really is a magic ring, Rose Rita said to herself. I wonder what it looks like. She also wondered who had taken it, and what they were going to do with it. She had walked into a real live mystery, and she was so excited about the whole business that she really wasn't scared at all.

It was nearly midnight when Rose Rita and Mrs. Zimmermann finally sat down to have their picnic supper. They laid out their meal on the kitchen table and fetched some dusty plates and tarnished silverware from the cupboard over the sink. After that it was time to turn in. There were two adjoining bedrooms at the top of the stairs, each with its own small dark oak bedstead. Rose

Rita and Mrs. Zimmermann rummaged in a linen closet at the end of the hall, and they found some sheets. The sheets smelled musty, but they were clean. They made up their beds and said good night to each other.

Rose Rita had trouble getting to sleep. It was a hot still night, and not a breath of air was stirring. The curtains on the open window hung still. She tossed and turned, but it was no use. Finally Rose Rita sat up and turned on the lamp on the bedside table. She dug into her valise for the copy of *Treasure Island* that she had brought along to read, and she propped her pillow up against the head of the bed. Now then, where had she left off? Oh, sure. Here it was. Long John Silver had captured Jim, and they and the pirates were searching for Captain Flint's treasure. It was an exciting part of the book. Jim had a rope around his middle and was being dragged along over the sand by Silver, who swung along jauntily on his crutch . . .

Tap, tap, tap. As she read, Rose Rita began to be aware of a sound. At first she thought it was in her head. She often imagined sights and sounds and smells when she was reading, and now maybe she was imagining the sound of Long John Silver's crutch. *Tap, tap, tap, tap* . . . it didn't sound like that, though . . . more like a coin being rapped on a desk top . . . and anyway, a crutch wouldn't make any noise on the sand. It would just . . .

Rose Rita's head drooped forward. The book fell

from her hand. When she realized what was happening, she shook herself violently. What a dope I am for falling asleep, she thought at first, but then she remembered that she was trying to read herself to sleep. I guess it worked, Rose Rita thought, with a grin. *Tap, tap, tap.* There was that sound again. Where was it coming from? It certainly wasn't in her head. It was coming from Mrs. Zimmermann's room. And then Rose Rita knew what the sound was. It was Mrs. Zimmermann rapping her ring on something.

Mrs. Zimmermann had a ring with a large stone set in it. The stone was purple, because Mrs. Zimmermann loved purple things. It wasn't a magic ring, it was just a trinket that Mrs. Zimmermann liked. She had gotten it at Coney Island. She wore it all the time, and whenever she was thinking about something, thinking really hard, she rapped the ring on whatever happened to be around, chairs or tabletops or bookshelves. The door was closed between the two rooms, but Rose Rita could see, in her mind's eye, a clear picture of Mrs. Zimmermann lying awake, staring at the ceiling and rapping her ring against the sideboard of the bed. What was she thinking about? The ring, probably—the other ring, the stolen one. Rose Rita really wanted to go in and talk the whole matter over with Mrs. Zimmermann, but she knew that was not the thing to do. Mrs. Zimmermann would shut up like a clam if Rose Rita tried to talk to her about Oley Gunderson's magic ring.

Rose Rita shrugged her shoulders and sighed. There was nothing she could do, and anyway she was nearly asleep. She fluffed her pillow up, turned out the light, and stretched out. In no time at all, she was snoring peacefully.

The next morning, bright and early, Rose Rita and Mrs. Zimmermann got their things together, locked up the house, and drove off toward Petoskey. They had breakfast in a café there and went to see Oley's lawyer. Then they drove on toward the Straits. That afternoon they crossed the Straits of Mackinac in a car ferry called *The City of Escanaba*. The sky was gray, and it was raining. The ferryboat heaved ponderously in the choppy waters of the Straits. Off on their right Mrs. Zimmermann and Rose Rita could just barely see Mackinac Island, a gray blurry smudge. The sun was coming out when *The City of Escanaba* reached St. Ignace. They were in the Upper Peninsula of Michigan now, and they were going to have two whole weeks to explore it.

The trip started off well. They saw Tahquamenon Falls and drove along the shore of Lake Superior. They saw the Pictured Rocks and snapped photos of each other. They drove through rolling oceans of pine trees and stopped to look at streams that ran red because there was so much iron in the water. They visited towns with strange names, like Ishpeming and Germfask and Ontonagon. At night they stayed in tourist homes. Mrs. Zimmermann hated the new motels that were springing up all over the place, but she loved tourist homes. Old white houses on shady back streets, houses with screened porches and green shutters and sagging trellises with morning glories or hollyhocks on them. Mrs. Zimmermann and Rose Rita would settle down for the night in a tourist home and sit out on the porch playing chess or cards and drinking iced tea while the crickets chirped outside. Sometimes there was a radio in Rose Rita's room. If there was, she would listen to the Detroit Tigers' night games until she got sleepy. And then in the morning breakfast in a diner or café, and then back on the road again.

On the fourth day of their trip something odd happened.

It was evening. Rose Rita and Mrs. Zimmermann were walking down the main street of a little town. The sun was setting at the end of the street, and a hot orange light lay on everything. They had had their dinner and were just stretching their legs after a long day of driving. Rose Rita was ready to go back to the tourist home, but Mrs. Zimmermann had stopped to look in the window of a junk shop. She loved to browse in junk shops. She could spend hours sifting through all sorts of trash, and sometimes she had to be dragged away by force.

As she stood by the window, Mrs. Zimmermann

noticed that the store was open. It was nine o'clock at night, but the owners of junk shops often keep odd hours. She went in, and Rose Rita followed her. There were old chairs with ratty velvet upholstery, and bookcases with a few books in them, and old dining room tables with an incredible assortment of junk laid out on them. Mrs. Zimmermann stopped in front of one of these tables. She picked up a salt and pepper set shaped like a fielder's mitt and a ball. The ball was the salt.

"How'd you like this for your room, Rose Rita?" she said, chuckling.

Rose Rita said she would love it. She liked anything that had to do with baseball. "Gee, could I have it for my desk, Mrs. Zimmermann? I think it's kind of cute."

"Okay," said Mrs. Zimmermann, still laughing. She paid the owner twenty-five cents for the set and went on browsing. Next to a dusty bowl full of mother-of-pearl buttons was a stack of old photographs. They were all printed on heavy cardboard, and, from the clothes that people in the pictures were wearing, they must have been pretty old. Humming, Mrs. Zimmermann shuffled through the stack. Suddenly she gasped.

Rose Rita, who had been standing nearby, turned and looked at Mrs. Zimmermann. Her face was pale, and the hand that held the photograph was trembling.

"What's wrong, Mrs. Zimmermann?"

"Come . . . come over here, Rose Rita, and look at this."

Rose Rita went to Mrs. Zimmermann's side and looked at the picture she was holding. It showed a woman in an old-fashioned floor-length dress. She was standing by the bank of a river, and she had a canoe paddle in her hand. Behind her a canoe was pulled up on the bank. A man in a striped jacket was sitting cross-legged next to the canoe. He had a handlebar mustache, and he was playing a banjo. The man looked handsome, but it was impossible to tell what the lady looked like. Someone had scraped the face of the lady away with a knife or a razor blade.

Rose Rita still didn't see what was bothering Mrs. Zimmermann. But as she stood there wondering, Mrs. Zimmermann turned the picture over. On the back these words were written: *Florence and Mordecai. Summer, 1905.*

"My gosh!" exclaimed Rose Rita. "Is that a picture of you?"

Mrs. Zimmermann nodded. "It is. Or rather, was, until someone . . . did that to it." She swallowed hard.

"How the heck did a picture of you get way up here, Mrs. Zimmermann? Did you used to live up here?"

"No, I did not. I've never seen this town in my life before. It's all . . . well, it's all very strange."

Mrs. Zimmermann's voice shook as she spoke. Rose Rita could see very clearly that she was upset. Mrs. Zimmermann was the sort of person who usually gave you the feeling that she had everything under control. She was a calm sensible sort. So when she got upset, you knew there was a reason.

Mrs. Zimmermann bought the photograph from the old man in the shop and took it back to the tourist home with her. On the way she explained to Rose Rita that witches and warlocks hacked up pictures that way when they wanted to get rid of somebody. Sometimes they let water drip on the photo until the face was worn away; or they might scrape the face off with a knife. Either way, it was like making a wax doll of somebody and sticking pins in it. It was a way of murdering somebody by magic.

Rose Rita's eyes opened wide. "You mean somebody's trying to do something to you?"

Mrs. Zimmermann laughed nervously. "No, no. I don't mean that at all. This whole thing, finding the picture of myself up here and finding it . . . damaged, well it's all just a funny coincidence. But when you fool around with magic the way I do, well, you get some strange ideas into your head. I mean, sometimes you have to be careful."

Rose Rita blinked. "I don't get what you mean."

"I mean I'm going to burn the picture," Mrs. Zimmermann snapped. "Now, I'd rather not talk about it any more, if you don't mind."

Late that night Rose Rita lay in bed, trying to sleep. Mrs. Zimmermann was downstairs in the guest parlor, reading—at least that's what she was supposed to be doing. On a hunch Rose Rita got up and went to the window. She remembered that she had seen an incinerator in the back yard. Sure enough, there was Mrs. Zimmermann, standing over the wire incinerator. Something was burning with a soft red glow at the bottom of the cage. Mrs. Zimmermann stood hunched over, watching it. The reddish light flickered over her face. Rose Rita felt afraid. She went back to bed and tried to sleep, but the picture of Mrs. Zimmermann standing there over her fire, like a witch in an old story, kept coming back to her. What was going on?

CHAPTER FOUR

The next morning at breakfast Rose Rita tried to get Mrs. Zimmermann to talk about the photograph, but Mrs. Zimmermann rather curtly told her to mind her own business. This of course made Rose Rita more curious than ever, but her curiosity wasn't getting her anywhere. The mystery would have to remain a mystery, at least for the time being.

A few days later Rose Rita and Mrs. Zimmermann were in a town over near the Wisconsin border. Once again they had settled down in a tourist home for the night. Rose Rita went out to mail a couple of postcards, and on her way back she happened to pass a high school gym where a Saturday night dance was in full swing. It was a hot night, and the doors of the gym were open. Rose Rita stopped a minute in the doorway and looked in at the kids who were moving slowly around on the dance floor. A big ball covered with little mirrors revolved overhead, scattering coins of light on the dancers below. The room was softly lit with blue and red light. Rose Rita stood and stared. It was really a beautiful scene, and she found herself thinking that maybe going to dances would be fun. But then she glanced along the wall and noticed some girls standing by the sidelines. No one was dancing with them. They were just standing there, watching. It didn't look like they were having a very good time.

A wave of sadness swept over Rose Rita. She felt tears stinging her eyes. Would she be in that wallflower line next year? It would be better to climb on a train and ride out to California and be a hobo. Did they let girls be hoboes? Come to think of it, she had never heard of a girl hobo. What a lousy deal girls had, anyway! They couldn't even be bums if they wanted to.

Rose Rita felt angry all the rest of the way home. She stomped up the steps of the tourist home and slammed the screen door behind her. There on the porch sat Mrs. Zimmermann. She was playing solitaire. As soon as she saw Rose Rita, she knew something was wrong.

"What's the matter, my dear? Is the world getting to be too much for you?"

"Yeah," said Rose Rita sullenly. "Can I sit down and talk to you?"

"Sure thing," said Mrs. Zimmermann as she gathered the cards into a heap. "This was getting to be a pretty dull game, anyway. What's on your mind?"

Rose Rita sat down on the glider, swung back and forth a bit, and then said abruptly, "If I keep on being friends with Lewis, am I gonna have to go out on dates with him and go to dances and all that stuff?"

Mrs. Zimmermann looked a bit startled. She stared off into space for a minute and thought. "No," she said slowly, as she rocked to and fro on the glider. "No, I don't see that you have to do that. Not if you don't want to. You like Lewis as a friend and not because he shows up at your door with a bunch of flowers in his hand. I think it should probably stay that way."

"Gee, you're great, Mrs. Zimmermann!" said Rose Rita, grinning. "I wish you'd talk to my mom. She thinks Lewis and I are gonna get married next year or something."

Mrs. Zimmermann made a sour face. "If I talked to your mother, it would make things worse, not better," she said, as she started laying out another hand of solitaire. "Your mother wouldn't like it much if I started butting in on her family's business. Besides, she may be right. In ninety-eight percent of the cases, a friendship like yours and Lewis's either breaks up or turns into a dating friendship. You may discover next year that you and Lewis are going different ways."

"But I don't want that to happen," said Rose Rita

stubbornly. "I like Lewis. I like him a whole lot. I just want things to stay the way they are."

"Ah, but that's just the trouble!" said Mrs. Zimmermann. "Things *don't* stay the same. They keep changing. You're changing, and so is Lewis. Who knows what you and he will think six months from now, or a year from now?"

Rose Rita thought a bit. "Yeah," she said at last, "but what if Lewis and me just decided to be friends the rest of our lives? What if I never got married, not ever? Would people think I was an old maid?"

Mrs. Zimmermann picked up the deck of cards and began to shuffle it slowly. "Well," she said thoughtfully, "some people would say that I've been leading the life of an old maid for some years now. Since my husband died, I mean. Most women would've remarried, quick as anything, but when Honus died, I decided to try single life—widowhood, call it what you like—for a while. And you know, it's not so bad. Of course, it helps to have friends like Jonathan. But the point I'm trying to make is, there isn't any one way of doing things that's the best. I was happy as a wife, and I'm happy as a widow. So try different things. See what you like best. There are people, of course, who can only do one thing, who can only function in one kind of situation. But I think they're pretty sad people, and I'd hate to think you were one of them."

Mrs. Zimmermann stopped talking and stared off into

space. Rose Rita sat there, with her mouth open, waiting for her to say more. But she said nothing. And when she turned and saw the anxious way Rose Rita was looking at her, she laughed.

"I'm through with my sermon," she chuckled. "And if you think I'm going to give you a handy-dandy recipe for how to live your life, you're crazy. Come on. How about a quick game or two of cribbage before bedtime? Okay?"

"You're on," said Rose Rita, grinning.

Mrs. Zimmermann got out her cribbage board, and she and Rose Rita played cribbage till it was time to go to bed. Then they went upstairs. As always there were two adjoining rooms, one for Rose Rita and one for Mrs. Zimmermann. Rose Rita washed her face and brushed her teeth. She threw herself down on the bed, and she was asleep almost before her head hit the pillow.

Later that night, around two in the morning, Rose Rita woke up. She woke up with the feeling that something was wrong. Very wrong. But when she sat up and looked around, the room looked absolutely peaceful. The reflection of the moon floated in the mirror over the bureau, and the streetlamp outside cast a puzzly black-and-white map on the closet door. Rose Rita's clothes lay neatly piled on the chair next to her bed. What was wrong then?

Well, something was. Rose Rita could feel it. She felt tense and prickly, and she could hear her heart beating

fast. Slowly she peeled back the sheet and got out of bed. It took her several minutes, but she finally got up the courage to go to the closet and yank the door open. There was a wild jangling of hangers. Rose Rita gave a nervous little yelp and jumped back. There was no one in the closet.

Rose Rita heaved a sigh of relief. Now she was beginning to feel silly. She was behaving like one of those little old ladies who peek under their beds every night before they turn out the lights. But as she was about to get back into bed, Rose Rita heard a noise. It came from the next room, and when she heard it, all her fear came rushing back. Oh come on, Rose Rita whispered to herself. Don't be such a scaredy-cat! But she couldn't just go back to bed. She had to go look.

The door between Mrs. Zimmermann's room and Rose Rita's room was ajar. Rose Rita crept slowly toward it and laid her hand on the knob. She pushed, and the door moved softly inward. Rose Rita froze. There was somebody standing by Mrs. Zimmermann's bed. For a long second, Rose Rita stared wide-eyed and rigid with terror. Suddenly she gave a wild yell and leaped into the room. The door crashed against the wall, and somehow Rose Rita's hand found the light switch. The bulb in the ceiling flashed on, and Mrs. Zimmermann sat up, disheveled and blinking. But there was no one standing by the bed. No one at all.

CHAPTER FIVE

Mrs. Zimmermann rubbed her eyes. Around her lay the rumpled bedclothes, and at the foot of the bed stood Rose Rita, who looked stunned.

"Good heavens, Rose Rita!" exclaimed Mrs. Zimmermann. "Is this some kind of new game? What on earth are you doing in here?"

Rose Rita's head was in a whirl. She began to wonder whether she might be losing her mind. She had been sure, absolutely sure, that she had seen someone moving about near the head of Mrs. Zimmermann's bed. "Gee, I'm sorry, Mrs. Zimmermann," she said. "I'm really awfully sorry, really I am! I thought I saw somebody in here."

Mrs. Zimmermann cocked her head to one side and

curled up the corner of her mouth. "My dear," she said dryly, "you have been reading too many Nancy Drew novels. What you probably saw was my dress on this chair. The window is open, and it must have been fluttering in the breeze. Now go back to bed, for heaven's sake! We both need some more shut-eye if we're to go gallivanting all over the Upper Peninsula tomorrow."

Rose Rita stared at the chair that stood next to Mrs. Zimmermann's bed. A purple dress hung limply from the chair's back. It was a hot still night. Not a breath of air was stirring. Rose Rita did not see how she could possibly have mistaken the dress on the chair for somebody moving around in the room. But then what had she seen? She didn't know. Bewildered and ashamed, Rose Rita backed toward the door. "G-good night, Mrs. Zimmermann," she stammered. "I . . . I'm really sorry I woke you up."

Mrs. Zimmermann smiled kindly at Rose Rita. She shrugged her shoulders. "It's okay, Rosie. No harm done. I've had some pretty wild nightmares in my time. Why, I remember one where . . . but never mind. I'll tell you some other time. Good night now, and sleep tight."

"I will." Rose Rita turned out the light and went back to her own room. She lay down on the bed, but she didn't go to sleep. She put her hands up behind her head and stared at the ceiling. She was worried. First there had been that photograph, and now this. Something was happening. Something was going on, but she couldn't for the life of her figure out what. And then there was that business of the break-in at Oley's farm, and the empty ring box. Did that have anything to do with what had happened tonight? Rose Rita thought and thought, but she didn't come up with any answers. It was like having two or three pieces of a large and complicated jigsaw puzzle. The pieces didn't make any sense all by themselves. Rose Rita figured that Mrs. Zimmermann must be as worried as she was. In fact, she was probably more worried, since the strange things were happening to her. Of course, Mrs. Zimmermann would never let on that she was upset. She was always ready to help other people, but she kept her own problems to herself. That was her way. Rose Rita bit her lip. She felt helpless. And she had a strong feeling that something really bad was going to happen soon. What would it be? That was another thing she didn't know.

Next day, toward evening, Mrs. Zimmermann and Rose Rita were bumping along a rutty back road about twenty miles from the town of Ironwood. They had been driving for about an hour on this road, and now they were about ready to turn back. Mrs. Zimmerman had wanted Rose Rita to see an abandoned copper mine that had once belonged to a friend of her family. At every turn in the road she had expected to see it. But the mine never appeared, and now Mrs. Zimmermann was getting discouraged.

The road was just plain awful. Bessie jounced and

jiggled so much that Rose Rita felt as if she were inside a Mixmaster. Every now and then the car would go banging down into a pothole, or a rock would fly up and hit the underside of the car with a sound like a muffled bell. And it was another hot day. Sweat was pouring down Rose Rita's face, and her glasses kept getting fogged up. Sandflies buzzed in and out of the open windows of the car. They kept trying to bite Rose Rita on the arms, and she slapped at them till her arms stung.

Finally Mrs. Zimmermann put on the brakes. She turned off the motor and said, "Darn it all anyway! I did want to show you that mine, but it must have been on another road. We'd better turn back if we're going to . . . oh, Oh Lord!"

Mrs. Zimmermann clutched the steering wheel and doubled over. Her knuckles showed white under her skin, and her face was twisted with pain. She clutched at her stomach. "My . . . God!" she gasped. "I've . . . never . . ." She winced and closed her eyes. When she was able to speak again, her voice was barely a whisper. "Rose Rita?"

Rose Rita was terrified. She sat on the edge of her seat and watched Mrs. Zimmermann. "Yeah, Mrs. Zimmermann? What . . . what's the matter? What happened? Are you okay?"

Mrs. Zimmermann managed a feeble smile. "No, I'm not okay," she croaked. "I think I have appendicitis."

"Oh my gosh!" When Rose Rita was in the fourth

grade, a kid in her class had died of appendicitis. His folks had just thought that he had a bad stomachache until it was too late. Then his appendix broke open, and he died. Rose Rita felt panicky. "Oh my gosh!" she said, again. "Mrs. Zimmermann, what are we gonna do?"

"We . . . we have to get me to a hospital quick," Mrs. Zimmermann said. "The only catch is . . . oh. Oh no, please no!" Mrs. Zimmermann bent over again, writhing with pain. Tears streamed down her face, and she bit her lip so hard that it bled. "The only catch . . ." Mrs. Zimmermann gasped, when she could talk again, ". . . the only catch is that I don't think I can drive."

Rose Rita sat perfectly still and stared at the dashboard. When she spoke, her lips barely moved. "I . . . I think I can, Mrs. Zimmermann."

Mrs. Zimmermann closed her eyes as another wave of pain swept over her. "What . . . what did you say?"

"I said, I think maybe I could drive. I learned to, once."

Rose Rita was not exactly telling the truth. About a year ago she had gone out to visit a cousin of hers who lived on a farm near New Zebedee. He was fourteen, and he knew how to drive a tractor. Rose Rita had pestered him until he finally agreed to teach her how to shift gears and let the clutch in and out. He taught her on an old wrecked car that sat in a field near the farmhouse, and after he had showed her the ropes, Rose Rita practiced by herself until she had all the gear positions straight in her head. But she had never actually been behind the wheel of a moving car, or even a car that just had the motor running.

Mrs. Zimmermann said nothing. But she motioned for Rose Rita to get out of the car. When she did, Mrs. Zimmermann dragged herself over into the seat where Rose Rita had been and slumped there against the door with her hand on her stomach. Rose Rita walked around and got in on the driver's side. She shut the door and sat there staring at the wheel. She was afraid, but a voice inside of her said, Come on. You've got to do it. She can't, she's too sick. Come on, Rose Rita.

Rose Rita slid forward until she was sitting on the edge of the seat. She would have moved the seat up, but she was afraid it would hurt Mrs. Zimmermann. Fortunately Rose Rita was tall for thirteen, and she had grown a lot in the past year. Her legs were long enough for her to reach the pedals. Rose Rita tapped the accelerator cautiously. Could she really do it? Well, she'd have to try.

Mrs. Zimmermann had left the car in first gear. But you couldn't start a car when it was in first gear, it had to be in neutral. At least that was what Rose Rita had heard from her cousin. Cautiously she pushed the clutch pedal in and eased the lever up into neutral. She turned the ignition key, and the car started instantly. Now, with her right foot on the gas and her left on the clutch, she pulled the gear shift lever forward and down. Slowly she began to let the clutch out the way she had been taught to do it. The car shuddered, and the engine killed.

"You've . . . got to . . . give it the . . . gas," Mrs. Zimmermann gasped. "When you . . . let the clutch out. . . give 'er the gun."

"Okay." Rose Rita was tense and trembling all over. She put the car back in neutral and started it up again. This time when she let the clutch out, she really floored the gas pedal. The car took a little jump forward and stopped again. Apparently too much gas was just as bad as too little. Rose Rita turned to ask Mrs. Zimmermann what to do now, but Mrs. Zimmermann had passed out. She was on her own.

Rose Rita gritted her teeth. She was getting mad now. "Okay, we're gonna try again," she said in a quiet firm voice. She tried and again the motor killed. It killed the next time, too. But the time after that she managed, somehow, to let the clutch out and press the gas pedal at just the right rate. The car moved slowly forward.

"*Yay, Bessie!*" Rose Rita yelled. She yelled so loud that Mrs. Zimmermann opened her eyes. She blinked and smiled feebly when she saw that the car was moving. "Atta girl, Rosie!" she whispered. Then she slumped over sideways and lost consciousness again.

Somehow Rose Rita managed to get the car turned around and headed back toward Ironwood. It was dark now, and she had to turn the lights on. The road was totally deserted. No farms, no homes. Rose Rita remembered one ruined shanty that they had passed, but it didn't seem likely that there was anyone living in it. No. Unless a car just happened to come along, there would be no help until they reached the two-lane blacktop that led back to Ironwood. Rose Rita swallowed hard. If she could just keep the car going, maybe everything would turn out all right. She glanced quickly at Mrs. Zimmermann. She lay slumped against the door. Her eyes were closed, and every now and then she would moan faintly. Rose Rita clenched her teeth and drove.

On Bessie crawled, up and down hills, over bumps and rocks, and in and out of potholes. Her pale headlight beams reached out before her into the night. Moths and other night insects fluttered past. Rose Rita felt as if she were driving along in a dark tunnel. Dark pine trees lined the road on either side. They seemed to press forward until Rose Rita felt hemmed in. An owl was hooting in the woods somewhere. Rose Rita felt lonely and frightened. She wanted to drive fast to get out of this awful place, but she was scared to. The road was so bumpy that she was afraid to speed up. It was frightening to have a big heavy car under her control. Every time the car hit a pothole, the wheel lurched violently to the right or the left. Somehow, though, each time Rose Rita managed to get straightened out. Oh, please, she prayed, get us there, Bessie. Please get us there before Mrs. Zimmermann dies. Please . . .

Rose Rita was not sure when, but after she had driven

along the dark winding road for some time, she began to have the feeling that there was someone else in the car with them. Rose Rita didn't know why she had this feeling, but it was there, and it was very persistent. She kept glancing up toward the rear-view mirror, but she never saw anything. After a while the feeling got to be so maddening that Rose Rita stopped the car. She put it in neutral, pulled on the emergency brake, and, as the car throbbed, she turned on the overhead light and glanced nervously into the back seat. It was empty. Rose Rita flipped off the light, put the car back in gear, and drove on. But the feeling kept coming back, and she found that it took a strong effort of the will to keep her eyes from wandering toward the rear-view mirror. The car was rounding a sharp curve when Rose Rita happened to glance up, and she saw, reflected in the mirror, the shadow of a head and two glittering eyes.

Rose Rita screamed and jerked the wheel violently to the left. With a screech of tires, Bessie swerved off the road and plunged down a steep bank. The car bounced and jounced wildly, and Mrs. Zimmermann's inert body slammed first against the door and then slid over across the seat to bump against Rose Rita. Rose Rita, panic-stricken, clutched the wheel and kept trying to find the brake with her foot, but she kept missing it. Down into darkness they went. Now there was a loud swishing, crackling sound outside the car, and a funny smell. In the fevered whirling of her brain Rose Rita found her-

self wondering, What is that smell? The crackling and swishing got louder, and finally Rose Rita got her foot on the brake. Her body lurched forward, and her head hit the windshield. She blacked out.

CHAPTER SIX

Rose Rita dreamed that she was clinging to a piece of wood that was floating in the sea. Someone was saying to her, "Are you all right? Are you all right?" That's a dumb thing to be saying, thought Rose Rita. Then she opened her eyes and found that she was sitting at the wheel of Bessie. A policeman was standing next to the car. He reached in the open window and touched her gently.

"Are you okay, miss?"

Rose Rita shook her head groggily. She touched her forehead and felt a swelling lump. "Yeah, I guess so, except for this bump on my head. I . . . my gosh! What happened?" She looked around, and saw that the car was embedded in a large clump of juniper bushes. Juniper! That was the smell! Daylight was streaming in through the dusty windows of the car. And there, on the seat beside her, lay Mrs. Zimmermann. She was asleep. Or was she . . . ?

Rose Rita reached over and started shaking Mrs. Zimmermann's shoulder. "Wake up, Mrs. Zimmermann!" she sobbed. "Oh, please! Wake up, wake—"

Rose Rita felt the policeman's firm hand on her arm. "Better not do that, miss. You don't know if she's got any broken bones or not. We've got an ambulance coming, and they'll check her over before they try to move her. What happened? Fall asleep at the wheel?"

Rose Rita shook her head. "I was trying to drive Mrs. Zimmermann back to the hospital after she got sick all of a sudden. I got scared and I drove off the road. I'm only thirteen, and I don't have any license. Are you gonna put me in jail?"

The policeman smiled sadly at Rose Rita. "No, ma'am. Not this time, anyway. But I think it wasn't very bright of you to try to drive, even if it was an emergency and all. You might of gotten yourself killed. As a matter of fact, if these bushes hadn't of been here, you *would've* been killed. And so would your friend there. But she's breathin' okay. I looked at her a minute ago. All we have to do is sit tight till the ambulance gets here."

A little while later a big white ambulance with a red cross on the side pulled up on the road next to the police car. Two men in white uniforms got out and edged their way down the embankment. They had a stretcher with them. By the time they got to the car, Mrs. Zimmermann was just coming to. The two men checked her over, and when they were sure she could be moved, they gently eased her out of the car and made her lie down on the stretcher. Up the hill they went with her, slowly. When they had her safe in the ambulance, they went back for Rose Rita. It turned out that she was a little bruised and shaken up, but otherwise okay. She climbed the hill on her own and got in the back of the ambulance with Mrs. Zimmermann. Off they went, siren screaming, toward Ironwood.

Mrs. Zimmermann spent the next three days in the hospital at Ironwood. The mysterious pains never returned, and the doctors informed her that they had been in the wrong part of the body for appendicitis. Mrs. Zimmermann was puzzled and frightened. Somehow it was worse not to know what had caused the pains, and the thought that they might return at any time was enough to make her very nervous. It was like living with a time bomb that might or might not go off.

So Mrs. Zimmermann, much as she disliked the idea, stayed in bed while the doctors at the hospital ran a series of tests. Nurses stuck needles into her and drew blood. They gave her vile-tasting potions to drink and made marks on charts. She was x-rayed and put in front of, and inside of, all sorts of strange science-fiction machines. Doctors stopped by every now and then to talk with Mrs. Zimmermann, but they never told her anything that she wanted to know.

Meanwhile, Rose Rita became a lodger at the hospital. Mrs. Zimmermann explained the situation to the doctors, and she showed them her insurance policy (which she always carried around with her in her purse, just in case), and it clearly stated that she was entitled to a private room. The private room had two beds, and Rose Rita slept in one of them. She played cards and chess with Mrs. Zimmermann and listened to night games with her on the radio. It so happened that the White Sox were playing at Detroit, and Mrs. Zimmermann was a White Sox fan because she had once lived in Chicago. So Rose Rita and she had fun rooting for opposite sides, and they even argued a bit, though not very seriously.

Some of the time, when sitting around in the hospital room got to be dull, Rose Rita went out and wandered around the town of Ironwood. She went to the public library and a Saturday afternoon movie. Some of the time she just explored. She got lost once or twice, but people were very nice to her, and she always managed to find her way back to the hospital.

On the afternoon of Mrs. Zimmermann's third day in the hospital, Rose Rita happened to be passing a vacant lot where some boys were playing move-up. They were getting tired of move-up, but they didn't have enough for teams. When they saw Rose Rita, they asked her if she wanted to play.

"I sure do!" Rose Rita yelled. "But whatever side gets me, they have to let me pitch."

The boys looked at each other for a minute, but after a hurried consultation, they decided that Rose Rita could pitch if she wanted to. Rose Rita loved to play baseball, and she really loved to pitch. She was the only girl in her school who could throw a curve with a softball. She had hesitation pitches, and blooper pitches, and she even had a knuckle ball, though it didn't work very well, because it's hard to hold a softball with your knuckles. Her underhand fast ball was famous—so famous, in fact, that she usually had to be persuaded just to lob it up there to weak hitters so they wouldn't strike out all the time.

So Rose Rita wound up playing softball with a bunch of boys she had never seen before. She got a lot of hits, and she grabbed off some hard line drives with her bare hands. She pitched, and she pitched pretty well until she happened to strike out a big husky kid with a crew cut. He thought he was a pretty good ball player, and he didn't like getting struck out by a girl. So he started getting on Rose Rita. He did all sorts of things: he kept calling her Four Eyes, and whenever her team took the field, he went out of his way to run past her just so he could give her a good hard shove and say "Oops, parm me, lady!" in a nasty sneering tone of voice. Finally, near the end of the game, Rose Rita hit a long drive that looked like it would be good for three bases. But as she dived into third, headfirst, there was the lug with the crew cut, and he had the ball in his hand. He could have tagged her on the shoulder or the arm or the back, but he shoved the ball right square into her mouth. It really hurt. The game stopped while Rose Rita pulled herself together. She checked her front teeth to make sure they weren't loose and cautiously rubbed her swollen upper lip. She felt like crying, but she fought down the urge. After a few minutes, Rose Rita went on playing.

In the ninth inning, when the crew-cut lug was pitching for the other side, Rose Rita hit a bases-loaded home run and won the game for her team. When she crossed home plate, all the boys on her side gathered around her and yelled "Yay, Rose Rita!" three times. It really made her feel great. But then she noticed that the guy who had been calling her names was standing there on the pitcher's mound and glaring straight at her.

"Hey, Four Eyes!" he yelled. "You think you're really somethin', doncha?"

"Yeah, I do," Rose Rita yelled back. "What's it to you?"

"Nothin' much. Hey, Four Eyes. How much do you know about baseball? Huh?"

"A heck of a lot more than you do," Rose Rita snapped.

"Oh yeah? Prove it."

"Whattaya mean, prove it?"

"I mean, let's have a contest to see who knows more about baseball, huh? How about it? You chicken? Chick-chick-chick, chick-chick-chick!" The boy flapped his arms like wings and did a rather poor imitation of a chicken.

Rose Rita grinned. This was too big a chance to miss. It so happened that Rose Rita was a real baseball nut. She knew all sorts of facts about baseball, like Ty Cobb's lifetime average and the number of unassisted triple plays that there were on record. She even knew about Smead Jolley's great record, four errors on a single played ball. So she figured that she would give this wiseacre kid a beating at the baseball fact game and get even with him for the fat lip he had given her.

Everybody gathered around to watch the contest. One of the other boys, a watery-eyed blond kid who talked through his nose, was chosen to think up questions. At first it was a pretty tough battle. The lug turned out to be pretty good at baseball facts. He knew the strikeout kings, and who the last thirty-game winner had been, and a lot of other stuff. But Rose Rita knew the stuff that the lug knew, so it turned into a tense nasty grudge fight that went on for some time, with neither one able to gain an inch on the other. In the end Rose Rita won, because she knew that Bill Wambsganss of the Cleveland Indians had pulled the only unassisted triple play ever to be pulled during a World Series game. The lug had a chance at the question first, but he didn't know the answer. Then it was Rose Rita's turn, and she knew it right away. Several of the boys yelled "Yay, Rose Rita!" and one even ran up to shake her hand.

The lug just got red in the face. He glowered at Rose Rita. If he had been mad before, he was furious now. "You think you're pretty damn smart, doncha?" he snarled.

"Yeah," said Rose Rita happily.

The lug put his hands on his hips and looked her straight in the eye. "Well, you wanna know what I think? I think you're a pretty funny kind of girl, that's what I think. A pret-ty damn funny kind of a girl."

It was a stupid remark, but it stung Rose Rita. It stung like a slap in the face. To the amazement of everyone, she burst into tears and ran off the field. *You're a pretty funny kind of a girl.* Rose Rita had heard people say this about her before, and what was worse, she had thought it about herself. She had often wondered if there was really something wrong with her. She acted like a boy, but she was a girl. Her best friend was a boy, but most of the girls she knew had girls for best friends. She didn't want to go on dates, even though some of the girls she knew had already started to date and had told her how much fun it was. A funny kind of a girl—Rose Rita couldn't get the phrase out of her head.

Rose Rita stopped on a street corner. She took out her hanky and dabbed at her eyes, and then she blew her nose. From the way people were looking at her as they passed by, she figured she must really be a mess. Her face felt hot and flushed. Now she was mad at herself, mad because she had let that dumb guy get her goat that way. As she walked along, she told herself that she had a lot to feel good about: she had practically won the game single-handed for her team, and she had won the baseball facts contest, in spite of what happened later. She started to whistle, and after two or three blocks of whistling, she felt better. She decided to go back to the hospital, just to see what was going on.

When Rose Rita walked into Mrs. Zimmermann's room, she walked in on an argument. Mrs. Zimmermann was sitting up in bed, and she was having it out with a worried-looking young doctor.

"But Mrs. Zimmermann," the doctor pleaded, "you're taking an *awful* chance with your health! If we had another day or so, we might be able to figure out—"

Mrs. Zimmermann cut him off contemptuously. "Oh, sure! If I were to stay here for a year, and if I were to lie very, very still, I'd get bedsores, and you'd know what to do about them, wouldn't you? Well, I'm sorry. I've wasted too much time as it is. Tomorrow morning, Rose Rita and I are hitting the road. You're just a bunch of quacks here, like most doctors."

"Now, Mrs. Zimmermann, I resent that. We've tried very hard to be nice to you, and we've also tried to find out about your pains. Just because all our tests have come out negative is no reason to . . ."

The doctor went on, and then Mrs. Zimmermann started in again. Rose Rita sat down in an armchair and hid behind a copy of *Ladies Home Journal*. She hoped that they wouldn't notice her. The argument went on for some time, and the doctor pleaded, and Mrs. Zimmermann was about as nasty and insulting as Rose Rita had ever seen her be. In the end Mrs. Zimmermann won. The doctor agreed that she could leave tomorrow morning if she wanted to.

Mrs. Zimmermann watched as the doctor gathered up his clip board, his stethoscope, and his medicine bag. When the door had closed behind him, she raised her hand and motioned for Rose Rita to come over to the bed.

"Rose Rita," she said. "We're in trouble."

"Huh?"

"I said, we're in trouble. I sent my dress out to be dry-cleaned. You know the one—the dress I was wearing when those pains hit me. The same dress that was draped over the chair by my bed, the night you thought you saw someone in my room. Remember?"

Rose Rita nodded.

"Well, the dress came back today, and look what came with it." Mrs. Zimmermann opened a drawer in the table that stood by the side of her bed. She took out a small brown Manila envelope and shook the contents out into Rose Rita's hand. Rose Rita looked down and saw a small golden safety pin and a little strip of paper.

There was writing in red ink on the paper, but she couldn't read it.

"What's this?"

"It's a charm. The cleaners found it pinned to the inside of my dress. Don't worry—it can't hurt you. Those things can only be rigged up to work on one person at a time."

"You . . . you mean . . ."

"Yes, my dear. That little strip of paper caused the pains I had the other night." Mrs. Zimmermann laughed grimly. "I wonder what Doc Smartypants there would say if I told him about *that!* I'm sorry, by the way, that I was so mean to him, but I had to be, so he'd let us go."

Rose Rita was frightened. She put the strip of paper and the pin on the table and backed away. "Mrs. Zimmermann," she said, "what are we gonna do?"

"I don't know, Rose Rita, I just don't know. Somebody is after me—that much is clear. But who it is or why they're doing it, I just don't know. I have some ideas, but I'd rather not share them with you right now, if you don't mind. I've told you all this because I don't want you to feel guilty about driving off the road that night. You had every right to be scared. The thing you saw in the back seat, it . . . well, it wasn't in your head. It was real."

Rose Rita shuddered. "What . . . what was it?"

"I'd rather not say anything more right now," said Mrs. Zimmermann. "But I will tell you this. We've got to get home, and we've got to get home fast. I've got to get hold of my copy of the *Malleus Maleficarum.*"

"The what?"

"The *Malleus Maleficarum.* It's a book that was written a long time ago by a monk. The title means The Hammer of Witches. That is, the book is a weapon to use in fighting off the attacks of those who fool around with black magic. It has a number of spells in it that will be of use to me. I should have memorized them long ago, but I didn't. So I need the book, and it's not the sort of thing you'd find at your friendly public library. We're going home the first thing in the morning, and I thought I ought to tell you why. I don't want to frighten you, but I figured you'd be frightened more if I went on being mysterious."

Rose Rita pointed at the strip of paper. "What're you gonna do with that?"

"Watch." Mrs. Zimmermann took a book of matches out of the drawer in the bedside table. She put the paper in an ashtray and lit it. While it burned, she made the sign of the cross over the ashtray and muttered a strange-sounding prayer. Rose Rita watched, fascinated. She felt scared, but she felt excited too, as if she had been suddenly swept out of her normal life and into an adventure.

That evening Rose Rita helped Mrs. Zimmermann pack. She got her own things together too. Mrs. Zimmermann informed her that Bessie was in the parking lot behind the hospital. A tow truck had pulled her up out of the juniper bushes, and the mechanics at a local garage had gone over her. She was all gassed and oiled and greased up, and ready to roll. A nurse came in with some papers for Mrs. Zimmermann to sign. The doctor paid one more visit, and said (rather coldly) that he hoped Mrs. Zimmermann had a good trip back. Everything was ready. Rose Rita and Mrs. Zimmermann crawled into bed and tried to get some sleep.

At first Rose Rita was too excited to sleep, but around midnight, she drifted off. Then, before she knew what was happening, she was awake again. Mrs. Zimmermann was standing by her bed. She was shaking her and shining a flashlight in her eyes.

"Come on, Rose Rita! Wake up!" Mrs. Zimmermann hissed. "We've got to go! Now!"

Rose Rita shook her head and rubbed her eyes. She fumbled for her glasses and put them on. "Wha . . . wha's the matter?"

"Wake up, I said! We're going to the farm. Now. We've got to!"

Rose Rita felt totally confused. "The *farm?* But I thought you said . . ."

"Never mind what I said. Get dressed and follow me. We're going back to the farm to . . . to get something I left there. Come on, you! Get a move on!" She shook Rose Rita again roughly, and flashed the light in her eyes. Rose Rita had never seen Mrs. Zimmermann act

this way before. Her voice was harsh, and her actions were rough and almost brutal. It was almost as if someone else had gotten inside of Mrs. Zimmermann's skin. And this business about going to the farm, instead of going straight home the way they had planned. What did it mean?

As Rose Rita dressed, Mrs. Zimmermann stood there, stiff and still, behind the white glaring halo of the flashlight. Rose Rita couldn't see her face, and she wasn't sure that she wanted to. When she was dressed, Rose Rita grabbed her valise and followed Mrs. Zimmermann. They tiptoed to the door, opened it a crack, and peered down the long dark hall. At the far end a nurse sat dozing behind a desk. An electric clock buzzed on the wall over her head. The whole hospital seemed to be asleep.

"Good!" said Mrs. Zimmermann, and she led the way down the hall to a set of stairs. The stairs led to the parking lot behind the hospital. There in the moonlight sat Bessie, the green Plymouth, staring patiently ahead as always. Rose Rita put the luggage in the trunk. Mrs. Zimmermann started the car, and they drove off.

It was a long hot dusty ride, all day, across the length of the Upper Peninsula. For Rose Rita, it was like a nightmare. Usually Mrs. Zimmermann was fun to travel with. She laughed and joked and sang songs, and talked a blue streak. When pestered, she even did little magic tricks, like snatching matches out of thin air, or throwing her voice into the weeds at the side of the road. But now, as they rode along, she was silent. She seemed to be brooding about something, but she wouldn't tell Rose Rita what it was. And Mrs. Zimmermann was nervous— very nervous. She glanced wildly from side to side, and sometimes got so jittery that she almost drove off the road. Rose Rita sat there rigid in her corner by the door, her sweaty hands at her sides. She didn't know what to do, or what to say.

The sun was going down over the Straits of Mackinac as Bessie chugged into the parking lot of the ferryboat landing at St. Ignace. A boat had just left, and Mrs. Zimmermann and Rose Rita had to wait a solid hour for the next one. They waited in silence, neither of them saying a word the whole time. Rose Rita went out and bought some sandwiches. It was her own idea—Mrs. Zimmermann had not stopped for lunch. Finally, though, the boat came in. It was called the *Grand Traverse Bay*. The sky was dark, and the moon was rising over the Straits, when Mrs. Zimmermann drove Bessie up the rattling gangplank and down into the black echoing hold of the ship.

When the car was parked, and the chocks had been placed under the wheels, Rose Rita started to get out, but then she discovered that Mrs. Zimmermann was just sitting there motionless behind the wheel.

"Mrs. Zimmermann?" Rose Rita called nervously. "Aren't you coming up?"

Mrs. Zimmermann gave a little start and shook her

head. She stared at Rose Rita as if she had never seen her before. "Come up? Oh . . . yes. Yes, of course. Be right with you." She got out of the car and, like a sleepwalker, clumped up the steps to the deck.

It ought to have been a very beautiful crossing. The moon shone down, silvering the decks and the ripply water of the Straits. Rose Rita tried to get Mrs. Zimmermann to walk around with her on the deck, but she wouldn't do it. She sat rigid on a bench and stared at her shoes. Rose Rita was frightened. This wasn't an adventure anymore. She wished, wished with all her heart, that they had never come on this trip. She wished they were back home in New Zebedee. Maybe if they were home, Uncle Jonathan, or Doc Humphries, or somebody, could figure out what was wrong with Mrs. Zimmermann and make her act like her old self again. Rose Rita didn't feel as if she could do anything for Mrs. Zimmermann. She felt utterly helpless. All she could do was tag along. Tag along, and wait.

An hour or so later Mrs. Zimmermann and Rose Rita were driving down the gravel road that led to Oley Gunderson's farm. They passed Gert Bigger's store and saw that it was closed. A tiny night light burned on the porch.

Rose Rita couldn't stand it any longer. "Mrs. Zimmermann," she burst out. "Why are we going to the farm? What's this all about?"

At first Mrs. Zimmermann was silent. Then she said,

in a slow dull voice, "I don't know why. There's something I have to do there, but I can't remember what it is."

They drove on. Gravel crackled and popped under the car's tires, and sometimes long leafy branches whipped across the doors or the roof. Now it began to rain. Big drops started to splat on the windshield, and Rose Rita heard the dull rolling of thunder. Flashes of lightning leaped out in front of the car. Now they were at the farm. As they drove into the yard, a bright flash lit up the front of the barn, showing the two staring window-eyes, and the yawning mouth of the door. It was like a monster mouth, opening to swallow them up.

Because it was raining outside, Rose Rita and Mrs. Zimmermann went into the house by way of the long covered walkway that ran from the house to the barn. But when they unlocked the door and tried to turn the lights on, nothing happened. Mrs. Zimmermann had forgotten to pay Oley's overdue electric bill, and the current had been shut off since their first visit. After digging around in a cupboard, Mrs. Zimmermann found a kerosene lamp. She lit it and put it on the kitchen table. Rose Rita opened up the picnic hamper, and they sat down to eat the sandwiches Rose Rita had bought. They ate in silence. In the smoky yellow light Mrs. Zimmermann's face looked haggard and worn. She also looked tense, very tense, as if she was waiting for something to happen. Rose Rita looked nervously over her shoulder. Beyond the circle of friendly lamplight the house lay in shadow. The staircase was a well of darkness. Rose Rita realized, with a sudden sick feeling, that she would have to go up those stairs to bed. She didn't want to go to bed. She didn't want to stay in Oley's house for another minute. She wanted to bundle Mrs. Zimmermann into the car and make her drive them back to New Zebedee, even if they had to drive all night. But Rose Rita didn't say anything. She made no move. Whatever the spell was that lay over Mrs. Zimmermann, it lay over Rose Rita too. She felt utterly totally powerless.

Outside it was pouring. There was a tin roof on the front porch, and the sound of the rain hitting it was a steady drumming roar. Finally, with an effort, Rose Rita pushed back her chair. She stood up.

"I think we . . . we oughta go to bed, Mrs. Zimmermann," she said hoarsely. Her voice was faint and seemed to be coming from deep down inside her.

"You go on, Rose Rita. I want to sit here and . . . and think a bit." Mrs. Zimmermann's voice was wooden and mechanical, and unbelievably weary. It almost sounded as if she were talking in her sleep.

Rose Rita backed away fearfully. She picked up her valise, took out her flashlight, and turned toward the stairs. As Rose Rita went up the steps, flashlight in hand, her shadow and the shadow of the railing danced weirdly on the wall next to her. Halfway up Rose Rita stopped and looked down. There sat Mrs. Zimmermann in the circle of yellow lamplight. Her hands were folded on the table, and she was staring straight ahead of her. Rose Rita had the feeling that, if she called to her, she wouldn't get any answer. She swallowed hard and went on up the stairs.

The bedroom with the black walnut bed was just as Rose Rita had left it. She began to peel back the spread, but halfway she stopped. She stopped because she had heard a noise from downstairs. A single small noise. Tap. The sound of Mrs. Zimmermann's ring. Now the sound was repeated, three times over. Tap . . . tap . . . tap. The sound was slow and mechanical, like the ticking of a big clock. Rose Rita stood there, flashlight in hand. She listened to the sound and wondered what it meant.

Suddenly a door slammed.

Rose Rita gave a little yelp and spun around. She dashed out of the room and down the stairs. On the landing she froze. There was the table, with the lamp burning on it. There was Mrs. Zimmermann's purse, and her cigar case. The front door was open. It banged gently in the wind. Mrs. Zimmermann was gone.

CHAPTER SEVEN

Rose Rita stood on the front porch of the farmhouse. Her flashlight dangled from one hand and made a pool of light at her feet. Slashes of rain cut across her shoes, and lightning lit up the wildly thrashing trees across the road. Thunder rolled. Rose Rita felt stunned. She felt as if she were walking in her sleep. Mrs. Zimmermann was gone. But where had she gone, and why? What had happened to her?

Cupping her hands to her mouth, Rose Rita called, "Mrs. Zimmermann! Mrs. Zimmermann!" but she got no answer. Slowly she picked her way down the steps, waving the flashlight in front of her. At the bottom of the steps she stopped and looked around. If Mrs. Zimmermann had run out the front door and down the front steps, it ought to have been easy to tell which way she went after that. The front yard was full of long grass, and Rose Rita and Mrs. Zimmermann had not touched it on the night before, because they had come into the house by using the covered walkway. Now, as Rose Rita moved her flashlight around, she saw a little patch of grass trampled down at the bottom of the steps. But no path led away, in any direction. The grass grew all around, tall and shiny and untouched. It was as if Mrs. Zimmermann had evaporated.

Panic seized Rose Rita. Yelling "Mrs. Zimmermann!" at the top of her voice, she thrashed through the wet grass till she came to the road. She looked to the right. She looked to the left. Nothing but darkness and rain. Rose Rita fell to her knees in a puddle and started to cry. She covered her face with her hands and sobbed bitterly. The cold rain poured down on her and soaked her to the skin.

At long last she got up. Staggering like a drunken person, half blinded by tears, she made her way back to the farmhouse. But on the front porch she stopped. She did not want to go back into that house. Not now, in the dark. With a shudder Rose Rita turned away. But where could she go?

Bessie. She thought of Bessie sitting in the barn. The barn was a dark spooky place, like the house, but Bessie was a friendly creature. Rose Rita really thought of the car as a living breathing person now. She could go and sleep in the car. It wouldn't hurt her—it would protect her. Rose Rita took a deep shuddering breath, clenched her fists, and started walking toward the barn. Rain slashed across her as she went.

The sound of the big white door rolling back echoed in the high raftered ceiling of the barn. There was Bessie, waiting. Rose Rita patted her hood and climbed into the back seat. She locked all the doors. Then she lay down and tried to sleep, but it was no use. She was too tense. All night Rose Rita lay there, wet and frightened and tired and alone. Once or twice she sat up suddenly when she thought she saw a face at the window of the car. But it was all her imagination—there was no one there.

As she lay staring at the ceiling of the car and listening to the storm, Rose Rita thought. Mrs. Zimmermann had disappeared. Disappeared as if by magic. In fact, there was no "as if" about it. Mrs. Zimmermann's disappearance had been caused by magic.

Rose Rita went over the sequence of events in her mind: first there had been Oley's weird letter about a magic ring, and then the empty ring box. Then came the mutilated photograph, and the shadow Rose Rita had seen moving around in Mrs. Zimmermann's bedroom that night. Then those horrible pains, and the slip of paper, and the strange way Mrs. Zimmermann had behaved on the trip back to the farm. But what was the key to the whole thing? Was the ring the key? Did somebody have it, and had they used it to do things to Mrs. Zimmermann? That seemed like a reasonable explanation to Rose Rita. But a heck of a lot of good reasonable explanations were going to do her. Mrs. Zimmermann was gone, and Rose Rita didn't know where to go to find her. Maybe she was dead. And as for the magic ring, if there was such a thing . . . well, Rose Rita didn't know who had it, and she hadn't the faintest idea of what she would do if she *did* know. So there she was.

Rose Rita thought like this, in endless circles, all the night long, while thunder rolled overhead and lightning lit up, now and then, the high dusty windows of the barn. Finally morning came. Rose Rita stumbled out into the sunlight to find everything looking sparkling and fresh and green. Blackbirds were gorging themselves on the mulberries in a crooked old tree in the front yard. Rose Rita felt a sudden burst of cheerfulness, but then she remembered Mrs. Zimmermann, and she burst into tears again. No, she said firmly to herself, blinking back her tears and brushing hair out of her eyes. You're not going to cry. That's not any good, you dumb dope. You've got to *do* something!

But what was she going to do? Here she was, alone, three hundred miles from home. For one wild instant she thought that she might drive Bessie all the way back to New Zebedee. After all she had driven the car for a little way, on that back road near Ironwood. But Rose Rita was scared. Scared of getting picked up by a policeman, scared of having an accident. Besides, driving home wouldn't help find Mrs. Zimmermann. She had to think of something else.

Rose Rita sat down on the front steps, put her head in her hands, and thought some more. Should she call up her folks and have them come and get her? She could hear what her father would say: "You see, Louise, that's what happens when you let Rose Rita run around with screwballs! The old bat flew off on a broom and left Rose Rita there to rot. Well, maybe the next time you think of letting our daughter go tooting off with a screwball you'll . . ." Rose Rita winced. She didn't want to face her father, not without Mrs. Zimmermann. Rose Rita thought some more.

Rose Rita racked her brains. She crossed and recrossed her legs and bit her lip and fumed. She was a real fighter, and she wasn't going to abandon Mrs. Zimmermann. Not if there was something she could do.

Rose Rita jumped up and snapped her fingers. Of course! What a dope she had been! Why hadn't she thought of this before? There was that book, that Mallet of Something, or whatever it was called. The book that Mrs. Zimmermann had been going home to get when she changed her mind—or somebody changed it for her. But Rose Rita didn't have the book. She didn't even know where she could get a copy. She sat down again.

Rose Rita thought about magic books for a while.

Rows of them, standing on shelves, books with spotted vellum covers and curly writing on their spines. *That was it!* Jonathan had magic books. He had a whole big collection of them. And what was more, he had the key to Mrs. Zimmermann's house. If he couldn't find that old Mallet Whatchmacallit, he could just go next door and dig it out of Mrs. Zimmermann's bookcase. Also, Jonathan knew about magic, because he was a wizard himself. Rose Rita could tell him what had happened, and he wouldn't think she had gone off her rocker. Good old Jonathan! He would know what to do.

Rose Rita got up and went into the house. There was an old-fashioned crank phone on the wall in the kitchen. Rose Rita took the receiver off the hook and gave the crank a few twirls. The bell inside the box rang, but the line was dead. Mrs. Zimmermann had forgotten to pay Oley's electric bill, and she had also forgotten to pay the phone bill.

Rose Rita hung up the receiver and stood there, feeling depressed. But then she remembered Gert Bigger's store. There was probably a phone there she could use. Rose Rita didn't want to have anything more to do with the crabby old woman who had cheated Mrs. Zimmermann that night they ran out of gas, but she didn't see any way around it. Gert Bigger's store was only a couple of miles down the road. Rose Rita sighed. She would just have to walk there and get help.

Rose Rita started out. It was already a hot day, even

though it was early in the morning, and the road was dusty. Steam rose from Rose Rita's clothing, which was still wet from the night before. She wondered if she would catch cold, but she didn't wonder very hard. Catching cold was the least of her worries right now.

It was farther to Gert Bigger's store than Rose Rita had thought it would be. Flies were buzzing around when Rose Rita rounded a bend and saw the store shimmering there in the heat. It looked pretty much the way it had when she saw it the first time. But as she got closer to the store, Rose Rita noticed one difference. There was a chicken in the chicken yard. Just one. A bedraggled-looking white hen. As soon as the chicken saw Rose Rita, it began to cluck excitedly and run back and forth. Rose Rita smiled. She had had a white hen for a pet once. It was called Henny Penny. This poor lonely chicken reminded her of it. Rose Rita wondered why the chicken was so excited, and then she noticed a stump in one corner of the yard. There was an ax leaning against it. It looked as if old Henry Penny was going into the pot before long. Poor thing, Rose Rita thought. It probably thinks I'm coming to chop off its head.

Rose Rita turned away and started up the steps to the store, but as she did so, she almost stepped on a small black dog. It was the same dog that had barked at her and Mrs. Zimmermann that other time. It must have been hunched down on the steps in the shadow, because Rose Rita could have sworn that the steps were empty when she glanced at them a second before. Imitating Mrs. Zimmermann, Rose Rita pulled back her foot as if she were going to kick the dog, and, as before, the dog ran off into the shubbery and disappeared.

Rose Rita walked up the steps. She opened the door and looked in. There was Gert Bigger, kneeling in the middle of the floor. She was unpacking cereal boxes and stacking them on a shelf.

"Well," she said, glaring at Rose Rita. "What do *you* want?"

"I . . . I have to make a phone call," said Rose Rita. Her voice was trembling as she spoke, and she was afraid she was going to burst into tears.

"You do, huh? Well, you better have some money handy. There's a pay phone over there on that wall." Gert Bigger pointed towards a scarred black phone at the end of the counter.

Rose Rita dug into her pocket and came up with a dime and a couple of pennies. She would have to make it a collect call.

As she walked down the aisle toward the phone, Rose Rita was aware that Gert Bigger was watching her. She wondered why. Oh, well, thought Rose Rita, she's just nosy. She dumped her coins on a little shelf in front of the phone and read the yellow sheet of instructions. For a collect call, she would have to dial O for the operator. Rose Rita put her finger in the O-hole and was just starting to dial, when she saw, out of the corner of her eye, that Gert Bigger was still staring at her. She had let her work go and was just kneeling there in the middle of the aisle, watching.

Rose Rita stopped in mid-dial. She took her finger out and let the little wheel click back into place. She had just had a very strange thought: What if Gert Bigger had done something to Mrs. Zimmermann? She had a grudge against Mrs. Zimmermann—Rose Rita knew that. And she lived close to Oley's farm. She might've broken in to steal that magic ring after he died. It was a crazy notion, and Rose Rita knew it was crazy. But she still wondered if she might be onto something.

She turned, and her gaze met Gert Bigger's.

"What's the matter now?" Gert Bigger growled. "You forget the number you were supposed to call?"

"Uh . . . yeah, I mean, no ma'am, er . . . never mind," Rose Rita stammered. She turned to the phone. This is dumb, she told herself. That crabby old lady isn't any witch. She doesn't have any magic ring. Just stop playing detective and make your crummy phone call and get it over with!

Rose Rita dialed O and got the operator. She told her that she wanted to make a collect call to New Zebedee, Michigan, to Mr. Jonathan Barnavelt. His number was 865. Rose Rita waited. She heard vague scratchy and fumbly sounds, and then she heard the buzzing sound that meant that the operator was ringing Jonathan's phone. *Bzz. Bzz. Bzz.*

"I beg your pardon," said the operator, "but the party does not answer. Would you—"

"Please try a little longer," said Rose Rita. "Please, ma'am. It's an emergency."

"Very well." The ringing went on.

As she waited, Rose Rita's eyes began to wander. On the wall next to the phone she saw an old photograph in a black frame. It was a picture of a man in an old-fashioned suit. He had a handlebar mustache . . .

Rose Rita froze. She knew who the man was. He was the man in the picture Mrs. Zimmermann had found in the junk shop. And now she remembered his name: Mordecai. Mordecai Hunks. He was the man Mrs. Zimmermann and Gert Bigger had fought over, a long time ago. He was the reason for Gert Bigger's hatred of Mrs. Zimmermann, her long-standing grudge. It was all beginning to fall together now . . .

Rose Rita turned her head slightly and glanced toward Mrs. Bigger. But at that moment a horn beeped outside. Somebody wanted gas. Gert Bigger heaved a discontented sigh, got up heavily, and stumped to the door.

"I'm sorry, Miss," said the operator, "but I cannot continue to ring the party's number. Would you care to call back at another time?"

Rose Rita was startled. She had forgotten about the phone call she was making. "Uh . . . okay," she mumbled. "I'll . . . uh, try later. Thanks."

Rose Rita hung up the phone and glanced quickly

around. Now was her chance. Behind the counter was a doorway covered by a heavy brown curtain. Rose Rita looked again toward the front of the store. Through the wide plate glass window, she could see Gert Bigger pumping gas. And now she saw another car pulling up on the other side of the pumps. The old bat would probably be out there for a while. Rose Rita took a deep breath, pulled the curtain aside, and ducked in through the doorway.

She found herself in an ugly little room with pale green walls. There was a coal company calendar on the wall and a bare bulb dangling from the ceiling. A small iron safe stood in one corner, and against the long wall was a high narrow shelflike desk. On the desk was a faded green blotter with columns of figures added up all over it. Arranged neatly next to the blotter were a bottle of Parker's Quink, a pile of wooden pens with rusty metal nibs, a brown gum eraser, and several well-sharpened pencils. On the other side of the blotter was an account book with a green cardboard cover. The date 1950 was printed on the cover. There was nothing here that looked in any way magical.

Rose Rita's heart sank. She felt foolish for doing what she was doing. But wait a minute. What were these? Rose Rita knelt down. Under the desk was a shelf, and on it were piled more green-covered account books. They looked just like the one on the desk, except that they were very dusty and had different dates. 1949,

1948, and so on back. Rose Rita opened one up. Just dull columns of figures. Debits, credits, receipts, and stuff like that. She was about to put the book back when she noticed something sticking out of the middle. She pulled it out and found that it was a folded piece of paper. When she opened the paper, she found a drawing done in pencil. It looked like this:

Rose Rita held the paper with trembling hands. She could feel her heart beating faster. She was no wizard, but she knew what this was, because she had once been allowed a closely supervised look into one of Uncle Jonathan's magic books. The drawing was a magic pentacle, one of those charms that witches and wizards use when they want good things or bad things to happen. Rose Rita stared at the drawing. She stared at it so long and so hard that she did not hear the soft tinkle of the bell as the front door of the store was quietly opened and carefully closed. A board creaked behind her. Suddenly the curtain was whipped aside, and Rose Rita turned to find Gert Bigger standing over her.

"Well now! What do you think you're doin'? Eh?"

CHAPTER EIGHT

Rose Rita knelt there on the floor and looked up at Gert Bigger's angry face. In her trembling hands she still held the piece of paper with the strange drawing on it.

Gert Bigger stepped into the little room and pulled the curtain shut behind her. "I asked you, Miss, what you think you're doing? There's a law against trespassing, you know, and there are reform schools for girls who steal things. Would you like your parents to know what you've been up to? Eh? Would you?"

Rose Rita opened her mouth to speak, but all that came out was "I . . . I . . . please . . . I didn't mean . . ."

Gert Bigger took a step forward. She reached down and snatched the paper from Rose Rita's numb fingers.

Silence fell while Gert Bigger stood there looking from the paper to Rose Rita and back to the paper again. She seemed to be trying to make up her mind.

At that moment the bell on the front door of the store jangled, and a voice yelled "Yoo-hoo, Gertie! Are you home?"

Gert Bigger turned and swore under her breath. Rose Rita jumped up and ducked out through the narrow curtained opening. She sprinted down the main aisle of the store, right past the surprised face of a middle-aged woman with a shopping bag in her hand. Slam went the door behind her. Rose Rita clattered down the steps and dashed across the road. She ran blindly, and she could hear herself crying as she ran. She cut across the corner of a cornfield, trampling the wrinkly green plants underfoot. Her feet found a pathway of green grass that ran along the edge of the cornfield and up over the top of a low hill. Rose Rita ran up it, ran as hard as she could, until she collapsed under a droopy elm tree that grew near a flat-topped boulder. She threw herself down on the grass, tore off her glasses, and cried.

Rose Rita lay there crying for a long time. She was tired and hungry and frightened and alone. She hadn't had any food at all since last night, and she had gotten almost no sleep. At first she was afraid that Gert Bigger would come after her. At any moment her hand would be on Rose Rita's shoulder. But Gert Bigger never came. Rose Rita went on crying, but she could feel her body

starting to relax. She didn't care about anything now . . . anything at all. It was a delicious feeling. Slowly her mind started to drift off. It was so nice lying here in the shade . . . so very, very nice . . . but it would be even nicer to be home. Home . . . in . . .

Rose Rita's eyes closed. A soft breeze rustled through the corn, and in the distance a fly was lazily buzzing. Rose Rita shook her head, fighting weakly against the drowsiness that was falling over her. She was trying to think of something. What was it? She never found out, because in a very few minutes she was fast asleep.

"Hey you, wake up! You better wake up! Don't you know it's bad to sleep on the wet ground? You might catch cold. Come on, wake up."

Rose Rita awoke to hear this worried insistent voice speaking to her. She shook her head and looked up. All she saw was a blur. Then she remembered her glasses. After fumbling a bit in the grass near her, she located them and put them on. When she looked up, Rose Rita saw a girl about her own age. She was wearing a short-sleeved plaid shirt and jeans, and muddy army boots. The girl had straight dishwater-blonde hair, and it was combed down on both sides of her head. Her face was longish, and it had a sad worried expression. The dark eyebrows curved up into worry lines. Rose Rita thought that she had seen this face somewhere before. But where?

When she remembered, she almost laughed. The girl looked just like the Jack of Clubs.

"Hi there," said the girl. "Gee, I'm glad you woke up! Didn't anybody ever tell you it was bad to sleep on the ground when it's wet? It rained last night, you know."

"Yeah, I know," said Rose Rita. She got up and put out her hand. "I'm Rose Rita Pottinger. What's your name?"

"Agatha Sipes. They call me Aggie for short. I live up that way, over that hill. This's my father's farm. By the way, are you the one that stomped all over those corn plants back there?"

Rose Rita nodded sadly. "Yeah, that was me. I'm sorry, but I was crying so hard that I didn't look where I was going."

The girl looked worried. "You oughtn't to do that kind of thing. Farmers work hard for their living." She added, in a less severe tone, "Why were you crying?"

Rose Rita opened her mouth, but then she hesitated. She wanted to tell her troubles to someone, but she wanted to be believed. "My friend Mrs. Zimmermann is lost, and I don't know where to find her. We were staying at a farm down the road last night, and she ran out the front door and just disappeared."

The girl rubbed her chin and looked wise. "Oh, I'll bet I know what happened. She probably went walkin' in the woods and got lost. It happens to lots of people up here in the summertime. Let's go up to my place, and we'll call up the sheriff's department, and they'll send out some people to look for her. They'll find her all right."

Rose Rita thought of the circle of trampled grass in front of the farmhouse. The circle with no path leading away. It was no use. She'd just have to tell the truth and risk the consequences. "Do . . . do you believe in magic?" she said suddenly.

The girl looked startled. "Huh?"

"I said, do you believe in magic?"

"You mean ghosts and witches and magic spells and stuff like that?"

"Yeah."

Agatha grinned shyly. "Yeah, I do. I know you're not supposed to, but I can't help it." She added, in a worried voice, "Sometimes I think there's a ghost in the cellar in our house, but Mom says it's just the wind at night. You don't think there's a ghost in our cellar, do you?"

"How would I know?" said Rose Rita, in an irritated voice. "Hey, do you want to hear about what happened to Mrs. Zimmermann or don't you?"

"Sure I want to hear. I really do. Tell me all about it."

Rose Rita and Agatha Sipes sat down on the grass under the elm tree. Rose Rita's stomach growled, and she remembered that she hadn't eaten since last night. She was terribly hungry. But she wanted to tell her story, and Agatha seemed eager to listen. Rose Rita began.

She told the whole story, as far as she knew it, from Oley's mysterious letter and the empty ring box, on through the very strange things that had been happening to her and Mrs. Zimmermann lately. When she got to the part about Mrs. Zimmermann's disappearance, Agatha's eyes grew wide. And when she described her run-in with Mrs. Bigger, Agatha's eyes got even wider, and her mouth dropped open. She glanced nervously in the direction of Gert Bigger's store.

"My gosh!" she said. "It's a wonder she didn't kill you! And you know what? I bet she's the one who made your friend disappear."

Rose Rita looked strangely at Agatha. "Do . . . do you know anything about her? Mrs. Bigger, I mean?"

"I sure do. She's a witch."

Now it was Rose Rita's turn to be flabbergasted. "Huh? How do you know?"

"How do I know? Because last year I worked in the Ellis Corners library, and she came in and took out every last book about magic that we had, that's how I know. Some of 'em were in the Reference Room, and she couldn't take 'em out, so she just sat there for hours and read. I asked Mrs. Bryer the librarian about her, and she said Mrs. Bigger had been doing that for years. Said she had library cards for all the libraries around here, and took out all the magic books she could find. Mrs. Bryer says she reads the covers off of 'em and never takes 'em back till the library starts houndin' her. Isn't that weird?"

"Yeah, it sure is." Rose Rita felt strange. She was wildly elated, because her hunch had been proved right —at least, she felt that it had been proved right. But at the same time she felt helpless and scared. If Mrs. Bigger really was a witch, what could she and Aggie do about it?

Rose Rita got up and paced around. Then she sat down on the flat-topped boulder and lapsed into deep thought. Aggie stood near her, looking uncomfortable. She shifted nervously from one foot to the other, and puckered up her eyebrows into the most worried frown she had produced yet. "Did I say something wrong, Rose Rita?" she asked, after several silent minutes had passed. "If I did, I'm sorry, I really am."

Rose Rita shook herself out of her trance and looked up. "No, Aggie, you didn't say anything wrong. Honest you didn't. But I just don't know what to do. If you're right, and old Mrs. Bigger is a witch, and she has done something to Mrs. Zimmermann, then . . . well, what can we do? Just the two of us, I mean."

"I don't know."

"Neither do I."

More silence. Silence for a good five minutes. Then Aggie spoke up again.

"Hey, I know what let's do. Let's go home to my house and have some lunch. My mom always fixes a lot of food, because we have a really big family, and I'm sure there'd be enough for you. Come on. After lunch maybe we can figure out what to do. You can't think good on an empty stomach. That's what my dad says, anyway."

Rose Rita looked reluctant, but she really didn't have any better ideas. On the way to the farmhouse Aggie talked a blue streak. She talked about things that she was worried about, like rabies and tetanus and electrical shock and mayonnaise that has been left out of the icebox too long. Rose Rita, however, was only half listening. She was still thinking, trying to make up her mind what to do. Should she give up playing Nancy Drew, girl detective, and call her folks and have them come and get her? No. Rose Rita was a stubborn girl, and she still thought she might be able to find Mrs. Zimmermann without the aid of her parents. What Aggie had told her about Mrs. Bigger and the magic books had made her more certain than ever that Mrs. Zimmermann had been carried off by witchcraft of some kind. So Rose Rita went back to her idea of calling Jonathan. She would do that as soon as she got to Aggie's house. With her mind racing along in high gear, Rose Rita tried to figure out what her next move would be. What should she say to Mrs. Sipes about what had happened?

They were within sight of the farmhouse when Rose Rita reached out and grabbed Aggie's arm. "Wait a minute, Aggie."

"Why? What's the matter?"

"We have to think up a story to tell your mother. I

can't tell her what I told you. She'll think I'm crazy. I can't even tell her my real name, because then she'd want to call up my folks, and I don't want her to call them up."

Aggie frowned. "I don't think you ought to lie to my mother. It's not nice to lie, and anyway I think you'll get caught. My mom is pretty smart. She'd see through it in a minute."

When people disagreed with Rose Rita, it usually made her mad. But in this case she was doubly mad, because she was proud of her ability to make up alibis and excuses. Making up excuses is hard, and it is not quite the same thing as telling tall stories. You have to be able to come up with a story that people will believe. And Rose Rita could really do that—most of the time.

Rose Rita threw an irritated glance at Aggie. "Your mom isn't the smartest person in the world, I bet. And anyway, I'm good at making things up. All we have to do is sit down and figure out a story. Then we both memorize it, so there won't be any slip-ups."

Now it was Aggie's turn to be crabby. "Oh yeah? What're we gonna tell her? Here's my new friend, Rose Rita, who just fell out of a flying saucer?"

"No, dope. We don't tell her something like that. We tell her something she'll think is true. And then we call Uncle Jonathan and get him to tell us what kind of spell to say to make Mrs. Bigger tell us what she did with Mrs. Zimmermann. Okay?"

Aggie bit her lip and wrinkled up her forehead. She took a deep breath and let it out. "Oh all right. But if we get caught, I'm gonna say it's all your fault. I'm not gonna get bawled out just because you think it's nice to lie to people."

Rose Rita gritted her teeth. "I don't think it's nice to lie. But we have to, that's all. Now come on. This is what we'll say . . ."

A bell began to ring. A little sharp clangy handbell was calling people in for lunch at the Sipes farmhouse. Aggie started forward, but Rose Rita grabbed her arm and dragged her over behind a forsythia bush. She put her lips to Aggie's ear and started to whisper.

CHAPTER NINE

The Sipes farmhouse was big and white, with a wide screened-in porch. Spirea bushes grew next to the porch, and there were peony bushes in the front yard. A large apple tree grew on one side of the house, and from one of its saggy limbs hung a tractor tire on a rope. There were kids' things scattered all over the yard. Baseball bats, bicycles, tricycles, puzzles, dolls, toy trucks, and plastic machine guns. Things like that. But when Aggie opened the front door, Rose Rita was struck by how neat and clean the house was inside. All the woodwork shone with polish, and there were doilies or embroidered runners on all the tables, chests, and shelves. There was a flowered carpet on the staircase, and a shelf clock ticking in the front hall. A pleasant smell of cooking was in the air.

Aggie took Rose Rita straight out to the kitchen and introduced her to her mother. Mrs. Sipes had the same long face and worry eyebrows that her daughter had, but she seemed friendly enough. She wiped her floury hands on her apron and greeted Rose Rita warmly.

"Hi! Glad to meet you! I wondered what was keeping Aggie. I rang the bell for lunch about five times, and I had just about given up on her. What did you say your name was?"

Rose Rita hesitated, just a second. "Uh, Rosemary. Rosemary Potts."

"What a nice name! Hi, Rosemary! How're you? Are you visiting in the neighborhood? I don't think I've seen you around before."

Rose Rita squirmed uncomfortably. "Uh, no, you haven't on . . . on account of I was just up here on vacation with . . . with Mrs. Zimmermann." Rose Rita paused. "She's a friend of my family, a real good friend," she added quickly.

"Yeah," Aggie added. "Mrs. Whatsername and Rose . . . uh, Rosemary's family are real good friends, they really are. Only Mrs. . . . Mrs. . . . ."

"Zimmermann," said Rose Rita, giving Aggie a dirty look.

"Oh, yeah. Mrs. Zimmermann. Well, old Oley—you

know him, Ma—he left Mrs. Zimmermann his farm, and she and Rosemary came up to look at it, and last night Mrs. Zimmermann wandered off into the woods out behind the farm, and she disappeared."

"Yeah," said Rose Rita. "I think she must've gotten lost. Anyway, I can't find her anywhere, and I'm getting scared."

Rose Rita held her breath. Would Mrs. Sipes believe this tale?

"Oh, Rosemary!" exclaimed Mrs. Sipes, putting her arm around her. "What an awful thing to happen! Look, I tell you what I'll do. I'll get on the phone and call up the sheriff's office and they'll get some of their men out there, right away quick, to search for her. There was someone who got lost in the woods up here only last year, and they found him before he got hurt. So don't worry. Your friend'll be all right."

Inwardly Rose Rita breathed a sigh of relief. She hated to lie about Mrs. Zimmermann's disappearance, and she was (in reality) worried sick about her. But she just didn't know what Mrs. Sipes would say if she were to tell her that Mrs. Zimmermann had disappeared right into thin air.

Later, after the call to the sheriff's department had been made, Rose Rita was sitting at a long dining room table with Aggie and seven other children and Mrs. Sipes. Rose Rita was sitting at the head of the table, in the place where Mr. Sipes usually sat. Mr. Sipes was away overnight in Petoskey, on business.

Rose Rita looked around the table. It was a worried-looking family. They all had those long faces and upturned eyebrows. There were tall kids and short kids, five boys and two girls (counting Aggie) and a baby in a highchair. On the table was a big platter of corned beef, potatoes, onions, and carrots, and there were more vegetables and some dumplings in the two smoking dishes that stood nearby. There was a cutting board with freshly baked bread on it, and there were two big pitchers of milk. Mrs. Sipes said grace, and then everybody dug in.

"Let Rosemary have some first," said Mrs. Sipes. "She's our guest, you know."

It took Rose Rita a second to recognize her new name. In fact she was startled when someone shoved a tureen of mashed carrots at her. "Oh . . . uh, thanks," she mumbled, and she helped herself to some.

Later on, when everyone had been served, Mrs. Sipes said in a loud clear voice, "Children, I think you should know that Rosemary here has had an accident. The friend she was traveling with got lost in the forest, and we're trying to find her. We've sent the sheriff's patrol out to look for her."

"I think anybody who gets lost in the woods over here must really be dumb," said a tall boy with black curly hair.

"Leonard!" said Mrs. Sipes in a shocked voice. "That will be *quite* enough out of you!" She turned to Rose Rita and smiled sympathetically. "I must apologize for my rude son. Tell us, Rosemary, where do you come from?"

"New Zebedee, ma'am. It's a little town way down near the bottom of the state. Probably you never heard of it."

"I think I know where it is," said Mrs. Sipes. "Now then. I really think we'd better notify your parents. They'll want to know what's happened. What is your father's name?"

Rose Rita stared at the tablecloth. She stuck out her lower lip and looked as sad as she could. "My folks are dead. Both of them. I live with my uncle Jonathan. He's my legal guardian, and his name is Jonathan Barnavelt, and he lives at 100 High Street."

Mrs. Sipes looked surprised and saddened. "My lord, you poor girl! What a string of misfortunes! First your parents dead, and now this to happen to you! Tell me, my dear. How did it happen?"

Rose Rita blinked. "How did what happen?"

"How did your parents happen to die? Excuse me for going into something so sad right at this present moment, but I couldn't help wondering what had happened to them."

Rose Rita paused. There was a mischievous gleam in her eye. She was beginning to enjoy her own lying. At first she had been afraid of being found out, but now that Mrs. Sipes had swallowed both the lost-in-the-forest story and the orphan story—not to mention Rose Rita's fake name—Rose Rita began to think that she would swallow anything. And inwardly she was chortling at her own cleverness in having made up the part about Jonathan being her guardian. There was a good one, since it would allow her to call up Jonathan and find out what she wanted to know, without any more fooling around. Rose Rita had intended to just say that her folks had been killed in a car accident, but now she decided to try for something fancy. It wouldn't do any harm.

"My folks got killed in a funny kind of way," she began. "You see, my dad used to be a forest ranger. He used to walk around in the woods a lot and make sure there weren't any forest fires, and that kind of thing. Well, one day he came across this beaver dam, and it was a really weird-looking kind of dam—all messy and screwed up. My dad had never seen a beaver dam that looked like it, not ever, and he wondered how come it looked the way it did. You see, what he didn't know was, the dam had been built by a beaver that had rabies. And then my dad brought my mom out to look at the dam, and the beaver bit 'em both, and they died."

Silence. Dead silence. Then Aggie's sister tittered, and one of the boys laughed.

"Gee," said Leonard in a loud sarcastic voice, "I

would've thought that if a beaver had the rabies, he would just run off into the woods and die. Wouldn't you think so, Ted?"

"Yeah," said the boy who was sitting next to Leonard. "I never heard of anyone gettin' bit by a beaver that had rabies. And anyway, if that's what really happened, how'd you ever find out? If your folks got bit and died, they wouldn't of told you nothin', would they?"

Rose Rita could feel her face getting red. Everyone was looking at her, and she felt as if she were sitting there without any clothes on. She stared hard at her plate and mumbled, "It was a real rare kind of rabies."

More silence. More staring. Finally Mrs. Sipes cleared her throat and said, "Uh, Rosemary, I think you'd better come into the other room with me for a minute, if you don't mind. And Aggie, you'd better come too."

Aggie got up and followed Rose Rita out of the room. With Mrs. Sipes leading the way, the glum little procession wound its way up the stairs and into a bedroom at the front of the house. Rose Rita and Aggie sat down side by side on the bed, and Mrs. Sipes closed the door softly behind her.

"Now then," she said, folding her arms and staring hard at Rose Rita. "I have heard incredible stories in my time, but this one just about takes the cake. I thought there was something odd about that orphan tale, but— Rosemary . . . by the way, is that your real name?"

Rose Rita shook her head. "No, ma'am," she said, in a tearful voice. "It's Rose Rita."

Mrs. Sipes smiled a faint little smile. "Well, at least it's fairly similar. Now listen, Rose Rita," she said, staring straight into her eyes, "if you're in some kind of trouble, I'd like to help you. I don't know what moved you to concoct that ridiculous story about the beaver, but you'll have to lie better than that if you want to grow up to be a con man, or a con girl, or whatever it is you want to be. Now do you suppose you could tell me, honestly and truly, what happened and why you're here?"

Rose Rita glared balefully at Mrs. Sipes. She wondered what Mrs. Sipes would say if she told her about the patch of trampled grass with no path leading away from it. "I told you, Mrs. Sipes," said Rose Rita stubbornly, "I told you that my friend Mrs. Zimmermann is lost, and I don't know where she is. Honest to God."

Mrs. Sipes sighed. "Well, my dear, I suppose *that* part of your story may be true. But I have never heard such an atrocious lie as that beaver story, really I haven't! Bit by a rabid beaver, indeed! And now you tell me that your real name is Rose Rita. All right, let's have some more of the truth. Are your parents dead, or, alive?"

"My folks are alive," said Rose Rita, in a dull hopeless voice. "And their names are George and Louise Pottinger, and they live at 39 Mansion Street in New Zebedee, Michigan. And I'm their daughter. I really am. Honest. Cross my heart and hope to die."

Mrs. Sipes smiled sympathetically at Rose Rita. "There now. Isn't it easier to tell the truth?"

Not much, thought Rose Rita, but she said nothing.

Mrs. Sipes sighed again and shook her head. "I don't understand you, Rose Rita. I honestly don't. If it's true that you were traveling with a friend of your family's named Mrs. Zimmermann—"

"It's true, all right," said Rose Rita, interrupting. "Her handbag is still on the kitchen table in that crummy old farmhouse, and it's probably got her driver's license and a lot of other stuff in it with her name on it. So there." She folded her arms and glared fiercely at Mrs. Sipes.

"Very well," said Mrs. Sipes calmly. "As I was saying, if that part of your story is true, why on earth did you try to hide your parents' identity?"

An answer sprang into Rose Rita's head, an answer that was partly true. "On account of my dad doesn't like Mrs. Zimmermann. He thinks she's a screwball, and if she turns up alive, my dad'll never let me go anywhere with Mrs. Zimmermann ever again."

"Oh, now, I think you're being rather hard on your father," said Mrs. Sipes. "I don't know him, of course, but it's hard to believe that he'd think Mrs. Zimmermann was a screwball just because she got lost in the woods. Lots of people get lost, every day."

Yeah, thought Rose Rita, but if he ever found out

Mrs. Zimmermann was a witch, he'd sure go through the roof. Besides he can't help us. Uncle Jonathan is the only one that can. Rose Rita wriggled impatiently and dug her heel into the rug. She felt like a prisoner. If only Mrs. Sipes would just go away so she could call up Uncle Jonathan and find out what to do about Mrs. Bigger! He could give her a magic formula to use, and then everything would be all right. It was all very frustrating. It was like almost having your hands on something and having someone slap your hands away every time you made a grab. She needed that book, the magic book with the funny name. But she couldn't do a thing until Mrs. Sipes left her alone.

While Rose Rita sat there stewing, Mrs. Sipes rattled on about responsibility and honesty, and how your parents were really your best friends if you gave them half a chance. When Rose Rita tuned back in on her, she was saying ". . . And so I think that what we have to do now is call your folks up and tell them what happened. They'll want to know that you're okay. Then I'll drive over to the Gunderson farm and see if everything is all right. You probably left everything wide open, and there are people who just walk in and take things, you know. After that all we can do is wait." Mrs. Sipes walked over and sat down next to Rose Rita on the bed. She put her arm around her. "I'm sorry to have been so hard on you, Rose Rita," she said softly. "I know you must be very upset because of what happened to your friend. But the police are out there now, combing the woods. I'm sure they'll find her."

Fat chance, thought Rose Rita, but again she said nothing. Now if only Mrs. Sipes would get in her car and go over to the farm and leave her here alone! *Go away, Mrs. Sipes! Go away.*

First, though, Rose Rita had to call her folks up. There was no getting around that. The three of them went downstairs, and Rose Rita called up her parents, long distance. Mrs. Pottinger answered the phone, and Rose Rita once again recited her story about how Mrs. Zimmermann had disappeared from the Gunderson farm in the middle of the night and had probably gotten lost in the woods. Mrs. Pottinger was the sort of person who got flustered easily, and when she heard of Mrs. Zimmermann's disappearance, she really got rattled. But she told Rose Rita not to worry, that she and Mr. Pottinger would be up there to get her as soon as they could, and she insisted on being called the moment there was any news about Mrs. Zimmermann. Then Mrs. Sipes took the phone, and she gave Mrs. Pottinger directions for getting to the Sipes farm. After that Mrs. Pottinger talked to Rose Rita a few minutes more, and then she hung up. And then, after a bit of fussing, Mrs. Sipes got into her car and drove off in the direction of the Gunderson farm.

Rose Rita stood by the front window watching Mrs.

Sipes's car as it disappeared over a hill. Aggie stood by her, watching, with her habitual worried expression.

"What're you gonna do now?" she asked.

"I'm gonna call up Lewis's Uncle Jonathan, right away quick. If he doesn't know what to do about old Mrs. Bigger, then nobody does!" Rose Rita felt excited. She already imagined herself armed with a spell and confronting Mrs. Bigger.

Rose Rita went back to the front hall and picked up the telephone. She glanced nervously around to make sure none of the other Sipes kids was in earshot. None of them was. Aggie stood by Rose Rita, anxiously waiting, as she asked for the long distance operator. "I want New Zebedee, Michigan, number 865, please, operator. The residence of Mr. Jonathan Barnavelt. This is a collect call."

Rose Rita and Aggie waited. They could hear the operator ringing Jonathan's phone. *Bzz. Bzz. Bzz.* Eight times she let it ring, and then she said, in that singsongy voice that Rose Rita knew so well, "I am sorry, but the party does not seem to answer. Would you care to call later?"

"Yeah," said Rose Rita, in a dull hopeless voice. "I'll call later. Thanks." She hung up the phone and sat down on the hassock next to the phone table. "Gosh darn!" she said angrily. "Gosh darn it all anyway! *Now* what are we gonna do?"

"Maybe they'll find Mrs. Zimmermann in the forest," said Aggie hopefully. She was having trouble keeping Rose Rita's lies separate from the true story in her head.

Rose Rita just looked at her. "We'll try again," she muttered. "He's got to be home sometime."

Rose Rita tried three more times in ten minutes, but each time the result was the same. After a little while Mrs. Sipes came back. She was beaming, because she had found Mrs. Zimmermann's handbag on the kitchen table in Oley's house, and in the handbag she had found Mrs. Zimmermann's driver's license, her car keys, and a lot of other identification. So now she was convinced that Rose Rita was telling her the whole truth. Rose Rita was glad she was convinced. Now if only Mrs. Sipes would go off to some far corner of her farm, so she could try Jonathan's number again!

But Mrs. Sipes stayed right at home the rest of the day. Rose Rita swung on the front porch swing, and played stickball with Aggie, and helped her feed the cows and slop the hogs. When she wasn't doing anything else, Rose Rita chewed her nails. *Why wouldn't Mrs. Sipes leave?* There was only one phone in the house, and since it was on a table in the front hall, it was hardly private. Mrs. Sipes was not the sort who would stand over Rose Rita while she called, but she might be in the other room, and what would she do if she heard Rose Rita asking Jonathan for a spell that would free Mrs. Zimmermann from Gert Bigger's enchantments? No, she would have to be alone to make a call like that, and Rose Rita knew it. She waited for her chance, but her chance never came.

That evening, as Rose Rita and Aggie helped Mrs. Sipes get dinner ready, the phone rang. It was Mrs. Pottinger. It seemed that their car had broken down on the road. Something had gone wrong with it—the differential, she thought it was. Whatever it was, they wouldn't be in until tomorrow morning. Was there any news about Mrs. Zimmermann? No, there wasn't. Mrs. Pottinger said they were sorry about the delay, but there was no help for it. They'd be there when they got the car running again.

Rose Rita felt like a prisoner who has gotten a stay of execution. Now she would have more time to try to get Uncle Jonathan! "Oh come on, Uncle Jonathan!" she prayed under her breath. "Next time, be home! Please be home! Please!"

Rose Rita spent the evening playing parcheesi and Michigan rummy with Aggie and some of the other Sipes kids. Before she knew it, it was time for bed. She took a bath, which she badly needed, and put on a clean pair of pajamas from her valise, which Mrs. Sipes had brought back from the farmhouse. When Rose Rita was all cleaned up, Mrs. Sipes told her that she was sleeping in the extra bed in Aggie's room. Aggie's room was all flouncy and frilly and pink, a regular girl's room. There was a big teddy bear in the rocking chair in the corner, and there was a vanity table with a round mirror and some perfume bottles on it. Even though she was a farm girl and wore jeans a good deal of the time, Aggie seemed happy to be a girl. She said she looked forward to going to Junior High, and dates and dances and proms and stuff like that. She said that it was a relief sometimes to get out of her jeans and the boots that smelled of manure and go to a square dance at the Four-H Building. Rose Rita wondered if she would think that way herself in the fall. Meanwhile, she had other things on her mind.

That night Rose Rita lay wide awake, listening to the sounds of the house. Her heart was beating fast, and she felt very nervous. The Sipes family went to bed at ten, because they had to be up at six in the morning to do chores. No exceptions were allowed. And considering the fact that there were eight children in the family, the house quieted down pretty fast. By ten-thirty you could have heard a pin drop in the hall.

"Are you awake, Rose Rita?" Aggie hissed.

"Of course I'm awake, you dope. I'm gonna go down in a few minutes and try Uncle Jonathan's number again."

"Do you want me to go with you?"

"No. It'd make too much noise if both of us go. Just sit tight, and wait."

"Okay."

Minutes passed. When Rose Rita was finally sure that the house was asleep, she got out of bed and tiptoed downstairs to the telephone. There was a hall closet near the phone, and fortunately the cord was long. Rose Rita took the phone into the closet, shut the door, and squatted there under the coats. Whispering as loudly as she dared, she asked for Jonathan's number again. Again the operator tried. Ten times, fifteen, twenty times. It was no use. He was away—probably gone for the night.

Rose Rita hung up the phone and put it back on the table. She tiptoed back up the stairs to Aggie's room.

"How'd it go?"

"No soap," Rose Rita whispered. "Maybe he's gone to visit his sister in Osee Five Hills. He does that every now and then, and I don't know her number. I don't even know what her name is. Oh gosh, what are we gonna do?"

"I dunno."

Rose Rita gripped her head with her hands and tried to think. If she could have shaken some thoughts out of her head, she would have done it. There had to be some way, there had to be . . .

"Aggie?"

"Shhh. Not so loud. My ma'll hear us."

Rose Rita tried whispering more softly. "Okay. I'm sorry. Hey, Aggie, listen. Does Mrs. Bigger live in her store? I mean, in back of it, or upstairs?"

"Nope. She lives about two miles down the road in a little house that sets way back from the road. How come you want to know that?"

"Aggie," said Rose Rita in a loud excited whisper, "how'd you like to help me break into Mrs. Bigger's store? Tonight!"

CHAPTER TEN

As soon as Aggie saw what Rose Rita's plan was, she
tried to back out. She thought up a thousand reasons for
not going to Mrs. Bigger's place, that night or any other
night. They might get caught and put in reform school.
Aggie's mom would catch them, and bawl them out, and
tell Rose Rita's folks. Mrs. Bigger might be there, hiding
in a closet and waiting for them. The store would be all
locked up, and they wouldn't be able to get in. They
might get bitten by Mrs. Bigger's dog. And so on and so
forth. But Rose Rita was not impressed by Aggie's arguments. She had only known Aggie for a short while, but
she knew by now that Aggie was a worrywart. Worry-
warts always imagine that terrible things are going to

happen. They imagine dangers where dangers don't exist. Lewis was a worrywart, and he was always fussing and fretting about something. Right now Aggie was acting just like Lewis.

To Rose Rita everything seemed clear. Mrs. Bigger was a witch, and she was always reading magic books. She probably had a copy of the Mallet of Whatever-it-was, the book that Rose Rita had to have if she was going to save Mrs. Zimmermann. It might be in her home, or it might be in her store somewhere. It was very likely to be in her store, since she spent a lot of time there and probably read while she worked. After all, Rose Rita argued, she had found that magic charm tucked away in one of Gert Bigger's account books. Well, if she had found that, she might find other things. Rose Rita ignored the holes in her argument. She didn't want to see them. Already she was beginning to be carried away by the idea of bearding Gert Bigger in her den. She imagined herself armed with a great book from which she read strange grim-sounding incantations, magic words that would bring Gert Bigger to her knees and make her bring Mrs. Zimmermann back from . . . from wherever Gert Bigger had sent her. It occurred to Rose Rita, of course, that maybe Mrs. Bigger had used her magic to kill Mrs. Zimmermann. Well, thought Rose Rita grimly, if she's done that, I'll make her bring Mrs. Zimmermann back—back from the dead. And if I can't do that, I'll make her pay for what she did. A tremendous anger was building in Rose Rita's mind. Righteous anger. She hated that big rawboned woman with the nasty sneering manner and the insults and lies and dirty rotten cheating ways. She was going to fix her, and fix her good. In the meantime, however, she had to persuade Aggie to go along with her plan. It wasn't easy. Rose Rita argued and wheedled, but Aggie was a stubborn girl—about as stubborn as Rose Rita. And Aggie was especially stubborn when she was scared.

"All right, Aggie," said Rose Rita, folding her arms and glaring. "If *that's* the way you're gonna be, I'll just go by myself!"

Aggie looked hurt. "You mean it? Really?"

Rose Rita nodded grimly. "Uh-huh. Try and stop me."

Actually, Aggie could have stopped Rose Rita easily, and Rose Rita knew it. All she had to do was shout, and Mrs. Sipes, who was a very light sleeper, would be down in the room asking them what all the racket was about. But Aggie didn't shout. She really did want to be in on the adventure. On the other hand, she was afraid.

"Come on, Aggie," Rose Rita pleaded. "We won't get caught, I promise you. And if we get our hands on a copy of that book I told you about, we can really fix old Mrs. Bigger's wagon. You'd like that, wouldn't you?"

Aggie's forehead wrinkled up. Her eyebrows got so worried that they almost met. "Gee, I still don't know, Rose Rita. Are you sure that whatchamacallit book'll be there?"

"Of course I'm not sure, dopey. But we'll never find out if we sit here all night. Come on, Aggie. Please!"

Aggie looked uncertain. "Well, how're we gonna get in? The doors and windows'll all be locked."

"We can figure that out when we get there. Maybe we'll have to break a window or something."

"It'd make a lot of noise," said Aggie. "And you might cut yourself on the glass."

"We'll pick the lock then. People do it all the time in the movies."

"This isn't the movies, this is real life. Do you know how to pick locks? Huh? Do you? I bet you don't."

Rose Rita felt totally exasperated. "Look, Aggie," she said, "if we get there and we can't find any way to get in, we can give up and come back. Okay? And if there is a way to get in, you won't even have to come inside with me. You can stay outside and be the lookout. Come on, Aggie. I really need you. How about it? Huh?"

Aggie scratched her head and looked uncertain. "You promise I won't have to come in with you? And if we can't get in, we'll come straight back here?"

Rose Rita drew a cross on her stomach with her finger. "I promise. Cross my heart and hope to die."

"Okay," said Aggie. "Wait'll I get my flashlight. We'll need it."

Working as quietly as they could, Rose Rita and Aggie got into their clothes and put on their sneakers. Aggie dug a long-barreled flashlight out of her closet and poked around in her dresser drawer till she found an old boy scout knife. It had a black wrinkly plastic handle, and inside a little glass bubble at one end of the handle was a compass. Aggie really couldn't say why she was taking along this particular piece of equipment, but she thought it might come in handy.

When they were all ready, the two girls tiptoed to the door of the bedroom. Aggie led the way. Carefully she opened the door, just a crack, and looked out.

"Okay!" she whispered. "Just follow me."

The two girls tiptoed down the hall and down the stairs. They walked softly through rooms that lay gleaming in moonlight till they reached the back door. The back door was propped open because it was a hot night, and the screen door was unhooked. They went out, closing the door softly behind them.

"Wow!" breathed Rose Rita. "That part was easy!"

Aggie smiled shyly. "Yeah. I've done it before. I used to go frog-spearin' with my brother down to the crick there, but my mom caught us and gave us heck. I haven't been out in the middle of the night since then. Come on."

Aggie and Rose Rita started walking down a rutty wagon road that ran between two plowed fields. They climbed a little fence and trotted along a grassy track that ran parallel to the main road. Rose Rita saw at once that they were going back by the way they had come on the previous day when Aggie found Rose Rita sleeping next to the cornfield. Now the field was on their left, rustling softly in the night breeze. Stars were clustered thick overhead, and crickets chirped in the tall grass.

Before long the girls passed the place where they had met. There was the droopy elm tree and the flat-topped boulder. They had been chattering excitedly, but now they grew quiet. They were not far from Mrs. Bigger's store.

At the edge of the gravel road the two girls paused. There was Gert Bigger's grocery store, shut up for the night. A yellow insect lamp lit up the front door, and through the wide plate glass window the girls could see a night light burning in the rear of the store. The sign with the flying red horse creaked gently in the wind, and the two gas pumps looked like soldiers on guard.

"Here we are," whispered Aggie.

"Yeah," said Rose Rita. She felt something tighten up in her stomach. Maybe this was a dumb plan after all. She was about to ask Aggie if she really felt like going ahead with their plan, but she swallowed her fears and crossed the road. Aggie followed, glancing about her nervously.

"It looks okay," said Aggie, when they were both on the other side of the road. "Her car's always parked over there when she's here, and it's gone."

"Good! Do you think we ought to try the front door?"

"Well, you can if you want to. But I'm sure it'll be locked."

Rose Rita trotted up the steps and rattled the door. It was locked. Locked tight. She shrugged and ran back down the steps.

"Come on, Aggie. That's one down, and a lot to go. It's such a hot night that she might have left one window open. Let's check the windows." Rose Rita could feel her courage and her habitual optimism coming back. Everything would work out all right. They'd find a way in.

Apparently Rose Rita's optimism was catching. Aggie brightened up and became—for her—confident. "Hey, that's an idea! Okay, we'll check."

As they passed around the side of the building, the girls heard a loud clucking sound. There behind the fence was that poor bedraggled white chicken. It looked even more beat-up and scrawny than it had when Rose Rita saw it the day before. Old Gertie oughta feed it, Rose Rita thought. As before, the hen was very excited. It ran back and forth behind the fence, clucking and flapping its wings.

"Oh be quiet!" Rose Rita hissed. "We're not gonna chop off your head! Just cool down, for heaven's sake!"

The two girls started to inspect the windows on the side of the house. The ones on the first floor were shut tight, and it was likely they were locked as well. Just to make sure Rose Rita got up on an orange crate and tried to move one of them. It wouldn't budge an inch.

"Darn it all anyway!" she grumbled as she got down off the crate.

"Oh, don't give up yet!" said Aggie. "We haven't tried the . . . oops. Watch out!"

Rose Rita whirled around in time to see a car pass by. Its headlights swept across the side of the store and were gone. If the driver had been paying attention, he would have seen the two figures standing next to the store. But, apparently, he had not noticed. Rose Rita felt exposed, as if she were in a fishbowl. She felt the danger of what she was doing.

"C'mon," she said, tugging nervously at Aggie's arm. "Let's go around to the back."

The two girls walked around to the rear of the store. The little white hen, which had never stopped squawking since the time they arrived, kept it up until they disappeared around the corner of the building. Rose Rita was glad when it finally shut up. It was beginning to make her nervous.

The two girls tried the back door. It was locked. Then they stepped back and surveyed the rear wall of the building. The first floor windows had heavy iron grills over them—probably they were the windows of the storeroom, where the groceries were kept. There was one window on the second floor, and—Rose Rita stepped back to make sure—yes, it was open! Not wide open, but open a crack.

"Wow!" said Rose Rita, pointing. "Do you see that?"

Aggie looked doubtful. "Yeah, I do, but I don't see how you could wiggle in through a crack like that."

"I'm not gonna wiggle in through the crack, dumbo! That crack means that the window isn't fastened. So if I climb up there, I can open it up."

"How you gonna do that?"

Rose Rita looked around. "I dunno yet. Let's see if there's anything to climb up on."

Rose Rita and Aggie poked around in the back yard of Gert Bigger's store for a while, but they didn't find any ladders. There was a toolshed, but it had a padlock on it. Rose Rita went back to the window and peered up at it owlishly. She rubbed her chin.

There was an apple tree growing near the store, and one of its branches nearly touched the sill of the window she wanted. But Rose Rita was an experienced tree climber, and she knew that the branch would start to bend as soon as she tried to climb out on it. By the time she got near the end of the branch, it would be bent way down. So that was no good. On the other hand there was a trellis nailed to the side of the house. It ran right up next to the window. If she could climb up on it, she might be able to get hold of the sill and swing herself over. It was worth a try.

Rose Rita took a deep breath and flexed her hands. She walked up to the trellis. It was covered with thick thorny vines, but there were places, here and there, where you could put your hands. Rose Rita put a foot on one slat and a hand on another. She swung herself up so her weight was on the trellis, and hung there, waiting to see what would happen. Nails skreeked as the trellis started to pull out from the wall.

"It doesn't look too good," said Aggie, screwing up her mouth into a very worried scowl. "If you climb any farther, you're gonna break your neck."

Rose Rita said nothing. The trellis was still attached to the wall, so she put another foot up. Then another foot, and another hand. With a loud splintering, crackling, rustling, and squeaking noise, the trellis leaned lazily sideways. Nails and broken pieces of wood dropped to the ground. Rose Rita leaped free of the wreckage and landed on her feet. Aggie, with a little cry, dropped the knife in the grass and ran to Rose Rita's side. She found her standing there, sucking a cut thumb and glaring hatefully at the ruined trellis.

"Darned thorns anyway!" Rose Rita grumbled.

"Gee, is she ever gonna be ticked off!" said Aggie. "Mrs. Bigger, I mean."

Rose Rita wasn't listening. She was wondering if maybe she could scale the side of the building. It wasn't very far up to the second story, and the white clapboard strips looked as though they might give her a handhold. She tried, but she slid down. She tried again, with the same result. She stood there, panting and redfaced. For the first time, she doubted the wisdom of her plan.

"Let's go home," said Rose Rita bitterly. She felt the tears stinging her eyes.

"Are you giving up already?" said Aggie. "Gee, I don't think that's a very good idea. We haven't looked at the other side of the store."

Rose Rita gave a start and looked at Aggie. She was right! Rose Rita had been so wrapped up in the problem of the upstairs window that she had forgotten all about the far side of the building, the one side that they hadn't checked out yet. Hope and optimism came flowing back.

"Okay. Let's go look," said Rose Rita, grinning.

On the far side of the store thick bushes grew up close to the windows, but there was a little tunnel in the shrubbery where you could sidle in if you hunkered down a bit. Rose Rita and Aggie bent over and edged their way in under the bushes. They looked up and saw that the windows on this side had grates and padlocks like the ones on the back of the store. But down at ground level was a cellar entrance. The old-fashioned kind, with two slanting wooden doors. Aggie shone her flashlight over the door. There was a pair of metal fixtures where the two doors met. Obviously they were meant to hold a padlock, but there was no padlock in the holes. The door was unlocked.

Cautiously Rose Rita gripped the handle of one of the heavy wooden doors. She lifted it, and a smell of earth and mold rose to her nostrils. It was like a breath from the grave. Rose Rita shuddered and stepped back. She

dropped the door. It fell with a loud clatter.

Aggie gave Rose Rita a frightened look. "What's wrong, Rose Rita? Did you see something?"

Rose Rita passed a hand over her forehead. She felt dizzy. "I . . . no, I didn't, Aggie, only . . . only I got scared. I d'no why, but I did. I guess I'm just a scaredy-cat, that's all."

"It's funny, isn't it?" Aggie mused, as she stared down at the door. "All those bars and locks on everything else, and she leaves this open. It's weird."

"Yeah. Maybe she didn't think anyone'd go pokin' around under these bushes." Rose Rita realized that this was a pretty weak explanation, but it was the only one she could come up with. There was something very strange about this open door. She just couldn't figure it out.

Suddenly Rose Rita thought of something. She picked up the cellar door again and opened it all the way. She opened the other door panel too. Then she took the flashlight from Aggie and stepped down into the dark opening. At the bottom of a short flight of stone steps Rose Rita found a black door with a dirty cobwebbed window. She put her hand on the porcelain knob and found that it felt surprisingly cold. Rose Rita turned the knob and pushed cautiously. At first she thought the door was locked, but when she pushed harder, it opened with a loud dismal rattle.

Inside the cellar it was pitch-dark. Rose Rita played the beam of her flashlight around and saw vague shapes hunched in the gloom.

"Are you okay?" called Aggie nervously.

"Yeah, I . . . I think so. Look, Aggie. You stay up here and keep watch. I'm goin' in and have a look around."

"Don't stay too long."

"Don't worry, I won't. See you later."

"Okay."

Rose Rita turned and flashed her light up. There stood Aggie with her worried frown. She was waving feebly. Rose Rita swallowed hard and thought about Mrs. Zimmermann. She turned and went in.

As she crossed the cold stone floor, Rose Rita glanced nervously from side to side. In one corner a furnace squatted. With its upraised metal arms, it looked like some kind of monster. Near it was a freezer. It reminded Rose Rita of a tomb. She laughed nervously. Why did everything seem so scary? This was a perfectly ordinary basement. There weren't any ghosts or monsters in it. Rose Rita walked on.

In a far corner of the basement she found a flight of wooden steps leading up. Slowly she climbed. The steps creaked loudly under her feet. At the top of the steps was a door. Rose Rita opened it and looked out. She was in the store.

Groceries stood piled in shadowy ranks. Cans, bottles,

jars, and boxes, half lit by the weak little bulb that burned over the cash register. Outside the wide front window a car passed. Rose Rita could hear a clock ticking slowly, but she couldn't see it. She walked across the room and opened a door. Here were steps leading up. She started to climb.

Halfway up the steps Rose Rita noticed something that made her stop: a picture hanging with its face turned to the wall. Curious, she reached up and turned it over. The picture showed a saint with a halo. He was clutching a cross and staring up toward heaven with wide unearthly eyes. Hurriedly Rose Rita turned the picture back toward the wall. A violent shudder passed through her body. Why had she been so frightened? She didn't know. When she had calmed down, she went on up the stairs.

At the top of the steps was an L-shaped hallway, and halfway along it was a paneled door. There was a key sticking out of the door. She turned it, and the door swung open. Rose Rita waved her flashlight around, and found that she was in a small bedroom.

There was a light switch just inside the door. Rose Rita's hand moved toward it, but then she stopped. Would it be a bad thing to turn the light on? She glanced toward the window. It was the only one in the room, the window she had tried to reach by climbing the trellis. The window looked out on the dark mass of trees behind the store. Gert Bigger was miles away. If I turn on the light, Rose Rita thought, people will just figure it's old Gertie up here counting her money. She snapped the switch and started looking around.

It was a very ordinary room. The only thing odd about it was its lived-in look, but it occurred to Rose Rita that maybe Gert Bigger stayed here during the winter, on nights when the weather was so bad that it was impossible to drive home. In one corner stood a small iron bed. It was painted green, and the wrought iron posies on the bars of the headboard were touched up in pink. Nearby was a closet without any door. Ordinary ladies' dresses hung on the rack, and wadded nylons lay on the floor near a heavy-looking pair of black ladies' shoes. There was a shelf in the closet, and something like a blanket lay folded up on it. Nothing unusual here.

Rose Rita walked across the room and examined the dresser. There was a mirror on top of it, and in front of the mirror was a collection of bottles and jars. Jergen's lotion, Noxzema, Pond's lotion, and a big blue bottle of Evening in Paris perfume. On the white linen runner lay tweezers and combs and brushes, and bits of tissue paper, and little curls of dark brown hair. There was a box of Kleenex, too.

Rose Rita turned and gazed around the room. Was there anything else here? There was. On a low table next to the bed was a large book. A big heavy book with a tooled leather cover. The pages were edged with gilt, and there were fussy gilded decorations on the spine and on the cover. A soiled red marker was sticking out of the book.

Rose Rita could hear her heart beating. She swallowed hard. Could this be it? She went closer, and opened the heavy front cover. Her face fell. It wasn't the book she wanted. It was something called *A Cyclopaedia of Jewish Antiquities*, by the Reverend Merriwether Burchard, D.D., Litt.D. Well, at least it was a book of some sort. Rose Rita started leafing through it.

The book was printed in double columns of tiny black print, and it was full of dark mysterious engravings. According to the captions, the pictures showed The Temple of Solomon, the Ark of the Covenant, the Brazen Laver, the Seven-Branched Candlestick, and things like that. Rose Rita knew what some of the things in the pictures were. There were engravings like these in her grandmother's family Bible. Rose Rita yawned. It looked like a pretty boring book. She looked around and sighed. This certainly wasn't any witch's den. Maybe she was wrong about Gert Bigger being a witch. Rose Rita realized, with a sinking heart, that her witch theory was based on a lot of guesswork. Mrs. Bigger might have had a picture of Mordecai Hunks on her wall, but what did that prove? As for the photo Mrs. Zimmermann had found, it might all have been just a coincidence. As for the strange drawing and Mrs. Bigger's odd reading habits, well, she might just be one of those people who want to be a witch. Mrs. Zimmermann had told Rose Rita once that there were lots of people who would love to have magical powers, although there wasn't chance in a million that they would ever get them. People like that would read magic books in hopes of getting to be magicians, wouldn't they? Well, wouldn't they?

Rose Rita began to wonder if she hadn't made a terrible mistake. Some strange things had happened to her and Mrs. Zimmermann, but that didn't mean that old Mrs. Bigger had made them happen. She picked up her flashlight off the bed and was about to go downstairs when she heard a noise. A faint scratching at the door of the bedroom.

Terror gripped Rose Rita for an instant, and then she remembered something that made her laugh. Mrs. Bigger had a dog. A small black dog. Probably she had locked it in the store for the night.

With a sigh of relief, Rose Rita opened the door. It was the dog, all right. It trotted across the room and hopped up on the bed. Rose Rita smiled and turned toward the door. But she stopped again, because the dog had made a very odd sound. A sound very much like a human being coughing. Animals sometimes make human sounds. The cries of cats are, on certain occasions, just like a baby's wails. Rose Rita knew that, but still the sound made her stop. The hair on the back of her neck stood up on end. She turned slowly around. There on the bed sat Gert Bigger. Her hard brutal mouth was set in the evilest of smiles.

CHAPTER ELEVEN

Rose Rita lay in darkness. She felt a slight pressure on her eyes and knew that there was something covering them, but she didn't know what it was. She would have reached up to uncover her eyes, but she couldn't. Her hands were crossed on her breast, and though she could feel them, she couldn't move them. She couldn't move any part of her body, nor could she speak, but she could hear, and she could feel. As she lay there, a fly—it felt like a fly—landed on her forehead and walked the length of her nose before buzzing away.

Where was she? Probably in the bedroom above Gert Bigger's store. It felt as if she was lying on a bed, anyway. And there was a blanket, or something like a blanket, drawn up over her body. It felt heavy, and the room was hot and still. Tiny rivulets of sweat ran down Rose Rita's body. Why couldn't she move? Was she paralyzed, or what? There came back to her now, like a bad dream, the terror she had felt when she saw Gert Bigger sitting on the bed, leering at her. She must have fainted then, because she could not remember anything after that.

Rose Rita heard a lock click. A door creaked open. Heavy footfalls crossed the room and stopped next to her head. A chair creaked.

"Well, well, well. And how are you, Miss Nosy? Hmmm? Not speaking to me? That's not nice. You know, I'm the one who ought to be insulted, the way you broke in here and rummaged around. Were you tryin' to find out if I was a witch? Well, you can relax. I am."

Gert Bigger laughed, and it was not at all the kind of laugh that you would expect to come out of a big husky woman like her. It was a high-pitched tinny giggle. Rose Rita thought it sounded like the laughter of a crazy person.

"Yes, sirree," Gert Bigger went on, "it all started when that old fool of a Gunderson dropped in here one night. He was half-crocked, and he started talkin' about this magic ring he had found on his farm. Well, at first I thought he was just foolin', but I got to thinkin' later—what if it's the truth? You see, I've always wanted to be able to work magic. I've studied up on it a lot. Well, after old Oley kicked off, I broke into his place and hunted around till I found the darned thing. It's on my finger right now. Did you read in that book what that fella Burchard said about it? It's all true, you know, every word. Here, let me read it to you."

Rose Rita heard the sound of fingers riffling through the pages of a book. "Here it is, where I stuck the marker. You must've seen it when you were pokin' around, though sometimes you nosy types don't see what's right under your nose." She giggled again. "Ready? Here it is. '. . . No account of Jewish antiquities would be complete without mention of the legendary ring of King Solomon. According to the great historian Flavius Josephus, King Solomon possessed a magic ring that enabled him to do many wonderful things. The ring gave him the power of teleportation, that is, the ability to be whisked from place to place, unseen. It conferred upon him the powers of sorcery and divination, and enabled him to humiliate his enemies by changing them into lowly beasts. In this manner, it is said, King Solomon brought low the king of the Hittites, when he turned him into an ox. The ring also enabled Solomon to change his own shape at will—his most favored form is said to have been that of a small black dog, in which shape he prowled about, spying on his enemies and finding out many secrets. But the greatest power of the ring was one which Solomon, wisest of men, never chose to use. The ring could, if the wearer desired it, give long life and great beauty. To obtain this gift, however, the wearer was obliged to call upon the demon Asmodai. It may be for this reason that Solomon refused to exercise this power of the ring. For, we are told, he who sups with the Devil . . .' "

The book slammed shut. "That's enough of you, Reverend," muttered Gert Bigger. "Well, there you are, Miss Nosy. Isn't that interestin'? But I'll tell you what is most interestin' of all. You came here at just the right time, you really did. I was goin' to do somethin' to you when I caught you pokin' around in my back room, but later, I says to myself, I says, 'She'll be back!' And you did come back, you did, you did!" Gert Bigger let out a peal of shrill laughter. "I left the padlock off of my cellar door, and you went right in, like the little fool that you are. Well, you're gonna find out what it's like to monkey around with witches. Florence found out, and I'm not through with her yet, not by a long shot." She paused and made an unpleasant spitting sound. "Phah! Oh, didn't I know, didn't I know what she was up to when she showed up here, pretendin' she was out of gas! I knew about her and all that magic monkey-do of hers, that college degree and all, and I says to myself, 'She's after the ring!' I was real worried then, because I didn't know how to handle the ring proper, cept'n for the black-dog trick. Well, after you folks went up north, I learned. I sent that photograft up there, and that was me you saw in Florence's room. I showed up in the back seat o' your car for a coupla seconds too. Scared the dickens out o'you, didn't I?" She laughed shrilly. Then, after another pause, she continued, in a grimmer tone, "Well, fun's fun, but I'm through playin' around. I've got Florence, and I'm gonna fix her good, so she'll never be able to get my ring from me, not ever!

"A course," she added, "I've got a special grudge against her for makin' my life miserable. If me'n Mordy had got married, my life would've been better. The old fool that I was married to used to beat me up. You don't know what it was like. You don't know at all." Gert Bigger's voice cracked. Was she crying? Rose Rita couldn't tell.

Gert Bigger rambled on, in her hard angry voice. She explained to Rose Rita that she had put her under a death spell. When dawn came, she would die. They would find her body here surrounded by the paraphernalia of Gert Bigger's magic. But Gert Bigger would be gone. In fact there would be no Gert Bigger, because she would be a young beautiful woman. She had it all figured out: she would go away to another place and change her name. She had drawn all her money out of the bank— it was in the safe downstairs. With a new name and a new life she could start making up for all the rotten things that had happened to her. And before she left, she would settle accounts with Florence Zimmermann, for good and for all.

After she had finished talking, Gert Bigger left the room and locked the door. Rose Rita stared hopelessly into the darkness that lay around her. She thought about Aggie. Aggie was her only hope. Rose Rita had no idea how much time had gone by since she left Aggie standing outside the cellar door. She hoped that Gert Bigger hadn't captured Aggie too. Rose Rita prayed, though her mouth stayed shut and no sound came out. Please, God, help Aggie to find me. Make her get help before it's too late. Please God please . . .

A long time passed. At least it seemed like a long time, though Rose Rita had no way of telling how long it was. Her wristwatch was still on her wrist, ticking, but it did her no good. How would she know when it was dawn? She would know when she was dead. Tick-tick-tick-tick. Rose Rita could feel her body growing numb. She couldn't feel her hands on her breast any more. She had a horrible vision of herself as a severed head lying on a pillow. It was such an awful thought that she tried to get rid of it, but it kept coming back. Please, God, send Aggie, send somebody. Tick-tick-tick-tick . . .

Brr-rrr-rrring. A doorbell was ringing. It rang several times, and then Rose Rita heard the muffled tinkling of the little bell above the door of the store. She heard nothing after that—if people were talking, she couldn't hear them. Silence. More time passed. Then Rose Rita heard the lock on the bedroom door click. Footsteps, and the creak of a chair as somebody heavy sat down.

"My lord, it takes all kinds to make a world!" said Gert Bigger. "Who do you suppose I've just been talkin' to? Guess. Give up? Mrs. Sipes, who lives down the road. Her and her daughter . . . Aggie I think is her name. They were all wrought up because Aggie said I kidnaped you. Imagine that!" Gert Bigger giggled. "They had even brought a cop along with 'em to search the place. Well, I know my rights. He didn't have no search warrant, and I told him so. I says to him, I know my rights and you can't come in, and no, I don't know nothin' about no little girl! So there! Imagine the nerve of 'em, comin' here like that!" Gert Bigger laughed again. The chair creaked as she rocked back and forth, laughing. The tiny flame of hope in Rose Rita's mind flickered out. She was going to die, and there was nothing that anyone could do about it.

Gert Bigger left the room, and there was another long dark silence. Rose Rita kept hearing little sounds, but she couldn't figure out what they were. Finally the door creaked open again, and she heard Gert Bigger walking around the room. She was humming to herself, and there was a sound of drawers opening and shutting. She was packing up, getting ready to leave. After what seemed like a long time, Rose Rita heard the latches of a suitcase snap shut. Gert Bigger walked over to her chair by the head of the bed and sat down again.

"How're you doin'? Hmm? Feel anything yet? This spell comes over you gradual-like, or so I'm told. But it

won't be over with till dawn, and that's still a ways off yet. Okay now. I'm all ready to go. I haven't taken care of Florence yet, but I think I'll do that on my way out. I want her to see what I'm like after I've been changed. And you know what? Seeing as how you've been so nice and quiet, I'm gonna let you watch me do my little quick-change act. Well, uh, of course I'm kiddin' in a way, because I really can't let you see me. I'd have to take those things off of your eyes, and that would break the spell, and we can't have that, can we? No sir-ree. But I tell you what I'll do. I'll sit right here in this chair and summon up old Asmodai, and you can hear his voice. How'll that be? Let me see now, what is it that I do? Oh yes . . ."

Gert Bigger clapped her hands three times and said in a loud commanding voice, "Send Asmodai to me! Now!"

At first nothing happened. Then, slowly, Rose Rita began to feel the presence of something evil. Feeling returned to her body. Her flesh was covered with goose bumps, and she felt cold. The air grew thick, and it was hard to breathe. Out of the darkness a harsh whispery voice spoke.

"Who calls upon Asmodai?"

"I do. I am wearing the ring of King Solomon, and I want to be changed. I want to be young and beautiful, and I want to live for a thousand years." Gert added quickly, "But I don't want to get old. I want to stay young, all the time."

"So be it," said the whispery voice.

As soon as the whispery voice had finished speaking, Rose Rita heard a small sound. It was a sound like somebody dropping a quarter on the floor. Then there was a sound like a strong wind roaring through the room. The room trembled, as if the ground underneath the building was quaking. Rose Rita heard all sorts of rattling clattering sounds. The bed shook, and whatever had been on her eyes slid off. She sat up and shook her head groggily. Rose Rita looked around. Where were her glasses? What had Gert Bigger done with them? She groped around on the nightstand and found them. She put them on and glanced around. Gert Bigger was gone. She had not heard her go out, and the key was sticking out of the inside of the door. On the bed next to her, Rose Rita saw two silver dollars. They must have been the things over her eyes. And she found that she was lying under a heavy black woolen blanket. It had a white border and a big white cross on it. Rose Rita knew what it was. She had been to a funeral at the Catholic church in New Zebedee, and she had seen a casket covered with a blanket just like this one. With a violent shudder she thrust the thing away from her and sat up.

Rose Rita felt sick. She felt like somebody who has been in bed with the flu for two weeks. When she tried to stand up, she sat down again suddenly. Sweat was pouring down her face. As she gazed woozily around the room, it occurred to her to wonder just what had happened to Mrs. Bigger. Probably she had had her wish granted, and she was out in Hollywood, living it up with Lana Turner and Esther Williams and all that crowd. Rose Rita didn't know, and she didn't care. She felt dizzy, and she couldn't stop shuddering. Her head was as light as a wicker basket. Finally, with an effort, she forced herself to stand up. Now she remembered something, something that had puzzled her. That sound, like a coin hitting the floor. What was it? Rose Rita got down on her hands and knees and looked under the bed. And at that moment she heard, from downstars, a terrific pounding and banging. The doorbell rang about eight times, and a muffled voice yelled, "Open up! Open up in the name of the law!" They were back! Aggie and her mom and the cops! Rose Rita glanced toward the door. What if Mrs. Bigger had left her ring behind? Wouldn't it be great to be able to run downstairs to meet Aggie with the ring of King Solomon in her fist? Rose Rita bent over and scrabbled in the dust under the bed. There it was! She reached out and hooked the ring with her finger. Now she drew the ring to her and closed her fist around it.

And with that something happened. A shudder ran through Rose Rita's body, and she felt . . . well, *strange*. She felt proud and bitter and angry, angry at the people who had come to drag her back to her old life.

"Okay, Mrs. Bigger," the voice boomed. "We're gonna give you a count of ten before we break the door down! One . . ."

Rose Rita got up and glared fiercely at the door. The expression on her face was so hateful that she hardly looked like herself at all. A wild light was in her eyes. So they were coming to get her! Well, they'd have to catch her first. She rushed to the door and unlocked it. With the ring still clutched tight in her fist, Rose Rita dashed out into the hall. At the far end of the hall was a half-opened door, and she could see stairs leading down. It wasn't the staircase she had come up by, it was another one, leading to the back of the building. Rose Rita ran toward it.

"Six . . . seven . . ."

Down the stairs she clattered. At the bottom was a door with a night lock and a chain. Working furiously, yet never letting the ring out of her hand for a second, Rose Rita undid the locks and chains and bolts.

"Ten!" There was a loud crash and a babble of voices shouting. In the middle of it all Rose Rita heard Aggie yelling "Rose Rita! Are you all right?" Rose Rita hesitated. She glanced waveringly toward the front of the store, where all the noise was coming from. Then her face hardened, and she gripped the ring tighter. Rose Rita turned and ran, out past the toolshed and the clothesline, toward the dark mass of trees that grew right up to the edge of Gert Bigger's back yard. The shadow of the pines seemed to reach out and swallow her up.

CHAPTER TWELVE

Rose Rita ran through the woods, her feet slapping the ground under her. Bits and pieces of scenery jolted past, branches and stumps, and fungi laddering tall dark trunks. She ran on a crooked path covered with brown pine needles, a path that wound deeper and deeper into the woods. Sometimes she fell or barked her shins on a stump, but each time she got up and kept on running. Faster and faster she ran. Branches whipped across her face and arms, leaving angry red marks, but the pain of the cuts just made her run faster. As she ran, her mind was filled with a wild jumble of thoughts. Images leaped before her, like flashes of lightning. Rose Rita saw them as clearly as if they had been printed on the air. She saw the boy with the crew cut who had yelled, "You're a pretty funny kind of a girl!" She saw the girls standing on the sidelines at the Saturday night dance. She saw the black prison-like junior high building where she had to go next fall. She saw girls in flouncy dresses, girls who wore nylons and lipstick and mascara, asking her, "What's the matter with you? Don't you want to go on dates? Dating is fun!"

As Rose Rita ran, she thought she could hear someone behind her, calling her name. The voice was faint and far-off, but she was sure she had heard it call to her once or twice. No, Rose Rita panted. You're not gonna get me. I've had about enough, I've had about enough, and I'm gonna get what I want . . .

On and on Rose Rita ran, pell-mell, through the dark pine forest. She left the path behind and half slid, half ran down a steep bank. The bank was covered with pine needles, and pine needles are slippery. She lost her footing and tumbled, head over heels. Over and over she rolled. When she got to the bottom, dazed and sick and shaken, the first thing she did was make sure that she had the ring with her. There it was, still clutched tight in her fist. Rose Rita opened her hand only long enough to make sure the ring was safe. Then she closed her fist tight, staggered to her feet, and started running again. There was something inside her head that kept driving her on, something relentless and mechanical, like a piston.

Go on, go on, it said. Keep going, keep going, keep going, keep going . . .

Rose Rita splashed across a shallow little stream and started to climb the bank on the other side. But the bank was steep, and it was hard climbing with one hand doubled up into a fist. Rose Rita paused, panting, half-way up. Why not put the ring on? She opened her hand and gaped stupidly at the small heavy object. It was too big—it would fall off her finger. How about putting it in her pocket? No, there might be a hole in the pocket. It might get lost. She had to know, all the time, that it was there. Rose Rita closed up her fist and climbed on, one-handed. She was a good climber, and there were roots here and there that could be used like the rungs of a ladder. Up she went. When she got to the top she paused to catch her breath.

"Rose Rita! Rose Rita! Stop!"

Rose Rita whirled. Who was that? It was a voice she knew. She was on the point of turning back when that driving piston in her head started up again. Go on, go on, go on, let's go, let's go, let's go. Rose Rita glared back across the stream. There was wild insane anger in her eyes now. "Come and get me!" she snarled through her teeth. Then she turned and ran on.

On into the forest Rose Rita plunged. But now her legs were starting to give out. They felt like rubber. Lying under that spell on Gert Bigger's bed had weakened her, the way a long illness would have. Her side hurt, and when she tried to catch her breath, watery bubbles kept bursting in her mouth. She was wringing wet with sweat, and her glasses were fogged up. Rose Rita wanted to stop, but the driving piston wouldn't let her. It forced her on until, finally, she reeled out into a little clearing. Rose Rita fell to her knees and looked around. Where was she? What was she doing? Oh, yes, she was going to . . . she was going . . . to . . . The world was starting to spin around her. Dark trees and starlit sky and gray grass whizzed past, like the things you see out of a car window when you're going very fast. Rose Rita fell down on her back and passed out.

The first thing that Rose Rita saw when she woke up, some time later, was a small cold pale moon shining down on her. She sat up and shook her head. All around her the dark trees stood, a ring of shadows cutting off escape. But she didn't want to escape, did she? No. She had come here to do something, but she couldn't for the life of her remember what it was. Rose Rita felt a pain in her left hand. She picked her fist up off the grass and stared at it as if it was something that belonged to somebody else. Slowly she opened her stiff cramped painful fingers. In her palm lay a large battered ring. She had been holding it so long, and so tight, that it had dug a deep red welt into her hand.

Wincing, Rose Rita turned the ring over with her fingers. It was made of gold—at least it seemed to be. And it was a signet ring. There was a design cut into the flat surface on the top. A face. A staring face with blank eyeballs and lips curled into a cold evil smile. Rose Rita was fascinated by the face. It seemed so lifelike. She half expected to see the lips part and to hear a voice speak.

And then she remembered why she was here.

Rose Rita stood up, swaying, in the gray moonlit clearing. She slid the ring onto the third finger of her left hand and held it there so it wouldn't fall off. Rose Rita gasped. The ring had shrunk to fit her hand! But she had no time to think of these things. A voice was in her head, telling her what to do. She clapped three times in weak imitation of Mrs. Bigger and said, in as loud a voice as she could manage, "I . . . I call upon As . . . Asmodai! Come to me! Now!"

A shadow fell across the gray starlit grass. And Rose Rita heard the harsh whispery voice that she had heard in Gert Bigger's room.

"I am called Asmodai. What do you want?"

Rose Rita shivered. She felt cold and frightened and alone. She wanted to rip the ring from her hand and throw it away. But she couldn't. An insistent angry voice, her own voice inside her head, went on talking. It told her what she had to do. It told her that she had to change, that she could solve all her problems now if only she had the courage. It also told her that she would only have this one chance, and that she'd never get another.

The whispery voice spoke again. It sounded faintly impatient. "I am called Asmodai. What do you want? You are the wielder of the ring of Solomon. What do you want?"

"I . . . I want . . . what I want to do is . . . what I want is . . ."

"Rose Rita, stop! Stop what you're doing and look at me!"

Rose Rita turned. There at the edge of the clearing stood Mrs. Zimmermann. The folds of her dress were filled with orange fire, and her homely wrinkled face was lit by the light of invisible footlights. A purple halo hovered about her, and its light fell upon the gray grass.

"Stop, Rose Rita! Stop what you're doing and listen to me!"

Rose Rita hesitated. She took the ring between her thumb and finger and started to take it off. It was on tight, but it could be moved. Now the voice in Rose Rita's head got louder. It told her not to listen to Mrs. Zimmermann. It told her that she had the right to be happy, to do what she wanted to do.

Rose Rita swallowed hard and licked her lips. She turned toward the shadow that waited, hovering, nearby. "I . . . I want to be a . . ."

Mrs. Zimmermann spoke again in a loud echoing com-

manding voice that seemed to fill the whole clearing. "I command you, Rose Rita, to give me that ring! Give it to me now!"

Rose Rita stood, hesitating. Her eyes were wide with fear. Then, like a sleepwalker, she turned and walked toward Mrs. Zimmermann. As she walked, she began working the ring loose from her finger. Up it slid, painfully, from one joint to the next. It was off now and lying in the palm of her right hand. Mrs. Zimmermann reached out and took it. She glanced at it scornfully and slipped it into the pocket of her dress. The halo faded and the footlights died. The folds of Mrs. Zimmermann's dress were just black creases now.

"Hi, Rose Rita," said Mrs. Zimmermann, smiling. "Long time no see."

Rose Rita looked nervously behind her, but the shadow was gone. Then she collapsed into Mrs. Zimmermann's arms and sobbed. Her whole body shook, and as she cried, she felt as if she were getting something poisonous and putrid out of her system. When she had cried herself out, Rose Rita stepped back and looked at Mrs. Zimmermann. Her face was pale and drawn, but her eyes were cheerful. She looked and talked like herself.

"What . . . what happened to you, Mrs. Zimmermann?" was all Rose Rita could think of to say.

Mrs. Zimmermann laughed softly. "I might ask you the same question, my dear. By the way, were you scared of me when I showed up just now?"

"I sure was. I was afraid you'd wave your wand and . . . hey!" Suddenly Rose Rita remembered. Mrs. Zimmermann's wand had been destroyed, and she had not made another. She was next-door to powerless as a witch. Then how . . . ?

Mrs. Zimmermann could tell what Rose Rita was thinking. She laughed again. It was a pleasant sound, and nothing like Gert Bigger's insane giggle. "Rose Rita," she said, chuckling, "you have been flimflammed. I bluffed you. You see, I can still make myself look pretty darned terrifying, with footlights and haloes and all, but if you had chosen to go on with what you were doing, I wouldn't have been able to do a thing to stop you. Not a blessed thing."

Rose Rita stared at the ground. "I'm glad you bluffed me, Mrs. Zimmermann. I almost did something awful. But . . . but what happened to you? The other night, I mean. Where did you come from just now?"

"From the chicken yard," said Mrs. Zimmermann, smiling wryly. "Haven't you guessed by now?"

Rose Rita's mouth dropped open. "You mean . . . you mean you were . . . ?"

Mrs. Zimmermann nodded. "Uh-huh. And I'll never be able to look a plate of chicken salad in the face again, as long as I live. Gertie did that to me with the ring. But in order for me to have been brought back to my proper shape, something must have happened to her. Do you know what it was?"

Rose Rita was utterly confused. "I . . . I thought maybe you had figured out some way to break the spell she put on you. Isn't that what you did?"

Mrs. Zimmermann shook her head. "No, my dear. Even in the days when I had my magic wand, I would not have been strong enough to defeat someone who had a ring like that one. No, Rose Rita. All I know is this: one minute I was behind that fence, leading my, uh . . ." (she coughed) ". . . my, uh, chickeny life, and the next minute, I was standing there like my old self. Something must have happened. Maybe you can tell me what."

Rose Rita scratched her head. "You got me, Mrs. Zimmermann. Mrs. Bigger was gonna kill me with a spell, but in the middle of it all, she disappeared. She was gonna use the ring to call on . . . to call on . . ." It was strange, but now that she didn't have the ring on her finger anymore, Rose Rita couldn't remember the name of the devil that Mrs. Bigger had called on.

"Asmodai?" said Mrs. Zimmermann.

"Gee. That's it. How'd you know?"

"I didn't get a doctorate in Magic Arts from the University of Göttingen for nothing. Go on."

"Well, she called on whatsisname, and she said she wanted to be young and beautiful and live for . . . for a thousand years, I think it was. Anyway, she disappeared, so I figure the magic must have worked. But I guess she didn't know there'd be an earthquake along with all the rest of the presto-chango. The coins slid off my eyes, and that's how I got loose."

"Lucky for you," said Mrs. Zimmermann. "I'm sure old Gertie didn't count on that happening. And there may have been some other things she wasn't counting on."

"Huh? What do you mean?"

"I'm not sure what I mean, just yet. Right now, however, I think we'd better be getting back to the store. When I ducked out of the chicken yard, there was an incredible ruckus going on inside the store. It sounded like they were turning the place inside out. But I figured you needed me more than they did. I just barely caught sight of you as you were hightailing it for the woods. I'm an old woman, and I can't run very fast, so you got ahead of me. But I didn't have any trouble following you. You left quite a trail in the underbrush. And anyway, I was a girl scout leader back in the old days. Come on."

As it was, Rose Rita and Mrs. Zimmermann didn't have much trouble finding their way back to the store. They followed the swath of trampled grass and broken branches and muddy footprints back to the little path, and from there on it was easy.

Later the two of them were trotting briskly along the needle-strewn path when all of a sudden Mrs. Zimmermann said, "Look!" She pointed off to the left, and there Rose Rita saw a young slender willow tree. It stood, all alone, amid tall pines.

"Look at what?" said Rose Rita, puzzled.

"That willow."

"Oh yeah. It's just a tree. What about it?"

"What about it? Well, for one thing, you don't usually see willows all by themselves in the middle of pine forests. You find them in willow groves, by the banks of rivers and lakes and streams. And there's something else wrong. Its leaves are trembling. Can you feel any wind?"

"Nope. Gee, that is weird. Do you think maybe it's blowing over there, but not here?"

Mrs. Zimmermann rubbed her chin. "Tell me, Rose Rita," she said suddenly. "Can you remember the exact words Mrs. Bigger used? When she got herself changed, I mean."

Rose Rita thought. "Gee, I don't think I can. Something about being young and beautiful and living a long time, like I said before."

"That tree is young, and it certainly is beautiful," said Mrs. Zimmermann quietly. "As for how long it will live, I really couldn't say."

Rose Rita looked at the tree, and then she looked at Mrs. Zimmermann. "You mean . . . you mean you think . . ."

"Like I said before, I don't know what I think. That is, I'm not sure. But something had to happen to return me to my present shape. If a witch is changed into something else—a tree, for instance—she isn't a witch any longer, and all her enchantments are broken. Come on, Rose Rita. Time's a-wasting. We'd better get back."

It was fully daylight when Rose Rita and Mrs. Zimmermann stepped out into the clearing behind Gert Bigger's store. They walked around to the front and found Aggie Sipes and her mother standing there. They were watching the two policemen, who, in turn, were staring at some things that lay piled on the front steps of the store. It was quite an odd collection. A funeral pall, a big wooden cross, some brown beeswax candles, a tarnished silver censer, a gilded incense boat, and an aspergillum—otherwise known as a holy water sprinkler. There was a big pile of books, too. Among them was the book that Rose Rita had found on Gert Bigger's bedside table.

As soon as Aggie caught sight of Rose Rita coming around the corner of the store, she gave a wild yell and ran toward her.

"Rose Rita, you're okay! Gee, I thought you were dead! Wow! Hooray! Whee!" Aggie hugged Rose Rita and jumped up and down. Mrs. Sipes came over too. There was a big smile on her face.

"Are you Mrs. Zimmermann?" she asked.

"I am," said Mrs. Zimmermann. The two women shook hands.

The two policemen walked over and joined the welcoming committee. They looked suspicious, as policemen often do. One of them had a note pad and a pencil in his hand.

"Okay," he said brusquely. "Are you the Mrs. Zigfield that got lost last night?"

"Yes. Zimmermann's the name, by the way. Please excuse my appearance, but I've been through quite a lot." Mrs. Zimmermann did indeed look as if she had spent the last two nights in the woods. Her dress was tattered and torn and had burrs all over it. Her shoes were wet and muddy, and her hair was a mess. There was pine pitch all over her hands and her face.

"Yeah," said Rose Rita. "We . . . we uh . . ." She realized with a sudden shock that she couldn't tell these people what had happened. Not and expect to be believed, that is.

"We, ah, had quite an experience, the two of us," Mrs. Zimmermann cut in quickly. "You see, I went walking out behind the Gunderson farm night before last, and I got lost in the woods. I know you'll think I was daffy for going out in the rain like that, but the fact is, I like walking in the rain. I love the sound of rain hitting the fabric of an umbrella—it's sort of a cozy sound, like rain on a tent roof. I hadn't intended to walk very far, but before I knew it, there I was, off the path and lost. Then, to make matters worse, the wind started blowing up a gale, and it blew my umbrella inside out, so I had to throw it away. Too bad too, because it was such a nice umbrella. But as I was saying, I got lost, and I've been wandering about for two days. Luckily I studied botany in college, and I know a little about what herbs and berries are safe to eat. So I'm a bit worn out, but otherwise okay, I think. Just by chance I ran into Rose Rita, and she guided me back to civilization. And from what she tells me, she's had quite a horrifying experience herself. It seems that the old lady who runs this store had her bound and gagged and locked in a closet. Then she gave her some drug and took her out into the woods and left her to starve. Fortunately Rose Rita knows a little wood-craft, and she was on her way back when she met me. Also," she added, reaching into her pocket, "we found this out in the woods, and when it got light, we were able to use it to help us find our way back."

It was Aggie's boy scout knife! The knife with the compass in the handle. Mrs. Zimmermann had found it where Aggie dropped it in Gert Bigger's back yard.

Rose Rita stared at Mrs. Zimmermann in pure admira-tion. She had told some good lies in the past, but never any quite as good as this one of Mrs. Zimmermann's. But then Rose Rita remembered Aggie. She knew the real story of how Mrs. Zimmermann had disappeared. And she knew about the knife, since she was the one who had dropped it. Would she spill the beans? Rose Rita glanced nervously at her and saw, to her surprise and irritation, that Aggie was trying hard to suppress a giggle. It was the first time Rose Rita had ever seen Aggie laugh.

But Aggie said nothing, and fortunately her mother did not notice the laughing fit that had come over her. The policeman with the note pad hadn't noticed either.

He had been busy jotting down every word Mrs. Zimmermann said. "Okay now," he said, looking up from his work. "Mrs. Zigfield, you got any idea what happened to the old lady that ran this store?"

Mrs. Zimmermann shook her head. "None whatsoever, officer. Can't you find her?"

"Nope. But we're gonna put out an all points bulletin for her arrest. Boy was she crazy! Did you see all this stuff?" He pointed toward the pile at the foot of the steps.

Mrs. Sipes looked at Mrs. Zimmermann with wide worried eyes. "Mrs. Zimmermann, what do you make of all this? Do you think Mrs. Bigger was a witch?"

Mrs. Zimmermann stared straight at her. "A *what?*"

"A witch. I mean, look at all these things. I can't imagine why else she would have . . ."

Mrs. Zimmermann put her tongue between her teeth and made a *tsk-tsk* sound. She shook her head slowly. "Mrs. Sipes," she said, in a shocked voice, "I don't know what you've been telling your daughter, but this is the twentieth century. There are no such things as witches."

CHAPTER THIRTEEN

When the Pottingers arrived at the Sipes farm later that morning, they found the Sipeses, their eight children, Mrs. Zimmermann, and Rose Rita, all huddled around a radio on the front porch of the farmhouse. They were listening to a radio report on what had come to be known as "the Petoskey witch case." The Pottingers were, of course, pretty tense to begin with, but when they found out that their daughter had, for a little while, been the prisoner of an elderly lunatic who imagined herself to be a witch—well, they really got the jitters. Mrs. Zimmermann did her best to calm them down. She pointed out that, after all, she and Rose Rita were safe, and the whole adventure—terrifying as it had been—was over. It seemed clear that if he could have found some way to do it, Mr. Pottinger would have blamed the whole affair on Mrs. Zimmermann's "screwballishness," but he didn't have time to do any blaming, what with all the fuss and flurry and tearful reunions going on around him. Mr. Sipes, who had come back from his business trip earlier that morning, took Mr. Pottinger out to show him the barn, and the Pottingers were invited to stay for lunch.

Around two that afternoon the Pottingers drove back to New Zebedee with Rose Rita. Rose Rita and Aggie had a tearful farewell at the car window, and they promised to write to each other a lot during the next year. The last thing that Aggie said as the Pottingers were about to drive away was, "I hope you don't get a flat tire. They're awful hard to fix." Mrs. Zimmermann stayed behind. She said, rather mysteriously, that she had some "business to attend to." Rose Rita figured that it had something to do with the magic ring, but she knew from past experience that Mrs. Zimmermann wouldn't tell her anything more until she was darned good and ready.

About a week after she got back to New Zebedee, Rose Rita received a purple-bordered letter in the mail. Inside was a piece of lavender-colored stationery, and on it this message was written:

My dear,

I'm back, and so is Lewis—for the time being. It seems that the pump that supplies the water to his camp broke down, and they're sending the kids home till they get it fixed. Sometime or other, Lewis will be going back for the rest of the camp session, but in the meantime, you are hereby invited to a coming-home-from-camp-for-now party for Lewis at my cottage on Lyon Lake next Saturday. Plan to stay overnight. If it's okay with your folks, I'll be around to get you in Bessie after lunch. It should be a lot of fun. Bring your swimming suit.

Yours,
Florence Zimmermann

PS: Don't bring any presents for Lewis. He's bringing home enough stuff from camp as it is.

Rose Rita had no trouble persuading her mother to let her spend the night at Mrs. Zimmermann's cottage. And so on Saturday off she went, valise in hand, to Lyon Lake. All the way out to the cottage Rose Rita tried to find out if Mrs. Zimmermann had discovered anything about the ring. But Mrs. Zimmermann said nothing. When they pulled into the driveway of the cottage, there was another car parked in front of them. Jonathan's car.

"Hi, Rose Rita! Gee, you look great!" There was Lewis. He was wearing his bathing suit.

"Hi, yourself," Rose Rita yelled, waving. "Where'd you get that sun tan? Out at the camp?"

Lewis grinned happily. He had been hoping she would notice. "Yeah. Hey, hurry up and get into your suit. Last one in is a wet hen!" Lewis reddened and covered his mouth with his hand. He had heard some of the story of Gert Bigger and the ring from Jonathan, and he knew what he had said.

Rose Rita glanced quickly at Mrs. Zimmermann, who was coughing rather loudly and trying to blow her nose at the same time.

As soon as Rose Rita had gotten her suit on, she ran down the long sloping lawn and dived into the water. Lewis was there ahead of her. He was swimming! Back and forth, up and down. It was only dog paddling, but for Lewis, that was something. For as long as Rose Rita had known him, Lewis had been scared of the water. Usually when he went in, he just stood around and splashed, or floated on an inner tube.

Rose Rita was overjoyed. She had always wanted for Lewis to know how to swim, so they could go swimming together. Of course, he was still scared of deep water, but he was getting more confident. Next year, he said, he'd get his Intermediate Swimmer's card for sure.

Later Rose Rita and Lewis were sitting on the lawn with towels wrapped around them. Nearby, on lawn chairs, were Jonathan and Mrs. Zimmermann. Jonathan was wearing his white linen suit, which he only wore on special occasions during the summer. The last special occasion had been V-J Day, so the suit was looking rather yellow, and it smelled of mothballs. Mrs. Zimmermann was wearing a new purple dress. She had thrown away the one she had been wearing on her vacation, because there were so many unpleasant memories associated with it. She looked rested and healthy. On a small table between her and Jonathan was a pitcher of lemonade and a plate heaped with chocolate chip cookies.

Lewis looked at Mrs. Zimmermann with awe. He was dying to ask her what it had felt like to be a chicken, but he couldn't think of any polite way of putting the question. Besides she was likely to be sensitive on the subject. So Lewis just ate his cookie and drank his lemonade and said nothing.

"All right, Florence," said Jonathan, puffing impatiently at his pipe. "We're all dying to know. What did you find out about the ring? Eh?"

Mrs. Zimmermann shrugged. "Almost nothing. I searched high and low in Oley's house, but all I found were these." She dug into a pocket of her dress and handed Jonathan three or four very rusty iron rings.

"What are these?" he said, turning them over. "Are they rejects from Oley's magic ring factory?"

Mrs. Zimmermann laughed. "No . . . at least, I don't think they are. I found them in a bowl in the back of the cupboard in Oley's kitchen. Do you really want to know what I think they are?"

"What?"

"Well, the Vikings used to wear leather breastplates with iron rings sewed to them. They called the breast-plates byrnies, I think. Anyway, these rings look like some I saw once in a museum in Oslo. I think Oley must have dug these up, along with the arrowheads—and the ring."

"Now wait a minute, Florence. I know I've got a beard, but it's not long and white, and I've still got most of my marbles. Are you trying to tell us that the Vikings brought that ring over to America with them?"

"I'm not trying to tell you anything, Weird Beard. I'm just showing you what I found. You can think what you like. I'm just saying that these rings *look* like Viking artifacts. The Vikings roamed all over the world. They even went to Constantinople. And a lot of the treasure of the ancient world found its way there. There are a thousand other ways they might have found the ring, of course. I don't know. As I say, you can think what you darned please."

Mrs. Zimmermann and Jonathan got into a long point-less argument over whether or not the Vikings ever came to America. In the middle of all this, Lewis interrupted.

"Excuse me, Mrs. Zimmermann, but . . ."

Mrs. Zimmermann smiled at Lewis. "Yes, Lewis? What is it?"

"Well, I was just wondering . . . are you sure it really was King Solomon's ring?"

"No, I'm not sure," said Mrs. Zimmermann. "Let's just say that I think it's likely. After all, the ring behaved the way Solomon's ring was supposed to behave. So it probably was that very same ring. On the other hand, there are lots of stories about magic rings that are supposed to have really existed. Some of the stories are true, and some of them are false. It might have been one of the other rings, like the ring of the Nibelungs. Who knows? I am, however, fairly sure that it was magic."

"What did you do with the darned ring?" asked Jonathan.

"Hah! I've been waiting for you to ask that! All righty. If you must know, I melted it down in Oley's cookstove. One of the properties of gold is that it will melt at a fairly low temperature. And from all I know about magic, once a magic ring loses its original shape, it loses its powers too. Just to be on the safe side, however, I put the ring (or what was left of it) in a baby food jar along with some lead sinkers. Then I rented a rowboat and rowed out on Little Traverse Bay, and dropped the jar into the drink. Good riddance to bad rubbish, as my father used to say."

Lewis could not contain himself any longer. He had heard from Rose Rita the story of how Mrs. Zimmermann had failed to remake her magic umbrella, and he felt bad about it. He wanted Mrs. Zimmermann to be the greatest magician in the world. "Mrs. Zimmermann!" he burst out. "How come you wrecked the ring? You could've used it, couldn't you? I mean, it wasn't really evil, was it? You could've done something really good with it, I'll bet!"

Mrs. Zimmermann gave Lewis a sour look. "You know who you sound like, Lewis? You sound like those people who keep telling us that the atomic bomb is a really wonderful thing, that it isn't really evil, though it has been put to evil purposes." Mrs. Zimmermann heaved a deep sigh. "I suppose," she said slowly, "I *suppose* that Solomon's ring—assuming that that's what it really was—could have been put to some good use. I thought about that before I melted the thing down. But I said to myself, 'Do you really think you're such an angelic creature that you could resist the urge to do nasty things with that ring?' Then I asked myself, 'Do you want to sit on the blamed thing for the rest of your life, always worrying and fidgeting for fear someone like Gert Bigger might grab it away from you?' The answer to both those questions was no, and that is why I decided to get rid of the ring. As you may know, Lewis, I don't have much magic power anymore. And you know what? It's a relief! I'm going to spend the rest of my days snapping matches out of the air and trying to beat Weird Beard over here at poker. Not," she added, with a sly glance at Jonathan, "that either of those things takes a great deal of talent to do."

Jonathan stuck out his tongue at Mrs. Zimmermann, and then both of them laughed. It was a happy relaxed sound, and Lewis and Rose Rita joined in.

There was more swimming, and more eating. After the sun went down, Jonathan built a bonfire down on the beach, and they all roasted marshmallows and sang songs. Lewis handed around presents. They were all things he had made at scout camp. He gave Jonathan a copper ashtray, and he gave Mrs. Zimmermann a necklace of purply-white seashells. To Rose Rita he gave a leather belt and a neckerchief slide that he had whittled. It was painted green with yellow spots, and the lump on the front was supposed to look like a toad. Well, at any rate, it had eyes.

Much later that evening, after Lewis and Jonathan had gone home, Rose Rita and Mrs. Zimmermann were sitting by the embers of the bonfire. Out across the darkened lake they could see the lights of other cottages. From somewhere came the sleepy drone of a motorboat.

"Mrs. Zimmermann?" said Rose Rita.

"Yes, my dear? What is it?"

"There's a couple of things I have to ask you. First of all, how come that ring didn't put the old whammy on you the way it did on me when I picked it up? When I gave it to you, you just looked at it as if you couldn't have cared less, and then you stuck it in your pocket. How come?"

Mrs. Zimmermann sighed. Rose Rita heard her snap

her fingers, and she saw the brief tiny flare of a match, and she smelled cigar smoke. "Why wasn't I affected?" said Mrs. Zimmermann, as she puffed. "You know, that's a good question. I guess it's because I'm really happy the way I am. You see, I think a ring like that can only exercise power over someone who isn't satisfied with himself. Or herself."

Rose Rita blushed. She still felt ashamed of what she had tried to do with the ring. "Did . . . did you ever tell Uncle Jonathan what . . . what I was gonna do when you stopped me?"

"No," said Mrs. Zimmermann softly. "I did not. As far as he knows, the ring dragged you off to some mysterious meeting with the devil. Remember, you never actually said what you wanted to do, though it wasn't hard for me to guess. And by the way, don't feel so bad. Lots of people would have wished for worse things than you wished for. Far worse things."

Rose Rita was silent for a while. Finally she said, "Mrs. Zimmermann, do you think I'll have a lousy time in school this fall? And what about when I'm a grownup? Will things be different then?"

"My dear," said Mrs. Zimmermann slowly and deliberately, "I may be a witch, but I'm not a prophet. Seeing into the future was never my line, even when I had my magic umbrella. But I will tell you this: You have a lot of wonderful qualities. When you tried to drive Bessie, for example. Lots of girls your age would've been too chicken even to try. That took guts. It also took guts to break into Mrs. Bigger's store in the hope that you might be able to rescue me. And another thing: The women who are remembered in history, women like Joan of Arc and Molly Pitcher, are not remembered because they spent all their time powdering their noses. As for the rest, you'll just have to wait and see how your life turns out. That's all I can say."

Rose Rita said nothing. She poked in the ashes with a stick while Mrs. Zimmermann smoked. After a while, the two of them got up, kicked some sand over the fire, and went to bed.

About the Author

Many of the events in John Bellairs's books are drawn from things that happened or that he wished *would* happen when he was growing up in Marshall, Michigan.

The Letter, the Witch, and the Ring is the third and final book in the *House with a Clock in Its Walls* trilogy. The two earlier books, *The House with a Clock in Its Walls* and *The Figure in the Shadows*, were both chosen by *The New York Times* as Outstanding Books of the Year.

John Bellairs is the author of several adult books, including *The Face in the Frost*. He lives in Haverhill, Massachusetts, with his wife Priscilla and their son, Frank.

About the Artist

Richard Egielski was born in New York City, where he still makes his home. He studied at Pratt Institute and Parsons School of Design, and is interested in both magazine and book illustration.

The Letter, the Witch, and the Ring is his first book for The Dial Press.

The SPORTS HEROES Library

Football's
SUPER BOWL
CHAMPIONS
I-VIII

Nathan Aaseng

 Lerner Publications Company • Minneapolis

ACKNOWLEDGMENTS: The photographs are reproduced through the courtesy of: pp. 4, 38, 49, 53, Wide World Photos, Inc.; p. 6, Pro Football Hall of Fame; pp. 8, 10, 12, 16, 18, 21, 23, 24, 30, 33, 34, 36, 41, 42, 44, 54, 59, 60, 73, 74, 77, 78, Vernon J. Biever; p. 27, New York Jets Football Club; p. 46, Baltimore Colts; pp. 56, 62 (Russ Russell Photography), 63, Dallas Cowboys; pp. 64, 67, 69, 70, Miami Dolphins.

Cover photograph: Vernon J. Biever

To Elizabeth Petersen

LIBRARY OF CONGRESS CATALOGING IN PUBLICATION DATA

Aaseng, Nathan.
  Football's Super Bowl champions, I-VIII

  (The Sports heroes library)
  Summary: Describes the winning performances of six football teams that have won the Super Bowl from 1967, when it was first played, to 1974.
  1. Super Bowl Game (Football)—History—Juvenile literature. [1. Super Bowl Game (Football)—History. 2. Football—History] I. Title. II. Series.
GV956.2.S8A18   796.332'72   81-13659
ISBN 0-8225-1072-3   AACR2

Manufactured in the United States of America

International Standard Book Number: 0-8225-1072-3
Library of Congress Catalog Card Number: 81-13659

2 3 4 5 6 7 8 9 10 92 91 90 89 88 87 86 85 84 83

Contents

Jan Stenerud's three field goals gave the Chiefs an early lead in Super Bowl IV. Here he boots one over a strong Minnesota rush.

Introduction

Every pro football player hopes to spend at least three hours of his life playing in a Super Bowl game. Each has confidence that he can come up with a key play to help win that glamorous event. And it is good that players have such confidence, because the pressure-filled Super Bowl is no place for the timid.

Football is one of the few major team sports in the United States that decides its champion in just one game. Super Bowl teams do not get a second chance, and one small mistake can ruin their hopes of a championship. Worse yet, the Super Bowl teams have to wait two weeks before they meet. Any athlete will tell you that the waiting is what is hardest on the nerves. After two weeks of answering questions, signing autographs, and thinking about the big game, some athletes are almost worn out before the game starts!

Hall of Famer Red Grange passes against the New York Giants. Except for two seasons, Grange played his entire professional career (1925-1934) with the Chicago Bears.

Because of its history, football's championship also includes an extra measure of rivalry. The National Football League (NFL) was formed in the 1920s. It struggled through hard times and took years to develop into a popular league. But gradually the NFL became a first-class organization with a history of stars such as Red Grange, Bronko Nagurski, and Sammy Baugh.

The American Football League (AFL) was formed in 1960. That was the fourth try at starting a league to compete with the NFL. At first the new league had trouble gaining respect. People laughed at the comical uniforms of the Denver Broncos with stripes running up and down on the socks.

And the New York Titans could only attract a few hundred fans in a city of millions. But the AFL was wealthy enough to outbid the NFL for top college stars like Alabama's Joe Namath, who signed in 1965.

Soon the AFL was claiming that its teams were as good as the NFL teams. But the NFL shrugged off the AFL as a "Mickey Mouse" league of second-rate teams. But since the two leagues never played each other, neither could prove they were right.

In 1966 the New York Giants of the NFL angered the AFL by signing one of their players, Buffalo kicker Pete Gogolak. So the AFL decided to get even by signing NFL stars. With the two leagues fighting over them, players started to command huge salaries. Then in June 1966, the owners avoided the price war by merging the two leagues. And it was decided that the champions of the leagues would meet at the end of the season to determine which was the better team in pro football.

At first this contest was called the AFL-NFL World Championship Game. But just one day before the game was to be played, Lamar Hunt, owner of the Kansas City Chiefs, happened to be watching his daughter bouncing a new toy called a Superball. That gave Hunt the idea of calling the championship

Football commissioner Pete Rozelle (left) presents Green Bay coach Vince Lombardi with the first Super Bowl championship trophy. From Super Bowl V on, the prize would be called the Vince Lombardi Trophy.

game the "Superbowl." Writers and fans started using the term, and the league officially named the title game "Super Bowl" in 1971. And finally fans had the chance to compare the AFL to the NFL.

Since the 1966 merger, there has been more interconference play between the AFL (now the American Football Conference) and the NFL (now the National Football Conference). But the Super Bowl remains a fight for conference pride as well as team pride. And the pressure of a Super Bowl grows even more as players look back on the role of luck in past games. Fumbles, penalties, an offical's error, or the bounce of a ball have all helped to wreck that most important game for the players. Bad breaks and mistakes would often seem to pile up on one team until the game became a one-sided romp.

All of the pressure has caused many teams to play cautiously in the Super Bowl, and that type of play resulted in some dull games. As far as producing exciting, well-played football, the Super Bowl has, in fact, rarely lived up to its name.

The Super Bowl, however, remains the showcase of the top teams and players in pro football. And it is still a tremendous test of players' abilities.

The following chapters introduce the teams and the players who faced the pressure, met the challenge, and won Super Bowl crowns in the first eight years of Super Bowl competition.

Packer quarterback Bart Starr barks out signals in Super Bowl II.

1
Green Bay
Packers
SUPER BOWL I
SUPER BOWL II

NFL teams were not fond of the Green Bay Packers in 1967. The Packers pushed everyone around, especially in championship games. But when it came to the first Super Bowl, the league's envy of the Packers turned to pride. The NFL could not have been happier when Green Bay was going to defend their league's honor against the AFL.

Ever since Coach Vince Lombardi's arrival in 1959, the Packers had played basic, tough football. They did nothing fancy. They simply blocked and tackled better than anyone else. Lombardi's young

Lombardi and Starr—the general and his field general—discuss game strategy against Cleveland in the 1965 title game. Together they led Green Bay to five NFL championships and two Super Bowl titles.

Packer team lost to the Philadelphia Eagles, 17-13, in the 1960 NFL championship. That was the last play-off game Lombardi ever lost. In 1961 the Packers creamed the New York Giants, 37-0, for the title. They repeated with a 16-7 win over the Giants in 1962 and a 23-12 thrashing of the Cleveland Browns in 1965.

By 1966 the Packer power runners Jim Taylor and Paul Hornung were losing some of their skills. But they could still make yardage by following

12

their fine linemen on sweeps around end. More and more, however, Green Bay relied on the skills of quarterback Bart Starr. Starr, who had been given little chance of making it as a pro when he had started out in 1956, was voted the NFL's Most Valuable Player in 1966. That year his accurate passing and skill at avoiding interceptions had led Green Bay to a 12-2 record. Then in the NFL championship against Dallas, Starr completely picked apart the Cowboy defense. He completed 19 of 28 passes for 304 yards and gave Green Bay enough of a cushion to hold on to a 34-27 win. In past years, such a win would have sent the Packers into a relaxing winter of celebration. But 1966 produced another champion, the AFL Kansas City Chiefs, who Green Bay would still have to beat. A loss to that new league would ruin the season for the proud Packers.

The Chiefs, meanwhile, could hardly wait for a chance to show how good they were. With nine All-Pro starters, Kansas City was by far the best team in their league. Quarterback Len Dawson could score quickly on strikes to ends Otis Taylor and Fred Arbanas. And the defense, anchored by 6-foot, 7-inch Buck Buchanon and swift linebacker Bobby Bell, could be overpowering.

The two weeks before the big game seemed to last forever as fans boasted about which team and which league were better. Then on January 15, 1967, the Chiefs and the Packers headed for Memorial Coliseum in Los Angeles for the kickoff. The Chiefs ran onto the field bursting with anger because of a clever plan by Coach Hank Stram. Just before kickoff, Stram had passed out hats with mouse ears to his players in the locker room. The team wore the hats while listening to the Mickey Mouse theme song. Every note reminded them of the sneers they had heard from the NFL for the last seven years.

The fired-up Chiefs went after the Packers on Green Bay's first offensive possession. Their pass rush smothered Bart Starr twice for losses, forcing Green Bay to punt. During that same series, Green Bay's best receiver, Boyd Dowler, hobbled off the field with an injury. His replacement, Max McGee, had caught only four passes all season long.

After stopping Kansas City's offense, Green Bay started to move the ball. They drove to the Chief's 37-yard line where they faced an important third-down play. The Packers needed a first down to get within scoring range. Starr drifted back to pass and spotted McGee bursting between two defenders. Starr hit McGee with a perfect pass, and Max never slowed down until he reached the end zone. Green Bay led, 7 to 0.

But before the NFL could say, "I told you so," the Chiefs marched back. Running back Mike Garrett wriggled away from three Packers on a screen pass and scampered for 17 yards. Dawson followed with a pass to fleet Otis Taylor, who raced to the Packer 7. From there Dawson faked a running play and looked to the end zone. There he saw Green Bay's Willie Wood left with two Chief receivers. Wood could not cover them both, and Curtis McClinton caught the 7-yard pass to tie the game.

The Packers struck back immediately as Starr connected with Carroll Dale on a 64-yard pass. But a penalty flag had been dropped, and the play was called back because of illegal procedure against Green Bay. Undisturbed, Starr took his time on a long drive to the Chief 24. On another key third down play, Starr flipped to Elijah Pitts for the first down. With the ball on the 14, Green Bay sent their most famous play into action. All-Pro guards Fuzzy Thurston and Jerry Kramer pulled out of the line and charged to the outside. Then bruising fullback Jim Taylor ran behind, waiting

Green Bay fullback Jim Taylor goes airborne through the Kansas City line in Super Bowl I.

for them to clear a path. The guards handled their men perfectly, and Taylor ran for the touchdown.

Just before halftime, Kansas City took to the air. Three passes covered 50 yards and set Mike Mercer up for a 31-yard field goal. The Chiefs went into halftime trailing only 14 to 10. But even more surprising to most fans was that the Chiefs had outgained Green Bay, 181 yards to 164.

At that point, Kansas City may have thought they had proved they could play as well as Green Bay. But there was still one half left to play, and Green Bay had found a soft spot in the Chiefs' defense— their cornerbacks. With a little better blocking and tackling, they knew they could handle this AFL team.

As the second half started, Len Dawson kept his team's hopes alive by scrambling into Green Bay territory. On the third down, he found himself surrounded by a fierce Packer pass rush. Dawson desperately hurled a pass near the left sidelines, but it was tipped by a linebacker and grabbed by safety Willie Wood. Wood raced toward the Chiefs' end zone, and he was not stopped until he reached the 5-yard line. One play later, Elijah Pitts, replacing Paul Hornung, burst into the end zone for a 21 to 10 Packer lead.

From then on, the Green Bay defense took over. Veteran linemen Willie Davis and Henry Jordan rushed Len Dawson into making poor second-half passes. Then when the Green Bay offense got the ball with the Packer blockers shutting down the Kansas City pass rush, Starr went to work on the Chief cornerbacks. Max McGee grabbed three tosses on one drive and finished up with a 13-yard

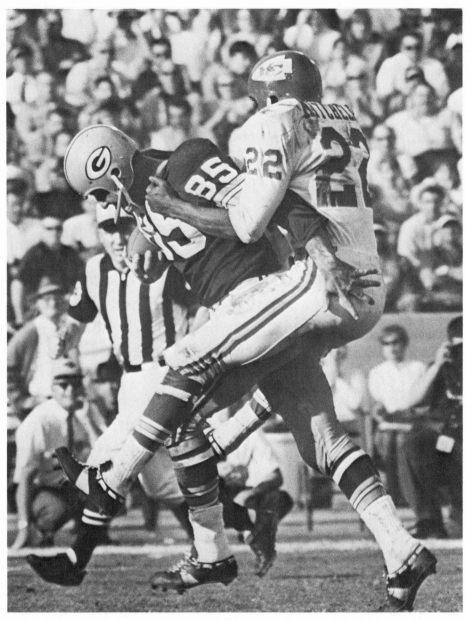

Max McGee, the unlikely hero of Super Bowl I, carries Chief corner-back Willie Mitchell with him after catching a Bart Starr pass. In the game, McGee grabbed seven passes for 138 yards and two touch-downs.

catch for a touchdown. Pitts ran one yard for the final points in the 35 to 10 victory.

The Packers felt as much relief as joy at beating the team from the unknown league. But few people were surprised that Bart Starr had done such a skillful job of moving his team. His 16 completions in 23 attempts for 250 yards earned him the game's Most Valuable Player Award and was a typical fine Starr performance. Far more incredible was Green Bay's other hero, Max McGee. McGee had caught seven passes for 138 yards and two touchdowns— almost twice as many passes as he had during the entire season!

To most people, the game had indicated that the AFL was not as close to the NFL in skill as they had thought. True, the Chiefs had some fine players, but they did not have enough of them. Kansas City had a few obvious weaknesses, and no team could afford *any* weaknesses when playing a Lombardi team!

The next year, there were a few new faces on the Packer team. Jim Grabowski and Donny Anderson took over most of the ball carrying. But for the most part, it was the same machine-like unit that had won the year before. Green Bay pulled out another tense win over the Cowboys to reach the Super Bowl. In the game's closing seconds, Starr's quarterback sneak on fourth down had won the game, 21-17, on the frozen Green Bay field.

Starr, however, was not quite up to form that season. Part of his problem may have been that his pass protection was breaking down. The Cowboys, for example, had tackled him behind the line eight times in the play-off game. This weak protection gave hope to Green Bay's Super Bowl opponent, the Oakland Raiders. The Raiders' defensive line—Ben Davidson, Tom Keating, Ike Lassiter and Dan Birdwell—had recorded an incredible record of 69 quarterback sacks in a season. And Oakland hoped that this bunch could destroy Green Bay's passing game when the two teams met in the Orange Bowl in Miami.

By game time on January 14, 1968, the Packers knew something that few people in football had suspected. Coach Lombardi had worked himself near exhaustion, and he was ready to retire. So the 1968 Super Bowl would be the last game for the Lombardi Packers. With that fact on the players' minds, there was no chance the Packers would take the game lightly.

Following the blocking of standout guard Gale Gillingham (68), Green Bay running back Travis Williams looks for an opening in Oakland's Super Bowl II defense.

During the game, Green Bay's linemen blocked so well that Starr was hardly bothered by Oakland's pass rush. On running plays, the Packers headed straight for the Raiders' strongest man, Ben Davidson. That was their way of daring the Raiders to stop them. Then Green Bay bulled downfield for 39- and 20-yard field goals by Don Chandler. Meanwhile the defense, led by the rock-hard middle linebacker Ray Nitschke, stopped the Raiders' running game. With tight coverage by defender Herb

21

Adderley on Oakland's fine end Fred Biletnikoff, the Raiders' passing game also stalled.

Frustrated by their surprising lack of a pass rush, Oakland sent their linebackers in on a blitz. Green Bay blocked the extra pass rushers, however, and Starr found end Boyd Dowler unguarded. Then Dowler took Starr's pass and raced 62 yards to make the score 13 to 0. But the Raiders desperately stayed in the game on a 23-yard touchdown pass to Bill Miller. The Raider defense then stiffened and forced Green Bay to punt. Roger Bird of Oakland fumbled the punt, and Green Bay recovered. Chandler turned the Raider mistake into a 16 to 7 half-time lead with a 43-yard field goal.

In the second half, the Packers drove steadily downfield. They bullied their way to the Raider 40-yard line where they faced a third down and a couple of yards to go for a first down. The Raiders braced themselves to bring down Donny Anderson as he ran into the line. But Anderson did not have the ball! One of Starr's trademarks was to try a pass when the defense expected a run on third down and short yardage, and that was one of those times. Starr passed 35 yards to Max McGee to set up a score by Anderson. Then Chandler booted a fourth field goal for 26-7.

The Packers' famous power sweep rumbles into action against the Raiders as Gale Gillingham (68) and Jerry Kramer (64) pave the way for Donny Anderson.

In the fourth quarter, Herb Adderley finished off the game in style. After holding Biletnikoff to only two catches for just 10 yards, he stepped in front of an Oakland pass. Herb caught the ball and found a clear field ahead. His 60-yard interception return for a score made the game a runaway at 33 to 7. Then Oakland added another touchdown pass to Miller to make the final score 33 to 14.

Starr again won respect for his fine leadership and for the second straight year was awarded the Most Valuable Player Award. He had gained 202 yards while completing 13 of 24 passes.

All-Pro linemen Forrest Gregg (left) and Jerry Kramer hoist Coach Lombardi to their shoulders to celebrate Green Bay's Super Bowl win over Oakland. Fourteen years later, Gregg would coach the Cincinnati Bengals in Super Bowl XVI.

The 1968 Super Bowl was a fitting end to Lombardi's Packer career. He had demanded perfection, and he had gotten it. Green Bay had made no mistakes. There had been no fumbles or interceptions. Although the game seemed to indicate that the NFL would continue to dominate the Super Bowl, Lombardi's retirement would spell both the end of Green Bay's success and the end of the NFL victories.

2
New York Jets
SUPER BOWL III

The New York Jets of 1968 had come a long way from the ragtag outfit that had started the 1960 season. A few players, such as wide receiver Don Maynard and linebacker Larry Grantham, had suffered through those difficult first years of the AFL. They remembered the laughter and the empty stands when their team had played as the Titans.

The big changes for the team started in 1963. Weeb Ewbank, who had coached the Baltimore Colts to NFL championships in 1958 and 1959, came over to lead the team. The new owner, Sonny Werblin, went after top college players and also found a respectable home for the games, Shea Stadium. Werblin wanted people to forget about the old days, so he changed the name of the team from Titans to Jets.

The new management quickly began to build their team. In 1964 they signed 220-pound fullback Matt Snell, linebacker Ralph Baker, defensive end Gerry Philbin, and kicker Jim Turner. Then the next season they made their most important trade ever. The Jets sent quarterback Jerry Rhome to Houston for the Oilers' Number One draft choice. With that choice, the Jets claimed Joe Namath, the fabulous quarterback from Alabama. Then they outbid the NFL for Joe's services, shelling out an unheard-of $400,000. New York also grabbed wide receiver George Sauer, defensive end Verlon Biggs, and defensive back Al Atkinson. Once they got those players, they were in business.

In 1968 the Jets won eight of their last nine games to finish with an 11-3 record. They relied heavily on Namath's passes to score points. Namath, in turn, counted on his determined linemen to give him time to throw. The Jets protected him so well that they were often called the "Mother Hens." That year New York beat the Oakland Raiders, 27-23, for a Super Bowl spot.

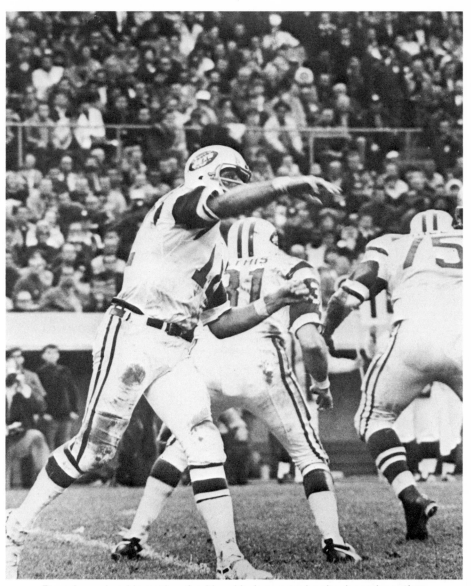

Broadway Joe Namath—the New York quarterback whose boasting made many NFL fans want the Colts to shut him up for good—fires a pass from behind a well-protected Jet pocket.

After Green Bay had taken apart the AFL's finest teams two years in a row, few gave the Jets a chance to win the Super Bowl. The Jets, after all, were not an overpowering team, even in the AFL. Their starting lineup had only three All-Pros—Namath, Sauer, and Philbin. And the Jets' Super Bowl opponent, the Baltimore Colts, seemed even stronger than the previous NFL champions.

Sprinkled with veterans from the old 1959 championship team, the Colts had won 13 of 14 games. And their iron defense had held three opponents scoreless during the year. Having seen the Colts wallop the Cleveland Browns, 34-0, for the NFL title, fans shuddered to think what they would do to the Jets.

The Jets' offense seemed to be easy pickings for the Colt defense. Baltimore could choke off a passing game with a zone defense manned by such greats as Bobby Boyd, Rick Volk, and Jerry Logan. Huge Bubba Smith could give quarterbacks fits with his pass rush, and hardhitting linebacker Mike Curtis patrolled the middle of the field. Most frightening of all was the Colts' eight-man blitz, which they had pulled off successfully against passing teams like New York all season long.

Surprisingly, the Jets were confident that they

would win. Joe Namath made headlines by guaranteeing a Jet victory, and he angered the Colts by saying that their quarterback, Earl Morrall, would be third-string on the Jets.

Namath, however, almost had to eat his words when the Jets and the Colts met in Miami's Orange Bowl on January 12, 1969. Led by the pass-catching of tank-like John Mackey and the running of Tom Matte, Baltimore drove down the field. They set up within easy field-goal range of Lou Michaels, but the kicker missed a 29-yard try.

"No problem," the Colts shrugged, as they recovered a Jet fumble on the New York 12. When Morrall dropped back to pass, he saw that Jet defender Randy Beverly had been beaten by Colt end Willie Richardson. Morrall threw, expecting a touchdown, but Jet Al Atkinson tipped the pass right into Beverly's arms for an interception.

New York then took the ball and surprised the Colts with their running game. They found a play that worked and ran it all afternoon. Rarely could the Colts stop a Matt Snell run to the left side of his line. There the blocks of one-time Colt reject Winston Hill almost always cleared a path for Snell. The Jets drove 80 yards with Snell banging the final 4 yards behind Hill for a 7 to 0 lead.

Namath hands off to Matt Snell, the powerful Jet fullback who scored the first touchdown in Super Bowl III.

Baltimore's Matte then brought his team to life, popping through the arms of a tackler at his own 26. He picked up speed and rumbled all the way to New York's 18. For the third time, the Colts had a great chance to score. But this time Jet defender John Sample killed the drive with a tumbling interception.

Baltimore's defense continued to get the ball back to their offense in good shape, and the Colts continued to threaten. Morrall tried for a quick score on a trick play. He pitched the ball to Matte, who ran toward the side, stopped, and tossed back to Morrall. The Jets, thinking Matte would run, were caught flat-footed. Colt receiver Jimmy Orr was left all alone by the goal line, screaming at Morrall to throw to him. But one of the few people in the stadium who did not see Orr was Morrall, the one who really counted. Instead Morrall threw off to the other side, where the ball was picked off by the Jets again.

At halftime the score read Jets 7, Colts 0. With all their scoring chances, the Colts could have wrapped the game up by then. Instead it was New York that held the upper hand. Then in the second half, Jet linebacker Ralph Baker jolted the Colts further when he recovered Matte's fumble at the Colt 33. Namath found openings in the Colts' zone defense and moved his team in close enough for a field goal by Jim Turner. Now it was Jets 10, Colts 0.

The Jet defense, growing in confidence, easily stopped the Colts on the next series. Then Namath went to work again. The Colts expected him to throw to his favorite target, Don Maynard. They did not know that Maynard had a bad leg and was just being used as a decoy. So while the Colts watched the injured Maynard, Namath pierced the

Colt zone defense with passes to George Sauer. Again they drew within range of Turner, who kicked a field goal for a 13-0 lead.

The desperate Colts then called on sore-armed veteran John Unitas to take over for the slumping Morrall. But it was obvious that the old Colt hero was not at his best. Unitas missed his receivers, and the ball went back to Namath. Again the Jets drove downfield. Snell ground out important first downs with his runs, and Namath again found Sauer in the clear for a long gain on a pass. Again the Jets drew within field goal range, and again Turner came through. Jets 16, Colts 0. The football experts looked on in amazement as the Jets kept building their lead over the 17-point favorites.

Finally Unitas passed the Colts downfield, where they plunged the final yard for a touchdown. With less than four minutes left, the Colts recovered the on-side kick and marched to New York's 19. At last it seemed the Colts had come to life. But the Jets' defense stopped Unitas and forced an incomplete pass on fourth down. The Jets took over, and Snell used up valuable time with his crunching runs. New York easily held on for a 16-7 victory.

Joe Namath's plays in the Super Bowl had shown that he could be an All-Pro in either league. He had

Snell breaks a Colt tackle en route to a big afternoon. His outstanding performance made Baltimore take note of New York's running attack and gave Namath more time to throw.

completed 17 of 28 passes for 206 yards and also won Most Valuable Player honors. Equally impressive was the work of Matt Snell, who had bulldozed through the stubborn Colt defense for 121 yards in 30 carries. Almost unnoticed in the Jet victory was the quiet work of Dave Herman. Herman was normally an offensive guard, but he had been asked to play tackle in the Super Bowl. Though he had no pro experience at that position, he limited Baltimore's great Bubba Smith to just one harmless quarterback sack.

Joe Namath could not understand why the game was called one of the great upsets in modern sports. After all, he *had* told everyone what was going to happen!

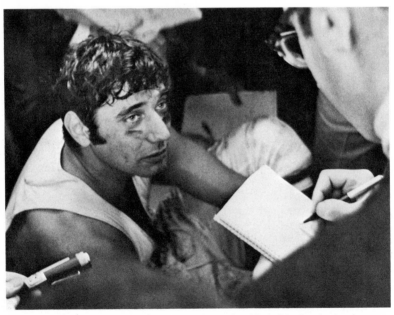

Joe had told them so! His guarantee of a New York win had come true, silencing many of his doubters.

3
Kansas City Chiefs
SUPER BOWL IV

The Kansas City Chiefs came into the 1970 Super Bowl with huge linemen, tiny running backs, and a score to settle. Most of their top players had been on the team that had lost the first Super Bowl game, and the memory of it still stung. The 290-pound Jim Tyrer still led a strong offensive line, and the equally large Buck Buchanan still took his place in the Chiefs' front wall of defense. Bobby Bell, Jim Lynch, Ed Budde, Otis Taylor, and Len Dawson all knew what it was like to lose that important game. This time they came armed with a few new weapons. Curly Culp and Aaron Brown made a huge defensive line even more awesome.

Chief quarterback Lenny Dawson calls a play in a Kansas City huddle during Super Bowl IV.

Willie Lanier plugged up the gaps from his middle-linebacker spot, and Jim Marsalis added much-needed help at defensive back.

Kansas City counted on its giant lines to over-power its opponent. Once the blocking paths had been cleared, a group of pro football's smallest runners—Mike Garrett, Warren McVea, and Robert Holmes—all under 5 feet, 10 inches, darted through the line. Kansas City liked to call its attack "the offense of the future." They used countless shifts of position, new formations, and trick plays. Their combination of brute strength and trickery helped them to become the first second-place team to play in the Super Bowl. The Chiefs had lost their division to the Oakland Raiders. But under a new play-off format system in which the divisional winners played the second-place teams, the Chiefs had been given a second chance. They had come back to defeat the Raiders in the AFL championship game, 17-7.

Kansas City's opponent that January 11, 1970, afternoon in New Orleans was the new NFL power, the Minnesota Vikings. While not exceptionally large, the Vikings' defense was made up of men so fast and so talented that they were considered the best unit in football. With quarterback Joe Kapp providing the offensive spark, the Vikings had blasted Cleveland, 27-7, to win the NFL title.

Kansas City quarterback Dawson had even more pressure on him than usual as the game started. It bothered him terribly that his name had been mentioned in rumors about gambling. Dawson also felt the rivalry between the AFL and NFL very deeply. Dawson remembered the day when he had been cut by the Pittsburgh Steelers back in 1958.

Minnesota's Joe Kapp tries an off-balance pass to Bill Brown while Ron Yary (73) tries to block Jerry Mays (75). Kapp's unusual passing style and wobbly passes had been good enough to take the Vikings to a 12-2 season and the NFL championship—but not to defeat the determined Chiefs in the Super Bowl.

Now he was determined to prove that the Steelers and the whole NFL had made a mistake in not giving him a chance to play.

In the game, Dawson avoided the Viking pass rush by throwing quick, short passes. Little by little, he chipped away at the Viking defense and brought his team into Minnesota territory. The drive stalled, though, and Jan Stenerud was called on to kick a difficult 48-yard field goal. It was a tough spot for the young Norwegian, who was more famous for his collegiate ski jumping than for his football playing. But he came through with a fine kick, and Kansas City led 3 to 0 after one quarter.

Meanwhile the Minnesota runners were being smothered by Kansas City's "stack" defense. The Chiefs were one of the first teams to move their defensive linemen into different positions, and Buck Buchanan often lined up straight across from the opposing center. Minnesota found it hard to move against this type of defense and had to punt back to the Chiefs. Again Dawson moved his team into field goal range, and Stenerud stretched the lead to 6-0.

Kansas City's next drive seemed to be going nowhere until the Chiefs tried a trick play. Wide receiver Frank Pitts circled around into the Chiefs' backfield and took a handoff. Then he continued running around right end behind fine blocking. The Vikings were caught unawares, and Pitts ran for 19 yards and a first down. For a third time, though, the Vikings' defense stiffened near the end zone, and Kansas City settled for a third Stenerud field goal.

The Chiefs received a huge lift when Minnesota's Charlie West fumbled the following kickoff. Kansas City recovered at the Viking 19, and this time the overworked Viking defense could not stop them. Garrett popped through for the final five yards behind Mo Moorman's block to open an incredible 16 to 0 halftime lead over the favored Vikings.

Minnesota then regrouped and came out fired up for the second half. They drove downfield against the Chiefs with Dave Osborn twisting and spinning for the touchdown from four yards away. With the score at 16-7, the Vikings seemed to be turning the game around. Their defense forced the Chiefs into another difficult third-down situation.

Again the Chiefs went to their bag of tricks. The end-around play with Frank Pitts worked once more, thanks to fine blocking by tackle Dave Hill, and the Chiefs had a key first down. At the Viking 46-yard line, quarterback Dawson hit Otis Taylor

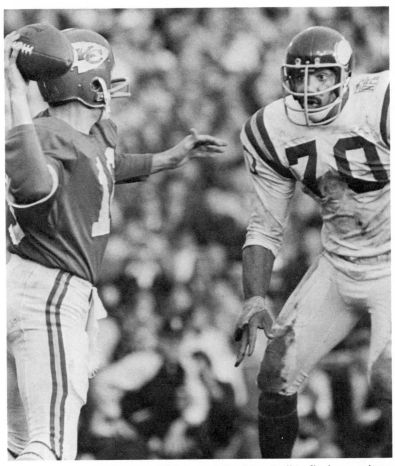

Lenny Dawson looks over Viking end Jim Marshall to find a receiver.

with another one of his quick passes. This time
Taylor broke away from Viking defender Earsell
Mackbee and raced down the right sidelines. He
avoided a last attempted tackle by Minnesota's
Karl Kassulke and ran for a touchdown.

The officials signal the touchdown that Otis Taylor just scored on a 46-yard pass from Dawson. Taylor, whose touchdown broke the game open for the Chiefs, caught six passes for 81 yards.

With a 23-7 lead, it was now up to the Kansas City defense to do its job. The Chiefs stopped the Vikings from any further scoring and finally sent quarterback Joe Kapp to the sidelines with a shoulder injury.

After the game, Len Dawson must have felt like a new man. His passing performance of 12 completions in 17 attempts for 142 yards made him the fourth quarterback in a row to win the Super Bowl's

Most Valuable Player Award. And shortly afterward, he was cleared of all rumors of gambling.

It was actually not the offense of the future that had stopped the Vikings as much as the *defense* of the future. Kansas City's stack had held the Vikings to 67 yards running, had forced three interceptions, and had recovered two fumbles. In that last game before the two leagues merged into one National Football League, Kansas City was proud to have finished their league's existence on a winning note.

Colt quarterback Earl Morrall can't get away from the Cowboy rush in Super Bowl V.

4
Baltimore Colts
SUPER BOWL V

Baltimore tackle Bob Vogel admitted that the 1970 Colt team was "far from the best" of the great Colt champions. That group did not have the talent that had won the NFL crown for Baltimore in 1958 on the overtime plunge by Alan Ameche. The team lacked the power of the group that had lost all of its quarterbacks in 1965 but had still come close to beating the champion Green Bay Packers. The great veterans of those teams were either retired—like football's top lineman Jim Parker —or getting old—like quarterback John Unitas. Only a handful of new stars were on hand to take their places. The best of these were linebacker

Hall of Famer Johnny Unitas sets up to throw. The 1971 Super Bowl would be Johnny U's last championship game.

Ted Hendricks—who at a slim 6 feet, 7 inches was called the "Mad Stork"—and Ray May.

But what the Colts lacked in talent, they made up for in courage and determination. That season the Colts had joined the Browns and the Steelers in moving to the American Football Conference with the old AFL teams. Still steaming over their embarrassing defeat in Super Bowl III, they went after their new conference rivals with a fury. In fact, they had eliminated the last remaining AFL team from the play-offs when they won the AFC championship. A 68-yard scoring pass from Unitas to wide receiver Ray Perkins helped down the Oakland Raiders, 27-17.

Because of their aging players, it seemed that this January 17, 1971, contest would be the Colts' last chance for a Super Bowl win. And as it turned out, they nearly bumbled the game away to their opponents, the Dallas Cowboys. The only thing that kept the Colts in the game was that Dallas was equally generous. The game was so filled with mistakes, turnovers, and blunders that it has been called the "Stupor Bowl." While the action on the artificial turf of Miami's Orange Bowl was sloppy, it also made for some strange and exciting plays.

Dallas linebacker Chuck Howley forced the first mistake when he intercepted a pass from Unitas in the first quarter and returned it to the Colt 46. But the great Colt defense not only held their ground, they pushed the Cowboys back. Linebacker Mike Curtis and 285-pound end Bubba Smith led the charge that swamped the Cowboy offense. Dallas was shoved all the way back to their own 31 and had to punt. Baltimore's Ron Gardin tried to return the punt, but the ball slipped out of his hands. Dallas recovered in perfect scoring position at the Colt 9. Again Baltimore's defense stopped the Cowboys, who settled for a 14-yard field goal by Mike Clark.

Minutes later, following a long pass to Bob Hayes, the former Olympic sprinter, the Cowboys threatened again at the Colt 12. But the stubborn Colts again pointed them in the other direction. Clark had to boot a 30-yard kick to give his team a 6-0 lead.

John Unitas then went to the pass to get his team moving. He aimed for wide receiver Eddie Hinton and fired. The pass sailed far too high, but Hinton jumped and got a finger on it. The ball then apparently tipped the hand of Cowboy defender Mel Renfro and fell into the arms of Colt tight end John Mackey. The big receiver sped down-field with his unexpected catch, untouched, and completed a 75-yard scoring play. Typical of that mistake-prone game, the Colts missed the extra point. So the score was tied at 6 to 6.

Unitas fumbled on the next Baltimore possession, and Dallas recovered on the Colt 29. For once

After scoring the Colts' first touchdown in Super Bowl V, John Mackey charges out of the end zone, holding the ball high.

the Cowboys started moving forward. Dan Reeves came up with a fine catch for 17 yards. This set up a 7-yard touchdown pass from Craig Morton to running back Duane Thomas. Now it was Dallas 13, Colts 6.

Shortly after that play, Unitas was knocked down as he tried to throw a pass. Mel Renfro intercepted the ball, and Unitas had to be helped from the field. When the Colts got the ball back, they sent Earl Morrall to replace Unitas. Morrall had been in the league a long time and had enjoyed several fine seasons. But all of this had been nearly for-gotten because of his poor game in Super Bowl III, and Morrall was eager to make up for that game.

As time ran out in the half, Morrall sped his team downfield. His first pass was good for 26 yards to Eddie Hinton. Then he connected with Roy Jefferson for 21. The Colts drove to a first down on the Cowboys' two-yard line. But three straight running plays went nowhere. Instead of trying for a field goal on fourth down, the Colts tried to tie the score with a pass. It fell incomplete, and the Colts came away with no points after their fine drive.

In the second half, the fans were treated to another series of "follow the bouncing ball" plays. Baltimore wasted no time in fumbling the kickoff. Then Dallas took over at the Colt 31, but they handed the ball right back on a Duane Thomas fumble. From there Baltimore drove within field-goal range and sent in rookie kicker Jim O'Brien to try for the three points. The kick fell short, but it put the Cowboys in poor position when the ball rolled dead only a foot from the Dallas end zone. Dallas tried to move the ball but was forced to punt, giving the Colts good field position. A 45-yard pass to Tom Nowatzke put them right on the Cowboys' doorstep. But Morrall's next pass was intercepted in the end zone by Chuck Howley, who was playing the finest game of his All-Pro career.

Although disappointed, the Colts did not give up, and they tried one of their trick plays after getting the ball back. Morrall pitched the ball to Sam Havrilak, a halfback with a good throwing arm. Then Havrilak stopped and threw a pass to Eddie Hinton, who was breaking for the end zone. Hinton caught the ball. But before he could reach the end zone, Dallas' Cornell Green knocked the ball out of his grasp. Colts and Cowboys leap-frogged over each other in a mad scramble after the ball, but it kept squirting away. Dallas finally recovered it in the end zone.

The Colts' extraordinary bad luck finally ended in the fourth period when their fine safety, Rick Volk, picked off a deflected Cowboy pass and ran it all the way to the Dallas three-yard line. This time big fullback Tom Nowatzke finally broke through Dallas' goal-line defense and barreled over for the score. At last Baltimore had broken through for a score to tie the game!

As the game drew to a close, however, it seemed like the Colts had wasted too many opportunities.

The Cowboys were driving for the winning score with two minutes left in the game. They reached the Colt 48 and needed only a first down or two to set up Mike Clark for the winning field goal. Instead the fierce Baltimore defense sent the Cowboys retreating again. A holding penalty and a quarterback sack dumped the Cowboys all the way back on their own 27!

From there it was almost hopeless for Dallas to try and get a quick score. Most fans thought they would play it safe, run out the clock, and wait for a chance to win in overtime. But Craig Morton spotted Dan Reeves in the open and threw the ball to him. The ball played one last slippery trick in the game and bounced off Reeves. Baltimore's All-Pro Mike Curtis caught the ball and returned it to the Cowboy 28.

By this time, Baltimore was convinced that it was foolish to take chances. They gave the ball to fullback Norm Bulaich on simple, straight-ahead plays. The 220-pounder clutched the ball tightly and squeezed out three yards.

With just a few seconds left, Baltimore sent their kicker, Jim O'Brien, into the game. Dallas knew that O'Brien was a rookie and would probably be very nervous about such an important kick.

So they called time-out to make him wait a little longer and get even more nervous. And O'Brien certainly *was* nervous. He even bent down to pick up some blades of grass to throw in the air to see from which direction the wind was blowing. O'Brien, unfortunately, had forgotten they were playing on artificial surface!

The holder for the kick was the old pro, Earl Morrall. He calmly told O'Brien not to worry about

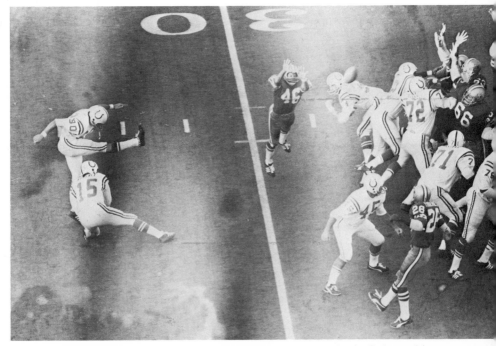

Under more pressure than he'd ever known before, Colt rookie kicker Jim O'Brien boots a 32-yard field goal in the final moments of Super Bowl V.

the wind and just kick the ball straight. O'Brien did, and the ball rose over a tower of Cowboys desperately trying to block the kick. That ball veered slightly to the right but stayed on target. And the Colts won 16 to 13!

The game, spoiled by six fumbles and six interceptions, might not have been a very well-played game. But the Colts' victory has ranked as the most thrilling Super Bowl in the game's history.

The kick is good! Kicker Jim O'Brien (80) and holder Earl Morrall (15) join their teammates in celebrating the kick that gave Baltimore the world championship.

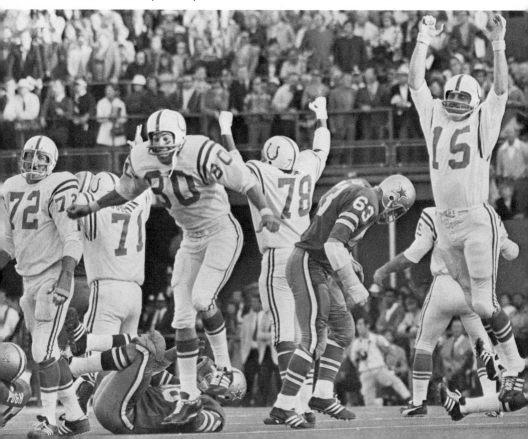

5
Dallas Cowboys
SUPER BOWL VI

The Dallas Cowboys of 1971 must have been the most frustrated team in football. Every year they came so close to being champions, but they always ended up being labeled losers. In both 1966 and 1967, a great Green Bay team had just squeaked past them to win the title. The following two years, they earned play-off spots but lost to the Cleveland Browns. In 1970 the Cowboys nearly won the Super Bowl before their mistakes cost them a win. Dallas' great defensive tackle, Bob Lilly, had best shown his team's feelings when he flung his helmet far downfield in disgust at the end of that Super Bowl loss.

Dallas coach Tom Landry built the Cowboys from an expansion team in 1960 to the NFL runner-up in 1966. Although they had been in the play-offs for six years in a row, second best was the most the Cowboys could accomplish until facing Miami in Super Bowl VI.

But the Cowboys' quiet, serious coach, Tom Landry, was not one to be discouraged. He kept studying ways to make his team better. In 1971 the Cowboys again reached the play-offs. Their "Doomsday Defense" smothered the San Francisco 49ers, 14-3, to win the NFC title and a spot in the Super Bowl.

Dallas' offense was led by Roger Staubach, their third starting quarterback in four years. "Roger the Dodger" had a habit of turning bad plays into long gains with his scrambling. Pass rushers would storm past the Cowboy blockers to pounce on Staubach, only to watch him scoot past and run downfield. When he had time to pass, Roger threw the ball so accurately that he was the NFC's top-rated passer.

Dallas' ground attack took advantage of three fine running backs. Duane Thomas, Calvin Hill, and Walt Garrison combined for almost 1,700 yards in 1971. Olympic gold medalist Bob Hayes led the pass receivers as he outsprinted defenders for eight touchdown passes and averaged 24 yards a catch.

That year it was a growing AFC power, the young Miami Dolphins, who stood in the way of a Dallas championship. The Dolphins had defeated Kansas City in the longest pro game ever played— a game that had gone into the second quarter of overtime—to gain the AFC finals against Baltimore. They then shut out the Colts, 21-0, to win a trip to the Super Bowl.

Landry and his assistants studied the Dolphin team carefully and decided that Miami was weakest in defending against running plays up the middle on first down. They found that if they sent center

Dave Manders and All-Pro guard John Niland to block middle linebacker Nick Buoniconti, they should be able to clear paths for their runners.

Landry did not need a computer to tell him how to stop Miami's offense. The Dolphins relied on powerful fullback Larry Csonka to blast up the middle for important first downs. And that happened to be where the Cowboys were the strongest. With tackle Bob Lilly, linebacker Lee Roy Jordan, and safety Cornell Green manning the inside, the Cowboys were happy to let Miami try to run.

On January 16, 1972, Miami's Mercury Morris waited in the end zone of New Orleans' Tulane Stadium for the kickoff. He hoped it would be the only time the Dolphins had to return a kickoff. But he and his teammates quickly discovered that it was not going to be their day. On Miami's second offensive drive, sure-handed Larry Csonka fell victim to the Super Bowl jinx. Csonka, who had not fumbled all season, dropped the ball on the Cowboy 48. Dallas linebacker Chuck Howley, one of the all-time great Super Bowl performers, recovered. In 1971 Howley had been the only member of a losing Super Bowl team to win the game's Most Valuable Player Award. And now it seemed he was on his way to another amazing performance.

Cowboy Cornell Green rides Miami's Paul Warfield to the turf as Dallas linebacker Chuck Howley (54) gives chase.

Staubach then led his team on a long drive to the Miami 2, with Thomas and Garrison piling up the yards. Then Mike Clark kicked an easy 9-yard field goal to give Dallas a 3-0 lead.

Miami then found the going tough against Dallas' well-disciplined defense. Late in the first quarter, quarterback Bob Griese found himself under a heavy rush from Dallas. He tried to scramble away from tacklers, but Bob Lilly stayed right on his heels. Lilly finally caught him for a 29-yard loss.

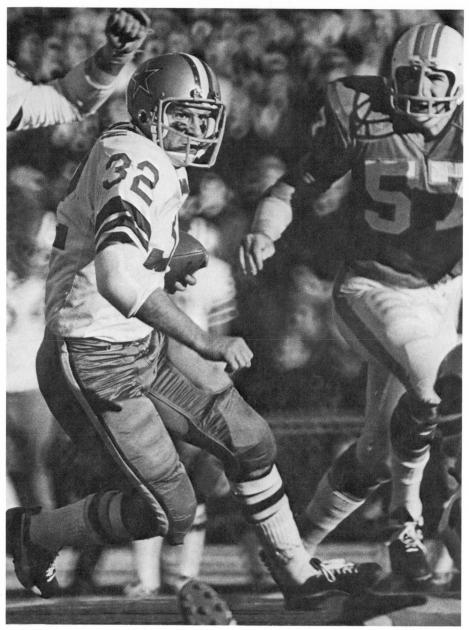

Veteran Cowboy Walt Garrison runs through the Dolphins. In Super Bowl VI, Garrison collected 74 of Dallas' rushing yards as the Cowboys' ground attack completely shredded Miami's defense.

60

In the second quarter, Dallas continued to march on the Dolphins. Manders and Niland were shutting off Buoniconti, and Cowboy runners Duane Thomas and Walt Garrison rushed through huge holes in the Dolphin defense. After moving to the Miami 7, Staubach completed a touchdown pass to receiver Lance Alworth to give them a 10-0 lead. The Dolphins then beat the clock to score on a 31-yard field goal by Garo Yepremian before halftime.

The Dolphins knew they had to do something to stop Dallas' running game. But whenever they tightened up the middle of their defense, the Cowboys ran around end. When they spread out their defense, the Cowboys charged up the middle with a 16-yard flanker reverse by Bob Hayes and tough inside running by Walt Garrison. Dallas took the second half kickoff and drove to the Dolphin 3. Duane Thomas did the honors from there with a fine run, and Dallas led, 17-3.

The Dolphins' hopes for a comeback were ruined by a third quarter in which they did not get a first down. As the Cowboys had expected, not even Csonka's power could make much yardage against the middle of their defense. And Miami's backs simply did not have the speed to run to the outside. Finally in the fourth period, they mounted a drive

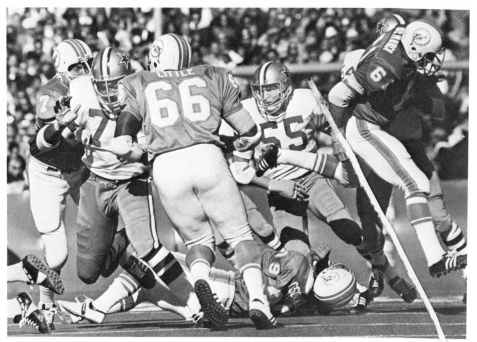

Cowboy defenders Jethro Pugh (left) and Lee Roy Jordan (55) burst through Miami's blockers on their way to a 24-3 rout of the Dolphins in Super Bowl VI.

and turned to one of their favorite plays to keep it going. This time, however, the wily linebacker Howley was ready for the short pass to Jim Kiick. He intercepted at midfield and would have scored a touchdown had he not tripped at the Miami 9. Two plays later, a pass from Staubach to tight end Mike Ditka finished the scoring. The Cowboys' punishing ground game used up most of the remaining time, and Dallas took home a 24-3 win.

The Cowboys had controlled the ball so well that Miami's offense was only on the field for 20 of the 60 regulation minutes. With silent running star Thomas and the rugged Garrison leading the way, the Cowboys had marched 252 yards on running plays, compared to Miami's 80. Typically, though, it was a quarterback, Staubach, who won Most Valuable Player honors. Roger had hit 12 of 19 passes for 119 yards and two touchdowns.

Roger "The Dodger" Staubach, MVP of Super Bowl VI, rolls out to look for a receiver. As the Cowboy offense overwhelmed a solid Dolphin team, Staubach led Dallas to 352 total yards, 23 first downs, and two touchdowns through the air.

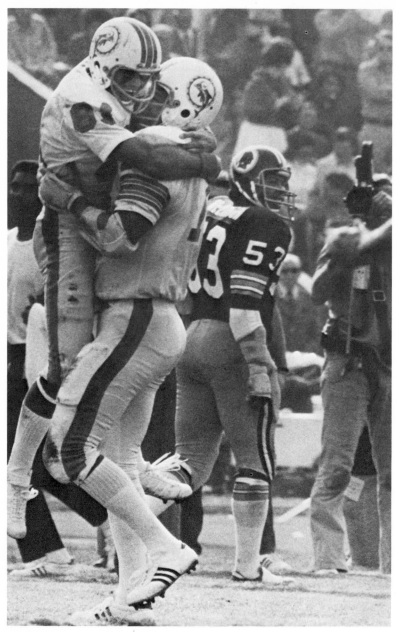

Small, slow, crafty Dolphin receiver Howard Twilley leaps for joy into the arms of tackle Norm Evans after Miami's defeat of the Washington Redskins in Super Bowl VII.

6
Miami Dolphins
SUPER BOWL VII
SUPER BOWL VIII

Some players have said that pro football play-offs are like playing a dice game: the teams are so even that luck plays the major role in deciding who goes to the Super Bowl. There have been, however, teams that have been so powerful that nothing short of a disaster could have kept them from pro football's most important game.

Probably the best example of a team that deserved to be in the Super Bowl was the Miami Dolphins. When a team went through an entire season un-defeated and played in three straight Super Bowls, there must have been more to it than luck. And Miami was the only team ever to record either of these successes.

Coach Don Shula took over a young team when he came to the Miami Dolphins in 1970. And in just one year, he changed Miami from a losing team into a winner. Miami had surprised football experts by sweeping aside the Baltimore Colts to win the AFC title in 1971. Their following Super Bowl loss must have bothered them terribly. But that would be the last time the Dolphins would lose for more than a year.

Miami's 14-0 record during the 1972 regular season was even more incredible considering they had to play most of the season without their star quarterback, Bob Griese. When Griese went out with an injury early in the season, it gave an old Super Bowl figure a chance to enter the Super Bowl picture for a third time. Earl Morrall came to join Shula, his former coach, and to take over the quarterbacking. Morrall kept the Dolphins' perfect string alive through the first game of the play-offs against Cleveland. By then Griese had healed. When Morrall and the Dolphins bogged down against the tough Pittsburgh Steelers in the AFC title game, Griese took over to help Miami win, 21-17.

When Miami's Super Bowl foe turned out to be the Washington Redskins, it set up an interesting contrast. The Redskins were the "Over the Hill

Coach Don Shula and quarterback Bob Griese—the masterminds of Miami's perfect 1972 season—confer on the sidelines.

Gang," a group of experienced pros. Players such as quarterback Billy Kilmer, tackle Walter Rock, and defensive aces Myron Pottios, Jack Pardee, and Roosevelt Taylor were all thought to be near retirement. Yet they had easily defeated Dallas for the NFC crown by a score of 26 to 3.

Miami's players, on the other hand, were still so young that fans were not yet familiar with their names. Their defense was even called the "No-Name" defense. Middle linebacker Nick Buoniconti was the only veteran player on defense. And the second oldest defender, safety Jake Scott, was only 27. At 26, tackle Manny Fernandez was the "old man" of the defensive line. Many thought that the Redskins' experience would be especially valuable in such a pressure-packed game.

It was an unusually hot and humid winter day on January 14, 1973, in Los Angeles when the two teams met. At first they pawed at each other with very basic, safe plays that were designed for short gains. Washington hoped that their halfback, All-Pro Larry Brown, could grind out enough yards to score. After that they could count on their solid defense to save the game.

But Brown got nowhere against Miami's fast-charging defense. Manny Fernandez clogged up the middle all by himself. And whenever the Redskins tried to run around end, they found a welcoming committee of sure-tackling Dolphins waiting for them.

Miami found a little better first-half success running Larry Csonka up the middle. The 235-

Miami tackle Manny Fernandez poses to pounce on Redskin All-Pro running back Larry Brown. In Super Bowl VII, the Dolphins held Brown to 72 yards in 22 carries.

pound fullback ran right over tacklers as he led his team to the Redskin 28-yard line. On third down with four yards to go for a first down, Bob Griese faded back to pass. His favorite target, Paul Warfield, was being closely guarded by Redskins, so he looked for his other wide receiver, Howard Twilley. Twilley was a slow runner, but he was clever at getting open and seldom dropped a pass.

In the same game, Dolphin fullback Larry Csonka chewed up Washington's defense for 112 yards on only 15 carries.

Griese threw to Twilley on the five-yard line, and Twilley fought his way into the end zone to give his team a 7-0 lead.

Miami nearly put Washington in a deep hole when Paul Warfield caught a touchdown pass of 47 yards. But an illegal procedure penalty on Miami wiped out the play, and Washington's defense forced them to punt. Late in the second quarter, Washington finally decided they were wasting their time sending Larry Brown into Miami's gang-tackling defense. Billy Kilmer started tossing some passes and moved his team into Dolphin territory for the first time in the game. Facing a third and 3 at Miami's 48, Kilmer went to a short pass to get the first down. This time Miami outsmarted him, however. They dropped into a new zone defense that Washington had not seen them use. So when Kilmer tossed the ball toward a running back, he did not see linebacker Buoniconti in his line of fire. Buoniconti intercepted the pass at his 41 and ran all the way back to Washington's 27.

The Redskin defense stiffened, and Griese was faced with a key third down and long yardage to go for a first down. This time the little quarterback went to his tight end, Jim Mandich, and covered 19 yards on the pass. This set up halfback

Jim Kiick for a 1-yard touchdown burst, and suddenly the Dolphins had a 14-0 halftime lead.

The second half was slow torture for the Redskins. First they put together their best offensive drive of the day, only to watch kicker Curt Knight miss a short field goal. Then Miami's Csonka took over, grinding steadily toward their goal line. When Dolphin kicker Garo Yepremian lined up for a fourth quarter field goal try, it appeared that Miami had the game won.

Only a strange and hilarious play involving the balding little kicker kept the game interesting. Yepremian attempted his kick from 42 yards away, but the kick was low and was blocked. The ball bounced back to Yepremian, who did not know what to do with it. As the Redskins charged at him, Garo's main thought must have been simply to survive. He tried to get rid of the ball by throwing it, but the ball flipped almost straight up in the air. Washington's Mike Bass gathered it in and romped 49 yards to cut the lead to 14-7.

Suddenly the Redskins, who had been beaten soundly most of the game, had a chance. With just over a minute left to play, they stopped Miami and got the ball back on their 30-yard line. But their comeback was stopped by an aroused Dolphin

After leading them to Super Bowl victory—his first in three tries—
Coach Don Shula gets an elevated joy ride from his players.

defense. The Redskins did not get even one yard
closer to the goal, and Kilmer was thrown to the
ground for a sack to end the game.

Miami celebrated their success as the first NFL
team to go through all 17 games unbeaten and

Throughout Super Bowl VII, safety Jack Scott troubled Redskin quarterback Billy Kilmer. Scott intercepted two of Kilmer's passes and helped to make Miami's defense scoreproof.

untied. Their defense had been so quick and effective that Washington's longest gain all day had been only 15 yards! Offensive hero Larry Csonka had run over Washington's proud defense for 112 yards in just 15 carries. But the Most Valuable Dolphin that day was safety Jake Scott. He had made two interceptions as well as some fine punt returns for his team. Dolphin teammates kidded Yepremian that he should have been voted the Redskins' Most Valuable Player!

74

Though Miami finally lost a couple of games in 1973, they looked even more awesome than they had the year before. They flattened the Oakland Raiders in the AFC championship game, 27-10. Miami's offensive line had handled the Raiders so easily that Griese had only tried six passes. With Larry Csonka doing most of the legwork, the Dolphins had stampeded through the Raiders for 266 yards rushing.

Standing in the way of a second straight Super Bowl win for Miami was the Minnesota Vikings. Minnesota still had Carl Eller and Alan Page from their respected defense of the past seven years, and they had clever quarterback Fran Tarkenton to get points for them. After the Vikings clobbered Dallas, 27-10, in the NFC title game, most experts predicted a close, exciting Super Bowl in Houston's Rice Stadium on January 13, 1974.

The Vikings' hopes, however, were dashed the first time Miami got the ball. Miami's brawny offensive line, led by guards Larry Little and Bob Kuechenburg and center Jim Langer, simply blew the Vikings off the line of scrimmage. They did so well that Bob Griese let his fullback Csonka choose the play he wanted to run. Csonka's favorite was a play in which some of the linemen would run to the right as if to block for an end sweep. When the defense started to run that way, Csonka would take the handoff and roar straight ahead through the spot that the defensive tackles had just left. That was the play that Csonka used to score from the 5 on Miami's first drive.

The Vikings could not make a first down when they went on offense, so the ball was turned over to the Dolphins. Their second drive was just like the first, with a lot of five- and six-yard runs by Csonka. This time Jim Kiick was given the scoring honors, and he dove into the end zone from a yard out. By then the first quarter was nearly over, and Minnesota found itself behind, 14-0, before it had even run its fourth play of the game! And Yepremian boosted the lead to 17-0 in the second quarter with a 28-yard field goal.

The Vikings finally recovered from their shock just before halftime. With Tarkenton throwing short, accurate passes, they moved to the Dolphin 7. The Vikings needed only two yards in three plays to get a first down inside the Dolphin 5. But the No-Name defense, led by Buoniconti, stopped Oscar Reed on three straight carries and finally recovered his fourth-down fumble to kill the drive.

In the second half, the Vikings not only had to

Viking running back Oscar Reed is thrown to the ground by Dolphins Nick Buoniconti (left) and Manny Fernandez (75). Miami held Minnesota to only 72 yards rushing in Super Bowl VIII.

contend with an unbeatable Miami team. They also had to battle a string of bad breaks. John Gilliam's 67-yard kickoff return was called back because of a penalty. Then after stopping Miami on a third down play, the Vikings were found guilty of defensive holding. That gave Miami an automatic first down. On that day the Viking defense gave Miami four free first downs due to penalties. Not that

Hard-driving Larry Csonka mauled the Vikings for 145 yards, setting a Super Bowl record and destroying Minnesota's second bid for a world championship.

Miami needed any help! Their ground game moved so well that Griese threw only seven passes and completed six of them. Miami's final touchdown was made possible by a graceful, diving catch by Paul Warfield, good for 27 yards. Though Minnesota finally scored on a run by Tarkenton, it was far too late to worry Miami.

Larry Csonka won the Most Valuable Player Award for gaining 145 yards in 33 carries. His workhorse running had kept the dangerous Tarkenton off the field for most of the game. The Dolphins' ground game was probably the best the game had seen in modern times. Despite running the least number of plays in their conference that season, they had scored the fifth most points. And the fact that the Dolphins could do that without relying on the long pass showed that their running plays almost always worked. Super Bowl VIII was indeed a classic illustration of what an ideal running attack should be.

It seemed that Miami's Coach Shula had built an unbeatable team. The champs were still young and expected to be writing Super Bowl history for years. But a last-minute pass beat them in the play-off the following year. Then Warfield, Csonka, and Kiick left to play in the new World Football League, and injuries further reduced the roster. Almost as suddenly as it had started, the Dolphin reign as Super Bowl champs was over.

Super Bowl Scores

SUPER BOWL I
January 15, 1967 / Memorial Coliseum, Los Angeles

Green Bay Packers (NFL)	7	7	14	7	**35**
Kansas City Chiefs (AFL)	0	10	0	0	**10**

Most Valuable Player Award: Bart Starr, Green Bay Packers

SUPER BOWL II
January 14, 1968 / Orange Bowl, Miami

Green Bay Packers (NFL)	3	13	10	7	**33**
Oakland Raiders (AFL)	0	7	0	7	**14**

Most Valuable Player Award: Bart Starr, Green Bay Packers

SUPER BOWL III
January 12, 1969 / Orange Bowl, Miami

New York Jets (AFL)	0	7	6	3	**16**
Baltimore Colts (NFL)	0	0	0	7	**7**

Most Valuable Player Award: Joe Namath, New York Jets

SUPER BOWL IV
January 11, 1970 / Tulane Stadium, New Orleans

Kansas City Chiefs (AFL)	3	13	7	0	**23**
Minnesota Vikings (NFL)	0	0	7	0	**7**

Most Valuable Player Award: Len Dawson, Kansas City Chiefs

SUPER BOWL V
January 17, 1971 / Orange Bowl, Miami

Baltimore Colts (AFC)	0	6	0	10	**16**
Dallas Cowboys (NFC)	3	10	0	0	**13**

Most Valuable Player Award: Chuck Howley, Dallas Cowboys

SUPER BOWL VI
January 16, 1972 / Tulane Stadium, New Orleans

Dallas Cowboys (NFC)	3	7	7	7	**24**
Miami Dolphins (AFC)	0	3	0	0	**3**

Most Valuable Player Award: Roger Staubach, Dallas Cowboys

SUPER BOWL VII
January 14, 1973 / Memorial Coliseum, Los Angeles

Miami Dolphins (AFC)	7	7	0	0	**14**
Washington Redskins (NFC)	0	0	0	7	**7**

Most Valuable Player Award: Jake Scott, Miami Dolphins

SUPER BOWL VIII
January 13, 1974 / Rice Stadium, Houston

Miami Dolphins (AFC)	14	3	7	0	**24**
Minnesota Vikings (NFC)	0	0	0	7	**7**

Most Valuable Player Award: Larry Csonka, Miami Dolphins